Perspectives on Las Américas

Global Perspectives

In a time of ever-increasing global phenomena, Blackwell Publishing's series *Global Perspectives* offers regionally focused volumes that attempt to move beyond the standard regional studies model. Each volume includes a selection of previously published articles and an extensive introduction by the volume editor, providing an overview of the history and cultures of the region under discussion. The articles are chosen to illustrate the dynamic processes by and through which scholars have described and understood regional history and culture, and to show how profoundly the ethnography of each region has influenced the direction and development of anthropological and social theory. The *Global Perspectives* series thus furnishes readers with both an introduction to the cultures of a vast array of world regions, and a history of how those cultures have been perceived and interpreted.

The contributors include anthropologists, historians, philosophers, and critics. Collectively they show the multiplicities of voice in regional studies, and reveal the interpenetration of ideas and concepts within and across disciplines, regions, and historical periods.

Published

1. Perspectives on Africa: A Reader in Culture, History, & Representation
   Edited and introduced by Roy Richard Grinker and Christopher B. Steiner
2. Perspectives on Las Américas: A Reader in Culture, History, & Representation
   Edited and introduced by Matthew C. Gutmann, Félix V. Matos Rodríguez, Lynn Stephen, and Patricia Zavella

In Preparation

Perspectives on Japan: A Reader in Culture, History, & Representation
Edited and introduced by William Kelly
Perspectives on the Middle East: A Reader in Culture, History, & Representation
Edited and introduced by Richard Tapper
Perspectives on Modern South Asia: A Reader in Culture, History, & Representation
Edited and introduced by Kamala Visweswaran and Ali Mir
Perspectives on the Caribbean: A Reader in Culture, History, & Representation
Edited and introduced by Philip Scher and Kevin Yelvington

Perspectives on Las Américas

A Reader in Culture, History, & Representation

edited and introduced by

Matthew C. Gutmann,
Félix V. Matos Rodríguez, Lynn Stephen,
and Patricia Zavella

Blackwell
Publishing

Editorial material and organization © 2003 by Blackwell Publishers Ltd
a Blackwell Publishing company

350 Main Street, Malden, MA 02148-5018, USA
108 Cowley Road, Oxford OX4 1JF, UK
550 Swanston Street, Carlton, Victoria 3053, Australia
Kurfürstendamm 57, 10707 Berlin, Germany

The right of Matthew C. Gutmann, Félix V. Matos Rodríguez, Lynn Stephen, and Patricia Zavella to be identified as the
Authors of the Editorial Material in this Work has been asserted in accordance with the UK Copyright, Designs, and
Patents Act 1988.

First published 2003 by Blackwell Publishers Ltd

Library of Congress Cataloging-in-Publication Data

Perspectives on Las Américas : a reader in culture, history, and representation / edited and introduced by Matthew C.
Gutmann . . . [et al.].
    p. cm.—(Global perspectives)
    ISBN 0–631–22295–2 (alk. paper)—ISBN 0–631–22296–0 (alk. paper)
    1. Latin America—History. 2. Hispanic Americans. 3. Latin Americans—United States. 4. Ethnicity. 5. Identity
(Psychology) 6. Sex role. 7. Popular culture. 8. Political culture. I. Gutmann, Matthew C., 1953- II. Series.
F1410 .P48 2003
980—dc21
                                                                                                    2002007335
A catalogue record for this title is available from the British Library.

Set in 9.5/11.5pt Ehrhardt
by Kolam Information Services Pvt. Ltd, Pondicherry, India
Printed and bound in the United Kingdom
by MPG Books Ltd, Bodmin, Cornwall

For further information on
Blackwell Publishing, visit our website:
http://www.blackwellpublishing.com

Contents

PART V Regional, National, and Transnational Political Cultures

List of Contributors

Editors

Matthew C. Gutmann is the Stanley J. Bernstein Assistant Professor of the Social Sciences – International Affairs at Brown University, where he teaches Cultural Anthropology, Ethnic Studies, and Latin American Studies. He is the author of *The Meanings of Macho: Being a Man in Mexico City* (University of California Press, 1996), *Mainstreaming Men into Gender and Development: Debates, Reflections, and Experiences* (with Sylvia Chant, Oxfam, 2000), and *The Romance of Democracy: Compliant Defiance in Contemporary Mexico* (University of California Press, 2002), and editor of *Changing Men and Masculinities in Latin America* (Duke University Press, 2003).

Félix V. Matos Rodríguez, a historian, is currently the Director of the Center for Puerto Rican Studies at Hunter College (City University of New York). He is the author of *Women and Urban Life in Nineteenth-Century San Juan, Puerto Rico (1820–62)* (University Presses of Florida, 1999); co-author of *"Pioneros:" Puerto Ricans in New York City, 1896–1948* (Arcadia, 2001); and co-editor of *Puerto Rican Women's History: New Perspectives* (M. E. Sharpe, 1998).

Lynn Stephen is professor and chair of the Department of Anthropology at the University of Oregon. She is the author of five books: *Zapotec Women* (University of Texas Press, 1991), *Class, Politics, and Popular Religion in Mexico and Central America* (with James Dow, University of Texas Press, 1990), *Hear My Testimony: María Teresa Tula, Human Rights Activist of El Salvador* (South End Press, 1994), *Women and Social Movements in Latin America: Power From Below* (University of Texas Press, 1997), and *Zapata Lives!: Histories and Cultural Politics in Southern Mexico* (University of California Press, 2002). Lynn Stephen's research focuses on gender, ethnicity, political economy, social movements, human rights, and nationalism in Latin America. She is currently working on two projects: (1) on immigration and Mexican farmworkers in Oregon and (2) the role of cooperatives and global marketing on the political, labor, and gender identities of Zapotec women in southern Mexico.

Patricia Zavella is Professor of Latin American and Latino Studies and Co-Director of the Chicano/Latino Research Center at the University of California, Santa Cruz. Significant publications include: *Women's Work and Chicano Families: Cannery Workers of the Santa Clara Valley* (Cornell University Press, 1987); *Telling to Live: Latina Feminist Testimonios*, co-authored with members of the Latina Feminist Group (Duke University Press, 2001), and *Chicana Feminisms: Disruption in Dialogue*, co-edited with Gabriela Arredondo, Aída Hurtado, Norma Klahn, and Olga Nájera Ramírez (Duke University Press, 2002).

Contributors

Norma Alarcón, Department of Ethnic Studies, University of California at Berkeley, Berkeley, CA 94720, USA.

Antonio Benítez-Rojo, Department of Spanish, Amherst College, 5 Barret Hall, Amherst, MA 01002, USA.

Lionel Cantú died in 2002. He taught in the Department of Sociology at the University of California at Santa Cruz.

Leo R. Chavez, Department of Anthropology, University of California, Irvine, CA 92697, USA.

Jane I. Collins, Women's Studies Center, University of Wisconsin, Madison, WI 53706, USA.

Karen Mary Davalos, Chicana/o Studies, Loyola Marymount University, One LMU Drive, Los Angeles, California 90045–2659, USA.

Marc Edelman, Department of Anthropology, City University of New York, The Graduate Center, 365 Fifth Avenue, New York, New York 10016, USA.

Arturo Escobar, Department of Anthropology, P.O. Box 3115, 301 Alumni Building, University of North Carolina, Chapel Hill, NC 27599-3115, USA.

Claudia Fonseca, Programa de Pós-Graduação em Antropologia Social, Instituto de Filosofia e Ciências Humanas, Universidade Federal do Rio Grande do Sul – Campus do Vale, Av. Bento Gonçalves 9500, Prédio 43311, Bloco AI, sala 104, Porto Alegre, RS, Brasil 91509–900.

Jeffrey Gould, Center for Latin American and Caribbean Studies, 1125 E. Atwater Avenue, University of Indiana, Bloomington, IN 47401, USA.

Libia Grueso, Proceso de Comunidades Negras (PCN), Carrera 2D, No. 57–14, Barrio Los Andes, Cali, Colombia.

Matthew C. Gutmann, Department of Anthropology, Brown University, Providence, RI 02912, USA.

Laurie Kroshus Medina, Department of Anthropology, 354 Baker Hall, Michigan State University, East Lansing, MI 48824, USA.

Félix V. Matos Rodríguez, Center for Puerto Rican Studies, Hunter College, 695 Park Avenue #E1409, New York, NY 10021, USA.

Frances Negrón-Muntaner, 9 Island Avenue # 1909, Miami, FL 33139, USA.

Ruben George Oliven, Programa de Pós-Graduação em Antropologia Social, Instituto de Filosofia e Ciências Humanas, Universidade Federal do Rio Grande do Sul – Campus do Vale, Av. Bento Gonçalves 9500, Prédio 43311, Bloco AI, sala 104, Porto Alegre, RS, Brasil 91509–900.

Américo Paredes died in 1999. He taught for several decades in the Departments of Anthropology and English at the University of Texas, Austin.

Richard Parker, Department of Sociomedical Sciences, Mailman School of Public Health, Columbia University, 722 West 168th Street, 9th Floor, New York, NY 10032, USA.

Néstor P. Rodríguez; Department of Sociology, 450 Philip Hoffman Hall, University of Houston, Houston, TX 77204–3012, USA.

Mark Rogers, Corporate Design & Usability, Eastman Kodak Co., 2400 Mt. Read Blvd., Rochester, NY 14650–3002, USA.

Carlos Rosero, Proceso de Communidades Negras (PCN), Carrera 2D, No. 57–14, Barrio Los Andes, Cali, Colombia.

Rubén G. Rumbaut, Department of Sociology, 316 Berkey Hall, Michigan State University, East Lansing, MI 48824–1111, USA.

Lynn Stephen, Department of Anthropology, 1218 University of Oregon, Eugene, OR 97403, USA.

Steve J. Stern, Department of History, 3211 Humanities Building, 455 North Park Street, University of Wisconsin, Madison, WI 53706–1483, USA.

Silvio Torres-Saillant, Latino–Latin American Studies Program, Syracuse University, Syracuse, NY 13244, USA.

Patricia Zavella, Department of Latin American and Latino Studies, Merrill College, University of California at Santa Cruz, CA 95064, USA.

Ana Celia Zentella, Department of Ethnic Studies, University of California, San Diego, La Jolla, CA, 92093–0522, USA.

Editors' Acknowledgments

Matthew C. Gutmann

Thanks to Felo, Pat, and Lynn for the pleasure of working together on this volume. My gratitude as well to colleagues at Brown University in Ethnic Studies, Anthropology, and Latin American Studies. I'd also like to acknowledge a Faculty Research Grant from the Center for the Study of Race and Ethnicity in America and a Richard B. Salomon Faculty Research Award, both from Brown, that were used to get this project started. In the Department of Anthropology at Brown, thanks for secretarial support to Kathy Grimaldi and Matilde Andrade. To Liliana and Maya, "*Este es su mundo. !Cuídenlo bien!*"

Félix V. Matos Rodríguez

To my Caribbean, Latino, and Latin American *colegas* at Northeastern University and at the Centro de Estudios Puertorriqueños at Hunter College for the constant support and exchange of ideas; to my co-editors, for the invitation to join them in this exciting and complex project; to Liliana Arabia and Lucas Andrés Matos, for your *cariño*.

Lynn Stephen

Thanks to former colleagues at Northeastern University who worked with me to build a program in Latino, Latin American, and Caribbean Studies and to begin to figure out how to build a dialogue between Latino and Latin American Studies. Collaborative projects with Oregon's farmworker union, Pineros y Campesinos Unidos del Nordoeste, helped me to see how to work on both sides of the border at once. UC Santa Cruz colleagues in the Hemispheric Dialogues 2 project (listed below) provided a stimulating space for working through questions in the introduction. A special thanks to Jonathan Fox for his helpful comments, to my co-editors for a truly collaborative and innovative project, and to my family – Ellen, Gabi and José – for their love and support.

Pat Zavella

Thanks to my colleagues at the University of California, Santa Cruz who have participated in the projects, Hemispheric Dialogue and Hemispheric Dialogues 2: Bridging Latin American and Latino Studies. These were joint projects between the Chicano/Latino Research Center and the Latin American and Latino Studies Department, funded by the Ford Foundation. The following faculty have been centrally involved in these dialogues: Sonia Alvarez, Pedro Castillo, Guillermo Delgado, Jonathan Fox, Wally Goldfrank, Susanne Jonas, Norma Klahn, Manuel Pastor, and Juan Poblete. Thanks also to Verónica López Duran, who provided admirable and timely research assistance.

From All the Editors

We would like to offer our editor at Blackwell, Jane Huber, our warmest gratitude for her enthusiastic support of this volume which, being neither "a Latino Studies Reader" nor "a Latin American Studies Reader," purposely sets out to span book markets in ways that would make more squeamish publishers shy away from the project. As we completed the final stages of editing this book we learned that one of our contributors, Lionel Cantú, had suddenly died. Lionel's passing is a terrible tragedy; his scholarship and enthusiasm will be missed in many ways.

This volume is dedicated to the people of Las Américas who have taught us the value of difference, dialogue, and collaboration.

Acknowledgments to Sources

Norma Alarcón, "Traddutora, Traditora: A Paradigmatic Figure of Chicana Feminism," from *Cultural Critique*, Fall 1989, pp. 57–87.

Antonio Benítez Rojo, "From the Plantation to the Plantation," from *The Repeating Island: The Caribbean and the Postmodern Perspective*, pp. 61–71 (excerpted). Durham, NC: Duke University Press, 1992.

Lionel Cantú, "A Place Called Home: A Queer Political Economy of Mexican Immigrant Men's Family Experiences," from *Queer Families, Queer Politics: Challenging Culture and the State*, edited by M. Bernstein and R. Reimann, pp. 112–36. New York: Columbia University Press, 2001.

Leo R. Chavez, "Immigration Reform and Nativism: The Nationalist Response to the Transnationalist Challenge," from *Immigrants Out! The New Nativism and the Anti-Immigrant Impulse in the United States*, edited by Juan F. Perea, pp. 61–77. New York University Press, 1997.

Jane I. Collins, "Transnational Labor Process and Gender Relations: Women in Fruit and Vegetable Production in Chile, Brazil and Mexico," from *Journal of Latin American Anthropology* 1(1), pp. 179–99, 1995. Reproduced by permission of the American Anthropological Association. Not for sale or further reproduction.

Karen Mary Davalos, "*La Quinceañera*: Making Gender and Ethnic Identities," from *Frontiers: A Journal of Women's Studies*, pp. 101–27. Copyright © 1996 by Frontiers Editorial Collective. Reprinted by permission of the University of Nebraska Press, Lincoln.

Marc Edelman, "A Central American Genocide: Rubber, Slavery, Nationalism, and the Destruction of the Guatusos-Malekus," from *Comparative Study of Society and History* 40(2), pp. 356–90, 1998. Cambridge University Press.

Claudia Fonseca, "Inequality Near and Far: International Adoption as Seen from a Brazilian *Favela*," from *Law and Society Review* 36(2), 2002.

Jeffrey Gould, "Gender, Politics, and the Triumph of *Mestizaje* in Early 20th-Century Nicaragua." Reproduced by permission of the American Anthropological Association from *Journal of Latin American Anthropology* 2(1), pp. 4–33, 1996. Not for sale or further reproduction.

Libia Grueso, Carlos Rosero, and Arturo Escobar, "The Process of Black Community Organizing in the Southern Pacific Coast Region of Colombia," from *Cultures of Politics/Politics of Cultures: Re-visioning Latin American Social Movements*, edited by Sonia E. Alvarez, Evelina Dagnino, and Arturo Escobar, pp. 196–219. Boulder, CO: Westview Press, 1998.

Matthew C. Gutmann, "For Whom the Taco Bells Toll: Popular Responses to NAFTA South of the Border," from *Critique of Anthropology* 18(3), pp. 297–315, 1998.

Laurie Kroshus Medina, "History, Culture and Place-Making: 'Native' Status and Maya Identity in Belize." Reproduced by permission of the American Anthropological Association from *Journal of Latin American Anthropology* 4(1), pp. 134–65, 1999. Not for sale or further reproduction.

Félix V. Matos Rodríguez, " '¿Quién Trabajará?': Domestic Workers, Urban Slaves, and the Abolition of Slavery in Puerto Rico," from *Workers, Slaves, and the Abolition of Slavery*, pp. 62–82. Armonk, NY: M. E. Sharpe.

Frances Negrón-Muntaner, "Jennifer's Butt," from *Aztlan* 22(2), pp. 181–94, 1997. Copyright © 1997 Frances Negrón-Muntaner.

Ruben George Oliven, "Two Sides of the Same Coin: Modern *Gaúcho* Identity in Brazil," from *Journal of Latin American Anthropology* 4(2)/5(1), pp. 106–25, 2000. Reproduced by permission of the American Anthropological Association. Not for sale or further reproduction.

Américo Paredes, "The United States, Mexico and *Machismo*," from *Folklore and Culture on the Texas–Mexican Border*," edited by Richard Bauman, pp. 215–34. Austin, TX: CMAS Books, 1993.

Richard Parker, "The Carnivalization of the World," from *The Gender/Sexuality Reader: Culture, History, Political Economy*, edited by R. N. Lancaster and M. di Leonardo, pp. 361–77. New York: Routledge, 1997.

Néstor P. Rodríguez, "The Real 'New World Order': The Globalization of Racial and Ethnic Relations in the Late Twentieth Century," from *The Bubbling Cauldron: Race, Ethnicity and the Urban Crisis*, by M. P. Smith and J. R. Feagin, pp. 211–25. Minneapolis: University of Minnesota Press, 1995.

Mark Rogers, "Spectacular Bodies: Folklorization and the Politics of Identity in Ecuadorian Beauty Pageants," from *Journal of Latin American Anthropology* 3(2), pp. 54–85, 1999. Reproduced by permission of the American Anthropological Association. Not for sale or further reproduction.

Rubén G. Rumbaut, "The Americans: Latin American and Caribbean Peoples in the United States," from *Americas: New Interpretative Essays*, edited by A. Stepan, pp. 275–307. Boston, MA: WGBH Educational Foundation, 1982.

Lynn Stephen, "The Construction of Indigenous Suspects: Militarization and the Gendered and Ethnic Dynamics of Human Rights Abuses in Southern Mexico," from *American Ethnologist* 26(4), pp. 822–42, 2000. Reproduced by permission of the American Anthropological Association. Not for sale or further reproduction.

Steve J. Stern, "New Approaches to the Study of Peasant Rebellion and Consciousness: Implications of the Andean Experience," from *Resistance, Rebellion, and Consciousness in the Andean Peasant World, 18th to 20th Centuries*, pp. 3–25. Copyright © 1987 by Steve J. Stern. Reprinted by permission of the University of Wisconsin Press, Madison.

Silvio Torres-Saillant, "Dominican Blackness and the Modern World," from *Dominican Studies Working Paper Series* 1, 1999. City College of New York, Dominican Studies Institute.

Patricia Zavella, "'Playing with Fire': The Gendered Construction of Chicana/Mexicana Sexuality," from *The Gender/Sexuality Reader: Culture, History, Political Economy*, edited by R. N. Lancaster and M. di Leonardo, pp. 392–408. New York: Routledge, 1997.

Ana Celia Zentella, "Returned Migration, Language, and Identity: Puerto Rican Bilinguals in Dos Worlds/Two Mundos," from *International Journal of the Sociology of Language* 84, pp. 81–100, 1990.

Introduction: Understanding the Américas: Insights from Latina/o and Latin American Studies

Lynn Stephen, Patricia Zavella, Matthew C. Gutmann, and Félix V. Matos Rodríguez

Global, transnational, hybrid, multilingual, multi-ethnic, deterritorialized – these words are often used to describe the reality of living on earth in the twenty-first century.[1] Just as often, we are also reminded that borders are concrete and material and that states stage both real and theatrical defense of their borders. For example, the U.S. government deploys the National Guard along with the U.S. border patrol to apprehend undocumented Mexican migrants, yet simultaneously has a de facto economic policy for commercial agriculture that encourages and depends on undocumented immigrant labor to harvest and process U.S. fruits and vegetables (Rosaldo 1997; Andreas 1998). States also have the power to intervene in the mobility and quality of human life (Sassen 1998; Chang 2000). Nations can deny full citizenship rights to those living legally within their limits and look the other way to abuses inflicted upon those who do not have a formally recognized legal status (Flores 1997). An accurate description of twenty-first-century life might include all of these ideas and experiences, particularly in the region we have come to call the Américas, an area of the world more conventionally carved up into North, Central, and South America, as well as the Caribbean.[2] Upon closer inspection, however, we see that

what we often think of as the ongoing tension between the integration of the peoples of the Americas and their simultaneous local, regional, and national Balkanization is not just a product of the twenty-first century, but has been an ongoing process for many centuries.

The articles in this interdisciplinary volume have been selected to provide a conceptual overview and concrete examples of research that examine the historical, cultural, economic, and political integration of the Américas in the present and recent past. They come primarily from the fields of anthropology and history. The selections include case studies in specific places at particular times. While several articles in Part I, "Colonialism and Resistance," deal with the colonial period in Latin America and the Caribbean, the bulk of the material in this volume is contemporary. The first intellectual purpose of this reader is to provide teachers and students with theoretical tools and concrete examples of how to think about culture, history, and representation in terms of (a) local realities in relation to transnational processes, (b) identities spread between multiple cultures and states, and (c) emerging identities that come through processes of migration from Latin America and settlement in the United States. Another way of thinking about these issues more broadly is through exploring how U.S. Latina/o Studies and Latin American/Caribbean Studies both present useful understandings of changes brought about through globalization of the Américas. The second intellectual goal of this reader is to initiate a discussion about ongoing differences in Latina/o and Latin American/Caribbean Studies approaches and to look for possibilities for dialogue and collaboration between the two fields. Both approaches are inherently interdisciplinary (particularly through emphasizing history, culture, and language), both involve narratives of origins and have their respective "national moments" within larger discussions of "Latin American" and "being Latino" (for example, the importance of being a Peruvian, Cuban, or Mexican in Latin America or being Chicano, Nuyorican, or Cuban-American within a discourse on being Latino). Both fields involve transnational imaginaries and have some history of community activism and solidarity with social movements. Latin American and Latina/o Studies use the notion of translation both linguistically and cross-culturally, and both fields decenter and question the United States as the primary political, economic, and social center of the Américas.

Changing Demographics, New Perspectives

Any discussion of the relationship between Latin American/Caribbean Studies and Latina/o Studies must be centered in the changing constructions of identity, current demographic realities, and histories of both fields. Both the United States and the countries of Latin America and the Caribbean have been significantly changed by the arrival of new populations from overseas as well as by internal migration, particularly since the 1970s. In Latin America migration from the countryside, along with reclassification of what constitutes rural and urban, caused about 40 percent of urban population growth from the 1950s to the 1970s and about 35 percent in the 1980s (Tam 1994; United Nations 1996). Now Latin America has become a major urban region of the world, with 75 percent of the popu-

lation living in cities (Gonzalez 2002:3). Urbanization rates are impressive in many countries – Venezuela (92 percent), Uruguay (90 percent), Argentina (88 percent), Chile (84 percent), Brazil (78 percent), Cuba (76 percent), and Mexico (75 percent) (United Nations 1995). Urbanization has taken longer in Central American countries because of smaller economies and a dependence on subsistence agriculture. However, it is estimated that, by 2010, 55 percent of Central America's population will live in cities as well (Gonzales 2002:3). This growth has been spurred by civilians who fled the countryside as a result of civil wars, as well as current development programs that offer little or nothing for farmers and concentrate on drawing foreign investment for low-paying factory jobs.

Rural–urban migration, in combination with the globalization of social movements in Latin America, has produced important realignments of ethnic identities and racial labels. For example, what historians have called in the past "Indians into Ladinos" in Guatemala (Grandin 2001) and "indigenous mestizos" in Peru (de la Cadena 2000; Paerregaard 1997) may still be happening at some level as a result of rural–urban migration and pressures to assimilate to national cultures in Latin American cities. The shift of rural population to the countryside, however, has also occurred in the context of regional and global congresses and campaigns by indigenous peoples. In some cases, this has resulted in the emergence of pan-indigenous movements within countries such as Mexico, Ecuador, and Guatemala, where distinct ethnic indigenous groups have come together in coalition to push back on exclusionary versions of nationalism that prevented them from demanding rights to territory, recognition of their culture and language, and the right to political participation (Warren 1998; Yashar 1999). National pan-indigenous movements have also participated in transnational networks and campaigns (see Brysk 2000:70). Many indigenous peoples in Latin America are also spread across national borders, such as the Aymara who live in Peru, Bolivia, Chile, and Argentina, forming a transnational population. In urban areas of Latin America the reconstitution of local cultures has also changed the meaning of categories such as "mestizo" and "Ladino" as the ethnic composition of urban areas is rapidly changing (see Weismantel 2001). Internal conflicts and civil wars such as those waged in Peru, Guatemala, and currently in Colombia have also produced large numbers of internal refugees who are "forced migrants."

Most migration in Latin America has been within the same country from rural to urban areas or out of the country, in large measure to the United States. Countries like Venezuela, Bolivia, Guatemala, Brazil, Colombia, Peru, and El Salvador all have negative net migration rates, indicating that they are losing population to other countries. Because of their economic success until recently, Chile and Argentina were attracting low levels of migrants, most from nearby countries. In 1998, Chile had an estimated 55,000 illegal immigrants, 40,000 of them from Peru. Most were in low-paying jobs (Gonzalez 1998).

While most migration in Latin America has been interregional, the United States has served as a major host country for migrants from Latin America and the Caribbean. Both the increase in the absolute number of Latin American migrants to the United States since the 1970s, as well as the changing composition of where those migrants come from within Latin America, have been reflected in the linguistic terminology and the identity politics of what it means to be a Latin American immigrant in the United States.

The use of multiple umbrella terms such as "Spanish," "Hispanic," or "Latino" indicates the tension among Latinas/os regarding their identities and coalitions with other groups. In the 1970 census, the Census Bureau used the term "people of Spanish origin," which pleased no one. Recognizing the need for a comprehensive term, the Census Bureau convened an advisory committee formed from representatives of various Chicano, Mexican, Puerto Rican, and Cuban political organizations. After heated debate, the committee eventually agreed to the term "Hispanic," which to many represented more mainstream political viewpoints. Beginning with the 1980 census, the term became a specially designated one including four subcategories: Mexican, Mexican American, or Chicano; Puerto Rican; Cuban; Other Spanish/Hispanic. Yet because the term lumped together groups with very disparate histories, socio-demographic characteristics, language capabilities and knowledge of Spanish, political interests, and treatment upon immigration to the United States, many activists and community members found Hispanic problematic. The term is a catchall that lumps together the categories of language, ethnicity, nationality, and the socially constructed notion of race (see Rodríguez 2000).[3]

The term "Hispanic" became popularized during the 1980s especially, with media hype about the "Decade of Hispanics" (Gómez 1992; Oboler 1995). The term "Latino" gained popular currency during the 1970s, reflecting an anti-assimilationist political consciousness arising from community-based organizing (Padilla 1985; Klor de Alva 1997). The aim was to be more inclusive of the multiple ethnic compositions of working-class communities, as well as the continued migrations from Latin America, especially Mexico and Central America, which remained high in large cities like Chicago, New York, or Los Angeles. The term "Latino" was included for the first time in the 2000 census. In that census, people of "Spanish/Hispanic/Latino" origin could identify as Mexican, Puerto Rican, Cuban, or "other Spanish/Hispanic/Latino." Though it emerged in opposition to the homogenized "Hispanic," "Latino" has also become exoticized and trendy, and potentially another form of commodification or what Eliana Rivero (1994) calls "the neutral soup of *Latinismo*." Even corporate interests and politicians' agendas now routinely include utilizing the Spanish language and national-ethnic identity markers (Dávila 1997, 2001).

Regardless of particular terms used by individuals to identify themselves, the overall Latino population is one of the fastest growing minority groups in the United States and is now equal to African Americans in size (Schmitt 2001). Latinization – the growing numbers and noticeable presence of Latinos – is occurring throughout the United States (Zavella 2000a), pushing scholars, government officials, and community members to reconceptualize what we mean by the Américas. Current demographic figures for the number of Latinos in the United States make a strong case for considering the country as as a significant part of Latin America and the Caribbean. The 2000 U.S. Census identified 35.3 million people as "Spanish/Hispanic/Latino." Recent estimates by demographers suggest that if those without documents were counted, the Latino population would be significantly larger. If the number of Latinos in the United States from the 2000 census (35,305,818) is compared with the populations of the largest Latin American countries – Brazil with 172,860,370, Mexico with 100,349,766, Colombia with 39,996,671, and Argentina with 39,685,655 – the United States would rank fifth.[4] Canada's last census was conducted in 1996 and showed 228,580 Spanish speakers and 222,870 Portuguese speakers out of a total population of 31,281,092, or 1.3 percent of the total (O'Mally et al. 2001).[5]

The ever-increasing presence of Latino immigrants in states like California, in combination with debates over cultural issues such as bilingual education and periodically higher unemployment rates, have resulted in ebbs and flows of nativist backlash (Perea 1997; Chavez 2001 and in this volume) and anti-immigrant legislation, such as Proposition 187 passed by California voters in 1994 (although rejected by nearly four out of five Latino voters).[6] Anti-immigrant physical and verbal violence has also been recorded in regions as different as Los Angeles, Chicago, and Long Island. Puerto Rican Congressman Luis Gutiérrez, for example, was harassed and humiliated by a guard at the visitors' entrance to the Capitol in 1996, who suggested that the Chicago-born congressman "go back to [his] country." Latin American immigration to the United States has promoted the economic, social, and cultural integration of the Américas–a point seen as the positive side of the "Latinization" of the United States through film, music, cuisine, dance and Spanish-language print and broadcast media networks (Gutiérrez 1998:315–316; Holston 1997). However, anti-immigrant cultural and political forces have simultaneously pushed back at Latin American immigrants, often portraying them as "different" from the dominant society because of racial, cultural, and linguistic characteristics that mark them as "other" (Flores 1997:256). Scholars (Comaroff 1992:60; Hall

1988:2; Omi and Winant 1987) point out that socially constructed categories such as race and ethnicity are perceived as impassible symbolic boundaries that become fixed in nature and take on the appearance of an autonomous force capable of determining the course of social and economic life. As Latinos become fixed and naturalized as "other" in broader American culture, one result is the homogenization of Latinos/as, the erasure of differences of history, identity, and culture tied to people's specific stories of immigration, settlement, or long-time history of living in the United States. At the same time, however, distinct groups of immigrants continue to construct nationalist-based identities through hometown associations, festivals, and other institutions that continue their specific ethnic and national identities.

The increasing numbers of people of Latin American origin who have migrated to the United States have stimulated a new theoretical perspective, from that of immigration to transnational migration. Immigration models often assume a linear model of change where migration and settlement entail discernible stages of liminality, transition, and adaptation to the host country by migrants. Instead, theorists of the "new transnationalism" argue that we should examine transnational circuits, spaces, or networks as people migrate from one country to another's borders (Glick Schiller et al. 1992, 1995; Rouse, 1992; Sassen 1988, 1988). Further, the current links between migrants and home societies are of a different order than previous generations, since people are pushed into the migrant stream by new circuits of capital which are sustained by transformations in technologies of transportation and communication. Thus transnational theorists make the useful suggestion that we have a "bifocal" orientation and examine the processes by which migrants construct links between their country of origin and their country of settlement.

With this transnational perspective in mind, Latinas/os who have migrated to the United States are transforming U.S. demographics as well as the culture, politics, and the economy, and provide a new set of relations that Latin American Studies and Latina/o Studies could explore. But first we will present histories of the two fields, to illustrate how such explorations will require new sets of lenses and means to explore common political agendas.

Latin American Studies: Foundations and Innovations

Dominant cultural attitudes in the United States that continue to view Latin American immigrants and second-, third-, fourth- and longer-generation Latinos as "outsiders" have, in part, a direct link to the way that Latin American Studies was originally framed from within the U.S. academy. The study of Latin American "others" originated from the vantage of U.S. political and economic hegemony in the region. U.S. cold-war ideology, which coincided with the destruction of the final structures of formal colonialism, framed history as the struggle between the "free West" led by the United States and the "Communist East," which could crop up anywhere, especially in Latin America after the "fall" of Cuba (Kearney 1996:31). Ironically, in this era that was supposed to mark a new world order (after colonialism), the United States continued to maintain a colonial presence in Puerto Rico and the Virgin Islands. Puerto Ricans have been U.S. citizens since 1917, yet the island continues as a U.S. territory and political debate between statehood, status quo, and independence is ongoing.

One of the paths for orchestrated efforts at preventing communism involved the invention of area studies – in this case, Latin American Studies: the creation of academic regional specialists and institutes devoted to the study of the history, economics, politics, sociology, and anthropology of Latin America, as well as the financial involvement of institutions like the Ford Foundation, the Social Science Research Council, and the American Council of Learned Societies in the region. Area specializations such as Latin American Studies coincided with the rise of a branch of economics known as development economics, focused on "the rescue of the poor countries from their poverty" (Galbraith 1979:26,30, cited in Escobar 1995:67). If poor countries could be rescued from their poverty, the reasoning went, then communist-inspired

governments and movements had a lesser chance of gaining a toehold in Latin America and elsewhere. Latin American countries, like others in the "Third World," were to be salvaged, managed, and fixed:

> In sum, the major ingredients of the economic development strategy commonly advocated in the 1950s were these: (1) capital accumulation; (2) deliberate industrialization; (3) development planning; and (4) external aid. The underdeveloped economies were thought to be characterized by a number of features that set them apart from the economies studied by orthodox economics... high levels of rural underemployment, a low level of industrialization, a set of obstacles to industrial development, and a disadvantage in international trade. (Escobar 1995:74–75)

Family planning was also seen as integral to ameliorating social problems that originated in the economy, and as early as 1965 a Pan-American Congress identified population increases in the region as too high compared to other regions (Stycos et al. 1971:26). Puerto Rico in particular also became a testing ground for contraceptive drugs and birth-control programs, informed by social science research in the region (López 1993).

In order to repair and control Latin American countries, great quantities of information had to be gathered and organized according to formulas for improvement. For some, Latin America and the Caribbean were viewed as post-World War II social science laboratories for U.S. academics to test out paradigms such as W. W. Rostow's (1960) stages of economic growth in Latin America, and ways to prevent "communist takeovers." One project in particular, described below, became famous and helped to move forward a current in Latin American Studies that was critical of U.S. foreign policy in the region.

Project Camelot, started in 1963 and funded through the Special Operations Research Organization (SORO – a campus-based contract research organization that serviced the Defense Department's research effort), was aimed at combating Soviet-inspired "wars of national liberation" and had a special focus on Latin America (Herman 1995:154–155). This non-profit organization was dedicated to conducting "non-material research in support of the Department of the Army's missions in such fields as counterinsurgency, unconventional warfare, psychological operations, and military assistance," and the research was aimed at producing a model of a "social system experiencing internal war accurate enough to be predictive, and therefore useful, to military policy planners" (Herman 1995:155, 156). Project Camelot was exposed when anthropologist Hugo Nutini lied to Chilean scholars about the funding for the project, and this information was contradicted by a Norwegian sociologist who provided information about the project's military funding to Chilean journalists. The project was publicly denounced in a special session of the Chilean senate and was eventually cancelled. This provided an ample political opening for Latin Americanist experts who disagreed with the interventionist nature of U.S. foreign policy to gain public attention and establish a position within the field of Latin American Studies.

In looking at the important trends in the first decades of the development of the field of Latin American Studies, it would be a mistake only to focus on the efforts coming out of the United States. The interdisciplinary focus of Latin American Studies was strengthened early on in Latin America through the founding of innovative research centers and organizations such as the Latin American Faculty for Social Sciences (FLACSO – founded in 1957) in Chile, Argentina, Brazil, Costa Rica, Cuba, the Dominican Republic, Ecuador, El Salvador, Guatemala, and Mexico; the Latin American Council of Social Sciences (CLACSO – founded in 1967) in Argentina; the Brazilian Center for Analysis and Planning (CEBRAP – founded in 1969) in Brazil; the Center for Research and Advanced Studies in Social Anthropology (CIESAS – founded in 1973) in Mexico; the Center for Social Investigations (CIS – founded in 1942) at the University of Puerto Rico, and Casa de las Américas in Cuba (founded in 1959), among others. These think-tanks often involved groups of scholars who theorized about the relationship between different aspects of social, cultural, political, and economic life. Influential theory developed within these research centers often made its way into the U.S. academy from the south to the north, although not always with its Latin American intellectual history intact.

For example, many U.S. academics identify dependency theory as a unified strand of theory that became accessible to North American readers through the work of Andre Gunder Frank (1967, 1969), Paul Baran (1957), and Theotonio Dos Santos (1970). In fact, the roots of "dependency theory" can be found in the late 1940s and early 1950s in Latin America through the analysis based on Prebisch, Furtado, and others before them who opposed "orthodox" theories "justifying the nonindustrialization of the region in view of the comparative advantages that might be obtained with agricultural production for export" (Cardoso 1977:9). In an article on the intellectual history of dependency theory in Latin America, Fernando Henrique Cardoso describes what he calls the U.S. "consumption of dependency theory" and documents how critiques of the developmentalist approach existed within the Economic Commission for Latin America, ECLA (founded in 1948, now called Comisión Económica para América Latina y el Caribe) itself, and also in the work of intellectuals who emphasized "not only the 'obstacles' and 'distortions' of capitalist development... but also the inequality of opportunities and wealth that was inherent in forms of development derived from the expansion of capitalism and the strengthening of imperialism" (1977:9). Cardoso points out that what became identified as "dependency theory" has continuity with earlier critiques of structural-functionalism and Keynesianism in Latin America.

As understood by most American academics, dependency theory turned the logic of underdevelopment economics on its head and looked at how the assumptions of development economics (capital accumulation, industrialization, development of markets) instead resulted in the extraction of economic value away from the periphery (Latin America) and directed it toward the core of the capitalist world system (the United States and Europe). Processes of underdevelopment often replicated those internal processes in Third World countries between the capital and outlying areas, and between European-oriented elites and indigenous peoples (Weismantel 2001). The results of this kind of "development" were dependency and, in fact, de-development accompanied by racialization and denigration toward rural, indigenous peoples.

Latin American and U.S. versions of dependency theory were not the only critiques leveled at the U.S.-centered vision of Latin American Studies, packaged in cold-war ideology. As early as the late 1950s and consolidated by the mid-1960s, a stream of scholarship critical of U.S. foreign policy in Latin America, beginning with Cuba, emerged within the field of Latin American Studies. Publications such as the *North American Congress on Latin America (NACLA)'s Report on the Americas* was founded in 1966 as a newsletter with the purpose of communicating major political, economic, and social trends in Latin America and their relationships to the United States. Early issues featured a strong critique of U.S. hegemony in the region and included pieces by prominent scholars in Latin American Studies as well as non-academics. In 1969 the NACLA newsletters featured articles such as "The Proletarianzation of the Puerto Rican," "The U.S. Media Empire in Latin America," and "USAID Spurs Population Relocation in Northeast Brazil." *Latin American Perspectives*, an academic areas studies publication, was founded in 1973 and first published in 1974 to provide a forum for debate on the political economy of capitalism, imperialism, and socialism in the Américas – also a perspective critical of U.S. foreign policy. The first issue contained articles titled "Socialism and Dependency" and "The Future of Latin America: Between Underdevelopment and Revolution," among others. In addition to publishing in these two critical venues, some Latin American Studies scholars were involved in founding and building solidarity organizations with links to labor, students, peasants, women, and political parties in Chile, El Salvador, Nicaragua, Guatemala, and elsewhere. Such political work also spilled over into Latin American Studies Association (LASA)

sessions in the 1970s and 1980s when the politicization of the Central American wars pushed LASA to the left. A multitude of academic sessions were devoted to critiquing the role of the United States in Central America and often brought Central American activists and politicians to meetings, as well as academics. Since the 1970s, some Latin Americanists were also involved in political work dedicated to Puerto Rican independence and promoted the concept of internal colonialism in their work.

Two developments in the 1980s were crucial to the further development of Latin American Studies in Latin America and its turn toward the study of history and culture in the social sciences in both the United States and Latin America – a key focus of this book. The first is the emergence of the field of Cultural Studies, in part as a response to the commodification of culture in late capitalism. As pointed out by John Beverly, "although Cultural Studies, particularly in its poststructuralist or Birmingham strands, has been politically connected with the Left and the new social movements, it also depends on the character and possibilities of capitalist production and circulation of commodities; it is something like a superstructural effect of economic deterritorialization" (1996:221). Thus the trajectory of capitalist development itself contributed to the integration of culture with political economy. In addition, the economic paradigm of what came to be called dependency theory, while certainly challenging modernist economic theory, did not work well in the realm of culture. Theorists such as Claudia Ferman (1966:ix) have pointed out that while terms such as "center" and "periphery" may describe some of the political and economic power of Latin American reality, they cannot express the nature of cultural production. "Cultural productions are neither 'central' nor 'peripheral' . . . from the standpoint of the producers and consumers of that cultural production, that product is always central" (1996:ix). Latin American Cultural Studies (as in other regions) not only decentered political economy as the main category of analysis in social sciences, but also redefined what is meant by culture. The distinction between "high culture," which usually represented the domain of European elite artistic traditions, has been blurred with "low culture," often designated as "handicrafts," "folklore," and "folk art." Discussions of culture in Latin American Studies now include a wide range of indigenous and hybrid cultural forms, from *corridos* (northern Mexican folk ballads) to comic books, to the art of Diego Rivera or Frida Kahlo.

The second development that was significant in refashioning the social sciences in Latin America was a questioning and redefining of the socialist political project in Latin America not only by intellectuals, but also by grass-roots movement activists such as feminists, indigenous groups, and others (see Escobar and Alvarez 1992; Slater 1985; Stephen 1997). In Latin American countries that lived under military dictatorships, such as Brazil, Chile, Argentina, and Uruguay in the 1970s, a key concern of social scientists became working toward and understanding processes of democratization, not the development of socialism under impossible conditions. Most evident in places like Pinochet's Chile, economic modernization – particularly in relation to a neo-liberal model – did not accompany democracy, as economic modernization proponents often argued. The cultural realm of politics and social conditions for democracy were deemed to be perhaps more important than economic models for dismantling military dictatorships. John Beverly and José Oviedo point out:

> What began to displace both modernization and dependency models, therefore, was an interrogation of the interrelation between the respective spheres (culture, ethnic, politics, etc.) of modernity, an interrogation that required of social scientists a new concern with subjectivity and identity as well as new understandings of, and tolerance for, the cultural, religious, and ethnic heterogeneity of Latin America. (1995:7)

As a part of the trend toward looking at issues of democratization and economic development, beginning in the mid-1970s, a significant group of women scholars emerged in the field of Latin American Studies who opened the door to later research focused on gender and sexuality. The seminal work of researchers such as Carmen Diana Deere and Magdalena Léon de Leal[7] in Peru and Colombia showed how monetization of local economies and the entrance of commercial capital affected different classes of women in distinct ways. Their work pushed others to look at women not just as a homogenous category, but also in relation to class and ethnicity. Two other major books, edited by June Nash and Helen Safa (1976, 1986), provided a comparative basis for understanding gender and class in Latin America. Other researchers built on this and integrated an analysis of ethnicity into their work, as well as taking on questions of gender and class (see Bourque and Warren 1981; Babb 1989; Silverblatt 1987; Stephen 1991). Since the mid-1980s, women's studies and gender studies have emerged as one of the strongest components of Latin American Studies, taking on masculinity and masculine sexuality (Gutmann 1996; Kulick 1998; Lancaster 1992; Prieur 1998; Quiroga 2001), as well as historically examining issues such as sexuality, marriage, gender roles, and nationalism (Dore and Molyneux 2000; Matos Rodríguez and Delgado 1998; Suarez-Findlay 1999; Summer 1991).

During the 1990s, social scientists working in Latin American Studies embraced a wide range of subjects that strongly confirmed the globalization of the subject. There is a concern with identities and subjectivities, a broad definition of politics that includes social movements and grass-roots organizations as well as the politics within the home, the community, and in formal political systems, a focus on transnational economies, and concerns about democracy and citizenship (Gutmann 2002). Perhaps more relevant to our anthology, recently Latin American Studies has become concerned with migration throughout the region, especially northward toward the U.S. and Canada (Bonilla 1992), although the consequences of Latino settlement are among many contemporary issues in an era of globalization.

Latina/o Studies: Foundations and Innovations

Latina/o Studies had its origins in student activism and identity politics of the 1960s, led by Chicanas/os and Puerto Ricans. In the late

1960s, the struggle of activists and scholars led to the creation of Chicana/o and Puerto Rican Studies departments, student support programs, and research centers within academia. By the 1990s, in response to the demographic and political shifts discussed below, some of these programs would broaden to include Latinas/os, or to focus on the Caribbean and/or Hispanic Studies more broadly.

In the late 1960s, student organizations such as the United Mexican American Students (UMAS), the Movimiento Estudiantil Chicano de Aztlán (MEChA), the Puerto Rican Student Movement (PRSM), and the Puerto Rican Student Union (PRSU) were active in campus politics, and they explicitly sought coalitions with student organizations from other racialized groups. Students demonstrated so that colleges and universities would offer courses that were relevant to their lives, recruit Latino faculty and staff who could serve as mentors and role models, facilitate open admissions, and commit to making college education accessible to students who had come from working-class barrios. Both MEChA and PRSU maintained ties to political organizations in Mexico and Puerto Rico, respectively, anticipating the cross-border perspective that would emerge later in Latina/o Studies (Muñoz 1989; Serrano 1998; Torres 1998).

The rationale for developing Chicana/o and Puerto Rican Studies departments and programs was to promote the link between knowledge and social action, especially addressing the socioeconomic problems faced by Chicana/o and Puerto Rican communities, and to study the particular experiences of these communities in the United States. The *Plan de Santa Bárbara*, for example, drafted by student and faculty activists in 1969, called for Chicano Studies programs throughout the Southwest and made explicit the connection between activism and scholarship through action research:

> How can the university contribute to the liberation of the Chicano people? In the long term, probably the most fundamental contribution it will make will be by producing knowledge applicable by the Chicano movement. The systemic character of

the racist relationship between *gabacho* [white] society and Chicanos will not be altered unless solid research becomes the basis for Chicano political strategy and action. (Chicano Council on Higher Education 1970:70)

However, the nationalism of the *Plan* and other movement documents, especially its model of *la familia* with its masculinist, heteronormative assumptions, were contested by those who called for broad-based political agendas that included women, gay men, and lesbians (Blackwell forthcoming; García 1989, 1997). In New York, the creation of Puerto Rican Studies departments and an open admissions policy were among the achievements of Puerto Rican students and activists within the City University of New York (CUNY). In 1973, CUNY's Center for Puerto Rican Studies was initiated to "create new knowledge and quickly and comprehensibly transfer it to a long denied community" (Committee for Puerto Rican Studies and Research 1972:3).

Chicana/o and Puerto Rican Studies programs were designed to push for the transformation of higher education, including through professional associations, from an elitist, racist, and hierarchical institution to one that served the concrete needs of these communities. The National Association for Chicana and Chicano Studies (NACCS), for example, founded in 1972, drew the connection explicitly between activism and research, which includes the critique of research paradigms and the importance of ideological struggle:

> NACCS recognizes the broader scope and significance of Chicana and Chicano research. We cannot overlook the crucial role of ideas in the construction and legitimization of social reality. Dominant theories, ideologies, and perspectives play a significant part in maintaining oppressive structures on theoretical, experiential, and policy levels. NACCS fosters the construction of theories and perspectives which attempt to explain the oppression and resistance of the Chicana and Chicano past, present, and future. Ideas must be translated into political

action in order to foster change. (National Association for Chicana and Chicano Studies website: http://latino.sscnet.ucla.edu/research/NACCS/)

Such goals could not be more different from the initial purpose of Latin American Studies, aimed to develop experts and institutes to collect information to maintain U.S. political and economic hegemony over Latin America and the Caribbean.

Eventually, over twenty-five programs in Chicano, Hispanic, Mexican American, or Puerto Rican Studies and fewer than ten joint programs that include one of these with a Latin American Studies program were established and contributed to the scholarly development of the field. For example, the Chicano Studies Department at the University of California, Santa Barbara (founded in 1969, based on the *Plan de Santa Bárbara* and thus one of the oldest programs) has an endowed chair, a research center, and a library collection devoted to Chicana/o Studies. The interdisciplinary curriculum focuses on gender, culture, and institutions, and in 2001 the department established the first Ph.D. program in Chicana/o Studies. Although there has been expansion and development in Chicano/Puerto Rican Studies, the current political climate has affected many departments. For example, the Puerto Rican Studies Department at City College (CUNY), which was founded in 1971 under the auspices of substantial student activism, was downsized to a small program in the 1990s.

There were some similarities in development and origins between Latin American Studies and Latina/o Studies. Both fields were multidisciplinary and had a primary focus on history and culture. Like Latin American Studies, Chicana/o and Puerto Rican Studies initially had a heavy emphasis on political economy and development. Influenced by Fanon (1963, 1965) and by Marxist historical materialism (Flores 1986), Chicana/o and Puerto Rican scholars interrogated the "internal colonies" theoretical paradigm which found structural similarities between Blacks, Chicanos, Puerto Ricans, and Native Americans (Almaguer 1975; Barrera et al. 1972; Bonilla and Campos 1981). Scholars began researching and

recovering histories left in the margins by dominant paradigms, and interpreting them from a revisionist perspective (Acuña 1972; Almaguer 1994; Camarillo 1979; Gutiérrez 1991; Gutiérrez 1995; Montejano 1987; Paredes 1958; Sánchez and Stevens-Arroyo 1987; Sánchez Korrol 1983). In addition to the mission of action research, Chicana/o and Puerto Rican studies were concerned early on with notions of borders. Indeed, within Chicana/o Studies, the notion that "we didn't cross the border, the border crossed us" (Acuña 1996:109; Paredes 1993), after the U.S.–Mexico war which ceded about half of Mexico to the United States, is paradigmatic. Contesting the masculine bias in the early revisionist historical and social scientific research, feminists began focusing on the experience of women (de la Torre and Pesquera 1993; Gonzalez 1999; Matos Rodríguez and Delgado 1998; MALCS 1993; Ortiz 1996; Pérez 1999; Ruiz 1987; Zavella 1987).

Literature also played a key role as a new generation of Chicano and Puerto Rican writers communicated their experiences through poetry and prose. This literature, often angry and abrasive, commented on and reflected on the problems of poverty, marginalization, and discrimination faced by Latinos/as. The students and scholars who founded Chicano and Puerto Rican Studies programs revered texts like Rodolfo "Corky" Gonzales's *Yo soy Joaquín* and Pedro Pietris's *Puerto Rican Obituary*. These authors had their counterparts in the writers of the "boom" generation in Latin America, such as Gabriel García Márquez, Julio Cortázar, and Alejo Carpentier, among others.

Similar to Latin American Studies, Latina/o Studies was also heavily influenced by the emergence of Cultural Studies, especially by feminists and gay and lesbian theorists. Lesbian feminist Gloria Anzaldúa (1987) offers a theory of *mestizaje*, hybridity, and the "borderlands" as a geopolitical site of poverty and racism, "*una herida abierta* [open wound] where the Third World grates against the first and bleeds," as well as fluid processes of consciousness and identity formation. Her work has been influential in Latin American Studies as well as Latina/o Studies (Mignolo 2000; Saldívar 1997; Saldívar-Hull

2000; Vélez-Ibáñez 1996). In another critical intervention, Rosa Linda Fregoso and Angie Chabram Denersesian critiqued the nationalist, masculinist assumptions implicit in Chicana/o movement discourse, that of a unitary subject:

> Our reframing of Chicano cultural identity draws from those theoretical insights elaborated by Hall and through which he reconstitutes cultural identity within the problematics of difference production, and positionality.... We seek therefore to recuperate that which was silenced by both the Chicano movement and cultural movements such as poststructuralism, and to give voice to historically persistent forms and practices of resistance of our own people. This enunciation is necessary if cultural studies are to begin to respond effectively to the complexities of a historical experience, fissured by race, class and gender, by linguistic discourses, and which are constructed by myriad cultural forms, some incorporated, others not fully incorporated. (1990:205, 207)

Puerto Rican scholars were also concerned with borders, fueled by the frequent migrations between the United States and Puerto Rico, as well as the great waves of migration and settlement of Puerto Ricans in the United States. Puerto Rican feminist scholars have also analyzed critically the rich cultural metaphors for the frequent moves between the island and the mainland, such as *la guagua aérea* ("airborne bus"), or "salsa" to name the style of Caribbean diasporic music based on mixture, hybridity, and creative energy that emerged in the late 1960s (Aparicio 1988).

Latina/o scholars have long been interested in diversity, notably among the experiences of migrants (Chavez 1991; Hondagneu-Sotelo 1994) and between migrants and those of multiple generations of settlement in the United States (Browning and De La Garza 1986; Portes and Rumbaut 2001). Another key issue has been how language use – whether Spanish-dominant, bilingual, or English-dominant – is constructed in response to locale, the presence of varied language groups, or assimilationist pressures in schools (Pedraza 1985; Zentella 1997 and in this volume). The imbrication of gender, race, ethnicity, class, sexual preference, generation, etc., makes for different social locations among Latinas/os (Zavella 1994), and there has been a wealth of work which interrogates this diversity or focuses on particular communities (Trujillo 1991).

Like Latin American Studies, Latino Studies was always interdisciplinary and inherently also challenged the ways that university bureaucracies defined the production and reproduction of knowledge outside of traditional departments. In particular, the experiences of the Chicana/o and Puerto Rican populations in the United States could not be understood without reconceptualizing the paradigms, methodology, and pedagogy inherited from traditional departments and from area studies.

Nonetheless, problems and tensions emerged within Latina/o Studies programs. As new groups migrated to the United States from Latin America – notably those from El Salvador and Guatemala to the west coast, and Colombia or the Dominican Republic to the east coast – students increasingly wanted Latina/o Studies to incorporate their experiences. Some programs eventually expanded their focus: the Department of Hispanic and Caribbean (formerly Puerto Rican) Studies at Rutgers University, or the Department of Raza (formerly Chicano) Studies at San Francisco State University are but two examples. At other universities, research institutes such as CUNY's Dominican Studies Institute (1994) emerged to help address the needs of Dominican students and scholars.

Other tensions are more endemic. Some of the migrants from South America or Cuba come from middle-class or elite-class backgrounds with more conservative political viewpoints, and often cannot relate to the Latino migrants from peasant or working-class origins who often are more radical in outlook. In multiethnic contexts like large cities, Latina/os from diverse national/ethnic backgrounds living in close proximity often have to negotiate stereotypes, prejudice toward, or differences in material resources accorded those who migrated earlier, even among members of their own group (Aparicio 2000; Torres 1998). Sexism and homophobia have been flash points of conflict, where feminists and gay and lesbian scholars and activists have had to push Latina/o Studies programs or professional associations to be more inclusive. In other cases, women have formed their own organizations, such as Mujeres Activas en Letras y Cambio Social (MALCS, "Activist Women in Letters and Social Change"), founded in 1983 in support of scholarship and professional development of Latinas. Indeed, some scholars question whether a common Latino experience really exists (Delgado 2001). Others, notably feminists of diverse backgrounds, have problematized differences and constructed a relational theoretical framework on Pan-Latina identities:

> [O]ur collaborative process, which used the method of *testimonio* [life story], ultimately, was framed by common political views about how to create knowledge and theory through our experiences.... Seeking to contest and transform the very disciplines that taught us the skills to recover our subjugated knowledges, we reclaimed *testimonio* as a tool for Latinas to theorize oppression, resistance, and subjectivity. Despite its complicated history, *testimonio* captures Latinas' complex, layered lives.... Our group histories and lived experiences are intertwined with global legacies of resistance to colonialism, imperialism, racism, anti-Semitism, religious fundamentalism, sexism and heterosexism. When theorizing about feminist *latinidades* [Latina/o identities], we reveal the interrelationships among these systems of power. Trained as critical thinkers, we are forced to acknowledge that occasionally institutions or discourses about which we are critical, such as religion or the family, produce contradictory effects on us, serving as sources of disempowerment and autonomy, repression and privilege. (Latina Feminist Group 2001:8, 17, 19)

Clearly the work of documenting and theorizing Latina/o experiences is producing innovations within academia beyond what the original student organizers had envisioned.

Dialogues and Collaboration between Latina/o and Latin American Studies: Possibilities and Limits

Despite the different histories and shifting concerns, there are a number of important reasons for Latin Americanists and Latina/o Studies scholars to collaborate. Perhaps the most important is the increase in migration from Latin America to the United States and Canada (as mentioned previously). Latinos and people in Latin America share common experiences under neo-liberal economic models, which have led to greater socioeconomic stratification within the United States and within Latin American countries. There is evidence, for example, that the North American Free Trade Agreement (NAFTA, implemented in 1994) led to an increase in the number of U.S. firms in some sectors that moved production to Mexico, which has led to increased unemployment and poverty among Latinas/os who worked in those sectors (Borrego 2000; Zavella 2000b). Increased globalization of the economy has led to concentration of more recent immigrants in the United States and within Latin America in the service sector, as well as the feminization of labor markets. Both fields consider it important to distinguish experience by race, ethnicity, class, gender, and sexuality. When particular types of migrants – young male workers, for example – move between the United States and Latin America, there are repercussions on both sides of the border. While return migration, and migration with Latin America has not been a high priority topic in Latin American Studies, it should be, and much could be learned from U.S. Latino/a Studies. Moreover, both approaches find it necessary to look at culture and political economy together. Through transnational cultural expressions such as music, dance, film, websites, magazines, etc., transnational community connections are constructed. Human rights activists in the United States increasingly must contend with discrimination and abuse endured by migrants, and grass-roots movements for social justice – environmental racism, labor, etc. – must negotiate working with multiracial coalitions that include migrants (Delgado 1993; Milkman 2000; Milkman and Wong 2000; Pulido 1996; Soldatenko 1991; Stephen 2001b).

The many changes brought on by globalization and transnational migration have led some analysts to reconceptualize the world of the Latino in the United States. As far back as 1958, for example, Américo Paredes suggested the concept of "greater Mexico" to illustrate how Mexicanos' cultural expressions transcend national boundaries. David Gutiérrez (1998:327) suggests that we consider Latino migrants as living in a "transterritorial third space carved out between the political and social worlds of the United States," in which cities such as Los Angeles in California, Las Cruces and Santa Fe in New Mexico, and Yuma in Arizona, and significant parts of Chicago and New York are firmly rooted in the circuits of Latin America. Indeed, De Genova suggests that south–north migration has led to the "reinvention of Latin America" in relation to racial categories and the use of space in places like "Mexican Chicago," where "something about Chicago itself has become elusive, even irretrievable, for the U.S. nation-state" and Chicago has a "proper place within Latin America" (1998:89–90). These new ways of thinking about Latinas/os and Latin America have led scholars to integrate scholarly work from both fields, and to problematize what a cross-border perspective entails (Romero et al. 1997; Darder and Torres 1998; Bonilla et al. 1998; Gutmann 1999, 2003).

Beyond globalization and transnationalization, there are other significant commonalities that should encourage dialogue between Latin American and Caribbean Studies. Both fields are inherently interdisciplinary and have consciously drawn on an integrated understanding of history, culture, language, and political economy in order to provide holistic perspectives on the lives of Latin Americans and Latinos. As interdisciplinary fields, both have had to defend their existence in the context of academic institutions that tend to support conventional disciplines and departments over interdisciplinary ones. In the words of Peter Smith, "interdisciplinary work has come to be viewed as 'undisciplined.' . . . We are jacks of all trades, but masters

of none . . . It is perhaps in reflection of this view that, at the end of the day, deans and provosts tend to support mainstream departments rather than interdisciplinary programs" (Smith 2002:8). While Smith does not advocate dialogue between Latino and Latin American Studies, his remarks suggest the importance of such programs working together within academic institutions to mutually support one another and emphasize the contributions of an interdisciplinary approach in two fields that now have some significant issues in common.

Possibilities for dialogue across Latino and Latin American Studies also depend on the willingness of academics in each field to learn each other's intellectual history and to look for common experiences. As discussed above, both Latin American Studies and Latino Studies have an intellectual history that involves academics also becoming activists and serving as "agents of solidarity" in movements within the United States and south of the border (see Arias 2002:3). Both fields also struggle with a dual tension between "nationalisms" that may pressure their disintegration from within and "transnationalisms" that can cause their validity as regions to be questioned from the outside. Some examples: the Latin American Studies Association long organized panels in relation to specific countries (Mexico, Peru, etc.), yet members pushed for sections organized around themes that cross national boundaries. The increasing diversity of Latin American immigration to the United States has forced Latina/o Studies to incorporate more national differences within what is labeled "Latina/o," to the chagrin of some nationalists. Thus both fields continue to deal with the issue of nationalism and national identity, despite the fact that population and cultural movements across regions and nations have muddled some nationalist categories. The nationalist tension within each field is further countered by "demographic shifts, diasporas, labor migrations, the movements of global capital and media, and processes of cultural circulation and hybridization that have brought into question the nature of areas' identities and composition" (Arias 2002:3).

This dual tension shared by Latina/o Studies and Latin American Studies has the further result of decentering the United States as the primary focus of economic, political, and cultural life in the Américas. Seeing Chicago and Los Angeles as part of Latin America (as now proposed by some in Latina/o Studies) and looking at how music created in the Caribbean has influenced Latin American and U.S. culture are strategies for counteracting U.S. influences in the Américas.

There are also issues that make it difficult to dialogue between Latina/o and Latin American Studies. The political history of U.S.–Latin American and Caribbean relations and the continued economic and political domination of the United States makes for privileges in the United States that are not equally shared in Latin America. And within the United States, Latino immigrants have often not shared equally in U.S. economic and political gains. For example, the history of how U.S. immigration policy often has been a labor policy clearly relates to the particular experience of Latinos in the United States and is an important part of Latino Studies. Latin American Studies has neglected the issue of immigration until recently, failing to look seriously at immigration within Latin America as well as the United States, what happens to return migrants, and the impact of outmigration on Latin American communities and cities.

Building historical memory in students and activists that acknowledges U.S. dominance in the region and the continuing internal colonialism of Latinos in the United States is important for students of Latina/o Studies and of Latin American Studies. The teaching of this history can involve different perspectives and tensions that can be difficult to translate across the two fields. The particular histories of Latina/o struggles and social movements, while sometimes linked, are distinct from those in Latin America and need to have a particular place in the history of the United States and of the Américas – they cannot be collapsed into other kinds of activism. In the same way, the history of social movements and struggles in Latin America cannot be fitted into categories and analysis based on a U.S. Latino experience. For example, the student movement in Mexico City in 1968 is distinct from the Chicano Student movement in the United States which occurred at the same time. Further, there is continued dis-

criminatory politics in the nation, seen in legislation in the United States against Latinos (such as California Proposition 187 and English-only proposals). The efforts on the part of universities and colleges to collapse Latina/o, Chicana/o, Puerto Rican Studies, etc., into "Ethnic Studies" and to move Latino student organizations into a "multicultural" center or institutes all reflect assimilation pressures in the academy. It is vital that Latina/o Studies and other similar programs remain alive and well to provide support for students and communities. Likewise, Latin American Studies programs are also going through difficult times and have to respond to other factors that may result in their demise – such as the end of the Cold War, the process of globalization, and the investment in traditional departments within universities (Smith 2002:8).

Nevertheless, the two fields have a common set of issues that suggest it is worthwhile for their practitioners to continue dialoguing with one another. What is needed to facilitate such a dialogue is a process of cultural and political translation, as stated by Sonia Alvarez:

> more productive hemispheric dialogues can only be fostered through sustained processes of cultural, political and disciplinary translation. It is all too easy for scholars and activists to have conversations in which they assume that they are speaking the same language (broadly defined), when subsequent misunderstandings reveal that they are not. A more deliberate focus on the recognition of different frameworks will help to overcome both linguistic differences (which remain a major issue) and to address conceptual translation needs that are often ignored or underestimated, affecting both scholarly conversations and activist-research dialogues. (2001:17)

In *Las Américas*, then, we include articles that illustrate the internal differences among Latinas/os and Latin Americans but also provide material for translating between the two fields and providing bridges for analyses of history, culture, and/or political economy that advance the dialogue between scholars of Latina/o and Latin American Studies. In that effort, we need to work to tease out the specific conceptual obstacles to translation between the two fields and look toward ways of talking across them. In this introductory article we do not provide the answers to how to engage in that process, but leave our readers with an invitation to do so as they read this book.[8]

The Readings: An Overview

Part I: Colonialism and Resistance

The integration of the region we are calling the Américas has resulted from a long historical process with profound roots in the legacy of colonialism. The readings in this Part I explore and analyze, in broad dimensions, this legacy. Some of the readings, such as those by Alarcón, Benítez Rojo, Rodríguez, and Stern, also document the strong elements of resistance that structures of political, economic, racial, and gender hierarchies have imposed in the region. In many cases, popular resistance has served as a mechanism to redefine, minimize, or rearticulate the oppression created by those hierarchies. Still, the structures of neocolonialism and global capital today are linked to the region's past and they continue to shape the most important contours of the region.

Norma Alarcón's article connects the organizing themes of Part I. She discusses the contemporary interpretations and the double etymology developed by Mexican and Chicano/a scholars regarding Malintzin or "La Malinche," as she is better known. Alarcón stresses how Malintzin's role as translator of Hernán Cortes and her relationship to language – her efforts to speak for and appropriate language for herself – have made her a scapegoat and a traitor to the Mexican people. Translation, the difficult art of redefinition and moving between two cultures, is often devalued as impure and corrupting. This is also what can happen when one represents an experience that has been marginalized or misrepresented. For Alarcón, Malintzin's story is a reminder of the mark of violence, particularly against women, in the origins of Mexico's history. "La Malinche" has also been a symbol that was rejected by leaders of the early Chicano movement and then more recently embraced and redefined by Chicana feminists. Connecting to

one of the themes of the reader – the areas of tension and possibility between disciplines and methodologies – Alarcón closes her article with a discussion of how postmodern analysis might not be an effective tool for those in solidarity with women of color, particularly with Chicanas.

The exploits of the "conquistadors" in the Andes and in Mexico in the sixteenth and seventeenth centuries caused the need for the redefinition of the strategic and economic value of the Caribbean within Spanish colonialism. Antonio Benítez-Rojo begins with a discussion of the different competing theories regarding the existence of the Caribbean as a coherent region. The plantation – with its hierarchies based on race, politics, ethnicity, and gender – serves as the central focus of analysis for demarcating both unity and diversity in the region. Although sugar and slavery serve as starting point for any coherent history of the Caribbean, Benítez-Rojo points out the importance of the timing of the development of large-scale sugar production as a key marker of difference and similarity in the region. The strength of "criollo" culture, and the level of Africanization in each Caribbean island, for example, are tied to the "epoch in which the Plantation took over within" each island. Finally, if the plantation and contraband trade could have served as potential organizing metaphors for the Caribbean in the seventeenth, eighteenth, and nineteenth centuries, perhaps the resort hotels and drug trafficking will serve that role in the twenty-first century.

Steve Stern's article provides a synopsis of the major trends in the study of peasantries and agrarian conflict in the Andes since the 1950s. Peasant societies in Latin America and elsewhere have been paradigmatic in the study of resistance to modernization. Stern discusses several of the key assumptions that most peasantry scholars have held, including the view that the modern political history of countries with large peasantries has been significantly affected by the political resolution of agrarian conflicts. One of the important contributions of Stern's article is his call to incorporate the analysis of preexisting patterns of "resistant adaptation" to any theories or explanations related to peasant behavior. Failure to do this leads to essentializing peasants and agrarian societies as parochial, defensive, and static. Stern makes several methodological suggestions for further study, including the need to conceptualize peasant consciousness as problematic and to scrutinize the local cultural history of the region studied. Finally, Stern's article encourages area study specialists to think out of the regional "boxes" to explore how the Andean experience can contribute to the study of peasants and agrarian unrest elsewhere in the world.

In his article, Néstor Rodríguez discusses the effects of economic globalization and international migration on intergroup racial and ethnic relations in the United States. He also calls for incorporating a global perspective into the sociological study of such relations. Rodríguez identifies at least three new developments affecting these: the creation of massive global diasporas moving from peripheral countries into the industrialized Western core; the new global–urban context of relations among ethnic and racial groups, particularly in cities and their suburbs; and the growth of a binational Latino immigrant community. One of the new features of this new global reality for Rodríguez is the role played by human agency. He sees this agency as dismissive of the efforts by states and intergovernmental programs to attempt to control migratory and labor flows, and as a sign of a popular struggle to reconfigure the spatial and economic divisions dictated by global capital. Finally, Rodríguez argues that any new intergroup relational theory that fails to address transnationalism will be unable to capture the complex and fluid situation of the United States.

We close Part I with an essay by Rubén Rumbaut documenting the history of Caribbean and Latin American immigration to the United States. Although some of the figures given by Rumbaut will be superseded by those released by the U.S. Census Bureau in the years 2002–2003, his analysis of the impact and trajectory of Latin American immigration remains highly relevant. Rumbaut also discusses the causes – social networks, state immigration policies, demography, economic inequality between countries, and U.S. expansion and intervention in the region, among others – that motivate the flow of people between the Americas. He also problematizes the terms "Hispanic" or "Latino/a" because they conceal great diversity in national, generation, class, and racial origins, legal status, mode of incorporation, and the reasons for migration and/or circulation. Still, he provides some socioeconomic data for the different Latino/a groups, such as education, income, and labor participation, and concludes with a discussion of Spanish language use and retention. Rumbaut's chapter also serves to contextualize many of the arguments presented in the introduction to this reader.

Part II: Global Political Economy

In Part II we provide a few examples of the global political economy of the Américas with a particular interest in the social economics of production and reproduction in the region. We also provide examples of how the insertion of different Latin American countries – Nicaragua (Edelman), Puerto Rico (Matos Rodríguez), and Chile, Mexico, and Brazil (Collins) – into different economic systems, such as slavery, industrial capitalism, and global capitalism, for example, had dramatic influences in their class, ethnic, racial, and gender structures. In Fonseca's chapter on Brazil, we also explore the way in which the political economy of the region affects structures, such as the family, often considered non-economic.

In his article, Matos Rodríguez analyzes the role that domestic work and urban slavery played in the process of the abolition of slavery in Puerto Rico. He discusses the importance that colonial authorities and the local urban elites gave to their perceived domestic labor shortage problem in San Juan and other cities. The evidence from continuous specific work regulations, the pro-abolition literature and propaganda, the struggles and frictions with colonial authorities, and the connections with the development of beneficent institutions all indicate that the concern regarding domestic work – although virtually forgotten in Puerto Rican historiography – was far from marginal in the island's economic, political, and social processes during the second half of the nineteenth century. In most debates regarding the reasons for the abolition of slavery in the Caribbean, gender dynamics are seldom discussed. In the case of Puerto Rico, Matos Rodríguez shows how urban slavery – a segment of the slave economy in which women were a majority – was an important consideration in the debate. The article also shows how gendered language and gender ideology were used by both sides of the abolition debate in Puerto Rico to advance their cause.

Marc Edelman explores the connection between emerging national discourses in Costa Rica and the insertion of Central America into the rubber boom of the mid-nineteenth century. In the region surrounding Lake Nicaragua many Guatusos were killed or enslaved by rubber tappers or *huleros*, as they were called in Spanish. Edelman's article shows how the Guatusos-Malekus indigenous people of southern Nicaragua became commodified as the demand for rubber and slaves intensified and, in the process, became part of the idyllic indigenous past of Costa Rica and a source of contention with Nicaragua. Edelman also shows that there was a convergence of secular, modernizing liberals and pro-clerical conservative forces in Costa Rica who helped to construct and reproduce the location of Guatusos in the national history at a time of border and navigation/commercial disputes with Nicaragua.

The importance of analyzing local structures of inequality and hierarchy in order to understand global dynamics in the structuring of labor markets is argued in Jane Collins's article. Her analysis of the very competitive export agro-industry in Brazil, Chile, and Mexico demonstrates how this industry has both imposed upon and learned from local practices to secure cheap labor. Collins also shows the importance of understanding gender relations to explain global issues in the current political economy of the Américas. Although the export agro-industry has thrived at the expense of cheap female labor, Collins also points out that there are other vulnerable groups – such as immigrants or minorities – who are also exploited, depending on the local labor, social, and political contexts. This article is an excellent example of how to integrate and conceptualize the local and global forces that shape labor relations.

Although most of the chapters in this part deal with specific commodities or with labor systems,

Claudia Fonseca brings in the difficult topic of children as commodities. Her article contrasts Brazil's new adoption policies – emerging from global legal discourses – and its longstanding local adoption practices, particularly among the poor. Fonseca shows how poor Brazilians have developed a system where children are placed in substitute households to accommodate family and individual hardships or crises. In this informal "Brazilian style" of adoption the birth mother is extremely involved in the process. In the legal, state-sanctioned system, birth mothers are asked to deliver their children and are then excluded from the rest of the process. The legal system is also disjointed from a Brazilian society in which legal papers – birth certificates, licenses, and other forms of identification – are rare for most poor people, particularly for children. The 1990 Children's Code, enacted by the Brazilian government as an example of comprehensive social legislation, is more geared toward the adoption by foreigners of Brazilian children and foreign sanction of Brazilian society than to the needs of Brazilian children. The Code's efficacy as a true mechanism to help children and to encourage Brazilians to adopt is severely questioned by Fonseca.

Part III: Identities, Practices, Hybridities

Using a variety of theoretical frameworks, the articles in Part III explore how people in the Américas create hybrid identities or practices in local sites in relation to macro-processes such as globalization, transnational migration, or hemispheric political formations. The impetus for changing identities and the formation of new social lives often are embedded within processes of migration and settlement, whether migrants move within Latin American or Caribbean societies, where historically the overwhelming majority of migrants remain, or make the trek north to the United States. These articles also illustrate human agency, where subjects construct identities in relation to the material and symbolic constraints upon their lives, including negotiating multiple uses of language or accepting/contesting repressive discourses with long histories to make for complex identity formations. Imbrications of difference on the basis of gender, sexuality, generation, race, ethnicity, class, or nation often come into play as individuals or communities negotiate identities and cultural expressions.

Laurie Kroshus Medina's article, "History, Culture, and Place-Making: 'Native' Status and Maya Identity in Belize," explores competing claims to native status by creoles, Garifuna (Afro-Caribs), and mestizos and the implications for the construction of a Pan-Maya identity by Mopan and Kekchi, who claim descent from the ancient Maya. She argues that the practices through which people produce history and place are simultaneously the processes through which they identify themselves as a people. In this complex contestation of identity, she suggests that cultural identification with the territory they have traditionally inhabited often can be seen through attention to the details of "dwelling" in and through particular landscapes. Traditional sustainable agriculture and ecotourism, designed to capitalize on the relatively "unspoiled" Belizean environment and Mayan culture, are moments of uneasy identity closure where differentiation crosscuts specific Mayan identities.

"The Carnivalization of the World," Richard Parker asserts, is a worldview that originates in Brazil's pre-Lenten *carnaval*. He argues that, for Brazilians and foreigners alike, the *carnaval* exemplifies the quintessential Brazilian spirit as well as moments when a "hidden tradition" of sensuality of the body comes into play and an entire society discovers and reinvents itself. The mixture of Amerindian, African, and European cultures influences the play of transvestism, merrymaking, and sensuality, to the point that individual reality and society are transformed so that the masses rule the streets. In this complex series of polymorphous pleasures, the *mulata* is the embodiment of sensuality and a symbol of Brazil itself in her performance of *samba*. Yet the utopian vision of *carnaval* reflects life as it might be rather than the reality of the daily *luta* (struggle).

In "Playing with Fire: The Gendered Construction of Chicana/Mexicana Sexuality," Patricia Zavella uses interviews to write women into the plot of sexuality. Problematizing the limitation of recall about practices that are forbidden, she finds that women's cultural poetics center on

two metaphors: "playing" contained meanings of teasing, testing, flirting, and challenging, while "fire" conveyed notions of passion, heat, a lack of control, and sanctions for indiscretions. She argues that Mexican women's cultural practices of sexuality entailed struggling with the contradictions of repressive discourses and social practices that were often violent toward women, and mixed messages about propriety and womanhood. Nonetheless, women express their human agency by exploring corporal pleasures and establishing relationships that are not always sanctioned.

Theorizing how subjects negotiate language use, Ana Celia Zentella presents the complex processes of identity formation and bilingualism by Puerto Ricans in "Returned Migration, Language, and Identity: Puerto Rican Bilinguals in *Dos* Worlds/Two *Mundos*." She argues that the revolving door of Puerto Rican migration creates bifurcated responses to the significance of code switching between English and Spanish, and the reception of English-dominant speakers. On the island where Spanish is dominant but English is the language of schooling and jurisprudence, both are seen as problematic, while in New York, Puerto Rican identity allows for more flexibility in language use. These general patterns are crosscut by gendered dynamics, where women are harbingers of changing language use and identity in Puerto Rican communities.

In "A Place Called Home: A Queer Political Economy of Mexican Immigrant Men's Family Experiences," Lionel Cantú presents a "queer materialist" analysis of identity formation by gay men who migrate from Mexico and settle in the United States. He views the family as a site where heteronormative constructions of gender and sexuality are reproduced and where the dynamics of migration are materially embedded prior to and after migration. He argues that these men's identities are fluid, socially constructed by migrants' changing social locations and political and economic contexts in which they are marginalized in multiple ways. Unexpectedly, migration provides opportunities for sexual expression, claiming a gay identity, and creating family with friends and other gays and lesbians.

In a fascinating discussion of "Dominican Blackness and the Modern World," Silvio

Torres-Saillant argues that we need to examine the historical background to provide a context for understanding existing racial attitudes in Dominican society. He unravels Dominicanos' complex structure of feelings in relation to the United States, the "deracialized social consciousness" that created contending discursive terrains. For him, the core of contemporary racial attitudes, deprecation of blackness by the ruling elite and ethnic self-affirmation by the masses, lies in the history of cultural dynamics in the Dominican Republic.

Part IV: Popular Cultures

With a mixture of astonishment and trepidation, *Time* magazine asked in 2001 whether "The American Century could give way to the Century of the Americas" (June 11, p. 5). Although popular cultures are hardly the only manifestations of what we call the Américas, they may provide especially palpable examples of what is common and different among Latinas/os in the Western Hemisphere. When addressing questions of authenticity and tradition, for example, popular cultures often make manifest the palpable sense of belonging to the same group of people who share a similar historical trajectory that in turn gives coherent expression to the notion of the Américas. Within specific countries (see the articles by Oliven on *Gaúcho* identity in southern Brazil and Rogers on beauty pageants in Ecuador in this part), in the expansive borderlands of particular countries like Mexico and the United States (see the articles by Paredes on *machismo* and Davalos on *La Quinceañera*), and certainly as shown in the emergence of Latinismo sensibilities in general (see Negrón-Muntaner's article on Latina/o bodies), popular cultures in the Américas are concentrated expressions of the coinciding and conflicting histories of classes, ethnicities, and genders in the region.

Frances Negrón-Muntaner's contribution engages the emergence of Pan-Latina/o, or Latina/o American identity through film and music. Utilizing a debate that ensued over the casting of the U.S.-born Puerto Rican actress Jennifer Lopez in the movie *Selena* (1997) about the murdered Tejana singer, Negrón-Muntaner notes that "Lopez argued that she was well-suited to play Selena because they shared an ethnic identity as Latinas beyond their 'national identities.'" Just as the Tejana Selena had through her selection of music, self-presentation, and performance become the Latina Selena, so, therefore, could Lopez justifiably represent Latinas of varying backgrounds. Playing with notions of divergent (stereotypical) body types *among* Latinas/os, Negrón-Muntaner examines the formation of ethnic identities not only through film and music but, just as significantly, in the very popular controversies generated by shifting cultural standards as embodied in depictions of Latinidad. Thus if Jennifer Lopez's big butt seemed to some unrepresentative of Tejana body types, for others its very un-gringo characteristics were symbolic of physical differences in which Latinas could feel pride.

Karen Mary Davalos considers some of the cultural and religious implications of transnational rites of passage in her study of *La Quinceañera* among Mexicanos living in Chicago. Whether legally or illegally resident in Chicago, and with or without the sanction of the Catholic Church there, the celebration by 15-year-old Mexicanas and their families and friends of the girl becoming a young woman provides the focal point of this examination of clashing gender, ethnic, and national identities. Ostensibly a matter of religious syncretism, of mixing and matching different religious and cultural traditions, as in the essay by Negrón-Muntaner we see here how controversy and debate over issues of popular culture become flash points and concentrations of broader cultural struggles such as those involving institutions like the Church, and illustrations of larger issues of change involving identities and social relations that are transforming, and being transformed, throughout the Américas.

In his ethnography of the modern *gaúcho* in southern Brazil, Ruben Oliven also shows how the cowboy figure has featured in the development of popular culture and identities in a very different part of Las Américas. Oliven sets out to explore and explain how a seemingly backward-looking regional popular movement based on middle-class, urban youth could arise at a time when globalization and nationalism are running amok in the world. Contrasting themes such as autonomy and integration with respect to regionalism and nation building, Oliven clearly demonstrates why, as he argues, the road to nationalism today runs through regions. In refusing to accept pat identification of the nation with either congealed diversity or homogeneity, Oliven shows clearly that the role of regions and regional identities is pivotal in tying together identity with and loyalty to broader geographic and classificatory boundaries.

The article by Américo Paredes is a pioneering study by one of the premier chroniclers of popular cultures in the Américas. Offering a thoroughly original account of *machismo*, Don Américo shows clearly that, contrary to nearly universal assumptions about the term, *machismo* does not have a long word history, nor is it correct to attribute it exclusively to Mexico or Latinas/os. Linking the notion of *machismo* to the history of cowboys/*vaqueros* on both sides of the Río Grande/Bravo, Paredes goes further by demonstrating the relationship between nation building and masculinity in the nineteenth-century United States and (a century later) in Mexico. Ultimately, he asks, "How Mexican is *machismo* and to what degree is it a Hispanic, a New World, or a universal manifestation?" Indeed, the history of machismo is replete with racist overtones that express the underlying power inequalities between the United States, Mexico, and other nations in the Américas, as well as between men and women in the region.

The matter of body types, and in particular "the use of women as emblems of various kinds of social groupings," is the subject of Mark Rogers's essay comparing white and indigenous beauty pageants in Ecuador. As concentrated displays of personhood, ethnicity, citizenship, and nationality, these beauty pageants contribute to the establishment and intensification of discrete indigenous and white identities in Ecuador. Rogers also notes that similar examples of ethnic reification and separation can be found in pageants in Bolivia, Colombia, Peru, the United States, and elsewhere in the Américas. The use of Quichua as well as Spanish in these beauty pageants, for example, helps to demarcate white from indigenous more generally, as well as to lay claim through the employment of specific popular cultural practices to authentic traditions, and in this way to trace contemporary beliefs and practices to "the image of historical continuity with past populations whose sovereignty was violated by the Spanish."

Among people living in particular regions of specific countries, among others who share their lives between two countries, and among those for whom culture has increasingly less to do with specific countries, through the study of popular Latina/o cultures today and historically we find ample evidence of the tension between the integration and Balkanization of peoples in the Américas.

Part V: Regional, National, and Transnational Political Cultures

Since the emergence of independent nations in Latin America there has been ongoing tension between the democratic demand for equal rights for citizens versus the recognition of the unique rights of indigenous peoples and others, often in the guise of collective rights. Historian Jeffrey Gould hones in on this tension, demonstrating how notions of nineteenth-century liberalism about democracy and equal rights for (male) citizens in Nicaragua promoted by national heroes such as Augusto Sandino delegitimized indigenous rights to communal land and political autonomy. Through tracing the emergence of a nationalist discourse of *mestizaje* in early twentieth-century Nicaragua, Gould provides important historical grounding to what he sees as a problematic celebration of cultural hybridity and *mestizaje* that can disguise assaults on indigenous communities and others.

Gould's discussion of the historical role of *mestizaje* and the construction of the "Indo-Hispanic" race in Nicaragua provides a useful foundation for the theme of assimilation that runs through all of the articles in this part. Notions of what indigenous, blacks, and others should assimilate toward have varied in the Américas, but the process of establishing a national cultural and racial norm has taken place throughout the region. Gould describes how in Nicaragua, unlike in Mexico, by 1940, official and popular discourse in El Salvador, Honduras, and Nicaragua not only described their societies as *mestizo*, "but moreover posited that Indians had ceased to exist at some time lost in the deepest recesses of historical memory." The building of national "cultures" such as *mestizaje* in the twentieth century have been challenged by the emergence of indigenous, black, and other ethnically-based movements that demand that nations such as Colombia and Mexico be truly multiethnic and multicultural as their constitutions now claim that they are.

In the United States the same type of struggle is being waged by immigrant rights groups who are seen by many as a threat to the "nation" that is conceived of as "a singular, predominantly Europe-American, English-speaking culture," in the words of Leo Chavez. Such a racially-based notion of U.S. nationalism can lead to statements such as that of Glen Spencer, founder of the Voice of Citizens Together, who proclaimed in the campaign for Proposition 187 that illegal immigration "is part of a reconquest of the American southwest by foreign Hispanics." While in Colombia, black movements such as the Process of Black Communities (PCN) described by Libia Grueso, Carlos Rosero, and Arturo Escobar have been fighting to receive political recognition of their territory and to weave together the ecological, cultural, and techno-economic in the face of regional, national, and international extractive capital, in the United States Mexican immigrants are struggling to receive basic health care, education, and nutrition. This is not unlike the kinds of basic demands for a minimal level of living and recognition of rights and dignity that were called for in 1994 by the Zapatista Army of National Liberation (Stephen 2002).

In Lynn Stephen's article, the struggle for reconstructing the sense of the national has been fueled by the Zapatista rebellion in the state of Chiapas, Mexico as well as by the larger indigenous movement for cultural and political autonomy that emerged in the political opening forged by the Zapatistas. Stephen traces the violation of the human rights of indigenous peoples in Oaxaca and Chiapas to colonial stereotypes of indigenous peoples that bled into nationalism in the twentieth century, and set up national norms about the correct behavior for indigenous men and women as either the incarnation of La Malinche (the whore) or La Virgen de Guadalupe (passive virgin mothers) and men as silent, passive individuals who do not have the ability to "speak" owing to their lack of Spanish. These historical tropes have been broken by indigenous movements that challenge the status quo politically, confront militarization in their communities, and mobilize the international discourse of human rights to rework top-down nationalism and couple it with self-determination for indigenous peoples in ways that offer an alternative to the marginalized position of many indigenous communities in Mexican history, in national and regional politics, and in economic development schemes.

The type of bottom-up nationalism that Stephen finds in indigenous movements in Oaxaca and Chiapas is also documented by Matthew Gutmann in his examination of cultural responses to the North American Free Trade Agreement (NAFTA) in urban popular neighborhoods of Mexico City. He finds discontent and frustration among Mexico's urban poor that signal an anti-Americanism, and anti-transnationalism that comes from those who have seen their standard of living and employment situations deteriorate since NAFTA came into effect in 1994. Gutmann finds that the urban poor, *los jodidos*, have taken it upon themselves to defend Mexico's national sovereignty because they feel the elites have relinquished all of their national loyalties. Thus like the indigenous of Mexico's south who are clamoring to be a part of the nation, the urban poor are also defending what they feel are the interests of the nation that have been sold down the river by a succession of presidents who promoted a neo-liberal economic model that benefited the few.

This pessimistic view of globalism and transnationalism makes an interesting contrast with Leo Chavez's rather upbeat assessment of the role of transnational Mexicans in the United States. While Chavez derides the assimilationist rhetoric of anti-immigrant groups in the United States, he finds the transnationalism of the "new immigrants" to the United States to be a positive element. Because transnational immigrants are people who maintain linkages in their home country, are not bound by national borders, and whose multiple identities are simultaneously situated in multiple nations and communities, they offer hope for a vision of the United States as inclusive and welcoming of cultural, national, and racial diversity. Thus for Chavez, the transnationalism of migrants such as the Mixtecs who have been living in transnational communities and families stretched between Oaxaca, Sinaloa, and Baja California, Mexico and the states of California, Oregon, and Washington in the United States (see Kearney 1996; Stephen 2001a; Zabin 1994; Zabin and Hughes 1995), offers hope for a new model of nationalism within the United States that moves away from assimilation to a false norm, and celebrates the richness of identities and connections brought by the new immigrants.

In their article on the process of black community organizing in Colombia, Grueso, Rosero, and Escobar offer an example of an effort to counter assimilationist politics and national culture and to unsettle the dominant project of national identity construction in Colombia. While Colombia's constitution was altered in 1991 to read that Colombia is now a multiethnic and multicultural nation, demands for territorial recognition and ethnic rights for black communities were not easily achieved. Out of a complex political process, a pluralistic network of more than 120 local organizations called the Proceso de Comunidades Negras, or PNR (Process of Black Communities) came forward to gain national political space for black communities through recognition of collective rights to traditional territories through Transitory Article 55, and through the creation of a new notion of politics that operated outside of the sphere of electoral politics and recognized alternative proposals for ethnic and cultural rights.

Grueso, Rosero, and Escobar offer a useful discussion of the "doubleness" of local and regional identities that are forged as a challenge to dominant scripts of national identity and the priorities of transnational capital. Their discussion gets at the key issue of how movements mobilize what some have called strategic essentialism (see Spivak 1989, 1990, 1993), while at the same time

emphasizing the flexibility that comes with the ongoing creation and re-creation of such identities. Their characterization of identity formation processes in relation to nationalism and transnationalism could be applied across the Américas to all dimensions of identity. Local, regional, national, and transnational identities are forged in relation to one another and incorporate a search for common roots and elements, yet are also constantly changing.

NOTES

1   See the work of Michael Kearney (1995a, 1995b) and Carole Nagengast and Michael Kearney (1990) on transnational indigenous migrants; for discussions of hybrid cultural formations and for processes of deterritorialization, see Néstor García Canclini (1995).

2   We use the term "Américas" to attempt to put everyone on a neutral footing and recognize all historical inhabitants and cultural contributions to the continent. Such an all-encompassing term has its own pitfalls, the greatest of which is the impossibility of covering all areas included in the Américas, either equally or at all. We have done our best to select a variety of articles that are both representative of different regions, but also illustrate the connections between them. While the "Américas" most certainly include Canada, our efforts to locate Canadian material relevant to this collection did not meet with success. We recognize this deficiency.

3   For example, the designation "Chicano" refers to an ethnic identity within the United States; Spanish may refer to language or national origin from Spain; Mexican and Cuban are nationalities and also often constructed as ethnic categories within the United States; Puerto Rican is a nationalist-based category, even though Puerto Rico does not exist as an independent nation but as a commonwealth of the United States. Most designations of national origin can also be understood as ethnic identities because of their assumptions of shared history and culture. In the U.S. Census, the category "Hispanic" is positioned relationally to racial categories based on color such as "white non-Hispanic" and "African American."

4 The population figures for Latin American countries are taken from the CIA *World Factbook 2000*. Individual states in the United States – such as California, with a Latino population of 10,966,556 (32.4 percent of the state's total) and Texas, with a Latino population of 6,669,666 (32 percent of the state's total) – are on a par with countries such as Cuba, with a population of 11,141,997 and El Salvador, with a population of 6,122,515. (The Latino population figures for individual states are taken from "Hispanic Population in the United States, March 2000, Ethnic and Hispanic Statistics Bureau, Population Division, U.S. Census Bureau. Http://www/census.gov/populations/www/socdemo/hisp. The national population of Cuba and ElSalvador are taken from the Central Intelligence Agency, CIA *World Factbook 2000*, http://www/odci.gov/cia/publications/factbook/.) Indeed, in an often-cited example, after Mexico City, the next largest concentration of Mexicans is probably in the greater Los Angeles area.

5 This small number suggests that the number of Latinos in Canada is still very small, even less than the 2.5 percent of "the Hispanic Population" found in the United States in 1945 (Suárez-Orozco 1998:5).

6 If enforced, the law would have denied public education, non-emergency health care, and other social services to undocumented immigrants and their children. The law also required public employees to report people they suspected of being in the United States without permission to immigration authorities. A federal judge ruled that most portions of Proposition 187 were unconstitutional and they have not been enforced.

7 See Deere 1979; Léon de Leal and Deere 1979, 1982a, 1982b.

8 For example, we need to look at different understandings of racialization that have occurred among Latino populations and others in the United States and compare that to Latin American Studies, where racialization had not been a focus until quite recently. We might also consider differences of transculturation that exist in Latin America against those among Latinos in the United States. Or explore the ways that both disciplines have different senses of the meaning of purity and essentialisation versus hybridity.

REFERENCES

Acuña, Rodolfo
1972 Occupied America: The Chicano's Struggle toward Liberation. San Francisco: Canfield Press.
—— 1996. Anything But Mexican: Chicanos in Contemporary Los Angeles. New York: Verso.

Almaguer, Tomás
1975 Class, Race, and Chicano Oppression. Socialist Revolution 25:71–99.
—— 1994 Racial Fault Lines: The Historical Origins of White Supremacy in California. Berkeley: University of California Press.

Alvarez, Sonia
2001 Hemispheric Dialogues 2. Research Cluster Report, CLRC (Chicano/Latino Research Cluster) News, University of California, Santa Cruz, Summer.

Andreas, Peter
1998 The U.S. Immigration Control Offensive: Constructing an Image of Order on the Southwest Border. *In* Crossings: Mexican Immigration in Interdisciplinary Perspectives. Marcelo M. Suárez–Orozco, ed. Pp. 343–356. Cambridge, MA: Harvard University Press.

Anzaldúa, Gloria
1987 Borderlands – La Frontera: The New Mestiza. San Francisco: Spinsters/Aunt Lute.

Aparicio, Frances
1988 Listening to Salsa: Gender, Latin Popular Music, and Puerto Rican Culture. Hanover, NH: University Press of New England.
—— 2000 Cultural Twins and National Others; Literacy Allegories of Interlatino/a Subjectivities. Working Paper 33. Chicano/Latino Research Center, University of California, Santa Cruz.

Appadurai, Arjun
1996 Modernity at Large: Cultural Dimensions of Globalization. Minneapolis: University of Minnesota Press.

Arias, Arturo
2002 President's Report. LASA Forum XXXII (4): 3–5.

Babb, Florence
1989 Between Field and Cooking Pot: The Political Economy of Marketwomen in Peru. Austin: University of Texas Press.

Baran, Paul
1957 The Political Economy of Growth. New York: Monthly Review Press.

Barrera, Mario, Carlos Muñoz, and Charles Ornelas
1972 The Barrio as Internal Colony. *In* People and Politics in Urban Society, Harlan Hahn, ed. Pp. 465–498. Urban Affairs Annual Review, Vol. 6. Los Angeles: Sage Publications.

Behar, Ruth
1993 Translated Woman: Crossing the Border with Esperanza's Story. Boston: Beacon Press.

Beverly, John
1996 On What We Do: Postmodernism and Cultural Studies. *In* The Postmodern in Latino and Latin American Cultural Narratives: Collected Essays and Interviews. Claudia Ferman, ed. Pp. 219–228. New York: Garland.

Beverly, John and José Oviedo
1995 Introduction. *In* The Postmodernism Debate in Latin America. John Beverly, José Oviedo, and Michael Aronna, eds. Pp. 1–17. Durham, NC: Duke University Press.

Blackwell, Maylei
forthcoming Contested Histories: las Hijas de Cuauhtémoc, Chicana Feminisms and Print Culture in the Chicano Movement, 1968–1973. *In* Chicana Feminisms: Disruptions in Dialogue, Gabriela Arredondo, Aída Hurtado, Norma Klahn, Olga Nájera-Ramírez, and Patricia Zavella, eds. Durham: Duke University Press.

Bonilla, Frank
1992 Racism and the Incorporation of Foreign Labor: Farm Labor Migration to Canada Since 1945. American Journal of Sociology 98 (1): 208–211.

Bonilla, Frank and Richard Campos
1981 A Wealth of Poor: Puerto Ricans in the New Economic Order. Daedalus 110: 133–176.

Bonilla, Frank, Edwin Meléndez, Rebecca Morales, and María de los Angeles Torres, eds.
1998. Borderless Borders: U.S. Latinos, Latin Americans, and the Paradox of Independence. Philadelphia: Temple University Press.

Bourque, Susan and Kay Warren.
1981. Women of the Andes: Patriarchy and Social Change in Two Peruvian Towns. Ann Arbor: University of Michigan Press.

Borrego, John.
2000. The Restructuring of Frozen Food Production in North America and Its Impact on Daily Life in Two Communities: Watsonville, Califor-
nia and Irapuato, Guanajuato. *In* Las Nuevas Fronteras del Siglo XXI: Dimensiones Culturales, Políticas y Socioeconómicas de las Relaciones México-Estados Unidos (New Frontiers in the Twenty First Century: Cultural, Political and Socioeconomic Dimensions of US–Mexico Relations), Norma Klahn, Alejandro Álvarez Béjar, Federico Manchón, and Pedro Castillo, eds. Pp. 397–424. La Jornada Ediciones: Centro de Investigaciones Colección: la democracia en México.

Browning, Harley L. and Rodolfo O. de la Garza, eds.
1986 Mexican Immigrants and Mexican Americans: an Evolving Relation. Austin: Center for Mexican American Studies, University of Texas.

Brysk, Alison
2000 From Tribal Village to Global Village: Indian Rights and International Relations in Latin America. Stanford, CA: Stanford University Press.

Caban, Pedro
1998 The New Synthesis of Latin American and Latino Studies. *In* Borderless Borders; U.S. Latinos, Latin Americans and the Paradox of Independence. Frank Bonilla et al., eds. Pp. 195–216. Philadelphia: Temple University Press.

Camarillo, Albert
1979 Chicanos in a Changing Society. Cambridge, MA: Harvard University Press.

Cardoso, Henrique Fernando
1977 The Consumption of Dependency Theory in the United States. Latin American Research Review XII (3): 7–24.

Central Intelligence Agency (C.I.A) 2000 World Factbook 2000. Washington D.C.: Central Intelligence Agency. Http://www.odci.gov/cia/publications/factbook/

Chang, Grace
2000 Disposable Domestics: Immigrant Women Workers in the Global Economy. Boston: South End Press.

Chavez, Leo R.
1991 Shadowed Lives: Mexican Undocumented Immigrants. New York: Harcourt Brace Jovanovich.
——2001 Covering Immigration: Popular Images and the Politics of the Nation. Berkeley: University of California Press.

Chicano Council on Higher Education
1970 El Plan de Santa Bárbara. Santa Barbara, CA: La Causa Publications.

Comaroff, John and Jean
1992 Ethnography and the Historical Imagination. Boulder, CO: Westview Press.

Committee for Puerto Rican Studies and Research
1972 A Proposal for Puerto Rican Studies and Research at the City University of New York. New York: CUNY, unpublished document.

Darder, Antonia, and Rodolfo D. Torres, eds.
1998 The Latino Studies Reader: Culture, Economy, and Society. Malden, MA: Blackwell.

Dávila, Arlene M.
1997 Sponsored Identities: Cultural Politics in Puerto Rico Philadelphia: Temple University Press.
—— 2001 Latinos Inc.: The Marketing and Making of a People. Berkeley: University of California Press.

Deere, Carmen Diana
1979 Changing Relations of Production and Peruvian Peasant Women's Work. *In* Women in Latin America: An Anthology from Latin American Perspectives. Pp. 36–46. Riverside, CA: Latin American Perspectives.

De Genova, Nicholas
1998 Race, Space, and the Reinvention of Latin America in Mexican Chicago. Latin American Perspectives 25 (5): 87–116.

de la Cadena, Marisol
2000 Indigenous Mestizos: The Politics of Race and Culture in Cuzco, Peru, 1919–1991. Durham, NC: Duke University Press.

de la Torre, Adela and Beatríz M. Pesquera, eds.
1993 Building with Our Hands: New Directions in Chicana Studies. Berkeley: University of California Press.

Delgado, Guillermo
2001 Existe América Latina? Working Paper 34, Chicano/Latino Research Center, University of California, Santa Cruz.

Delgado, Héctor L.
1993 New Immigrants, Old Unions: Organizing Undocumented Workers in Los Angeles. Philadelphia: Temple University Press.

Dore, Elizabeth and Maxine Molyneux, eds.
2000 Hidden Histories of Gender and the State in Latin America. Durham, NC: Duke University Press.

Dos Santos, Theotonio
1970 The Structure of Dependence. American Economic Review 40(2): 231–236.

Escobar, Arturo
1995 Encountering Development: The Making and Unmaking of the Third World. Princeton, NJ: Princeton University Press.

Escobar, Arturo and Sonia E. Alvarez, eds.
1992 The Making of Social Movements in Latin America: Identity, Strategy and Democracy. Boulder, CO: Westview Press.

Fanon, Frantz
1963 The Wretched of the Earth. Constance Farrington, trans New York: Grove Press.
—— 1965 A Dying Colonialism. Haakon Chevalier trans.; Adolfo Gilly, intro. New York: Grove Press.

Ferman, Claudia
1996 Introduction. *In* The Postmodern in Latino and Latin American Cultural Narratives: Collected Essays and Interviews. Claudia Ferman, ed. Pp. vii–xiv. New York: Garland.

Flores, Estevan T.
1986 The Mexican-Origin People in the United States and Marxist Thought in Chicano Studies. *In* The Left Academy: Marxist Scholarship on American Campuses. Bertell Ollman and Edward Vernoff, eds. Pp. 103–138. New York: McGraw-Hill.

Flores, William V.
1997 Citizens vs. Citizenry: Undocumented Immigrants and Latino Cultural Citizenship. *In* Latino Cultural Citizenship: Claiming Identity, Space and Rights. William V. Flores and Rina Benmayor, eds. Pp. 255–277. Boston: Beacon Press.

Frank, Andre Gunder
1967 Capitalism and Underdevelopment in Latin America. New York: Monthly Review Press.
—— 1969 *Latin America: Underdevelopment or Revolution*. New York: Monthly Review Press.

Fregoso, Rosa Linda and Angie Chabram Dernersesian
1990 Chicana/o Cultural Representations: Reframing Alternative Critical Discourses. Cultural Studies, Special issue 4(3): 203–212.

Galbraith, John Kenneth
1979 The Nature of Mass Poverty. Cambridge, MA: Harvard University Press.

García, Alma
1989 The Development of Chicana Feminist Discourse, 1970–1980. Gender and Society 3(2): 217–238.

García, Alma M., ed.
1997 Chicana Feminist Thought: The Basic Historical Writings. New York: Routledge.

García Canclini, Néstor
1995 Hybrid Cultures: Strategies for Entering and Leaving Modernity. Minneapolis: University of Minnesota Press.

Glick Schiller, Nina, Linda Basch, and Cristina Blanc-Szanton
1995 From Immigrant to Transmigrant: Theorizing Transnational Migration. Anthropological Quarterly 68 (1): 48–63.

Glick Schiller, Nina, Linda Basch, and Cristina Blanc-Szanton, eds.
1992. Towards a Transnational Perspective on Migration: Race, Class, Ethnicity, and Nationalism Reconsidered. New York: New York Academy of Sciences.

Gómez, Laura E.
1992 The Birth of the "Hispanic" Generation: Attitudes of Mexican-American Political Elites toward the Hispanic Label. Latin American Perspectives 19 (4): 45–58.

Gonzalez, David
2002 Central America's Cities Grow Bigger, and Poorer. New York Times, 17 March: 3.

Gonzalez, Deena J.
1999 Refusing the Favor: the Spanish-Mexican Women of Santa Fe, 1820–1880. New York: Oxford University Press.

Gonzalez, Gustavo
1998 Migration-Chile: Illegal Migration Leads to Labor Abuse. World News, Inter Press Service, July 13. www.oneworld.org/isp2/jul98/15 27 057.hmtl

Grandin, Greg
2001 A More Onerous Citizenship: Illness, Race, and Nation in Republican Guatemala. In Reclaiming the Political in Latin American History: Essays from the North. Gilbert Joseph, ed. Pp. 205–230. Durham, NC: Duke University Press.

Green, James
1999 Beyond Carnival: Male Homosexuality in Twentieth Century Brazil. Chicago: University of Chicago Press.

Gutiérrez, David G.
1995 Walls and Mirrors: Mexican Americans, Mexican Immigrants and the Politics of Ethnicity. Berkeley: University of California Press.

—— 1998 Ethnic Mexicans and the Transformation of "American" Social Space: Reflections on Recent History. In Crossings: Mexican Immigration in Interdisciplinary Perspectives. Marcelo M. Suárez-Orozco, ed. Pp. 307–340. Cambridge, MA: Harvard University Press.

Gutiérrez, Ramón A.
1991 When Jesus Came the Corn Mothers Went Away: Marriage, Sexuality and Power in New Mexico, 1500–1846. Stanford, CA: Stanford University Press.

Gutmann, Matthew C.
1996. The Meanings of Macho: Being a Man in Mexico. Berkeley and Los Angeles: University of California Press.

—— 1999 Ethnicity, Alcohol, and Acculturation. Social Science and Medicine 48 (2): 173–184.

—— 2002 The Romance of Democracy: Compliant Defiance in Contemporary Mexico. Berkeley: University of California Press.

—— 2003 Dystopian Travels in Gringolandia: Engendering Ethnicity among Mexican Migrants to the United States. Ethnic and Racial Studies.

Hall, Stuart
1988 New Ethnicities. In ICA Document 7. Pp. 27–31. London: Institute for Community Arts (ICA).

Herman, Ellen
1995 The Romance of American Psychology: Political Culture in the Age of Experts. Berkeley: University of California Press.

Holston, Mark
1997 Rock en Español. Hispanic (Jan./Feb.): 46, 48, 50, 52.

Hondagneu-Sotelo, Pierrette
1994 Gendered Transitions: Mexican Experiences of Immigration. Berkeley: University of California Press.

Kearney, Michael
1995a The Effects of Transnational Culture, Economy, and Migration on Mixtec Identity in Oaxacalifornia. In The Bubbling Cauldron: Race, Ethnicity, and the Urban Crisis. Michael Peter Smith and Joe R. Feagin, eds. Pp. 226–243. Minneapolis: University of Minneapolis Press.

—— 1995b The Local and the Global: The Anthropology of Globalization and Transnationalism. Annual Review of Anthropology 24: 547–565.

—— 1996 Reconceptualizing the Peasantry: Anthropology in Global Perspective. Boulder, CO: Westview Press.

Klor de Alva, J. Jorge
1997 The Invention of Ethnic Origins and the Negotiation of Latino Identity, 1969–1981. *In* Challenging Fronteras: Structuring Latina and Latino Lives in the U.S. Mary Romero, Pierrette Hondagneu-Sotelo and Vilma Ortiz, eds. Pp. 55–74. New York: Routledge.

Kulick, Don
1998 Travesti: Sex, Gender and Culture among Brazilian Transgendered Prostitutes. Chicago: University of Chicago Press.

Lancaster, Roger
1992 Life is Hard: Machismo, Danger, and the Intimacy of Power in Nicaragua. Berkeley: University of California Press.

Latina Feminist Group
2001 Telling to Live: Latina Feminist Testimonios (Luz del Alba Acevedo, Norma Alarcón, Celia Alvarez, Ruth Behar, Rina Benmayor, Norma E. Cantú, Daisy Cocco de Filippis, Gloria Holguín Cuádraz, Liza Fiol-Matta, Yvette Flores-Ortiz, Inés Hernández-Avila, Aurora Levins Morales, Clara Lomas, Iris López, Mirtha N. Quintanales, Eliana Rivero, Caridad Souza, and Patricia Zavella). Durham, NC: Duke University Press.

León de Leal, Magdalena and Carmen Diana Deere
1979 Mujer y capitalismo agrario. Vol. 1. Bogotá: Asociación Colombiana para el Estudio de la Población.

—— 1982a. Las Trabajadoras del agro. Debate sobre la mujer en América Latina y el Caribe. Bogotá: Asociación Colombiana para el Estudio de la Población.

—— 1982b. Sociedad, subordinación, y feminismo. Debate sobre la mujer en América Latina y el Caribe. Bogotá: Asociación Colombiana para el Estudio de la Población.

López, Iris
1993 Sterilization and Reproductive Freedom among Puerto Rican Women in New York City. *In* Latino Ethnography. Special issue on Urban Anthropology 22 (3–4): 299–324.

Matos Rodríguez, Félix and Linda Delgado, eds.
1998 Puerto Rican Women's History: New Perspectives. Armonk, NY: M. E. Sharpe.

Mignolo, Walter D.
2000 Local Histories/Global Designs: Coloniality, Subaltern Knowledges, And Border Thinking. Princeton, NJ: Princeton University Press.

Milkman, Ruth, ed.
2000 Organizing Immigrants: The Challenge for Unions in Contemporary California. Ithaca, NY: ILR Press.

Milkman, Ruth and Kent Wong
2000 Voices from the Front Lines: Organizing Immigrant Workers in Los Angeles. Los Angeles: Center for Labor Research and Education, UCLA.

Montejano, David
1987 Anglos and Mexicans in the Making of Texas, 1836–1986. Austin: University of Texas Press.

Mujeres Activas en Letras y Cambio Social Editorial Board (MALCS) 1993 Chicana Critical Issues. Berkeley, CA: Third Woman Press.

Muñoz, Carlos, Jr.
1989 Youth, Identity, Power: The Chicano Movement. London: Verso.

Nagengast, Carole and Michael Kearney
1990 Mixtec Ethnicity: Social Identity, Political Consciousness, and Political Activism. Latin American Research Review 23:61–91.

Nash, June and Helen Safa, eds.
1976. Sex and Class in Latin America. South Hadley, NY: J. F. Bergin Publishers.

—— 1986 Women and Change in Latin America. South Hadley, NY: Bergin & Garvey.

Nieves, Josephine et al.
1987 Puerto Rican Studies: Roots and Challenges. *In* Towards a Renaissance of Puerto Rican Studies: Ethnic and Area Studies in University Education. Maria E. Sánchez and Antonio Stevens-Arroyo, eds. Pp. 3–12. Highland Lakes, NJ: Atlantic Research and Publications.

Oboler, Suzanne
1995 Ethnic Labels, Latino Lives: Identity and Politics of (Re)presentation in the United States. Minneapolis: University of Minnesota Press.

O'Mally, Martin, Jennifer Chen, and Gary Graves
2001 Making Sense of the Census. Backgrounder. CBS News, Canada, Online, May. http:cbc.ca/news/indepth/background/census1.html

Omi, Michael and Howard Winant
1987 Racial Formation in the United States: From the 1960s to the 1980s. New York: Routledge & Kegan Paul.

Ortiz, Altagracia, ed.
1996 Puerto Rican Women and Work: Bridges in Transnational Labor. Philadelphia: Temple University Press.

Padilla, Felix M.

1985 Latino Ethnic Consciousness: The Case of Mexican Americans and Puerto Ricans in Chicago. Notre Dame, IN: University of Notre Dame Press.

Paerregaard, Karsten

1997 Linking Separate Worlds: Urban Migrants and Rural Lives in Peru. London: Berg.

Paredes, Américo

1958 "With His Pistol In His Hand," A Border Ballad And Its Hero. Austin: University of Texas Press.

—— 1993 Folklore and Culture on the Texas-Mexican Border. Richard Bauman, ed. Austin: Center for Mexican American Studies, University of Texas.

Pedraza, Pedro

1985 Labor Maintenance among New York Puerto Ricans. In Spanish Language Use and Public Life in the U.S.A. Lucia Elias-Olivares, Elizabeth A. Leone, Rene Cisneros, and John Gutiérrez, eds. Berlin: Mouton.

Perea, Juan, ed.

1997 Immigrants Out!: The New Nativism and the Anti-Immigrant Impulse in the United States. New York: New York University Press.

Pérez, Emma

1999 The Decolonial Imaginary: Writing Chicanas into History. Bloomington: Indiana University Press.

Portes, Alejandro and Rubén G. Rumbaut

2001 Legacies: The Story of the Immigrant Second Generation. Berkeley: University of California Press.

Prieur, Annick

1998 Mema's House, Mexico City: On Transvestites, Queens, and Machos. Chicago: University of Chicago Press.

Pulido, Laura

1996 Environmentalism and Economic Justice: Two Chicano Struggles in the Southwest. Tucson: University of Arizona Press.

Quiroga, Jorge

2001 Tropics of Desire: Interventions from Queer Latino America. New York: New York University Press.

Rivero, Eliana

1994 Fronteraisleña, Border Islander. In Bridges to Cuba/Puentes a Cuba. Ruth Behar, ed. Special issue. Michigan Quarterly Review 33 (fall): 672.

Rodríguez, Clara

2000 Changing Race: Latinos, the Census, and the History of Ethnicity in the United States. New York: New York University Press.

Romero, Mary, Pierrette Hondagneu-Sotelo, and Vilma Ortiz, eds.

1997 Challenging Fronteras: Structuring Latina and Latino Lives in the U.S. New York: Routledge.

Rosaldo, Renato

1997 Cultural Citizenship, Inequality, and Multiculturalism. In Latino Cultural Citizenship: Claiming Identity, Space, and Rights. William V. Flores and Rina Benmayor, eds. Pp. 27–38. Boston: Beacon Press.

Rostow, W. W.

1960 The Stages of Growth: A Non-Communist Manifesto. Cambridge: Cambridge University Press.

Rouse, Roger

1992 Making Sense of Settlement: Class Transformation, Cultural Struggle, and Transnationalism among Mexican Migrants in the United States. Annals of the New York Academy of Sciences 645 (July): 25–52.

Ruiz, Vicki L.

1987 Cannery Women, Cannery Lives: Mexican Women, Unionization, and the California Food Processing Industry 1980–1950. Albuquerque: University of New Mexico Press.

Saldívar, José David

1997 Border Matters: Remapping American Cultural Studies. Berkeley: University of California Press.

Saldívar-Hull, Sonia

2000 Feminism on the Border: Chicana Gender Politics and Literature. Berkeley: University of California Press.

Sánchez Korrol, Virginia E.

1983 From Colonia to Community: The History of Puerto Ricans in New York City, 1917–1948. Westport, CT: Greenwood Press.

Sánchez, María E., and Stevens-Arroyo, Antonio M., eds.

1987 *Towards a Renaissance of Puerto Rican Studies: Ethnic and Area Studies in University Education.* Boulder, CO: Social Science Monographs; Highland Lakes, N.J.: Atlantic Research and Publications; New York: Distributed by Colombia University Press.

Sassen, Saskia
1988 The Mobility of Labor and Capital: A Study in International Investment and Labor Flow. New York: Cambridge University Press.
—— 1998 Globalization and Its Discontents: Essays on the New Mobility of People and Money. New York: Free Press.

Schmitt, Eric
2001 New Census Shows Hispanics Now Even with Blacks in U.S. New York Times, March 8: A1.

Serrano, Basilio
1998 "Rifle, Cañón, y Escopeta!": A Chronicle of the Puerto Rican Student Union. In The Puerto Rican Movement: Voices from the Diaspora. Andrés Torres and José E. Veláquez, eds. Pp. 124–143. Philadelphia: Temple University Press.

Silverblatt, Irene
1987 Moon, Sun, and Witches; Gender Ideologies and Class in Inca and Colonial Peru. Princeton, NJ: Princeton University Press.

Slater, David
1985 New Social Movements and the State in Latin America. Amsterdam: CEDLA.

Smith, Michael Peter
1994 Can You Imagine? Transnational Migration and the Globalization of Grassroots Politics, Social Text 38 (Summer): 15–33.

Smith, Peter H.
2002 Area Studies in a Global Age. LASA Forum XXXII (4): 7–9.

Soldatenko, Maria A.
1991 Organizing Latina Garment Workers in Los Angeles. Aztlan, a Journal of Chicano Studies, Las Obreras: The Politics of Work and Family, ed. V. Ruiz, special issue, 20 (1–2): 73–96.

Spivak, Gyatri C.
1989 In a Word: An Interview. Differences 1:124–156.
—— 1990 Postcolonial Critic: Interviews, Strategies, Dialogues. New York: Routledge.
—— 1993. Inside the Teaching Machine. New York: Routledge.

Stephen, Lynn
1991 Zapotec Women. Austin: University of Texas Press.
—— 1997 Women and Social Movements in Latin America: Power From Below. Austin: University of Texas Press.
—— 2001a Globalization, The State, and the Creation of Flexible Indigenous Workers: Mixtec Farmworkers in Oregon. Urban Anthropology and Studies of Cultural Systems and World Economic Development 30 (2–3): 189–214.
—— 2001b The Story of PCUN and the Farmworker Movement in Oregon. Eugene: Department of Anthropology, University of Oregon.
—— 2002 Zapata Lives: Histories and Cultural Politics in Southern Mexico. Berkeley: University of California Press.

Stycos, J. Mayone, et al.
1971 Ideology, Faith, And Family Planning in Latin America: Studies in Public and Private Opinion on Fertility Control. New York: McGraw-Hill.

Suarez-Findlay, Eileen
1999 Imposing Decency: The Politics of Sexuality and Race in Puerto Rico, 1870–1920. Durham, NC: Duke University Press.

Suárez-Orozco, Marcelo M.
1998 Introduction: Crossings: Mexican Immigration in Interdisciplinary Perspectives. In Crossings: Mexican Immigration in Interdisciplinary Perspectives. Marcelo M. Suárez-Orozco, ed. Pp. 3–52. Cambridge, MA: Harvard University Press.

Summer, Doris
1991 Foundational Fictions: The National Romances of Latin America. Berkeley: University of California Press.

Tam, L.
1994 Urban Migration in Bolivia and Peru: Association with Child Mortality, Breastfeeding Cessation, Maternal Care, and Contraception. DHS Working Paper No. 8. 29 pp. Calverton, MD: Macro International, March.

Torres, Arlene
1998 La Gran Familia Puertorriqueña "Ej Prieta de Beldá" (The Great Puerto Rican Family is Really Really Black). In Blackness in Latin America. Vol. II. Arlene Torres and Norman E. Whitten, Jr., eds. Pp. 285–306. Bloomington: Indiana University Press.

Trujillo, Carla ed.
1991 Chicana Lesbians: The Girls Our Mothers Warned Us About. Berkeley, CA: Third Woman Press.

United Nations (UN)
1995 World Urbanization Prospects: The 1994 Revision. New York: UN
—— 1996. World Economic Survey. New York: UN.

U.S. Census Bureau
2000 Hispanic Population in the United States. Ethnic and Hispanic Statistics Bureau, Population Division. Washington, D.C.: U.S. Census Bureau. http://www.census.gove/populations/www/socdem/hisp

Vélez-Ibáñez, Carlos G.
1996 Border Visions: Mexican Cultures of the Southwest United States. Tucson: University of Arizona Press.

Warren, Kay
1998 Indigenous Movements and Their Critics: Pan-Maya Activism in Guatemala. Princeton, NJ: Princeton University Press.

Weismantel, Mary
2001 Cholas and Pishtacos: Tales of Race and Sex in the Andes. Chicago: University of Chicago Press.

Yashar, Deborah
1999 Democracy, Indigenous Movements, and the Postliberal Challenge in Latin America. World Politics 52 (1): 76–104.

Zabin, Carol
1994 The Effects of Economic Restructuring on Women: The Case of Binational Agriculture in Baja California and California. Economic Development Quarterly 8 (2): 186–196.

Zabin, Carol and Sallie Hughes
1995 Economic Integration and Labor Flows: Stage Migration in Farm Labor Markets in Mexico and the United States. International Migration Review 29 (2): 395–422.

Zavella, Patricia
1987 Women's Work and Chicano Families: Cannery Workers of the Santa Clara Valley. Ithaca, NJ: Cornell University Press.

—— 1994. Reflections on Diversity among Chicanas. In Race. Steven Gregory and Roger Sanjek, eds. Pp. 199–212. New Brunswick, NJ: Rutgers University Press.

—— 2000a Latinos in the USA: Changing Socio-Economic Patterns. Social and Cultural Geography 1 (2): 155–167.

—— 2000b Engendering Transnationalism in Food Processing: Peripheral Vision on Both Sides of the U.S.–Mexico Border. In Las Nuevas Fronteras del Siglo XXI: Dimensiones Culturales, Políticas y Socioeconómicas de las Relaciones México-Estados Unidos (New Frontiers in the Twenty-First Century: Cultural, Political and Socioeconomic Dimensions of U.S.–Mexico Relations). Norma Klahn, Alejandro Álvarez Béjar, Federico Manchón, and Pedro Castillo, eds. Pp. 397–424. La Jornada Ediciones: Centro de Investigaciones Colección: la democracia en México.

Zentella, Ana Celia
1997 Growing Up Bilingual: Puerto Rican Children in New York. Malden, MA: Blackwell.

Part I

Colonialism and Resistance

1

Traddutora, Traditora: A Paradigmatic Figure of Chicana Feminism

Norma Alarcón

When the Spanish conquistador appears, this woman [a Mayan] is no more than the site where the desires and wills of two men meet. To kill men to rape women: these are at once proof that a man wields power and his reward. The wife chooses [sic] to obey her husband and the rules of her own society, she puts all that remains of her personal will into defending the violence [of her own society] of which she has been the object.... Her husband of whom she is the "internal other,"... leaves her no possibility of asserting herself as a free subject.

Tzvetan Todorov, *The Conquest of America*

In his splendid book *Quetzalcóatl and Guadalupe*, Jacques Lafaye gives a fascinating account of the roles those two divine and mythic figures played in the formation of the Mexican national consciousness.[1] Quetzalcóatl was an Aztec god whose name, so the missionaries argued, was the natives' own name for the true Messiah. Guadalupe, on the other hand, was the emerging Mexican people's native version of the Virgin Mary and, in a sense, substituted for the Aztec goddess Tonantzin. By the time of Mexican independence from Spain in 1821, Guadalupe had emerged triumphant as the national patroness of Mexico, and her banner was often carried into battle. In a well-known article which may have inspired Lafaye, Eric R. Wolf comments that

the Mexican War of Independence marks the final realization of the apocalyptic promise ... [T]he promise of life held out by the supernatural mother has become the promise of an independent Mexico, liberated from the irrational authority of the Spanish father-oppressors and restored to the chosen nation whose election had been manifest in the apparition of the Virgin at Tepeyac.... Mother, food, hope, health, life; supernatural salvation from oppression; chosen people and national independence – all find expression in a single symbol.[2]

There is sufficient folklore, as well as documentary evidence of a historical and literary nature, to suggest that the indigenous female slave Malintzin Tenepal was transformed into Guadalupe's monstrous double and that her "banner" also aided and abetted in the nation-making process or, at least, in the creation of nationalistic perspectives. On Independence Day of 1861, for example, Ignacio "El Nigromante" Ramírez, politician and man of letters, reminded the celebrants that Mexicans owed their defeat to Malintzin – Cortés's whore.[3] Moreover, Malintzin may be compared to Eve, especially when she is viewed as the originator of the Mexican people's fall from grace and the procreator of a "fallen" people. Thus, Mexico's own binary pair, Guadalupe and Malintzin, reenact within this dualistic system of thought the biblical stories of our human creation and condition. In effect, as a political compromise between conquerors and conquered, Guadalupe is the neorepresentative of the Virgin Mary and the native goddess Tonantzin, while Malintzin stands in the periphery of the new patriarchal order and its sociosymbolic contract.[4]

Indeed, Malintzin and the "false god" and conqueror Hernán Cortés are the countercouple, "the monstrous doubles," to Lafaye's Quetzalcóatl and Guadalupe. These two monstrous figures become, in the eyes of the later generations of "natives," symbols of unbridled conquering power and treachery, respectively.[5] Malintzin comes to be known as *la lengua*, literally meaning the tongue. *La lengua* was the metaphor used, by Cortés and the chroniclers of the conquest, to refer to Malintzin the translator. However, she not only translated for Cortés and his men, she also bore his children. Thus, a combination of Malintzin-translator and Malintzin-procreator becomes the main feature of her subsequently ascribed treacherous nature.

In the eyes of the conquered (oppressed), anyone who approximates *la lengua* or Cortés (oppressor), in word or deed, is held suspect and liable to become a sacrificial "monstrous double." Those who use the oppressor's language are viewed as outside of the community, thus rationalizing their expulsion, but, paradoxically, they also help to constitute the community. In *Violence and the Sacred*, René Girard has observed that the religious mind "strives to procure, and if need be to invent, a sacrificial victim as similar as possible to its ambiguous vision of the original victim. The model it imitates is not the true double, but a model transfigured by the mechanism of the "monstrous double."[6] If in the beginning Cortés and Malintzin are welcomed as

saviors from, and avengers of, Aztec imperialism, soon each is unmasked and "sacrificed," that is, expelled so that the authentic gods may be recovered, awaited, and/or invented. While Quetzalcóatl could continue to be awaited, Guadalupe was envisioned, and her invention was under way as the national Virgin Mother and goddess only twelve years after Cortés's arrival. Guadalupe, as Lafaye himself suggests, is a metaphor that has never wholly taken the place of Tonantzin. As such, Guadalupe is capable of alternately evoking the Catholic and meek Virgin Mother and the prepatriarchal and powerful earth goddess. In any case, within a decade of the invasion, both Cortés and Malintzin begin to accrue their dimensions as scapegoats who become the receptacle of human rage and passion, of the very real hostilities that "all the members of the community feel for one another."[7] In the context of a religiously organized society, one can observe in the scapegoating of Cortés and Malintzin "the very real metamorphosis of reciprocal violence into restraining violence through the agency of unanimity."[8] The unanimity is elicited by the chosen scapegoats, and violence is displaced onto them. That mechanism then structures many cultural values, rituals, customs, and myths. Among people of Mexican descent, from this perspective, anyone who has transgressed the boundaries of perceived group interests and values often has been called a *malinche* or *malinchista*. Thus, the contemporary recuperation and positive redefinitions of her name bespeak an effort to go beyond religiously organized Manichaean thought. There is nothing more fascinating or intriguing, as Lafaye demonstrates, than to trace the transformation of legends into myths that contribute to the formation of national consciousness. However, by only tracing the figures of transcendence – the recovered or displaced victims of the impersonators – we are left without a knowledge of the creation process of the scapegoats – whether it be through folklore, polemics, or literature. An exploration of Cortés's role as monstrous double shall be left for another occasion. It is clear that often his role is that of the conqueror, usurper, foreigner, and/or invader.[9] In the course of almost five centuries Malintzin has alternately retained one of her three names – Malintzin (the name given her by her parents), Marina (the name given her by the Spaniards), or Malinche (the name given her by the natives in the midst of the conquest). The epithet *La Chingada*[10] has surfaced most emphatically in our century to refer to her alleged ill-fated experience at the hands of the Spaniards. The epithet also emphasizes the sexual implications of having been conquered – the rape of women and the emasculation of men.

Guadalupe and Malintzin almost always have been viewed as oppositional mediating figures, though the precise moment of inception may well elude us. Guadalupe has come to symbolize transformative powers and sublime transcendence and is the standard carried into battle in utopically inspired movements. Always viewed by believers as capable of transforming the petitioner's status and promising sublime deliverance, she transports us beyond or before time. On the other hand, Malintzin represents feminine subversion and treacherous victimization of her people because she was a translator in Cortés's army. Guadalupe and Malintzin have become a function of each other. Be that as it may, quite often one or the other figure is recalled as being present at the "origins" of the Mexican community, thereby emphasizing its divine and sacred constitution or, alternately, its damned and secular fall. The religiously rooted community, as Girard notes, "is both attracted and repelled by its own origins. It feels the constant need to re-experience them, albeit in veiled and transfigured form . . . by exercising its memory of the collective expulsion or carefully designated objects."[11] Though Guadalupe is thought to assuage the community's pain due to its fall from grace, Malintzin elicits a fascination entangled with loathing, suspicion, and sorrow. As translator she mediates between antagonistic cultural and historical domains. If we assume that language is always in some sense metaphoric, then, any discourse, oral or written, is liable to be implicated in treachery when perceived to be going beyond repetition of what the community perceives as the "true" and/or "authentic" concept, image, or narrative. The act of translating, which often introduces different concepts and perceptions, displaces and may even do violence to local

knowledge through language. In the process, these may be assessed as false or inauthentic.

Traditional nonsecular societies, be they oral or print cultures, tend to be very orthodox and conservative, interpreting the lifeworld in highly Manichaean terms. It is common in largely oral cultures to organize knowledge, values, and beliefs around symbolic icons, figures, or even persons, which is a characteristic of both the Spanish and the natives at the time of the conquest, and one that in surprising numbers continues to our day in Mexican/Chicano culture.[12] In such a binary, Manichaean system of thought, Guadalupe's transcendentalizing power, silence, and maternal self-sacrifice are the positive, contrasting attributes to those of a woman who speaks as a sexual being and independently of her maternal role. To speak independently of her maternal role, as Malintzin did, is viewed in such a society as a sign of catastrophe, for if she is allowed to articulate her needs and desires she must do so as a mother on behalf of her children and not of herself. Because Malintzin the translator is perceived as speaking for herself and not the community, however it defines itself, she is a woman who has betrayed her primary cultural function – maternity. The figure of the mother is bound to a double reproduction, *strictu sensu* – that of her people and her culture. In a traditional society organized along metaphysical or cosmological figurations of good and evil, cultural deviation from the norm is not easily tolerated nor valued in the name of inventiveness or "originality." In such a setting, to speak or translate on one's behalf rather than the perceived group interests and values is tantamount to betrayal. Thus, the assumption of an individualized nonmaternal voice, such as that of Chicanas during and after the Chicano movement (1965–75),[13] has been cause to label them *malinches* or *vendidas* (sellouts) by some, consequently prompting Chicanas to vindicate Malinche in a variety of ways, as we shall see. Thus, within a culture such as ours, if one should not want to merely break with it, acquiring a "voice of one's own" requires revision and appropriation of cherished metaphysical beliefs.

The Mexican poet and cultural critic Octavio Paz was one of the first to note – in his book *The*

Labyrinth of Solitude[14] – a metonymic link between Malintzin and the epithet *La Chingada*, which is derived from the Hispanicized Nahuátl verb *chingar*. Today *La Chingada* is often used as a synonym for Malintzin. Paz himself reiterates the latter in his introduction to Lafaye's book by remarking that "entre la Chingada y Tonantzin/Guadalupe oscila la vida secreta del mestizo" (The secret life of the mestizo oscillates between La Chingada and Tonantzin/Guadalupe).[15]

Although Paz's views are often the contemporary point of departure for current revisions of the legend and myth of Malintzin, there are two previous stages in its almost five-hundred-year trajectory. The first corresponds to the chroniclers and inventors of the legends; the second corresponds to the development of the traitor myth and scapegoat mechanism which apparently comes to fruition in the nineteenth century during the Mexican independence movement.[16] In this study I would like to focus on the third, modernistic stage which some twentieth-century women and men of letters have felt compelled to initiate in order to revise and vindicate Malintzin.

In writing *The Labyrinth of Solitude* to explicate Mexican people and culture, Octavio Paz was also paying homage to Alfonso Reyes's call to explore and discover our links to the past as put forth in *Visión de Anáhuac (1519).*[17] In that work Reyes suggested that Doña Marina, as he calls her, was the metaphor par excellence of Mexico and its conquest, oppression, and victimization, all of which are very much a part of Mexican life and "historical emotion."[18] Though Reyes's vision was somewhat muted by the decorous language of the beginning of the century, Paz exploits the modernistic break with the sacred in order to expand and clarify Reyes's Doña Marina by transfiguring her into *La Chingada*. In the now-famous chapter "The Sons of La Malinche," Paz argues, as Reyes did before him, that "our living attitude . . . is history also"[19] and concludes that La Malinche is the key to our Mexican origins. In his view Malintzin is more properly our historically grounded originator and accounts for our contemporary "living attitude." However, Paz is not interested in history per se but in the affective and imaginary ways in which that history is/has been experienced and the ways in

which we have responded to it. Paz explores the connections between Malintzin and *La Chingada*, that is, the sexual victim, the raped mother. He argues that as taboo verb (and noun), *chingar* lacks etymological documentation, yet it is part of contemporary speech. Independent of any historical record, the word's existence and significance seem phantasmagorical, illusory. In Terry Eagleton's terms, then, Paz goes to work on the apparently illusory, "the ordinary ideological experience of men,"[20] and tries to demonstrate its connection to historical events and, by implication, men's attitudes towards the feminine. In doing so, however, he transforms Malintzin into the Mexican people's primeval mother, albeit the raped one. To repudiate her, he argues, is to break with the past, to renounce the "origins." Paz believes that he is struggling against "a will to eradicate all that has gone before."[21] He concludes by saying that Cortés's and Malintzin's permanence in the Mexican's imagination and sensibilities reveals that they are more than historical figures: they are symbols of a secret conflict that we have still not resolved. Through the examination of taboo phrases, Paz makes Malintzin the Muse/Mother, albeit raped and vilified – hence, also *La Chingada*. In calling attention to the fact that Malintzin and Cortés are more than historical figures, Paz in effect is implying that they are part and parcel of Mexican ideology – our living attitude; thus they have been abducted from their historical moment and are continuing to haunt us through the workings of that ideology. In a sense, by making Malintzin the founding mother of Mexicans, Paz has unwittingly strengthened the ideological ground that was there before him while simultaneously desacralizing our supposed origins by shifting the founding moment from Guadalupe to Malintzin. Paradoxically, Paz has displaced the myth of Guadalupe, not with history, but with a neomyth, a reversal properly secularized yet unaware of its misogynistic residue. Indeed, Paz's implied audience is male – the so-called "illegitimate mestizo" who may well bristle at the thought that he is outside the legitimate patriarchal order, like women! In Paz's figurations illegitimacy predicated the Mexican founding order. It is a countersuggestion to the belief that Guadalupe legitimized the Mexican founding order. The primary strategy in Paz's modern (secular) position is to wrest contemporary consciousness away from religious cosmologies.

Unlike Reyes, Paz mentions that "the Mexican people have not forgiven Malinche for her betrayal."[22] As such, he emphasizes the ambivalent attitude towards the origins despite the need for acceptance and a change of consciousness. Carlos Fuentes, too, pleads for acceptance of the "murky" and knotted beginnings of the Mexican people in *Todos los gatos son pardos.*[23] However, if Paz implicitly acknowledges the asymmetrical relationship between that of slave (Malintzin) and master (Cortés) by saying that our neosymbolic mother was raped, Fuentes privileges Malintzin's attributed desire for vengeance against her people – hence her alliance with Cortés. Subsequently, Fuentes has Malintzin reveal herself as a misguided fool, thus becoming the ill-fated Mother-Goddess/Muse/Whore, a tripartite figure who possesses the gift of speech. The gift, in the end, makes her a traitor. She self-consciously declares herself *la lengua*, "Yo sólo soy la lengua," adding that objects ultimately act out the destiny that the logos proposes.[24] In this instance, Fuentes, along with such contemporaries as Rosario Castellanos, Elena Poniatowska, José Emilio Pacheco, and Octavio Paz, is portraying through Malintzin the belief that literature is the intention, through the power of language, to recover memory by recovering the word and to project a future by possessing the word.[25] The underlying assumption is that history, insofar as it obeys ideological and metaphysical constraints, does not truly recover human events and experience, nor is it capable of projecting change – thus literature is allocated those functions. Simultaneously, however, and perhaps unknowingly, this point of view ironically suggests that literature (language) also narrates ideological positions that construct readers. In suggesting that their literary production is a theory of history, these Mexican writers also appear to suggest that it is capable of effecting historical changes. It is clear that both Paz and Fuentes view themselves as catalysts, as movers and shakers of the "academic" historians of their time and country. From a secular perspective Paz and Fuentes see themselves as more

radical and as providing a cultural critique. They explode myths with countermyths, or narrative with counternarrative.[26]

In Fuentes's play, Malintzin is the narrator who is in possession of speech. She is, as a result, given the task of recovering the experience of the conquest by spanning the confrontation between powers – that of Cortés and Moctezuma. Thus, for Fuentes, narration is a feminine art in opposition to the masculine "arts of power," a bridge for disparate power brokers, who thus make use of Malintzin's mediating image. One can observe here a romantic artifice – woman the Mother-Goddess/Muse/Whore who is knowledge itself – if only the male artists can decipher it; in this Fuentes falls in line with many other writers from Goethe to Paz. It is, of course, ironic that the narrative should be viewed even symbolically as a feminine art, or an art embedded in the feminine, since few women have practiced it throughout history. But as the fallen goddess in Fuentes, Malintzin recalls patriarchy's Eve, the first linguistic mediator and the primeval biblical mother and traitor, who, of course, is later replaced by the Virgin Mary, alias Guadalupe – the "go-between" mediating two cultural spaces that are viewed as antithetical to each other.

To suggest that language itself, as mediator, is our first betrayal, the Mexican novelist and poet José Emilio Pacheco writes a deceptively simple yet significant poem entitled "Traddutore, traditori" ("Translator, Traitor"). In the poem, Pacheco names the three known translators involved during the time of the conquest – Jerónimo Aguilar, Gonzalo Guerrero, and Malintzin. Pacheco claims that we are indebted to this trio for the knot called Mexico ("el enredo llamado México").[27] For Pacheco, what might have been "authentic" to each cultural discourse before the collision has now been transformed by language's creative and transformative powers. The translators, who use language as their mediating agent, have the ability, consciously or unconsciously, to distort or to convert the "original" event, utterance, text, or experience, thus rendering them false, "impure." The Mexican cultural and biological entanglement is due to the metaphoric property of language and the language traders. By translating, by converting, by transforming

one thing into another, by interpreting (all meanings suggested by the dictionary), the "original,"
supposedly clear connection between words and
objects, is disrupted and corrupted. The
"corruption" that takes place through linguistic
mediation may make the speaker a traitor in the
view of others – not just simply a traitor, but a
traitor to tradition which is represented and
expressed in the "original" event, utterance,
text, or experience. In Pacheco's poem the treacherous acts are rooted in language as mediator,
language as substitution, that is, as metaphor.

It is through metaphor and metonymy that
Reyes, Paz, Fuentes, and Pacheco have been
working to revise, reinterpret, or reverse Malintzin's significations. In the twentieth century, they
are the first appropriators "rescuing" her from
"living attitudes." To cast her in the role of
scapegoat, monstrous double, and traitor as
other men have done is to deny our own monstrous beginnings, that is, the monstrous beginnings of the mestizo (mixed-blood) people in the
face of an ethic of purity and authenticity as
absolute value. By recalling the initial translators
and stressing the role of linguistic mediation,
Pacheco's revisions are the most novel and diffuse
the emphasis on gender and sexuality that the
others rely on for their interpretive visions. Paz
and Fuentes have patently sexualized Malintzin
more than any other writers before them. In
so doing they lay claim to a recovery of the
(maternal) female body as a secular, sexual, and
signifying entity. Sometimes, however, their perspective hovers between attraction and repulsion,
revealing their attitudes towards the feminine and
their "origins." For Fuentes, Malintzin's sexuality is devouring, certainly the monstrous
double of Guadalupe, the asexual and virginal
feminine.

Chicano writers have been particularly influenced by Paz's and Fuentes's revisions of Malintzin. The overall influence can be traced not
only to the fascination that their writings exert
but to the fact that their work was included in
early texts used for Chicano Studies. Two such
texts were *Introduction to Chicano Studies* and
Literatura Chicana: Texto y Contexto.[28] The Chicanos, like the Mexicans, wanted to recover the
origins. However, many Chicanos emphasized

the earlier nationalistic interpretations of Malintzin as the traitorous mediator who should be
expelled from the community rather than
accepted, as Paz and Fuentes had suggested. In
their quest for "authenticity" Chicanos often
desired the silent mediator – Guadalupe, the
unquestioning transmitter of tradition and deliver
from oppression. Thus, it should not have come
as a surprise that the banner of Guadalupe was
one of those carried by the Chicano farm workers
in their strike march of 1965.[29]

In discussing woman's role in traditional
cultures, anthropologist Sherry Ortner has stated,

> Insofar as woman is universally the primary
> agent of early socialization and is seen as
> virtually the embodiment of the functions of
> the domestic group, she will tend to
> come under the heavier restrictions and
> circumscriptions surrounding the unit. Her
> (culturally defined) intermediate position
> between nature and culture, here having the
> significance of her mediation (i.e. performing
> conversion functions) between nature and
> culture, would account not only for her
> lower status but for the greater restrictions
> placed upon her activities.... [S]ocially en-
> gendered conservatism and traditionalism of
> woman's thinking is another – perhaps the
> worst, certainly the most insidious – mode of
> social restriction, and would clearly be related
> to her traditional function of producing well-
> socialized members of the group.[30]

The woman who fulfills this expectation is more
akin to the feminine figure of transcendence, that
is, Guadalupe. In a binary, Manichaean society,
which a religious society is almost by definition,
the one who does not fulfill this expectation is
viewed as subversive or evil and is vilified
through epithets the community understands. If
one agrees with Adrienne Rich, not to speak of
others since Coleridge, that the imagination's
power is potentially subversive, then, for many
Chicanas, "to be a female human being trying to
fulfill traditional female functions in a traditional
way [is] in direct conflict"[31] with their creativity
and inventiveness, as well as with their desire to
transform their cultural roles and redefine themselves in accordance with their experience and

vision. If literature's intention is, in some sense, the recovery or projection of human experience, as the Mexican writers discussed also suggest, then linguistic representation of it could well imply a "betrayal" of tradition, of family, of what is ethically viewed as "pure and authentic," since it involves a conversion into interpretive language rather than ritualized repetition. It is not surprising, then, that some of the most talented writers and intellectuals of contemporary Chicana culture should be fascinated with the figure most perceived as the transgressor of a previous culture believed to be "authentic." It is through a revision of tradition that self and culture can be radically reenvisioned and reinvented. Thus, in order to break with tradition, Chicanas, as writers and political activists, simultaneously legitimate their discourse by grounding it in the Mexican/Chicano community and by creating a "speaking subject" in their reappropriation of Malintzin from Mexican writers and Chicano oral tradition – through her they begin a recovery of aspects of their experience as well as of their language. In this way, the traditional view of femininity invested in Guadalupe is avoided and indirectly denied and reinvested in a less intractable object. Guadalupe's political history represents a community's expectations and utopic desires through divine mediation. Malintzin, however, as a secularly established "speaking subject,"[32] unconstrained by religious beliefs, lends herself more readily to articulation and representation, both as subject and object. In a sense, Malintzin must be led to represent herself, to become the subject of representation, and the closest she can come to this is by sympathizing with latter-day speaking female subjects. Language, as Mikhail Bakhtin has noted,

> becomes "one's own" only when the speaker populates it with her own intention, her own accent, when she appropriates the word, adapting it to her own semantic and expressive intention. Prior to this moment of appropriation, the word does not exist in a neutral and impersonal language (it is not, after all, out of a dictionary that the speaker gets her words!), but rather it exists in other people's mouths, in other people's contexts, serving

other people's intentions: it is from there that one must take the word, and make it one's own.... Language is not a neutral medium that passes freely and easily into the private property of the speaker's intentions; it is populated – overpopulated with the intentions of others. Expropriating, forcing it to submit to one's own intentions and accents, is a difficult and complicated process.[33]

Expropriating Malintzin from the texts of others and filling her with the intentions, significances, and desires of Chicanas has taken years. Mexican men had already effected the operation for their own ends; it was now women's turn. (Though in this essay I only deal with the efforts of Chicanas, some Mexican women writers such as Juana Alegría and Rosario Castellanos have also worked with this figure and have contested male representations.)

One of the first to feel the blow of the masculine denigration of Malintzin was Adelaida R. del Castillo. It was a blow that she apparently felt personally on behalf of all Chicanas, thus provoking her to say that the denigration of Malintzin was tantamount to a defamation of "the character of the Mexicana/Chicana female."[34] For Chicanas, as del Castillo implies, Malintzin was more than a metaphor or foundation/neomyth as Paz would have it; she represented a specific female experience that was being misrepresented and trivialized. By extension, Chicanas/Mexicanas were implicated: del Castillo's attempt to appropriate Malintzin for herself and Chicanas in general involved her in vindication and revision. It is not only Malintzin's appropriation and revision that is at stake, but Chicanas' own cultural self-exploration, self-definition, and self-invention through and beyond the community's sociosymbolic system and contract. The process, however, is complicated by Chicanas' awareness that underlying their words there is also a second (if not secondary) sociosymbolic order – the Anglo-American. She leaves herself open to the accusation of "anglicizing" the community, just as Malinche "hispanicized" it, because her attempts at self-invention are "inappropriate" to her culture and her efforts are viewed as alien to the tradition. In other words, changes wreak havoc with the perceived "authenticity." Each writer, as we shall see, privileges a different aspect of Malintzin's "lives" – that is, the alleged historical experience and/or the inherited imaginary or ideological one.

Adaljiza Sosa Riddell, in "Chicanas in El Movimiento,"[35] an essay written in the heat of the Chicano movement of the early seventies, views Malintzin as a cultural paradigm of the situation of contemporary Chicanas. She thinks that the relationship of Chicanas to Chicanos in the United States has paralleled Malintzin's relationship to the indigenous people in the light of the Spanish conquest. Riddell concludes that Chicanas, like Malintzin before them, have been doubly victimized – by dominant Anglo society and by Mexicano/Chicano communities. In turn, these factors account for some Chicanas' ambiguous and ambivalent position in the face of an unexamined nationalism. Riddell's passionate attempt at revision and appropriation is both a plea for understanding some women's "mediating" position and an apology – an apologia full of irony, for it is the victim's apologia!

Victimization in the context of colonization and of patriarchal suppression of women is a view shared by Carmen Tafolla in her poem "La Malinche."[36] Tafolla's Malintzin claims that she has been misnamed and misjudged by men who had ulterior motives. In Tafolla's poem Malintzin goes on to assert that she submitted to the Spaniard Cortés because she envisioned a new race; she wanted to be the founder of a people. There are echoes of Paz and Fuentes in Tafolla's view, yet she differs by making Malintzin a woman possessed of clear-sighted intentionality, thus avoiding attributions of vengeance.

As Tafolla transforms Malintzin into the founder of a new race through visionary poetry, Adelaida R. del Castillo effects a similar result through a biography which is reconstructed with the few "facts" left us by the chroniclers. In her essay del Castillo claims that Malintzin "embodies effective, decisive action. . . . Her actions syncretized two conflicting worlds causing the emergence of a new one, our own. . . . [W]oman acts not as a goddess in some mythology"[37] but as a producer of history. She

goes on to say that Malintzin should be "perceived as a woman who was able to act beyond her prescribed societal function (i.e., servant and concubine) and perform as one who was willing to make great sacrifices for what she believed to be a philanthropic conviction."[38] Del Castillo wants to avoid the mythmaking trap by evading "poetic language" and by appealing to "historical facts." In a sense, unlike the male Mexican writers reviewed, she privileges history as a more truthful account than literature. (This may spell the difference between del Castillo's Anglo-American education and experience and that of Mexican nationals for whom history often is reconstructed anew with each new regime, thereby encouraging a cynical attitude. Perspectives on the disciplines of history and literature differ according to our location, experience, and education.) However, notwithstanding her famed translating abilities, Malintzin has left us no recorded voice because she was illiterate; that is, she could not leave us a sense of herself and of her experience. Thus our disquisitions truly take place over her corpse and have no clue as to her own words, but instead refer to the words of the chroniclers who themselves were not free of self-interest, motive, and intention. Thus, all interpreters of her figure are prey to subjectivized mythmaking once they begin to attribute motives, qualities, and desires to her regardless of the fact that they have recourse to historical motifs regarding her role, a role seen through the eyes of Cortés, Bernal Díaz del Castillo, Tlaxcaltecas, and many others present at the time. For Adelaida R. del Castillo, then, Malintzin should be viewed as a woman who made a variety of *choices* (sic) due to a "philanthropic conviction," that is, her conviction that Cortés was Quetzalcóatl and, subsequently, that Christ was the true Quetzalcóatl, or that the true Quetzalcóatl was Christ – hence Malintzin's role in converting the indigenous population and her "sense of deliverance when she recognized that the Spaniards resembled Quetazalcóatl."[39] In other words, Malintzin initially fell victim to a mistaken identity but subsequently recognized Quetzalcóatl in Christ and displaced her devotion onto Cortés, onto Christ, and, subsequently, onto the child who would represent the new race. I think there is as much a revision of Paz and Fuentes as of history (i.e., the chroniclers) in del Castillo's interpretation, as well as a repudiation of Paz's views of woman's passive sexuality. In short, as del Castillo revises a "mythology" (as she names it in opposition to history) with which she feels implicated, she appears to be reading two texts at once, the purported "original" one (the chroniclers) and the "mythology of the original" (Paz and Fuentes). These texts are separated by almost five centuries; however, del Castillo wants to appropriate Malintzin for herself, as one whose face reflects her vision – Malintzin as agent, choice-maker, and producer of history. Actually, the whole notion of choice, an existentialist notion of twentieth-century Anglo-European philosophy, needs to be problematized in order to understand the constraints under which women of other cultures, times, and places live. In trying to make Malintzin a motivated "producer of history," del Castillo is not so much reconstructing Malintzin's own historical moment as she is using her both to counter contemporary masculine discourse and to project a newer sense of a female self, a speaking subject with a thoroughly modern view of historical consciousness.

A similar strategy is used by Cordelia Candelaria in the essay "La Malinche, Feminist Prototype."[40] For Candelaria, Malintzin is the feminist prototype because she "defied traditional social expectations of woman's role."[41] Candelaria enumerates a variety of roles that she enacted: "liaison, guide to region, advisor on native customs, and beliefs, and strategist . . . [T]he least significant role was that of mistress."[42] Though the roles described by the chroniclers may fit within such a description, the verb "defied" does not. It is difficult to know to what extent it was possible to defy either native or Spanish cultures since both adhered to the trinitarian worldview of Authority, Religion, and Tradition. The defiance Candelaria speaks of is rooted in contemporary existentialist philosophy, which has been as yet an unfinished revolt against the former worldview.[43] In revising the image of Malintzin, Candelaria privileges a self capable of making choices and of intellectual acumen over a self-manifesting sexuality and polyglotism, thus

avoiding in effect the two most significant charges against her. Since sexuality, especially as ascribed to the maternal, and language are such powerful aspects of culture, it is in my opinion inadvisable to avoid them; they must be kept in view by the newer sense of a self who challenges traditions.

It is as a redeeming Mother/Goddess that Sylvia Gonzáles awaits Malintzin's return in her poem "Chicana Evolution."[44] In this poem Gonzáles views the self as a "Chicana/Daughter of Malinche."[45] Gonzáles claims to await Malinche's return so that she may deny her traitorous guilt, cleanse her flesh, and "sacrifice herself" in "redemption of all her forsaken daughters"[46] – the New World's Demeter, perhaps, who shall rescue all Chicana Persephones. Whereas Fuentes will have Malintzin redeem the latter-day sons/Quetzalcóatl, Gonzáles will have her redeem the daughters. This redemptory return will empower Gonzales's creativity, who admires those women who have stripped themselves of passivity with their "pens."[47] At present, however, she feels over whelmed by her definitions – "a creation of actions/as well as words."[48] For Gonzáles, writing itself is empowering, yet she postpones the daughters' actual enablement, as if the appropriation of language were still to take place. As a result, her revision is gloomy – we still await. Our deliverance is viewed in apocalyptic terms, but Malinche has been substituted for Guadalupe.

The intertextual debate between women and men raises the following question implicitly: does Malintzin belong to the sons or the daughters? Each answers for him- or herself, narrowing the quarrel to a struggle for the possession of the neomaternal figure. Malintzin's procreative role is privileged in one way or another by most of these writers. Who shall speak for her, represent her? Is she now the procreator of the new founding order? Who will define that order?

In the face of patriarchal tradition, Malintzin as Mother-Goddess/Muse/Whore is viewed by some as the daughters' own redemptress. In the recently published three-part poem called *La Chingada*, Alma Villanueva envisions Malintzin as the displaced and desecrated prepatriarchal goddess who has returned to redeem and empower her daughters and to transform the sons. Villanueva states in a short preface to the poem:

"This poem is a furious response centuries later to masculine culture, that is, a patriarchal destructive power that threatens all existence . . . "; the destructiveness emanates from "a strange, disembodied, masculine God" through whom men first "discredited, the first raped woman, when the feminine was forced to abdicate its sacred power."[49] In the previsionary section, Villanueva suggests that the Mexican/Chicana Malintzin, also known as *La Chingada*, is a recent reenactment and parody of the more ancient routing of the Goddess, one of whose names was Demeter.

Within the poem itself, the goddess Malintzin/Demeter calls upon the sons to transform themselves into "loving men capable of reinventing love." That feat can only be achieved by evoking the "girlchild inside" of them, by healing all the nameless wild animals that they killed and watched die due to some masculine quest or ritual.[50] In Part II, titled "The Dead," in opposition to Part I which was titled "The Living," the Goddess, who is now conflated with *La Llorona/Mater Dolorosa*,[51] mourns her dead daughter. The daughters were prepared for their defeat through socialization. The malediction "*Hijos de La Chingada*" is reserved for the sons, who in profound irony have been birthed to kill the mourned daughters. Subsequently, the Goddess calls upon the daughters to give birth to themselves, to renew their being. Both sons and daughters are forbidden to look back to old religious models and are urged to re-create themselves with her help. She is willing to sacrifice herself so that "You are born, at last, unto/yourself!"[52] In her representation of Malintzin, Villanueva tries to fulfill Adrienne Rich's view of the daughter's desire for a mother "whose love and whose power were so great as to undo rape and bring her back from death."[53]

Villanueva's interpretation of Malintzin draws on elements from Paz who, along with Rich in *Of Woman Born: Motherhood as Experience and Institution*,[54] is one of the epigrammatic voices preceding the poem. She also borrows elements from Fuentes; however, she replaces his view of a vengeful Malintzin with a redeeming one, who will not be still until she is recognized as patriarchy's suppressed woman, the one upon whose body Western civilization has been built – hence, the call for erasing religious models which hold daughters and sons back from newer senses of self. In her feminist revision Villanueva differs from Paz and Fuentes in that she does not "plead" for acceptance of Malintzin as Goddess/Raped Mother. On the contrary, Malintzin speaks on her own behalf and is enraged over her suppression, desecration, and rape, all of which have disenabled the female line. A crime has been committed against the Mother/Goddess, and she demands retribution and justice. Villanueva addresses directly the sexual and linguistic aspects of Malintzin's so-called betrayal, precisely what Candelaria avoids in her representation. In reading Villanueva's poem, one is made aware of the powerful charge effected when the speaking subject appropriates language and expresses her rage at the suppression of maternal self-representation.

Lucha Corpi refers to Malintzin by her Spanish name, Marina. This factor is significant because Corpi inscribes Marina into biblical discourses rather than pre-patriarchal ones. Thus, it follows that she should be called Marina as the Spaniards baptized her. For Corpi, Marina is a parody and reenactment of Eve and Mary, a woman who has sacrificed herself for the latter-day daughter and who, because of her experience, presages a renewing and enabling cycle. In four poems, or one poem consisting of four parts, which are in turn titled "Marina Mother," "Marina Virgin," "The Devil's Daughter," and "She (Distant Marina)," Corpi revises the story of Marina/Malintzin.[55] Marta Sánchez, in *Contemporary Chicana Poetry: A Critical Approach to an Emerging Literature*, views Corpi's cycle of poems accurately, I think, when she observes that "Corpi's cultural paradigm leaves readers no alternative but to accept a passive Marina who can do nothing about her situation."[56] "Marina Madre" is perceived as victim of her own feminine condition. That is, insofar as women are women and mothers, they are incommensurably vulnerable. Using images that allude to the Old and New testaments, Corpi imagines a Marina made of the "softest clay" by the Patriarchs ("los viejos"): in biblical inscription and creation as either Eve ("her name written on the patriarchal tree") or as Mary ("the fruit of her womb stolen") and, nearer to us in time, the Marina abandoned and vilified by father, husband, and son. The latter three may be seen as an allusion to the male triad in one God – Father, Son, and Holy Ghost – as the Catholic tradition holds. By planting her soul in the earth, Corpi's latter-day Marina reinscribes herself and awaits her own renewal. The "she" in the fourth poem – "She (Distant Marina)" – is that contemporary daughter who is imagined as a "mourning shadow of an ancestral figure" crossing a bridge leading to a new time and space, a reconstructed self. The passive, victimized Marina of the first two poems is left behind. Marta Sánchez has also suggested that the bridge is the boundary crossed "between Mexico and the United States."[57] Both Corpi's reinscription and Sánchez's interpretation of it continue to emphasize the mediating function assigned to Marina, though from a Chicano point of view in which the Spaniards, harbingers of a different existence, are now replaced by Anglo-Americans. It is important to reiterate the value placed by many Chicanas on a primary identification with the indigenous people or recuperations of that identity and the rejection of a Spanish one, despite the use of the language. However, these rhetorical strategies are now often undertaken to underscore our differences from Anglo-Americans.

For Gonzáles, Villanueva, and Corpi the forced disappearance of the Mother/Goddess leads to the daughter's own abjection. The daughter is doomed to repeat the cycle until the ancient powers of the goddess are restored. Of the three, however, Villanueva is the only one who, in appropriating Malintzin, makes her a speaking subject on her own behalf and on behalf of the daughters in a truly powerful way. Gonzáles and Corpi objectify her and leave us with a promise of vindication.

Cherríe Moraga also explores the significations of Malintzin in her recent book *Loving in the War Years: lo que nunca pasó por sus labios*.[58] Moraga feels, on the one hand, a need to recover the race of the biographical mother so that she may recover her ethnosexual identity and, on the other, a need to appropriate her political and literary voice.[59] Simultaneously, however, a search for

the identity of, and relation between, self and mother also requires an exploration of the myth of Malintzin who is our "sexual legacy."[60] That legacy is inscribed in cruel epithets such as "*La Chingada*," "*La Vendida*," "Traitor." These epithets are in turn used on women to stigmatize, to limit the quest for autonomy, and to limit "The Chicana imagination ... before it has a chance to consider some of the most difficult questions."[61] Moraga points to the double bind of the Chicana who defies tradition; she is viewed either as a traitor to her race or a lesbian. As such, not only is the lesbian in the Chicano imagination *una Malinchista*, but vice versa. Feminism, which questions patriarchal tradition by representing women's subjectivity and/or interjecting it into extant discursive modes, thereby revising them, may be equated with *malinchismo* or lesbianism. Even as she recognizes the double bind, Moraga proceeds to identify herself as a lesbian who, as such, represents the "most visible manifestation of a woman taking control of her own sexual identity and destiny, who severely challenges the antifeminist Chicano/a."[62] Moraga thinks that if she were not a lesbian she would still be viewed as one by a culture that does not understand the pursuit of a sexual identity beyond heterosexism.[63] In a sense, for Moraga, lesbianism in our culture is the ultimate trope for the pursuit of newer gender identities, for anything that smacks of difference in the face of traditional gender values. Rather than try to revise the myths of Malintzin, Moraga accepts them and labels them male myths whose purpose is to exercise social control over women. To escape the double bind, Moraga has no choice but to declare that, indeed, she comes "from a long line of vendidas."[64] One could, however, opt for Lorna D. Cervantes's sarcastic view of the usual male perception of Malintzin's figure by stating ambiguously, as does the title of her poem, "Baby, you cramp my style."[65] Baby is, of course, a double allusion – to him who would impose his notions on her and to Malinche, whose historical existence and subsequent interpretations are a burden. Moraga and Cervantes, in a sense, become the heroines of their own individualized vision and revision, for it is through their appropriations that we proceed beyond Malinche.

However, have they truly integrated the "treacherous" Malintzin whose ascribed attributes are the source of contention – the speaking subject and procreator? Cervantes's sarcasm is a dismissal of the subject in favor of her own future self-creation. On the other hand, if one follows Moraga's reasoning and takes it one step further, then one would have to say that the ultimate trope for the pursuit of new gender identities is not so much lesbianism as it is the speaking subject who is also a lesbian mother, or perhaps one who articulates and visualizes herself and procreation beyond heterosexism. If newer racial and gendered identities are to be forged, the insight arrived at in writing needs to be communicated to millions of women who still live under such metaphoric controls. How are they to be persuaded to accept these insights if they still exist under the ideology "Guadalupe-Malintzin"?

If for the Mexican male writers the originating rape is of paramount importance because it places in question their legitimacy as sons, Chicanas – with the exception of Villanueva, who accepts Paz's view – do not even mention rape in connection with Malintzin. Paz, as far as I can discern, was the first writer to advance forcefully the metonymic relations between three terms – Malintzin, La Chingada, and rape. Though pillage and rape are almost by definition factors of conquest and colonization, there is no trace of evidence that Malintzin suffered the violent fate of other indigenous women, strictly speaking – though her disappearance from the record is troublesome and puzzling. One may even argue that she performed as she did to avoid rape and violence upon her body, to "choose" negatively between lesser evils. Clearly, in patriarchal and patrilineal societies – which these were – sons stand to lose a great deal more if they are the illegitimate offspring of rapes. Daughters, like their mothers, would still have to struggle to protect themselves from rapists. "Legitimacy" under these circumstances at best grants a female protection from rape; it does not make a woman her father's heir nor even give her a sure claim to her offspring. For the men, the so-called rape is largely figurative, a sign of their "emasculating" loss; for the women, it is literal. There is irony in Paz's insistence that Malintzin should also serve as the figure for "our" rape since it may well be that she saved herself from such a fate through diligent service. There are no choices for slaves, only options between lesser evils.

Because Malintzin's neosymbolic existence in the masculine imagination has affected the actual experience of so many Mexicanas and Chicanas, it became necessary for "her daughters" to revise her scanty biography. Through revisions, many undertaken in isolation, contemporary Chicana writers have helped to lay bare Malintzin's double etymology which until recently appeared illusory and hallucinative: one privileges the sociosymbolic possibilities for signification; the second, the existential and historical implications. Some of the writers discussed have actually, as speaking subjects, reemphasized the patriarchal view of the maternal/feminine as mediator, even though they wish to represent her themselves. Others have transformed her into the neo-myth of the goddess. Still others have foregrounded qualities such as "choice-maker," "history producer," and "self-aware" speaking subject, all of which are part of modern and contemporary experience and desire. In a sense, they sidestep the image of Malintzin as raped mother and part of the feminine condition. Except for Villanueva, who follows Paz in this respect, no one has explored the full impact – imaginary or not – that such an image may have for us. It emphasizes that our beginnings, which took place barely half a millennium ago, are drenched in violence, not simply symbolic but historically coinciding with European expansionist adventures. It implies that the object of that violence was/has been feminine (or feminized) and that it barely begins to be recovered as subject or even object of our history. Since the European expansionists of the time were Christians, it implies that indeed the ancient putative suppression of the goddess was reenacted; the missionaries did not have a problem assimilating Quetzalcóatl into their discourse but suppressed Tonantzin. However, since Chicanas have begun the appropriation of history, sexuality, and language for themselves, they find themselves situated at the cutting edge of a new historical moment involving a radical though fragile change in consciousness. It is an era in which we live in simultaneous time zones from the pre-Colombian to the ultra-modern, from the cyclical to the linear. The latter is certainly a theme in the work of Carlos Fuentes, Rosario Castellanos, Octavio Paz, and other contemporary Mexican writers. However, I think that the objectified thematics have now passed onto a more consciously claimed subjectivity in the work of Chicanas such as Gloria Anzaldúa's *Borderlands/ La Frontera: The New Mestiza*.[66] Moreover, such subjectivity is capable of shedding light upon Chicanas' present historical situation without necessarily, in this newer key, falling prey to a mediating role but, rather, catching stunning insights into our complex culture by taking hold of the variegated imaginative and historical discourses that have informed the constructions of race, gender, and ethnicities in the last five hundred years and that still vibrate in our time. Issues of "class" and "color" (i.e., race and ethnicity) per se have not entered the appropriation because, I think, the historical person and textual figure of Malintzin (indigenous female slave in her own society as well as in the one taking shape under the Spaniards) implicitly subsume those as part of her condition – hence the possibility of her suppression as feminine/maternal speaking subject. It could very well signify that anyone *completely* deprived of voice within the Anglo-European and Spanish imperialist projects has by definition been an impoverished and/ or enslaved woman of color. Here, then, is a powerful reason why the notion of the "literature of women of color" in the United States is one of the most novel ideas to have arisen in the Anglo-European imperialist context. Such a notion is yet to be part of Mexican or Latin American criticism; we have yet to see how women there begin to resolve their struggle for self-representation. Mexican writers Elena Poniatowska and Rosario Castellanos have many a heroine who is a woman of color. Consciously or unconsciously they have tried, as upper-class Mexican writers, to understand the complexity of the relationship between a woman of color (or native one) and Anglo-European patriarchal history and thought. It is in the vibrations of that distance between them that the appropriation of the many transformations of a woman of color lies.

In a more recent appropriation of Malintzin, Tzvetan Todorov appears to agree with some of the Chicanas discussed, which is an interesting phenomenon since for each the work of the other was unavailable at the time of writing. The agreement appears coincidental for those of us who have been forced for historical, political, and economic reasons to become perennial migrants in search of "home." For Todorov, Malintzin is the

> first example, and thereby the symbol, of the cross-breeding of cultures; she thereby heralds the modern state of Mexico and beyond that, the present state of us all, since if we are not invariably bilingual, we are inevitably bi- or tri-cultural. La Malinche glorifies mixture to the detriment of purity ... and the role of the intermediary. She does not simply submit to the other ... ; she adopts the other's ideology and serves it in order to understand her own culture better, as is evidenced by the effectiveness of her conduct (even if "understanding" here means "destroying").[67]

The reconstruction of ourselves as women or as exiles from "home" due to subjugations is fraught with paradox, contradiction, and unlikely partners, such as Mexican male writers and Todorov. Though Todorov does not mention the role of gender and sexuality in his interpretation, he also readily finds a point of identification for himself.

As historical subject Malintzin remains shrouded in preternatural silence, and as object she continues to be on trial for speaking and bearing the enemy's children and continues to be a constant source of revision and appropriation – indeed, for articulating our modern and postmodern condition. The "discovery" and colonization of what is presently called the Third World could just as well be said to have started when the Spaniards conquered Mexico as at any other moment – and also at a time when a significant portion of Europe was about to inaugurate the modern epoch, that is, the Reformation, Copernicus, Galileo, Cartesian philosophy, etc. Thus the quarrel over the interpretation of Malintzin serves not only as a heuristic device for the assumption of feminism in a traditionalist and essentialist setting where men refuse to let

women speak for themselves, or women feel constrained from speaking, but also as the measure-
ment of discursive maneuvers in the effort to
secularize or appropriate thought for oneself. It
is noteworthy that these have to be undertaken
under the auspices of a woman – the one who did
not remain the "internalized other" of the European's other. And what about the women who
remain the "internalized others," that is, the ones
who submit or are "offerings" to the colonizers?
What can we make of such gifts? Do they become
like the Mayan women in the epigram, a woman
in the service of violence against herself?

Much of the Chicana feminist work of the
seventies, like Anglo-American feminist work,
was launched around the assumption of a unified
subject organized oppositionally to men from a
perspective of gender differences. The assumption that the subject is autonomous, self-deter-
mining, and self-defining often has been a critical
space shared by many feminists because it opens
up vistas of agency for the subject. Often that
critical space has generated the notion, especially
among Anglo-Americans, that women's oppression can be described universally from the perspective of gender differences, as if boundaries of
race, ethnicities, and class had not existed. The
fact that Todorov also shares that critical space
makes it possible for him to project onto La
Malinche observations similar to those of some
Chicanas, ironically even more similar than those
of Mexican men. The Mexican men do not forget
that she is an Indian and a woman, thus making it
possible for them to understand the "betrayal" on
the grounds that she would not want to remain
"in the service of violence against herself." However, to the extent that we know it, the story of La
Malinche demonstrates that crossing ethnic and
racial boundaries does not necessarily free her
from "violence against herself"; moreover, once
her usefulness is over she is silenced and disappears from the record, precisely because she is an
Indian and a woman. She crosses over to a site
where there is no "legitimated" place for her in
the conqueror's new order. Crossings over by
"choice" or by force become sporadic individual
arrangements that do not necessarily change the
status of Indian women or women of color, for
example. The realization that the "invitation" to

cross over, when it is extended, does not ameliorate the lot of women of color in general has led, in
the eighties, to a feminist literature by Chicanas
and women of color which demonstrates that,
despite some shared critical perspectives, boundaries exist and continue to exist, thus accounting
for differential experiences that cannot be contained under the sign of a universal woman or
women. Yet for Mexicans, Guadalupe is a symbol
that continues to exist for the purpose of
"universalizing" and containing women's lives
within a discrete cultural banner that may be
similar to those of other cultures. On the other
hand, the diverse twentieth-century interpretations of La Malinche rupture the stranglehold
of religion by introducing the notion of historical,
sexual, and linguistic agency, though not necessarily available to La Malinche herself at the
beginning of the Mexican colonial period.

Postmodern feminist theories have arisen to
supplant gender standpoint epistemology and to
diffuse explanatory binarisms. However, the critical question arises: do they free women of color
from the "service of violence against themselves,"
or do they only rationalize it well? For those of us
who simultaneously assume a critical position and
a kinship with "native women" and women of
color, the "philosophical bases of political
criticism"[68] and cognitive practices are as important as the deployment of critical theories: do they
also function to help to keep women from doing
service against themselves – if not, why not?

NOTES

1   Jacques Lafaye, *Quetzalcóatl y Guadalupe: La
    Formación de la conciencia en México (1531–
    1813)*, trans. Ida Vitale (México: Fondo de Cul-
    tura Económica, 1983).
2   Eric R. Wolf, "The Virgen de Guadalupe: A
    Mexican National Symbol," *Journal of American
    Folklore* 71, no. 279 (January–March 1958): 38.
3   Cited in Gustavo A. Rodríguez, *Doña Marina*
    (Mexico: Imprenta de la Secretaría de Rela-
    ciones Exteriores, 1935), 48.
4   I borrow the notion of "sociosymbolic contract"
    from Julia Kristeva. She uses the notion in the

essay "Women's Time," trans. Alice Jardine and Harry Blake, *Signs* 7, no. 1 (Autumn 1981): 13–35. I take it to mean a kind of contract within which the social life of women (and some men) is expected to conform or live up to a metaphysical (essential) configuration of who we ought to become in the socialization process. These metaphysical configurations are accompanied by culture-specific "semantic charters." Pierre Maranda suggests that "[s]emantic charters condition our thoughts and emotions. They are culture-specific networks that we internalize as we undergo the process of socialization." Moreover, these charters or signifying systems "have an inertia and momentum of their own. There are semantic domains whose inertia is high: kinship terminologies, the dogmas of authoritarian churches, the conception of sex roles." See his essay "The Dialectic of Metaphor: An Anthropological Essay on Hermeneutics," in *The Reader in the Text: Essays on Audience and Interpretation*, ed. Susan R. Suleiman and Inge Crosman (Princeton: Princeton University Press, 1980), 184–85.

5 The "natives" that came to hate Cortés and Malintzin are the mestizos – the mixed-blood offspring – since the indigenous people at the time of the conquest often welcomed them as liberators. It is of interest to note that throughout the Mexican colonial period the missionaries staged secular plays for the indigenous population in which Cortés and Malintzin were represented as their liberators. Some parishes, even today, continue to reenact these plays in dispersed communities. I draw the preceding comments from Norma Cantú's work in progress, "Secular and Liturgical Folk Drama," presented at the National Association of Chicano Studies, Los Angeles, March 29–April 1, 1989.

6 René Girard, *Violence and the Sacred*, trans. Patrick Gregory (Baltimore: Johns Hopkins University Press, 1977), 273.

7 Ibid., 99.

8 Ibid., 96.

9 Cortés's misfortunes with the Spanish Crown may be linked to the need of the successor colonizers and the colonized to extirpate him from their relations with Spain. Certainly, he has been expelled from public life in Mexico where no monuments or mementos to his role in the conquest may be seen. Ironically, he is very much in everyone's mind.

10 *La Chingada* is used to refer, literally, to a woman who is "fucked" or "fucked over." Thus, Paz and others suggest a metonymic relation to rape. When used in the past participle, passivity on her part is implied. The verb and its derivatives imply violent action, and much depends on context and the speaker's inflection. To refer to a masculine actor, the term *chingón* is used.

11 Girard, *Violence and the Sacred*, 99.

12 I draw on the work of Walter J. Ong for parts of this discussion, especially *The Presence of the Word: Some Prolegomena for Cultural and Religious History* (New Haven: Yale University Press, 1967) and *Orality and Literacy: The Technologizing of the Word* (New York: Methuen, 1982).

13 These dates are highly arbitrary, especially the closing date. There is consensus among Chicano critics that the production of contemporary Chicano literature began in conjunction with César Chávez's National Farm Workers' Association strike of 1965, noting the fact that Luis Valdez's Teatro Campesino was inaugurated on the picket lines. See Marta Sánchez's *Contemporary Chicana Poetry: Critical Approaches to an Emerging Literature* (Berkeley and Los Angeles: University of California Press, 1985), 2–6. For the recuperation of the term *vendida* (sellout), see Cherríe Moraga's essay "A Long Line of Vendidas," in her *Loving in the War Years: Lo que nunca pasó por sus labios* (Boston: South End Press, 1983), 90–117.

14 Though the Spanish original was published in 1950, I use the Lysander Kemp translation of Octavio Paz, *The Labyrinth of Solitude: Life and Thought in Mexico* (New York: Grove Press, 1961).

15 Lafaye, *Quetzalcóatl y Guadalupe*, 22.

16 These stages have suggested themselves to me in reviewing Rachel Phillips's essay "Marina/Malinche: Masks and Shadows," in *Women in Hispanic Literature: Icons and Fallen Idols*, ed. Beth Miller (Berkeley and Los Angeles: University of California Press, 1983), 97–114. See also Rodríguez's *Dona Marina* and the work of Norma Cantú, "Secular and Liturgical Folk Drama."

17 Though the work was originally published in 1915, I use Alfonso Reyes, *Visión de Anáhuac (1519)* (México: El Colegio de Mexico, 1953).

18 Reyes, *Visión de Anáhuac*, 61–62.

19 Paz, *Labyrinth of Solitude*, 71.

20 Terry Eagleton, *Marxism and Literary Criticism* (Berkeley and Los Angeles: University of California Press, 1976), 19.

21 Paz, *Labyrinth of Solitude*, 87.

22 Ibid., 86.

23 Though originally published in 1970, I use Carlos Fuentes's *Todos los gatos son pardos* (Mexico: Siglo XXI, 1984).

24 Ibid., 64, 99.

25 Ibid., 5–6.

26 An interesting study of Paz's and Fuentes's work is presented by Edmond Cros, *Theory and Practice of Sociocriticism*, trans. Jerome Schwartz (Minneapolis: University of Minnesota Press, 1988), 153–89.

27 José Emilio Pacheco, *Islas a la deriva* (México: Siglo XXI, 1976), 27–28.

28 For example, Octavio Paz's "The Sons of La Malinche" may be found in *Introduction to Chicano Studies: A Reader*, eds. Livie Isauro Durán and H. Russell Bernard (New York: Macmillan, 1973), 17–27, and Carlos Fuentes's "The Legacy of La Malinche," in *Literatura Chicana: Texto y Contexto*, eds. Antonia Castañeda Shular, Tomas Ybarra-Frausto, and Joseph Sommers (New York: Prentice-Hall, 1972), 304–06.

29 For a perspective on men's implicit or explicit use of oppositional female figures whose outlines may be rooted in Guadalupe-Malintzin, see Juan Bruce-Novoa, "One More Rosary for Doña Marina," *Confluencia* 1, no. 22 (Spring 1986): 73–84. In the eighties some Chicana visual artists have begun experimenting with the image of Guadalupe. Ester Hernández, for example, depicts the Virgin executing a karate kick. Santa Barraza depicts a newly unearthed Coatlicue (Mesoamerican fertility goddess) pushing Guadalupe upward and overpowering her. The contrastive images tell the story of the difference between them – the one small, the other huge. See reproductions of these works in *Third Woman* 4 (1989): 42, 153, respectively. Yolanda M. López has portrayed "Guadalupe Walking" in high-heel sandals. The reproduction that *Fem* 8, no. 34 (Junio–Julio 1984) carried on its cover provoked a large number of hate mail, accusing the editors of being "Zionists." According to Hernández's personal communication, the exhibit of her Guadalupe ink drawing caused a minor scandal in a small California town. She had to leave the exhibit to avoid violent attack. Community leaders had to schedule workshops to discuss the work and the artist's rights. Modern revisions of Guadalupe are fraught with difficulty and may well be the reason why Chicana writers have bypassed her. She still retains a large, devoted following.

30 Sherry B. Ortner, "Is Female to Male as Nature is to Culture?," in *Woman, Culture, and Society*, ed. Michelle Zimbalist Rosaldo and Louise Lamphere (Stanford: Stanford University Press, 1974), 85.

31 Adrienne Rich, *On Lies, Secrets and Silence: Selected Prose, 1966–1978* (New York: Norton, 1979), 43.

32 For the notion of the "speaking subject" I am guided by Julia Kristeva's work, especially "The Ethics of Linguistics," in *Desire in Language: A Semiotic Approach to Literature and Art*, trans. Thomas Gora, Alice Jardine, and Leon S. Roudiez, ed. Leon S. Roudiez (New York: Columbia University Press, 1980), 23–25.

33 I have taken the liberty of changing all of the he's in Bakhtin's text to she's (Mikhail M. Bakhtin, *The Dialogic Imagination: Four Essays*, trans. Caryl Emerson and Michael Holquist, ed. Michael Holquist [Austin: University of Texas Press, 1981], 293–94).

34 Adelaida R. del Castillo, "Malintzin Tenepal: A Preliminary Look Into a New Perspective," in *Essays on La Mujer*, ed. Rosaura Sánchez and Rosa Martínez Cruz (Los Angeles: Chicano Studies Center Publications, University of California, Los Angeles, 1977), 141.

35 Adaljiza Sosa Riddell, "Chicanas and El Movimiento," *Aztlán* 5, nos. 1–2 (1974): 155–65.

36 Carmen Tafolla, "La Malinche," in *Five Poets of Aztlán*, ed. Santiago Daydi-Tolson (Binghamton, N.Y.: Bilingual Press, 1985), 193–95.

37 del Castillo, "Malintzin Tenepal," 125.

38 Ibid., 126.

39 Ibid., 130.

40 Cordelia Candelaria, "La Malinche, Feminist Prototype," *Frontiers* 5, no. 2 (1980): 1–6.

41 Ibid., 6.

42 Ibid., 3.

43 The unfinished revolt is discussed by Hannah Arendt, *Between Past and Future: Eight Exercises in Political Thought* (London: Penguin Books, 1978).

44 Sylvia Gonzáles, "Chicana Evolution," in *The Third Woman: Minority Women Writers of the United States*, ed. Dexter Fisher (Boston: Houghton Mifflin, 1980), 418–22.

45 Ibid., 420.

46 Ibid., 420.

47 Ibid., 420.

48 Ibid., 419.

49 Alma Villanueva, "La Chingada," in *Five Poets of Aztlán*, ed. Santiago Daydi-Tolson (Binghamton, N.Y.: Bilingual Review Press, 1985), 140.

50 Ibid., 153.

51 In "La Llorona, The Third Legend of Greater Mexico: Cultural Symbols, Women, and the Political Unconscious," *Renato Rosaldo Lecture Series Monograph*, no. 2 (1984–85) (Tucson: Mexican American Studies and Research Center, University of Arizona, Spring 1986): 59–93, José Limón has argued that La Llorona (The Weeping Woman) would make a more effective feminist cultural symbol for women of Mexican descent. In fact, he argues that Chicanas have failed to recognize her potential feminist political importance. In my view, La Llorona fails to meet some of the modern and secularizing factors that Chicanas have felt they've needed in order to speak for themselves. The so-called second wave of global feminism forces contemporary women to deal with the notion of the self and subjectivity that previous feminisms have often by passed in favor of women's rights on the basis of being wives and mothers. The current debate on La Malinche goes beyond that.

52 Villanueva, "La Chingada," 163.

53 Ibid., 142.

54 Adrienne Rich, *Of Woman Born: Motherhood as Experience and Institution* (New York: W. W. Norton, 1976).

55 Lucha Corpi, "Marina Mother," "Marina Virgin," "The Devil's Daughter," and "She (Distant Marina)" in her *Palabras de Mediodía/Noon Words: Poems*, trans. Catherine

Rodríguez-Nieto (Berkeley: El Fuego de Aztlán Publications, 1980), 118–25.

56 Sánchez, *Contemporary Chicana Poetry*, 190.

57 Ibid., 194.

58 Cherríe Moraga, *Loving in the War Years*.

59 For a complementary essay on the way Chicana writers have reconstructed the relationship between self and mothers in order to redefine their feminine/feminist identity, see Norma Alarcón, "What Kind of Lover Have You Made Me, Mother?," in *Women of Color: Perspectives on Feminism and Identity*, ed. Audrey T. McCluskey (Bloomington, In.: Women's Studies Monograph Series, no. 1, 1985), 85–110.

60 Moraga, *Loving in the War Years*, 99.

61 Ibid., 112.

62 Ibid., 113.

63 In charging the Chicano community with heterosexism, Moraga relies on Adrienne Rich's sense of the term in "Compulsory Heterosexuality and Lesbian Existence," in *Women – Sex and Sexuality*, ed. Catharine R. Stimpson and Ethel Spector Person (Chicago and London: University of Chicago Press, 1980), 62–91.

64 Moraga, *Loving in the War Years*, 117.

65 Lorna D. Cervantes, "Baby, You Cramp My Style", *El Fuego de Aztlán* 1, no. 4 (1977): 39.

66 Gloria Anzaldúa, *Borderlands/La Frontera: The New Mestiza* (San Francisco: Spinsters/Aunt Lute, 1987).

67 Tzvetan Todorov, *The Conquest of America: The Conquest of the Other*, trans. Richard Howard (New York: Harper and Row, 1985), 101.

68 The gulf between criticism and politics or criticism and cognitive practices is examined by S. P. Mohanty, "Us and Them: On the Philosophical Bases of Political Criticism," *Yale Journal of Criticism* 2, no. 2 (1989): 1–31; Mary E. Hawkesworth, "Knowers, Knowing, Known: Feminist Theory and Claims of Truth," *Signs* 14, no. 3 (Spring 1989): 533–57; Edward W. Said, *The World, The Text, and the Critic* (Cambridge: Harvard University Press, 1983); and Chandra T. Mohanty, "Under Western Eyes: Feminist Scholarship and Colonial Discourse," *Boundary 2* 12, no. 3, and 13, no. 1 (Spring and Fall 1984): 333–58.

2

From the Plantation to the Plantation (Excerpt)

Antonio Benítez-Rojo

The Plantation and the Africanization of Culture

The history of the non-Hispanic possessions in the Caribbean is complex in the extreme. In any event, this book does not hope to cover the history of the different colonial blocs. It is of interest nonetheless that the presence of Spain's rival powers in the area coincided, almost from the first years, with the sustained and dizzying increase in the demand for sugar and other tropical agricultural products, thanks to the increase in consumer demand that capitalism aroused. With rapid enrichment as their incentive, the Caribbean colonies belonging to England, France, and Holland began to exploit the land with total abandon according to the model of the slave plantation. In fact, after a brief period characterized by the presence of the small landholder and the European artisan, attended by servants of the same race and creed whose services were contracted for a fixed number of years, the plantation economy, with its continuous slave importations, burst upon the Caribbean scene.

Spain, in a state of total economic, political, and social decadence during the last years of the Hapsburg rulers and embroiled in successive wars with the nations that had the most influence upon the European world system, did not participate actively in this stage of commercial expansion and

capital accumulation. Moreover, its Caribbean colonies were the objects of uninterrupted attack from privateers and pirates, as likewise was the traffic in riches transported from the Indies to Seville. We must bear in mind that the first of these attacks materialized in 1523, and that the so-called age of piracy ended at about 1720; that is to say after two centuries of constant boardings, combats, burnings, and sackings. All of that without even counting the many official wars in which the Caribbean found itself involved, from Valois's to Teddy Roosevelt's. This is why the efforts of the colonial governments were to be centered, especially from the sixteenth to the eighteenth century, on the construction of forts and the adoption of defensive measures to protect not just the port cities but also the galleons that circled the Caribbean picking up loads of gold and silver in Cartagena, Portobelo, and San Juan de Ulúa.[1] Thus the Greater Antilles – what remained of them after the French and English occupations – if they in fact did keep on producing some sugar within a system of trading posts, stayed apart from a true plantation economy and therefore apart from the massive introduction of slaves. At the start of the eighteenth century, when the machinery of the plantations had been installed firmly in the English, French, and Dutch colonies, the Spanish islands presented demographic, economic, and social panoramas that were very different from those that predominated in the rest of the Caribbean.

The fact that Spain was not to undertake to build a politics of the plantation in its Antillean colonies until the end of the eighteenth century had consequences of such importance as to differentiate historically the Hispanic from the non-Hispanic islands. If we compare the demographic figures corresponding to the different colonial blocs, it will be seen that the percentage of slaves relative to the rest of the population was much lower in the Spanish Antilles than in the rival powers' colonies; at the same time it will be observed that the free Negro and mulatto population is much more important in the former than in the latter, as can be seen in table 2.1.

The demographic and social structure of Spain's colonies in the Caribbean, with a smaller proportion of slaves and a greater number of whites and freedmen, is a reflection of its late exposure to the transformative dynamics of the plantation economy. The possibilities for analysis that figures of this kind offer are of incalculable value to the full appreciation of the differences that come into play in the Caribbean region. The difference that Froude noticed between Havana and Kingston can be explained in large part by the fact that at the beginning of the eighteenth century the island of Cuba was more a colony of settlement than of exploitation, and that its economic activity was limited by a monopolist, restrictive mercantile regime that had yet to implant the plantation structure firmly. The situation in Jamaica, however, was becoming very different. After a period characterized by the protection of privateers and pirates who raided the Spanish colonies, a period dominated by the interests of the Brotherhood of the Coast and by Henry Morgan's presence in Port Royal, the colonial administration broke away from the buccaneers and set its eye on perfecting the plantation system. By 1800, as table 2.1 shows, 88.2 percent of its population consisted of slaves, and "white power," made up of planters, employees, traders, functionaries, and military men, counted for a mere 4.4 percent of the total number of inhabitants. I mean by this that while Havana grew like a city similar to those in Spain – as Froude would observe – Kingston grew like a

city of the Plantation; that is, scarcely more than an urban precinct dominated by sugar warehouses, commercial offices, the governor's house, the fort, the docks, and the slave shacks. When the creoles of Havana in those years were to feel like setting the stages for an expansion of the sugar industry, it was a matter of people who were born there, people who came from the oldest families, who had lived there for years in relation to civic institutions like the Church and the school, the book industry and the press, the patriotic society and the university, the consulate and the department of public works, the botanical garden and the theater, etc. Consequently, Havana was transformed into a city of plazas, esplanades, towers, walls, palaces, and theaters, all this before it was to turn out to be the capital of the Plantation. When the latter started to materialize, it had to adapt itself to the model of settlement that we have just described.

The differences that existed among the Caribbean colonies, and even the differences that we now perceive, were created in large part by the epoch in which the Plantation took over within each. Thus, in Froude's time, one could observe in the British colonies, in relation to the Spanish ones, a lesser degree of economic diversification, a smaller number of smallholders and artisans, a more restricted internal market, a poorer system of transportation and communications, a more reduced middle class, a weaker institutional life, a more deficient system of education, a greater conflict with the language of the mother country, and a tardier appearance of arts and letters.

Hence the differences that Froude saw between the cities in the Spanish colonies and those of the English ones were owing mainly to the epochs in which they had set themselves as capitals of the Plantation. Some had sprung up in a more or less normal fashion and others were marked, almost from their founding, by slave-holding despotism, impermanence, absentee ownership, and price instability on the international sugar market. Froude did not realize that cities such as Kingston, Bridgetown, Georgetown, Cayenne, Fort-de-France, Paramaribo, etc. had been built in fact as Plantation ports; they answered the requirements of societies where, on average, nine out of every

Table 2.1   Caribbean Population by Castes, Early 19th Century

Colony	Year	Total population	Slave population	As % of colony's total	As % of non-white
			Slave population		
British Antilles					
Anguilla		?			
Antigua	1832	35,412	29,537	83.4	89.3
Bahamas	1810	16,718	11,146	66.7	87.4
Barbados	1834	100,000	80,861	80.6	92.5
Barbuda		?			
Berbice	1811	25,959	25,169	97.0	99.0
Bermuda	1812	9,900	4,794	48.4	91.4
Demerara	1811	57,386	53,655	93.5	96.0
Dominica	1811	26,041	21,728	83.4	87.9
Essequibo	1811	19,645	18,125	92.3	96.0
Grenada & Carriacou	1811	31,362	29,381	93.6	96.0
[Br.] Honduras	1790	2,656	2,024	76.2	84.5
Jamaica	1800	340,000	300,000	88.2	89.5
Montserrat	1812	7,383	6,537	88.5	94.2
Nevis	1812	10,430	9,326	89.4	93.9
St. Christopher	1812	23,491	19,885	84.6	90.9
St. Lucia	1810	17,485	14,397	82.3	88.5
St. Vincent	1812	24,253	22,020	90.8	94.0
Tobago	1811	17,830	16,897	94.8	98.0
Tortola		?			
Trinidad	1811	32,664	21,143	64.7	73.8
Virgin Islands					
Danish Antilles					
St. Croix	1841	–	20,000		
St. John		?			
St. Thomas	1841	7,000	5,000	71.4	76.9
Dutch Antilles					
Saba		?			
St. Eustatia	1850	2,500	2,000	80.0	95.2
St. Martin	1850	3,600	3,000	83.3	
Curaçao	1833	15,027	5,894	39.2	47.4
Surinam	1830	56,325	48,784	86.6	90.6
Spanish Antilles					
Cuba	1827	704,487	286,942	40.7	32.9
Puerto Rico	1860	583,181	41,738	7.1	14.8
Santo Domingo	1791	125,000	15,000	12.0	?
Swedish Antilles					
St. Bartholomew	1840	7,000	?		
French Antilles					
Guadaloupe	1836	107,810	81,642	75.7	
Martinique	1789	96,158	83,414	86.7	94.0
Saint-Domingue	1791	520,000	452,000	86.9	94.0
Guiana					
St. Martin (part)	1836	3,869	2,925	75.6	
Marie Galante	1836	13,188	10,116	76.7	
Saintes	1836	1,139	569	49.9	
Desirada	1836	1,568	1,070	68.2	

Free non-white population				White population		
Number	As % of total	As % of all non-whites	As % free	Number	As % of colony's totals	As % free
3,531	10.0	10.7	64.0	1,980	5.6	36.0
1,600	9.6	12.6	29.2	3,872	23.0	70.8
6,584	6.5	7.5	33.9	12,797	12.7	66.1
240	1.0	1.0	30.3	550	2.0	69.7
451	4.6	8.6	8.7	4,755	48.0	91.3
2,223	3.9	4.0	51.3	2,108	3.6	48.7
2,988	11.4	12.1	69.3	1,325	5.2	30.7
757	3.9	4.0	50.0	763	3.9	50.0
1,210	3.9	4.0	61.0	771	2.5	39.0
371	14.0	15.5	58.7	261	9.8	41.3
35,000	10.2	10.5	70.0	15,000	4.4	25.0
402	5.4	5.8	47.5	444	6.1	52.5
603	5.8	6.1	54.6	501	4.8	45.4
1,996	8.5	9.1	55.4	1,610	6.9	44.6
1,878	10.7	11.5	60.8	1,210	7.0	39.2
1,406	5.7	6.0	62.9	827	3.4	37.1
350	2.0	2.0	37.5	583	3.2	62.5
7,493	22.9	26.2	63.3	4,353	13.3	36.7
?				3,200		
?				?		
1,500	21.4	23.0	75.0	500	7.2	25.0
?				?		
100	4.0	4.8	20.0	400	16.0	80.0
?	–	–	–	600	16.6	–
6,531	43.5	52.6	71.4	2,602	17.3	28.6
5,041	8.9	9.4	66.8	2,500	4.4	33.2
106,494	15.1	27.1	25.5	311,051	44.1	74.5
241,037	41.3	85.2	44.5	300,406	51.5	55.5
?						
?						
5,235	5.4	6.0	33.3	10,636	11.0	66.7
28,000	5.3	6.0	41.0	40,000	7.6	59.0

Source: Franklin W. Knight, *The Caribbean: The Genesis of Fragmented Nationalism* (New York: Oxford University Press, 1978).

ten inhabitants had been slaves at one time, and this fact made it superfluous to think about adopting measures that would contribute to raising, to a degree greater than that which was strictly necessary, levels of urbanization, institutionalization, education, public services, and recreation. Although slavery had already disappeared when Froude visited the Caribbean, the Plantation continued to exist, and the region's cities still showed the marks of their recent slaveholding past. One should also consider that, for many years, the ethnocentric and colonialist thinking of the European mother countries refused to admit that the Caribbean population of African origin had any need of living standards as dignified as those prevailing in their own societies. From this viewpoint and the reactionary opinions that it engendered, of which Froude was one of the best known purveyors, the Afro-Caribbean was a lazy being, unenterprising, irresponsible, and likely to acquire all sorts of social defects; a collective being incapable of governing himself and of properly constituting a state; in sum, a second-class citizen who had to be kept at a distance and who would have to be content with very little.

One ought to ask whether the difference that Froude saw extended analogously into the cultural sphere. I think that they did. But I also think that these differences are closely related to the processes that transformed the plantation into the Plantation. To show this we may begin with an accepted premise, let's say, the fact that if it's quite easy to find African cultural features within each of the Caribbean nations, it is no less certain that those features present themselves in each case with a unique extension and depth. For example, it is generally agreed that Haiti, Cuba, and Jamaica are, in this order, the islands whose cultures show a greater degree of Africanization. Moreover, among the Antillean islands with the least African culture, Barbados is usually presented as the first example.

Our demonstration's second step would be, naturally, to elaborate a satisfactory explanation of this phenomenon using the plantation/Plantation conversion, or better, to offer a hypothesis applicable not just to these four islands but to all the Antilles. Let's start with Haiti.

In 1804, when the Haitian nation was formally constituted under the government of Dessalines, about 90 percent of the adult population had been slaves. If one takes into account that in the latest years of colonization the Plantation was absorbing 40,000 new slaves,[2] and that the life expectancy of a slave under the conditions of intense exploitation did not reach ten years, one has to conclude that the great majority of this population had been born in Africa. That is to say that when Haiti emerged as a free nation the African components of its culture not only dominated over the European ones, but were more active, or if you like, on the offensive, as they had been exalted during the revolutionary process in the struggle against the slaveholding power of the whites. Even more, the revolts led by Boukman, Jean François, and other leaders . . . were organized under the influence of the *loas* of voodoo, a belief whose supersyncretism is dominated by African elements. Later on, after Dessalines – a former slave – was assassinated, the country stayed divided with Christophe in the north and Pétion in the south, reunifying in 1818 under Boyer's government. The fact that both Pétion and Boyer represented the group of rich, Catholic, and enlightened mulattos made it turn out that hundreds of thousands of Negroes fell under the control of the new "mulatto power," not as slaves, certainly, but surely in a position of servitude that kept them from leaving the plantations on which they worked. Thus the Plantation reorganized itself anew in Haiti, although under other work and power relations. It is easy to suppose that this vast population of hundreds of thousands of men and women of African origin maintained many of their customs, among them the cults that the Church prohibited. These old slaves – like Ti Noel of *El reino de este mundo* – were the ones who kept alive the cults devoted to Damballah, to Papa Legba, to Ogun, the voodoo and petro cults, with their ritual sacrifices, to whose sacred drums the greater part of the Haitian population, especially in the countryside, still responds.[3]

If the former slaves had known a more complete liberty in Boyer's time, the Africanness of the culture would surely be even greater now. In any case, I think that it is possible to sustain the argument that the rapid and intense expansion of the plantation system in French Saint-Domingue, perhaps the most accelerated model of the Plantation that the world has ever seen, brought as its consequence an unusual density of African population. As it was liberated within the span of a single generation, its members had scarcely become acculturated toward European ways – voodoo shows this clearly – and the cultural components that they brought with them prevailed in the interplay over those that came from Europe via the mulattos. It is rather significant that the new republic rejected the name Saint-Domingue to adopt that of Haiti, which was the Taino name for Hispaniola when Columbus arrived; and also that Haitian *Créole* should take a considerable number of words from the aboriginal language. To my mind, this indicates that as far as the past was concerned there was a popular preference for what was aboriginal over what had come from Europe.

But how do we explain Cuba's having now a more Africanized culture than those of Barbados or Jamaica? If we look at ... table 2.1, we shall see that its slave population was less than 41 percent, while Jamaica's, in 1800, was more than 88 percent. Moreover, if we compare the cultural life on the two islands throughout our century, we see that Cuban religious beliefs, music, dance, painting, literature, and folklore show an African influence unequaled in any other Antillean nation except Haiti. What happened in Cuba that didn't happen in Jamaica or in Barbados? I think that many factors come in to play here to differentiate one island from another, but I believe that one of the most important is the late date at which the Plantation was first set up in Cuba. The number of Negroes introduced upon the island between 1512 and 1761 is estimated at 60,000, which puts the annual average at some 250 slaves. The majority of them did not work on sugar plantations – Cuba exported the product in very limited amounts at that time – but were distributed within the leather economy, produce cultivation, public works, and domestic service. We already know that in the eastern provinces the Negro participated actively in the formation of the early Antillean culture that we have called creole culture; from there, at least in its magical-religious

beliefs, its music and its dances, it moved on to Havana, where it would adapt itself to the specificities of the local culture.

There is proof that there existed, in the seventeenth century, what we would call a creole culture in Havana and in other important localities, each of them different from the others. This would have been nurtured by feasts to various patron saints or Virgins – sequences of days in which people made music, danced, ate certain dishes, and entertained themselves with all kinds of games and pastimes. In 1714, for example, the Virgen de Regla (Yemaya in the syncretic cult) was consecrated as Havana's patron, setting off festivals that lasted for eight days and in which whites, slaves, and free Negroes participated.[4] But this also happened with the patrons of any other place, not even counting dates such as the one dedicated to the Virgen de la Caridad, whose prolonged festivals were celebrated throughout Cuba in different ways.[5] On these dates, the so-called *cabildos*, which were associations of slaves and free Negroes grouped together according to their African nations of origin, played an important role. I mean to say by all this that, before the formation of what we could call a Cuban national culture – a phenomenon that occurred later under the Plantation – it is possible to imagine a type of creole culture characterized by the variety of its local manifestations but also, above all, by the participation of the Negro, slave or not, in conditions advantageous to him as an acculturating agent. It should be noted how high the percentage of free Negroes was in Cuba; in 1774, for example, they made up 20.3 percent of the entire population, a figure that tells of their mobility and their being in position to exert cultural influence in the process of Africanization. At the end of the eighteenth century, when the machinery of the plantation began to extend itself into the environs of Havana, there already existed a kind of creole culture, considerably Africanized, in many places on the island.[6]

In Jamaica's case, the most interesting comparison is with Barbados, which is taken today – as I've said – as one of the least Africanized islands in the Caribbean. Let's take a brief look at each island's plantation history. The English landed on Barbados in 1625. The island's early labor force was made up of colonists, Carib Indians, white slaves, criminals, deported political prisoners, and indentured servants. In 1645 there were 18,300 whites, of which 11,200 were landowners, and 5,680 Negro slaves – there whites for every Negro – in an economy based on small-holding cultivation of tobacco. In 1667, though, there were 745 owners and 82,023 slaves.[7] What had happened? The sugar Plantation had arrived and, displacing the tobacco small holdings, took up nearly all the land on the island. In 1698, a mere thirty years later, there was a ratio of nearly eighteen slaves for each white man.

Concerning Jamaica, the first thing to take into account is that it was colonized by Spain at the beginning of the sixteenth century, and it fell into England's hands in 1655; that is, it lay for 150 years within the Spanish colonial system and its northern zone was a depository of creole culture of the Windward Passage type. When the Spaniards left the island, many slaves ran off and stayed for years in the country's inland mountains. As we know, during the earliest years of English rule the city of Port Royal replaced Tortuga as home of the buccaneers of the Brotherhood of the Coast. England, and France and Holland as well, used their services in making war on Spain. Their best-known leader was Henry Morgan, who was without a doubt the most popular man in Jamaica during the decade of the 1660s. Morgan sacked cities in Cuba, Nicaragua, Mexico, Venezuela, and Panama, leaving behind an entire cycle of legends. . . . The sack of Portobelo yielded 100,000 pounds sterling, and in the capture of Maracaibo 260,000 doubloons were taken.[8] It is no exaggeration to say that in the Jamaica of those years there was an economy based on privateering, in which the Negro participated. But Charles II's restoration brought peace with Spain, and in the last decades of the century the investors' interest turned to the already existing plantation business. During the eighteenth century Jamaica completed its transition to the Plantation and surpassed Barbados as a sugar exporter. It is calculated that more than 600,000 slaves entered the colony between 1700 and 1786.[9]

Now having both islands' history sketched out before us, we can observe the phenomenon that the greater or lesser Africanness of the islands' present-day cultures does not necessarily correspond to the Negro population's demographic importance, but may be explained rather by the epoch at which the Plantation machinery was set up. The later it was implanted, as happened in Jamaica when compared to Barbados, the Africans already living there, slaves or not, would have had occasion actively to bring their cultural influence to bear on European things for a more prolonged period of time. In Plantation conditions, in spite of the enormous percentages reached by the numbers of slaves in relation to the total population, the African was reduced to living under an incarcerating regimen of forced labor, which stood in the way of his being able to exert a cultural influence upon the European and creole population. Still more, he was living under a deculturating regimen that took direct action against his language, his religion, and his customs, as African practices were looked upon with suspicion and many of them were controlled or prohibited. Furthermore, the plantation owners would spread out their slave contingents according to place of origin so that communication between them would be more difficult in case of revolt. One should add to all this the fact that slave children born on the plantation were very soon separated from their mothers, thus impeding the transmission of cultural components through a maternal tie. Finally, we must remember that one of every three slaves died during his first three years of intense exploitation. In more general working conditions, half of Barbados's slave population had to be renewed every eight years, and of Jamaica it has been observed that 40 percent of the slaves died in a period of three years.[10] In my opinion, one has to conclude that the Negro slave who arrived at a Caribbean colony before the Plantation was organized contributed much more toward Africanizing the creole culture than did the one who came within the great shipments typical of the Plantation in its heyday.

In reality, the key to Africanization lay, to my way of thinking, in the degree of mobility that the African possessed when he came to the Caribbean. A state of rebellion allowed the freest cultural expression, as was the case with the Haitian slave. He is followed in order by the *cimarrón* (runaway slave) – an important factor in Jamaica – since in the *palenques* (settlements of runaways) a kind of life was lived that was characterized by the interplay of African components exchanged among men and women coming from different regions of Africa; these components were carried throughout their lives by the *palenques*'s members, and they could be communicated to the outer world in various ways.... After the *cimarrón*, there came in successive order the freedman, the urban slave, the smallholder's slave, the slave who worked on non-sugar-growing plantations, and finally, the so-called *esclavo de ingenio* (mill slave). In spite of the natural differences of opinions held by different investigators of the Caribbean, the judgment that the slave on the sugar plantation was the most intensely exploited and repressed seems to be 100 percent unanimous. In my opinion, consequently, this slave would have been the least active African agent in the process of communicating his culture to the creole social milieu.

We also observe, in each Caribbean nation, cultural differences with respect to Asian components. There were colonies, such as Santo Domingo and Puerto Rico, that had no Asian immigration in the last century, owing to their relative abundance of local labor in relation to their plantations' requirements. Nevertheless, in the majority of the area's island and mainland territories, the scarcity of African manpower – or its high price – made the planters turn their eyes toward southern Asia in search of new sources of cheap labor. Thus there arrived in the Caribbean vast contingents of workers contracted under an arrangement similar to that of the previous *engagés* or indentured servants. These immigrations, nevertheless, did not issue from a single cultural womb, but rather from the most diverse Asian territories, such as India, China, and Java. Furthermore, they were not distributed evenly among the region's different colonial blocs. For example, the great majority of the Indians went to the English colonies, while the Chinese and the Malays were concentrated, respectively, in Cuba and Surinam. So that the notable Asian cultural influences in the Caribbean, in line with their diverse origins, show

themselves through very different codes. One should not forget, however, that it was the Plantation that demanded their incorporation into the area.

The Plantation: Sociocultural Regularities

As we have seen, the Plantation proliferated in the Caribbean basin in a way that presented different features in each island, each stretch of coastline, each colonial bloc. Nevertheless – as Mintz would see – these differences, far from negating the existence of a pan-Caribbean society, make it possible in the way that a system of fractal equations or a galaxy is possible. The different sugar-producing machines, installed here and there through the centuries, can be seen also as a huge machine of machines in a state of continuous technological transformation. Its inexorable territory-claiming nature made it – makes it still – advance in length and depth through the natural lands, demolishing forests, sucking up rivers, displacing other crops, and exterminating the native plants and animals. At the same time, ever since it was put into play, this powerful machine has attempted systematically to shape, to suit to its own convenience, the political, economic, social, and cultural spheres of the country that nourishes it until that country is changed into a *sugar island*. Of this subject, Gilberto Freyre and Darcy Ribeiro, respectively, referring to the case of the plantation of the Brazilian northeast (which, insofar as it shows these and other effects, might be taken simply as another Caribbean island), say:

> The *Casa Grande* [planter's residence], together with the slave cabins, represents in itself an economic, social, and political system: a system of production (*latifundio*, monoculture); a system of labor (slavery); a transportation system (oxcart, sedan chair, palanquin, horse); a religious system (familial Catholicism, with a cult of the dead, etc.); a system of family and sexual life (patriarchal polygamy); a system of domestic and personal hygiene (urinal, banana grove, bath in the river or standing with a washbasin); a political system (bossism, cronyism). The *Casa Grande* was at once a fortress, a bank,

a hospital, a cemetery, a school, an asylum for widows, orphans, and the elderly . . . [11] It was the sincere expression of the needs, interests, and the broad rhythms of patriarchal life, made possible by the sugar revenues and the slaves' productive work.[12]

The *fazenda* [hacienda] constitutes the basic structuring model for Brazilian society. Around it the social system is organized as a body of auxiliary institutions, norms, customs, and beliefs whose purpose is to safeguard its being and persistence. So also do the family, the people, and the nation spring out of and develop from the *fazenda*'s effects and as such are defined by it.[13]

The extraordinary effects of the sugar-making machine's dynamics in colonial societies – to the point where these latter seem almost an enlarged reflection of the former – do not end with the abolition of slavery. Certainly there are changes and adjustments to go with this new situation, but the plantation machine in its essential features keeps on operating as oppressively as before. For example, the sugar expansion that the Antilles experienced in the first decades of the twentieth century unleashed dynamics similar to those seen a century or two earlier. The best lands were appropriated or controlled by the planting companies, and the peasants and smallholders were displaced violently to the marginal zones, unserved by the improved methods of transport and communication that the planting interests introduced. On this subject, Mintz writes: "During the transformation of the plantation sectors into modern factories in the field, particularly after 1900, the peasant sectors fell farther behind, as modern roads, communications systems, and company stores developed in the coastal zones. Thus the contrast between peasants and plantations has to some extent become even sharper in this century."[14]

In a way similar to what occurred in Barbados in the seventeenth century, sugarcane became the *primera agricultura*, in opposition to other forms of agricultural business. This peculiarity, combined with the practice of monoculture, determines the contradictory fact that an essentially agricultural country finds itself having to import food. In generalized conditions of low productivity and relative scarcity of manpower, this factor has disastrous consequences, since the great plantation machine – its sectors involving agriculture, industry, transport, communications, administration, and commerce – needs enormous masses of material and labor resources, snatching them cyclically from the country's other economic activities. In critical situations of this kind, it is not uncommon to resort to the rationing of food products. In 1970, when the Cuban government tried to produce ten million tons of sugar, the country was virtually paralyzed, or, if you like, changed into an enormous state-run plantation on which the cane harvest lay down the law.

The sugar-milling complex – the plantation's heart – created to hold perpetual dominion, would tend to subsist in the most adverse external market conditions, competing there with prices lower than the cost of production if need be. This situation fits the type of social structure that we observe in the statistical table. Clearly, this hierarchized structure will always seem ideal to the small group that holds the economic power by force, and thus its rigidity and disproportion will essentially persist under more modern work relations, and will continue to exert a similar influence in all of the different spheres of the national life.

If we bear in mind that the Plantation was a proliferating regularity in the Caribbean sphere, it becomes difficult to sustain the idea that the region's social structures cannot be grouped under a single typology. It is true that the Plantation's model differs from one island to another, and that sugar's hegemony begins in Barbados, passes to Saint-Domingue, and ends in Cuba, spreading itself out in time and space over three centuries. But it is precisely these differences that confer upon the Plantation its ability to survive and to keep transforming itself, whether facing the challenge of slavery's abolition, or the arrival of independence, or the adoption of a socialist mode of production.

Nonetheless, our agreeing with Mintz that the Caribbean may be defined in terms of a *societal area* is far from affirming, necessarily, the existence of a common pan-Caribbean culture. It is true that I have spoken here about the presence of an early creole culture around the Windward

Passage, of a variegated creole culture in the different locales, and even of a national culture. But in all this I have in no way meant to suggest that these cultures are *unities*, in the sense that they admit a stable and coherent reading. In my opinion, any expression of culture – a myth, a song, a dance, a painting, a poem – is a kind of impersonal message, at once vague and truncated; an obscure and previous desire that was already moving around here and there and that can never be interpreted entirely by a performer or read completely by a reader; every effort by the one or the other to fill this essential gap will fail to lead him toward a goal, but will issue into lateral movements, spiralings, steps that go forward but also backward – let's say, different styles of dancing the rumba. And so, nothing and nobody can provide us with the absolute truth about what a local culture is, much less a national culture. How then can we presume that it's possible to define with any precision what lies within or without the culture of our extremely complicated archipelago?

In any case, for the present-day observer it is more or less evident that in the expressions that manifest themselves in the diffuse Caribbean zone there are components that come from many places around the globe, and that these, it seems, are not constant, stable, homogeneous, or even parallel among the nations, regions, and localities that claim the title of being Caribbean. It was precisely this state of chaos that moved Mintz to look for a form of Caribbeanness not within the cultural sphere but rather in the economic and social patterns. I think also that there is considerable truth in Moya Pons's opinion with respect to a lack of any pan-Caribbean consciousness, and in his alternative of taking the Caribbean as a series of Caribbeans situated next to each other, which offers a certain analogy with Froude's observations. But Labat's testimony is also self-evident: "It is no accident that the sea separating your lands establishes no differences in the rhythms of your bodies." And we must pay attention to that statement, above all because it refers directly to the question of culture, which is what concerns us. What does Labat point to as a regular feature common to the entire Caribbean? One element: rhythm. It is rhythm that, in his

words, puts all the Caribbean peoples in "the same boat," over and above separations imposed on them by "nationality and race"; it is rhythm – not a specific cultural expression – that confers Caribbeanness. So that if Mintz defines the region in terms of a "societal area," one must conclude that Labat would have defined it in terms of a "rhythmical area."

How does Labat demonstrate this special rhythmic quality? He looks at performances. It's true that his opinions concerning the creoles' dances are not those of a specialist – although they have been credited by Fernando Ortiz, Janheinz Jahn, and others – but it happens that they, even though empirical and hastily written down, are largely confirmed in the eighteenth century by Moreau de Saint-Méry, one of the most serious and enlightened authorities on everything Caribbean of his time. For example, Labat speaks of the existence of a dance (or rhythm) called the *calenda* which enjoys the greatest popularity in the entire area, and which is danced as much by the Negro slaves and the free Negroes as by the white creoles, even the nuns, in the Spanish colonies. Labat offers the following description of this dance:

> What pleases them the most and is their most common diversion is the *calenda*, which comes from the Guinea coast and, judging by all its antecedents, from the kingdom of Ardá ... The dancers array themselves in two lines, facing each other, the men on one side, the women on the other. The spectators form a circle around the dancers and drummers. The most gifted sings a *tonadilla*, improvised to deal with some current matter, and the tune's refrain is repeated by all the dancers and spectators, and accompanied by clapping hands. The dancers raise their arms, as if they were playing castanets, they jump, turn, and spin, they approach to within three feet of each other and then they move backward following the beat, until the sound of the drum tells them to join together, with the thighs of some beating against those of others, that is, the men's with the women's. On seeing them, it seems that their bellies are beating together, when in truth their thighs alone are joined. They soon back

away, pirouetting, to repeat the movement with supremely lascivious flourishes ... They dance the *calenda* in their churches and Catholic processions, and the nuns do not stop dancing it even on Christmas eve upon a raised theater in the choir, facing the railings, which are open so that the populace may have the aid of these good souls in celebrating the Savior's birth. It is true that no men are let in with them... And I would like to think even that they dance it with a very pure intent, but how many spectators would judge them as charitably as I do?[15]

A century later, Moreau de Saint-Méry writes of the same dance, calling it the *kalenda*,[16] which has not changed much since Labat's time. It is still an extremely popular and widespread dance, and it continues with its same format of two lines divided by sex that come together in the center and then separate, while the chorus claps and repeats the singer's improvisations. In Moreau de Saint-Méry's opinion the dance takes the name *kalenda* from one of the drums – the largest and most deep-sounding – that enter the rhythm, although it is very probably the other way around, since Fernando Ortiz, in his *Nuevo cat-auro de cubanismos*, has listed this dance under the name *caringa* or *calinda*, deriving the word from that of an ancient region and river in the Congo. In any case, this dance's rhythm and its circular and antiphonal style were spread out through the entire region in the seventeenth and eighteenth centuries, and the dance was a permanence from which a variety of folk dances may have sprung, such as the *chica*, the *yuka*, the *zarabanda*, etc.[17] But here we are not interested in trips to the origins of things, for no matter how pleasant they may be they usually lead to the vertigo that comes with a desire to explain what can't be explained. We are interested, nevertheless, in establishing that, at least since the seventeenth century, there are rhythms common to the entire Caribbean, rhythms that follow a kind of poly-rhythmic and polymetric percussion very different from European percussive forms, and which are impossible to write down using conventional notation. Of this mysterious property of Caribbean music, Ortiz informs us:

The usual tools of "white" musicology are insufficient. "The famous violinist Bohrer has confessed to me that he tried vainly to decipher a contrabass part performed every night in 'La Habanera' by a black man who couldn't read a single note" (N. B. Rosemond de Beauvallon, *L'ille de Cuba*, Paris, 1844). Emilio Grenet thinks correctly that, "properly speaking a *habanera*... has never been written down... It could be said that its creative principle is its rhythmic structure, but if the musician is not imbued with 'Cuban feeling' the musical product will never be a *habanera* in the strictest sense of the word" (*Popular Cuban Music*, Havana, 1939). Torroella, the popular composer and pianist, told us: "Music that is most characteristically Cuban can not be written down or put inside a musical staff. And it is natural that this should be the case, because much of it comes to us from the Negroes, and they, when they came to Cuba, did not know how to write, either." "But many Negroes now can write," we argued. And he answered us: "Yes, but don't you know that among the blacks there is always a secret being kept?" At the end of the last century, the great musician "of color" Raimundo Valenzuela also taught this when, asked how to read and perform the extraordinary figure called the *cinquillo*, so intriguing to students of Afro-Cuban music, he said that he would never explain it because the *cinquillo* was "a secret"... When the maestro Amadeo Roldán conducted the Orquesta Filarmónica in performing his *Rebambaramba*, upon reaching a certain moment in the piece he left the drummers free of his baton so that they could execute certain complicated rhythms in their own fashion... Today we hardly balk at accepting the impossibility of placing Negro music within the staff. "I doubt that it's possible with the present method of notation to set down an absolutely faithful transcription of all of the peculiarities of African music, for its true nature is to resist all setting down." (W. D. Hambly, *Tribal Dancing and Social Development*, London, 1926)[18]

But to think that Afro-Caribbean rhythms apply only to percussion would be to simplify enormously their importance as a common cultural element. Regarding the rhythms that come into play in the dance, and even in song, Ortiz continues to inform us:

> With regard to the transcription of the dances and their steps and figures, we find ourselves facing the same obstacles ... To the classical ballet's way of thinking there is a choreographic vocabulary in which each step has its name ... But it is as yet impossible to put to music paper the rapid and extremely complex movements of the African dance, in which feet, legs, hips, torsos, arms, hands, head, face, eyes, tongue, and finally all human organs take part in mimetic expressions that form steps, gestures, visages, and uncountable dance figures ... Furthermore (with regard to song), "it is essential to recognize that transcriptions and analyses of phonograph records, no matter how carefully done, can never tell the whole story of the relation between the musical styles of the New World and of Africa, nor can it establish the differences between the musics of different regions of the New World, since, as Hornbostel observes, the problem also includes a consideration of the intangible aspects of singing technique and the habitual practices behind the accompaniments and the key changes. (Melville J. Herskovits, "El estudio de la música negra en el Hemisferio Occidental," *Boletín Latinoamericano de Música*, V, 1941)[19]

But even to restrict the Caribbean's rhythms to the dance and to song is to be flagrantly reductive. Consider a paragraph written by E. Duvergier de Hauranne on the occasion of his visit to Santiago de Cuba in the last century:

> The alley that runs behind the market presents a lively spectacle every morning: carts drawn by oxen or mules, grotesquely loaded donkey trains, horsemen wearing huge straw hats who, on nervous, rearing horses, open a difficult passage through crowds of Negroes and people of color. Vigorous men come and go carrying barrels and baskets; others carry bundles of goatskins, cages filled with chickens. The Negresses, dressed in light cotton and scandalous kerchiefs, let themselves be seen for an instant before the tumult, balancing, on their heads, the basket of fruits or vegetables that they steady at times with their arm rounded like a pitcher's handle; some, beneath their balanced loads, parade through the crowd with the flexible movements of untamed cats; others, their hands on their hips, advance with little steps, swaying in humorous insouciance. On the market's patio and along the length of the porch roofs that surround it, squatting vendors peddle their wares laid out on tables or on the ground itself: fruits, flowers, plants, pottery, brilliant swatches of silk, red and yellow silken handkerchiefs, fish, shellfish, casks of salt fish and meat; there are piles of oranges, pineapples, watermelons, crested cabbages, hams, golden cheeses, layers of plantains and onions, of mangoes and yams, lemons and potatoes spread out confusedly beside bunches of flowers. The walkway is so elevated that it almost reaches the level of the displays, so that with any misstep an old Negress could be spilled upon on a basket of eggs crushed. The buyers buzz about like a swarm of flies; they haggle, they gesticulate, they laugh, they babble in the harmonious colonial *patois*.[20]

Notice that the center of this picture is held by the Negresses of Santiago who open paths, with their bundles and baskets, through the marketplace. What are the words that the writer uses to characterize their movement? No others, certainly, than ones that attempt a representation of inner rhythms: "balancing, on their heads, baskets of fruits.... they parade through the crowd with the flexible movements of untamed cats.... they advance in little steps, swaying in humorous insouciance." It's clear that Hauranne, a foreigner, saw that these Negresses walked in a "certain kind of way," that they moved in a way entirely different from that of European women. And it is not only movement that differentiates them, but also plastic immobilities – silences – such as "carrying their hands on their hips," or balancing baskets on their heads "with their arm rounded like a pitcher's handle." But Hauranne goes even further in his description. It is easy to see that he makes an effort to communicate an overall rhythm that can be

broken down into separate, more or less autonomous rhythmic planes – polyrhythm: the rhythm
of the oxcarts, together with the donkeys and
horses; the rhythm of the Negresses, which we
have just seen, together with the rhythm of the
men who come and go carrying bundles and
burdens and chicken cages; finally the heteroclitic,
variegated, and seething plane of colors, odors,
tastes, tactile sensations, and sounds where Hauranne inscribes fruits, fish, cheeses and hams, silk
swatches and pottery, eggs and flowers, flies
swarming and buzzing, laughter and gesticulation
and babbling in an undecipherable but lilting language. These are rhythms that can be "seen" and
even "heard" in the manner of Afro-Caribbean
percussion.

What Hauranne tried to represent with his pen,
his compatriot Mialhe and the Spaniard Land-
aluze tried to communicate through painting and
lithography, also in the past century. Their respective compositions *Día de Reyes (La Habana)*
and *Día de Reyes en La Habana* work to capture
the rhythms of the drums, of the dances, of the
songs, of the fantastic dress and colors that this
annual holiday, where the slaves were freed for
one day, set out upon Havana's streets in an
enormous carnivalesque spectacle. It is precisely
this rhythmic complexity, rooted in the forms of
the ritual sacrifice and directed toward all of the
senses, that gives pan-Caribbean cultures a way of
being, a style that is repeated through time and
space in all its differences and variants. This
polyrhythm of planes and meters can be seen
not just in music, dance, song, and the plastic
arts, but also in the cuisine – the *ajiaco* – in
architecture, in poetry, in the novel, in the
theater, in bodily expression, in religious beliefs,
in idiosyncrasies, that is, in all the texts that
circulate high and low throughout the Caribbean
region.

Let's hear Carpentier as he speaks of colonial
window gratings:

We would have to make an immense inventory of gratings, an endless catalog of iron-
work, to define fully the baroque features that
are always implicit and present in the Cuban
town. There is, in the houses of the *Vedado*,
of Cienfuegos, of Santiago, of Remedios, the

white and intricate grating, almost plantlike
in its abundance and in the tangles of its
metal ribbons, with pictures of lyres, flowers,
vaguely Roman vases, amid infinite spirals
that form, in general, the letters of the
woman's name that was also given to the
villa over which she ruled, or a date, a
succession of historically significant numbers . . . The grating also is home to rosettas,
peacock tails, interwoven arabesques . . . enormously luxuriant in this displaying of bolted,
crossed, and interwoven pieces of metal
. . . And there is also the austere grating,
barely ornamented . . . or the one that
presumes to make itself unique with a gothic
figuration, a florid pattern never seen before,
or a style derived surprisingly from that of St.
Sulpice.[21]

And there is not just the polyrhythmic chaos of
window gratings, but also of columns, balconies,
panes of glass that crown doors and windows with
their fabulous semicircles. That deafening conjunction of architectonic rhythms, Carpentier
says, was giving Havana "that style without a
style that over the long term, through a process
of symbiosis, of amalgamation, establishes itself
as a peculiar baroqueness that stands in for a
style, inscribing itself within the history of
urban behaviors."

Rhythms, rhythmic planes that mix together
like the sacred *batá* drums. And nevertheless
within this forest of sounds and turbulences
there are meaningless regularities that act as
vehicles for the drummers and dancers to unleash
their violence and reach the trance, or better, the
transition, to a world without violence. I haven't
found a definition of rhythm better than the one
given by the African poet Léopold Senghor:

Rhythm is the architecture of being, the inner
dynamic that gives it form, the pure expression of the life force. Rhythm is the vibratory
shock, the force which, through our senses,
grips us at the root of our being. It is
expressed through corporeal and sensual
means; through lines, surfaces, colors,
and volumes in architecture, sculpture, or
painting; through accents in poetry and
music, through movements in the dance.
But, doing this, rhythm turns all these con-

crete things toward the light of the spirit. In the degree to which rhythm is sensuously embodied, it illuminates the spirit...Only rhythm gives the word its effective fullness; it is the word of God, that is, the rhythmic word, that created the world.[22]

In commenting on the polymeters and polyrhythms in African cultures, Janheinz Jahn says:

Common to both basic forms is the principle of *crossed rhythms*; that is, the main accents of the basic forms employed do not agree, but are overlaid in criss-cross fashion over one another, so that, in polymetry for example, the particular basic meters begin not simultaneously but at different times.[23]

It is precisely this crossed or chaotic rhythm that makes Hauranne's description of the marketplace attractive. Does this mean that the Caribbean rhythm is African? If I had to answer this question, I would say not entirely. I would say that the crossed rhythm that shows up in Caribbean cultural forms can be seen as the expression of countless performers who tried to represent what was already here, or there, at times drawing closer and at times farther away from Africa. The marketplace that Hauranne describes is a coming together of rhythms in which there is much of the African, but also the European; it is not a "mulatto" mixture, if that term is meant to convey a kind of "unity"; it is a polyrhythmic space that is Cuban, Caribbean, African, and European at once, and even Asian and Indoamerican, where there has been a contrapuntal and intermingled meeting of the biblical Creator's *logos*, of tobacco smoke, the dance of the *orishas* and *loas*, the Chinese bugle, Lezama Lima's *Paradiso*, and the *Virgen de la Caridad de Cobre* and the boat of the Three Juans. Within this chaos of differences and repetitions, of combinations and permutations, there are regular dynamics that coexist, and which, once broached within an aesthetic experience, lead the performer to re-create a world without violence, or – as Senghor would say – to reach the Effective Word, the elusive goal where all possible rhythms converge.

NOTES

1   See Paul E. Hoffman, *The Spanish Crown and the Defense of the Caribbean* (Baton Rouge: Louisiana State University Press, 1980), pp. 175–212.

2   Eric Williams, *From Columbus to Castro: The History of the Caribbean, 1492–1969* (London: André Deutsch, 1970), p. 245.

3   The presence of blood sacrifices in Caribbean beliefs ought to be related in the first place to the cultures of black Africa, but it would be senseless to discount the influences in this regard brought by other cultures that emigrated to the Caribbean, let's say, the Sephardic, the Chinese, the Canarian, and in general the substrata of certain European cultures that, like the Galician, brought over important pagan components that were assimilated by the local form of Christianity. In any case, the signal presence of the sacrifice within the present state of Caribbean culture presupposes a collective desire for the conservation of these rituals, all this without mentioning the numerous symbolic forms that, like the carnival or the burning of the *juif* (Haiti), refer directly to the sacrifice of the scapegoat. Although I have already noted it, I take this opportunity to underline the idea that such an idea of conservation obeys the conditions of acute social violence, still in effect, in which Caribbean society was set up. The relations between sacrifice and public violence have been studied by René Girard in his *La violence et le sacré* (Paris: Bernard Grasset, 1972)/*Violence and the Sacred*, trans. Patrick Gregory (Baltimore: Johns Hopkins University Press, 1977). Here Girard expounds clearly the hidden function of sacrifice: to discharge in the death of the scapegoat, in a channeled and foreseeable way, the participants' individual violence (originating in insecurity, fear, rivalry, etc.), toward the end of avoiding the collective violence that would endanger the public order. Thus it could be said that, in repeating the ritual sacrifice, Caribbean society tries to sublimate the danger of a blind sociocultural dissolution whose results are impossible to anticipate, or, if you like, to control the regime of tensions and differences, deferring the moment of the system's explosion.

Colony	Year	Slaves	Freedmen	Proportion
Jamaica	1787	256,000	4,093	1:64
Barbados	1786	62,115	838	1:74
Grenada	1785	23,926	1,115	1:21
Dominica	1788	14,967	445	1:33
Saint-Domingue	1779	249,098	7,055	1:35
Martinique	1776	71,268	2,892	1:25
Guadaloupe	1779	85,327	1,382	1:61
Cuba	1774	44,333	30,847	1:1.5
Cuba	1787	50,340	29,217	1:1.7

4   Unlike what ocurred with the slave in the sugar mill, it often happened that these Negroes bought their freedom through a legal provision called *coartación* (which limited the owner's right of possession). This contributed, in Cuba, to the proportion of slaves to freedom being much lower than in the non-Hispanic colonies. Williams, in *From Columbus to Castro* (p. 190), assembles the table shown above:

Notice that as the number of plantations in Cuba kept increasing, between 1774 and 1787, the proportion of slaves increases as well. Nevertheless, in the year 1787 itself, Jamaica had one freedman for every sixty-four slaves, while in Cuba the proportion did not even reach one to two.

5   Lydia Cabrera, *Yemayá y Ochún* (New York: Chicherukú, 1980), pp. 9–19.

6   In the city of Santa Clara, for example, the feast of the Virgen de la Caridad was celebrated by the Negroes in the following manner:

They came from all of the mills in the district, and in ... the bare land that surrounded the church, the eve of September 8, in the morning, to the sound of the drums ... they cut the grass, which the Negresses collected, in small baskets, dancing and drinking rum. In the afternoon, in procession, the King and the Queen of the Council of the Congolese (who predominated there) filed past beneath an enormous parasol four meters in diameter which they called the *tapasolón* and behind them, under another *tapa-solón*, those who were called the princes. They were followed by a great number of their retinue or vassals. All of the men were dressed in frock coats and trousers and sported derby hats; at their waists were toy sabers and they wore leather shoes. The cortège was led, in front of the great parasol, by the drums, rustic wooden trunks a meter and a half long. [Also there were] four or five drums of different sounds, which

were carried between the legs. The Council had its seat in a piece of land of its own near the church ... There the Negroes danced a kind of Lancer; lined up in two rows, the men facing the women, they executed dance figures and moved to the drumbeats ... To play a rumba figure was absolutely forbidden. When the creoles in the congos' line insinuated a rumba figure – that was profane music – the indignation of the elders could be felt. It was typical ... to share among the Negro participants who attended with their Kings, and also the white devotees – all in the greatest harmony – the Agualoja, a drink made from water, sweet-basil, and burnt maize. (Cabrera, *Yemayá y Ochún*, p. 57.)

It should be pointed out that if indeed the Plantation brought down the proportion of free to enslaved Negroes in the island's total population, their number continued to be much greater than in any other, non-Hispanic, colony. For example, owing to the massive slave importations, the percentage of freedmen between 1774 and 1827 went down from 20.3 percent to 15.1 percent. But this last figure was not even remotely equaled by the English, French, and Dutch colonies.

7   Williams, *From Columbus to Castro*, pp. 136–37.

8   Ibid., p. 83.

9   Ibid., p. 145.

10   Ibid., p. 146.

11   Gilberto Freyre, *Casa grande & Senzala* (Rio de Janeiro: Schmidt, 1936), pp. xxxiii. There is an English edition, *The Masters and the Slaves: A Study in the Development of Brazilian Civilization*, trans. Samuel Putnam (New York: Alfred A. Knopf, 1966).

12   Ibid., p. xii.

13   Darcy Ribeiro, *As Américas e a Civilização* (Rio de Janeiro: Civilização Brasileira, 1970), pp. 262–63.

14 Mintz, "The Caribbean as a Socio-cultural Area," *Cahiers d'Histoire Mondiale* 9, no. 4: 916–41, at p. 922.

15 Quotation taken from Fernando Ortiz, *Nuevo catauro de cubanismos* (Havana: Editorial de Ciencias Sociales, 1974 [1923]), pp. 127–28.

16 M. L. E. Moreau de Saint-Méry, *Description topographique, physique, civile, politique, et historique de la partie Française de L'Île Saint-Domingue* (Philadelphia: 1797–1798), vol. 1, pp. 44–45.

17 See, for example, Moreau de Saint-Méry, *Dance*, trans. Lily and Baird Hastings (Brooklyn: 1975 [Philadelphia 1796]), pp. 66–73; Fernando Ortiz, *Los instrumentos de la música afrocubana* (Havana: 1952–55), vol. 4, p. 196; *La africania de la música folklórica de Cuba* (Havana: 1950), p. 2; Janheinz Jahn, *Muntu: Las culturas neoafricanas*, trans. Jasmin Reuter (Mexico: Fondo de Cultura Económica, 1978 [German ed., 1958]), pp. 118–19.

18 Fernando Ortiz, *La música afrocubana (La africania de la música folklórica de Cuba)* (Madrid: Júcar, 1974), pp. 166–67. In the last few decades special methods have been developed to annotate African percussion, but this, far from negating what Ortiz had said, reinforces him in that it is the music of the West that has had to adapt itself to the African and neo-African elements of the Caribbean.

19 Ibid., pp. 167–69.

20 E. Duvergier de Hauranne, "Cuba las Antillas," *Santiago* 26–27 (1977):299.

21 Alejo Carpentier, "La ciudad de las columnas," *Tientos y diferencias* (Havana: Ediciones Unión, 1966), pp. 55–56.

22 Léopold Sédar Senghor, "L'esprit de la civilisation ou les lois de la culture négro-africaine," *Présence Africaine* 8–10 (1956). Quotation taken from Jahn, *Muntu*, p. 277. There is an English edition, *Muntu: An Outline of the New African Culture*, trans. Marjorie Grene (New York: Grove Press, 1961).

23 Ibid., p. 229.

3

New Approaches to the Study of Peasant Rebellion and Consciousness: Implications of the Andean Experience

Steve J. Stern

The non-European world exploded after World War II, and the combined effects of decolonization, revolution, and the Cold War provoked a torrent of studies on agrarian unrest and political mobilization.[1] The new preoccupation – in certain respects a "rediscovery" – was especially evident among social scientists in the United States.[2] After all, it was the United States that assumed leadership of the West in the Cold War, financed a huge and expanding university system, and agonized over policy failures in China, Cuba, and Vietnam.

By the 1960s, as scholars struggled to understand the turbulence of the non-European world, and wrestled with their own political consciences, the agrarian question came to assume an ever more prominent place in our understanding of modern world history. Normally irrelevant or secondary to the contemporary political life of industrialized societies such as the United States, England, and (to a lesser extent) France, the "traditional" agrarian classes – landlords and peasants – suddenly played pivotal roles on the stage of contemporary history. Students of modernization and political mobilization, for example, saw in the Third World the final death throes of archaic classes and values as once traditional societies awakened painfully to contemporary urban

values and expectations. The agrarian sector nurtured the historic values, traditions, and social relations that held non-Western societies back from a more rapid modernization of their economies and political institutions, and that made the transition to modern life more difficult and politically explosive.[3] Those who took a more critical stance toward the industrialized West discovered that the agrarian question was central to an understanding of the Western and non-Western worlds alike. Barrington Moore (1966) demonstrated that contemporary political cultures, whether democratic or authoritarian, rested on a historical foundation of agrarian violence and transformation. It was in an earlier world of lords, peasants, and nascent bourgeois strata, and in the political paths their societies took to revamp the agrarian sector, that Moore found the keys to the "democratic" or "authoritarian" features of political life in contemporary England, France, Germany, the United States, China, and Japan. Eric R. Wolf (1969) focused more pointedly on the "Third World" and argued that the great revolutions of the twentieth century were fundamentally "peasant wars." In various parts of the world, peasantries – subsistence-oriented agricultural producers subjected to the authority and economic exactions of a state, or a landed class of overlords, or both – faced the destructive advance of capitalist relations and values. Capitalism's advance undermined the peasants' access to the land, resources, and socio-political mechanisms they normally needed to sustain their way of life. In Mexico, Russia, China, Vietnam, Algeria, and Cuba, peasantries rose up in great defensive mobilizations that made revolution both necessary and possible. (In fairness to Wolf, his superb analysis of specific case studies illuminated the limits and variations that qualify the general interpretation. See, for example, his handling of the idiosyncrasies of the Cuban case.) The irony was that, in shattering the old order, the peasants facilitated the rise to power of revolutionary groups, political parties, and states whose interest in social transformation might, in the end, hasten the peasants' own destruction or subjugation.[4]

By the 1970s, the study of peasantries and agrarian conflict had become a well-established and vital field of scholarly inquiry. The field is now sufficiently mature and self-sustaining to produce theoretically and empirically interesting work for decades to come. Whether the issue is the impact of "modernization" on peasants, the transition to capitalism in the countryside, the structural causes of agrarian rebellion and its role in regime breakdown and revolution, or the internal differentiation of the peasantry into strata of varying economic welfare and political proclivities, we can now point to a cluster of studies rich in sophistication.[5] Within peasant studies, the subject of agrarian rebellion continues to command the attention of talented intellectuals, and the more interesting attempts to generalize about "peasants" often focus implicitly or explicitly on agrarian conflict and rebellion. To the list of early classics by Hobsbawm (1959), Moore (1966), and Wolf (1969), we can now add more recent landmark works by Scott (1976), Paige (1975), Tilly (1978), Popkin (1979), and Skocpol (1979). And these are simply works that aspire to high levels of generalization. Any area studies specialist could easily add a list of pioneering efforts for his or her culture area.

The study of peasants and agrarian conflict is a field too sophisticated, diverse, and politically charged to descend into stale uniformity. Yet, despite notable dissents (to be discussed later), one can identify several widespread assumptions and assertions that shape our overall image of peasants and agrarian rebels. First, most scholars now agree that the incorporation of predominantly peasant territories into the modern capitalist world economy had a destructive impact on peasant life, at least in the medium run. Even those who see "modernization" as ultimately beneficial would now be inclined to concede that it first exacts a heavy price (see, for example, Clark and Donnelly 1983: 11). Traditional values and social relations come under assault; local institutions that once provided a measure of economic security and income redistribution become ever more precarious; time-tested political strategies vis-à-vis lords or the state prove increasingly obsolete. The net result breaks down the viability of an earlier way of life, and provokes political unrest and mobilization. Second, scholars tend to agree that the penetration of capitalism accentuates the internal differentiation of peasant society into rich and poor strata. More precisely, capitalism breaks down institutional constraints that pressured wealthy peasants and villagers to channel their resources into "redistributive" or prestige-earning paths that blocked the free conversion of wealth into investment capital. In the most extreme cases, such a process polarizes peasant society into bourgeois farmers and proletarianized paupers, and subjects the remaining "middle peasants" to an insecure and problematic future. Political analysis of agrarian movements requires explicit attention to internal differentiation among the peasantry. Third, the political resolution of agrarian conflict and crisis is held to have had a strong, sometimes decisive, impact on the modern political history of countries with an important peasant tradition. In these countries' histories, the "agrarian question" looms large in the structural breakdown of colonial and *ancien régime* states. . . .

Fourth, and most questionable . . . are the assumptions about peasants as political actors. Peasants are frequently depicted as parochial and defensive "reactors" to external forces, and their political behavior, in this view, tends to reflect their objective "structural" position in society. Agrarian rebels "react" to changes dictated by forces outside the peasant sector itself – price cycles in the world market, the spread of capitalist plantations, the policies of the landed upper class or the state, and so on. Their economic base and social relations fragment the peasantry into separate and highly localized "little worlds" – the parochial world of a community, or a landed estate – and frequently pit peasants against one another as competing clients of the state's or lords' patronage. Limited in their political horizons, structurally divided amongst themselves, unable to understand national-level politics, let alone forge effective political strategies beyond the immediate locale, peasants succumb to the appeal of a millenarian redemption when searching for a means to transform society as a whole. To the extent that peasants either develop or benefit from effective political initiatives at the national level, such successes reflect not the peasants' historic capacity to analyze and respond to national-level politics, but instead rather recent changes: the peasants' political modernization; the leadership and influence of urban groups, rural-to-urban migrants, and intellectuals allied with the peasants; the ability of revolutionaries to channel rural mobilization against foreign invaders into a national political movement.

In short, when peasants rebel, they are held to do so in reaction to changes determined by all-powerful external forces or "systems." Their modes of consciousness, even in rebellion, are generally seen as quite limited and predictable, and logically derivative from their "structural" position in society. These assumptions about peasants as political actors are not simple figments of intellectuals' imagination. Enough evidence exists to demonstrate that the "parochial reactor" phenomenon is not only real, but that it also represents at least one powerful tendency in peasant political life. The problem in view of . . . the argument made later in this introduction is that a tendency which is partial and in many cases offset by other tendencies has been taken to represent *the* essential character of peasant political behavior and consciousness.

The four sets of assumptions and assertions mentioned above do not exactly add up to a unified theory of agrarian conflict and peasant rebellion,

nor do they command uniform consensus among scholars. The literature includes explicit dissents from these views. Popkin (1979), for example, presents a sweeping challenge to assertions about the destructive impact of capitalism on peasants, and their alleged mobilization to defend the crumbling "moral economy" associated with a precapitalist way of life. Macfarlane's (1978) portrait of rural folk in medieval and early modern England likewise stresses their individualism and calculating entrepreneurship – although his typically British preoccupation is not to challenge our theoretical notions of "peasants" so much as to establish "peculiarities" that set England apart from truly peasant regions of the world. The weight of population and life cycle trends in analyzing the causes and limits of internal differentiation is a subject of some dispute rooted in the distinctive perspectives of Chayanov (1986) and Lenin (1964) (cf. Shanin 1972). More recent and ongoing researches into "everyday forms of peasant resistance" (Scott 1985, *JPS* 1986; cf. Cooper 1980, Isaacman et al. 1980, Isaacman 1985) will undoubtedly drive us to reconsider our views of peasants as political actors, and is at least partly compatible with . . . approaches to peasant resistance and consciousness . . . . Nonetheless, the dissenters swim upstream against a formidable tide, and the new areas of inquiry are only beginning to recast deeply held assumptions and interpretations. The images sketched above – the destructive impact of capitalism, the boost given by capitalism to the internal differentiation of peasant strata into rich and poor, the major impact of the agrarian question on national political life more generally, and the parochial character of peasants as political actors – continue to constitute a common core of "prevailing wisdoms" that permeate both general theory and particular case studies.

The experience of native Andean peoples in the highlands of Peru and Bolivia is highly relevant to the literature on peasants and agrarian rebellion. In highland Peru–Bolivia, large majorities of the population have historically earned their sustenance as peasant cultivators. Andean peoples have for centuries been sharply affected by the North Atlantic economies in the vanguard of world capitalist transition and development.

The ethnic division between Andean "Indians" and creole "nationals" has made the assumption of peasant parochialism pervasive and intense. Moreover, Andean rebellions of varying scope and ambition have erupted frequently since the eighteenth century – first in relation to the breakdown of the Spanish colonial order in the late eighteenth and early nineteenth centuries, later in relation to creole attempts at nation-building during the late nineteenth and twentieth centuries. These Andean rebellions provide a thick set of historical materials with which to reconsider the paradigms and methods we use to understand agrarian and peasant unrest more generally.

Yet despite the pertinence of the Andean experience, it has not played an important role in developing or evaluating general theory on peasants and peasant rebellion. Although research in Andean history and anthropology has crackled with intellectual innovation and excitement in recent decades, the sense of *implication* drawn from such research has been largely restricted to the Andean culture area itself. (For important exceptions, however, see Orlove and Custred 1980.) At least three factors account for this somewhat insular sense of implication. First, within the Andean field, specialists have struggled to liberate the Andean experience from the shadow of other culture areas and political discourses. In an earlier era, and even to this day, some writers have viewed the ancient Incas and their contemporary descendants as examples of the virtues or defects of socialism, welfare states, or totalitarianism, or as mere variations on a general theme such as "irrigation civilizations." To discover the real nature of Andean civilization and its achievements it has been necessary to react against earlier manipulations and superficiality by emphasizing unique aspects of the Andean experience not easily subsumed under general categories. John V. Murra's pioneering and influential interpretations of Andean "verticality" and Inca-peasant political relations may be understood in these terms.[6] Second, outside the Andean field, political events in Bolivia and Peru have not generated the kind of sustained political obsessions provoked by political conflicts in China, Cuba, Vietnam, and Chile. The Bolivian revolution of 1952 and the

Peruvian revolution of 1968 each provoked intellectual interest and valuable studies, but each defied the usual Cold War categories, each erupted at times when other revolutions and upheavals loomed larger in political debate (China and Korea in the early 1950s, Vietnam and Chile in the late 1960s and early 1970s), and each fizzled to a murky denouement that reduced political interest. Finally, the ethnic issue is unavoidable in the Andean agrarian experience, and introduces complicating and awkward complexities to general discussions of "peasants." Uncertainty about the role that indigenous, ethnic, and racial issues should have in theoretical debates about "peasantry" – a category usually defined and theorized in ethnic-blind terms – has probably impeded explicit intellectual dialogue between Andean specialists and students of peasantry in general.

The articles in this book largely avoid explicit engagement of theory, yet they add up to something more than an original contribution to Andean history and studies. Of course, the Andean world is a worthy scholarly subject in its own right. Moreover, any serious attempt to analyze the Andean experience must address its singular, even idiosyncratic, features. The essays in this book contribute provocative findings and reevaluations to problems in the history of Andean rebellion and consciousness. In doing so, they add depth to and substantially revise, sometimes radically revise, the historiography of Andean peoples. This contribution alone justifies the publication of this collection, and each of the book's four sections will include brief introductory remarks highlighting the essays' specific significances for the history of Andean rebellion and resistance. The remainder of this general introduction will focus not on this book's contributions to Andean historiography as such, but rather on its implications for the study of "peasants" and agrarian unrest in general.

Taken as a whole, the essays in this book plead for a rethinking of assumptions and paradigms in four areas: the role of peasants as continuous initiators in political relations; the selection of appropriate time frames as units of analysis in the study of rebellion; the diversity of peasant consciousness and political horizons;

and the significance of ethnic factors in explaining "peasant" consciousness and revolt. In each of these four areas, I will point to essays and findings in this book that recast our perspectives during three different Andean historical conjunctures: the late colonial crisis of the eighteenth century, political conflicts and wars of the nineteenth-century republics, and agrarian conflict and political mobilization in Bolivia since the 1940s. I will also suggest why the perspectives taken in these essays apply broadly, not to the Andean cases alone. And finally, in each of these four areas, I will conclude with a methodological suggestion that illustrates the practical implications of these essays for students of peasant rebellion more generally.

Let us begin with peasants as *continuous initiators* in political relations among themselves and with nonpeasants. For all the advances made in the field of agrarian studies, we are still only beginning to understand the manifold ways whereby peasants have continuously engaged their political worlds – in apparently quiescent as well as rebellious times, as initiators of change as well as reactors to it, as peoples simultaneously disposed to "adapt" to objective forces beyond their control and to "resist" inroads on hard-won rights and achievements. Peasant political action tends still to be reduced to its most dramatic and abnormal moments – moments of rupture, defensive mobilization against harmful change, collective violence against authority. Although the literature recognizes that peasants have placed their own stamp on the political histories of their regions and countries, it shrinks such impact to moments of crisis leading to rebellion. During more "normal" times, peasants recede from the political picture. Politically speaking, they are an inert force – dormant, traditional, or ineffectual. This reductionism fits nicely with the image of peasant rebels as parochial "reactors" to external forces, and with the assumption that such defensive and limited political behavior is largely inherent in the objective, "structural" condition of peasants.

The problem with this approach is not only that it fails to understand peasant politics during "normal" or quiescent times, but also that it leads to superficial explanations of the causes of rebel-

lion. Such is the case, at least, for Andean history. For the late colonial period, for example, my essay and that by Mörner and Trelles demonstrate the danger of attempts to deduce insurrectionary behavior from "structural" variables, or to explain insurrection as defensive reactions to destructive external forces. Significantly, my essay's attempt to propose an alternative explanation of late colonial insurrection requires that we look seriously at the evolution of *preexisting* patterns of "resistant adaptation" that entailed innovative political engagement of the state by peasants. In this perspective, the relevant question becomes not why a politically dormant and traditionalist peasant mass suddenly became insurrectionary, but rather why, at specific moments, ongoing peasant resistance and self-defense increasingly took the form of collective violence against established authority. In this context, Campbell's vivid discussion of Andean political splits and choices during the wars of the 1780s analyzes not a sudden effort by peasants to forge effective political relations and strategies, but rather the continuation of such efforts in a new and insurrectionary context.

Similarly, this book's essays on republican history point to the importance of peasants' ongoing and sometimes innovative political involvement. Platt's and Mallon's analyses of nineteenth-century politics invert our conventional understanding of peasant–state relations. For Bolivia, Platt shows how peasants tried, with mixed results, to *impose* their conception of peasant–state relations on state officials, and explains rebellion in terms of the history of this peasant initiative. For Peru, Mallon shows how a particular group of peasants developed a "national project" of their own, one sufficiently vital to sustain the creation of an independent "peasant republic" and sufficiently threatening to oligarchical state-building to invite repression. . . . the political dilemmas and decisions faced by Bolivian peasant rebels since the 1940s take on new meaning. The Andean political strategies and evaluations studied by Albó and by Dandler and Torrico for the contemporary period represent not a sudden "awakening" of political consciousness, but the continuing experimentation and accumulation of experience by peasants in their political relations with the state and with nonpeasants.

For the modern as well as colonial periods, it is when we assume a prior history of "resistance" and peasant self-defense – a history that embraces apparently tranquil periods and that places peasants in a position of active, sometimes innovative political engagement – that we are able to arrive at a more profound appreciation of the moments when peasants turned to outright rebellion. It is when we study the bases of apparent and real accommodations to authority, consider the patterns of resistant assertion and self-protection incorporated into such accommodations, the ways such "resistant adaptation" made accommodation partial and contingent, and the values and ongoing political evaluations that lay behind partial accommodations, that we discern more clearly why peasants sometimes became rebels or insurrectionists.

The essays in this book study native Andean peoples in terms that see them as continuously involved in the shaping of their societies, sometimes in a role as political initiators, not mere reactors, and often exerting an important limiting impact on their local superiors and on "external" actors or systems. This perspective, in turn, serves as a prerequisite for understanding the causes and character of political unrest in the Andes. Although such an approach has not yet made much of an impact on theory, a growing body of area studies literatures on peasants and slaves suggest the applicability of this perspective to rural culture areas beyond the Andean region.[7] Our first methodological suggestion follows directly from this perspective: *explicit analysis of preexisting patterns of "resistant adaptation" is an essential prerequisite for any adequate theory or explanation of peasant rebellion.* Only by asking why, during what period, and in what ways earlier patterns of "resistance" and defense proved more compatible with and "adaptive" to the wider structure of domination, and perhaps even its partial legitimation, do we understand why resistance sometimes culminated in violent collective outbursts against authority. (In some cases, "resistant adaptation" may have included occasional acts of violence, and the necessary analysis would therefore include study of transformations in the uses of violence, rather than imply a pure or simple transition from nonviolent to violent forms of resistance.) Successful analysis

of the "resistant adaptation" that preceded the outbreak of rebellion or insurrection requires, in turn, that one see peasants as continuously and actively engaged in political relations with other peasants and with nonpeasants.

This approach views rebellion as a short-term variant within a long-term process of resistance and accommodation to authority, and therefore raises our second area of rethinking: the selection of time frames as units of analysis. Whether studying a local rebellion or a full-scale insurrection of regional or supraregional proportions, how far back in time need the analyst go to discern correctly the causes and internal dynamics of the rebellion?

Again and again, . . . Andean case studies . . . suggest that we must look at multiple time frames simultaneously – relatively short time frames ("conjunctural" and "episodic") to understand the recent changes that make rebellion or insurrection more likely and possible, and to appreciate dynamic changes that emerge during the course of violent conflicts; and longer time frames spanning centuries to understand the historic injustices, memories, and strategies that shape the goals, consciousness, and tactics of the rebels. For the colonial period, the essays by Salomon and Szemiński and the ongoing researches of Manuel Burga . . . demonstrate that a deep familiarity with late-eighteenth-century culture history and memory is essential if we are to grasp the categories and concepts of late colonial rebels. My essay's speculation on the breakdown of "resistant adaptation" makes seventeenth-century history an indispensable building block, not mere "background," in the explanation of civil war in the 1780s. Similarly, despite notable differences between them, Bonilla, Platt, and Mallon all invoke continuities and legacies from distant colonial times to explain, in part, the character of nineteenth-century rebellions. And for modern Bolivia, Albó demonstrates that politically engaged Aymara peoples and their opponents think in terms of memories spanning two centuries' time. In each of these cases, limiting the relevant historical unit of analysis to a forty- or fifty-year period preceding rebellion is perilously myopic, and violates the historical memory and consciousness of the rebels themselves.

Obviously, the need to incorporate long time frames into the relevant units of analysis does not imply that short-term events and changes are irrelevant. Campbell's account of tupamarista–katarista relations during the civil war of the 1780s, Mallon's study of the unfolding of peasant nationalism in the midst of war and foreign occupation, and Dandler and Torrico's close account of the commitment established between President Villarroel and Cochabamba's peasants, provide eloquent and convincing proof that so-called episodic events matter enormously, above all in fluid moments of crisis and rebellion. The challenge faced by scholars is not to *replace* short- or medium-term units of analysis with the *longue durée*, a procedure that risks burying real changes, moments of fluidity and rupture, and their causes under a picture of long continuities and glacially paced change. The challenge is, rather, to develop an analysis that successfully incorporates multiple time scales into its vision of rebellion and its causes.

Unfortunately, social scientists and theoreticians are somewhat disposed to look at the shorter time frames alone and to restrict "history" to decades rather than centuries. If long-term phenomena are mentioned, they may be presented as mere historical "background" to orient the reader, not as a source of explanatory tools explicitly incorporated into the analysis. Whether the long-term view is omitted altogether, or included pro forma, the resulting myopia can lead to erroneous, even absurd conclusions. As Theda Skocpol (1979: 41) has noted for studies of the Chinese Revolution: "it seems remarkably short-sighted in historical terms to regard it as a new-nation-building revolution of the mid-twentieth century. China had an imperial Old Regime with a cultural and political history stretching back many hundreds of years." Peasants, almost by definition, interact with state structures and overlords, and in many culture areas this political inheritance embraces centuries and partly defines the issues at stake in rebellion. When the Mexican revolutionary Emiliano Zapata was asked why he and his peasant armies were fighting, he pointed to a box of old colonial land titles.[8] For the peasants of revolutionary Morelos, the relevant time scales included not only the changes intro-duced under the recent rule by Porfirio Díaz (1876–1910), not only the immediate policies of their Constitutionalist contemporaries, who betrayed the peasants' version of the revolution, but also a centuries-long struggle over land that defined the peasants' aspirations and understandings of proper rights and obligations in their relations with the state.

Our second practical suggestion, then, is that *the method used to study peasant rebellion should incorporate long-term frames of reference explicitly into the analysis.* The precise definition of the relevant long-term frame of reference will depend on the particular case at hand, but it should at least include the period considered relevant in the rebels' own historical memory, and the period during which the last enduring strategy of "resistant adaptation" was developed. It is difficult to imagine a time scale less than a century long that meets these criteria. A method which studies multiple time scales, including long-term ones, will not only explain better the causes and ideological characteristics of particular rebellions and insurrections. It will also enable the student to distinguish more clearly between genuinely new patterns of collective violence and grievance, and repetitions of historic cycles of resistance and accommodation that occasionally included some forms of collective violence.

We have already attached importance to the historical memory of peasants, but historical memory is itself but a slice of the larger pie called peasant consciousness. In this area, too, this book calls for a reassessment of common theoretical assumptions. For the Andean case, the expectations of ideological parochialism and predictability do not stand up under scrutiny. The forms of consciousness and the breadth of political horizons uncovered . . . are too diverse and flexible to fit into the usual straitjacketed category of "peasant consciousness" described earlier in this essay. The peasants' aspirations and ideological commitments go beyond narrow obsessions with local land, subsistence guarantees, or autonomy (i.e., the desire simply to be left alone). Nor can we say that the peasants' material experience, social connections, and political understandings were largely bounded by the "little worlds" of communities and haciendas. For the late colonial period, both directly and through intermediaries, peasants moved in social, economic, and ideological orbits that stretched considerably beyond their principal locales of residence and work. Mobilization to install a new Inca-led social order reflected not a simple yearning for local subsistence and autonomy, but an effort to forge a new macrolevel polity that blended more successfully local peasant needs and aspirations with supraregional political order. True, one could dismiss the struggle for an Inca-led Andean renaissance as an example of the "prepolitical" millenarianism to which peasants desperate to overcome their fragmentation are prone. But in this case, one would have to confront Alberto Flores Galindo's inversion of our usual assumptions. Flores shows that the search for an Inca liberator was not an aspiration confined only to peasants or Indians. The dream of an Inca-led resurgence was a political idea whose appeal was so compellingly "universal," in the late colonial Andean world, that it fired the imagination of more "cosmopolitan" individuals, and made it possible for Andean peasants to envision a social order that allied them with nonpeasants and nonindigenous peoples under Inca auspices.

Similarly, our nineteenth- and twentieth-century materials depict an awareness of political worlds beyond the immediate locale, a willingness to deal with states, and a flexibility of consciousness far more complex than the predictable parochial obsessions with land, subsistence, or autonomy. Platt introduces notions of peasant-state reciprocities; Mallon argues for a bottom-up peasant nationalism *before* a bourgeoisie imposes "nationalism" on a citizenry integrated by an internal market; Dandler and Torrico provide eloquent testimony of peasant interest and commitment to populist political pacts; Albó explores the painful reevaluations that led Aymara peasants, in particular, to reject paternal political pacts, and to search for new forms of *national-level* political action. In all these depictions, Andean peasants are no more inherently parochial than other political actors; their consciousness does not conform to a priori assumptions; their political behavior is nurtured by a long historical experience dealing with states and macrolevel political forces; and their ideological

history is an important variable in its own right in the explanation of rebellious activity.

The particular values, memories, and vision of the world that define the content of Andean rebel consciousness may be in important respects uniquely Andean, but the same cannot be said of the failure of Andean peasant consciousness to conform to a priori categories. One must recall that most peasantries have had long experience with states and with nonpeasants. Moreover, most peasantries have resided in well-defined "culture areas" (Mesoamerica, Mediterranean Europe, Islamic North Africa, China, Indochina, etc.) with complex internal histories defining cultural notions of social identity and aspiration, order and disorder, justice and vengeance, continuity and change, and the like. These cultural notions are products of a history shaped by both peasants and nonpeasants; more important, their spread has not been restricted only to nonpeasant elites, even if peasants have imposed their own partial variation on broad cultural themes.[9] Under these circumstances, deducing from the general "structural" features of peasantries their characteristic form(s) of consciousness is hopelessly one-dimensional and ahistorical. Deducing, in addition, that peasants are characteristically parochial, backward, and defensive merely adds insult to injury. It is quite instructive that sensitive students of *particular* peasantries find the history and complexity of their consciousness far richer than our theoretical postures would imply. Frances Fitzgerald's analysis of "Marxism-Leninism in the Vietnamese Landscape" (1973: 284–304; based in good measure on Mus 1952), for example, is a stunning example of the way specific historical traditions and values in Vietnamese culture provided a foundation for a rebel-peasant consciousness compatible with Marxist notions of revolution and justice. To take a more narrowly defined example, Arturo Warman found that Mexican peasants' resistance, in the 1970s, to state attempts to "collectivize" the management of their communal lands (*ejidos*) did not reflect the ignorance, parochialism, and traditionalism intellectuals commonly used to explain the peasants' "reactionary" stance. On the contrary, the peasants shrewdly recognized that behind the rhetorical masks of progress and material reward lay an attempt by the state to organize and control modern agrarian enterprises in ways that would destroy economic options the peasants needed to survive (Warman 1980: 61–83).[10] The peasants were neither ignorant about macrolevel politics, nor inherently opposed to "progress" or to collective forms of economic organization.

Our third methodological suggestion, then, is that studies of peasant rebellion *should treat peasant consciousness as problematic rather than predictable, should pay particular attention to the "culture history" of the area under study, and should discard notions of the inherent parochialism and defensiveness of peasants.* From this perspective, parochialism and defensive obsessions with local rights may indeed prevail among particular rebellious peasantries at particular times and places, but these patterns could not be explained away as a near-universal phenomenon inherent in the situation of being a peasant threatened by external overlords, state authorities, or markets. This perspective also allows the analyst to assess more dynamically the interplay of material and ideological variables (since the latter do not always "reflect" the former in simple or direct ways), and to consider in what ways explicit attention to peasant consciousness changes our understanding of the causes and issues at stake in rebellion. It will encourage us, too, to develop the new theoretical tools needed to explain the multiple contours peasant consciousness can take. Mallon's theoretical explanation of the development of nationalist consciousness before the consolidation of a dominant bourgeoisie and internal market is an instructive and exciting example.

If one takes peasant consciousness seriously in the Andes, one must immediately weigh the significance of ethnicity in "peasant" consciousness and revolt. Here, too, the Andean experience provokes a reassessment of assumptions and paradigms. By ethnicity, I mean the use of presumed cultural and physical attributes (race or color, biological or cultural ancestry, religion, language, work habits, clothing, etc.) – attributes considered to adhere strongly to the persons involved rather than to be easily renounced, adopted, or transferred – to draw social boundaries that place people into distinctive groupings within the

larger world of social interaction. To the extent that ethnic boundaries do *not* coincide with class boundaries, ethnic relations and identification may serve to link the grievances and world views of peasants and nonpeasants. Such was the case, for example, in the insurrectionary mobilizations that sought to install an Inca-led order in the late colonial Andes. A shared sense of ethnic identification and grievance served as a bridge, in at least some areas, uniting the loyalties of native Andean peasants, and Andean elites whose class privileges (ownership of haciendas, investment in mercantile enterprises, participation in tribute incomes, etc.) sharply distinguished them from peasants. To the extent, on the other hand, that ethnic boundaries *do* coincide with class boundaries, the language, ideology, and causes of peasant rebellions are difficult to understand in ethnic-blind terms. An ethnic component is built into the oppressions, patterns of adaptation and resistance, sense of grievance, and aspirations that will loom large in the explanation and analysis of revolt. Such ethnic bases of revolt are particularly important, for example, in the rebellions studied by Salomon and Platt for the eighteenth and nineteenth centuries. (Cf. the research of Gonzales...) It is precisely the ethnic dimension of Andean peasant consciousness in Peru that leads Bonilla to dismiss Mallon's finding of peasant nationalism in Peru's central highlands as atypical at best. In most other areas, Bonilla argues, the ethnic question loomed larger and would have made peasant nationalism impossible.

Clearly, the ethnic dimension is unavoidable in any broad discussion of rebellion and consciousness by Andean peasants. This has held true, for the Andean area, in regions and time periods when ethnic and class boundaries virtually coincided, and when they have not. The findings of Dandler and Torrico, Albó, and Cárdenas... make emphatically clear both how significant ethnicity is in contemporary peasant politics, and also how easily it has tripped up those who perceive Bolivian class conflicts in ethnic-blind terms.

But is the weight of ethnic-racial issues in Andean peasant history peculiar and atypical? If so, the tendency to theorize and explain peasant revolts in ethnic-blind terms is not seriously mistaken. The ethnic question, however, has sharply affected the history and probably the consciousness of many peasantries. Especially in the Third World, the spread of North Atlantic capitalism has been closely associated with various forms of colonial domination – formal colonial rule, warfare and informal rule, missionary religion, and so on. The assault on the material underpinnings of peasant life has inevitably brought with it the divisions of language, religion, culture, and race that nurture ethnic relations and consciousness. Under these conditions, we should be surprised if an ethnic-national component does *not* loom significantly in peasant rebellion and consciousness. European peasants may be the exception rather than the rule in this instance, even though one need only look to British Ireland, or to the Christian "reconquest" of Islamic Spain, to find analogies in the European experience.

In addition, even when the division between colonizer and colonized is set aside, internal ethnic matters may be indispensable to any serious analysis of peasant politics, consciousness, or rebellion. Campbell's discussion of late colonial insurrection shows clearly that Andean insurrectionaries were internally divided amongst themselves, and that intra-Andean ethnic boundaries figured significantly in such divisions. Anyone remotely familiar with the religious question in Ireland, or the historic stereotypes that North and South Vietnamese have used to characterize their differences (see Fitzgerald 1973: 64–66), or the tendency of many peasant communities to turn "inward" and claim an identity and interest distinctive from that of rival communities as well as that of nonpeasants (Wolf 1957; Stern 1983), will appreciate the potential significance of ethnic conflicts and consciousness among peasants.

Finally, even when obvious ethnic divisions are not applicable, the protagonists of class conflict may tend to attach more subtle sorts of ethnic accouterments to themselves or to other social classes. (This process is sometimes described as "classism.") The Zapatista peasants of Morelos, for example, were mainly mestizos, not Indians, and they were in any event relatively "acculturated" compared to peasants from other parts of Mexico. Nonetheless, landowners and

urban elites could not help but attach a derogatory ethnic label to their class enemies, and considered the Zapatistas barbaric "Indians" engaged in wild and destructive race war. Even urban workers were influenced by the tendency to ascribe ethnic characteristics to other social classes. When the Zapatistas occupied Mexico City, workers were stunned and to some extent alienated by the respectful social style and evident religiosity of the peasants. The characteristics that adhered to the peasants *as a distinctive kind of people* introduced an ethnic element into the controversial decision of the workers to reject a peasant–worker coalition with the Zapatistas, and to ally instead with the peasants' Constitutionalist enemies (Hart 1978: 131–33). It would be naive to believe that the tendency of nonpeasants to dismiss the peasants as barbaric, ignorant, or superstitious did not have an important hand in the peasants' own sense of grievance and aspiration.

If, as I have argued, the significance of ethnic factors in peasant consciousness and revolt is not peculiar to the Andes, we are in a position to make a fourth methodological suggestion. In theory as well as particular studies of peasant revolt, even when ethnic matters are not obviously relevant (as they are, say, in Ireland or Peru), *ethnic-blind analysis should be justified rather than used as a point of departure*. In some cases and for some purposes, ethnic variables may not be important to the understanding of rebellion. But this needs to be demonstrated explicitly. Ethnic-blind categories are probably a mistake for many parts of the Third World in recent centuries, and may seriously limit the usefulness of general theory.

This essay has sought to break with the tendency of Andean historians and anthropologists to restrict the sense of implication we draw from Andean case studies. It also issues a challenge to theorists and to students of other peasantries to incorporate the Andean experience into their paradigms and methodologies. The specific purposes of this introductory essay should not be taken to detract, however, from the importance of the Andean experience in its own right. Each of the essays that follow offers an original and significant twist on one or another theme essential to the history of Andean rebellion.

Taken together, they offer eloquent testimony of the varied ways in which Andean peasants have struggled to better their lot, transform aspiration into reality, even take destiny into their own hands. To this history we now turn.

NOTES

1   This assertion is almost self-evident to anyone who has studied the literature on peasants, agrarian revolution, or political mobilization. See, for example, the dates of the literature on peasants and on revolution reviewed by Clark and Donnelly (1983) and by Skocpol (1979: 3–33), or the works cited in notes 3–5. A content analysis of articles published in major scholarly journals, and of the subject areas of new journals (such as *Journal of Peasant Studies* or *Peasant Studies*), would almost certainly support the same assertion.

2   I borrow the term "rediscovery" from Shanin (1971a: 11). As Shanin points out, the late 1950s and 1960s hardly witnessed the rise of the *first* significant scholarly or political interest in peasants and agrarian issues. Debate in Germany and Russia in the late nineteenth and early twentieth centuries, for example, provoked classic works by Chayanov (1986; orig. 1923), Kautsky (1974; orig. 1899), and Lenin (1964; orig. 1899). The weight of agrarian issues in the history and political polemics of particular countries such as France, England, and Mexico, moreover, produced important historical literatures on agrarian matters well before the 1960s, even though these literatures tended not to generalize or theorize beyond the particular country's experience. And, of course, Mao Zedong's great political innovation was to place peasants and agrarian conflict at the heart of the theory and praxis of the Chinese revolution.

Nonetheless, it was the late 1950s that witnessed a resurgence of interest in peasants and political mobilization in the Western scholarly world, especially the United States, and an emphasis on theoretical and comparative perspectives facilitating broad generalization. It is no accident that it was precisely during the 1960s and 1970s that "old" classics were rediscovered and reprinted in Western editions.

3   See, for somewhat varied examples of the literature on modernization and political mobilization, Black 1960, 1976; Deutsch 1961; Eisenstadt 1966; Huntington 1968; C. Johnson 1964, 1966; J. Johnson 1958; Lambert 1967; Landsberger 1969; Lipset 1967; Rogers 1969; Shanin 1971b. Influential works by Parsons (1951) and Smelser (1963) had an important impact on much of the literature cited above. For a perceptive critical review of theories of revolution – a literature which partly overlaps that on modernization and political mobilization – see Aya 1979.

4   For influential works critical of the industrialized West, and bearing significant similarities to the perspectives of Moore (1966) and Wolf (1969), see Hobsbawm 1959; Polanyi 1957; Scott 1976; Skocpol 1979; Stavenhagen 1975; Thompson 1971; Wallerstein 1974; Worsley 1968.

5   The characterization of the literature in this and the following four paragraphs draws on the literature cited in notes 1 to 4, my own familiarity with the extensive literature for Latin America, and the following major works not emphasizing Latin America: Adas 1979; Alroy 1966; Blum 1961, 1978; Chesneaux 1973; Cohn 1970; Cooper 1980; Dunn 1972; C. Johnson 1962; Migdal 1974; Paige 1975; Shanin 1966, 1972; Stinchcombe 1961; Tilly 1978; Wolf 1966. Those readers wishing further orientation to the literature on Latin American peasants are advised to consult such journals as *Latin American Research Review* and *Latin American Perspectives*, or to consult the following recent works: Bauer 1979; de Janvry 1982; Duncan and Rutledge 1978; Mallon 1983; and Roseberry 1983. See also Landsberger 1969; Stavenhagen 1970.

7   See Murra 1975: esp. 23–115, 193–223; cf. Murra 1956. For an extensive and recent consideration of Murra's ideas, and Murra's own retrospective, see Masuda et al. 1985.

8   For Latin American and Caribbean cases, see Larson 1983; Mintz 1977; Mintz and Price 1976; Stern 1981. For Africa, see Isaacman and Isaacman 1977; Isaacman et al. 1980; Isaacman 1985. For the U.S. South, see Genovese 1974; Hahn 1983. For Southeast Asia see Scott 1985; *JPS* 1986.

9 The incident was first recounted and explained by Sotelo Inclán (1943: 201–3), and subsequently the subject of further perceptive discussion by Womack (1969: 371–72) and Fuentes (1969). I am very grateful to Eric R. Wolf for graciously drawing my attention to the "scholarly genealogy" of this event. For example, one could argue that in Mesoamerican cultures, the notion that human sacrifice to the gods was necessary to sustain the cosmos served elite interests and was most fully elaborated by ruling priests and intellectuals. Note, for example, Padden's charge (1967) that the Aztecs encouraged and manipulated such beliefs as part of their imperial strategy. Nonetheless, it is also clear that such notions of the relation between humans, gods, and the continuity of life were long diffuse in Mesoamerican cultures, and that peasants shared such notions, even if they did not always draw the same conclusions as elites regarding the necessity and effects of particular sacrificial practices and institutions. Similarly, in Vietnam, the cultural notion that real social transformation could only occur under a "mandate from heaven" might have been elaborated by Vietnamese elites, but peasants could also partake of such notions, might bend them to suit peasant needs and understandings, and in some instances resist or attack elites under the auspices of a heavenly mandate. To cite another example, in Mediterranean Europe, peasants might absorb much of the paternal values inculcated by the Catholic Church, but use their "religiosity" to forge special bonds with patron saints so uniquely responsible to the peasants' communities that the saints seemed to overshadow Jesus. In each of these examples, the peasants' rebelliousness or lack thereof might be affected by values and understandings shaped by nonpeasants as well as peasants, and the nature of the peasants' rebelliousness or lack thereof might be affected by values and understandings shaped by nonpeasants as well as peasants, and the nature of the peasants' consciousness and political proclivities could not be derived exclusively from "structural" variables (community peasant versus hacienda serf, independent yeoman farmer versus sharecropper or tenant, hacienda peon versus plantation laborer, and so on).

10 Cf. the remarkably complex and sensitive interpretation of peasant consciousness in Mexico in Meyer 1973. Scott's recent book (1985) is also extremely provocative in this regard.

REFERENCES

ADAS, MICHAEL
1979 *Prophets of Rebellion: Millenarian Protest Movements Against the European Colonial Order*. Chapel Hill: University of North Carolina Press.

ALROY, GIL CARL
1966 *The Involvement of Peasants in Internal Wars*. Princeton: Center of International Studies.

AYA, ROD
1979 "Theories of Revolution Reconsidered: Contrasting Models of Collective Violence." *Theory and Society: Renewal and Critique in Social Theory* 8 (Elsevier-Amsterdam, July): 39–99.

BAUER, ARNOLD J
1979 "Rural Workers in Spanish America: Problems of Peonage and Oppression." *Hispanic American Historical Review* 59 (Feb.): 34–63.

BLACK, CYRIL E., ed.
1960 *The Transformation of Russian Society: Aspects of Social Change since 1861*. Cambridge: Harvard University Press.
1976 *Comparative Modernization: A Reader*. New York: Free Press.

BLUM, JEROME
1961 *Lord and Peasant in Russia: From the Ninth to the Nineteenth Century*. Princeton: Princeton University Press.
1978 *The End of the Old Order in Europe*. Princeton: Princeton University Press.

CHAYANOV, A. V.
1986 *The Theory of Peasant Economy*. Originally published 1923. Madison: University of Wisconsin Press.

CHESNEAUX, JEAN
1973 *Peasant Revolts in China, 1840–1949*. Translated by C. A. Curwen. New York: W. W. Norton & Company.

CLARK, SAMUEL, AND JAMES S. DONNELLY, JR.
1983 "General Introduction." In Clark and Donnelly, eds., *Irish Peasants: Violence and Political Unrest, 1780–1914* (Madison: University of Wisconsin Press). Pp. 3–21.

COHN, NORMAN

1970 *The Pursuit of the Millennium: Revolutionary Millenarians and Mystical Anarchists of the Middle Ages*. Rev. ed. New York: Oxford University Press. Original edition published in 1957.

COOPER, FREDERICK

1980 *From Slaves to Squatters: Plantation Labor and Agriculture in Zanzibar and Coastal Kenya, 1890–1925*. New Haven: Yale University Press.

DE JANVRY, ALAIN

1982 *The Agrarian Question and Reformism in Latin America*. Baltimore: Johns Hopkins University Press.

DEUTSCH, KARL W.

1961 "Social Mobilization and Political Development." *American Political Science Review* 55 (Sept.): 493–514.

DUNCAN, KENNETH, AND IAN RUTLEDGE, eds.

1978 *Land and Labour in Latin America: Essays on the Development of Agrarian Capitalism in the Nineteenth and Twentieth Centuries*. Cambridge: Cambridge University Press.

DUNN, JOHN

1972 *Modern Revolutions: An Introduction to the Analysis of a Political Phenomenon*. Cambridge: Cambridge University Press.

EISENSTADT, S. N.

1966 *Modernization: Protest and Change*. Englewood Cliffs, N. J.: Prentice-Hall.

FITZGERALD, FRANCES

1973 *Fire in the Lake: The Vietnamese and the Americans in Vietnam*. New York: Vintage Books.

FUENTES, CARLOS

1969 "Viva Zapata." *The New York Review of Books* (13 March): 5–11.

GENOVESE, EUGENE D.

1974 *Roll, Jordan, Roll: The World the Slaves Made*. New York: Random House.

HAHN, STEVEN

1983 *The Roots of Southern Populism: Yeoman Farmers and the Transformation of the Georgian Upcountry, 1850–1890*. New York: Oxford University Press.

HART, JOHN M.

1978 *Anarchism and the Mexican Working Class, 1860–1931*. Austin: University of Texas Press.

HOBSBAWM, ERIC J.

1959 *Primitive Rebels: Studies in Archaic Forms of Social Movement in the 19th and 20th Centuries*. Manchester: Manchester University Press.

HUNTINGTON, SAMUEL P.

1968 *Political Order in Changing Societies*. New Haven: Yale University Press.

ISAACMAN, ALLEN

1985 "Chiefs, Rural Differentiation and Peasant Protest: The Mozambican Forced Cotton Regime, 1938–1961." *African Economic History* 1, 4: 15–56.

ISAACMAN, ALLEN, AND BARBARA ISAACMAN

1977 "Resistance and Collaboration in Southern and Central Africa, ca. 1850–1920." *International Journal of African Historical Studies* 10, 1: 31–62.

ISAACMAN, ALLEN, ET AL.

1980 "'Cotton is the Mother of Poverty': Peasant Resistance to Forced Cotton Production in Mozambique, 1938–1961." *International Journal of African Historical Studies* 13, 4: 581–615.

JPS

1986 *Journal of Peasant Studies* 13 (Jan.): Special Issue on "Everyday Forms of Peasant Resistance in South-East Asia."

JOHNSON, CHALMERS A.

1962 *Peasant Nationalism and Communist Power: The Emergence of Revolutionary China, 1937–1945*. Stanford: Stanford University Press.

1964 *Revolution and the Social System*. Stanford: Hoover Institution.

1966 *Revolutionary Change*. Boston: Little, Brown, and Company.

JOHNSON, JOHN J.

1958 *Political Change in Latin America: The Emergence of the Middle Sectors*. Stanford: Stanford University Press.

KAUTSKY, KARL

1974 *La cuestión agraria*. Mexico City: Ediciones de Cultura Popular. Originally published in 1899.

LAMBERT, JACQUES

1967 *Latin America: Social Structure and Political Institutions*. Berkeley: University of California Press. Originally published in French in 1963.

LANDSBERGER, HENRY A., ed.

1969 *Latin American Peasant Movements*. Ithaca, N.Y.: Cornell University Press.

LARSON, BROOKE

1983 "Shifting Views of Colonialism and Resistance." *Radical History Review* 27: 3–20.

LENIN, V. I.

1964 *The Development of Capitalism in Russia*. Moscow: Progress Publishers. Originally published in 1899.

LIPSET, SEYMOUR MARTIN

1967 "Values, Education, and Entrepreneurship." In Lipset and Aldo Solari, eds., *Elites in Latin America* (New York: Oxford University Press). Pp. 3–60.

MACFARLANE, ALAN

1978 *The Origins of English Individualism: The Family, Property, and Social Transition.* New York: Cambridge University Press.

MALLON, FLORENCIA E.

1983 *The Defense of Community in Peru's Central Highlands: Peasant Struggle and Capitalist Transition, 1860–1940.* Princeton: Princeton University Press.

MASUDA, SHOZO, ET AL.

1985 *Andean Ecology and Civilization.* Tokyo: University of Tokyo Press.

MEYER, JEAN

1973 *La cristiada.* 3 vols. Mexico City: Siglo XXI.

MIGDAL, JOEL S.

1974 *Peasants, Politics, and Revolution: Pressures Toward Political and Social Change in the Third World.* Princeton: Princeton University Press.

MINTZ, SIDNEY

1977 "The So-Called World System: Local Initiative and Local Response." *Dialectical Anthropology* 2: 253–70.

MINTZ, SIDNEY, AND RICHARD PRICE

1976 "An Anthropological Approach to the Afro-American Past: A Caribbean Perspective." Occasional Paper in Social Change No. 2, Institute for the Study of Human Issues (ISHI). Philadelphia: ISHI.

MOORE, BARRINGTON, JR.

1966 *Social Origins of Dictatorship and Democracy: Lord and Peasant in the Making of the Modern World.* Boston: Beacon Press.

MURRA, JOHN V.

1956 "The Economic Organization of the Inca State." Ph.D. diss., University of Chicago. Also available as *La organización económica del estado Inca.* Mexico City: Siglo XXI, 1978.

1975 *Formaciones económicas y políticas del mundo andino.* Lima: Instituto de Estudios Peruanos.

MUS, PAUL

1952 *Viêt-Nam: Sociologie d'une guerre.* Paris: Editions du Seuil.

ORLOVE, BENJAMIN S., AND GLYNN CUSTRED, eds.

1980 Land and Power in Latin America: Agrarian Economies and Social Processes in the Andes. New York: Holmes & Meier Publishers, Inc.

PADDEN, R. C.

1967 *The Hummingbird and the Hawk: Conquest and Sovereignty in the Valley of Mexico, 1503–1541.* Columbus: Ohio State University Press.

PAIGE, JEFFREY M.

1975 *Agrarian Revolution: Social Movements and Export Agriculture in the Underdeveloped World.* New York: Free Press.

PARSONS, TALCOTT

1951 *The Social System.* Glencoe, Ill.: Free Press.

POLANYI, KARL

1957 *The Great Transformation.* Boston: Beacon Press.

POPKIN, SAMUEL L.

1979 *The Rational Peasant: The Political Economy of Rural Society in Vietnam.* Berkeley: University of California Press.

ROGERS, EVERETT M.

1969 *Modernization Among Peasants: The Impact of Communication.* New York: Holt, Rinehart and Winston, Inc.

ROSEBERRY, WILLIAM

1983 *Coffee and Capitalism in the Venezuelan Andes.* Austin: University of Texas Press.

SCOTT, JAMES C.

1976 *The Moral Economy of the Peasant: Rebellion and Subsistence in Southeast Asia.* New Haven: Yale University Press.

1985 *Weapons of the Weak: Everyday Forms of Peasant Resistance.* New Haven: Yale University Press.

SHANIN, THEODOR

1966 "The Peasantry as a political factor." *Sociological Review* 14: 5–27.

1971a "Introduction." In Shanin 1971b: 11–19.

1971b (Ed.) *Peasants and Peasant Societies.* Baltimore: Penguin Books.

1972 *The Awkward Class: Political Sociology of Peasantry in a Developing Society: Russia, 1910–1925.* Oxford: Clarendon Press.

SKOCPOL, THEDA

1979 *States and Social Revolutions: A Comparative Analysis of France, Russia, and China.* New York: Cambridge University Press.

SMELSER, NEIL J.

1963 *Theory of Collective Behavior.* New York: Free Press of Glencoe.

SOTELO INCLÁN, JESÚS

1943 *Raíz y razón de Zapata.* Mexico City: Editorial Etnos.

STAVENHAGEN, RODOLFO
1970 (Ed.) *Agrarian Problems and Peasant Movements in Latin America*. New York: Doubleday and Anchor.
1975 *Social Classes in Agrarian Societies*. New York: Doubleday and Anchor.

STERN, STEVE J.
1981 "The Rise and Fall of Indian-White Alliances: A Regional View of 'Conquest' History." *Hispanic American Historical Review* 61 (Aug.): 461–91.
1983 "The Struggle for Solidarity: Class, Culture, and Community in Highland Indian America." *Radical History Review* 27: 21–45.

STINCHCOMBE, A. L.
1961 "Agricultural Enterprise and Rural Class Relations." *American Journal of Sociology* 67 (Sept.): 165–76.

THOMPSON, E. P.
1971 "The Moral Economy of the English Crowd in the Eighteenth Century." *Past & Present* 50 (Feb.): 76–136.

TILLY, CHARLES
1978 *From Mobilization to Revolution*. Reading, Mass.: Addison-Wesley.

WALLERSTEIN, IMMANUEL
1974 *The Modern World-System: Capitalist Agriculture and the Origins of the European World-Economy in the Sixteenth Century*. New York: Academic Press.

WARMAN, ARTURO
1980 *Ensayos sobre el campesinado en México*. Mexico City: Nueva Imagen.

WOLF, ERIC R.
1957 "Closed Corporate Peasant Communities in Mesoamerica and Central Java." *Southwestern Journal of Anthropology* 13: 1–18.
1966 *Peasants*. Englewood Cliffs, N. J.: Prentice-Hall.
1969 *Peasant Wars of the Twentieth Century*. New York: Harper and Row.

WOMACK, JOHN, JR.
1969 *Zapata and the Mexican Revolution*. New York: Alfred A. Knopf.

WORSLEY, PETER
1968 *The Trumpet Shall Sound: A Study of "Cargo" Cults in Melanesia*. 2d ed. New York: Schocken Books.

4

The Real "New World Order": The Globalization of Racial and Ethnic Relations in the Late Twentieth Century

Néstor P. Rodríguez

Introduction

The late twentieth century has witnessed an increasing globalization of racial and ethnic relations in the United States. Since the mid-1960s, world developments, transnational migration, and the emergence of binational immigrant communities have significantly affected the character of intergroup relations in U.S. society. Perhaps not since the initial European colonization of the Americas has the global context been such a prominent macrostructural background for evolving racial and ethnic relations in the United States. Domestic and foreign capitalist expansion, technological advances in communication and transport, antisystematic movements and counterinsurgency campaigns abroad, and growing global strategies in the structuration of everyday life among third-world working classes have been major social forces affecting the globalization of intergroup relations in the United States and in other Western capitalist societies.

Increasing Globalization of Racial and Ethnic Relations

Since its inception in the "long" sixteenth century, capitalist world development has influenced relations – especially power relations – among racial and ethnic populations in many world regions. The subjugation of indigenous populations in the Americas, the harnessing of African slave labor in the West Indies, and the subordination of immigrant labor in Western industrial societies are examples of the historical capitalist influence on intergroup relations. The state has played a crucial role in the formation and maintenance of racial-ethnic structures in contexts of capitalist development. In the United States, the state has played an important function in the racial formation of society through such means as designating racial categories (for example, "white," "Negro," and "Indian" in the nineteenth century), implementing racial policies (for example, "separate but equal" education), and equilibrating the racial order (for example, through civil rights acts).[1] Through their institutional capacities, including religious positions, northern European white males were the primary architects of the initial structures of capitalist-related domination, that is, the intertwined structures of race, class, and state relations. To a considerable extent, the racist ideological foundations laid by northern European white males continue to frame issues of race relations today.

Given the historical continuance of world-capitalist influence on evolving racial and ethnic relations, what has to be explained are the present era's different relational dimensions between global capitalist development and evolving intergroup relations. To the extent that new dimensions evolve out of fundamental changes in the global structuration of capitalism, they represent discontinuities, and thus new moments of advanced capitalism. As I will argue later, human agency among working-class peoples in less-developed regions, and not just the impersonal structural growth of capital, is very much at the root of this development.

Global Diasporas

One dimension is the massive movements of people between different regions of the world. While earlier periods of the capitalist world system involved the voluntary and forced movement of populations, in the late twentieth century international migration reached a watershed in the massive numbers of migrants and in the great diversity of sending and receiving communities. Another major characteristic, and one prefigured by the nineteenth-century Irish emigration, is the migration from peripheral regions (Africa, Asia, and Latin America) to core societies of the capitalist world system. Starting in the age of industrial capitalism and accelerating in the era of advanced capitalism, this migration significantly affects racial and ethnic relations in Western societies.

In the United States, by the mid-1970s undocumented Mexicans alone reached the high mark of 1.3 million immigrants per year recorded in 1907, during a decade of heavy European influxes.[2] Affected by a change in U.S. immigration law, the period from the 1960s through the 1980s saw a dramatic shift in the origin of legally arriving immigrants: the number of legally arriving European immigrants decreased by 52.1 percent, while the number of legally arriving Asians and Latinos increased by 456.7 percent and 88.4 percent, respectively.[3] While European immigrants came from a number of different cultural backgrounds, together Asian and Latino immigrants represented a much broader cultural spectrum.

Equally important, some Asian and Latino immigrants (for example, Hmong, Montagnard, Garifuna, and Maya) represented cultural backgrounds new to U.S. society.

Global Urban Contextualization

A second world development affecting today's racial and ethnic relations is the increasing global-urban context of racial and ethnic intergroup relations. As major urban centers become increasingly incorporated into the world economy, relations among racial and ethnic populations in these centers become increasingly sensitive to international developments. Since the beginning of the capitalist world system, major urban centers in core societies have played various roles in providing resources for world economic exchange and development. In specific historical periods, some cities have owed much of their population growth to their specialization as financial or production centers in the global economy.[4] Often the growth of these specialized cities has included substantial immigration as investment or work opportunities attract foreigners.[5] This pattern has accelerated in the present era of high-tech communications and rapid travel.

In the United States, world cities have substantial foreign-born populations. For example, 28.4 percent of New York City's population and 38.4 percent of Los Angeles' population was foreign-born in 1990.[6] Miami, a banking center and entrepôt for the Caribbean and Latin America, had a 1990 foreign-born rate of 59.7 percent.[7]

International developments can quickly affect racial and ethnic relations in U.S. world cities strongly linked to a global system. Problems abroad that reduce markets or in other ways constrain industrial growth in the metropolises of world cities can lead to tensions among economically stressed racial and ethnic groups in these areas. For example, when dropping world oil prices paralyzed Houston's economy in the mid-1980s, anti-Latino and antiblack sentiments increased among many white homeowners in the city's west side. Settling by the thousands in west-side apartments vacated by unemployed white office workers, Latino immigrants and black in-migrants dramatically changed the char-

acter of many previously all-white neighborhoods, which were also experiencing shrinking
property values with the collapse of the city's
real estate market.[8]

The international stimulus of evolving intergroup relations in urban areas may also be
political. For instance, Central American refugee
influxes during the 1980s created new Latino-
Anglo relations in U.S. cities through the sanctuary movement. Latino and Anglo activists crossed
ethnic and class lines in many urban localities to
weld political alliances in community-based organizations that fed, housed, and transported
Central Americans on the run from U.S. government agents. The story of this Anglo-Latino
alliance has yet to be written, but its development
can be traced in the newspapers, newsletters, and
other documents of community-based organizations working with Central American newcomers.

In a second example, supportive relations
between the Cuban government and the African
National Congress (ANC) strained relations
between African Americans and Cuban Americans
in Miami. During a visit by Nelson Mandela, the
city's Latino mayor refused to meet the African
leader because of his praises for Fidel Castro's
support for the ANC – a definite taboo among the
city's Cuban-origin population. Offended by this
Latino ostracism of Mandela, some African
American leaders called for a boycott of the city
by outsiders. This was but an additional case in a
lengthy series of problematic developments
between African Americans and Latinos (Cuban
Americans) in Miami.[9] The killing of black men
by Latino police officers precipitated three major
riots in the 1980s in the city's poor black areas. A
mayoral election in the 1980s demonstrated the
souring of Miami's black–Cuban relations: 95
percent of black voters voted against the Cuban
American candidate.[10]

Binational Immigrant Communities

A third global factor presently affecting U.S.
racial and ethnic relations is the growth of binational Latino immigrant communities. Taking
advantage of modern technology, many Latino
immigrants have a binational existence, enjoying
social reproduction in their new settlements *and*

in their communities of origin.[11] Some Central
American families have evolved trinational
households as members exist and interact across
Central America, the United States, and Canada.
Transcending spatial barriers with rapid
communication and transportation, Latino immigrant families evolve transnational households
that concentrate income-earning activities in the
United States and maintain considerable social
and cultural nurturing in their communities of
origin.

From the East Coast to the West Coast, the
binational social reproduction of Latino immigrants is highly evident. The constant crisscross-
ing of the country in immigrant journeys between
U.S. settlement areas and hometowns in Mexico
and Central America, the rapid growth of Latino
satellite communication businesses and fast-cour-
ier companies that reach even remote village areas
in Central America, the high-wattage beaming by
Mexican AM stations to the United States, the
proliferation of Latino-international television
and newspaper media in U.S. cities – all are
part of the immigrants' binational reproduction.
Latino bus and van businesses have emerged to
transport immigrants to localities in Mexico and
the United States. In the same neighborhoods
where these transport businesses are located can
be found courier services to take letters and pack-
ages to immigrant communities of origin in
Mexico and Central America. Some of these businesses also offer telephone service directly to
many communities in Mexico and Central America. La Ranchera de Monterrey, a high-wattage
radio station (1050 AM) in Monterrey, Mexico,
transmits nightly throughout Mexico and many
parts of the United States. The station plays
songs dedicated across the U.S.-Mexico border
and sends messages concerning family emergen-
cies to Mexican immigrants in the United States.

Binational existence affects intergroup relations
in immigrant settlement areas by reinforcing the
immigrants' internal social and cultural infrastructure, reducing dependency on mainstream social
resources. Indeed, the binational residency of many
Latino immigrants has helped foster a new set
of intergroup dynamics: *intra*group relations between long-term residents and new immigrants.[12]
Especially among first-generation immigrants,

incorporation into the mainstream or into established ethnic groups of English-speaking Latinos becomes optional in the presence of a highly viable binational social structure.

Recent Impact of Globalization on U.S. Racial and Ethnic Relations

In *The Disuniting of America*, noted historian Arthur M. Schlesinger Jr. bemoans the loss of the vision of America (the United States) as a melting pot creating a people with a unifying American identity.[13] According to Schlesinger, a number of recent developments – for example, the end of the cold war, mass migrations, and faster modes of communication and transport – have brought changes, especially the "cult of ethnicity," that threaten to segment, resegregate, and retribalize U.S. society. Resurgent ethnicity, according to Schlesinger, is disintegrating nations across the world: "What happens when people of different ethnic origins, speaking different languages and professing different religions, settle in the same geographical locality and live under the same political sovereignty? Unless a common purpose binds them together, tribal hostilities will drive them apart. Racial and ethnic conflict, it seems evident, will now replace the conflict of ideologies as the explosive issue of our times."[14] The future of U.S. intergroup relations in the next century thus "lies darkly ahead," according to Schlesinger.[15]

My own view is that the ethnic dynamics that Schlesinger perceives to be decomposing the United States are but one subprocess of a multitude related to the increasing global contextualization of U.S. intergroup relations. Many of the major patterns of presently evolving racial and ethnic relations can be grouped into the following three categories: intergroup competition and conflict, intergroup incorporation, and intergroup labor replacement. These intergroup processes can transpire at two levels: between established racial and ethnic groups (for example, between African Americans and Anglos), and between established and new-immigrant groups (for example, between Mexican Americans and new Mexican immigrants).

Intergroup Competition and Conflict

On a daily basis newspapers in large U.S. cities carry stories of intergroup competition and conflict. The reconfiguration of political districts, elections for single-district representatives, the redrawing of neighborhood-school boundaries, physical assaults by hate groups, police brutality in minority neighborhoods, outbreaks in the inner city – all are contemporary instances of problematic intergroup relations. The long history of racial and ethnic conflict in our society, as well as in other societies, suggests that it is a basic mode of societal organization, especially in determining the distributions of societal resources (educational, health, and the like) among groups differentiated by power.[16]

White racism, the original and still central racism in the United States, for example, flourished in the post-Civil War era when blacks started to make social, economic, and political gains. In southern cities, for instance, when black workers made sizable percentage gains in the building trades in the late 1800s, white racism in trade unions acted to systematically eliminate blacks from skilled jobs. In an August 1906 diatribe against blacks who were used by Chicago employers to replace striking white workers, trade union leader Samuel Gompers referred to the black workers as "hordes of ignorant blacks... possessing but few of those attributes we have learned to revere and love...huge strapping fellows, ignorant and vicious, whose predominant trade was animalism."[17] By 1950, black workers accounted for only 1 percent to 3 percent of the workforces in building trade occupations.[18]

The history of capitalist development is replete with the use of ethnic divisions to structure economic activity. This practice continues in the present era. As a multicultural society, the United States is an exaggerated case of this structuration. U.S. industrialists and other business owners frequently segmented or replaced workforces by recruiting ethnics, especially immigrants.[19] Needless to say, this fostered tensions between U.S.-born and immigrant workers.[20]

In the recessive times of the late twentieth century, large and small capitalists have seized upon immigrant labor with special vigor. Economic restructuring strategies contained in the great U-turn of the U.S. economy have given immigrant labor critical status in some cases. Sociologist Rebecca Morales has shown how employers in Los Angeles' automobile manufacturing industry used Mexican immigrant workers in the late 1970s to restructure production.[21] In the 1980s, the Houston area showed a novel immigrant role in capitalist recomposition strategies: using immigrants to restructure consumption.[22] Facing a sharp decline of middle-class tenants during the city's recession, apartment complex owners turned to newly arriving immigrants, mostly undocumented Latinos, to rebuild their tenant populations. This initially nondivisive strategy had the latent effect of antagonizing many white homeowners in surrounding neighborhoods.

Obviously, capitalist economic strategies do not account for all intergroup tensions. As illustrated above, political developments also may lead to racial-ethnic tension. In addition, in settlement communities, intergroup relations at times lapse into sharp competition or conflict as the arrival of new groups leads to the redefinition of sociospatial boundaries.

Intergroup Incorporation

In many cases throughout the United States, settlement communities that have witnessed intergroup tensions have also witnessed efforts to enhance intergroup incorporation, often simultaneously. A host of sources (educational, political, religious) promote the incorporation of ethnically and racially different groups.[23] This is especially true concerning recently arrived immigrants. Perhaps more than before, attempts to incorporate newcomers sometimes include measures to maintain their culture and integrate part of it into the mainstream, semiotic structure.

Across many U.S. localities, formal activities currently undertaken to promote the value of diversity and the goal of intergroup incorporation include Diversity Week on university campuses, Unity conferences, cultural-awareness training seminars in private and public organizations, International Day in places of worship, and ethnic commemoration months in grade schools. Two

concerns drive participants in formal, incorporating activities. One concern is that society's growing diversity must be managed to ensure constructive results; the second concern is that racial minority groups must learn to work together as they ascend politically in the inner city.[24]

The promotion of intergroup incorporation through informal activities (for example, family celebrations, sandlot games, and ganging) no doubt has a much greater impact, as neighbors, co-workers, and friends spin intergroup webs with primary relationships, forming interpersonal bonds across group boundaries. Especially among ordinary people, commonality is an important stimulus for informal social interaction that promotes intergroup incorporation. For example, the Changing Relations Project, which investigated relations between established residents and newcomers in the late 1980s, found that common social space (such as apartment complexes and workplaces) sometimes created opportunities for informal intergroup interaction.[25]

What is different about intergroup incorporation in the present era is that the process can be multidirectional, in contrast to the mostly Anglo-conformity trends of earlier times. Across social, cultural, economic, and political dimensions, mainstream actors (business owners, elected officials, religious organizations, and so on) can be found incorporating the interests of newcomers, helping to maintain the newcomers' cultural distinctiveness.[26] For many business owners in large cities, multidirectional, intergroup relations create new markets and strategies. In a Houston case, for example, Korean investors opened a restaurant and hired Mexican immigrant workers to cook Chinese food for mainly African American customers. In California and Texas cities, Asian investors have ventured into Mexican businesses, learning Spanish better than English in some cases.

Intergroup Labor Replacement

U.S. race and ethnic relations have involved a long history of intergroup labor replacements. Capitalists in a variety of industries (agricultural, construction, manufacturing, and so forth) have constantly replaced groups of workers with different groups of workers. The growth of agri-business on the West Coast, the founding of manufacturing on the East Coast, and the building of the country's railroad system involved a multitude of cases where capitalists reconstituted their workforces with ethnically or racially different workers.[27] In particular, new immigrant groups replaced established labor groups as employers found special qualities among newcomer workers, such as self-recruitment, less work resistance, and the acceptance of lower pay.

Intergroup replacement in the labor force is not a matter of job competition. It is not a situation in which newcomers compete with, and take jobs away from, U.S. workers. It is a racial-ethnic structural recomposition of the labor market, *eliminating* intergroup job competition. In time, certain job sectors become visibly immigrant, and U.S. workers do not even bother to look for work in those sectors' industries, creating a sort of reserved labor market for immigrant workers.[28] Things can quickly turn around, however. For example, when office-cleaning Central American crews voted to unionize in downtown Houston, their corporate employer called in the Immigration and Naturalization Service and turned to U.S. workers to rebuild its workforce.

In many urban and rural labor markets throughout the United States today, new Latino immigrant workers (men and women) have replaced established black and Latino workers as the preferred workforce in low-skilled, low-wage industries. Especially in the most labor-intensive industries of the service sector, many employers have turned to new Latino immigrant workers to fill their labor needs. In some cases, employer racism against blacks is at the root of the new-found preference for immigrant labor, while in other cases new-immigrant labor is just too good a bargain to pass up, even in the face of employer sanctions.[29]

As employers find new immigrant labor more attractive, the work opportunity structure of unskilled, low-wage U.S. workers suffers a relative decline, if not an absolute one.[30] The impact of intergroup labor replacement is especially severe in inner cities with large poverty concentrations, settings in which the center of gravity of the labor market keeps moving farther and farther away from the masses of unemployed and under-employed people.

The plurality of racial-ethnic relations (competition and conflict, incorporation, labor replacement) reflects the increasing diversity of influencing sources, which at times contradict each other. Within capital, for example, employers in workplaces may promote intergroup tension as a strategy to divide and control workers, while corporate executives in city growth machines may promote intergroup harmony as a strategy to attract and settle businesses. Moreover, while economic segmentation (for example, stratified labor markets) may keep groups apart, noneconomic institutions (for example, places of worship) may bring them together.[31] The multiplicity of existent intergroup scenarios reflects not an indeterminacy of racial and ethnic relations, but highly dynamic matrices of classes, institutions, subcultures, networks, and individuals.

A large volume of immigration has contributed significantly to the dynamism of intergroup relations in U.S. society. In the following section, I will discuss how growing globalization of everyday life in peripheral regions of the capitalist world system has affected this change.

The Globalization of Everyday Life

A factor influencing the globalization of U.S. racial and ethnic relations is a growing globalization of everyday life in less-developed countries. For many families in the bottom socioeconomic strata of these countries, the fulfillment of everyday-life activities (such as housing, schooling, clothing, eating) has become dependent on the transnational income-producing strategy of international migration.[32] In the late twentieth century, guest workers in Western Europe and Latino immigrant workers in the United States illustrate this development.

Global structural context

Structural developments of the capitalist world system have given rise to conditions that promote international income-producing strategies in many less-developed regions. Periodic economic crises resulting from increased national integration into the world market, austere social policies dictated by foreign financial agencies, insurgent movements against economic and political elites, and counterinsurgency programs are examples of developments that severely constrain masses of urban and rural workers in less-developed regions and lead many of them to seek global survival strategies.

My observations in one Mayan *municipio* in the western highlands of Guatemala exemplify this development.[33] Facing increasing economic hardships – for example, rising food prices, unemployment, and reduced artisan marketplaces – and almost no viable economic alternatives in a national context of severe economic recession and civil war, over two thousand of the *municipio's* fourteen thousand inhabitants left during the 1980s to look for work in the United States. Having grown up in the *municipio's* small town or in its surrounding villages, only a few of the undocumented Mayan migrants had traveled long distances prior to their migration. After finding work in the United States, many of the Mayan immigrants remitted wage earnings to their families back home, helping them to survive and even prosper in some cases. Remittances from the United States have affected the *municipio's* social structure by creating degrees of social mobility, village-to-town migration, and land price inflation.

Decades of intervention by the United States, the World Bank, and other international financial organizations have laid the transnational structural context that restricts the capacity of many Maya and other Guatemalans to survive economically. Since the U.S.-planned coup against the democratically elected government of Jacobo Arbenz in 1954, the United States has supported (if not actually organized) political and economic activities in Guatemala to ensure the country's openness to foreign investors. The United States has supported Guatemalan government actions against popular movements and has obtained international funding for Guatemalan infrastructural projects to attract private investors into the country's export sector.[34] As part of a project to convert the Central American Pacific Coast into an export zone, the World Bank provided mil-

lions of dollars for highway construction in Guatemala's coastal areas at a time when many of the country's rural population (the majority of the population) lived in isolated communities lacking adequate road linkages.[35] Opening up roads in the Mayan highlands would have created a potential for growth in the area's farming and artisan economy, a family-centered economy where economic health depends on travel to marketplaces.

Structural developments in Western core societies of the capitalist world system also promote international income-producing strategies among working-class families in less-developed regions. In the United States, the institutionalized use of immigrant labor throughout the lower echelons of the labor market created a permanent attraction for foreign workers, including the undocumented. Through several programs (student and temporary visas, green cards, H-2 certifications, braceros, amnesty and legalization, temporary protective status, and so on), the U.S. government has directly and indirectly assisted the creation and reproduction of foreign-worker labor markets, which help sustain families in less-developed regions.

Human agency

Systemic, structural developments create the need to migrate, but it is reflective and willful human action that organizes and carries out the migration. In the Guatemalan *municipio* described above, arguments pro and con illustrate the reflective assessment of migration as an income-producing strategy. Indeed, many economically stressed households in the *municipio* refuse to adopt this strategy, or show only minimal and sporadic interest in migrating. In some cases, immigrants return to their *municipio*, disappointed with immigrant life or eager to restart their artisan business. Some of these migrate again to the United States after reconsidering their decision to return or after suffering new economic setbacks.

The enormous surge of undocumented immigrants in the United States in the late twentieth century demonstrates a growing popular autonomy among working-class peoples in the sending communities.[36] The autonomy consists of implementing transnational, sustaining strategies (organized from the individual to the community level) independent of intergovernmental migrant-labor programs. As a class act, the state-free movement of undocumented migrants challenges the U.S. border's legitimacy as a socio-political boundary, not by seeking to redefine it, but by making it irrelevant. In many U.S. urban areas the result of this autonomous human action has been the formation of binational communities. This autonomous, transnational development has been nothing short of remarkable, with millions of undocumented men and women significantly reshaping social structures across national boundaries completely independent of direct state support.

Within the larger framework of global capitalism, much like the worker organizing that attempted to overcome capital's divisions in industrial societies, the autonomous migration of millions of undocumented workers represents a popular struggle to overcome capital's divisions in the world economy. The struggle is not to escape capitalism, but to relocate in its prosperous, core areas.

Conclusion

The globalization of U.S. racial and ethnic relations seriously challenges intergroup relational theories that fail to address transnational contexts. Social scientists need to wake to evolving intergroup changes in the 1990s affected by global events and contrasting sharply with assumed prevailing patterns of intergroup convergence. For example, more attention should be given to how immigration in the past decade and a half created conditions of intergroup divergence, as newcomers developed alternative social structures or as established residents responded with resistance and withdrawal. The latter occurrence raises a crucial question of how new social divisions affect a society still riddled by racism and other forms of subordination against peoples of color and women.

Bringing the global into sociological research is always a challenge. It is an especially important challenge in intergroup research at a time when large proportions, the majority in some cases, of residents in racial and ethnic concentrations are foreign-born and maintain social-reproductive ties to communities abroad.

Incorporating a global perspective into intergroup research requires reexamining conceptualizations derived mainly from a national or local unit of analysis and searching for their global significance. For example, it requires going beyond conceptualizing the ethnic enclave as an alternative, economic opportunity structure and seeing its interstitial role of globalizing the local and the familiar in immigrant settlement areas. The global perspective also requires a more comparative and relative research approach, one that explores and compares the diverse, and at times competing, views of different actors involved in intergroup activities. The task here is to understand how different worldviews generate intentions that aggregate into the visible social order. This is a crucial task in further understanding the ancillary capacity of the globalized social to transform heterogeneous ambiences into homogeneous experiences or into organic pluralities.

By far the biggest conceptual challenge of the global perspective is to reconcile the global with the local. This challenge is more than providing a global contextualization or a global causal factor for local developments. The challenge is to explore the capillary agencies (formal and informal institutions, communities, households, networks, individuals, etc.) transforming the local and the global into each other.

NOTES

1   Michael Omi and Howard Winant, *Racial Formation in the United States* (New York: Routledge and Kegan Paul, 1986), chap. 5.
2   In 1975 the U.S. Border Patrol apprehended 579,400 "deportable" Mexicans. If we assume that at least two or three Mexicans entered successfully for every one apprehended, then over 1.4 million undocumented Mexicans entered in 1975. For the 1975 number of apprehended Mexicans, see U.S. Bureau of the Census, *Statistical Abstract of the United States, 1989*, 109th ed. (Washington. D.C.: GPO, 1989), table 297.

3 U.S. Bureau of the Census, *Statistical Abstract of the United States: 1992*, 112th ed. (Washington, D.C.: GPO, 1992), table 8.

4 Néstor P. Rodríguez and Joe R. Feagin, "Urban Specialization in the World-System," *Urban Affairs Quarterly* 22, no. 2 (December 1986): 187–220.

5 Ibid., 194–211; Japanese cities with banking and manufacturing international activities are an obvious exception to this historical pattern.

6 U.S. Bureau of the Census, *1990 Census of Population and Housing Summary*, CPH-5-1 (Washington, D.C.: GPO, 1992), table 1.

7 Ibid.

8 Néstor P. Rodríguez and Jacqueline Maria Hagan, "Apartment Restructuring and Latino Immigrant Tenant Struggles," *Comparative Urban and Community Research* 4 (1992): 175–76.

9 Joe R. Feagin and Clairece Booher Feagin, *Racial and Ethnic Relations*, 4th ed. (Englewood Cliffs, N.J.: Prentice-Hall, 1993), 324–26.

10 Ibid., 325.

11 Leo R. Chávez, *Shadowed Lives* (New York: Harcourt Brace Jovanovich, 1992), chap. 7; Reynaldo Baca and Dexter Bryan, "Mexican Undocumented Workers in the Binational Community," *International Migration Review* 15, no. 4 (1980): 737–48.

12 Louise Lamphere, ed., *Structuring Diversity* (Chicago: University of Chicago Press, 1992). Also see Robert L. Bach, *Changing Relations* (New York: Ford Foundation, 1993).

13 Arthur M. Schlesinger Jr., *The Disuniting of America* (New York: Norton, 1992).

14 Ibid., 10.

15 Ibid., 10.

16 Feagin and Feagin, *Racial and Ethnic Relations*; Anthony H. Richmond, *Immigration and Ethnic Conflict* (New York: St. Martin's Press, 1988).

17 Quoted in Philip S. Foner, *History of the Labor Movement in the United States*, vol. 3 (New York: International, 1975), 242.

18 Ibid., 238.

19 For example, see David M. Gordon, Richard Edwards, and Michael Reich, *Segmenting Work, Divided Workers* (Cambridge: Cambridge University Press, 1982).

20 Foner, *History of the Labor Movement in the United States*, vol. 1.

21 Rebecca Morales, "Transnational Labor," *International Migration Review* 21 (1987): 4–26.

22 Rodríguez and Hagan, "Apartment Restructuring," 167–69.

23 Lamphere, *Structuring Diversity*; Bach, *Changing Relations*, chaps. 2 and 4.

24 Some Latino established leaders have yet to see the value of working together in the political ascension of minority groups in Houston's inner city: see Rob Gurwitt. "Collision in Brown and Black," *Governing* 6, no. 4 (January 1993): 32–36.

25 Bach, *Changing Relations*, chaps. 2 and 4.

26 Ibid., chap. 4.

27 Carey McWilliams, *Factories in the Fields* (Hamden, Conn.: Archon Books, 1969); Foner, *History of the Labor Movement*, vol. 2; Stanley Feldstein and Lawrence Costello, eds., *The Ordeal of Assimilation* (Garden City, N.Y.: Anchor Press, 1974).

28 For a case study discussion of this situation, see Néstor P. Rodríguez, "Undocumented Central Americans in Houston," *International Migration Review* 21, no. 1 (Spring 1987): 4–26.

29 The Immigration Reform and Control Act of 1986 made the hiring of undocumented workers a federal criminal offense for the first time in the country's history.

30 Vernon M. Briggs Jr., *Mass Immigration and the National Interest* (Armonk, N.Y.: Sharpe, 1992), chap. 7.

31 Bach, *Changing Relations*, chap. 4.

32 For example, see Chavez, *Shadowed Lives*, 72, and Douglas S. Massey, Rafael Alarcón, Jorge Durand, and Humberto Gonzales, *Return to Aztlan* (Berkeley: University of California Press, 1987). In visits in the late 1980s and early 1990s to a *municipio* in the western highlands of Guatemala, I have also witnessed this transnational income strategy.

33 From 1988 to 1992 I made yearly visits with migrants who return to the *municipio* during its annual patron saint fiesta in late July. The *municipio* is located in the department of Totonicapan.

34 David Landes with Patricia Flynn, "Dollars for Dictators," in *The Politics of Intervention*, ed. Roger Burbach and Patricia Flynn (New York: Monthly Review Press, 1984), 133–61.

35 Ibid.

36 "Autonomy" is a central concept in some Marxist analyses of working-class struggles; see Harry Cleaver, *Reading Capital Politically* (Austin, Tex.: University of Texas Press, 1979), 45–66.

5

The Americans: Latin American and Caribbean Peoples in the United States

Rubén G. Rumbaut

The development of caste and class relationships stratified by racial and ethnic status has been a central theme of U.S. history, shaped over many generations by the European conquest of indigenous peoples and by massive waves of both coerced and uncoerced immigration from all over the world. Indeed, immigration, annexation, and conquest – by hook or by crook – have been the originating processes by which American ethnic groups have been formed and through which, over time, the United States itself has been transformed into arguably the world's most ethnically diverse society. The familiar Anglocentric story of the origins of the nation typically begins with the founding of the first permanent English settlement in America at Jamestown, Virginia, in 1607, and the arrival of the Pilgrims at Plymouth, Massachusetts, in 1620. Until very recently the "Hispanic" presence in what is now the United States was little noted (the term itself was not used by the Census Bureau until 1970), although that presence antedates by a century the creation of an English colony in North America and has left an indelible if ignored Spanish imprint throughout Florida and the Southwest.[1] Today the Hispanic presence has emerged, seemingly suddenly, as a pervasive fact of American life. History is filled with unintended consequences, and one of the ironies (a "latent destiny"?) of the history of a nation that expanded its influence and

"manifest destiny" into Latin America and the Caribbean is that, in significant numbers, their diverse peoples have come to the United States and themselves become "Americans."

U.S. Expansion, Immigration, and the Formation of Ethnic Minorities

In 1790, the first census ever taken in the newly established United States of America counted a population of 3.9 million people, including 757,000 African Americans (more than 90 percent of whom were slaves). Excluded from those census figures were some 600,000 Native Americans, their numbers already decimated since the Europeans' arrival. Three-fourths of the nonslave population was of British origin, either immigrants or descendants of immigrants from the colonial center. Germans were the largest non-English-speaking immigrant group, concentrated in Pennsylvania, where their presence was occasionally viewed with alarm. Indeed, as early as 1751 the redoubtable Benjamin Franklin had put the matter this way: "Why should *Pennsylvania*, founded by the *English*, become a Colony of *Aliens*, who will shortly be so numerous as to Germanize us, instead of our Anglifying them?"

Much has changed since then; much has not. Today's public alarm has focused on Hispanics and their presumed lack of Anglo-conformity, as argued by former Colorado governor Richard Lamm in his book *The Immigration Time Bomb: The Fragmenting of America*, and by nativist organizations, such as U.S. English. In late 1991, in the middle of a prolonged recession, California governor Pete Wilson singled out the cost of providing public services to immigrants as a major cause of the state's budget deficit; and columnist Pat Buchanan announced his candidacy for the Republican presidential nomination on an "America First" platform that singled out immigration as a key political issue, arguing that ease of assimilation, based on language, culture, and background, should be the criterion for immigrant admissions: "I think God made all people good. But if we had to take a million in, say Zulus next year or Englishmen, and put them in Virginia, what group would be easier to assimilate and would cause less problems for the people of Virginia?"[2]

In 1790, the original 13 colonies, on the periphery of a world system dominated by European powers, covered 891,000 square miles. During the nineteenth century, the territory of the fledgling nation soon doubled with the Louisiana Purchase (1803) and the acquisition of Florida (1819). It doubled again by midcentury with the annexation of Texas (1845) and the entire Southwest (roughly half the territory of Mexico) at the end of the U.S.–Mexico War (1848), and with the acquisition of the Oregon Territory (1846) and Alaska (1867). By the end of the century the United States had acquired Puerto Rico, the Philippines, and Guam in the aftermath of the Spanish-American War (1898), and had annexed Hawaii and American Samoa. The peoples of these regions came with the territory. (Territorial expansion in the twentieth century has been limited to the purchase of the Virgin Islands from Denmark in 1917, and the acquisition after World War II of the Palau and Northern Mariana islands in the western Pacific.)

Today, the territory of the 50 states exceeds 3.7 million square miles, and, after two world wars and the end of the Cold War, the United States is the unrivaled hegemon – politically, militarily, culturally, and to a declining extent economically – at the center of the world system. Concomitantly, following the passage in the 1920s of re-strictive national-origins immigration quotas, the Great Depression, and World War II, the United States has again become a nation of immigrants. By the 1980s it had attracted two-thirds of all immigrants worldwide, primarily from the developing countries of Asia and Latin America, who are transforming anew its ethnic mosaic.

In 1990 the U.S. census officially counted a population of 249 million (follow-up surveys suggested that 5 million may have been missed by census takers). About three-fourths were of European origin, most descendants of the largest transoceanic immigration in world history, which brought some 40 million Europeans to the United States in the century from the 1820s to the 1920s. Twenty-nine million African Americans accounted for another 12 percent of the total (in sub-Saharan Africa, only Nigeria and Ethiopia have larger African populations). Together with the 1.9 million American Indians and Alaska Natives, who compose less than 1 percent of the U.S. population, they actually formed the country's oldest resident ethnic groups. The census also counted more than 7 million Asian Americans and Pacific Islanders – who doubled their numbers since 1980. Among them were some of the newest ethnic groups in the country, whose large-scale immigration dates to the 1965 abolition of the national-origins laws that had barred Asians from entry, and to the largest refugee resettlement program in U.S. history, which has brought over 1 million refugees from Vietnam, Laos, and Cambodia since the end of the Indochina War.

More significantly, the census counted 22.4 million Hispanics, or 9 percent of the total U.S. population, up 53 percent from 14.6 million in 1980 and nearly six times the estimated 1950 estimate of 4 million. (This official total is not adjusted for an estimated undercount of 1 million Hispanics, and excludes the 3.5 million Spanish-speakers living in Puerto Rico, as well as all non-Hispanic nationalities from Latin America and the Caribbean.) This sharp increase has been largely due to recent immigration from Latin America and the Caribbean; these migrants now form the largest non-English-speaking immigrant group. Indeed, only Mexico, Argentina, and Colombia have larger Spanish-origin populations. If current trends continue, Hispanics as a whole may well exceed African Americans in population size sometime in the next decade.

About 60 percent – 13.5 million – of all U.S. Hispanics are of Mexican origin; 12 percent are Puerto Ricans (2.7 million on the mainland, not including the more than 3 million in Puerto Rico)[3] – making them the nation's largest ethnic minorities after African Americans. Only four other groups had populations above 1 million in 1990: American Indians; the Chinese (the nation's oldest and most diversified Asian-origin minority, originally recruited as laborers to California in the midnineteenth century); Filipinos (colonized by the United States in the first half of this century and also recruited to work in Hawaiian and Californian plantations until the 1930s); and Cubans (who account for 5 percent of all Hispanics and whose immigration is also tied closely to the history of U.S.–Cuba relations). The original incorporation of these sizable groups, except the oldest, American Indians, and the newest, Cubans, was characterized by processes of labor importation. While the histories of each took complex and diverse forms, the country's four largest ethnic minorities – African Americans, Mexican Americans, Puerto Ricans, and American Indians – are peoples whose incorporation originated involuntarily through conquest, occupation, and exploitation (followed, in the case of Mexicans and Puerto Ricans, by mass immigration during the twentieth century, much of it initiated by active labor recruitment by U.S. companies), setting the foundation for subsequent patterns of social and economic inequality. The next three largest groups – the Chinese, Filipinos, and Cubans – today are largely composed of immigrants who have come to the United States since the 1960s but have built on structural linkages established much earlier.[4]

Indeed, while today's immigrants come from more than 100 different countries, the majority come from two handfuls of developing countries located either in the Caribbean basin or Asia, all variously characterized by significant historical ties to the United States. The former include Mexico – still by far the largest source of both legal and illegal immigration – Cuba, the Dominican Republic, Jamaica, and Haiti, with El Salvador emerging prominently as a source country for

the first time during the 1980s. Asia contributes immigrants primarily from the Philippines, South Korea, Vietnam, China (including Taiwan), and India.[5] Each country's historical relationship with the United States has given rise to particular social networks that serve as bridges of passage to the United States, linking places of origin and destination, opening "chain migration" channels, and giving the immigration process its cumulative and seemingly spontaneous character.[6] Regarding Mexico and Puerto Rico, Alejandro Portes has argued cogently in this vein that

> [T]he countries that supplied the major Spanish-origin groups in the United States today were, each in its time, targets of [an] expansionist pattern [of] U.S. intervention. . . . In a sense, the sending populations were Americanized before their members actually became immigrants to the United States. . . . The rise of Spanish-speaking working-class communities in the Southwest and Northeast may thus be seen as a dialectical consequence of past expansion of the United States into its immediate periphery. . . . Contemporary migration patterns tend to reflect precisely the character of past hegemonic actions by regional and global powers.[7]

The Mexican-American writer and filmmaker Luis Valdés put it plainly, if pithily: "We did not, in fact, come to the United States at all. The United States came to us."

Many factors – economic, political, cultural, demographic – help explain contemporary immigration to the United States, but none can adequately do so outside its concrete historical context. Consider geographical proximity as an impetus to immigration. For example, half of all recent legal immigration and most of all illegal immigration originates in nearby Caribbean basin countries, with Mexico accounting for the greatest share. But five of the top 10 sending countries are in Asia, half a world away (the Philippines has ranked second only to Mexico over the past 30 years). Next-door neighbor Canada is not among the top sending countries. Cheap airplane travel has greatly reduced distances, but Europeans are no longer coming by the millions, as they did a century ago when ocean travel was far more difficult. More undocumented immigrants come from Mexico than any other country, but at least 100,000 Irish immigrants settled illegally (by overstaying their visas) in Boston and New York during the 1980s. Shorter distance does not explain why Salvadorans and Colombians are arriving and Costa Ricans and Venezuelans are not; nor why until fairly recently Jamaicans went to Great Britain and Surinamese to the Netherlands instead of to the United States (when Suriname achieved independence from the Netherlands in 1975, the new government could not halt the emigration of skilled Surinamese, most of them Hindus, to the Dutch metropole).

Economic inequality – especially wage differentials – between sending and receiving countries is also a factor. Since midcentury, less-developed countries (LDCs) have dominated international immigration flows, reflecting the nature of unequal exchanges in a global economy (labor flows from LDCs to more-developed countries [MDCs], capital from MDCs to LDCs). Thus Europeans and Canadians, who had composed the majority of immigrants to the United States until the early 1960s, now account for just over 10 percent of the total. The 2,000-mile U.S.–Mexico border, by contrast, is the biggest point of North–South contact in the world, and a Mexican worker can earn more in a day in the United States than in a week in Mexico. But if wage differentials alone determined migration patterns, we would expect far greater numbers of Mexican immigrants than the relatively tiny fraction of the potential pool who actually cross the border. We would also expect sizable flows to the United States from the world's poorest countries, yet none are significantly represented (except for Vietnamese, Laotians, and Cambodians, who were admitted under special legal provisions as Cold War refugees).

Population size is another factor. Certainly China and India, with more than 20 percent of the world's population, have a huge pool of potential immigrants. Yet very few immigrants come to the United States from other very large countries, such as Brazil and Indonesia, while some very small countries, including the Dominican Republic, Jamaica, Haiti, and Guyana, now send a large proportion of their populations. Demographic pressures must be considered: immigration serves as an escape valve to reduce overpopulation, but many countries with severe population growth and density problems are not main sources of U.S. immigration. Political instability in countries of origin must also be taken into account, but war and violence alone do not explain immigration to the United States. In fact, more than 90 percent of the world's refugees are people who have fled from one Third World country to another.

State immigration policies regulating exit and entry influence but do not determine the size, composition, and direction of immigrant flows. The very existence of substantial numbers of illegal immigrants underscores the limits and defeasibility of legal rules. Certainly the 1965 Immigration Act eliminated racist quotas barring Asians and others from entry to the United States and opened the door to immigrants from all countries on an equal basis (within specific numerical and other criteria, emphasizing primarily family reunification, but occupational skills as well). Yet less than a dozen countries account for the majority of today's newcomers. At the time when legislation was passed, it was widely expected that Southern Europeans would be favored over Asians and Africans, since they had few family members in the United States who could take advantage of the law's preference system. Yet what happened was precisely the opposite of what was intended by the lawmakers. The fact that Cubans have faced exit restrictions at home has not impeded their exodus. Incredibly, a 17-year-old successfully crossed the shark-infested Florida Straits riding a windsurfer in 1990, and in 1991 some 2,000 persons made the crossing on inner tubes and makeshift rafts. The fact that persons in most MDCs (excluding Japan) face no exit restrictions has not fueled their immigration.

Still, state policies have important effects. For example, Jamaican and other West Indian immigrants "switched" destinations from the United Kingdom to the United States and Canada in the 1960s, with the passage of the 1962 Commonwealth Immigration Act, which "slammed the

door" on black immigration to the United Kingdom, and the passage in 1965 of the Hart–Celler
Act in the United States, which benefited them
because of their nations' new status as independent countries.[8] The U.S. Immigration Act of 1990,
which increases authorized immigration by 40
percent annually, nearly triples – from 54,000 to
140,000 – the number of visas each year for immigrant professionals, executives, and other skilled
persons of exceptional ability. It also provides
another 10,000 visas per year to immigrant entrepreneurs who invest a minimum of $1 million in a
new U.S. commercial enterprise employing at
least 10 full-time workers. While leaving family-
sponsored immigration basically unchanged, the
intent of the new law is to compete in a global
immigration market in which skilled people have
become commodities. But its effects cannot be
fully anticipated. For instance, in seeking to lure
the best and the brightest, the new law will further
limit the legal entry of low-wage, unskilled
workers (nannies, maids, restaurant workers) to
10,000 annual visas, and will increase the waiting
period to more than 10 years (in 1990 the
waiting list had 126,442 applicants for such "sixth
preference" visas). The new law will thus unwittingly increase pressures for illegal immigration
among the less skilled and will deepen class inequalities among newcomer groups.[9]

While these and other factors have consequences that are not always intended, large-scale
immigration flows to the United States are not
simply a function of state policies or of individual
costs and benefits calculations. Nor can immigration be reduced to simple push-pull or supply-
demand theories. It must be understood in the
macrocontext of historical patterns of U.S. expansion and intervention, and in the microcontext of
social networks created and consolidated in the
process, which help sustain continued immigration and ethnic group formation. This process is
illustrated by some of the largest contemporary
Asian immigrant groups, including Filipinos
(following 48 years of U.S. colonial rule, the pervasive Americanization of Filipino culture, development of a U.S.-style educational system,
adoption of English as an official language, heavy
dependence on U.S. trade and foreign investment,
direct recruitment of Filipinos into the U.S. Navy,

and establishment after World War II of the largest U.S. military bases in the Pacific), Koreans
(following the Korean War), and Vietnamese
(following the Vietnam War).

The countries of the Caribbean basin – particularly Mexico, Puerto Rico, and Cuba – perhaps have felt most strongly the weight and lure
of the U.S. hegemonic presence. Since the days
of Benjamin Franklin (who in 1761 suggested
Mexico and Cuba as goals of American expansion) and Thomas Jefferson, the Caribbean countries were viewed as belonging, as if by some
"laws of political gravitation" (as John Quincy
Adams said in 1823), to the "manifest destiny"
of the United States. The Caribbean, then, was
viewed as "the American Mediterranean," as
Alexander Hamilton called it in *The Federalist* in
1787.[10] Ironically, it is precisely the people from
these countries who are visibly emerging as a
significant component of American society.
They are not, however, a homogeneous lot;
rather, they reflect different histories, settlement
patterns, immigrant types, and modes of incorporation into the United States.

Hispanics in the United States:
Histories and Patterns of Settlement

Mexicans, Puerto Ricans, and Cubans trace their
main historical ties to the United States to the
nineteenth century, with Mexicans by far the
largest and oldest of Hispanic ethnic groups.
Overwhelmingly, Mexicans became incorporated
into the the U.S. economy as manual laborers.
When the Treaty of Guadalupe–Hidalgo ceded
the Southwest territories to the United States in
1848, perhaps 80,000 inhabitants of Mexican and
Spanish origin were residing in that territory –
nearly three-fourths of them lived in New
Mexico, with smaller numbers of *Tejanos* and
Californios. Toward the end of the century, with
the rapid expansion of railroads, agriculture, and
mining in the Southwest and of the U.S. economy generally, and the exclusion in 1882 of Chinese workers and later the Japanese, Mexicans
became the preferred source of cheap and mobile
migrant labor. This occurred at about the same
time that capitalist development in Mexico under
the government of Porfirio Díaz was creating a

landless peasantry. By the early 1900s railroad lines – which expedited deliberate labor recruitment by U.S. companies – had linked the Mexican interior with other states, particularly Texas, which became the major center of Mexican settlement, though under harsh, castelike conditions.[11] In other parts of the United States, from the copper and coal mines of Arizona and Colorado to the steel mills and slaughterhouses of Chicago, to Detroit and Pittsburgh, large numbers of Mexicans were working as manual laborers.

Not all these *braceros* returned to Mexico, and settler communities formed and grew. As many as 1 million Mexicans – up to one-tenth of the Mexican population – crossed the U.S. border at some point during the violent decade of the Mexican Revolution of 1910. Demand for their labor in the United States increased during World War I and the 1920s. The 1910 U.S. census counted some 220,000 Mexicans; that number more than doubled by 1920, and tripled to more than 600,000 by 1930. Largely at the urging of American growers, the restrictive national-origins immigration laws passed in 1921 and 1924 placed no limits on Western Hemisphere countries, in order to allow the recruitment of Mexican workers when needed – and their deportation when not. This happened during the 1930s, when about 400,000, including many U.S. citizens, were repatriated to Mexico, and again during the even larger deportations of "Operation Wetback" in the mid-1950s.

The large increase in the Mexican-origin population in California dates to the World War II period, which saw the establishment of the Bracero Program (1942–64) of contract-labor importation. The end of the Bracero Program prompted increased flows of illegal immigration, which peaked in 1986 when the Immigration Reform and Control Act was passed, then declined briefly but increased and stabilized again in 1989. Despite the large flows of legal and illegal Mexican immigration in recent years, the 1980 census found that 74 percent of the Mexican-origin population was U.S.-born. Though the Chicano experience and consciousness has gone through distinct psychohistorical generations and differed markedly from that of recent immigrants, the formation of the nation's second-largest ethnic group still retains the stamp of its working-class origins and history of exploitation and discrimination.[12]

Puerto Rico, a rural society based on subsistence agriculture and coffee exports, was occupied by the United States in 1898 and formally acquired as part of the Treaty of Paris, which settled the Spanish-American War. The islanders' status was left ambiguous until the passage of the Jones Act in 1917, which gave Puerto Ricans U.S. citizenship and made them eligible for the military draft. These provisions essentially remained after 1947, when a new constitution defined commonwealth status for Puerto Rico. This status defines the island's relationship with the United States and distinguishes Puerto Ricans fundamentally from other Latin American and Caribbean peoples. As U.S. citizens by birth, Puerto Ricans travel freely between the island and mainland – just as one would travel from Hawaii to California – without having to pass through screenings of the Immigration and Naturalization Service or Border Patrol, as would foreign-born immigrants.

Puerto Rican migration has been viewed as an exchange of people for capital. Soon after the military occupation, U.S. capital began flowing into Puerto Rico. This was especially true of the new and rapidly growing sugar industry, which displaced subsistence peasants into the cities and combined with high population growth to create urban unemployment. The island's capital-intensive industrialization and urbanization rapidly accelerated after the introduction of "Operation Bootstrap" in 1948, but failed to solve urban unemployment and population growth problems and intensified internal economic pressures for migration to the mainland. Though it never reached the extent it did with Mexican workers, labor recruitment began in 1900 when a large group of workers went to sugar cane plantations in Hawaii, and later to farms on the mainland. Labor recruitment became widespread among industrial employers only during and after World War II – at the same time that cheap air travel was instituted between San Juan and New York (a one-way ticket cost less than $50). Mass immigration to New York reached its peak at this time and made Puerto Ricans the first "airborne" migration in U.S. history. The Puerto Rican population on the mainland grew from about 12,000 in 1920, to 53,000 in 1930, to 301,000 in 1950, and tripled to 888,000 in 1960. Net Puerto Rican migration to the mainland during the 1950s – about 470,000 – was higher than the immigration totals of any country, including Mexico. Although net migration has since decreased, travel back and forth is incessant, averaging more than 3 million people annually in the 1980s. The pattern of concentration in New York City, which accounted for more than 80 percent of the total Puerto Rican population in the U.S. mainland in 1950, gradually declined to 62 percent in 1970 and to under 40 percent in 1990. About 45 percent of the more than 6 million Puerto Ricans now reside on the U.S. mainland.[13]

Unlike Mexico, the first nation in the Americas to achieve independence from Spain, and Puerto Rico, the only territory that has never become an independent state, Cuba was the last Spanish colony. It became formally independent in 1902, following three years of U.S. military occupation at the end of the second Cuban War of Independence (1895–98) and the Spanish-American War (1898).

A notable Cuban presence in the United States goes back to the early nineteenth century, when Cuban exiles began a tradition of carrying out their political work from bases in New York and Florida. Throughout the nineteenth century, Cuba was the target of repeated annexation efforts by the United States and a main focus of U.S. trade and capital investment. However, it never became a recruiting ground for agricultural workers, as did Mexico and Puerto Rico. U.S. economic penetration of the island increased sharply after the war and the military occupation at the turn of the century, expanding U.S. control over sugar production and other sectors of the Cuban economy, including transportation, mining, construction, and public utilities. By 1929 U.S. direct investment in Cuba totaled nearly $1 billion; this was more than one-fourth of all U.S. investment in Latin America as a whole, and more than that invested by U.S. capital in any Latin American country, both in absolute terms and on a per capita basis.

Moreover, Cuba became a virtual "protectorate" of the United States after 1902 under the terms of the Platt Amendment, attached by the U.S. Congress to the Cuban constitution. Not rescinded until 1934, the Platt Amendment formalized the right of the United States to intervene in Cuban internal affairs and lease the Guantánamo Bay naval base, which the United States has held ever since. These actions have bred deep resentment of U.S. domination in various sectors of the Cuban population. Nonetheless, an informed observer could write that, at least in the cities, "it is probably fair to say that by 1959, no other country in the world, with the exception of Canada, quite so resembled the United States."[14]

At that time the Cuban population in the United States was just over 70,000. The waves of exiles that began in earnest in 1960 in the context of the East–West Cold War have continued to the present in several phases: the daily flights, suspended after the 1962 missile crisis; the orderly "freedom flights" between 1965 and 1973; boat flotillas from Camarioca in 1965 and Mariel in 1980; and the increasingly desperate crossings with the deepening economic and social crisis in Cuba after 1989. Despite U.S. government efforts to resettle the exiles away from Miami, many eventually drifted back, making the city a majority-Cuban community. At over 1 million, the Cuban-American population in 1990 represents about 10 percent of the island's population. One of the many ironies of the history of U.S.–Cuba relations is that Fidel Castro, anti-Yankee par excellence, may have done more to deepen structural linkages between Cuba and the United States than anyone else in Cuban history.[15]

Table 5.1 presents data from the 1990 census on the Hispanic population: its size and concentration in major states and countries of settlement. From 1980 to 1990, the U.S. population grew by 9.8 percent, and that of Hispanics by 53 percent, a growth rate that was significantly exceeded in several states and metropolitan areas. While Hispanics now constitute 9 percent of the total population, their impact is much more notable due to their concentration in particular localities. Nearly three out of four Hispanics in the United States reside in just four states: California, with over a third of the total; Texas,

Table 5.1 States and Counties of Principal Hispanic Settlement in the United States, 1990

State/County	Total 1990 His-panic Population	% Hispanic Pop. Growth, 1980–1990	% Hispanic of State or County Pop.	% of U.S. His-panic Population	Percent of Each Group's U.S. Population				
					Mexican	Puerto Rican	Cuban	Other Hispanic
U.S. TOTAL	22,354,059	53.0	9.0	100.0	60.4	12.2	4.7	22.8
STATES:								
California	7,687,938	69.2	25.8	34.4	45.3	4.6	6.9	26.9
Texas	4,339,905	45.4	25.5	19.4	28.8	1.6	1.7	7.6
New York	2,214,026	33.4	12.3	9.9	0.7	39.8	7.1	18.9
Florida	1,574,143	83.4	12.2	7.0	1.2	9.1	64.6	9.7
Illinois	904,446	42.3	7.9	4.0	4.6	5.4	1.7	2.3
New Jersey	739,861	50.4	9.6	3.3	0.2	11.7	8.2	6.0
Arizona	688,338	56.2	18.8	3.1	4.6	0.3	0.2	1.2
New Mexico	579,224	21.4	38.2	2.6	2.4	0.1	0.1	4.9
Colorado	424,302	24.9	12.9	1.9	2.1	0.3	0.2	2.6
COUNTIES								
Los Angeles, CA	3,351,242	62.2	37.8	15.0	NA	NA	NA	NA
Dade (Miami), FL	953,407	64.1	49.2	4.3	NA	NA	NA	NA
Cook (Chicago), IL	694,194	39.0	13.6	3.1	NA	NA	NA	NA
Harris (Houston), TX	644,935	74.7	22.9	2.9	NA	NA	NA	NA
Bexar (San Antonio), TX	589,180	27.8	49.7	2.6	NA	NA	NA	NA
Orange (Santa Ana), CA	564,828	97.3	23.4	2.5	NA	NA	NA	NA
The Bronx, NY	523,111	32.0	43.5	2.3	NA	NA	NA	NA
San Diego, CA	510,781	85.6	20.4	2.3	NA	NA	NA	NA
Kings (Brooklyn), NY	462,411	17.9	20.1	2.1	NA	NA	NA	NA
El Paso, TX	411,619	38.6	69.6	1.8	NA	NA	NA	NA
New York (Manhattan), NY	386,630	15.0	26.0	1.7	NA	NA	NA	NA
Queens, NY	381,120	45.2	19.5	1.7	NA	NA	NA	NA
San Bernardino, CA	378,582	128.2	26.7	1.7	NA	NA	NA	NA

Source: U.S. Bureau of the Census, "Persons of Hispanic Origin for the United States and States: 1990," and "Hispanic Origin Population by County: 1990 and 1980," 1990 *Census of Population* (1991). Data for specific ethnic groups by county not yet available.

accounting for nearly one-fifth; and New York and Florida, with one-sixth combined.

By contrast, less than one-third of the total U.S. population resides in these states. Indeed, Hispanics now account for more than 25 percent of the populations of California and Texas. Concentration patterns are even more pronounced for specific groups: three-fourths of all Mexican Americans reside in California and Texas, half the Puerto Ricans are in the New York–New Jersey area; and nearly two-thirds of the Cubans are in Florida. Significant numbers of Mexican Americans and Puerto Ricans are also in Illinois, overwhelmingly in Chicago. The category "Other Hispanic" used by the census includes both long-established groups and recent immigrants. The long-established groups trace their roots to the region prior to the Southwest annexation after the U.S.–Mexico War and live notably in New Mexico, where Hispanics still account for more than 38 percent of the state's population, despite comparatively little recent immigration. Recent immigrants come from Central and South America and the Spanish Caribbean, with a quarter in California, another quarter in New York–New Jersey, and a tenth in Florida.

These patterns of concentration are even more pronounced in metropolitan areas, and in particular communities within metropolitan areas. Moreover, different immigrant groups concentrate in different metropolitan areas and create distinct communities within them. The main reason is that immigrants, especially working-class groups and ethnic entrepreneurs, tend to concentrate in urban areas where coethnic communities have been established by past immigration. Such spatial concentrations provide newcomers with significant sources of social, cultural, and economic support unavailable to more dispersed immigrants, such as professionals, whose settlement decisions are more a function of their credentials and job offers than of pre-existing ethnic communities.

Dense ethnic enclaves also provide immigrant entrepreneurs with access to cheap labor, working capital, credit, and dependable markets. Over time, as immigrants become naturalized citizens and voters, local strength in numbers also provides opportunities for political representation of ethnic minority group interests. Ethnic social networks thus shape not only migration but also adaptation and settlement processes in areas of final destination. Table 5.1 lists the 13 largest U.S. countries of Hispanic concentration (out of more than 1,200). There were 3.4 million Hispanics in Los Angeles County alone, accounting for 15 percent of the national Hispanic population and 38 percent of the total Los Angeles population. Three other countries shown in table 5.1 – Orange, San Diego, and San Bernardino – are adjacent southern California areas that reflected the highest rates of Hispanic population growth over the decade. Combined with Los Angeles, they account for 21.5 percent of the U.S. total. Adding Riverside, Ventura, Kern, and Imperial counties, also in southern California, would increase the proportion to 25 percent.

Nearly 8 percent of the total Hispanic population resides in four boroughs of New York City: the Bronx, Kings (Brooklyn), New York (Manhattan) and Queens counties. (However, their growth rates, while high, were below the national Hispanic average.) Half the populations of Dade County (Miami) and Bexar County (San Antonio) are Hispanic – principally of Cuban and Mexican origin, respectively – as are more than two-thirds of El Paso's population (on the Mexican border) and nearly a quarter of Houston's. Indeed, Los Angeles's Mexican-origin population today is exceeded only by that of Mexico City, Guadalajara, and Monterrey; Havana is the only city in Cuba larger than Cuban Miami; San Salvador and Santo Domingo are slightly larger than Salvadoran Los Angeles and Dominican New York; and twice as many Puerto Ricans reside in New York City as in Puerto Rico's capital, San Juan.

New Immigrants from Latin America and the Caribbean: National and Class Origins

The focus on "Hispanics" as a generic category is misleading, since it conceals both substantial generational differences among groups so labeled and contemporary immigrants' enormous diversity – in national origins, racial-ethnic and class origins, legal status, reasons for migration, modes of exit, and contexts of reception.

Table 5.2 New Neighbors: Foreign-born Persons Counted in the 1980 U.S. Census, by Year of Arrival, and Legal Immigrants Admitted in 1981–1990, by Region and American Countries of Birth

Region/Country of Birth	No. of 1980 Foreign-Born in the U.S.	% of 1980 Population of Origin	Year of Immigration to the U.S.			Immigrants Admitted in 1981–90
			Pre-1960 (%)	1960–69 (%)	1970–80 (%)	
WORLDWIDE:	14,079,906	0.3	38.2	22.2	39.5	7,338,062
Europe and USSR	5,149,355	0.7	65.6	18.0	16.3	705,630
Latin America	4,372,487	1.2	16.1	30.5	53.5	3,460,683
Asia	2,539,777	0.1	12.5	18.0	69.4	2,817,426
Africa	199,723	0.04	15.7	19.2	65.1	192,212
NORTH AMERICA:						
Canada	842,859	3.5	64.7	20.2	15.2	119,204
Mexico	2,199,221	3.1	17.5	18.9	49.7	1,653,250
CARIBBEAN:	1,258,363	4.3	11.9	45.5	42.7	892,703
Cuba	607,814	6.3	12.8	60.4	26.8	159,257
Jamaica	196,811	8.8	11.6	29.7	58.6	213,805
Dominican Republic	169,147	2.9	6.1	37.2	56.8	251,803
Haiti	92,395	1.7	4.6	30.8	64.6	140,163
Trinidad and Tobago	65,907	6.2	7.4	30.8	61.8	39,533
Barbados	26,847	10.7	19.8	24.4	56.3	17,482
CENTRAL AMERICA:	353,892	1.6	13.7	25.7	60.6	458,753
El Salvador	94,447	2.0	6.1	16.8	77.2	214,574
Guatemala	63,073	0.9	6.4	24.3	69.3	87,939
Panama	60,740	3.1	29.0	31.5	39.6	29,045
Nicaragua	44,166	1.6	18.5	20.6	60.9	44,139
Honduras	39,154	1.0	15.6	32.2	52.2	49,496
Costa Rica	29,639	1.3	14.3	38.9	46.8	15,490
SOUTH AMERICA:	560,616	0.2	10.7	37.0	56.2	455,977
Colombia	143,508	0.5	7.9	37.2	55.0	124,436
Ecuador	86,128	1.1	7.6	39.1	53.2	56,026
Argentina	68,887	0.2	16.5	40.3	43.2	25,717
Peru	55,496	0.3	9.7	30.9	59.4	64,381
Guyana	48,608	6.4	7.0	20.6	72.4	95,374
Brazil	40,919	0.03	20.6	31.3	48.1	23,772
Chile	35,127	0.3	11.3	26.9	61.9	23,439
Venezuela	33,281	0.2	10.6	16.1	73.2	17,963
Bolivia	14,468	0.3	11.8	33.6	54.5	12,252

Source: U.S. Bureau of the Census, "Foreign-Born Population in the United States – Microfiche," *1980 Census*, table 1 (1985); *Statistical Abstracts of the United States, 1990*; and U.S. Immigration and Naturalization Service, *1990 Statistical Yearbook*.

It is true that persons from Spanish America have dominated immigrant flows, averaging about 80 percent of the Latin American/Caribbean total in recent decades (not including Puerto Ricans, who, as U.S. citizens, are not counted in official immigration statistics). But sizable flows have also come from the non-Spanish-speaking Caribbean basin. Table 5.2 presents 1980 census data on the U.S. foreign-born population. (Detailed 1990 census data will not be available until 1993.) At 14.1 million persons, it is the world's largest immigrant population, although it constitutes only 6.2 percent of the total U.S. population, much lower than its proportion at the turn of the century. The table, supplemented by INS data on all immigrants legally admitted during 1981–90, is broken down by world region, all major sending countries in Latin America and the Caribbean, and by decade of arrival.

As of 1980, Europeans still composed the largest foreign-born population in the United States (5.1 million), but two-thirds were older persons who had immigrated well before 1960. The relatively small number of 1981–90 immigrants from Europe reflects their declining trend over the past three decades. Canadians exhibited a similar pattern. The number of Asian and African immigrants doubled during the last decade. More than two-thirds of their 1980 populations had arrived only during the 1970s, reflecting the fact that their immigration has largely taken place since the passage of the 1965 Act. Latin America accounted for 4.4 million foreign-born persons in 1980, more than half coming just in the previous decade. The enormous number of immigrants admitted during 1981–90 (3.5 million)[16] meant that *by 1990, for the first time in U.S. history, Latin American and Caribbean peoples composed the largest immigrant population in the country.*

Mexico's 1980 immigrant population in the United States was 2.2 million, of whom about 900,000 were estimated by the Census Bureau to be undocumented. Mexican immigrants accounted for half the total from Latin America and the Caribbean. Another 1.7 million were legally admitted during the 1980s, again, accounting for half the total number of Latin American and Caribbean immigrants admitted during the decade. The Cuban-born population in 1980 – 608,000 – was by far the next largest immigrant group, and the only one that arrived preponderantly during the 1960s. All other Latin American and Caribbean immigrants as of 1980 had arrived primarily during the 1970s.

However, the number of Cubans admitted during the 1980s – including most of the 125,000 who came in the 1980 Mariel boatlift, which occurred shortly after the 1980 census was taken – was surpassed by that of Dominicans, Salvadorans, and Jamaicans, with Haitians not far behind. The INS totals for Dominicans and

especially Salvadorans and Guatemalans for the 1980s surely undercount their actual numbers: the majority of Salvadorans and Guatemalans entered illegally during the decade, most after the 1981 date required to qualify for the Immigration Reform and Control Act's amnesty provisions.

From South America the largest flow has continued to be from Colombia, although significant numbers of Ecuadorans and Peruvians came during the 1980s. The biggest increase was registered by the Guyanese, making them, surprisingly, the second-largest immigrant group from South America. Indeed, as table 5.2 shows, the Guyanese share a common pattern with other English-speaking groups in the Commonwealth Caribbean, principally Jamaica, Trinidad, and Barbados: the percentage of immigrants from these countries relative to their 1980 homeland populations was very high, ranging from 6.2 to 10.7 percent. The proportions grew significantly from 1981 to 1990 for Jamaicans, who more than doubled their 1980 total, and the Guyanese, who tripled it by 1990. Similarly, although not shown in table 5.2, the 14,436 English-speaking immigrants from Belize in the United States in 1980 constituted 10 percent of Belize's population. During the 1980s over 18,000 more emigrated to the United States. Only Cuba had sent a similarly high proportion – 6.3 percent, or 7.6 percent if the 1980 Mariel "entrants" were added to the totals.

By contrast, the percentage for next-door neighbors Canada and Mexico was just over 3 percent, with Dominicans and Salvadorans just under. The proportions from Argentina, Peru, Chile, Venezuela, and Bolivia were minuscule, and that from Brazil was by far the lowest of all in Latin America (0.03 percent), lower even than that from Asia and Africa. Also minuscule were the 1980 proportions for Uruguay – 0.4 percent, based on 13,278 immigrants in the United States[17] – and Paraguay – 0.08 percent, based on 2,858 immigrants, the lowest total by far from any sizable Latin American country.

Table 5.3 extends this general picture with detailed 1980 census information on social and economic characteristics of all these immigrant groups, ranked in order of proportion of college graduates, which may serve as a proxy for social class origins. These data, compared against the norms for mainland Puerto Ricans and total U.S. population, reveal immigrants' extraordinary socioeconomic diversity in general, and those from the Americas in particular.

One point that stands out is the extremely high degree of educational attainment among immigrants from Asia and Africa: about 40 percent are college graduates, compared with 16 percent for the total U.S. population, and they are well above the norm in proportion of professionals. For some countries such as India (not shown in the table), the proportions are much higher than the continental averages. For example, more than 90 percent of Indian immigrants to the United States in the late 1960s and early 1970s had professional and managerial occupations in India prior to immigration, as did four-fifths in the late 1970s and two-thirds during the 1980s. This was true despite the fact that over time most of these immigrants were admitted under family reunification preferences. By the mid-1970s there were more Filipino and Indian medical graduates in the United States than there were American black physicians. By the mid-1980s one-fifth of all engineering doctorates awarded by U.S. universities went to foreign-born students from Taiwan, India, and South Korea alone. It has been estimated that since the early 1950s, fewer than 10 percent of the tens of thousands of students from China, Taiwan, Hong Kong, and South Korea who came to the United States for training on nonimmigrant visas ever returned home. Rather, many adjusted their status and gained U.S. citizenship through occupational connections with American industry and business, thus becoming eligible to send for family members later.

These data document a classic pattern of "brain drain" immigration. Indeed, although they come from developing countries, these immigrants as a group are perhaps the most skilled ever to arrive in the United States. This helps explain the class origins of the recent popularization of Asians as a "model minority," as well as to debunk nativist calls for restricting immigrants to those perceived to be more "assimilable" on the basis of language and culture.[18] Canadians and Europeans, though they are much older resident groups – as reflected in their low labor force participation rates and high naturalization rates – show levels of education slightly below the U.S. average, an occupational profile slightly above it, but much lower poverty rates. By contrast, Latin Americans as a whole have well-below-average levels of educational attainment, the highest rates of labor force participation, with high concentrations in lower blue-collar employment, and higher poverty rates.

However, a different picture emerges when the data are broken down by national origin, underscoring that these populations cannot sensibly be subsumed under the supranational rubric of "Hispanic" or "Latino," except as a catchall category. Among Latin Americans, the highest socioeconomic status (SES) is reflected by Venezuelans, Bolivians, and Chileans, also the smallest of the immigrant groups, and by Argentineans, who have the highest proportion of professionals among all immigrants from the Americas. This suggests that these groups consist substantially of highly skilled persons who have entered under the occupational preferences of U.S. immigration law. Peruvians and Cubans reflected levels of educational attainment slightly above the U.S. norm, and their occupational and income characteristics put them at about the national average. Occupying an intermediate position were groups from the English-speaking Caribbean – Jamaica, Trinidad, Barbados, Guyana – with SES patterns quite similar to each other and slightly below U.S. norms. The lowest SES is found among Mexicans, Dominicans, and Salvadorans, who were also the largest groups of immigrants entering both legally and illegally in the 1980s. Their characteristics approximate those of mainland Puerto Ricans, except the poverty rate for Puerto Ricans is much higher than that of any other Latin American or Caribbean immigrant group. Guatemalans, Ecuadorans, Hondurans, Nicaraguans, Haitians, and Colombians also reflected a much higher ratio of lower blue-collar to upper white-collar employment.

The Venezuelan case is puzzling and bimodal, because it shows extraordinarily low rates of labor force participation and the highest level of college graduates, but also high poverty rates. Brazilians

Table 5.3 Social and Economic Characteristics of the U.S. Foreign-born Population, 1980, in Rank Order of College Graduates, by Region and American Countries of Birth, Compared to Total U.S. Population

Region/Country of Birth	Education[1] % College Graduates	Labor Force[2] Participa- tion Rate %	Occupation[3] % Upper White-Collar	Occupation[3] % Lower Blue-Collar	Income % Families in Poverty	Citizenship % U.S. Naturalized
REGION OF ORIGIN:						
Africa	38.7	60.8	36.1	12.9	13.0	38.0
Asia	37.9	62.6	31.1	15.3	11.2	34.8
Canada	14.3	50.2	29.7	12.2	4.6	61.0
Europe	12.1	47.4	23.9	18.4	5.2	72.1
Latin America	8.9	66.0	11.2	31.3	18.3	29.0
LATIN AMERICA AND CARIBBEAN:						
Venezuela	31.4	34.4	27.4	11.7	22.7	17.3
Bolivia	30.7	68.3	27.7	11.9	8.5	32.4
Chile	24.4	70.3	25.4	16.4	7.8	27.7
Argentina	24.2	69.1	28.5	15.4	8.3	38.8
Peru	20.3	70.5	21.1	22.1	10.7	28.8
Cuba	17.1	66.9	19.3	23.9	10.9	45.1
Panama	16.0	68.6	22.3	13.3	11.9	55.1
Guyana	15.0	71.0	19.6	15.9	14.4	31.2
Colombia	14.6	69.7	15.1	29.8	12.5	24.9
Haiti	13.4	72.0	12.1	28.6	19.5	26.1
Costa Rica	12.9	64.1	14.4	22.6	14.0	29.9
Trinidad and Tobago	12.4	71.7	16.3	13.1	14.3	29.3
Nicaragua	12.2	63.5	13.3	28.9	18.6	24.3
Jamaica	11.0	72.8	15.7	14.7	12.4	36.3
Brazil	10.8	58.3	24.9	17.6	8.2	35.3
Honduras	9.6	66.7	10.6	27.3	14.9	35.0
Ecuador	9.3	68.5	11.5	36.9	15.7	24.7
Barbados	8.5	70.0	14.8	14.7	10.9	42.4
Guatemala	6.9	72.2	7.5	32.4	17.5	17.9
El Salvador	6.5	72.9	5.8	32.6	18.8	14.3
Dominican Republic	4.3	62.1	6.9	33.5	31.0	25.5
Mexico	3.0	64.2	5.4	33.1	22.1	23.6
Puerto Ricans in U.S.	5.6	54.9	12.2	30.9	34.9	NA
Total U.S. Population:	16.2	62.0	22.7	18.3	9.6	NA

1 Persons 25 years or older.
2 Persons 16 years or older.
3 Occupation of employed persons 16 years or older; "Upper white-collar": professionals, executives, and managers; "Lower blue-collar": operators, fabricators, and laborers.
Source: U.S. Bureau of the Census, "Foreign-Born Population in the U.S. – Microfiche," 1980 Census, tables 2, 4, 7, 10–11 (1985).

too show below-average participation in the labor force but, by contrast, have lower-than-average levels of poverty. The reasons for the patterns of these two groups are unclear and cannot be accounted for by available demographic data.[19]

The last column of table 5.3 provides data on the percentage of each group naturalized as U.S. citizens as of 1980. As would be expected, immigrant groups that had resided longer in the United States – Europeans and Canadians, most of whom came before the 1960s – had a higher proportion of naturalized citizens. Recent arrivals – Asians, Africans, and Latin Americans, most of whom had come only in the 1970s and who are just beginning to make their way in the United States – were much less likely to have initiated the citizenship acquisition process. However, Latin American immigrants as a whole had the lowest proportion of naturalized citizens (29 percent), despite the fact that Asians and Africans were the most recently arrived groups (as shown earlier in table 5.2).

Clearly, time spent in the United States does not alone explain why different groups become U.S. citizens at different rates. But this is an important question, since, along with higher numbers and greater concentration, citizenship acquisition and effective political participation go to the heart of ethnic politics and the ability of these groups to make themselves heard in the larger society. Among legal immigrants, the research literature has shown that the motivation and propensity to naturalize is higher among upwardly mobile younger persons with higher educational levels, occupational status, English proficiency, income, and property, and whose spouses or children are U.S. citizens. A study of all immigrant cohorts arriving in the United States between 1970 and 1979 – thus controlling for length of residence in the country – found that higher-SES Asian immigrants had the highest rates of naturalization, as did political refugees, such as Vietnamese and Cubans, whose return options were blocked. The lowest propensities were found among Mexicans and Canadians, economic (not political) immigrants for whom return is relatively simple and inexpensive. In fact, the combination of three variables alone – educational levels, geographical proximity, and political origin of migration – largely explained differences in citizenship acquisition among immigrant groups.[20]

Finally, table 5.4 presents 1980 census data on the U.S. foreign-born population's level of English-language proficiency, broken down by region and for all the largest Latin American and Caribbean immigrant groups. As a whole, Latin American and Caribbean immigrants exhibit a much lower degree of English proficiency than do Asians, Africans, and Europeans, reflecting

previously noted differences in socioeconomic status and time spent in the United States. But again, even among "Hispanic" groups, as much diversity exists in their patterns of language competency as in their socioeconomic characteristics. Quite obviously, nearly all immigrants from the Commonwealth Caribbean are English monolinguals (a much higher proportion than Canadians, in fact). Among all other Latins, Panamanians – the oldest resident Latin American immigrant group, nearly a third of whom had arrived in the United States prior to 1960 – were the most English proficient. In fact, about a third were already English monolinguals. Immigrants from Bolivia, Argentina, Venezuela, and Chile, the highest-SES groups from Latin America, followed in English proficiency. The least proficient, with approximately half reporting an inability to speak English well or at all, were immigrants from the Dominican Republic, Mexico, and El Salvador. As seen earlier, these were also the largest immigrant cohorts entering in the 1980s, as well as the lowest-SES groups from Latin America.

In addition to education and time in the United States, age and residence within dense ethnic enclaves were also factors in the development of English proficiency. Cuban refugees, whose median age is the oldest of any immigrant group, are the best example: nearly 40 percent reported speaking English not well or at all. On closer inspection, they reveal themselves to be older or elderly persons residing in areas of high ethnic concentration, such as Miami. Still, the data in table 5.4 are remarkable in showing that even among the most recently arrived groups, large proportions already report being able to speak English well or very well, and indeed, that significant proportions of the foreign-born speak English *only*. This fact notwithstanding, English-language competency – particularly among Hispanic immigrants in the United States who allegedly harbor a Spanish "retentiveness" and "unwillingness" to assimilate – has become a highly charged sociopolitical issue, with nativist organizations warning about cultural "balkanization" and Quebec-like linguistic separatism in regions of high Hispanic concentration. This issue will be addressed further below.

Table 5.4   English Proficiency of the U.S. Foreign-born Population, 1980, in Rank Order, by Region and American Countries of Birth[1]

Region/Country of Birth	% Speak English Only	% Speak Very Well	% Speak Well	% Speak Not Well	% Speak Not at All
REGION OF ORIGIN:					
Canada	79.5	13.7	5.3	1.4	0.1
Africa	27.2	45.2	20.4	5.9	1.3
Europe	40.0	30.0	19.3	8.6	2.2
Asia	11.6	36.5	30.2	16.6	5.1
Latin America	13.1	24.2	23.0	23.3	16.4
LATIN AMERICA AND CARIBBEAN:					
Barbados	96.8	2.4	0.6	0.1	0.0
Trinidad and Tobago	93.2	5.0	1.5	0.3	0.0
Jamaica	94.0	4.0	1.5	0.4	0.1
Guyana	93.3	4.6	1.5	0.5	0.2
Panama	33.5	44.0	16.5	4.8	1.2
Brazil	16.3	41.5	29.3	10.8	2.1
Bolivia	7.9	45.4	29.9	13.6	3.2
Argentina	9.1	44.3	29.0	13.6	4.0
Venezuela	9.3	39.5	32.0	14.8	4.4
Chile	8.7	38.9	31.7	15.9	4.9
Costa Rica	10.0	41.7	27.6	15.5	5.2
Peru	7.6	37.5	31.3	18.2	5.5
Haiti	4.6	35.1	36.8	18.5	5.0
Honduras	14.6	33.5	26.1	18.6	7.1
Colombia	6.2	30.8	30.5	8.4	10.0
Ecuador	3.9	29.2	29.5	25.5	11.9
Nicaragua	5.1	30.1	27.3	23.6	13.9
Cuba	3.1	34.1	23.1	21.4	18.3
Guatemala	4.3	25.7	29.5	27.8	12.7
El Salvador	2.7	20.9	27.0	32.2	17.3
Mexico	2.4	21.3	24.6	29.5	22.1
Dominican Republic	2.3	21.1	23.9	29.2	23.5

[1]Persons five years of age and older.
Source: U.S. Bureau of the Census, "Foreign-Born Population in the United States – Microfiche," *1980 Census*, table 12 (1985).

Hispanics in the United States Today: A Socioeconomic Portrait

The preceding section focused attention on the diversity of *immigrant* groups from Latin America and the Caribbean, given the importance of the contemporary, and rapidly increasing, immigration to the United States. The 1980 census data presented above are the most recent and, for that matter, the only available national data set that breaks down such information by country of origin. But those data are limited to the foreign-born, which by definition excludes all Puerto Ricans, as well as nearly three-fourths of Mexican Americans and almost one-fourth of Cuban Americans, who are U.S.-born.

No similarly detailed data by ancestry or national origin are available for native-born populations. For such coverage, we must rely on the U.S. Census Bureau's ethnic classification of "Hispanic-origin" groups, which is limited to five categories – persons of Mexican, Puerto Rican, Cuban, "Central/South American," and "other Hispanic" origin – and excludes all non-Spanish-speaking nationalities from Latin America and the Caribbean, such as Jamaicans,

Haitians, Guyanese, and Brazilians. The category "Central/South Americans" thus lumps together groups as diverse as Dominicans, Guatemalans, Colombians, Peruvians, and Argentineans. Analyses of these data thus cannot be meaningfully interpreted. The category "other Hispanic" includes persons who trace their origins in the United States over many generations; mixed-ethnicity and residual cases that could not be clearly coded into one of the other categories; and a relatively small number of immigrants from Spain. Despite these limitations, the data do cover all members of the three largest U.S. Hispanic ethnic groups, including both immigrants and native-born, thus permitting a fuller comparative assessment of their social and economic situation. As noted previously, detailed information from the 1990 census will not become available until 1993, but equivalent current population survey data collected in March 1990 from a national sample are instructive. These are summarized in table 5.5 for all five Hispanic-origin groups and are compared to descriptive statistics for the total U.S. population.

As table 5.5 shows, significant differences exist in the socioeconomic position of Hispanic-origin ethnic minorities. Compared with the median age of 32.8 years for the total U.S. population in 1990, Cubans are notably older – 39.1 years – and Mexicans, younger – 24.1 years. This in part reflects below-average and above-average fertility, respectively. About 20 percent of adult Americans are college graduates – the same proportion as Cubans – but only 5 percent of Mexican Americans[21] and almost 10 percent of Puerto Ricans are college graduates. Indeed, on every measure of socioeconomic performance listed in table 5.5 – labor force participation rates, occupations of men and women, family income and poverty rates, and the percent of female-headed families – Cubans were the only Hispanic ethnic group that had essentially reached parity with norms for the U.S. population as a whole. Only with respect to home ownership are Cuban Americans still lagging behind the national norm (47 percent to 64 percent).

Other Hispanic groups exhibit patterns of socioeconomic attainment generally below that of the U.S. average. Among them Puerto Ricans are in the worst socioeconomic situation, though they are all U.S. citizens and more highly educated than Mexican Americans. Puerto Rican men and especially women have much lower rates of labor force participation – 69 and 41 percent, respectively, compared with 75 and 57 percent for the total U.S. population. This is partly a reflection of the fact that 39 percent of Puerto Rican families are female-headed, compared with the U.S. average of 16.5 percent, and have higher poverty rates, lower mean family incomes, and fewer home owners.

Mexican men, and Central/South American men and women, exhibit the highest rates of labor force participation, although Mexican men and women also have the highest unemployment rates. Mexicans and Central/South Americans are disproportionately concentrated in lower blue-collar occupations (operators, fabricators, laborers), as are Mexican men in agricultural work, and Mexican and particularly Central/South American women in the low-wage service sector. Despite their high poverty rate (25.7 percent), 45 percent of Mexican families in the United States own their homes and only about 19 percent are female-headed. Both these figures compare proportionately to the Cubans, and the latter percentage is close to the national average. Since Mexicans compose 60 percent of the national Hispanic population, their characteristics tend to dominate aggregate figures when presented for the Hispanic population as a whole (which, as the data in table 5.5 clearly show, should not be taken as a homogenous unit). An issue posed by these data, then, is how to explain the significant socioeconomic differences among the various groups.

Cubans' general socioeconomic advantage relative to other Hispanic groups can be accounted for by the upper-and middle-class origins of the first waves of exiles, who left after the 1959 revolution. But their upper-and middle-class origins do not account for research findings showing Cubans maintaining above-average occupations and family incomes, even after controlling for their educational levels and other "human capital." Similarly, Mexicans' and Puerto Ricans' general socioeconomic disadvantage relative to Cubans and others can be accounted for by their

Table 5.5 Social and Economic Characteristics of Hispanic Ethnic Groups in the United States, Compared to the Total U.S. Population, 1990

Characteristic	Total U.S. Population	Mexican Origin	Puerto Rican Origin	Cuban Origin	Central/ South American	Other Hispanic*
Age						
Median age	32.8	24.1	27.0	39.1	28.0	31.1
% 55 years and over	20.6	8.7	12.8	28.5	8.0	19.4
Education[1]						
% College graduates	21.3	5.4	9.7	20.2	15.6	15.2
%<5 years of school	2.4	15.5	9.7	5.8	8.8	3.9
Labor Force Status[2]						
Men (% in labor force)	74.6	81.2	69.2	74.9	83.7	75.3
Men (% unemployed)	5.9	8.6	8.2	6.3	6.9	6.2
Women (% in labor force)	57.2	52.9	41.4	57.8	61.0	57.0
Women (% unemployed)	5.1	9.8	9.1	5.1	6.3	5.9
Occupation (men):[3]						
% Upper white-collar	26.0	8.3	11.2	25.9	12.2	16.6
% Lower white-collar	20.5	12.6	19.4	20.2	17.1	18.6
% Upper blue-collar	19.4	21.2	22.0	20.9	17.0	21.1
% Lower blue-collar	20.3	31.7	24.5	20.9	31.3	23.3
% Service occupations	9.8	15.1	20.6	11.3	19.8	17.7
% Farming, fishing	4.0	11.2	2.6	1.1	2.6	2.8
Occupation (women):[3]						
% Upper white-collar	26.4	14.2	23.1	22.1	14.1	20.3
% Lower white-collar	44.9	38.1	43.5	47.5	31.4	42.3
% Upper blue-collar	2.2	3.2	1.9	1.3	1.9	2.6
% Lower blue-collar	8.1	18.8	12.0	10.4	17.4	10.5
% Service occupations	17.4	23.9	18.8	18.3	35.0	23.6
% Farming, fishing	1.0	1.8	0.3	0.4	–	0.3
Economic Status						
Mean family income ($)	41,506	27,488	26,682	38,497	32,158	33,388
% Families in poverty	10.3	25.7	30.4	12.5	16.8	15.8
% Female-headed families	16.5	19.6	38.9	18.9	25.0	24.5
% Own–buying home	64.1	44.9	28.4	46.7	24.4	54.4

*See text for definition of "Other Hispanic."
[1]Persons 25 years or older.
[2]Persons 16 years or older.
[3]"Upper white-collar": professionals, executives, managers; "Lower white-collar": technical, sales, and administrative support; "Upper blue-collar": precision production, craft, and repair; "Lower blue-collar": operators, fabricators, and laborers.
Source: U.S. Bureau of the Census, *The Hispanic Population of the United States: March 1990* (Current Population Reports, 1991).

particular histories of discrimination and exploitation. But the histories do not account for the significant differences between Mexicans and Puerto Ricans in their present circumstances.

With regard to the Cuban advantage, the Cubans' mode of incorporation was assisted by the favorable governmental reception given them as political exiles fleeing a Communist revolution (although other Cold War refugees in the United States, notably the Indochinese, have received much greater levels of public assistance without comparable socioeconomic gains).[22] The consolidation of an ethnic enclave economy by south Florida's Cuban entrepreneurs has been more significant. This helps explain how successive cohorts of Cuban immigrants have been able to exceed expected levels of socioeconomic attainment. In Miami, Cuban-owned enterprises increased from about 900 to 25,000 between the late 1960s and the late 1980s. By 1985 Hispanic-owned firms in Dade County reported $2.2 billion in sales, pushing the area to first place in gross receipts among all Hispanic firms nationwide. A longitudinal survey of Cuban refugees who arrived in Miami in 1973 showed, that by 1979, 21.2 percent were self-employed and another 36.3 percent were employed in businesses owned by Cubans. These figures were quadruple and double, respectively, the proportionate figures in a parallel sample of Mexican immigrants who arrived in the United States at the same time. A subsequent survey of Mariel Cubans who arrived in Miami in 1980 found that 28.2 percent were self-employed by 1986, and another 44.9 percent were employed by co-nationals.[23]

Regarding the Mexican and Puerto Rican situations, available analyses point to different modes of incorporation in different labor markets and ethnic hiring queues. Briefly stated, these analyses suggest that Mexican low-wage workers in the Southwest and Midwest have been employers' preferred sources of pliable labor, not least because many are immigrants and a substantial proportion are undocumented. In contrast, Puerto Ricans, who are U.S. citizens by birth and not subject to deportation, often entered the Northeast's highly unionized labor markets, but massive industrial restructuring over the past two decades has resulted in the rapid decline or elimination of jobs in which they were disproportionately concentrated. The Puerto Ricans appear to have been displaced, as employers shift to other immigrant groups – especially Dominicans, Colombians, and other undocumented immigrants – willing to work in low-wage jobs and under poor working conditions. During this period many have migrated back to Puerto Rico,

and those remaining in the Northeast have experienced unemployment levels, withdrawal from the labor force, and disrupted family structures characteristic of the inner-city "underclass."

Significantly, a study by Marta Tienda found that Cuban workers in the New York–New Jersey area during the same restructuring period did not have similar experiences, despite their disproportionate representation in some of the same labor markets as Puerto Ricans. This suggests that Cubans may have been ranked higher in employment queues or were more successful in finding alternative employment by moving to Miami. In any case, this scholarship underscores the import of structural factors and historical contexts of reception and incorporation in shaping socioeconomic outcomes among different ethnic groups. It also debunks an undue "culture of poverty" emphasis on inner-city residents' individual attributes or Hispanics' supposed lack of "assimilability."[24]

Language and the Politics of Linguistic Assimilation

In the context of a recent and broader public debate over "multiculturalism" in American life, much attention has been focused on concerns raised by nativist organizations, including U.S. English, the Federation for American Immigration Reform (FAIR), and others. They are worried about the "fragmenting of America" by new immigrants, primarily Spanish-speakers from Latin America, and what they see as the impending demise of the English language in areas of immigrant concentration. By planting concern that today's immigrants, unlike yesterday's, do not want to assimilate, these groups have focused the discussion on the survival of English as the nation's only language and as its cultural centerpoint. As reflected by the passage of "English Only" measures in several states, pressures against bilingualism in America are rooted in more fundamental social and political concerns that date back to the origins of the nation (as reflected by Benjamin Franklin's comments cited at the beginning of this essay). The point was underscored by Theodore Roosevelt during the peak immigration years at the turn of the century: "We have room but for one language here, and that is the English language; for we intend to see that the crucible turns our people out as Americans, and not as dwellers in a polyglot boarding-house."

The paradox is that, while the United States has probably incorporated more bilingual people than any other nation in the world since Franklin's time, American history is notable for its near mass-extinction of non-English languages. A generational pattern of progressive anglicization is clear: first-generation immigrants learn survival English but speak their mother tongue to their children at home; the second generation in turn speaks accentless English at school and work, where its use is required and its social advantages are unmistakable. Meanwhile, the use of the mother tongue atrophies (for example, Spanish quickly becomes "Spanglish" and Vietnamese, "Vietglish"); with very few exceptions the third generation grows up as English monolinguals. This process explains why the United States has been called a "language graveyard."

For all the alarm about Quebec-like linguistic separatism in the United States today, the last census suggests that this generational pattern remains as strong as in the past. In 1980 well over 200 million Americans spoke English only, including substantial proportions of foreign-born (as shown in Table 5.4). Among new immigrants who had arrived in the United States between 1970 and 1980, 84 percent spoke a language other than English at home, but over half, adults as well as children, reported being able to speak English well. Among pre-1970 immigrants, 62 percent still spoke a language other than English at home, and the overwhelming majority of them – 77 percent of the adults, and 95 percent of the children – spoke English well. Among native-born, less than 7 percent spoke a language other than English at home, and more than 90 percent of them, both adults and children, spoke English well.

More detailed studies have confirmed that in all American ethnic groups, without exception, children consistently prefer English to their mother tongue. With any ethnic group, the use of English increases in direct ratio to the proportion of U.S.-born. Table 5.6 presents related findings from a unique 1976 data set on patterns of monolingualism and bilingualism among all adults and children for the main Hispanic ethnic groups (including both the native-born and foreign-born). Among Mexican Americans, the largest Hispanic group, 20 percent of adults spoke Spanish only, 21 percent spoke English only, and the remaining three-fifths spoke both languages, although a majority usually spoke English. Among the children, 40 percent were already English monolinguals, and a minuscule 3 percent, mainly preschoolers, spoke Spanish only. Tiny percentages of Spanish monolinguals also characterized the children of all other Hispanic groups. Cuban adults in this 1976 sample, overwhelmingly recent immigrants, were the least likely Hispanic group to have shifted to English, yet they were also the most successful among Hispanic ethnic groups in socioeconomic terms. At the same time, three-fourths of Cuban children aged 5 to 17 already spoke English only or usually – a proportion similar to that seen for Mexican, Puerto Rican, and Central and South American children (the proportion for "other Hispanic" was nearly nine-tenths).

As pointed out earlier, immigrant groups vary significantly in their rates of English-language ability, reflecting differences in educational and occupational levels. But even among Spanish speakers, who are considered the most resistant to language shift, the trend toward anglicization is present. Language loyalty among them, especially Mexicans, is due largely to the effect of continuing high immigration to the United States. For example, a recent study of a large representative sample of Mexican-origin couples in Los Angeles found that among first-generation women, 84 percent used Spanish only at home, 14 percent used both languages, and 2 percent used English only. By the third generation there was a complete reversal, with 4 percent speaking Spanish only at home, 12 percent using both, and 84 percent shifting to English only. Among the men, the pattern was similar, except their shift to English was even more marked by the second generation.[25] Indeed, in U.S. immigrant families, grandparents and grandchildren often cannot communicate with one another except through bilingual relatives, usually the parents.[26]

Table 5.6 Monolingualism and Bilingualism among Hispanic Adults and Children in the United States, 1976

Current Language Spoken (%)	Mexican Origin	Puerto Rican Origin	Cuban Origin	Central/South American	Other Hispanic
Adults (18 years and older):					
Spanish Only	20	21	33	25	10
Spanish Usually (also English)	23	36	40	29	18
English Usually (also Spanish)	35	32	25	30	24
English Only	21	10	1	15	48
Children (5–17 years old):					
Spanish Only	3	5	1	7	1
Spanish Usually (also English)	19	17	26	19	12
English Usually (also Spanish)	38	52	62	34	27
English Only	40	25	11	40	60

Source: David E. López, Language Maintenance and Shift in the United States Today, vol. 1 (Los Alamitos, Calif.: National Center for Bilingual Research, 1982), tables II-D and II-E. Data from the 1976 Survey of Income and Education.

English proficiency has always been a key to immigrants' socioeconomic mobility and full participation in their adoptive society. It is worth noting that in 1986, with the passage of Proposition 63, the initiative declaring English California's official language, more than 40,000 immigrants were turned away from ESL classes in the Los Angeles Unified School District alone: the supply of services could not meet the vigorous demand for English training. The efforts of linguistic nativists to compel immigrants to shed their foreign languages contrast sharply and ironically with the efforts of elite native youth to acquire a halting command of often the same foreign languages in U.S. universities.

English-language dominance is not threatened in the United States today – or for that matter in the world, where it has become already firmly established as the premier international language of commerce, diplomacy, education, journalism, aviation, technology, and mass culture. What is threatened is a more scarce resource: the survival of languages brought by immigrants themselves, which, in the absence of social structural supports, are destined to disappear. Given the immense pressure for linguistic conformity put on immigrant children by peers, schools, and the media – and later through exogamous marriages and integration into the mainstream economy and society – the preservation of fluent bilingualism beyond the first generation is an exceptional outcome. It is dependent on parents' intellectual and economic resources, their efforts to transmit the mother tongue to their children, and on the presence of institutionally complete ethnic communities where literacy in a second language is taught in schools and is valued in business and the labor market (such as that found in large entrepreneurial enclaves). The combination of these factors is rare: Miami may provide the closest approximation in the United States today, but even there the rapid and progressive anglicization of the Cuban second generation is evident.

Where such supports for bilingualism are lacking, the outcome is not only rapid English acquisition but the equally rapid loss of the home language. Such enforced linguistic homogeneity is an undesirable goal at a time when the United States finds itself enmeshed in global economic competition – including competition for skilled talent in a global immigration market, as reflected in the new Immigration Act of 1990. The need for Americans who fluently speak foreign languages becomes increasingly compelling, and the second generation now growing up in many American cities could fulfill such a need. In any event, far from posing a social or cultural threat, the existence of areas where foreign languages are fluently spoken enriches American culture, in the full sense of the phrase, and the lives of natives and immigrants alike.

The Europeans who founded and in large part dominated the United States have finally stopped coming, except in relatively small trickles. Latin Americans, and increasingly Asian Americans, are now beginning to remake it. While the immediate future augurs an acceleration of present trends, they too, like the Europeans, will at some point cease coming. All such passages contain their own internal contradictions, albeit in forms that defy safe or sage predictions. Europeans who came to the United States in the peak period of immigration in the nineteenth and early twentieth centuries helped transform the country, but not in their own image. They were transformed by American society more than the other way around. The peoples of Latin America and the Caribbean, and of Asia, who are now coming to the United States in this new peak immigration period that will most probably continue into the twenty-first century, are also helping transform America. But, as in the past, they will not do so in their own image.

NOTES

1   See, for example, Rubén G. Rumbaut, "The Hispanic Prologue," in David Cardús (ed.), *A Hispanic Look at the Bicentennial* (Houston: Institute of Hispanic Culture, 1978), 5–22; Carlos M. Fernández-Shaw, *Presencia Española en los Estados Unidos* (Madrid: Edicióones Cultura Hispánica, 1972); and Joseph P. Sánchez, "Hispanic American Heritage," in Herman J. Viola and Carolyn Margolis (eds.), *Seeds of Change: A Quincentennial Commemoration* (Washington, D.C.: Smithsonian Institution Press, 1991), 173–85. Indeed, half a dozen states bear Spanish names, and several of the largest U.S. cities and most of the cities of its most populous state are named in Spanish after Catholic saints and symbols. The presence of hundreds of "Indian" tribes comprising perhaps 5 million people in the territory of what is now the United States at the time of the arrival of the European colonists has also been largely ignored, and it has probably never occurred to most Americans that the names of 26 of the 50 states – from Alabama and Alaska to Texas, Wiscon-

sin, and Wyoming – have indigenous names; and one, Indiana, reflects also the fact that Columbus's mistake has not yet been corrected after 500 years.

2   Richard D. Lamm and Gary Imhoff, *The Immigration Time Bomb: The Fragmenting of America* (New York: Dutton, 1985). On Wilson's views, see Robert Reinhold, "In California, New Discussion on Whether to Bar the Door," *New York Times*, Dec. 3, 1991, A-1. For Buchanan's remarks, see the *San Diego Union*, Dec. 9, 1991, A-11; and Cathleen Decker, "Buchanan Uses Whatever It Takes in Long-Shot Bid," *Los Angeles Times*, Jan. 14, 1992, A-1.

3   Although Puerto Ricans are U.S. citizens by birth, the U.S. Census only includes Puerto Ricans living on the mainland in reporting U.S. population totals. A separate count is kept for Puerto Rico, as well as Guam and other territories.

4   In the case of Cuba, consider this extraordinary excerpt from President William McKinley's State of the Union message on December 5, 1899: "The new Cuba yet to arise from the ashes of the past must needs be bound to us by ties of singular intimacy and strength if its enduring welfare is to be assured. Whether those ties shall be organic or conventional, the destinies of Cuba are in some rightful form and manner irrevocably linked with our own, but how and how far is for the future to determine in the ripeness of events." Cited in Louis A. Pérez, Jr., *Cuba and the United States: Ties of Singular Intimacy* (Athens: Univ. of Georgia Press, 1990), ix.

5   For an analysis of contemporary (including Asian) immigration to the United States, see Alejandro Portes and Rubén G. Rumbaut, *Immigrant America: A Portrait* (Berkeley: Univ. of California Press, 1990); David M. Reimers, *Still the Golden Door: The Third World Comes to America* (New York: Columbia Univ. Press, 1985); and Rubén G. Rumbaut, "Passages to America: Perspectives on the New Immigration," in Alan Wolfe (ed.), *America at Century's End* (Berkeley: Univ. of California Press, 1991), 208–44. It is beyond the scope of this essay to provide a comprehensive listing of the voluminous literature that has accumulated on contemporary immigration to the United States; the reader is referred to the extensive references cited in the above.

6 On social networks in the immigration of Mexicans and Dominicans to the United States, see Douglas Massey, Rafael Alarcón, Jorge Durand, and Humberto González, *Return to Aztlán: The Social Process of International Migration from Western Mexico* (Berkeley: Univ. of California Press, 1987); Sherri Grasmuck and Patricia Pessar, *Between Two Islands: Dominican International Immigration* (Berkeley: Univ. of California Press, 1991). See also Guillermina Jasso and Mark R. Rosenzweig, *The New Chosen People: Immigrants in the United States* (New York: Russell Sage Foundation, 1990).

7 Alejandro Portes, "From South of the Border: Hispanic Minorities in the United States," in Virginia Yans-McLaughlin (ed.), *Immigration Reconsidered: History, Sociology, and Politics* (New York: Oxford Univ. Press, 1990), 160–94. For a critical historical assessment of two centuries of U.S. expansion and intervention in Latin America, see Frank Niess, *A Hemisphere to Itself: A History of US-Latin American Relations* (London: Zed, 1990).

8 See Dawn Marshall, "A History of West Indian Migrations: Overseas Opportunities and 'Safety-Valve' Policies," in Barry B. Levine (ed.), *The Caribbean Exodus* (New York: Praeger, 1987), 15–31. See also Ransford W. Palmer (ed.), *In Search of a Better Life: Perspectives on Migration from the Caribbean* (New York: Praeger, 1990); Franklin W. Knight and Colin A. Palmer (eds.), *The Modern Caribbean* (Chapel Hill: Univ. of North Carolina Press, 1989); and Robert A. Pastor (ed.), *Migration and Development in the Caribbean: The Unexplored Connection* (Boulder, Colo.: Westview Press, 1985).

9 For a discussion of the 1990 Act, see Francesco Isgro, "The New Employment-Based Immigration Selection System," *Migration World* 19: 5 (1991), 34–37.

10 See Niess, *A Hemisphere to Itself;* Eric Williams, *From Columbus to Castro: The History of the Caribbean* (New York: Random House, 1984); Franklin W. Knight, *The Caribbean: The Genesis of a Fragmented Nationalism*, 2d ed. (New York: Oxford Univ. Press, 1990).

11 See David Montejano, *Anglos and Mexicans in the Making of Texas, 1836–1986* (Austin: Univ. of Texas Press, 1987); David J. Weber, *The Mexican Frontier, 1821–1846: The American Southwest Under Mexico* (Albuquerque: Univ.

of New Mexico Press, 1982); Sarah Deutsch, *No Separate Refuge: Culture, Class and Gender on an Anglo-Hispanic Frontier in the American Southwest, 1880–1940* (New York: Oxford Univ. Press, 1987). For a comparative historical study of Mexican Americans in San Antonio, Santa Fe, Tucson, and Los Angeles, see Richard Griswold del Castillo, *La Familia: Chicano Families in the Urban Southwest, 1846 to the Present* (Notre Dame, Ind.: Univ. of Notre Dame Press, 1984).

12 See Lawrence A. Cardoso, *Mexican Immigration to the United States, 1897–1931* (Tucson: Univ. of Arizona Press, 1980); Mario Barrera, *Race and Class in the Southwest* (Notre Dame, Ind.: Univ. of Notre Dame Press, 1979); Rodolfo Alvarez, "The Psycho-Historical and Socio-economic Development of the Chicano Community in the United States," in Carol A. Hernández, Marsha J. Haug, and Nathaniel N. Wagner (eds.), *Chicanos: Social and Psychological Perspectives* (St. Louis: Mosby, 1976), 38–51; Mario T. Garcia, *Mexican Americans: Leadership, Ideology, and Identity, 1930–1960* (New Haven: Yale Univ. Press, 1989); Juan Gómez Quiñones, *Chicano Politics: Reality and Promise, 1940–1990* (Albuquerque: Univ. of New Mexico Press, 1990).

13 See Portes, "From South of the Border"; Joan Moore and Harry Pachón, *Hispanics in the United States* (Englewood Cliffs, N. J.: Prentice-Hall, 1985); Virginia E. Sánchez Korrol, *From Colonia to Community: The History of Puerto Ricans in New York City, 1917–1948* (Westport, Conn.: Greenwood Press, 1983); Frank Bonilla and Ricardo Campos, "A Wealth of Poor: Puerto Ricans in the New Economic Order," *Daedalus* 110 (1981), 133–76; Joseph P. Fitzpatrick, *Puerto Rican Americans: The Meaning of Migration to the Mainland*, 2d ed. (Englewood Cliffs, N.J.: Prentice-Hall, 1987).

14 Wayne S. Smith, *Portrait of Cuba* (Atlanta: Turner Publishing, 1991), 63. See also Pérez, *Cuba and the United States*; Niess, *A Hemisphere to Itself;* Hugh Thomas, *Cuba: The Pursuit of Freedom* (New York: Harper & Row, 1971).

15 For a provocative essay on the subject, see Carlos Alberto Montaner, *Cuba: Claves para una Conciencia en Crisis* (Madrid: Editorial Playor, 1983); see also Carlos Alberto Montaner, "The Roots of Anti-Americanism in Cuba:

Sovereignty in an Age of World Cultural Homogeneity," *Caribbean Review* 13 (1984), 13–46. Cf. Portes and Rumbaut, *Immigrant America*, and Portes, "From South of the Border."

16   As noted, the figure of 3,460,683 immigrants from Latin America and the Caribbean refers only to persons *legally* admitted as permanent residents during 1981–90 and does not include an estimate of illegal immigration. However, the figure does include 1,359,186 formerly illegal immigrants (of whom 71 percent were Mexican nationals) who qualified for legalization of their status in 1989 and 1990 under the amnesty provisions of the Immigration Reform and Control Act (IRCA). INS immigration data for 1991 and 1992 will add to the regular immigration totals another 1.7 million persons who qualified for legalization under IRCA as they complete the bureaucratic process of obtaining a "green card," the majority of them being from Mexico and other Latin American countries. A total of 3.1 million undocumented immigrants were found eligible for legalization under IRCA; most of them had resided in the United States since 1981 or earlier (the remainder were Special Agricultural Workers who could demonstrate that they had worked in the United States during 1985–86). See Rumbaut, "Passages to America"; cf. Leo R. Chávez, *Shadowed Lives: Undocumented Immigrants in American Society* (Fort Worth: Harcourt Brace Jovanovich, 1991).

17   This does not mean that Uruguayans do not emigrate. On the contrary, according to recent reports, the Uruguayan "brain drain" may be the largest in Latin America; there are nearly 1 million Uruguayans living outside their country, about a fourth of the population (another 3 million reside in Uruguay). They have gone not to the United States but to Mexico and elsewhere. See Isgro, "The New Employment-Based Immigration Selection System," 37; and the essay . . . by M. Patricia Fernández Kelly and Alejandro Portes in *Americas: New Interpretative Essays*, ed. A. Stepan (Oxford: Oxford University Press, 1982).

18   See Rumbaut, "Passages to America," for a comparative analysis of the class origins of contemporary Asian and Latin American immigrant nationalities in the United States. For a

contemporary local assessment, cf. David Rieff, *Los Angeles: Capital of the Third World* (New York: Simon & Schuster, 1991).

19   For a related detailed analysis based on public use samples of the 1960, 1970, and 1980 censuses, see Frank D. Bean and Marta Tienda, *The Hispanic Population of the United States* (New York: Russell Sage Foundation, 1987). With respect to the Venezuelan case, Bean and Tienda "suspect that a large share of this group consists of individuals who are independently wealthy individuals and not compelled to work" (294). A similar explanation may apply in part to the Brazilians (who, as non-Hispanics, were not included in their study).

20   For a comparative-historical analysis of generational patterns of ethnic identity, citizenship acquisition, and political participation among immigrant and ethnic groups, with a focus on the diverse experiences of Mexicans, Cubans, Dominicans, Colombians, and other groups from Latin America – and the unlikely prospects for a nationwide "Hispanic" politics, at least in the short term, based on efforts to mobilize groups of different national and class origins under a common generic label – see Portes and Rumbaut, *Immigrant America*, chap. 4. Like African Americans, Mexican Americans reflect a reactive political history marked by institutionalized discrimination and disenfranchisement, but differ in their proximity to and strong identification with the country of origin – factors that have presented added obstacles to effective political organization and participation in the United States, despite the watershed of the Chicano movement of the late 1960s and early 1970s. Cf. Garcia, *Mexican Americans*; and Gómez Quiñones, *Chicano Politics*.

21   An earlier study found that as of the early 1970s out of 24 million African Americans there were 2,200 who had earned Ph.D.'s, while among the 8 million Mexican Americans only 60 individuals had earned a Ph.D., when a similar level of disadvantage would have yielded about 730. This may be taken as an indicator of the level of available technical expertise (that is, one can infer the number of doctors, lawyers, and master's and bachelor's degrees from it), and it underscores the fact that

"Mexican Americans were almost entirely lacking in certification for middle-class status" until very recently. See Alvarez, "Psycho-Historical and Socio-economic Development."

22 On the import of government aid to the Cuban exiles, see Silvia Pedraza-Bailey, *Political and Economic Migrants in America: Cubans and Mexicans* (Austin: Univ. of Texas Press, 1985). On the case of the Indochinese, see Rubén G. Rumbaut, "The Structure of Refuge: Southeast Asian Refugees in the United States, 1975–1985," *International Review of Comparative Public Policy* I (1989), 97–129.

23 See Alejandro Portes and Robert L. Bach, *Latin Journey: Cuban and Mexican Immigrants in the United States* (Berkeley: Univ. of California Press, 1985); Alejandro Portes and Leif Jensen, "The Enclave and the Entrants: Patterns of Ethnic Enterprise in Miami Before and After Mariel," *American Sociological Review* 54 (Dec. 1989), 929–49; Alejandro Portes, "The Social Origins of the Cuban Enclave Economy of Miami," *Sociological Perspectives* 30 (Oct. 1987), 340–72.

24 Marta Tienda, "Puerto Ricans and the Underclass Debate," *The Annals* 501 (Jan. 1989), 105–19. See also the articles collected in Edwin Meléndez and Clara Rodríguez (eds.), "Puerto Rican Poverty and Labor Markets," *Hispanic Journal of Behavioral Sciences* (special issue) 14

(Feb. 1992); Portes, "From South of the Border"; Nicholas Lemann, "The Other Underclass," *The Atlantic*, Dec. 1991, 96–110.

25 David E. López, "Chicano Language Loyalty in an Urban Setting," *Sociology and Social Research* 62 (1978), 267–78. See also Portes and Rumbaut, *Immigrant America*, chap. 6; Calvin Veltman, *Language Shift in the United States* (Berlin: Mouton, 1983); Melvyn C. Resnick, "Beyond the Ethnic Community: Spanish Language Roles and Maintenance in Miami," *International Journal of the Sociology of Language* 69 (1988), 89–104; Ray Hutchison, "The Hispanic Community in Chicago: A Study of Population Growth and Acculturation," *Research in Race and Ethnic Relations* 5 (1988), 193–229. The appearance of widespread Spanish-language loyalty is not typically presented in the popular media as a function of high levels of contemporary immigration and tends to leave the impression that English is being gradually supplanted; cf. Claudia Puig, "The Explosion of *Radio en Español:* Why Southern California's Spanish-Language Stations Are Zooming Off the Charts," *Los Angeles Times*, April 7, 1991, Calendar-9.

26 See Michael Quintanilla, "The Language Gap: Third-Generation Minorities Learn There's Sometimes a Price to Be Paid for 'English Only,'" *Los Angeles Times*, June 9, 1991, E-1.

Part II
Global Political Economy

6

"¿Quién Trabajará?": Domestic Workers, Urban Slaves, and the Abolition of Slavery in Puerto Rico

Félix V. Matos Rodríguez

This essay analyzes the role that domestic work and urban slavery played in the process of the abolition of slavery in Puerto Rico. Puerto Rico's historiography has shown the significance that economic, demographic, and social changes among rural slaves played in the demise of slavery. In this essay, on the other hand, I will discuss the importance that colonial authorities and the local urban elites gave to their perceived domestic labor shortage problem in San Juan and other cities. The evidence from continuous specific work regulations, the pro-abolition literature and propaganda, the struggles and frictions with colonial authorities, and the connections with the development of beneficence institutions all indicates that the concern regarding domestic work – although virutally forgotten in Puerto Rican historiography – was far from marginal in the Island's economic, political, and social processes during the second half of the nineteenth century.

Puerto Rico's historians have written extensively on the events leading to the abolition of slavery in 1873.[1] Recently, there has been growing interest in exploring not only the transition from slave labor into so-called "free" labor, but also the processes through which different agents defined complementary and contradictory notions of the concept of "freedom."[2] The exploration of these themes is not an isolated phenomenon in Puerto Rico's historiography but part of a larger dialogue regarding the forces that led to the eradication of slavery in the Americas and the behavior and expectations of the different groups involved in the process, including masters, slaves, merchants, and politicians.[3]

My interest in domestic work comes from the need to add new elements to the debates about slavery and its eventual abolition in Puerto Rico. Furthermore, domestic work has begun to be studied more cautiously given the developments in the fields of women's and gender studies.[4] Historically, domestic work in Latin America has been done by women, and nineteenth-century Puerto Rico was no exception to this rule. Recent research has stressed the importance of domestic work to the general economy, particularly in relation to the development of capitalism and urbanization in different regions.[5] In urban enclaves, domestic services, paid or not – such as washing, cooking, ironing, cleaning, and supervising children, ill people, and the elderly – have been key to the growth and development of other sectors of the economy. Although the chores we traditionally associate with domestic work apparently have not changed much over the years – with the exception, perhaps, of technological innovations that have supposedly simplified the work – it is important

Table 6.1 Domestic Workers by Race in San Juan: 1846 (Santa Bárbara, Santo Domingo, and San Francisco barrios)

	White	Black	Parda	Mulatto	Totals
Laundresses	19	158	81	101	359
Cooks	2	78	12	8	100
Servants	10	460	115	57	642
Totals	31	696	208	166	1,101

Source: AGPR, Censos San Juan, Barrios Santa Bárbara, Santo Domingo y San Francisco, 1846.

Table 6.2 Domestic Workers by "Status" in San Juan: 1846 (Santa Bárbara, Santo Domingo, and San Francisco barrios)

	Free	Slave	Totals
Laundresses	265	94	359
Cooks	23	77	100
Servants	67	575	642
Totals	355	746	1,101

Source: AGPR, Censos San Juan, Barrios Santa Bárbara, Santo Domingo y San Francisco, 1846.

to recognize that, as with many other sectors of the economy, domestic work has a history. The development and historical evolution of domestic work must be problematized in order to appreciate its contribution to the socioeconomic transformations in Caribbean and Latin American history. This essay is a contribution to re-evaluating the importance of domestic work in Puerto Rico's history.

There was a direct connection between domestic work and urban slavery in nineteenth-century Puerto Rico. If it is true that not all urban women slaves were domestics, it is also true that a majority of urban women slaves performed domestic chores such as being servants, cooks, laundresses, nannies, and maids.[6] Given the lack of interest in domestic work in Puerto Rican and Caribbean historiography, it should not be surprising that urban slavery is also understudied in the region.[7] In most Puerto Rican and Caribbean slavery studies, the emphasis has been on plantation work and sugar processing. In this essay, I will regard domestic work and urban slavery as virtually synonymous, even when aware that not all urban slaves worked as domestics and that in rural plantations the distinctions between domestic and field slaves were often murky.

The selection of San Juan as the focus for this study is based on several important criteria. During the first two-thirds of the nineteenth century, San Juan was the Island's most important political, intellectual, and economic urban center.[8] Throughout the first half of the nineteenth century the importation of slaves increased in Puerto Rico, and also in San Juan. Halfway through the century, the processes that led to the abolition of slavery started. At the time of abolition, San Juan was the city with the highest number of domestic slaves.[9] This is particularly significant considering that other cities such as Mayagüez and Ponce had far higher total numbers of slaves, both rural and urban. San Juan is, therefore, an appropriate place to analyze the role played by domestics and urban slaves in the abolition process during the second half of the nineteenth century in Puerto Rico.

Domestic Work in the Capital

My first inquiry is: Who were domestics and urban slaves in San Juan? We can obtain a description of the characteristics of the women who performed domestic chores in mid-nineteenth-century San Juan through the use of census data and notarial records. Unfortunately, information regarding the lives of domestics is not abundant.[10] Census data, however, allows us to determine the geographic, racial, and marital status distribution of domestics. The only surviving mid-century manuscript census in San Juan is the one taken in 1846.[11] In that census, there is information about three of the four *barrios* (quarters) that composed the walled city: Santa Bárbara, Santo Domingo, and San Francisco. There is also a slave registry for 1872, which has been studied by Negrón Portillo and Mayo Santana.[12] This registry, unfortunately, does not have information regarding free women of color.

Who were San Juan's mid-nineteenth-century domestics and what kinds of jobs did they perform? Table 6.1 shows the number of domestics in the three San Juan quarters included in the 1846 census data.[13] Almost all the individuals listed as domestics in the 1846 census were women. Servants or maids were the most common type of domestics, followed by laundresses. The number of domestics, 1,101, is significant, particularly if we consider that San Juan's total population at that time was around 13,000 inhabitants.[14] Domestics, then, comprised at a minimum 8 percent of San Juan's population in 1846. These numbers, however, must be taken with caution because they could be affected by several factors. One can assume, for example, that many men and women classified as slaves in the census perhaps performed domestic chores in their masters' homes, even if they were not classified with any occupation. Thus, the number of domestics in 1846 was probably higher than the census figures indicate.

Tables 6.1 and 6.2 show the racial composition and the *condición* (free or slave status), respect-

ively, of San Juan's domestics. There was a marked difference among domestics in the city: the majority of the laundresses were free women (73 percent), while the majority of the servants or maids (90 percent) and the cooks (77 percent) were slave women. In 1846, slaves comprised about 20 percent of San Juan's total population.[15] Given the data provided above, it should not be unexpected to find that a high percentage of the cooks (78 percent) and the maids (72 percent) in San Juan were black. Among domestics, only laundresses had a less polarized racial breakdown: 49 percent of them were black, 23 percent were *pardas*, and 28 percent were mulattos.[16] Irrespective of the racial differences found among the laundresses and other domestics, it is clear that a majority of San Juan's domestics were black or colored (97 percent) and that a high percentage of them were slaves (68 percent).

The 1846 census also allows us to explore other characteristics of San Juan's domestics. The census data show that most domestics were between 10 and 44 years of age.[17] Servants or maids tended to be younger than cooks and laundresses. Table 6.3 shows the marital status of San Juan's domestics. The great majority of the city's domestics were single (93 percent). Almost all the servants were single (99 percent). These servants usually lived in the residence of their master or employer. Most of the cooks were also single (91 percent). Finally, among the laundresses, four out of five were single. In the case of laundresses, even though most were single, there was a high percentage of heads of household.[18] Thirty-eight percent of the laundresses and 13 percent of the cooks were heads of household. These figures contrast with those of the servants, given that not one servant was a head of household in

Table 6.3 Domestic Workers by Marital Status in San Juan: 1846 (Santa Bárbara, Santo Domingo, and San Francisco barrios)

	Married	Single	Widows	Totals
Laundresses	30	291	39	360
Cooks	5	94	4	103
Servants	4	657	1	662
Ironer	–	1	–	1
Totals	39	1,043	44	1,126

Source: AGPR, Censos San Juan, Barrios Santa Bárbara, Santo Domingo y San Francisco, 1846.

1846. The percentage of heads of household among laundresses points to a high number of single mothers among them.

The 1872 data from San Juan's slave registry confirms some of the trends identified in the 1846 data, even when the 1872 data do not include free domestics. In 1872, a majority of the domestic slaves in San Juan were women between 10 and 40 years of age.[19] Although by 1872 the total number of slaves in the city had decreased compared to the mid-century numbers, it seems that the characteristics of domestic slaves had not changed much.

The work done by domestics was quite arduous. In the case of laundresses, for example, their work required much physical strength. Laundresses could be employees or slaves working full-time in a single residence, military barrack, or monastery, or they could sell their services to multiple clients. In the latter case, laundresses probably collected clothes from their clients and took them to wash in their own homes or to one of the public water fountains in the city. Among these itinerant laundresses one could find slaves who, although mostly responsible for washing and folding their masters' family clothes, also rented their services – or were rented out by their masters – to other families.[20] This system of slave rentals was pretty frequent in the city, to the extent that it drew heavy criticism, censure, and requests for its eradication from the both the *Cabildo* (city council) and the central government.[21]

Washing clothes was not a simple task in a city lacking easy access to fresh water. In other Puerto Rican towns or cities, women took their wash to the nearest river, usually located at the outskirts of the town or city. San Juan had no such nearby rivers. San Juan's residents depended on three water fountains and several wells to supply them with water. The fountain with the highest volume and best quality of water was located in the Condado area near the San Antonio bridge – a considerable walk from the city's walls.[22] Another well was located in the Puntilla area, but the water quality there was poor and city residents stopped using it during the mid-nineteenth century. The Miraflores islet, located even farther away than the Condado fountain, had water of

excellent quality. The city also had three intramural wells located in the plazas facing the Carmelite and Franciscan convents and the San Justo gate. These wells were opened at the onset of the nineteenth century, but their water supply and volume were unreliable. The intramural wells were closed in the 1860s after repeated complaints from religious leaders regarding the noise, public scandals, and general unruly behavior of the people who used the wells located in front of churches and convents.[23]

Many laundresses took their wash to the Condado fountain or the wells located within the city walls. Other laundresses took water to their homes or used water collected in cisterns. Some had access to the cisterns at the military garrisons or the city's hospital. In all cases, the laundresses' work required carrying a heavy load of either clothes or water for a considerable distance. Laundry work ended with the task of drying the washed clothes so that they could be ironed and returned to their owners. In many cases, the laundresses' children helped collect the soiled clothes and with the drying and ironing processes. The Condado fountain and the other intramural wells were public gathering places for the laundresses and their children.

Very little is known about the work performed by other domestics. Most cooks and servants in San Juan were slaves and lived in the master's residence. These domestics were in proximity to their masters' families, a situation that invited greater intimacy, and at the same time, greater friction with the family. The intimacy, for example, that allowed some slaves to receive their manumission given "good and admirable services" made other domestic slaves the victims of suspicious accusations by their masters, including, for example, poisoning of food.[24] Although domestic chores required many hours of work, San Juan's urban setting and the errands masters often required of their domestics allowed these slaves to spend a considerable amount of time on their own and outside their masters' residences. Some domestic slaves even rented their services to others outside their masters' families.

Slavery remained an active institution in San Juan and the rest of the Island until abolition. During the decade prior to abolition, slaves were still being bought and sold in San Juan.[25] Many of these slaves were later sold to the haciendas in San Juan's periphery as the demand for agricultural slaves remained high and hacienda owners paid higher prices to obtain them. Although the sale of slaves continued in Puerto Rico, statistics show that the slave population decreased in the decade prior to abolition. In San Juan's case, the number of slaves decreased from 1,334 in 1869 to 890 in 1872.[26] The decreasing number of slaves in San Juan was certainly a factor affecting the demand for domestic work in the city.

Domestic Work and Urban Slavery in the Abolitionist Debate

The debates regarding the potential abolition of slavery in Puerto Rico, debates that gathered momentum and intensity in the second half of the nineteenth century, made few references to the situation of domestic slaves. From the perspective of hacendados, merchants, politicians, and intellectuals, the key concerns of the abolition debate were: Will the sugar industry survive? Will we have a cheap and abundant workforce? What will the repercussions of abolition be in the social and political realms? Will masters get compensated for their slaves? What will the diplomatic and international fallout be? How will such a process be handled? Slaves, for their part, also articulated their own visions of what a post-slavery Puerto Rico would be like.

Although the future of domestic and urban slaves was not a central theme in the abolitionist debates, it is important to acknowledge that domestic slaves did figure in the rhetorical strategies of the warring sides of the debate. In the first place, pro-abolition groups used the figures of the total number of domestic slaves to argue that Puerto Rico's agriculture would not be affected by the elimination of slavery. *El Abolicionista*, the propaganda newspaper of the pro-abolition forces, gave the following rationale in Madrid's press:

Of the 30,000 slaves that exist in the tiny Antille, 25,000 are dedicated to domestic service and their manumission will not affect agricultural production at all. Agriculture right now is done with free laborers, except

for the 8,000 slaves that complete the total number of slaves for the entire Puerto Rico.[27]

The manipulation of numbers (not always exact or reliable) and the arbitrary designation of slaves as either agricultural or domestic were some of the ways in which the supporters of abolition presented their argument to minimize fears of a financial and agricultural disaster in Puerto Rico resulting from abolition.

Other pro-abolitionist leaders used the numbers of domestics and the nature of domestic work not to mitigate fears of a potential economic crisis following abolition, but to mitigate fears of a social revolt. For many, their opposition to abolition stemmed not from financial considerations but from social order concerns. The racial hierarchy that slavery provided Puerto Rico could be altered or inverted with the end of slavery, something that worried members of the white elite. Others feared the potentially damaging effects on society of the supposed intellectual and moral inferiority of slaves. To appease those fears, pro-abolitionists used domestic slaves as an example of the docility and obedience that the ruling elite wanted to see perpetuated in a post-abolition Puerto Rico. To this end, the famous Puerto Rican abolitionists Segundo Ruiz Belvis, José Julian Acosta, and Francisco Mariano Quiñones wrote in 1867:

Of the 41,000 total slaves, the 28,000 employed in mechanical tasks and in domestic service have always seen public authority over the master's authority, respecting both. If this situation keeps the slaves today away from any idea of disturbance, with more reason will it keep it away the day they obtain their freedom.[28]

With explanations such as this, abolitionist leaders tried to dissipate fears of a freedmen's revolt or of any other kind of racial disturbance. The abolitionists manipulated the images associated with domestic slaves – their supposed docility and loyalty toward their masters – to minimize the threats suggested by the anti-abolitionist forces.

One last argument used by the promoters of abolition was to accentuate the lack of employment and work options the domestics would face once slavery disappeared. Abolitionists, again, used domestic slavery to counter the arguments of their antagonists. The pro-slavery forces argued that abolition would create a major havoc in the labor market given that former slaves would seek only well-paid jobs, or they would filter to the countryside to engage in subsistence agriculture.[29] Although abolitionists like Acosta and Ruiz Belvis acknowledged that some alteration in the labor supply was likely once slavery ended, these leaders emphasized the volume of domestics that would probably end up working in the same kind of jobs they had as slaves. Acosta and Ruiz Belvis presented their views in the *Proyecto para la abolición de la esclavitud* (1867):

> Because it has occurred to no one that domestic slaves, most of them women, and those dedicated to mechanical tasks in the towns, will abandon their ordinary tasks when they become free, given that their actual situation is far more benign than that of slaves living in the countryside. The transition from slavery to freedom will be, therefore, less violent.[30]

The abolitionist leaders promoted the image of an orderly and pacific transition after abolition. In the quotation above, abolitionists used the strategy of feminizing domestic slavery by accentuating that the majority of the domestic slaves were women. This feminization attempted to conjure images of docility and submission destined to appease those fearful of the effects of abolition. Pro-abolition leaders utilized the nature of domestic slavery itself, the apparent lack of employment options for the new freedmen and women, and the myth of the domestic slave as a loyal and docile subject in order to promote the eradication of slavery in Puerto Rico.

The Labor "Crisis" and the Struggle to Control the Supply of Domestics in San Juan

Aside from the manipulation in the propaganda in favor of and against the abolition of slavery in Puerto Rico, the colonial authorities and the commercial and agricultural elite had faced what they described as a *crisis de brazos* (labor crisis) since the mid-nineteenth century. Governor López de Baños instituted a registry for wage-laborers (*jor-*

naleros) in 1938, forcing every landless person age 16 through 60 to register with the municipal vagrancy juntas and list his or her occupation.[31] The so-called labor crisis did not occur because there were not enough workers in Puerto Rico, but because the government and the elite wanted to dictate working conditions and wages on the Island.[32] Social and labor control regulations of those without land continued all through the nineteenth century as profits in the sugar sector dwindled and the possibilities of reproducing a slave labor force decreased. Perhaps the best known of these regulations was the *jornalero* legislation issued by Governor Juan de la Pezuela in 1849. Pezuela's regulations combined all labor control laws approved by previous governors and added a new requirement that forced *jornaleros* to carry a notebook or passbook in which information regarding their labor history was kept. Although labor control mechanisms were applied all through the Island, in San Juan's case repressive and preventive regulations were issued around the reproduction, access, and control of domestic workers.

The apparent shortage of workers affected San Juan in the second half of the nineteenth century. Not only did the abolition of slavery debate cause concerns and re-negotiations, but also the city's elite faced the problem of recruiting domestics in order to keep their privileged lifestyle. The problem was not that there were not enough women ready to work as domestics, but that given demographic and economic changes in San Juan there were fewer women willing to accept the elite's terms of remuneration and working conditions. Among the factors that affected the supply of domestic workers in San Juan were demographic changes (fewer women and fewer people of color), the effects of the cholera epidemic in 1855, the rise in the price of slaves given the end of the slave trade, and the fears rising out of the impending abolition of slavery on the Island.[33]

On the economic side, urban slavery in San Juan – as well as on the rest of the Island – entered a crisis beginning in the second half of the nineteenth century. Rising inflation, ever increasing prices of basic goods, the shortage of domestic slaves, and the difficulty in providing for those slaves directly affected the viability of urban slavery in San Juan. This crisis, similar to the ones that affected several other Caribbean and Latin American urban centers, combined with the changing demographic patterns in San Juan, marked not only the limits of the attempts at regulating domestic work but also the terms of the supply of and demand for domestic work in the capital.[34]

Faced with the difficulty of obtaining domestics, Spanish authorities initiated a campaign of identifying and controlling workers. In 1858, for example, the central government prepared a list of domestics, agricultural workers, and unemployed people in each town.[35] Lists such as this indicated the importance the insular government placed on domestic work – it was, after all, one of the categories of the list – although most official communiqués and contemporary accounts privileged the work of agricultural workers. In 1864, San Juan's Cabildo started another listing of women and men over fourteen years of age who "rent themselves for permanent domestic work in someone else's home, cooking, washing, cleaning and taking care of a home or family or analogous occupations."[36] This municipal listing, created from an Island-wide one, included information regarding all the work contracts issued to domestics. The 1864 regulations required "obedience, fidelity and respect" from the domestics to their employers, a requirement that was not expected to be reciprocated by employers. Violations to the regulations – which included losing your work passbook or not having updated information in the passbook – were only stipulated for the domestic workers. The penalties were: "If you were male you faced six days of correction working in public works in the region at half-pay, and if female a fine of four reales or a day in jail."[37] The only punishment to the employers mentioned in the 1864 regulations was that they were to go to court if they were behind in their payments to the domestic worker. The 1864 regulations were part of ongoing Island-wide efforts throughout the 1860s to reinstate and reinforce some of the coercive labor measures designed in the 1830s and 1840s given the perceived failure to increase the supply of workers.[38] In 1871, the government enacted another set of regulations pertaining to domestic work. Official

authorities themselves recognized that these 1871 regulations were not enforced, "perhaps because at that time domestic work was still performed for the most part by slaves."[39]

The impact of the abolition of slavery on the supply of workers in Puerto Rico after 1873, particularly in urban centers, needs to be studied with more care. Nevertheless, it is clear that both Spanish authorities and the local elite were convinced that there was a shortage of domestics in San Juan. The Spanish governor, for example, commented on the negative effects of abolition a few years after it was enacted. He said:

> after the abolition of slavery, [there was] the need to mitigate one of its effects, in the Capital particularly, which was the shortage of domestics, even for the most necessary chores. There were not then, as now, any available replacements.[40]

The governor's commentary referred to a petition to transfer twenty-five inmates from the local jail to perform domestic chores in San Juan due to the difficulty experienced by the elite in finding workers willing to perform domestic services.

In 1876 – three years after the abolition of slavery in Puerto Rico – the city regulated domestic work by forcing domestics to carry a passbook, and to register at the local town hall.[41] City authorities justified the new regulations not just because of the so-called shortage of domestics, but also to defend the rights of both workers and employers during contracting. The registry had information regarding the conduct, physical traits, place of birth, marital status, and names of the parents of each domestic.[42] Besides the standard regulations of movement, scheduling, and residency, the 1876 law also attempted to limit the pool of domestics to city residents and thus avoid encouraging immigration into San Juan from other parts of the Island. Domestics not complying with the passbook and the registry were fined three pesos for the first infraction. In the case of a second infraction, the fine increased to six pesos, and the domestic was exiled to her/his city of origin.[43]

It is ironic that city officials complained about a shortage of domestic employees at the same time that they were legislating to ship potential workers out of San Juan. This points to the real purpose behind all the domestic work regulations: to control and manipulate the supply of domestics and dictate the terms of the working conditions of those domestics in the city. Also, the 1876 regulations coincided with the last year of the mandatory contracting of the slaves "liberated" in 1873. Although there are no clear data about the effects of the actual abolition of slavery in San Juan, studies from towns such as Guayama showed a significant increment of former slaves, particularly women, migrating to cities seeking employment as domestics.[44] The 1876 regulations in San Juan were perhaps destined not only to dictate the terms of employment in the city but also to prevent a massive migration of *libertos* (freedmen and women) who might become a safety and economic hazard to the colonial officials and the urban elite.

The different domestic service regulations issued by the colonial government, starting in the 1850s and continuing in various years after slavery was abolished, show similar patterns. First, all regulations were drafted to ameliorate the so-called labor crisis among domestics in San Juan and other parts of Puerto Rico. Second, the regulations copied the mechanisms – registries, passbooks, spatial and geographical restrictions, punitive measures ranging from fines to forced hard labor – employed by insular authorities in the legislation regulating *jornaleros* and other landless people on the Island. Third, the passbooks subordinated workers to the bureaucratic whims and fancies of colonial officials and employers. Given that any improper conduct, from the employers' perspective, had to be recorded in the passbook, domestics were vulnerable to their employers' caprices, in addition to the control the employers had in the areas of contracting and determining wages. Finally, the continuous passing of regulations indicated that even if Puerto Rico's historiography has neglected the importance of domestic work, that was not the case with Spanish authorities and the dominant classes in nineteenth-century Puerto Rico.

Beneficence – Social and Labor Control

Another response by colonial Spanish officials and Puerto Rico's elite to the problem of securing an abundant, cheap, and docile supply of domestics was the proliferation of public and semi-private beneficence institutions in the nineteenth century. The liberal conception of beneficence superseded old notions of charity, which had shaped the way the state, church, and dominant classes had responded to the needs of the poor on the Island.[45] Beneficence institutions became the locale where liberal and modernizing discourses in Puerto Rican society merged with social engineering projects destined to make economic and medically marginal individuals into productive members of society. It was in the *casas de amparo*, the asylums and hospitals, where the elite and the government experimented with their recipes for rehabilitation, vocational instruction, discipline, and job placements in order to, among other objectives, guarantee the reproduction of domestic workers and artisans who could be lost as a result of the abolition of slavery.

The Casa de Beneficencia in San Juan was inaugurated in 1844. From the specific original intent to serve as a "*casa de recogidas, amparo o reclusión*," the Casa was turned into a multi-purpose establishment by the time of its opening.[46] In the Casa, mental patients were committed, slaves and women awaiting trial were "deposited," prostitutes and indigent people were cloistered, and vocational instruction was provided to poor children to turn them into artisans and domestics. On several occasions, the Casa also housed and distributed so-called *emancipados* – slaves illegally shipped into Puerto Rico after the slave trade was abolished – to hacienda owners in need of agricultural or domestic workers.[47] In order to generate its operating revenue, the Casa relied on the profits made by interns who did laundry for the nearby hospitals and military garrisons. This type of arrangement – in which the institution generated its own revenue, women learned domestic service skills that would make them "useful" and productive in the future, and the Spanish bureaucracy's domestic service needs were supplied – was considered ideal by the colonial authorities. It is not surprising, then, to discover multiple petitions by elite city members requesting to house a domestic from the Casa in their residences in the period between 1844 and 1873. Doña Ana María Crosas de Vidal, for example, asked the Cabildo for an orphan girl from the Casa to be employed as a domestic. Crosas de Vidal promised "to take care of and provide for her as if she were one of our own family," and the Cabildo accepted her petition.[48]

The Casa de Beneficencia was not the only institution created in San Juan that combined the rhetoric of beneficence with the training, placement, and control of domestic workers during the decades of the so-called labor shortage prior to abolition. In 1859, for example, a group of ladies in San Juan requested permission to create a beneficence asylum to provide elementary and vocational education to poor children. In 1861, after an intense struggle between San Juan's bishop and the Island's governor regarding who would have jurisdiction over the institution, the Asilo de San Ildefonso opened its doors.[49] The Asilo, administered by a board of elite women and staffed by nuns and volunteers, provided elementary and religious education to poor girls. As in other beneficence institutions established in Puerto Rico at the time – in Ponce, for example, the Asilo de Damas was opened in 1866 and the Asilo Tricoche in 1868 – elite women organized institutions that guaranteed a reliable, accessible, and trained supply of domestic workers.[50]

Beneficence in San Juan, like in the rest of Puerto Rico, emerged partly as a response from the colonial authorities and the elite to the labor shortage problems they thought affected the Island starting at mid-century. In San Juan, beneficence establishments were oriented toward recruiting, training, and placing domestic workers. The city's elite women played an important role in creating and administering these institutions, which helped to guarantee their privileged lifestyle and kept them in charge within the public sphere of the domestic staff they supervised in the private sphere of the home. Although much remains to be researched and studied regarding the emergence of beneficence institutions during the second half of the nineteenth century, it is clear that their emergence concurs with the attempts by the dominant class to mitigate the repercussions of the so-called labor crisis on the Island and to prepare themselves for the eventual labor market changes caused by the impending abolition of slavery.

Domestic Workers and Their Conflicts with City Officials

The perception of a lack of domestic workers and their even greater shortage once slavery was abolished was not the only reason why colonial authorities and the elite attempted several labor and social control strategies. Although it is not easy to recover the responses and the activities of nineteenth-century domestics, there is evidence that they fought to improve their working conditions and the remuneration they received for their services. The colonial bureaucracy and the municipal policing authorities had constant clashes with domestics from the mid-nineteenth century on. These clashes were another reason why new mechanisms of labor and social control were tried in San Juan during the second half of the nineteenth century.

Of all the domestic workers in San Juan, it was the laundresses with whom city officials had the most problems and frictions. The reasons for these frictions were many. First, laundresses, for the most part, were black, mulatto, or parda. This, added to their access to visible public spaces (such as water fountains and plazas) and to private spaces (the homes and the bedrooms of their masters or clients), made laundresses highly suspicious in the eyes of city officials. It must be kept in mind that, until the 1850s, San Juan was a demographically black and colored city and that the Creole and Spanish elites were always fearful of a slave and colored revolt.[51] For public safety officials – all of them male – it must also have been uncomfortable and difficult to operate in predominantly female public spaces, such as a water fountain crowded with laundresses and their children.

The fears regarding the behavior of laundresses in San Juan were not merely abstract. At several junctures, city laundresses challenged colonial and police officials. The laundresses at the Hospital de la Caridad, for example, complained and organized work stoppages on several occasions to protest the lack of access to water and the poor working conditions at the hospital.[52] In one of their disputes, the laundresses requested from the Cabildo in 1842 permission to use the water cisterns at the military barracks in Ballajá. A Laundresses' Guild existed in 1876, although there is not much information regarding its activities or membership.[53]

Another incident that shows the repeated frictions between city officials and laundresses occurred in 1857 at Condado's water fountain. The *alcalde* (municipal judge) of Cangrejos – a small suburb outside San Juan – chastised several laundresses at the Condado fountain not only for the noise and bustle they were causing but also for encroaching on private property as they washed and dried their clothes. The *alcalde* argued that his job was

> To prevent, as it is expected by the government, all causes of scandal and disorder in the section of the territory to the right of the road leading to San Juan and in the fountain's surroundings, which were being committed by the mentioned laundresses who behaved without any respect to my authority or to the property. Since the laundresses were invading all the land, I asked them to leave the premises given that it was not political nor convenient that they stayed there, particularly when their presence there had led others, not interested in earning a precarious subsistence washing clothes but in creating a scandal and demoralizing the general public and those who traveled near the fountain with their improper and unruly behavior disregarding the provisos of the island's government.[54]

After a heated exchange, the laundresses replied that they did not recognize the *alcalde*'s jurisdiction because the water fountain was located in San Juan and not in Cangrejos. The dispute between the laundresses and the *alcalde* ended up on the governor's desk.

If the clashes with colonial officials did not enhance the laundresses' poor reputations, their status as women who earned a living working in the city's streets did not help them either. Their public persona excluded laundresses from the considerations and respect of men. Laundresses were not protected like other women who did not venture into the streets without an escort and otherwise stayed behind closed doors. The laundresses who worked outside their homes were frequent victims of physical, verbal, and sexual abuse. Not only were they targets of these kinds of abuse, but their condition as public women limited their attempts at vindicating themselves after the abuse was committed. The documentation from the civil courts provides ample evidence of the "presumption of guilt" in cases against women whose work forced them out to the streets escorted only, perhaps, by their children or by fellow domestics, or against women whose work forced them in and out of their clients' homes. Her status as a laundress, for example, was enough for the court to dismiss Juana de Dios González's lawsuit against Pasqual García. González was suing García, a soldier, for "seduction and rape" under the pretension and promise of marriage.[55] González claimed that García visited her house, promised to marry her, and had given her a child; therefore, he had to marry her. In these kinds of cases it was usually enough to know that a man had visited a woman's house for the court to rule in favor of the woman, forcing the man either to marry her or to provide her with an adequate dowry. García defended himself by arguing that it was well known that González and her mother were laundresses, and that it was logical to assume that his ins and outs of their house had nothing to do with romance, but with his laundry. The public nature of González's work had cost her her day in court.

Another laundress, Ysabel Avilés, faced a similar fate. She was sued by the soldier Don Julián Gutiérrez for having insulted him publicly. Gutiérrez argued that Avilés, who normally took care of his laundry, had entered his house and told him that "it was enough for him to be a soldier to be indecent, a scoundrel and a thief."[56] Avilés, in her defense, accepted having insulted Gutiérrez, but only after explaining that since he owed her money, she went to his house to collect her payment, only to be publicly insulted by Gutiérrez and violently thrown out of his house into the street. The judge accepted Gutiérrez's version of the story and asked Avilés for a public apology. Avilés did not accept the judge's decision.

Colonial and ecclesiastical authorities both complained about the lack of decorum and order present in San Juan's public plazas. As the nineteenth century advanced, uneasiness grew among the elite regarding the possible abolition of slavery and the potential challenges to the social and economic hierarchy it could unleash. Furthermore, by mid-century, San Juan was beginning to feel the first European influences regarding urban beautification, decoration, and hygiene in open public spaces.[57] This combination of factors led city officials to approve in the late 1860s the construction of a public washing area to move all the laundresses into Puerta de Tierra, an extramural barrio.[58] In Puerta de Tierra, the laundresses would be sufficiently near the city to be able to provide adequate laundry services and sufficiently far away not to be a public safety, hygiene, and beauty problem. Under the mask of beautification, decoration, and hygiene, Spanish officials and the city elite's hid their fears and insecurities regarding the dislocations and changes that the post-abolition world would bring to San Juan.

Conclusion

The access to and control of domestic work in San Juan played an important role during the 1840–73 period as shown by the multiple regulatory attempts and by the recurring conflicts between domestics and city officials. Although it did not play a leading role, domestic work did figure in the comments and strategies of the two sides in the abolition of slavery debate in Puerto Rico. Even when the Island's historiography has marginalized the study of domestic work in the Island, it is clear that these workers worried many in Puerto Rico during the second half of the nineteenth century.

I have identified three responses to the socioeconomic transformations occurring just prior to the abolition of slavery, particularly as it related to the supply of domestics. The first one was the attempt at increasing the social and spatial control over domestics using lists, registries, and punitive legislation, in response to what the government and the elite saw as a labor shortage. This was not a new pattern in the history of the Spanish colonial government's ongoing struggle to guarantee a cheap, docile, and abundant labor force in Puerto Rico. These attempts trace their ideological roots to the insular laws of the 1840s and the parallel

campaigns to eradicate vagrancy and common-law marriage on the Island.[59] Instead of visionary public policy solutions targeted at improving and modernizing the Island's economy, Spanish officials and their allies opted for a tough policing stand to face their perceived labor shortage problems.

The second response was a struggle to control the city's public and private spaces. This struggle had been going on in San Juan, if in a less intense manner since the beginning of the nineteenth century. The city elites' policies effectively pushed significant numbers of people of color (the majority of them women) out of the city and into the surrounding extramural barrios.[60] The idea of the public washing area in Puerta de Tierra, although it was never constructed, shows the way in which San Juan's upper classes wished to reconfigure the city's social, economic, and racial space. In terms of private spaces, more research is still needed regarding the struggles for control and distance in these spaces. The renegotiations between domestics and their masters or employers that occurred as abolition got nearer and the uncertainty grew regarding the rules that would apply in the post-slavery world await the careful scrutiny of future Puerto Rican historians.

The third response was provided through the creation of beneficence institutions. The advocates of beneficence pointed to the intellectual and public policy currents in Europe to rally support for the establishment of beneficence institutions. The ironic twist of this influence is that the elite still needed domestic work to carry out its modernizing agenda. Domestics guaranteed the free time that elite and the new professional classes needed to dedicate themselves to their modernizing social, economic, and cultural projects. Public and semi-private beneficence was a mechanism by which new forms of social control, vigilance, job placement, rehabilitation, and vocational and religious training were experimented with.

A significant part of this essay has focused on analyzing some of the reactions of San Juan's elite to the changes in the mid-nineteenth-century labor market. Unfortunately, I have not been able to document with equal precision the domestics' reactions to the transformations mentioned above. Logically, the mere existence of all the registries and regulations indicates that there was some resistance to doing domestic work under the conditions dictated by the upper classes. Perhaps other sources – diaries, letters, or court testimonies – will allow the exploration of domestic workers' quotidian engagement or distancing from this process. If the experiences of the laundresses are an indicator, one can argue that the Spanish authorities and the elite faced groups of women intent on defining, to the best of their abilities and resources, the terms of their working conditions.

Another element that could shed some light on the development of domestic work in Puerto Rico during the second half of the nineteenth century would be the experience of other Caribbean and Latin American urban centers. In Barbados, for example, Pedro Welch has shown how the experiences with urban slaves in Bridgetown prepared the governmental and commercial elite to consolidate control mechanisms for the period after abolition. Among the mechanisms they instituted were the control and regulation of emigration and the creation of a city police corps to monitor and punish the new freedmen and women.[61] The attempts to regulate post-slavery domestic work in San Juan with mechanisms from the pre-1873 world indicate that in Puerto Rico the colonial authorities also learned from their experiences with the mobility and resistance of urban slaves and *libertos*. It is also likely that the authorities in Puerto Rico were acquainted with the various mechanisms of social and labor control employed in the British and French Caribbean possessions after slavery was abolished in 1833 and 1848 respectively. The experiences in other urban areas of Puerto Rico, such as Ponce, Mayagüez, and Arecibo, could help to corroborate this hypothesis.

San Juan's domestics, many of them urban female slaves, were part of the cast of characters that worried colonial officials, elite members, and those debating the wisdom of abolition. This essay has attempted to highlight the importance of domestic service to the urban economy of San Juan at a time of transition from slave labor to so-called "free" labor. I have also analyzed how domestic service was linked to other develop-

ments in San Juan such as the institutionalization of public and semi-private beneficence establishments. Many questions emerge from the evidence presented here regarding San Juan, and they merit further study. What can be learned from the evidence of other urban centers in Puerto Rico? How do they compare with San Juan's experiences? Why have domestic labor and urban slavery attracted so little attention in Puerto Rican historiography? How can the history of abolition and slavery in Puerto Rico begin to be rewritten considering the experiences of urban centers? I hope that this study stimulates further historical research regarding domestic work and its connections with the significant socioeconomic transformations of Puerto Rico, such as the abolition of slavery.

NOTES

Abbreviations

AGPR	Archivo General de Puerto Rico
AHD	Archivo Histórico Diocesano
AHN	Archivo Histórico Nacional
C	Caja
CP	Fondo Colecciones Particulares
E	Expediente
f	folio
FAT	Fondo Audiencia Territorial
FGEPR	Fondo Gobernadores Españoles
FMSJ	Fondo Municipal San Juan
FOP	Fondo Obras Públicas
FPN	Fondo Protocolos Notariales
L	Legajo
P	Pieza/Parte
S	Serie
Se	Sección
v	vuelto

This article was originally published as "'¿Quien Trabajará?' Trabajo doméstico, esclavitud urbana y abolición en San Juan en el siglo XIX", in the journal *Revista de Ciencias Sociales*, and is translated with their permission.

The author wishes to thank Emilio Kourí, Luis Figueroa, Eileen Findlay, Jorge Duany, Pedro

San Miguel, and Joan Krizack for their helpful commentaries and suggestions.

1 See, among others, Centro de Investigaciones Históricas, *El proceso abolicionista en Puerto Rico: Documentos para su estudio*, 2 vols. (San Juan: Instituto de Cultura Puertorriqueña, 1974–78); José Curet, "About Slavery and the Order of Things: Puerto Rico, 1845–1873," in *Between Slavery and Free Labor: The Spanish Speaking Caribbean in the Nineteenth Century*, ed. Manuel Moreno Fraginals, Frank Moya Pons, and Stanley L. Engerman (Baltimore: Johns Hopkins University Press, 1985), 117–40; Luis M. Diaz Soler, *Historia de la esclavitud en Puerto Rico*, 3d ed. (Río Piedras: Editorial Universitaria, 1981); Arturo Morales Carrión, *Auge y decadencia de la trata negrera en Puerto Rico (1820–1860)* (San Juan: Centro de Estudios Avanzados de Puerto Rico y el Caribe & Instituto de Cultura Puertorriqueña, 1978); Benjamin Nistal-Moret, "Problems in the Social Structure of Slavery in Puerto Rico During the Process of Abolition, 1872," in Moreno Fraginals, Moya Pons, and Engerman, *Between Slavery and Free Labor*, 141–57; and Andrés Ramos Mattei, *La hacienda azucarera: Su crecimiento y crisis en Puerto Rico (siglo xix)* (San Juan: Centro de Estudios de la Realidad Puertorriqueña [CEREP], 1981).

2 See Curet, "About Slavery"; Andres Ramos Mattei, ed. *Azucar y esclavitud* (Rio Piedras: Editorial Universitaria, 1982); and Luis Figueroa, "Facing Freedom: The Transition from Slavery to Free Labor in Guayama. Puerto Rico, 1860–1898" (Ph.D. diss., University of Wisconsin–Madison, 1991).

3 This literature is quite extensive. See, among others, Robin Blackburn, *The Overthrow of Colonial Slavery, 1776–1848* (London: Verso Books, 1988); Arthur F. Corwin, *Spain and the Abolition of Slavery in Cuba, 1817–1886* (Austin: University of Texas Press, 1967); David Brion Davis, *The Problem of Slavery in the Age of Revolution, 1770–1823* (Ithaca: Cornell University Press, 1975); Seymour Drescher, *Capitalism and Slavery: British Mobilization in Comparative Perspective* (New York: Oxford University Press, 1986); William A. Green, *British Slave Emancipation: The Sugar Colonies and the Great Experiment, 1830–1865* (Oxford: Oxford University Press, 1976); Thomas C. Holt, *The Problem of*

Freedom: Race, Labour and Politics in Jamaica and Britain, 1832–1938 (Baltimore: Johns Hopkins University Press, 1992); Moreno Fraginals, Moya Pons, and Engerman, *Between Slavery and Free Labor;* Rebecca Scott, *Slave Emancipation in Cuba: The Transition to Free Labor, 1860–1899* (Princeton: Princeton University Press, 1985); "Comparing Emancipations: A Review Essay," *Journal of Social History* 20, no. 3 (1987): 565–83; "Exploring the Meaning of Freedom: Postemancipation Societies in Comparative Perspective," *Hispanic American Historical Review* 68, no. 3 (1988): 407–28; Dale W. Tomich, *Slavery in the Circuit of Sugar: Martinique and the World Economy* (Baltimore: Johns Hopkins University Press. 1990); and Pedro L. Welch, "Notes from the Bridgetown Underground: Control and Protest in Post-Emancipation Barbados," paper presented at the 28th Annual Meeting of the Society of Caribbean Historians, Bridgetown, Barbados, April 17, 1996.

4 See, for example, Elsa Chaney and May G. Castro, eds., *Muchachas No More: Household Workers in Latin America and the Caribbean* (Philadelphia: Temple University Press, 1989); Sandra L. Graham, *House and Street: The Domestic World of Servants and Masters in Nineteenth-Century Rio de Janeiro* (Cambridge: Cambridge University Press, 1988); Mary Romero, *Maid in the USA* (New York: Routledge, 1992); and Heidi Tisman, "The Indispensable Services of Sisters: Considering Domestic Service in Latin America and the Caribbean," *Journal of Women's History* 4, no. 1 (1992): 37–59.

5 Tera Hunter, "Household Workers in the Making: Afro-American Women in Atlanta and the New South, 1861 to 1921" (Ph.D. diss., Yale University, 1990); Elizabeth Kuznesof, "A History of Domestic Service in Spanish America, 1492–1980," in Chaney and Castro, *Muchachas No More*, 17–36; and Tisman, "The Indispensable Services."

6 Mariano Negrón Portillo and Raúl Mayo Santana, *La esclavitud urbana en San Juan: Estudio del Registro de Jornaleros de Esclavos de 1872* (Rio Piedras: Ediciones Huracán, 1992), 80–81.

7 Rubén Carbonell Fernández, "Las compra-ventas de esclavos en San Juan, 1817–1873" (M.A. thesis, Department of History, University of Puerto Rico-Río Piedras); Félix V. Matos

Rodríguez, "Street Vendors, Shop-Owners and Domestics: Some Aspects of Women's Economic Roles in 19th Century San Juan, Puerto Rico," in *Engendering History: Caribbean Women in Historical Perspective*, ed. Verene Shepherd, Bridget Brereton, and Barbara Bailey (Kingston: Ian Randle Publishers, 1995), 176–96; Negrón Portillo and Mayo Santana, *La esclavitud urbana*; and Pedro L. Welch, "The Urban Context of the Slave Plantation System: Bridgetown, Barbados, 1680–1834" (Ph.D. diss., University of the West Indies, 1994).

8 Luis Aponte-Parés, "Casas y Bohios: Territorial Development and Urban Growth in XIXth Century Puerto Rico" (Ph.D. diss., Columbia University, 1990), 291–99; and Aníbal Sepúlveda Rivera, *San Juan: Historia ilustrada de su desarollo urbano, 1508–1898* (San Juan: Carimar, 1989), 222–24.

9 Centro de Investigaciones Históricas, *El proceso*, 2d vol., 181–82.

10 Aixa Merino Falú, "El Gremio de Lavanderas de Puerta de Tierra," in *Historias vivas: Historiografía puertorriqueña contemporánea*, ed. Antonio Gaztambide Géigel and Silvia Alvarez Curbelo (San Juan: Asociación Puertorriqueña de Historiadores & Editorial Postdata), 74–79.

11 Félix V. Matos Rodríguez, "Economy, Society and Urban Life: Women in Nineteenth Century San Juan, Puerto Rico (1820–1870)" (Ph.D. diss., Columbia University, 1994), 32; 96–97.

12 Negrón Portillo and Mayo Santana, *La esclavitud urbana*, 9–14.

13 The 1846 census is the first one providing the occupation or employment of women in San Juan. The 1846 data come from three out of the four quarters that made up the city of San Juan then. AGPR, FMSJ, Censos San Juan (Santa Barbara, Santo Domingo and San Francisco barrios), 1846.

14 Adolfo De Hostos, *Historia de San Juan, cuidad murada* (San Juan: Instituto de Cultura Puertorriqueña, 1983), 21.

15 Matos Rodríguez, "Economy, Society," 105.

16 *Pardo/a* usually refers to light-skinned mulattos.

17 AGPR, FMSJ, Censos San Juan, 1846.

18 I have included as "heads of households" those individuals listed in the 1846 censuses as *jefe*

(head) or *inquilino* (tenant). The data come from AGPR, FMSJ, Censos San Juan, 1846.

19 Negrón Portillo and Mayo Santana, *La esclavitud urbana*, 114–17.

20 Ibid., 81–89.

21 Díaz Soler, *Historia*, 158–61.

22 De Hostos, *Historia de San Juan*, 477–79.

23 Sepúlveda Rivera, *San Juan*, 288–90.

24 An example of this type of accusation can be found in the testament of Don Patricio Fogarty. Fogarty accused his *mulata* cook of poisoning his food. AGPR, FPN, San Juan, José María León de Urbina, February 21, 1827, C-442, 84f-85v.

25 Carbonell Fernández, "Las compra-ventas," 29–32.

26 Negrón Portillo and Mayo Santana, *La esclavitud urbana*, 97.

27 Centro de Investigaciones Históricas, *El proceso*, 2d vol., 437. This and all subsequent direct block citations have been translated by the author. The discrepancy in the numbers appears in the original document.

28 Segundo Ruiz Belvis, José J. Acosta, and Francisco M. Quiñones, *Proyecto para la abolición de la esclavitud*, 2d ed. (Río Piedras: Editorial Edil, 1978), 70.

29 Díaz Soler, *Historia*, 278–79.

30 Ruiz Belvis, *Proyecto*, 70–71.

31 Fernando Picó, *Historia general de Puerto Rico*, 2d ed. (Río Piedras: Ediciones Huracán, 1986), 170.

32 Francisco Scarano, "Labor and Society in the Nineteenth Century," in *The Modern Caribbean*, ed. Franklin Knight and Colin Palmer (Chapel Hill: University of North Carolina Press, 1989), 51–84.

33 Matos Rodríguez, "Economy, Society," 88–129.

34 Maria Odila Silva Dias, *Power and Everyday Life: The Lives of Working Women in 19th Century Brazil* (New Brunswick, NJ: Rutgers University Press, 1995).

35 AGPR, FGEPR, Censo y Riqueza, 1858, C-16.

36 AGPR, FMSJ, Actas del Cabildo, C-24, 19 de mayo de 1864, 93f-v.

37 "Reglamento que ha de observarse en la locación del trabajo personal para el servicio doméstico," Chapter 5, Article 6. AGPR, FGEPR, S-Municipios, C-480, June 8, 1964.

38 Gómez Acevedo, *Organizatión y reglamentación*, 117–23.

39 AGPR, FMSJ, L-24G, E-941, April 3, 1876.

40 AHN, Se-Ultramar, Serie-Gobierno de Puerto Rico, L-5113, E-60, September 5, 1879.

41 De Hostos, *Historia de San Juan*, 81.

42 Article 4, AGPR, FMSJ, L-24G, E-941, April 3, 1876.

43 Article 1, AGPR, FMSJ, L-24G, E-941, April 3, 1876.

44 Figueroa, "Facing Freedom," 359–64.

45 Teresita Martínez Vergne, "The Liberal Concept of Charity: Beneficencia Applied to Puerto Rico, 1821–1868," in *The Middle Period in Latin America: Values and Attitudes in the 17th-19th Centuries*, ed. Mark d. Szuchman (Boulder, CO: Lynne Rienner, 1989), 167–84.

46 Matos Rodríguez, "Economy, Society," 272–73.

47 Teresita Martínez Vergne, "The Allocation of Liberated African Labour Through the Casa de Beneficencia – San Juan, Puerto Rico, 1859–1864," *Slavery and Abolition* 12:3 (1991): 200–216.

48 AGPR, FMSJ, Actas del Cabildo, C-24, December 23, 1864, 216v.

49 Matos Rodríguez, "Economy, Society," 295–97.

50 Ramón Marín, *Las fiestas populares de Ponce*, 1875 reprint (Río Piedras: Editorial de la Universidad de Puerto Rico, 1994), 227–28.

51 Matos Rodríguez, "Economy, Society," 102–07.

52 See, for example, AGPR, FMSJ, Actas del Cabildo, May 4, 1842, 88v, and June 30, 1842, 122f.

53 Merino Falú, "El Gremio de Lavanderas", 74.

54 The *alcalde*'s version is found in AGPR, FOP, Obras Municipales, L-62LL, E-13, C-236, July 14, 1857. Unfortunately, the record does not contain the governor's decision regarding the controversy. It is interesting that the chief naval officer of the Island testified in favor of the laundresses, arguing that the property in question was within his jurisdiction.

55 AGPR, FMSJ, L-73E, (P.I.), E-3, December 22, 1822.

56 AGPR, FMSJ, L-73E, (P.I.), E-12, October 10, 1841.

57 Ángel G. Quintero Rivera, *Patricios y plebeyos. Burgueses, hacendados, artesanos y obreros (Las relaciones de clase en el Puerto Rico de cambio de siglo)* (Río Piedras: Ediciones Huracán, 1988), 23–98; and Sepúlveda Rivera, *San Juan*, 158–91.

58 The public facility was never constructed, although discussion regarding its possible construction lasted into the 1880s. See AGPR, FOP, Obras Municipales, L-62LL, E-15, C-326.

59 Picó, *Historia*, 173–74. Also, Antonia Rivera Rivera, "El problema de la vagancia en el Puerto Rico del siglo XIX," *Exegesis* 5, no. 14 (1992): 12–19.

60 Matos Rodríguez, "Economy, Society," 130–32.

61 Welch, "Notes from the Underground," 20–21.

7

A Central American Genocide: Rubber, Slavery, Nationalism, and the Destruction of the Guatusos-Malekus

Marc Edelman

Hulero [rubber tapper]. – A person who extracts rubber. Those involved in this lucrative industry in the North of the country are nearly all Nicaraguans and for a long time they were the terror of the poor Guatuso Indians, whom they killed without pity or hunted to sell as slaves in the neighboring Republic.

Carlos Gagini, *Diccionario de costarriqueñismos* (1919:159–60).

In 1919, when Carlos Gagini penned this two-sentence definition of *hulero* for a dictionary of "Costa Rican-isms," he matter of factly specified murderousness, slaving, terrorism, and Nicaraguan nationality as intrinsic characteristics of rubber tappers. Few other entries in Gagini's compilation reveal so tellingly a key implicit objective of the country lexicons that Central American intellectuals (for example, Membreño 1982 [1895]) began to publish in the late nineteenth century: the specification, through Spanish dialectology, of a still emergent national identity vis-à-vis neighbors who – until recently – had not been clearly distinct Others but simply fellow subjects first of one or another province of the Spanish Captaincy General of Guatemala and later, briefly, of the Mexican Empire (1821–23) and the independent Central American Federation (1823–38). And none of the other generally concise entries in Gagini's dictionary hints so directly at the links between processes of com-

modity creation, physical and cultural death, and the construction of nations.

This essay examines the encounter between the Guatuso-Maleku indigenous people and tapper-slavers intent on appropriating a new geographical space in order to meet international demand for rubber and local demand for human slaves (more than three centuries after the abolition of Indian slavery in Spain's colonies and five decades after the abolition of all slavery in independent Central America). The main source it employs is a report by the German-born Bishop of Costa Rica, Bernardo Augusto Thiel, on an 1882 mission to "the territory of the Guatusos" in the forests south of Lake Nicaragua. It also explores the ways in which the experience of commodification of rubber and then of human beings was narrated and reinterpreted as part of an emerging ideology of Costa Rican distinctiveness and nationalism. Specifically, the essay argues that, first, the Costa Rican elite's demonization of Nicaragua was a key aspect in the formation of national identity and that border disputes between the two countries became opportunities for sharpening previously weak or non-existent national distinctions. Second, that attempts to consolidate remote and contested border regions – and to incorporate indigenous peoples beyond the control of the state – imbued nationalist ideology and practice with the very conquest-oriented and proselytizing rhetoric and procedures which post-independence elites claimed to reject as part of the hated colonial heritage. Third, that even for an elite which stressed "European-ness" as a defining Costa Rican characteristic vis-à-vis "barbaric" non-white Others, unassimilated Indians could serve – in the absence of a historical "imagined community" – to elaborate "guiding fictions of pre-existing peoplehood and national destiny."[1] Finally, and fourth, that in late nineteenth-century Central America, "civilizing" projects involved considerable collaboration and ideological agreement between the modernizing, secular Liberals usually associated with nation buillding and the proclerical Conservatives whose evangelizing (and ethnographic) expeditions played a significant part in articulating legitimating narratives for emerging states.

Bishop Thiel's crusade to the Guatusos-Malekus was a kind of peculiar hybrid: part colonial-style evangelizing mission, with friars planting giant crucifixes in desolate jungle clearings (Thiel 1882f); part scientific ethnological expedition, with the Bishop and his party recording detailed observations about aboriginal lifeways and language, unearthing burials, and interrogating leery natives about their experiences; and part a horrifying encounter with genocide and exploitation that, like so much of Latin American history, nonetheless unfolded with tragicomic novelistic episodes, such as when Nicaraguan soldiers took the Bishop himself prisoner, believing him to be a Costa Rican general impersonating a high Church official in order to seize disputed territory along the border.[2]

Within two decades of Charles Goodyear's 1839 discovery of how to "vulcanize" latex, making a sticky or brittle substance malleable and elastic, world demand for rubber soared. By the 1860s, vulcanized natural rubber had become essential for machine gaskets, belts, tubes, and railway car bumpers and, soon after, for wire insulation and bicycle and then automobile tires (Dean 1987:9; Schultes 1993:481–3). Central America was one of the first regions that responded to the growing demand. Because of its proximity to U.S. industries and the abundance of rubber trees throughout its largely forested terrain, budding entrepreneurs – large and small – began to extract and export latex and to explore and claim concessions in promising pieces of virgin forest.

As in the Amazon boom (Barham and Coomes 1994a, 1994b; Coomes and Barham 1994), a wide variety of tenure systems and relations of production (or extraction) characterized the Central American rubber sector.[3] In Guatuso-Maleku territory, however, as elsewhere along the Costa Rican–Nicaraguan border, the rubber tappers were primarily non-Indians who received supplies on credit from merchant-rubber exporters (*habilitadores*), many of them North American (Belt 1874:4, 32–33; Dozier 1985:116). The tappers generally worked in groups of two to four on expeditions that lasted one to three months. Paul Lévy, a French traveller who published a detailed report on the Nicaraguan economy in 1873, noted dryly that "the huleros, because of the extraordinarily unsettled lives they lead, in the middle of forests full of harmful animals, form an especially active part of the population, entrepreneurial and hardened in their work" (1873:480–1).

The slaving that accompanied the rubber boom in Guatuso-Maleku territory did not, in contrast to the situation in parts of the Amazon (Muratorio 1991; Taussig 1987), involve enslavement of indigenous tappers. Instead, "entrepreneurial" huleros kidnapped Guatuso women and children for sale as household servants and forced the men to serve as unpaid bearers in the forest.

Despite the Central Americans' many attempts to insert themselves in the world rubber economy, the region remained a minor player. Nicaragua, by far the largest exporter, earned over one-third of its foreign exchange from rubber by the mid-1870s, but this was more a reflection of the weakness of other sectors than of the dynamism of rubber; the country never came close to exporting one million dollars worth of rubber in a year (Schoonover 1991: Table 71). In part this was simply a matter of scale: All the Central American countries together were roughly three-quarters the size of Texas, while the Amazon basin occupied a large proportion of the South American continent. Species of the genus *Hevea* – especially *Hevea brasiliensis*, the source of the highest quality "Pará rubber" (Schultes 1993:479–80) and of the overwhelming bulk of exports from Brazil, by far the largest producer – were native only to the central and southern Amazon (Dean 1987:2–3, 38). Central American production derived exclusively from species of the genus *Castilla*, colloquially known as *caucho*, and commanded lower prices.[4] Until 1858, when U.S. companies sent experts to evaluate Central American rubber species and Nicaragua made its first shipment of latex to New York, most specialists thought the *Castilla* varieties useless, as some indeed were (Dozier 1985:116; Pittier 1910:265). In contrast to *Hevea*, bleeding latex from *Castilla* species generally killed the trees.[5]

The San Juan River, the most promising rubber zone in Central America, flowed from Lake Nicaragua to the Atlantic. Because only a thin strip of land separated the lake from the Pacific, the San Juan became a key artery for trans-isthmian transport early in the colonial period and a major focus of geopolitical contention, first between England and Spain, later between England and Nicaragua, and then between Nicaragua and Costa Rica (Obregón Quesada 1993; Sibaja Chacón 1974).[6] During the California gold rush, thousands of aspiring miners from the eastern United States travelled the San Juan route, then the fastest way to reach San Francisco. By the late nineteenth century, it was widely believed that the Río San Juan would be the site of a Central American canal. Prior to the start of construction on the Atlantic railroad in the 1880s, northeastern Costa Rican rivers, especially the Sarapiquí and San Carlos, were also of great interest to those seeking a route to transport coffee to the Caribbean coast (González 1976). The Guatuso-Maleku Indians had the poor fortune to live very close to all of this activity, along the Río Frío, a smaller river system that flows north from the volcanic cordillera in Costa Rica and meets the San Juan right as it leaves Lake Nicaragua (see map in Figure 7.1).

The Guatuso-Maleku Indigenous People

On a clear day in 1780, Father Antonio Jáuregui and don José Ynsarraundiaga climbed to the top of the volcano near the colonial Costa Rican capital of Cartago. Pointing their telescope to the north, they endeavored to see if they could "discover the place where the Guatuso Indians live":

> And observing from the highest point of this volcano [3,432 meters], they were able to see and discover toward the North some immense plains [covered with] forests and three large rivers which, originating in different districts, joined in the middle of the plain; and although they saw both the North [Atlantic] and South [Pacific] seas, they were unable to see smoke or gardens, which is what they had desired (de la Fuente 1938 [1785]:546).

Two interrelated concerns apparently prompted Jáuregui and Ynsarraundiaga to ascend the volcano: a fervent yearning to "discover," "conquer" and "settle" pagan Indians; and a growing number of reports over the preceding three decades that these Indians lived in the jungles east of the continental divide and south of the Río San Juan, specifically on the "plains of Guatusa" (a name which means agouti [*Dasyprocta punctata*], an animal similar to, but larger than the guinea pig). Most of these accounts probably concerned indigenous groups other than the people today known as Guatusos-Malekus (Betancourt and Constenla 1981:20; Conzemius 1930:94).[7] But two years before Jáuregui and Ynsarraundiaga ascended the volcano, a Spanish priest, Tomás López, paddled up the Río Frío in the company of natives from Orosí, a volcano just south of Lake Nicaragua, and Ometepe, an island in the Lake. As soon as these Indians, from areas near the Frío basin, spotted Guatuso rafts on the riverbanks, they "were filled with fear" and adamantly refused to proceed any further, thus aborting the expedition (de la Fuente 1938 [1785]:547).

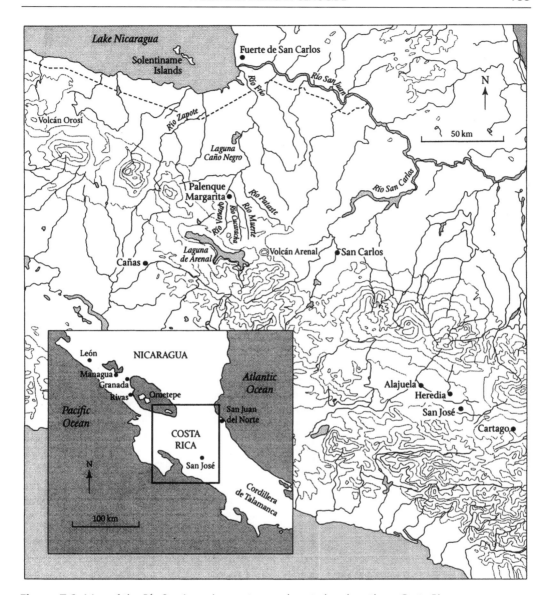

Figure 7.1. Map of the Río San Juan river system and central and northern Costa Rica

In 1783, Padre López joined another effort to find the Guatusos, this time under the direction of the Bishop of Nicaragua and Costa Rica, don Estéban Lorenzo de Tristán. When the missionaries had advanced up the Río Frío, and after the zealous López had gone on with just a servant and an "interpreter" from Solentiname, the Indians attacked "with many arrows." Tristán and his group, including several wounded, fled to Granada, assuming López to be dead, since they had last seen him marching alone into the forest, crucifix in hand, in the midst of the Guatuso attack and "he has not come out and there has been no more news of him" (de la Fuente 1938 [1785]:547; see also Betancourt and Costenla 1981:30–32; Thiel 1927:110).

In 1850, Trinidad Salazar, the Commander of the Fort of San Carlos, situated where the Río San Juan leaves Lake Nicaragua, tried to ascend the Río Frío into Guatuso territory. On the sixth day, a large group of Indians attacked his unit, severely wounding him and provoking a rapid retreat. A few months later, speaking with U.S. diplomat Ephraim Squier, "he gave . . . a glowing account of the beauty of the stream [Río Frío], and the fertility and luxuriance of its shores." He lamented "that a stream of this size, and the wide extent of country around it, are wholly unknown, [which] would seem to show how much remains to be discovered in Central America" (Squier 1852:117).

The Río Frío remained "wholly unknown," of course, largely because of its inhabitants' fierce determination to repel outsiders. Six years after Salazar's defeat at the hands of the Guatusos, nineteen Costa Rican troops under the command of Pío Alvarado travelled down the Río Frío in an effort to reach the San Juan river and reconnoiter the Fort of San Carlos, which had been captured by William Walker's pro-slavery filibusters during their invasion of Central America. When Alvarado's soldiers had almost reached the mouth of the River, he sent twelve men on ahead and

> was suddenly attacked by a band of Indians. At a distance of some 15 paces, a savage bellow was heard, similar to the roar of a howler monkey, and immediately came a veritable rain of arrows. The attackers formed a phalanx of some 80 men, who all appeared young and who had at their head a chief who wore a feathered ornament. . . . As soon as they felt themselves wounded by the Indians' arrows, two of Pío's most valiant companions threw themselves on the Indians with their machetes and killed several, causing the rest to flee. . . . The fear of a second attack gave those in the expedition so much speed that they did not stop day or night, which was quite difficult, since Pío himself was ill with fever and the two men wounded by the Indians' arrows had to be carried (von Frantzius 1893 [1862]:34).[8]

Squier's description of the Guatusos in 1850 as "wholly unknown" was echoed by Bishop Thiel more than three decades later as he prepared his own expedition to Christianize the Indians.[9] Nonetheless, despite abundant myths about "light-skinned, red-haired" Indians of "enormous strength" and valiant woman warriors "as white as Englishwomen" (Gabb 1875:484; Gagini 1917:81; Lothrop 1926:17), by the 1870s a certain amount was known about the Guatusos' problems with the huleros. In 1874, for example, British mining engineer and naturalist Thomas Belt, who travelled several times down the San Juan River, described "the wild Indians of the Rio Frio" (1874:32) with that strange combination of biologized racism, empiricist detachment, and empathic indignation so typical of nineteenth-century European and North American scientists in Latin America:

> [The] most fabulous stories have been told about the Rio Frio and its inhabitants; stories of great cities, golden ornaments, and light-haired people. . . . They are called Guatuses [sic], and have been said to have red or light-coloured hair and European features . . . ; but, unfortunately for these speculations, some children, and even adults, have been captured and brought down the river by the Ulleros [sic], and all these have the usual features and coarse black hair of the Indians. One little child that Dr. Seemann and I saw at San Carlos, in 1870, had a few brownish hairs amongst the great mass of black ones; but this character may be found amongst many of the indigenes, and may result from a very slight admixture of foreign blood. I have seen altogether five children from the Rio Frio, and a boy about sixteen years of age, and they had all the common Indian features and hair; though it struck me that they appeared rather more intelligent than the generality of Indians (1874:37–38).

Belt added that some of the "more adventurous" huleros, "ascended the Rio Frio, and being well provided with firearms, which they mercilessly used, they were able to defy the poor Indians, armed only with spears and bows and arrows, and to drive them back into the woods. . . . The Ulleros," he continued,

> rush on shore and seize everything that the poor fugitives have left behind them; and in some cases the latter have not been able to carry off their children, and these have been

brought down in triumph to San Carlos. The excuse for stealing the children is that they may be baptized and made Christians (1874:39–40).[10]

A few years later, William Gabb, a U.S. geologist who spent nearly two years prospecting in the southeastern region of Talamanca, published a study of indigenous groups in Costa Rica. While he never actually visited the Guatusos, he did go to considerable effort to interview those who had. Denouncing the "bad treatment, robbery and massacre" visited on the Indians, he also referred to "a [Guatuso] boy, now dead, [who] lived for a while in Alajuela [Costa Rica]." Alajuela residents, describing the boy as "sullen," noted that when asked "the names in his language of things with which he was familiar, such as plantain or banana, he always remained silent, and neither coaxing nor threats could extort a word" (Gabb 1875:485).

Before he departed on his 1882 mission to the Guatusos, Bishop Thiel was undoubtedly aware of Gabb's and others' accounts of the unfolding tragedy along the Río Frío and its tributaries, if only because his friend, lawyer León Fernández, had prepared a Spanish translation of Gabb's work for his multivolume anthology of Costa Rican historical documents, the first tome of which appeared in 1881. In a preface to Gabb's essay, Fernández painted a grim picture of the trade in Guatuso slaves and estimated that "today nearly three hundred of these Indians exist, sold in different towns of Nicaragua." He went on to assert that "the traffic in slaves would have continued if it had not been for the efforts and activity of our philanthropic and enlightened bishop of this diocese, don Bernardo Agusto [sic] Thiel" (in Gabb 1883 [1875]:306–7).

Even as late as 1882, however, after more than a decade of rubber tapper forays, the Guatusos-Malekus seemed to have been in only sporadic contact with outsiders. Bishop Thiel, who took ethnographic description with the seriousness befitting a German-trained intellectual of his time, noted that their only metal tools appear to have been "some broken iron machetes, which the Indians had probably stolen from the huleros and, in order that two could use them, had split in two" (1882f).[11] The rest of their material cul-

ture was traditional and indigenous: large nets, baskets, gourd and ceramic vessels, and hammocks, all made by women; wooden machetes and digging sticks; various kinds of medicinal plants; and huge dwellings or *palenques* with well-constructed thatched roofs. Various sources (for example, von Frantzius 1893 [1862]:33) indicate that they used plantain fibers dipped in raw latex as torches or candles. They had sizable plantations of cassava, maize, cacao, and sugarcane, some cultivated cotton and tobacco (which participants in the 1882 mission smoked "out of curiosity"), and "immense" groves of plantains, from which they brewed fermented *chicha* in three-foot tall ceramic vessels (Thiel 1882d, 1882f).

Thiel's account of the Guatusos was like many other contemporary depictions of "primitives" in its assumption that they suffered lives of arduous, unrewarding toil. Describing trees over one yard thick that Guatusos had felled with "thousands of machete blows," he declared, "It is incredible the amount that these unhappy souls work!" (1882f). At the same time, Thiel's narrative hints at what may have been something of an "original affluent society," with plentiful food and abundant leisure (cf. M. Sahlins 1972:1–39).[12] "The Indians," he reported, "work the plantain groves in common, in groups of 40 to 50 individuals. They divide in two groups which alternate, [each] always working two hours and [then] resting another two" (1882f).

Despite Thiel's imaginative attribution of unvarying work shifts to the natives, life in Guatuso territory was probably not as "hard" or "unhappy" as the Bishop portrayed it – at least prior to the arrival of the rubber tappers. Game and fish were undoubtedly abundant. And plantains require so little attention that in Nicaragua and in nearby areas of Costa Rica around this time elites considered them (and cassava) the prototypical crop of lazy "vagrants" and even contemplated banning their cultivation (Barahona 1981:379; Belt 1874:40; Valverde 1907:20).[13]

Whether or not Thiel's ethnology is reliable in all its details, his descriptions, as well as more recent scholarship (Costenla 1993:4; Fonseca and Cooke 1993:221; Johnson 1963:55–56), suggest that Guatuso-Maleku culture shared many features with traditional indigenous groups of lowland South America.[14] They were almost certainly matrilocal (Thiel 1927:140), which would help account for their ability to mobilize large defense teams composed of related males from different villages. And, like other relatively isolated Amerindian populations, they had little or no immunity to the diseases to which they were exposed after rubber tappers and then missionaries invaded their territory.

The Crusade of His Most Illustrious Lordship, Bernardo Augusto, Bishop of Costa-Rica

Who was the "philanthropic and enlightened bishop" who, according to León Fernández, ended the traffic in Guatuso slaves? Born in the Rhineland and educated in a rigorous German gymnasium, Bernardo Augusto Thiel (1850–1901) joined the Order of St. Lazarus just in time to be banished from Germany in Bismarck's 1873 Kulturkampf campaign against the Catholic Church. The following year he received a post in Ecuador, but after three years an anti-clerical Liberal revolution there forced him to leave for Costa Rica, where he was named bishop in 1880 (Sanabria 1941:14–40). Twice exiled before he was thirty (he would be expelled yet again, from Costa Rica, in 1884, returning two years later), Thiel apparently developed an especially strong loathing for "masonry and Liberalism," which fueled an intense missionary zeal (Sanabria 1941:26).

Shortly after his installation as bishop, Thiel began a series of expeditions to outlying regions of Costa Rica where unassimilated indigenous peoples still lived (Sanabria 1941:445–51). His successes on these first crusades may have made him overconfident about his capacity as a missionary, just as his fluency in various European languages and his familiarity with the few existing indigenous Costa Rican lexicons may have led him to overestimate his ability to speak Guatuso and other native languages. On a January 1882 excursion to southern Costa Rica, as he reported without a hint of irony or self-consciousness, he encountered two Viceita (Talamanca) Indians, and greeted them "in their own tongue," asking

them where they were from and what they were doing. One Viceita answered the Bishop's questions in Spanish. The other responded, "*yo no hablar inglés*" (Thiel 1882n:2).

Thiel had learned about the precarious situation of the Guatusos from the work of Gabb and Fernández, as well as from the Quesada family, whose properties bordered the Indians' territory (Betancourt and Constenla 1981: 21).[15] The inspiration for his first expedition to the Guatusos derived not only from the success of his previous missions to southern Costa Rica but from a symbolic factor that had a powerful resonance for Thiel: In 1882 it would be exactly 100 years since Bishop Tristán's ill-fated incursion, in which Padre Tomás López had vanished into the forest after telling his servant and interpreter to flee in the midst of a Guatuso attack (Betancourt and Constenla 1981:30–31; Thiel 1882b).

In preparation for the expedition to the Guatusos, Thiel assigned Ramón Quesada, an hacendado from the outlying settlement of San Carlos, Alajuela, to blaze a trail to the northwest, where it would "lead infallibly to the Indian settlements" (Thiel 1882b). Late in the dry season, on Easter Monday, April 10, Thiel departed San José. Two days later his party passed through the last of Quesada's "beautiful pastures," crossed the Peñas Blancas River, and entered Guatuso territory, where they found a rubber tapper's hut in which to spend the night (1882c).

The expedition included 37 people: Bishop Thiel; León Fernández, a lawyer and historian "in charge of the scientific part;" José María Figueroa, a gifted illustrator in charge of geographical study; San Carlos hacendado Ramón Quesada and eight members of his family; Francisco Pereira, a priest and Thiel's secretary; Colonel Concepción Quesada and a military unit consisting of 10 privates, a bugler, and an orderly; 3 "Indians" from Tucurrique, an indigenous community near Cartago pacified and Hispanicized shortly after the sixteenth-century conquest, who were "armed with arrows and spears to provide the expedition with fresh fish";[16] a Guatuso – unnamed – who was to serve as interpreter;[17] a rubber tapper "knowledgeable about the byways and paths of the Indians"; and two mule drivers in charge of the expedition's 17 horses and 8 mules. The group was well-armed, with 14 rifles and 12 shotguns. "For protection against nocturnal attack," the band brought along "six dogs accustomed to the forest" (1882c).

In its first day beyond civilization, the expedition became lost and ended up proceeding no more than 3 miles. The following day, after Sunday mass, it advanced further, despite having to construct a 15-foot bridge over one of the many streams, a task to which all contributed, "even His Most Illustrious Lordship" the Bishop. On Monday they found the first Indian trails and one member of the party shot and wounded a peccary which, "pursued by the dogs, darted onto the path on which all were coming; it passed right between the feet of the Most Illustrious Lord Bishop," whereupon it was summarily dispatched by "several machete blows from the soldiers." This provided meat for the evening meal, prepared at an abandoned shelter found in the forest (1882c).

At 4 in the afternoon on Tuesday, after advancing 8.5 miles through difficult terrain, the expedition arrived at the Pataste River, where it found an Indian plantain grove and numerous pit traps, one of them 3.5 yards deep and 1.5 yards in diameter and all concealed "with such care that one member of the party would have fallen in one of these holes if another, better acquainted [with the traps], had not warned him" (1882d).[18]

A day later the expedition reached the end of the path that Ramón Quesada had carved through the jungle (Thiel 1882d). Leaving the horses and mules behind, Thiel advanced first with an escort of 10 and then with just Colonel Quesada and the Guatuso interpreter. Eventually they encountered several large houses with some 20 cooking hearths and "fresh signs" of the natives. Rejoining other members of the advance party, the Bishop threw himself full force into the explorer role, blazing the trail by slashing the trees, and in the process giving himself "quite a deep wound." Soon, from atop a small hill, they spotted 3 large *palenques* or houses. Finding the community abandoned, they took advantage of the inhabitants' absence to brew coffee, recite a prayer, and examine and measure the buildings and utensils.

Only on Thursday, its sixth day out, did the expedition finally see any Guatusos. First, the rubber tapper guide reported that "he smelled the odor of Indians who had recently passed by" (1882d). Then, following his directions, the explorers found a new plantain grove and hair left by an Indian who had recently had a haircut. Soon they located a group of 10 small houses, with some 30 fires still burning and huge piles of plantains. A single Indian who had been left to guard the place fled and although "we called to him in his tongue to approach, it was impossible [and] he disappeared" (1882d).

A day later, at 5:30 in the afternoon, Thiel, accompanied by the two Hispanicized Indians from Tucurrique, returned from an exhausting exploratory trek through the forest. Passing through a wide grassy field, they heard

> the cries and songs of Indians who were having a fiesta, playing drums and drinking *chicha*; others were pounding bark for cloth a short distance away; the Indian who was on watch fled across the field and disappeared. His Lordship, alone with the two Tucurriques, did not judge it prudent to approach the Indians, who might have received him poorly (1882e).

On Saturday, April 22, Thiel continued his search for the elusive Guatusos, accompanied by lawyer-historian León Fernández, Colonel Quesada, and 4 other members of their party; other expedition participants set off to reconnoiter the area where drums and singing had been heard the day before. Thiel's group passed through "interminable plantain groves" and found recently abandoned, half-eaten Indian "lunches." On the banks of the Río Muerte – near the place where Guatusos had killed Padre Tomás López exactly 100 years earlier – they spied 2 Indians, "completely naked, tall and robust, who were crossing to the other side of the river" (Thiel 1882e).

Although they signalled the Indians to approach and even dove into the river in pursuit, the members of the expedition were unable to overtake them. Later the expedition found yet another large community, empty of its inhabitants but with 21 blazing cooking fires and huge quantities of plantains and chicha. Bowls of boiled green tobacco lay next to each of the many hammocks. Later that afternoon, returning to camp, the expedition caught sight of a Guatuso "spy" who escaped into the forest. At 10 at night they heard Indians coming near their campsite. Thiel acknowledged that "almost everyone spent the night nearly without sleeping," though he attributed their insomnia not to any danger from natives lurking in the woods but to the "swarms of mosquitoes that made it impossible to rest even for a moment" (1882e).

By this time the morale of the group with Thiel had deteriorated so much that the Bishop lamented:

> The last days' expeditions proved to us that it was impossible to get close to the Indians, or even to speak with one of them; and all [of us] fell into a deep sadness, despairing for the happy conclusion of the expedition for which so many sacrifices and expenses had been incurred.

Despite what Thiel already knew about the depredations of the hueleros in Guatuso territory, he remarked that

> it was impossible for us to understand the reasons for the Indians' constant flight, something that His Lordship had never found, either among the Viceitas or the Chirripoes [southern Costa Rican indigenous groups], and we resolved to return to San Carlos [in Costa Rica] (1882e).

Early on Sunday morning, Thiel and his party met up with the other crusaders who had gone to the site of Friday's Guatuso fiesta. "These," he wrote, "had been happier in their expedition, having been able to take (*tomar*) two Indians. Great was the happiness of all on seeing the first Guatusos. Now there was hope of entering into contact, through them, with the rest of the Indians" (1882e). Rubber tappers had seized one of the Indians, a father of three, intending to sell him in Nicaragua, and had turned him over "voluntarily" to the missionary-explorers when they heard that the Bishop was in the area. The other Indian, who had been fishing in the Río Pataste, was detained near Friday's fiesta site after a brief chase through the forest.

Though Thiel insisted that the captives be handled with caution, he appears to have rationalized that they were willing to stay with him, since they promised to provide guide services in return for trade goods (1882e). In any case, the captive Guatusos confirmed for the Bishop the urgency of saving their people from what was clearly a desperate situation:

> One of the Indians told us of the great travails they all experienced because of the *hueleros'* mistreatment; an *hulero* had killed his father, [who] had been cutting a rubber tree in his plantain grove in order to make a dress from the bark, when one of the *hueleros* secretly approached him and split his head open with a machete; all had been forced to flee to the forest when the *hueleros* came near, leaving their houses and provisions and living from roots and palm hearts; that the *hueleros* had stolen very many children; that moreover many children had died in the forest fleeing from the *hueleros* and that some had been devoured by jaguars, and others had died from snake bites; that moreover, many adult men and women had died from the diseases they caught when they were forced to live in the forest during the rainy months, without shelters or food (1882e).

Despite the Indians' dramatic recounting of their suffering, it is hardly obvious that they made a sharp distinction between the noble missionaries and the evil rubber tappers. In spite of their assurances of collaboration, they refused to take Thiel to their communities and declared that if they did so they would be beaten to death with clubs by their "*paisanos*" (Thiel 1882f). In order to inspire the two Guatusos' confidence, Thiel set out alone with them, ordering the rest of the expedition to follow a short distance behind:

> Hardly had the Bishop left with the two Indians, when they attempted to flee; they pushed the Bishop strongly [and] he nearly fell to the ground. One ran to the forest and the other restrained His Lordship, who had quite good presence of mind at that moment; the noise brought the others and after one-quarter of an hour they [re]captured the Indian who had fled (1882f).

"The Indians took us all day on little-trafficked paths," Thiel continued, "always avoiding those that led to their communities." He also reported that

they completely deceived us. . . . All of us were very irritated with the Indians. . . . And so, we walked and fell over trees, vines and roots, some [of us] armed with smoldering torches, crossing streams and the Pataste River on tree trunks, until we arrived at eight-thirty at camp, overcome with exhaustion from nearly twelve hours of continuous marching (1882f).

From Barbarism to Civilization?

By now the missionaries had spent two enervating weeks in Guatuso territory. On Tuesday, April 25, they prepared to return to civilization, "convinced that it was impossible to use the Indians to reconnoiter the communities and that there was thus no longer any reason to remain among the Guatusos" (Thiel 1882f).[19] Nonetheless, Thiel and ten members of his party decided to leave the area by travelling down the Río Frío toward Lake Nicaragua in a rowboat rented from some rubber tappers, hoping along the way "to find some Guatuso Indians stolen and sold by the *huleros*" (1882f). The other members of the expedition set off overland for central Costa Rica.

The launch carrying the eleven crusaders was so heavily laden that "with the slightest movement it filled with water" (Thiel 1882f). The journey nonetheless passed without incident until the afternoon of Thursday April 27, when Thiel and his party reached a point near the border, six miles from where the Río Frío flows into the Río San Juan and Lake Nicaragua (1882g). There they encountered several houses and an hacienda, where the travellers received a cordial welcome. Two hacienda workers rowed downriver to advise the Nicaraguans at the San Carlos Fort of the imminent arrival of the Bishop. That night there were so many mosquitoes that the travellers had to walk around while eating, and nearly everyone found it impossible to sleep. In the morning, Thiel wrote, having travelled just one-quarter of an hour,

we encountered a boat with the señora who was owner of the hacienda. . . . She told us that in San Carlos everyone was in a hubbub over the arrival of the Bishop and that the Commander had dispatched people to meet us; [and] one of the workers whom we had sent the previous afternoon informed us that all men capable of bearing arms had been called to duty (1882g).

Soon a launch with several men in military uniforms pulled alongside and inspected everything in the Bishop's boat. The soldiers fired four shots in the air which, Thiel said, his party "considered a sign of happiness, such as is the custom when a Bishop arrives in a village" (1882g). Then another boat appeared flying the Nicaraguan flag and carrying more soldiers and a bugler. As Thiel continued downstream with his new escorts, he gave the soldiers some small gifts from the expedition's scarce provisions, the bugler played a march, and the soldiers yelled, "Long live the Government of Nicaragua!" The Nicaraguans fired more rounds in the air and, wrote Thiel, "since we thought they were shots of happiness, we responded" [with shots of our own] (1882g). A while later yet a third vessel came into view, "full of soldiers armed with 'Chassepot' [breech-loading rifles]" (1882g).

At this moment, it seems that a growing sense of the absurd began to infect Thiel, at least as he subsequently narrated the events.

This now seemed to us rather ridiculous and for that reason we resolved to calm down the Nicaraguan *Señores*. At Tablazo Point, where we encountered the third boat, we saw lying in ambush by a small pond a fourth boat with armed soldiers, which continued along with the other boats; after three-quarters of an hour we reached a point called "Coloradito," two miles from the Lake and, considering this place the border between Costa Rica and Nicaragua, His Lordship said that we ought to ask permission to go on. Here there were some soldiers on land; the Nicaraguan boats tied up on shore and we stayed in the middle of the river, calling in loud voices to ask permission to pass. In a little while the one called "Major" answered us, "Go ahead!" and others yelled "go ahead" (1882g).

Though border formalities – and the border's very location – seem to have been of more concern to Thiel than to the Nicaraguans, the latter rapidly took charge once in their own territory.

Again all the Nicaraguan boats joined together and they told us that since we were many and to advance faster, it would be good if some of us went in their boats. . . . Then a launch came and the Major told His Lordship to get in. His Lordship responded that . . . he was not in a hurry to reach San Carlos; the people repeated their urgings and an officer said *that it was necessary to get into the launch.* His Lordship said, "very well, if you please," and with another companion embarked in the launch (1882g, emphasis in original).

When the boats reached the Fort of San Carlos, the town priest came to the dock to greet the Bishop and to take him to his lodgings in the home of a local notable. Everywhere Thiel encountered crowds of well-wishers who wanted to kiss his ring. Spotting many people who appeared to be Guatusos, he spoke a few words in their language and was quickly surrounded by Indians, mostly children between six and fourteen years old.

He asked them how many of them there were in the Fort of San Carlos and they told fifty to sixty; then His Lordship asked the owner of the house who was seated at his side, the priest and various gentlemen if it were true that there were so many Guatusos and they answered that it was so and that perhaps there were more than sixty in the Fort of San Carlos. . . . A little Indian, about four years old, did not want to separate from the Bishop; the Bishop asked a girl of about fifteen years who said she was the little boy's sister how she had come to San Carlos; then she told her story: that one day the men had gone to work in a plantain grove, leaving the women and children in the *palenque*, when suddenly the *huleros* arrived; that she did not want to flee with the others for love of her little brother, who then was barely four months old, and thus they captured her and her brother and sold her in San Carlos. Immediately His Lordship asked several Indians how they had been taken and all told the story of their sufferings (1882g).

In the middle of the conversation with the Guatusos, at 12:30 PM, an officer arrived with a letter from the Fort's Commander, Pedro Rojas, directing Thiel and the others to prepare, on the basis of "higher orders from His Excellency the President," to leave San Carlos immediately on the 4:00 PM steamer to Granada, on the other side of Lake Nicaragua. Thiel read the message to himself, informed the officer that he would soon send a reply to the Commander, and continued his discussion with the Indians. At lunch, speaking in French to assure privacy, he described the letter to lawyer León Fernández and asked him to respond verbally to the Commander (Thiel 1882g; Rojas 1882).

Fernández went to Commander Rojas's office and told him that it was an illegal act to take the Bishop and the others prisoner and bring them against their will to Granada. The expedition was, he declared, entirely pacific and there was no reason to be alarmed. The three firearms in their luggage were "for defending themselves in the forest against attack by ferocious animals and for hunting" (Thiel 1882h). Rojas, he remarked, could easily ascertain that the rest of their gear consisted of an altar, miters, holy oils, and other "ecclesiastical utensils," as well as blankets, clothes, and food.

After Fernández returned, he and Thiel asked San Carlos residents what suspicions the Commander could possibly harbor about them. "Since the night before," they were told, "the town had been very alarmed, fearing an attack from the Costa Rican side; that a rumor had spread that the Bishop who was coming was nothing more than a General in disguise and the Priest, a Captain; that all people capable of bearing arms had been called up" (Thiel 1882h).

The sense of the surreal that began to invade Thiel when Nicaraguans with Chassepot rifles pulled alongside his boat on the Río Frío clearly intensified on hearing that he was thought to be a general masquerading as a bishop.[20] It was, he wrote, "cause for not a little laughter" and reminiscent of "several well-known episodes of '*Don Quijote de la Mancha*'; it really seemed to us that here another '*Cervantes*' would have found new, original characters for another work in the style of '*Don Quijote*'" (1882h).

Thiel sent Fernández back to Commander Rojas "to see" – as he put it, employing an uncharacteristically blunt double entendre – "if it were possible to straigten out this *tuerto*," a term referring to both "a wrong" and "a person blind in one eye" (1882h). Apparently it was not, because the Commander sent Fernández back with "express orders from the President of the Republic" that the Bishop's party "had to leave for the interior [of Nicaragua] without delay." Thiel then went to the Commander's office in a last-ditch attempt to have the order rescinded. "I have not come to ask favors, sir," he lectured him,

> but to protest against your order and the outrage that you commit against citizens of a neighboring Republic and moreover against the Bishop of the Catholic Church of Costa Rica. You commit an act that dishonors Nicaragua beyond measure and I will be certain to make it known to the entire civilized world.... I profoundly regret this arbitary and barbarous act; I regret it for the ashes of one of my ancestors, the unforgettable Bishop of Nicaragua and Costa Rica Don Lorenzo Esteban Tristán, who one hundred years ago, leaving from this place, made an expedition to the territory of the Guatusos, suffering a thousand travails from those Indians; and I, his successor, find myself trampled by those who ought to follow his virtues. With which, Señor Comandante, goodbye (1882h).

After his "*adios*," Thiel offered his hand to the Commander and left the office. Back at the Costa Ricans' quarters, the steamer's accountant came to collect the passengers for the trip across the Lake to Granada. The Bishop, Fernández and the others refused to go, however, without a written directive from the Commander. Finally an officer arrived who informed Thiel and his party that they would have to board the boat "willingly or by force" and the Bishop, "in order to avoid greater abuses and violence," complied (Thiel 1882h; Thiel *et al.* 1882). The boat's accountant then reappeared to inform the Bishop and his companions that even though as prisoners they were supposed to travel second-class, the captain would permit them to occupy first-class quarters (Thiel 1882h).

When the steamer reached Granada on the morning of April 29th, Thiel sent lawyer Fernández to find "a foreign consul" or a notary public (Costa Rica apparently did not yet have a consul in this, the major city of southern Nicaragua). The city prefect came to the dock to let Thiel know that he considered Commander Rojas's detention of the Bishop and his companions a "dishonor" for Nicaragua and that they were now in "complete liberty" (Thiel 1882i). Thiel insisted that they would not disembark until they had registered a formal protest with a notary. After a long wait, the notary arrived, and the ten injured parties dictated their complaint. The notary then accompanied the two legal witnesses to the nearby house of President Joaquín Zavala, but he declined to receive them. The Bishop and lawyer Fernández went next to protest verbally. President Zavala, who reportedly made a number of "disagreeable observations," told them that he had refused to admit the notary because one of the witnesses "was a barefoot man and could not thus be admitted to his home." Ironically, both of the witnesses were shoemakers (Thiel 1882i; Thiel *et al.* 1882).[21]

On Monday May 1st, Thiel went to the house of ex-President Pedro Joaquín Chamorro to visit with the Bishop of Nicaragua, who had come to express his profound regrets and bitterness over the unexpected occurrence that had stranded the Costa Rican prelate in Granada (Thiel 1882j:1). At Chamorro's house,

> he was introduced to three Guatuso Indians from twelve to fifteen years old. His Lordship spoke a few words to them in their native tongue and then asked how these Indians had been acquired. He was answered: they were purchased for a price of fifty pesos each from the *huleros*.... Since one of the Indians was wounded, one of His Lordship's party asked him the cause of his wounds and the Indian answered: that the *huleros* had burned his legs with rubber torches to prevent him from fleeing to the forest. His Lordship was informed that the number of Indians in Granada was some fifty to sixty and that there were others in Rivas, San Juan del Norte, in Managua, in León and in other cities of the Republic; that in all there could be 200 to 250, but that the *huleros* had taken

out many more; that the Indians were so delicate that more than half had died; ... It was learned that two Guatuso Indians had even been taken to New York (1882j:1).

From Chamorro's house, Thiel and Fernández went directly to ask President Zavala to order the Commander of the Fort of San Carlos to turn over some Indians to them on their return. Zavala responded that he would be pleased to give them a dozen Indians and would even provide funds to compensate their "owners." Thiel – at this point more the zealous missionary than the good Samaritan – replied that "with four Indians he would have enough, that his objective was to put them in school and use these to catechize the others" (1882j:1).

On May 3, Thiel and his companions arrived back in the Fort of San Carlos, "this time travelling first class" (1882k). Even though the authorities in Granada had promised to dismiss the Commander who had taken Thiel prisoner (Gaceta Oficial 1882:4; Medina 1882), he was still at his post. In response to the Bishop's request to provide him with some Guatusos, "The Commander answered that he had not received such instructions from the President and that moreover these Indians were *property* of the persons who had purchased them" (Thiel 1882k, added emphasis in original).

An Indian woman with a baby boy, who said she had been captured and sold for forty pesos, showed the Bishop scars left by her mistress's beatings. "This," Thiel wrote, "was sufficient to fill us with compassion and for us to resolve to take her with us at any cost [to Costa Rica],

> even without the consent of the woman who had bought her. ... The woman who said she was the Indian's owner came, demanding two hundred pesos for her, forty for the purchase and one hundred sixty for four months of maintenance since December. His Lordship told her that all this money would be reimbursed by the Government of Nicaragua. ... [Our aim] was to return her to the land of her birth and to her family, from which she had been so cruelly separated (1882k).

On his last day in the Fort of San Carlos, the Bishop also met a younger Indian woman who complained that townspeople "called [the Guatusos] monkeys and wild animals" and that, although she wanted to accompany him to Costa Rica, she was too weak from disease to make the journey (1882k).[22] In a mass just before his departure, Thiel exhorted the town's residents to feel compassion for the Guatusos and to turn over "two or three" so that he could educate them as missionaries. "All were moved by the Bishop's words," he reported, "but nothing was obtained" (1882k).

Curiously, considering that "nothing was obtained," the Bishop reported arriving in San José, the capital of Costa Rica, on the evening of May 13, "with his Guatuso Indians" (1882l). Nothing in his narrative indicates who precisely these Indians were or how he acquired them. It seems, however, that he retained the men "taken" on the way to Nicaragua and that he thought the better of returning the Guatuso woman he met in the Fort of San Carlos "to the land of her birth and her family." In the final installment of his story, Thiel noted that he had brought to San José "three [male] Guatuso Indians and *an Indian woman with her little son*. In my house, moreover, is the Guatuso who served as interpreter" (1882p, emphasis added). The mystery of where Thiel obtained "his" Indians came to light more than four decades after his crusade. In 1923, another Bishop, Antonio del Carmen Monestel, visited Guatuso and met

> people nearly a century old who remember how much they fled when Bishop Thiel *conquered* them. And there are others who were caught by attack dogs, the only way the Prelate [Thiel] could apprehend them and study their language, in order to teach them other customs and so that they could be his interpreters on future visits (Céspedes 1923:67, added emphasis in original).

After returning from Guatuso territory to San José, Thiel received numerous adulatory letters that claimed the Indians as proto-Costa Ricans. They were "our lost brothers" (ACM 1882b), "children of God and moreover Costa Ricans" (ACM 1882c), and "new sons given to the nation who will contribute with their hands to exploit the lands that were, in a way, foreign to the very nation" (ACM 1882e). Thiel's Guatusos were not part of a formal exposition or "exhibitionary complex" (Bennett 1988), although one can wonder about the fate of the Guatusos who, according to Thiel, had been taken to New York.[23] Nonetheless, their conspicuous presence in a close-knit capital "city" with barely 30,000 inhabitants (Hernández 1985:61) demonstrated the efficacy of a national project that the elite – and others – increasingly conceived as a virtual imperial conquest of outlying regions beyond the country's densely populated central valley.[24]

In Thiel's eyes, "his" Guatusos – who could hardly have had a developed notion of nationhood – became strategic instruments in a nation-building project. They would help Christianize their benighted brethren along the Río Frío and form civilized towns along the frontier, especially, he remarked in 1882, if the Costa Rican government could win the release from Nicaragua of more Guatuso captives (1882p). They would personally attest to the barbarism of Nicaraguans and would serve as an instructive example of the humane qualities that differentiated Costa Ricans from their northern neighbors.

The Bishop's Guatusos also played a key role in connecting the new Costa Rican nation to its remote, "primitive" roots and in highlighting its progressive present and future. Like the native peoples exhibited around this time in European and North American world's fairs, museums, and circus sideshows (Rydell 1984, 1993), the arrival in San José of unevangelized, "savage and barbarous" Indians permitted urban Costa Ricans to imagine their nation's romantic roots in the pre-Columbian past and to envisage hurtling back in time to the allegedly formative moment of the conquest. Thirteen priests from Cartago, flattering the Bishop in a letter which compared him to "Orpheus taming tigers with his lyre," clearly expressed this widespread sentiment, albeit with a set of rather muddled analogies:

> Upon seeing you and your respectable party the aborigines fled to the forests, as in one of the scenes of the barbarians' incursions against the Romans, or if you wish, and while it pains us to say it, as in the conquest of America by the Europeans. ¡Ah! it was as if the neighboring civilization had gone back to

the world of three centuries before, and [as if] Costa Rican territory had its Hottentot-land, a seedbed of slaves (ACM 1882c:238).

Continuing Death on the Northern Frontier

Following his first expedition to Guatuso territory, Bishop Thiel succeeded in having the Costa Rican government pass a law prohibiting the persecution of the Indians and banning rubber and timber extraction (Hall 1984:75). Many huleros, though not all (ACM 1882f), did leave, at least for a time. On one occasion, some Indians apparently felt empowered enough to tie up an hulero and bring him to the justice of the peace in San Carlos, where they accused him of stealing fruit and wounding one of them on the hand (ACM 1882f, 1882i). The judge received their complaint, however, "with indifference" (ACM 1882i). One observer noted, furthermore, that "the Indians have suffered some abuses from the bad conduct of the soldiers" sent to protect them and that "they did not come out [of the forest] until after the soldiers had left the place" (ACM 1882h).[25]

Four years later the state established what was supposed to be a permanent military presence in the Guatuso zone, consisting initially of some forty soldiers (Céspedes 1923:46), in order to repress the remaining huleros, save the Indians, and protect national sovereignty. Subsequent interpretations of these events (for example, Montero 1892:200; Noriega 1923:125) suggest that Thiel's missionary and lobbying efforts effectively ended the genocide.[26] But did the "philanthropic and enlightened" Bishop Bernardo Augusto Thiel really put an end to the traffic in slaves or the destruction of the Guatusos?[27]

Thiel returned three times to the Guatusos in the early 1880s (with several of "his" Indians in tow), and again in 1896 (Sanabria 1941:450–1), though the only detailed published account is from the latter expedition (Theil 1927:99–151). It is clear from this 1896 narrative that in the fourteen years since Thiel's first visit, the Guatusos experienced extreme physical and cultural devastation. The Guatusos customarily buried their dead in shallow graves in the floors of their large dwellings. In 1882, the Bishop and his companions reported only two burials in the many settlements they visited (Thiel 1882f). In 1896, in contrast, they visited eleven communities where the smell of death was literally everywhere. "It is impossible to live among the Guatusos," a disgusted Thiel commented, "due to the bad odor which rises from the shallow burials that they have in their houses" (1927:121).

In the *palenque* of Tojifo, they found a population of 26 men, 12 women and nine children – and no fewer than 15 recent burials. Margarita – the largest palenque, some 35 by 16 meters – had 24 men, 13 women, 17 children, and more than 60 recent interments. The total population for the eleven communities was 267 – 133 men, 70 women, and 64 children. The total number of recent burials was 298, more than the number of people who remained alive (Thiel 1927:151). The skewed sex ratio and the top-heavy age structure of the surviving population suggests that many women and children had been captured and taken away. In 1882, Thiel had commented that the Guatusos were "tall and robust" (1882e). Fourteen years later, they suffered from mortal pulmonary diseases, sores, fevers and anemia, as well as lice infestations (Thiel 1927:115, 130). They were, Thiel observed, "very thin and very weak, with faces etched with discouragement, sadness and suffering" (1927:149–50).

By the 1890s, depression and cultural decomposition were clearly taking a toll. Suicide was said to be very common among the Indians (Montero 1892:200). Some communities lacked pots for brewing chicha and nets for fishing (Thiel 1927:130). In several settlements, "civilized" Indians who had managed to return home after years in captivity were beginning to abandon customary subsistence patterns (Thiel 1927:149). Guatusos travelled to San José and other towns where they begged in order to buy shirts, firearms, and machetes (Thiel 1927:113). Thiel encouraged them to become involved in the market by bringing small quantities of cacao to the capital, where his administrator traded it for machetes and rifles (Thiel 1927:117–8). Even the Guatusos' festive, traditional chicha-based alcoholism seems to have taken on grotesque and

pathetic features. In the Tojifo palenque, Thiel encountered

> a strange and ridiculous . . . thinly mustached Indian, shirtless, but wearing a faded frock-coat and a breech cloth, a Tyrolian hat on his head and a staff in his hand . . . , with his face, legs, arms, belly and chest painted red, performing courteous pirouettes and telling us that he was leaving to drink chicha in the other palenque (1927:116).

Nor had the hulero raids ceased in 1896.[28] Thiel found Indians with machete wounds inflicted by huleros, heard of women who had just been raped and of men murdered for refusing to serve as unpaid bearers of contraband rubber. Passing through the palenque of Margarita for a second time, he found it abandoned, with an old suitcase lying on the ground, the owner of which was pursuing Indians in the woods (1927:139, 143, 148). Not long after the departure of the inebriated Indian in the frock coat and breech cloth, Thiel came face-to-face with him at a bend in the trail,

> with a huge load on his shoulders that he could scarcely carry. On seeing us he threw down everything and thrust himself into our midst, saying "*ichicete! ichicete!* (hulero, hulero)," pointing to a rubber tapper . . . who wanted to force him to carry the cargo to the Lake (1927:118).

The dozens of soldiers that the government had sent ten years earlier were apparently no longer on the scene. Thiel's 1896 report repeatedly mentions the "lack of police," of "an authority who commands respect," and of "a permanent authority" (1927:143, 139, 144). Curiously, though, he was not above according at least some of the blame for the plight of the Guatusos to the Indians themselves: "Without courage to defend themselves, they prefer to give themselves up to the caprices of their tyrants, like vile slaves" (1927:139).

Not all Guatusos, however, "preferred to give themselves up." Although Thiel was fond of mentioning that the Guatusos now revered him as a "*saca*," or friend, those that the Bishop had told to meet him in Cañas at the start of the expedition to serve as bearers had failed to appear

(Thiel 1927:99). Even as late as 1923, when another ecclesiastical chronicler visited the Guatusos, the Indians were still compelled to perform labor, probably unremunerated, for non-Indians: "The children are not afraid of white people, but the old people often flee, when for some reason they are forced to work" (Céspedes 1923:52).

Conclusion: Between the Lines of the Nationalists' Projects

It is hardly necessary to read very far between the lines of Thiel's (and others') writings to glimpse an alternative to later glowing accounts of successful evangelization of the Guatusos and of his saving them from genocide. The rubber boom ended in the early twentieth century, as low-cost Asian plantation rubber supplanted rubber gathered in the wild. The genocide against the Guatusos appears to have diminished by then too, as the Indians' numbers plummeted to less than 200 souls, from a pre-boom population of well over 1,000.[29]

Thiel's 1882 report makes no mention of any Guatuso calling him saca, or friend. The Indians' constant flight, even as late as the 1920s, suggests the limits of their fondness for outsiders and the depths of their terror, including a fear of the attack dogs that His Most Illustrious Lordship had used to chase down potential interpreters and guides in 1882. Yet within a decade of Thiel's first expedition, the saca theme had become a staple of nationalist historiography and ethnology and part of a Manichean discourse about national differences. Writing of the Guatusos in an 1892 geography textbook, for example, Francisco Montero declared that, "the Indians show as much affection for Costa Ricans as they do hatred for Nicaraguans. They call us sacas, which means brothers in their dialect. And they try always to be of service and to give things to people from the interior [of Costa Rica]" (1892:200; compare Noriega 1923:125).

It is perhaps necessary, in light of this widespread assumption that barely acculturated natives could easily distinguish nicas from Costa Ricans, to ask whether the dreaded huleros were all Nicaraguans, as León Fernández felt compelled to state, or "nearly all Nicaraguans," as

Gagini's dictionary indicated. In the early 1880s, just before the rise of the banana sector, rubber was Costa Rica's most important export after coffee (Hernández Alarcón 1977:243).[30] Over the continental divide, just west of Guatuso country, rubber (mainly *Castilla nicoyensis*) grew (or was cultivated) throughout the Costa Rican province of Guanacaste, although it was becoming scarce by the turn of the century (Nutting 1882:383; Valverde 1907:38).[31] There it was gathered by itinerant huleros who formed – together with fishers, hunters, squatters, and cattle rustlers – what large landlords viewed as a dangerous "vagabond" class; "theft of rubber" constituted a significant enough problem that hacienda owners called for requiring those selling it to prove the "legitimate origin" of their product (Valverde 1907:35, 38–39, 57).[32] The majority of the huleros in Guatuso territory were certainly Nicaraguans. But to claim that "nearly all" were would require demonstrating that Guanacastecans – who to Costa Ricans from the interior looked and spoke like Nicaraguans – almost never crossed the continental divide, even as the rubber trees to the west, in their area of origin, were "exterminated."

The story about Costa Rican sacas, or friends, and evil Nicaraguan huleros also prompts us to take another look at León Fernández, the lawyer-historian who accompanied Thiel on his first expedition and who later did so much to establish the institutions and the myths of Costa Rican history. At first glance, Fernández's participation in the Guatuso campaign is peculiar; as a Liberal intellectual and a Mason (Meléndez 1975:9), he was likely at least somewhat anti-clerical and at best disinterested in evangelizing "barbaric" Indians.[33] Fernández did, however, have more than a passing interest in border questions, a consideration which makes his presence among Thiel's crusaders rather more comprehensible.[34]

New narratives of national history often emerge concurrently with the consolidation of national territories, projecting processes back in time on a space that is always coextensive with the later, modern boundaries of the state. These new nationalist historiographical traditions – for they quickly become entrenched "traditions" – posit the nation as a timeless, generic entity, with a fixed territory that acts as the permanent arena for its history (Chatterjee 1993:110). They entail "characteristic amnesias" (Anderson 1983:204) about earlier allegiances and borders.

In Costa Rica – which became independent as a province of the Captaincy General of Guatemala, then a part of the Mexican Empire and then of the Central American Federation – national identity was embryonic at best in the early 1880s. Indeed, it was only in the 1850s that the terms *Nación* and *nacional* began to be used at all to refer to Costa Rica rather than to the whole of Central America (Acuña 1995:67). Nicaragua was scarcely different in this regard: some "proto-nationalist expressions" occurred in connection with the invasion of U.S. filibusters in the 1850s, but it was only in the 1870s that Conservative regimes took the first steps to construct a specifically Nicaraguan national identity. Prior to the Liberal reforms that began in Guatemala in the 1870s, isthmian governments still represented themselves as embodying the will of the *pueblos* (that is, as the political apex of a group of localities) rather than of their citizenries. Liberal elites were enamored of secular developmentalism and the Central American *Patria Grande* (large fatherland), while Conservatives mixed localism and Catholicism with nostalgia for the *Madre Patria* (Spain) (Acuña 1994:147–8, 1995:67).[35] As elsewhere in Spanish America, nations emerged

> in areas that had no guiding fictions for autonomous nationhood. The process of concept preceding political reality found in the United States and much of Europe was in large measure reversed; guiding fictions of national destiny had to be improvised after political independence was already a fact (Shumway 1991:2)

Inventing or improvising nations where before there had been none involved naturalizing new categories of identity and de-historicizing or forgetting prenational processes and phenomena.[36] If nationalism is fundamentally "a theory of political legitimacy" (Gellner 1983:1), it is also often a "continuous process of defining 'friend' and 'enemy,' . . . of maintaining boundaries between 'us' and 'them'" (P. Sahlins 1989:270–1). "Pilgrim

creole functionaries and provincial creole printment" (to use Anderson's term [1983:65]) played key roles in articulating the necessary "guiding fictions." Refining the raw material for this process of invention and improvisation involved lexicographers, self-taught ethnologists and a newly professionalized corps of historians.

The methods, concerns, institutions, and personnel of the new *historia patria* ("fatherland history" or, less literally, patriotic historiography) were also inextricably linked to the definition of the country's political and cultural boundaries (Quesada 1988; Palmer 1993). Border disputes with Colombia and Nicaragua led lawyers working on government commissions, of whom León Fernández was the most prominent, to mine the archives and libraries of Guatemala, Madrid, Seville, Paris, and London in search of documents that might buttress Costa Rica's territorial claims. These lawyers-turned-historians devoted much of their energy to the compilation of anthologies of documents that focused on territorial issues. León Fernández's more ambitious ten-volume magnum opus provided materials not just on frontiers and not just for the new National Archives founded in 1881 but – like Thiel's captive Guatusos – for imagining "an ancient political community that extended back to Columbus, where there had been virtually no knowledge of the area prior to the gaining of independence in 1821" (Palmer 1993:62).[37]

Could it be that a lawyer expert in border issues, such as Fernández, was as indispensable for Bishop Thiel's expedition as the interpreter, soldiers, or guard dogs? The Costa Ricans' tone of wounded innocence when taken prisoner at the Fort of San Carlos and their representation of the Nicaraguan Commander's actions as the work of an irrational madman conceal a more complex reality. In the 1858 Cañas-Jérez Treaty, Nicaragua received jurisdiction over the Río San Juan, but Costa Rica was guaranteed unimpeded navigation on it. Tensions between Costa Rica and Nicaragua had been high since 1876, when Nicaragua limited Costa Rican shipping on the San Juan and signed a treaty with France that would have blocked Costa Rican participation in any future interoceanic canal that might be built using the San Juan route. War appeared imminent, and the two countries broke diplomatic relations for two years (Obregón Loría 1981:176–81). Nicaraguan sensitivities about the Río San Juan were magnified because Britain continued (until 1894) to exercise a much-resented protectorate over the "Mosquito Reserve," which constituted a large portion of eastern Nicaragua (Hale 1994:37–45).

Around the time of Thiel's first expedition to the Guatusos these conflicts were still unresolved, and some of the Costa Rican lawyer-historians were raising the possibility that their country might claim "with perfect justice, not just free navigation on the San Juan, which nobody can legally challenge, but its entire right bank from where it exits Lake [Nicaragua] to the [Caribbean] sea," (Peralta 1882:15–16). In this context of territorial disputes and diplomatic tension, both the presence of Fernández in Thiel's party and the seemingly demented actions of Nicaraguan Commander Rojas make considerably more sense.

In bringing to a provisional close the complex story behind this essay's epigraph, Carlos Gagini's curiously charged definition of hulero, it might be useful to say a few words about the production of the dictionary in which it appeared. The definition cited in the epigraph is from the second, 1919 edition of Gagini's work, published when its author was director of the National Library (and not long before he would take over the National Archives, another key institution of the emerging nation, founded by León Fernández). Gagini's first edition, titled *Diccionario de barbarismos y provincialismos de Costa Rica*, contained a more anodyne definition of hulero ("an individual who extracts rubber"), even though it appeared more than a decade after Bishop Thiel's mission to Guatuso territory, when the depredations of the rubber tappers were well known (1893:383). Like most of the 1893 edition's other entries Gagini considered the term hulero a quaint "provincialism" or perhaps even a "barbarism", revealing keywords which suggest a conception of Costa Rica as a province rather than a nation and an elite view of commonalities between the "*indios bárbaros*" described by Bishop Thiel and the other "bárbaros" who spoke Costa Rican Spanish, "a grotesque carica-

ture of that divine speech of Garcilaso, Calderón and Cervantes" (Gagini 1893:i).[38] By 1919, when Gagini published a second edition called *Diccionario de costarriqueñismos*, the nationalist project was well consolidated and the lamentable "barbarisms" had become picturesque "Costa-Ricanisms," "natural result[s] of the phonetic and semantic evolution to which all living languages are subject" (1919:i).[39] The huleros' extermination of the Guatusos appeared in Gagini's second edition as one more object lesson in a crescendoing chorus about Nicaraguan malevolence and Costa Rican virtue.

NOTES

I greatly appreciate the encouragement, critical comments, and leads to relevant sources received from Philippe Bourgois, Mac Chapin, Les Field, Jeffrey Gould, Charles R. Hale, Mary Helms, Iván Molina, Débora Munczek, Steven Palmer, K. Sivaramakrishnan, Joel Wallman, and *CSSH*'s anonymous reviewers, as well as the artistry of Doug Williamson, who prepared the map.

1 Palmer (1995) provides a succinct discussion of how late nineteenth-century Costa Rican elites propagated a "homogeneous" white national self-image among a population with considerable indigenous and African ancestry. The notions of "imagined community" and "guiding fictions" are, respectively, from Anderson (1983) and Shumway (1991).

2 Thiel's secretary on the journey, Francisco Pereira, priest and vicar of Alajuela, wrote most of the report. Thiel, however, appears as author (Thiel 1882c), which is amusing, given the frequent, exalted third-person references to him ("His Most Illustrious Lordship"). Pereira's name appears at the end of the account of Thiel's Guatuso visit (1882l). León Fernández inserted Thiel's 1882 chronicle as a lengthy running footnote to the Spanish translation of U.S. geologist William Gabb's 1875 article on Costa Rica indigenous peoples (Gabb 1883 [1875]:309–24). A 1927 version of Thiel's account, edited by Henri Pittier, modifies or omits a number of key sections of the 1882 text, including most of the days in which the Nicaraguan Commander

forced the Bishop and his party to travel to Granada against their will.

3   In Guatemala, Honduras, and Nicaragua, governments granted concessions to foreign companies which extracted rubber on huge expanses of state lands (Dozier 1985:158; Fomento 1913a, 1913b; Lanuza 1983:54; Nicaragua 1882; Schwartz 1990:110). In Guatemala's Petén and in Nicaragua's Mosquitia merchants extended credit to Indian and mestizo laborers, who then had to work off their debts (Helms 1971:22–23; Schwartz 1990:110; von Oertzen, Rossbach and Wünderich 1990:51–52). In southeastern Costa Rica, Indians gathered rubber and sarsaparilla which they bartered in Limón Port for shotguns, metal tools, and cacao (Gabb 1875:525; Thiel 1882n). In El Salvador, mayors distributed rubber plants to peasants whose communal lands were undergoing privatization (Lindo-Fuentes 1990:135). In Nicaragua and Honduras, foreign investors started rubber plantations, sometimes with as many as one million trees (Crespo 1912:310; Dozier 1985:158–59; Sánchez 1912:503); one Honduran municipality in Colón Department classified all propertied residents as "first-class capitalists," "second-class capitalists" or "proprietors" and obliged every individual to plant respectively 1,000,600 or 300 rubber trees each year, a strategy which produced a rather paltry annual output of 2,000 or so pounds of rubber (Balfate 1911; Crespo 1912).

4   The genus *Castilla* was first proposed in 1793 by a Spanish botanist posted in Mexico, Vicente Cervantes (an 1805 English translation of Cervantes' report termed the genus Castilloa, an error which still frequently appears in the literature). Cervantes called the Mexican species he described *Castilla elastica*. In the late nineteenth and early twentieth centuries, as the rubber boom gathered steam, botanists identified at least ten more species, some of them previously believed to have been *Castilla elastica* Cervantes. The principal species in the Río Frío and Río San Juan basins was *Castilla costaricana* Liebmann (Pittier 1910:249, 272).

Hevea tappers in the Amazon also collected latex from *Castilla* species, which were found throughout the Amazon and north into Central America and Mexico (Barham and Coomes 1994b:46; Weinstein 1983:26; Yungjohann

1989:50–54). Amazon tappers, alone or in small groups, generally worked *Hevea* trees, which usually grew on river flood plains, only during the dry season; if tapped properly, the trees would provide decent yields year after year. In the Amazon region, *Castilla* trees grew in interfluvial upland forests and in northern zones beyond the range of *Hevea*, and could be worked, usually by teams of tappers, during the entire year (as was the case in Central America). This year-round extraction pattern was one factor that made the exploitation of indigenous populations more intense in *Castilla* zones than in *Hevea* zones.

5   British naturalist Thomas Belt explained that the tree died after being tapped because the harlequin beetle (*Acrocinus longimanus*) laid its eggs in cuts made by the tappers, and the grubs then bored "great holes all through the trunk" (1874:34).

"It . . . is an almost universal complaint, from Africa, America, and Asia," wrote A.W. Greeley in the *National Geographic Magazine*, "that the greed and carelessness of the native collectors, who seek to obtain the greatest immediate quantity by the least laborious methods, are rapidly destroying the rubber-bearing plants. Trees are either felled or so deeply and roughly incised as to speedily die" (1897:83). That Greeley, a General and the U.S. Army's Chief Signal Officer, was concerned about rubber suggests an early preoccupation on the part of the military with strategic materials. His condemnation of the "natives' greed" did not, of course, extend to those who purchased, financed, or refined the raw latex.

6   Rubber ignited state interest in remote jungle frontiers throughout the Americas, causing violent territorial conflicts between Brazil and Bolivia (and between the Brazilian states of Pará and Amazonas), as well as lesser disputes involving Venezuela, Colombia, and Peru (Hennessy 1978:99–102; Weinstein 1983:192–212). While rubber figured to some degree in Costa Rican–Nicaraguan contention over the San Juan basin, particularly in relation to the huleros' kidnapping of Guatuso slaves, the river's potential as an interoceanic transport artery and canal route was certainly more significant (and indeed, geopolitical competition over the area predated the rubber boom by centuries). In both South and

Central America, however, these border contro-versies became opportunities for creating or re-inforcing the national identities of both frontier and "interior" populations.

7 Gagini suggests that the Indians were called "Guatusos" because they were believed to have red hair like the agouti or *guatusa*. In the mid-eighteenth century, several missionaries ex-plored forested regions inhabited by Guatusos (Thiel 1983:134, 186, 192). Around the same time, residents of the Costa Rican town of Esparta pursued Indians believed to have taken cattle from a place called "Guatusa pasture" (*potrero de la Guatusa*) on "Guatusa hill" (*Cerro Guatuso*) (de la Fuente 1938 [1785]:546; Gagini 1917:80–81). Near the Río Zapote they found cattle hides and bones, as well as assorted items of European technology, including "seven poorly made guitars" (Información 1907 [1756]:518). Another explanation for the Gua-tuso Indians' name derives from the capture, on Cerro Guatuso in 1761, of four Indian women, who were called *Guatusas* (some sources [Thiel 1983:192] describe them as *zambas*, suggesting they were of mixed indigenous and African des-cent). They affirmed that they had been Chris-tianized by Clemente Adán, a priest who years earlier fled into the forest after quarreling with his superiors (Prado 1983 [1925]:318–20).

These Indian rustlers and Christian zambas, though, were almost certainly not Guatusos-Malekus. Until about 1930 and the work of Conzemius (1930) the term Guatuso was applied not only to the Guatusos-Malekus, but to an-other, now extinct group of Ramas in the zone of Río Zapote. This was west of the Río Frío, more accessible to Spanish settlements and closer to most of the sites of the alleged rustling. The Guatusos-Malekus' language and technology, even in the late nineteenth century, suggest a surprisingly high degree of isolation from both whites-mestizos and nearby indigenous groups. Genetic and linguistic evidence gathered during the last two decades strongly suggests that the Guatusos-Malekus were not, as some historians (e.g., González 1989:112–13) have claimed, recent descendants of other indigenous groups that sought refuge along the Río Frío following the conquest (Fonseca and Cooke 1993:219–21). Nor is there any substantiation for the existence of "white and bearded" Guatusos, said (e.g., by

Quijano 1939:401) to be descendants of Span-iards who fled inland following seventeenth-century pirate attacks on the coast.

8 See also Fernández's editorial note in Gabb (1883 [1875]: 304–5). In 1869, one later partici-pant in Thiel's 1882 expedition, Colonel Ques-ada, entered Guatuso territory from the slopes of the Tenorio Volcano but was also attacked and quickly withdrew (Thiel 1882b).

9 Nearly a century after Thiel's expedition Frank-lin Loveland (1976: 166) wrote in a similar vein: "We know very little about the Guatuso and the peoples of northeastern Costa Rica. It is impera-tive that we strive to gain a basic knowledge of these peoples before their languages and life-styles are transformed as a result of accelerated contact and rapid social change."

It is a sad comment on the ahistorical procliv-ities of much contemporary anthropology that unbeknownst to Loveland, the "accelerated contact and rapid social change" he feared had thoroughly "transformed" Guatuso "lifestyles" over 100 years before. Nonetheless, Thiel's ac-count and the other sources used here, while permitting greater understanding of the Guatu-sos' tragic experience, have a number of obvious limitations, not the least of which is that "history" still arrives with outside penetration of native territories.

10 Belt also noted that one Colonel M'Crae, a naturalized Nicaraguan of British origin resi-dent in El Castillo, on the San Juan River, had "distinguished himself during the revolution-ary outbreak of 1869 [the Martínez-Jérez mili-tary uprising]. He collected the rubber men and came to the assistance of the [Nicaraguan] gov-ernment, helping greatly to put down the insurrection" (1874:32). This militarization of the rubber tappers was likely the precursor to the organized forays up the Río Frío that sub-jugated the Guatusos-Malekus.

11 Reports about the Costa Rican soldiers that penetrated Guatuso territory in 1856 while searching for the Río San Juan do not mention metal tools at all, although they do allude to stone axes and numerous other items, many similar to those later described by Thiel (Von Frantzius 1893 [1862]:33). Belt (1874:41) reported obtaining "a rude stone hatchet, set in a stone-cut wooden handle" that rubber tappers had "pillaged" from the Indians

("Well figured," he said, "in Evan's 'Ancient Stone Implements,' p. 140, but erroneously stated in the text to be from Texas"). Gabb (1875:485) wrote that the Guatusos "had stone axes set in wooden handles [and] good steel machetes (all agree that they have seen these, but where do they get them?)."

12 In 1896, in an account of his fifth and last visit to Guatuso territory, Thiel remarked not that the Indians' worked hard, but that "all live a life of idleness, content to be dressed poorly and nourished even worse" (1927:108).

13 Thiel seemed to recognize later that the Guatusos did not have to work very hard, though he did not recognize this as a positive quality; in recounting his 1896 visit to the Guatusos, he repeatedly described them as "slothful" (1927:127, 141, 149). "They know no kind of money, nor any class of commerce, contenting themselves with plantains and cassava, [crops] which require no effort beyond harvesting them" (1927:117). He also commented that, while the men lived "a life of idleness," the women "do not rest," cooking (which in 1882 he said was the men's job), carrying heavy loads, and taking care of children (1927:128).

14 These included a Chibcha language, distantly related to those spoken in northern Colombia; tuber- and plantain-based horticulture and consumption of copious fermented beverages; large, multi-family dwellings; burials in or near the houses of the deceased; and a wide range of hunting and fishing techniques.

15 In the 1870s Fernández passed through San Juan del Norte (Meléndez 1975:9), where he may well have heard firsthand about the situation of the Guatusos-Malekus.

16 In the early 1870s, President Tomás Guardia quarreled with León Fernández, his brother-in-law, and sent him into internal exile in Tucurrique, where he may have met the "Indians" who accompanied the Bishop to Guatuso territory.

17 This Guatuso individual is not only unnamed but also unexplained. He was probably one of the handful of partially Hispanicized Guatusos, largely former captives, who ended up in Costa Rican towns in the years before Thiel's expedition departed (Betancourt and Costenla 1981:21).

18 In 1856, members of the Costa Rican military unit that passed through Guatuso territory frequently fell into these traps (von Frantzius 1893 [1862]:33).

19 In the 1927 edition of Thiel's account (p. 32) this passage substitutes the phrase "our prisoners" (*nuestros presos*) for "the Indians."

20 In this part of his account, Thiel does not mention anything about Concepción Quesada, a member of his party who was a colonel in the Costa Rican Army. The Nicaraguan Commander appears not to have been aware of Quesada's rank or even that he was an army officer, since in his note to Thiel he only describes the group as consisting of the Bishop, a priest and "nine more secular individuals," without mentioning the colonel or his military status (Rojas 1882). When the group later reached Granada and dictated a complaint to a notary, however, Quesada identified himself as a "colonel in active service" (ACM 1882a:200).

21 Another source describes the witnesses as a shoemaker's son (*hijo zapatero*) and a tailor (ACM 1882a:202).

22 While Thiel reported this racism with outrage in 1882, in an account of his 1896 trip to the Guatusos, he nonetheless refers to the Indian children as "little monkeys" (*pequeños micos*) (1927:128). As late as 1923, prominent intellectuals still exoticized and dehumanized the Guatusos, resulting in preposterous claims such as the following:

> At certain times of year the women go into heat, in a similar fashion to some of our domestic animals. And even stranger, with the most repugnant practices of the canine race, the Indian women in that state withdraw from society and *rise up*, going to the forest followed by some Indian men, and there they stay at risk for weeks at a time, exhibiting in the middle of the lonely woods the most immoral scenes (Noriega 1923:124, added emphasis in original).

23 "The Indians are becoming an object of curiosity," hacendado Ramón Quesada informed Thiel in October 1882:

> Many ask about them, others claim to have an express authorization from the President to meet them, others are only waiting for the dry season to go and explore the [Guatuso] area, and the only things talked about are the cacao, fruit and profit that can be taken out of there.

But nobody is concerned about whether this favors [the Guatusos] or not; nobody thinks about that (ACM 1882j).

24 Several of the congratulatory letters and municipal council declarations that followed Thiel's expedition to Guatuso territory refer to the mission as a "conquest" (ACM 1882d, 1882e). That this was part of a broader conception of central Costa Rica imposing itself on its peripheries is suggested by the comment of prominent lawyer-politician Eusebio Figueroa who, in 1876, suggested that the planned railroad to the Caribbean coast would be like the French conquest of Cochin China (Palmer 1995:76).

25 "The memory is still alive among us," several Indian leaders declared in a 1996 legal writ, "of how our parents and grandparents had to suffer the humiliation of passing hours and days in holes in the ground, with stocks on their feet, which was a punishment imposed by the first police authorities on the Malekus for practicing their culture" (Blanco et al. 1996:4).

26 Even later specialists have uncritically accepted this dubious interpretation. Costenla, for example, writes that "on creating a permanent military presence, the huleros, so as not to attract the attention of the Costa Rican authorities . . . had to abandon the persecution of the surviving Indians" (1993:3–4).

27 One also might ask why there was considerable demand for Guatuso slaves in Nicaragua, but apparently little or none in Costa Rica. Part of the reason is that wealthy Costa Ricans had an alternative source of unpaid labor and of the prestige that apparently went with having exotic valets and household servants. At the same time that slaving was occurring in Guatuso territory, the Atlantic Railroad Company began to sell Chinese indentured laborers who had gone on strike for 350–400 pesos each to members of the Costa Rican elite. Technically, purchasers did not acquire the Chinese as chattel, but simply bought their obligation to work – usually as cooks, household servants, and farm hands – for the remaining period of their contracts, generally eight years. By mid-1874, the railroad company had sold over 400 Chinese to wealthy Costa Ricans and foreigners, including President Tomás Guardia,

who acquired 14 (Casey 1975; Fallas 1983:208–14).

28 Some two dozen rubber firms still operated in San Juan del Norte in 1897, though the volume of exports was down considerably compared with the 1880s (Niederlein 1898:70).

29 The genocide appears to have ended some time between Thiel's 1896 expedition and the 1899 visit of German geologist Karl Sapper, who reported that the Costa Rican authorities had a permanent command post in the area and that hulero attacks had ceased (Sapper 1942:81–96). Nearly a century later, the Guatusos-Malekus faced severe poverty and continuing threats to their existence as a distinct people. Estimates of their population today range from 449 (Mejía et al. 1994:1) to 590 (Blanco et al. 1996:2), well under half the pre-rubber boom level. Spanish is rapidly supplanting the Maleku language (Baeza and Froehling 1973; Costenla 1988, 1993). In the late 1950s, the Guatusos-Malekus lived in a territory of approximately 11,000 hectares (Blanco et al. 1996:5). The Guatuso-Maleku Indigenous Reserve contained just under 3,000 hectares when it was founded in 1976. Twelve years later the Indians had lost all but 411 hectares to non-indigenous farmers and ranchers who flooded into the region in the 1980s, responding to government incentives to settle underpopulated zones near the Nicaraguan border (the Costa Rican state also removed 250 hectares from the Reserve in 1977). Protests and land occupations in 1990 succeeded in recovering only about 200 hectares of the lost territory (Blanco et al. 1996; Guevara and Chacón 1992:99). In 1996 the Malekus filed suit against the Costa Rican government to recover the Reserve (Blanco et al. 1996).

30 Virtually all the rubber from Guatuso territory was exported via San Juan del Norte and showed up, if at all, in Nicaraguan, not Costa Rican, trade statistics. Much Costa Rican rubber, from the Guatuso zone and elsewhere, came down the Río San Carlos, rather than the Río Frío. Because the Río San Carlos entered the Río San Juan below the last customs house at El Castillo, and because San Juan del Norte was a free port, the Nicaraguan government was unable to collect its export duties (Dozier 1985:116).

31 According to Pittier, *Castilla nicoyensis* "is a
    good rubber producer, the milk being particu-
    larly abundant toward the end of the dry
    season, and to this fact is due its almost com-
    plete extermination in the western forests of
    Costa Rica" (1910:277). This destruction of
    Castilla nicoyensis trees likely increased land-
    owners' concerns about "rubber theft."

32 Probably the biggest plantation belonged to Dr.
    Pánfilo Valverde and was on the southwestern
    side of Tenorio Volcano, the eastern slope of
    which was Guatuso territory (Pittier 1910:277).
    Valverde, who as Interior Minister in 1907 was
    in the forefront of efforts to repress rustlers,
    "furtive   hunters,"   huleros,   and   other
    "vagrants," probably suffered thefts of rubber
    on his Hacienda Tenorio; at very least, his prop-
    erty – remote, forested and "invaded" by squat-
    ters – was one of those most affected by cattle
    rustlers (Valverde 1907). In the 1890s, Costa
    Ricans who colonized the edges of Guatuso ter-
    ritory also planted rubber. Retired military offi-
    cer, Juan Alvarez, for example, had 500 rubber
    trees, as well as cacao and coffee, on his farm on
    the bank of the Río Frío (Thiel 1927:143).

33 The presence in the expedition of illustrator
    José María Figueroa is similarly odd, given his
    iconoclastic sympathies and history of scandal-
    ous behavior, which were almost certainly
    known to Bishop Thiel. As a youth, he was
    charged with having surreptitiously affixed
    "obscene" sketches of the daughters of an elite
    family to the exterior walls of houses in his
    native Cartago (one of these confiscated draw-
    ings survives, depicting a Rubens-esque,
    smiling young woman in petticoats, whose
    raised leg reveals her genitalia). He was also
    said during the trial to be operating a "Masonic
    lodge" in his home (see Malavassi 1995).

34 According to Meléndez (1975:10), "Shared
    interests in history led . . . [Fernández] to main-
    tain a cordial relation with the erudite
    Bishop . . . Thiel." Ironically, however, Fernán-
    dez was a key figure in events which precipi-
    tated the expulsion of the Bishop from Costa
    Rica. In 1883 Foreign Minister Eusebio Fig-
    ueroa, thinking he had been insulted by Fer-
    nández, challenged him to a duel. Fernández
    killed him (according to some accounts without
    waiting for the count of "three") and the
    Bishop refused to bury Figueroa because he

had perished as "a victim of the barbarous
custom of duels." At the funeral, a mob broke
into the locked burial ground and interred Figueroa in his family's mausoleum. Soon after,
the government decreed the secularization of
cemeteries, hospitals, marriage and education,
broke relations with the Vatican and expelled
Thiel and the Jesuits from Costa Rica (Obregón
Loría 1981:204–17; Sanabria 1941:65–66).
Thiel was permitted to come back in 1886, as
long as the the church played a subordinate role
in politics. His reinstatement was emblematic
of a reconciliation between pro-clerical and
Liberal factions of the elite (Palmer 1995:84).
A year after Thiel's return, Figueroa's son
avenged his father by ambushing and shooting
Fernández, whose last words were reportedly
directed at his assassin: "Good son, bad gentleman" (Meléndez 1975:10).

35 Thiel highlighted the old loci of identity even
    as he articulated the new nationalism. When
    listing the leading members of his expedition,
    the Bishop specified the town of residence of
    each (though not those of the soldiers or mule
    drivers), thus suggesting both the salience of
    local identity and the narrow bounds of his
    view of citizenry (1882c).

36 In the 1880s in Costa Rica the new nationalism
    also involved the creation of a national origin
    myth and heavily mythologized national heroes
    (Palmer 1993).

37 One case relevant to this essay illustrates Fer-
    nández's penchant for projecting a naturalized
    Costa Rican nation onto a distant past when no
    such entity existed. In Guatemala Fernández
    consulted Bishop Tristán's 1783 chronicle of
    his trip from Granada to Guatuso territory, a
    manuscript that was subsequently lost until the
    discover of a colonial-era copy in a Madrid
    library (and its publication in 1981 by Betan-
    court and Costenla). After Fernández's death,
    his son found his notes on the document, which
    were limited to a transcription of the days the
    expedition spent on what years later became
    Costa Rican territory (Betancourt and Costenla
    1981:22).

38 Gagini refers to the three giants of the six-
    teenth-   and   seventeenth-century   Spanish
    Golden Age: poet Garcilaso de la Vega, drama-
    tist Pedro Calderón de la Barca, and novelist
    Miguel de Cervantes.

39 Anderson (1983:71) points out that "the nineteenth century was, in Europe and its immediate peripheries, a golden age of vernacularizing lexicographers, grammarians, philologists, and literateurs. The energetic activities of these professional intellectuals were central to the shaping of nineteenth-century European nationalisms in complete contrast to the situation in the Americas between 1770 and 1830."

This aspect of the Latin American nationalisms emerged somewhat later in the nineteenth century, but they too had their lexicographers, Gagini and Thiel (1882q) among them.

REFERENCES

ACM [Archivo de la Curia Metropolitana, San José]
1882a. "Protesta hecha por varios vecinos de Costa Rica contra el Comandante de San Carlos" (29 April 1882). Caja 433, folios 200–202 vuelto.
——. 1882b. "Carta de 104 mujeres al Obispo Thiel" (24 June 1882). Caja 433, folios 233–234.
——. 1882c. "Carta del Clero de Cartago al Obispo Thiel" (26 June 1882). Caja 433, folio 238.
——. 1882d. "Sesión ordinaria del Cantón General de Heredia" (3 July 1882). Caja 433, folios 247–248.
——. 1882e. "Carta de la Vicaría Foránea de la Provincia de Heredia al Obispo Thiel" (6 July 1882). Caja 433, folios 249–251.
——. 1882f. "Carta de Ramón Quesada al Obispo Thiel" (12 July 1882). Caja 433, folios 257–259.
——. 1882g. "Telegrama al Sr. Obispo de Ramón Quesada E." (11 August 1882). Caja 433, folio 284.
——. 1882h. "Carta de Grecia al Obispo" (19 August 1882). Caja 433, folios 292–293.
——. 1882i. "Carta de Ramón Quesada al Obispo Thiel" (19 August 1882). Caja 433, folios 295–297.
——. 1882j. "Carta de Ramón Quesada al Obispo Thiel" (28 October 1882). Caja 433, folios 340–341.
Acuña Ortega, Víctor Hugo
1994. "Nación y clase obrera en Centroamérica durante la época liberal (1870–1930)," in Iván Molina Jiménez and Steven Palmer, eds., *El paso del cometa: Estado, Política social y culturas populares en Costa Rica (1800/1950)*, 145–65. San José: Editorial Porvenir-Plumsock Mesoamerican Studies.

——. 1995. "Historia del vocabulario político en Costa Rica: Estado, república, nación y democracia (1821–1949)," in Arturo Taracena Arriola and Jean Piel, eds., *Identidades nacionales y Estado moderno en Centroamérica*, 63–74. San José: Editorial de la Universidad de Costa Rica.
Anderson, Benedict
1983. *Imagined Communities: Reflections on the Origin and Spread of Nationalism*. London: Verso.
Baeza Flores, Alberto; and Heino Froehling
1973. *Costa Rica: patrones culturales de comunidades indígenas*. San José: CEDAL.
Balfate, Municipalidad de
1911. "Nuevo patrimonio: cultivo del hule. Actas de la Municipalidad de Balfate Departamento de Colón." *Boletín de la Secretaría de Fomento, Obras Públicas y Agricultura* [Honduras] 1:2 (September), 82–88.
Barahona Portocarrero, Amaru
1981. "Breve ensayo sobre la historia contemporánea de Nicaragua," in Pablo González Casanova, ed., *América Latina: historia de medio siglo*, vol. 2: *Centroamérica, México y el Caribe*, 377–404. Mexico: Siglo XXI.
Barham, Bradford L.; and Oliver T. Coomes
1994a. "Reinterpreting the Amazon Rubber Boom: Investment, the State, and Dutch Disease." *Latin American Research Review*, 29:2, 73–109.
——. 1994b. "Wild Rubber: Industrial Organisation and the Microeconomics of Extraction During the Amazon Rubber Boom (1860–1920)." *Journal of Latin American Studies*, 26 (February), 37–72.
Belt, Thomas
1874. *The Naturalist in Nicaragua*. London: J. Murray.
Bennett, Tony
1988. "The Exhibitionary Complex." *New Formations*, 4 (Spring), 73–102.
Betancourt de Sánchez, Helia; and Adolfo Constenla Umaña
1981. "La expedición al territorio de los guatusos: una crónica colonial hispana y su contraparte en la tradición oral indígena." *Revista de Filología y Lingüística de la Universidad de Costa Rica*, 7:1–2, 19–34.
Blanco et al. [Antonio Blanco Rodríguez, Luciano Castro Castro, José Aniceto Blanco Vela, Bienvenido Cruz Castro]
1996. "Recurso de amparo contra el Poder Ejecutivo, el Ministro de Gobernación, el Instituto de

Desarrollo Agrario y la Comisión Nacional de Asuntos Indígenas." Manuscript.

Boletín
1912. "Plantaciones de hule en el Depto. de Olancho." *Boletín de la Secretaría de Fomento, Obras Públicas y Agricultura* [Honduras] 1:9 (April), 559.

Casey, Jeffrey J.
1975. "Sección documental: la inmigración china." *Revista de Historia* (Costa Rica), 1:1, 145–65.

Céspedes Marín, Amando
1923. *Crónicas de la visita oficial y diocesana al Guatuso.* San José: Imprenta Lehmann (Sauter and Co.).

Chapman, Anne
1992. *Masters of Animals: Oral Traditions of the Tolupan Indians–Honduras.* Philadelphia: Gordon and Breach.

Chatterjee, Partha
1993. *The Nation and Its Fragments: Colonial and Post-Colonial Histories.* Princeton: Princeton University Press.

Conzemius, Edward
1930. "Une tribu inconnue du Costa Rica: les indiens Rama du rio Zapote." *L'anthropologie,* 40:93–108.

Coomes, Oliver T.; and Bradford L. Barham
1994. "The Amazon Rubber Boom: Labor Control, Resistance, and Failed Plantation Development Revisited." *Hispanic American Historical Review,* 74:2, 231–57.

Costenla Umaña, Adolfo
1988. "El guatuso de Palenque Margarita: su proceso de declinación." *Estudios de Lingüística Chibcha,* 7:7–37.

——. 1993. *Laca majifijica: la transformacín de la tierra.* San José: Editorial de la Universidad de Costa Rica.

Crespo, Salvador
1912. "Departmento de Colón." *Boletín de la Secretaría de Fomen to, Obras Públicas y Agricultura* [Honduras], 1:6 (January), 306–19.

Dean, Warren
1987. *Brazil and the Struggle for Rubber: A Study in Environmental History.* Cambridge: Cambridge University Press.

de la Fuente, Antonio
1938 [1785]. "Don Antonio de la Fuente, Síndico General de los Conventos de San Francisco, pide que se levante una información sobre los trabajos realizados por los misioneros en el descubri-

miento de los indios Guatusos. – Año de 1785." *Revista de los Archivos Nacionales* [Costa Rica], 2:9–10, 545–8.

Dozier, Craig
1985. *Nicaragua's Mosquito Shore: The Years of British and American Presence.* Tuscaloosa: University of Alabama Press.

Fallas Monge, Carlos Luis
1983. *El movimiento obrero en Costa Rica 1830–1902.* San José: Editorial Universidad Estatal a Distancia.

Fomento, [Ministerio de]
1913a. "Cuadro sinóptico de concesiones otorgadas por el Estado a contar desde 1877." *Boletín de la Secretaría de Fomento, Obras Públicas y Agricultura* [Honduras], 2:4–6 (April–June), 212–3.

——. 1913b. "Cuadro sinóptico de concesiones otorgadas por el Estado a contar desde 1877." *Boletín de la Secretaría de Fomento, Obras Públicas y Agricultura* [Honduras], 2:4–6 (August), 436–37.

Fonseca, Oscar M.; and Richard G. Cooke
1993. "El sur de América Central: contribución al estudio de la región histórica chibcha," in Robert M. Carmack, ed., *Historia general de Centroamérica, tomo I historia antigua,* 217–82. Madrid: FLACSO.

Gabb, William M.
1875. "On the Indian Tribes and Languages of Costa Rica." *Proceedings of the American Philosophical Society,* 14:483–602.

——. 1883 [1875]. "Tribus y lenguas indígenas de Costa-Rica," in León Fernández, ed., *Documentos para la Historia de Costa Rica,* vol. III, 303–486. San José: Imprenta Nacional.

Gaceta Diario Oficial
1882. "Editorial." *La Gaceta Diario Oficial,* 5:1265 (May 20), 5.

Gagini, Carlos
1893. *Diccionario de barbarismos y provincialismos de Costa Rica.* San José: Tipografía Nacional.

——. 1917. *Los aborígenes de Costa Rica.* San José: Trejos Hermanos.

——. 1919. *Diccionario de costarriqueñismos, segunda edición.* San José: Imprenta Nacional.

Gellner, Ernest
1983. *Nations and Nationalism.* Ithaca: Cornell University Press.

González, Paulino
1976. "Ruta Sarapiquí: historia sociopolítica de un camino." *Avances de Investigación* (Instituto de Investigaciones Sociales, Universidad de Costa Rica), 15:1–99.

——. 1989. "La conquista," in Jaime E. Murillo, ed., *Las instituciones costarricenses: de las sociedades indígenas a la crisis de la república liberal*, 77–120. San José: Editorial de la Universidad de Costa Rica.

Greeley, A. W.
1897. "Rubber Forests of Nicaragua and Sierra Leone." *National Geographic Magazine*, 8:3 (March), 83–88.

Guevara Berger, Marcos; and Rubén Chacón Castro
1992. *Territorios indios en Costa Rica: orígenes, situación actual y perspectivas*. San José: García Hermanos.

Hale, Charles R.
1994. *Resistance and Contradiction: Miskitu Indians and the Nicaraguan State, 1894–1987*. Stanford: Stanford University Press.

Hall, Carolyn
1984. *Costa Rica: una interpretación geográfica con perspectiva histórica*. San José: Editorial Costa Rica.

Helms, Mary W.
1971. *Asang: Adaptaions to Culture Contact in a Miskito Community*. Gainesville: University of Florida Press.

Hennessy, Alistair
1978. *The Frontier in Latin American History*. Albuquerque: University of New Mexico Press.

Hernández, Hermógenes
1985. *Costa Rica: evolución territorial y principales censos de población 1502–1984*. San José: Editorial Universidad Estatal a Distancia.

Hernández Alarcón, Eduardo
1977. "Comercio y dependencia en Costa Rica durante los años 1880–1890." *Anuario de Estudios Centroamericanos*, 3:235–65.

Información
1907 [1756]. "Información hecha con motivo de la entrada de fray José Miguel Martínez y fray José de Castro á las montañas de los indios Guatusos. – Año de 1756," in León Fernández, ed., *Documentos para la Historia de Costa Rica*, vol. IX, 510–23. Barcelona: Imprenta Viuda de Luis Tasso.

Johnson, Frederick
1963. "Central American Cultures: An Introduction," in Julian H. Steward, ed., *Handbook of South American Indians*, vol. 4: *The Circum-Caribbean Tribes*, 43–68. New York: Cooper Square Publishers.

Lanuza, Alberto
1983. "La formación del Estado nacional en Nicaragua: las bases económicas, comerciales y financieras entre 1821 y 1873," in A. Lanuza *et al.*, *Economía y sociedad en la construcción del Estado en Nicaragua*, 7–138. San José: Instituto Centroamericano de Administración Pública.

Lévy, Pablo
1873. *Notas geográficas y económicas sobre la República de Nicaragua*. Paris: Librería Española de E. Denné Schmitz.

Lindo-Fuentes, Héctor
1990. *Weak Foundations: The Economy of El Salvador in the Nineteenth Century 1821–1898*. Berkeley: University of California Press.

Lothrop, Samuel Kirkland
1926. *Pottery of Costa Rica and Nicaragua*, vol. I. New York: Museum of the American Indian-Heye Foundation.

Loveland, Franklin O.
1976. "Afterward: Anthropological Research in Lower Central America," in Mary W. Helms and Franklin O. Loveland, eds., *Frontier Adaptations in Lower Central America*, 165–70. Philadelphia: Institute for the Study of Human Issues.

Malavassi, Paulina
1995. "Dibujos obscenos en el Cartago de 1843." *Actualidades del CIHAC* [Centro de Investigaciones Históricas de América Central, Universidad de Costa Rica], 2:5 (December), 1–4.

Medina, F. J.
1882. "Ministerio de Relaciones Exteriores de Nicaragua." *La Gaceta Diario Oficial*, 5:1265 (May 20), 2.

Mejía Marín, Noemy; Raúl I. Bolaños Arce; Juan de Dios Ramírez Gatgens; Rocío Alvarado Cruz
1994. *Historias malecus*. Heredia: Editorial de la Universidad Nacional and Centro Cultural de la Embajada de España.

Meléndez, Carlos
1975. "Introito," in León Fernández, *Historia de Costa Rica durante la dominación española 1502–1821*, 2ª ed., 7–13. San José: Editorial Costs Rica.

Membreño, Alberto
1982 [1895]. *Hondureñismos*, 3ª ed. Tegucigalpa: Editorial Guaymuras.

Montero Barrantes, Francisco
1892. *Geografía de Costa Rica*. Barcelona: Tip. Lit. de José Cunill Sala.

Muratorio, Blanca
1991. *The Life and Times of Grandfather Alonso: Culture and History in the Upper Amazon*. New Brunswick: Rutgers University Press.

Nicaragua
1882. *Concesion par la République de Nicaragua a M. Aristide-Paul Blanchet d'un canal pour le transit interocéanique par les lacs du Nicaragua: et de 353*

kilóm. carrés de terrains pour la culture de caou-
tchouc, 4 mars 1882. Bourges, France: H. Sire.

Niederlein, Gustavo
1898. *The State of Nicaragua of the Greater Republic*
of Central America. Philadelphia: Philadelphia
Commercial Museum.

Noriega, Félix F.
1923. *Diccionario geográfico de Costa Rica*, segunda
ed. San José: Imprenta Nacional.

Nutting, C. C.
1882. "On a Collection of Birds from the Hacienda La
Palma, Gulf of Nicoya, Costa Rica." *Proceedings of*
the United States National Museum, 5:382–409.

Obregón Loría, Rafael
1981. *Hechos militares y políticos.* Alajuela: Museo
Histórico Cultural Juan Santamaría.

Obregón Quesada, Clotilde
1993. *El Río San Juan en la lucha de las potencias*
(1821–1860). San José: Editorial Universidad
Estatal a Distancia.

Palmer, Steven
1993. "Getting to Know the Unknown Soldier: Official Nationalism in Liberal Costa Rica, 1880–
1900." *Journal of Latin American Studies*, 25 (February), 45–72.
——. 1995. "Hacia la 'auto-inmigración': el nacionalismo oficial en Costa Rica 1870–1930," in
Arturo Taracena Arriola and Jean Piel, eds., *Iden-*
tidades nacionales y Estado moderno en Centroamér-
ica, 75–85. San José: Editorial de la Universidad
de Costa Rica.

Peralta, Manuel M. de
1882. *El Río San Juan de Nicaragua: derechos de sus*
ribereños. Madrid: Librería de M. Murillo.

Pittier, Henry
1910. "A Preliminary Treatment of the Genus
Castilla." *Contributions from the United States Na-*
tional Herbarium, 13:7, 247–79.

Prado, Elado
1983 [1925]. *La orden franciscana en Costa Rica*, 2ª
ed. San José: Editorial Costa Rica.

Quesada C., Juan Rafael
1988. "El nacimiento de la historiografía en Costa
Rica." *Revista de Historia* (número especial), 51–81.

Quijano Quesada, Alberto
1939. *Costa Rica de ayer y hoy 1800–1939.* San José:
Editorial Borrasé Hermanos.

Rojas, Pedro
1882. "N°. 2 Ilustrísimo Señor Obispo de la Diócesis
de Costa-Rica." *La Gaceta Diario Oficial*, 5:1265
(May 20), 2.

Rydell, Robert W.
1984. *All the World's a Fair: Visions of Empire at the*
American International Expositions, 1876–1916.
Chicago: University of Chicago Press.
——. 1993. *World of Fairs: The Century-of-Progress*
Expositions. Chicago: University of Chicago Press.

Sahlins, Marshall
1972. *Stone Age Economics.* Chicago: Aldine.

Sahlins, Peter
1989. *Boundaries: The Making of France and Spain in*
the Pyrenees. Berkeley: University of California
Press.

Sanabria, Víctor M.
1941. *Bernardo Agusto Thiel, segundo obispo de Costa*
Rica (apuntamientos históricos). San José: Imprenta
Lehmann.

Sánchez, Rubén
1912. "Departamento de Choluteca." *Boletín de la*
Secretaría de Fomento, Obras Públicas y Agricul-
tura [Honduras], 1:9 (April) 499–506.

Sapper, Karl
1942. *Viajes a varias partes de la República de Costa*
Rica 1899 y 1924. San José: Imprenta Universal.

Schoonover, Thomas; and Ebba Schoonover
1991. "Statistics for an Understanding of Foreign
Intrusions into Central America from the 1820s
to 1930, Part III." *Anuario de Estudios Centroa-*
mericanos, 17:2, 77–119.

Schultes, Richard Evans
1993. "The Domestication of the Rubber Tree: Economic and Sociological Implications." *American*
Journal of Economics and Sociology, 52:4 (October)
479–85.

Schwartz, Norman B.
1990. *Forest Society: A Social History of Petén, Guate-*
mala. Philadelphia: University of Pennsylvania
Press.

Shumway, Nicolas
1991. *The Invention of Argentina.* Berkeley: University of California Press.

Sibaja Chacón, Luis F.
1974. *Nuestro límite con Nicaragua.* San José: Instituto Tecnológico Don Bosco.

Squier, E. G.
1852. *Nicaragua: Its People, Scenery, Monuments and*
the Proposed Interoceanic Canal. New York:
D. Appleton and Company.

Taussig, Michael
1987. *Shamanism, Colonialism and the Wild Man: A*
Study in Terror and Healing. Chicago: University
of Chicago Press.

Thiel, Bernard Augusto
1882a. "Nº. 4 Señor Prefecto Don Manuel Lacayo." *La Gaceta Diario Oficial*, 5:1265 (May 20), 2–3.
——. 1882b. "Secretaría de Culto." *La Gaceta Diario Oficial* (Costa Rica), 5:1276 (June 2), 1.
——. 1882c. "Secretaría de Culto." *La Gaceta Diario Oficial* (Costa Rica), 5:1277 (June 3), 1.
——. 1882d. "Secretaría de Culto." *La Gaceta Diario Oficial* (Costa Rica), 5:1278 (June 4), 1.
——. 1882e. "Secretaría de Culto." *La Gaceta Diario Oficial* (Costa Rica), 5:1279 (June 6), 1.
——. 1882f. "Secretaría de Culto." *La Gaceta Diario Oficial* (Costa Rica), 5:1280 (June 7), 1.
——. 1882g. "Secretaría de Culto." *La Gaceta Diario Oficial* (Costa Rica), 5:1281 (June 8), 1.
——. 1882h. "Secretaría de Culto." *La Gaceta Diario Oficial* (Costa Rica), 5:1282 (June 10), 1.
——. 1882i. "Secretaría de Culto." *La Gaceta Diario Oficial* (Costa Rica), 5:1283 (June 11), 1.
——. 1882j. "Secretaría de Culto." *La Gaceta Diario Oficial* (Costa Rica), 5:1284 (June 13), 1–2.
——. 1882k. "Secretaría de Culto." *La Gaceta Diario Oficial* (Costa Rica), 5:1285 (June 14), 1.
——. 1882l. "Secretaría de Culto." *La Gaceta Diario Oficial* (Costa Rica), 5:1286 (June 15), 1.
——. 1882m. "Secretaría de Culto." *La Gaceta Diario Oficial* (Costa Rica), 5:1287 (June 16), 1.
——. 1882n. "Secretaría de Culto." *La Gaceta Diario Oficial* (Costa Rica), 5:1288 (June 17), 1–2.
——. 1882o. "Secretaría de Culto." *La Gaceta Diario Oficial* (Costa Rica), 5:1289 (June 18), 1.
——. 1882p. "Secretaría de Culto." *La Gaceta Diario Oficial* (Costa Rica), 5:1291 (June 21), 2.
——. 1882q. *Apuntes lexicográficos de las lenguas y dialectos de los indios de Costa Rica*. San José: Tipografía Nacional.
——. 1900. *Carta pastoral del Illmo. y Revmo. Señor D. Bernardo Augusto Thiel, Obispo de Costa Rica:*

"Para el fin del siglo XIX y principio del siglo XX". San José: Tipografía de San José.
——. 1927. *Viajes a varias partes de la República de Costa Rica*. San José: Imprenta y Librería Trejos Hermanos.
——. 1983. *Datos cronológicos para la historia eclesiástica de Costa Rica*, 2ª ed. San José: Comisión Nacional de Conmemoraciones Históricas.
Thiel, Bernardo Augusto et al. [Thiel, Bernardo Augusto, León Fernández y Bonilla, Francisco Pereira, Concepción Quesada, José María Figueroa, Ramón Quesada, Mercedes Quesada, Baltasar Quesada, Joaquín País, Jesús País, and Raimundo Hernández]
1882. "Nº. 1. Protesta hecha por varios vecinos de Costa-Rica, contra el Comandante de San Carlos, con motivo de ultrajes que éste les hizo." *La Gaceta Diario Oficial*, 5:1265 (May 20), 2.
Valverde, Pánfilo J.
1907. *Industria pecuaria: la cría de ganado y el abigeato en la Provincia de Guanacaste*. San José: Tipografía Nacional.
von Frantzius, A.
1893 [1862]. *La ribera derecha del Río San Juan (una parte casi desconocida de Costa Rica)*, P. Biolley, trans. San José: Tip. Nacional.
von Oertzen, Eleonore; Lioba Rossbach; and Volker Wünderich, eds.
1990. *The Nicaraguan Mosquitia in Historical Documents 1844–1927*. Berlin: Dietrich Reimer Verlag.
Weinstein, Barbara
1983. *The Amazon Rubber Boom 1850–1920*. Stanford: Stanford University Press.
Yungjohann, John C.
1989. *White Gold: The Diary of a Rubber Cutter in the Amazon 1906–1916*. Oracle, AZ: Synergetic Press.

8

Transnational Labor Process and Gender Relations: Women in Fruit and Vegetable Production in Chile, Brazil and Mexico

Jane I. Collins

The more we understand about the development of capital itself, the more we understand that...alongside the drive to commodify everything...is another critical part of its logic which works in and through specificity. Capital has always been quite concerned with the question of the gendered nature of labor power.   (Hall 1991:29)

To superimpose the categories developed by Labor Market Segmentation proponents and radical economists upon the conditions that exist in underdeveloped countries is a theoretically sterile exercise.   (Fernández-Kelly 1983:99)

In recent years, anthropologists whose research focuses on labor have faced a series of challenging questions. We have attempted to follow the changing ways in which workers are being incorporated into an increasingly complex international division of labor. We have sought to document the effects of the adoption of neoliberal economic policies on labor. And, in a more introspective and methodological vein, we have looked for new models that will help us analyze local-level changes in labor relations stemming from global economic change. For researchers working in Latin American contexts, where the strength of labor movements was undermined or destroyed by repressive regimes of the 1960s, 1970s and 1980s, and where neoliberalism has been widely embraced, these issues have been especially pressing.

The literature devoted to these questions is massive, and this article will examine only one small part of it – labor dynamics within the export fruit and vegetable industry. Yet the story of this particular sector has implications for research on Latin American labor in other contexts. In part, this is because export fruit and vegetable production tends to be extremely labor intensive. Therefore, labor in this sector faces corporate strategies aimed at wage reduction and "casualization" that parallel strategies in other labor-intensive industries, such as textiles and electronics (Collins 1995a; Pugliese 1991). In part, the broader implications are methodological, as all anthropologists working on labor issues struggle with questions of how to integrate the local and global forces that structure labor relations, and how to broaden our understanding of labor markets to take into account the "extra-economic" institutions that affect their form and function. This article will provide a brief overview of the recent growth of export fruit and vegetable production, and of labor dynamics within the industry. It will then review the ways in which research on this sector in Latin America has extended our theoretical understanding of the functioning of local labor markets harnessed to the production of exports for national and transnational capital.

The Fresh Fruit and Vegetable Industry in Latin America

While the fresh fruit and vegetable industry has always been global, several recent trends have fostered its growth and transnational integration. One is the increased consumption of fresh produce in industrialized nations (Cook 1990), an increase facilitated by the development of new cold-chain technologies for long-distance distribution and marketing (Friedland 1994:174). In 1990, fruits and vegetables constituted 13% of world agricultural exports. They were exceeded in volume of international trade only by grain and oilseeds, and were a more significant proportion of total trade than either agricultural raw materials or sugar (Islam 1990). U.S. imports for all fruits and vegetables more than doubled from 1979 to 1989 – from just over two billion to 4.8 billion dollars (1982 dollars). The value of Mexico's exports increased 167% during this period, while Brazil's increased 262% and Chile's 367% (FAO 1985, 1989). In addition to an overall increase in consumption, there has been a shift toward consumption of fresh – rather than processed – fruits and vegetables and toward reduced pesticide and chemical residues (Lopez 1989). These changing consumer preferences require a more labor intensive production process and often entail new modes of controlling work regimens (Collins 1995b).

Within the fruit and vegetable industry, globalization has taken a number of forms. In some cases, transnational firms have become involved in production, either on their own account, or through sub-contracting. While the industry is dominated by five large conglomerates,[1] smaller

firms of diverse origins have also become involved in direct production. Even in regions where transnationals control only a small proportion of total output, their presence changes the competitive environment for all firms. In the Chilean case, Valdés has noted that the established agrarian elite of the fruit-producing zones has responded to the "wake-up call of the transnationals," becoming integrated into international circuits of finance capital and monitoring international markets (1992:71).

When *national* firms produce for export, they must frequently rely on the services of specialized brokers, jobbers and agents to locate their produce on world markets (Friedland 1994:180). Their success depends as much on their ability to obtain reliable access to these post-harvest services as it does on their competitiveness at the point of production (Jaffee 1992). Extremely specialized transport and storage facilities are required to maintain an unbroken cold chain from the packing house to the point of purchase. The timely availability of transportation and other facilities is crucial to the quality of the product. While small farmers have successfully gained access to export services in some cases, larger firms characteristically have an advantage in utilizing these channels (Carter et al. 1993). For this reason, while small farms can often produce export fruits and vegetables at a lower cost than larger operations, they are at an overall disadvantage in entering export markets (Collins n.d.).

Within neoliberal discourse, many fruits and vegetables have been characterized as "non-traditional exports." This perspective argues that "new" fruits and vegetables – often destined for upscale niche markets in Europe, the United States and Japan – can contribute to the foreign exchange earnings of debt-strapped nations. It resurrects arguments about comparative advantage to suggest that climate and cheap labor make Third World production sites particularly appropriate for these crops (Goldin 1990; Sarris 1984). Yet as several observers have noted, these crops possess many of the disadvantages of more traditional agricultural exports, including low levels of fixed capital investment, volatility in terms of trade, and high levels of competition.

As Llambi notes, "For most Latin American countries, to become specialized fruit and vegetable exporters may be no more than an updated version of former divisions of labor that reduced them to raw material exporters and manufactured goods and basic food importers" (1994:211). Raynolds (1994) has emphasized the need for strong state regulation in order to stabilize investment and obtain benefits from growth in this sector.[2]

The role of labor within the fruit and vegetable industry has been less studied, though as the arguments about comparative advantage suggest, the competitiveness of these firms is premised on their ability to pay a low wage. Because the production of high quality fruits and vegetables for export is extremely labor intensive, firms in this sector are continually interested in tapping new, lower-cost pools of workers. The case studies that are available demonstrate how firms use the political and social arrangements in which labor markets are embedded to both cheapen and discipline local labor forces.

One of the major ways that the fruit and vegetable industry has "cheapened" its labor supply is through the employment of women. In almost all contexts of production, the labor force in fruit and vegetable production is predominantly female (Collins 1995a). In some places, women work mostly in packing (Arizpe and Aranda 1981; Feder 1978; Roldán 1982), while in other places they work in the fields (Barrón 1990; Collins 1993; Venegas 1992). In some cases, firms employ women almost exclusively as temporary workers (Rodríguez and Venegas 1989; Valdés 1992) while in others they hire them on a quasi-permanent basis (Collins 1993). Firms may employ older women with families for some tasks and young unmarried women for others (Roldán 1982; Venegas 1992). Gender never operates simply, or in isolation, in these labor markets, but in connection with a host of other factors, including race, ethnicity, citizenship status and migrancy (Krippner n.d.; Thomas 1985). These factors intersect in determining the economic vulnerability of workers, and the value that will be attributed to their labor, as well as their susceptibility to regulation by state institutions and to control by household and family structures.

Theories of Workforce Structure: The Failure to Account for Heterogeneous Outcomes

Fruit and vegetable firms clearly attempt to design labor regimes that accommodate the high labor requirements of the production process, as well as the need for labor that is disciplined enough to meet the stringent quality standards set for fruit and vegetable import. Labor costs are often the single most important element of a firm's cost structure. Research conducted by the author in the São Francisco Valley of Northeastern Brazil revealed that labor could account for as much as 60% of production costs for export grapes (Collins n.d.). The importance to firms of strategies to obtain cheap labor is revealed in the following quote from a document prepared for the Chilean fruit industry:

> A final element, of no less relevance, is the availability of cheap labor, given the importance of this item in the cost structure of producing and commercializing the fruit. The advantages derived from this factor have accentuated in the last few years, to the degree that high rates of unemployment have tended to discourage migration to the large centers. There has thus been generated a contingent of surplus labor, which has permitted us to achieve higher levels of production... without any significant degree of pressure for salary increases. (Gana and Romaguera 1987:50, translation by author)

A Brazilian brochure designed to attract foreign investment echoes these strategic concerns:

> The Northeast of Brazil, where most of the São Francisco River Valley lies, is considered a poor region, afflicted with periodic droughts, and with a large number of under- or unemployed. It has become a tradition, during the droughts, for the population to migrate to the Mid-South of the country in search of employment. The irrigation projects now underway have attracted part of this contingent. Thus, the labor force that is found right in the region has helped reduce production costs. (CODEVASF, n.d., translation by author)

While cheap labor is obviously of tremendous concern, firms do not obtain it in the relatively straightforward way that existing theories would predict. One body of theory that should have something to say about the structure of the workforce in the fruit and vegetable industry focuses on the "new international division of labor." Beginning with the work of Fröbel, Heinrichs and Kreye (1980), this research has focused on the internationalization of the circuits of productive capital, particularly recent shifts of industrial production from core to peripheral nations in the world economy. These arrangements are held to differ from more traditional international trading arrangements in the degree of functional integration they involve, with the increasing fragmentation of many production processes and their relocation on a global scale (Dicken 1992). Theories of the new international division of labor have emphasized the search by transnational corporations for cheap, controllable labor with the goal of minimizing labor costs. Proponents have discussed the way this search has been facilitated by developments in production technologies that permit fragmentation and standardization of processes (Henderson and Castells 1987). Some researchers have also pointed to the impact of falling rates of profit and labor mobilization in the industrialized countries (Jenkins 1984). If the theory of comparative advantage says that Third World nations *ought* to be producing labor intensive crops and manufactures, proponents of the new international division of labor say that transnational corporations have recognized the advantages of cheap labor and are globalizing their production operations in response to this fact.

Another body of theory which should have implications for the study of a globalizing fruit and vegetable industry is labor force segmentation theory. Researchers working within this tradition have emphasized the distinction between a primary sector of relatively high waged, secure jobs with benefits and a secondary sector of lower-waged jobs requiring less skill and education and offering less security, fewer benefits and little opportunity for advancement (Reich, Gordon and Edwards 1973). While originally devised to explain the structure of the labor force in

the U.S. and Western Europe, some researchers have argued that by transferring unskilled and semi-skilled operations abroad, "multinational corporations transform foreign labor markets into an extension of the secondary sector in core countries; that is they transfer abroad certain features present in the secondary sector of the U.S. labor market in order to embrace foreign workers" (Fernández-Kelly 1983:100).

Feminist researchers who have sought to revise theories of the new international division of labor and labor force segmentation have argued that if Third World labor is "cheap" in the international context Third World women's labor is cheaper (Chapkis and Enloe 1983; Fuentes and Ehrenreich 1983). This body of work has shown that rates of female employment have increased with the shift from import-substitution industrialization in the Third World to export-oriented approaches (Chinchilla 1977; Safa 1981). It has shown how the constraints of home responsibilities, as well as cultural constructions of domesticity and motherhood, have shaped women's entrance into labor markets as well as the recruitment strategies of firms (Stichter and Parpart 1990). Many authors have emphasized the importance of employer demand in structuring the positions that women occupy in the workforce (Scott 1990) and have noted the concentration of women in certain labor-intensive branches of industry (Elson and Pearson 1981; Lim 1978; Milkman 1983).

These bodies of theory point to the fact that firms involved in labor intensive production seek ways to reduce the cost of that labor. They suggest that relocation to Third World production sites and hiring women are important ways of accomplishing that reduction. As previously indicated, this is clearly an important factor impelling the globalization of the fruit and vegetable industry. But none of these theories explains the specificity of workforce outcomes within Third World settings. As Fernández-Kelly has pointed out for the manufacturing sector, they fall short of explaining why, within the secondary segment of the labor market, and even within particular sectors, women are hired by particular industries and concentrated in certain occupations (1983:96). In the specific context of fruit and vegetable production, they do not explain why women form a semi-permanent labor elite in some regions, while they are among the most disenfranchised temporary workers in others. They do not explain why women of particular ages are preferred for particular jobs. And they are silent on the ways that workers whose ethnicity, migrancy and citizenship status make them especially vulnerable are incorporated into the workforce (Krippner n.d.).

Fernández-Kelly suggests that in order to obtain a more fine-grained analysis of workforce outcomes we need a framework which identifies the ways that local labor markets are inserted into a broader economic and political context – that is, that looks at both local and global forces as they come together in a concrete institutional setting. In her research on the *maquiladora* industry on the U.S.-Mexican border, Fernández-Kelly notes an important difference in the recruitment patterns of apparel and electronics firms. Garment manufacturers tend to employ women who are older and less educated, many of whom are single mothers or have unemployed spouses. Electronics firms tend to hire younger, more educated women, who are often still living as daughters in their parental homes. These "demographic" differences subdivide the local labor market in subtle but important ways, creating a more elite sector (in electronics) with jobs that are generally of short duration (averaging three years) and a less privileged sector with longer term jobs. While both types of jobs fall within the secondary sector, their differential hiring practices operate to reduce wage rates and prevent the emergence of entitled workers.

Fernández-Kelly sees local and global forces as intersecting in local labor markets. It is in these labor markets that the needs of firms for a particular kind of labor at a particular price intersect with the needs of a local population for jobs. Just as the firms' needs are conditioned by aspects of the competitive environment within the industry, the form and scale of capital investment, supply and demand fluctuations and available technology (1983:3), the local population's need for jobs is conditioned by prevailing wages, unemployment rates for men and women, and unwaged opportunities to contribute to family income. In addition, local labor markets are the sites where a particular community's understandings of gender, ethnicity and work interact with the understandings held by capitalist firms.

The interplay between local and global forces in local labor markets can have a range of outcomes. As Hall (1993), Appadurai (1990) and others have noted, the impact of global investment patterns is not inevitably "homogenization" of local patterns to some dominant western norm. While a restructuring of local economies results from foreign investment and export production, local populations have often played an important role in shaping and/or resisting the new social forms that result. At times, Fernández-Kelly notes, multinational corporations can "benefit from and accentuate preexisting imbalances in labor markets" (1983:101). In these cases, they appropriate and deepen existing gender and ethnic divisions and enhance the illusion of their naturalness. In other cases, they may contradict prevailing notions of social order, "employing sectors of the population who were not previously part of the work force [such as most women] while excluding those who were [such as men]" (Fernández-Kelly 1983:101). Ong's research on employment in the export-processing zones of Malaysia demonstrates the resistance that may arise when the gender norms imposed by firms in the work environment contradict those held by workers (1987). In an example from the agricultural sector, Stolcke has shown how the employment of women under new wage labor regimes in coffee-producing zones of southern Brazil cracked the structure of the patriarchal families that had formerly sharecropped together in that region (1984).

The variability in the structure of the workforce in export fruit and vegetable production attests to the need for a framework like that used by Fernández-Kelly. It reveals the need to understand the strategies of firms as more than a search for undifferentiated cheap labor, and to look at the ways that firms mobilize local institutions and patterns of ethnic and gender discrimination to "cheapen" an already low-cost labor pool. It shows the power of local institutions in facilitating the entry of capital. Finally, it reveals the importance of attending to the power and agency of workers as they seek new ways of mobilizing to protect their interests, in contexts where syndical traditions have been eroded by authoritarian rule, and where ethnic and gender divisions are salient in the workplace.

Recent Studies

Chilean fruit workers: las temporeras

All analysts of Chilean fruit production have commented on the prevalence of temporary workers in the industry (cf. Gómez and Echenique 1982). Generally this pattern is held to be technically determined by the seasonality of the enterprise (Gana and Romaguera 1987:12–13). A 1986 study of grape production in Chile's Aconcagua Valley reveals a more complex pattern, however. While women provide over 40% of all work-days in the region, only 6% of the permanent workers hired by fruit firms are female (Rodríguez 1987: 260, 177). Among semi-permanent workers (workers legally contracted as temporaries, but whose contracts are systematically renewed so that they work most of the year) only 2% are female (Rodríguez and Venegas 1989:159). The vast majority of women working within the industry are thus employed for the six-month period of the harvest in field work and in packing houses.

In a study of seven grape firms in the Aconcagua Valley, Rodríguez (1987), Rodríguez and Venegas (1989), and Venegas (1992) have documented the gender and age composition of the workforce involved in various tasks associated with fruit production and post-harvest handling. The majority of women employed as temporary fruit workers are married; a large proportion (around 30%) are also heads of households (Venegas 1992:102). Many women who work in fruit see advantages in the "flexibility" of temporary contracts and feel that they could not continue working at the intense pace of the harvest throughout the year (Medel et al. 1989:52–56). Others, classified by Venegas as "multi-occupational" women, move from fruit packing during the harvest to a range of other temporary jobs during the rest of the year. These women are predominantly heads of household, or come from

families where men are unemployed or underemployed[3] (see also Valdés 1987:39–41 and 1988:419). In fact, a major focus of women's organizing within the fruit and vegetable sector in Chile has been the establishment of community kitchens to assist those who are without food during the period when work is not available (Valdés 1992:134–135).

Competition between men and women for temporary jobs in fruit production is allayed somewhat by the allocation of different positions in a highly specific technical division of labor. The 82% of men who work in the fields are assigned tasks such as maintenance of vines, cleaning, tying and planting. The 45% of women who work in the fields are generally only involved in harvest activities. In packing, women predominate. The 55% of women who work in the packing houses are assigned tasks in cleaning and packing, while the 13% of men who work in this context mainly construct boxes and move fruit into refrigerated spaces (Valdés 1992:102–106).

Valdés describes how this technical division of labor – which is highly arbitrary – acquires the characteristics of a sexual division of labor over time. Much of the literature on women's work in labor-intensive production systems argues that they possess unique capacities (whether innate or socialized) for painstaking work. Valdés' distinction between these two concepts makes it possible to see how a rather arbitrary assignment of tasks (with only tenuous links to real physical differences) becomes rationalized in terms of prevailing gender norms. For example, women's jobs are held to be repetitive, manual tasks that require delicacy and efficiency. Where employers require women to monitor and make judgements about the quality of the fruit, this is held to be akin to "'cosmetology' demanded by the consumer in the external market" (Valdés 1992:109, translation by author). Men's tasks, in contrast, are said to require "qualification" – they perform a "job" while women perform "tasks."

In addition to the gendered ways in which work is divided, Valdés shows that "every task carried out by men or women has distinct prestige, a different salary, different forms of payment and distinct working conditions (1992:110, translation by author). Men's jobs involve greater spatial mobility, greater use of tools of all sorts, and their positions are more likely to offer opportunities for advancement. While women who work in packing may earn more than men during their months of employment, Valdés reminds us that they are paid at piece rates, are often working 12-hour days, and that they only receive this income five to six months per year. Perhaps most importantly, men are allocated 100% of positions involving control and monitoring of other workers (Valdés 1992:109–111). This highly gendered division of labor within the firm, when combined with men's and women's distinct responsibilities in the home, leads Valdés to conclude that men and women in the fruit sector must mobilize through independent unions in order to represent their very different interests and to prevent men's greater public power from eclipsing women's agendas (1988:423).

The Chilean case is perhaps the most "classical" of the three to be reviewed here, in the sense that it fits best with prevailing theory. In an overall context of low wages, women have been tapped as a "new" source of labor[4] whose entry into the labor market creates a surplus of workers. As Fernández-Kelly notes, this kind of increase in the number of potential laborers "tends to diminish the bargaining power of the local working class" (1983:101), lowering wages for everyone. Lago (1987) has suggested that Chilean fruit firms have strategically shifted from employing male workers to employing women (often from the same households) at a lower wage. The "increase in production" without "pressure for salary increases," which Gana and Romaguera (1987:50) described as characteristic of the 1980s and 1990s, has resulted as much from the incorporation of women into the agricultural labor force as from any downturn in rural–urban migration in recent years.

Women have not been incorporated into the workforce randomly, however, but in accordance with cultural patterns that devalue women's labor. Fruit firms hire women in the most unstable and lowest paid positions. These positions, which in a technical sense require careful work and some skill, are gendered according to cultural norms largely shared by employers and employees. These norms draw a connection between women's tasks and their unremunerated and unvalued work in the home, thus justifying lower rates of pay and poorer working conditions. In addition, women are excluded from positions of power in the social division of labor of the firm – that is, from positions involving control or monitoring, and those with possibilities of upward mobility.

Northeastern Brazil: elite grape workers

If one believed that fruit firms assign tasks to women in accordance with the technical demands of the production process or women's innate propensities and abilities, one would only have to compare the Chilean and Brazilian cases in order to be dissuaded from this view. Research conducted in newly irrigated zones of Brazil's São Francisco Valley has revealed an extremely complex pattern of labor recruitment to the wide range of crops grown there (Collins 1993). Among the most surprising findings is the fact that women who work in grapes are among the most stably employed agricultural workers in the region.[5] Because climatic conditions are stable throughout the year, and because of the availability of irrigation, grape producers in the São Francisco Valley can obtain two harvests annually. Jobs in vineyards run for approximately 11 months of the year, and are thus among the most highly sought after jobs in the region. Unlike in Chile, women hold 65% of these jobs.

Grape exporters in the São Francisco Valley see the employment of women as helping them to resolve a contradiction between two important goals – producing a high quality product that can meet export standards and reducing the cost of labor. They argue that women are more willing to work under the heavy supervision required to insure consistent levels of quality,[6] and that they are socialized to perform tasks with "high interactive labor intensity" – that is, tasks involving the constant monitoring of plant health and growth, including careful weeding, pruning and irrigation and harvesting based on assessment of when individual pieces of fruit are ripe.[7] Unlike the Chilean case, on Brazilian grape farms women performed the entire range of tasks involved in caring for grapes over the productive cycle, as well as harvesting grapes and working in the packing houses. As in Chile, however, women did not operate machinery or work with irrigation technology and they did not perform tasks involving the monitoring or supervision of other workers.[8]

The arguments of firm managers that women are "better suited" to these production tasks in grapes do not seem to tell the whole story, however, given that managers in Chile found women workers to be inappropriate for many of these same jobs. Clues to some possible alternative explanations can be drawn from case studies of workforce segmentation in the United States. Oppenheimer (1970), Baran (1990) and others have shown that women are frequently recruited into new skilled jobs in order to establish low wage levels with the new skilled area. Baran, in particular, has shown how, in the U.S. insurance industry, women were recruited to jobs at the same time that those jobs were undergoing a process of "responsibilitization" – that is, as certain aspects of decision-making and quality control were shifted onto those jobs. In this way, employers gained access to a segment of the workforce that was both skilled and cheap. The literature on clerical work in the United States has shown a pattern of women and machinery being introduced into the labor process simultaneously, in order to retain a low valuation and low wage levels for jobs that have become more skilled and technical (Baran 1990; Crompton and Jones 1984).

If women were employed for a similar purpose in the São Francisco Valley, then one would expect the wage rate of permanent women to be less than that of permanent men. This is indeed the case. Women are routinely paid the minimum monthly wage – the same wage received by seasonal laborers. Men who work as permanent employees are paid one-and-a-half times the monthly minimum wage. The explanation that managers give for this differential is that permanent male employees are performing more responsible tasks, such as managing and monitoring irrigation equipment. Women's tasks – pruning and tying grape vines, even occasionally grafting them, and most quality control operations – are

considered less skilled. That is, skill – for these women – is recast as dexterity. Thus, a position in the workforce that might otherwise be construed as "elite" due to the skill levels required and the year-round nature of the work, is devalued by its classification as "women's work" and is remunerated accordingly.[9]

Another very important aspect of the structure of the workforce in the Brazilian case is the presence of large numbers of migrants from other drought-stricken areas of the Northeast in the irrigation zones. Firms hire these workers in temporary positions in a range of crops, usually on a day-by-day basis. They work without signed work cards, and therefore receive no benefits from the employer or the state. They are the "reserve army" of workers who flood the labor market, lower wages, and undermine the bargaining power of labor in the region. One could argue that it is in part because of their availability that women can be recruited to perform other functions within the workforce.

Mexican tomatoes: gender and ethnicity

Evidence from tomato-producing regions of Mexico reveals an even more complex structuring of the workforce than that described for grapes in Chile or Brazil. Roldán's (1982) early account of women's work in tomatoes noted the heterogeneity of the workforce. She observed that firms hired both younger women living in their parental households and older women who were partially or fully responsible for the support of their families. Her survey results did not indicate a clear pattern, however, in how these women were distributed among various tasks in tomato production.

More recent work on export tomato production in Sinaloa has related the structure of the workforce to changing competitive pressures as the Mexican tomato industry seeks to retain a position in U.S. markets. Krippner (n.d.:10–16) has shown that, because of high marketing costs (commissions, transport and tariffs), low labor costs are critical in allowing Sinaloan producers to compete with their counterparts in Florida. A series of strikes among tomato workers in the 1970s threatened to undermine the cost competitiveness of Sinaloan firms, and led these firms to experiment with a range of ways for lowering their wage bills.

Krippner describes a three-tiered system of labor recruitment which began to emerge in the late 1970s. The lowest tier of the system is field labor. To fill these jobs, firms recruit and transport indigenous families from other regions of Mexico. Field labor represents the largest portion of labor costs for firms, thus a reduction of wages in this area is significant. Importing labor artificially creates the "labor surplus" that was described in the Brazilian and Chilean cases. The use of family labor means that children can be employed at a lower wage (or in some cases, no wage) and that the activity is marked as "unskilled" by the presence of women and children. In addition, the ethnicity of workers and their dislocation render them especially vulnerable to the control of the firm in the regions where they are working (Krippner n.d.: 22–24). Krippner disagrees with accounts that have argued that workers are imported in order to deal with a labor shortage in zones of tomato production (Thompson 1987:206). She argues instead that this "is not so much a question of absolute labor shortages, but rather *labor at what cost* . . . local workers from Culiacan and surrounding communities have been priced out of the market by migrants. Moreover, what is really in short supply is not labor in general but labor which is politically vulnerable and without alternatives" (Krippner n.d.: 24).

The second tier of the labor system described by Krippner entails packing jobs, which are largely filled by young, unmarried women who are transported from production site to production site, following the tomato harvest. Because of this migratory pattern, these women are employed over a large portion of the year (ten months). The tasks involved in packing are highly specialized, and are paid at piece rate. Barrón (1990, 1992) has described these women as "professionals" because of their skill and specialization. Krippner notes that cultural constructions of gender which portray these young women's income as "supplementary" prevent them from translating specialization and skill into claims on higher salaries, job security or

benefits. In addition, continual migration between production sites also erodes their attempts to exercise the claims of more permanent workers (Krippner n.d.: 24–25).

A third group of tomato workers are the selectors, or sorters, who must accurately distinguish between grades of tomatoes based on criteria such as color, shape, firmness, blemishes and presence of disease. This is a complex task which requires significant experience to perform quickly and accurately. Tomato firms hire local women in the areas of production for this task. These women are hired for relatively short periods each year, but because of their experience, are rehired on a regular basis. Selectors are unable to parlay their significant skills into higher wages or benefits, however. This is due to the seasonality of their employment, their status as married or female household heads having limited labor market experience, and less propensity to migrate in search of employment (Barrón 1990:160; Krippner n.d.:27).

The case of tomato production in Sinaloa, Mexico reveals a strategy that combines elements of the Chilean and Brazilian cases. Women, within indigenous families, form part of a surplus labor force imported into the region in order to reduce wages for field labor. At the same time, because of the existence of this surplus labor, local women can be employed – as they are in Brazil – to devalue positions that would otherwise be marked as "elite" due to the regularity of employment or the skill required. As Krippner notes, "what emerges from this analysis is a picture of a highly differentiated and complex labor system in which gender plays a critical role in *articulation* with other worker characteristics" (n.d.: 6).

Conclusions

A recent (1991) advertisement run by Del Monte in *The Packer* (the trade magazine for fruit and vegetable growers and packers) showed two Hawaiian women standing in a pineapple field. The accompanying text referred to the women as "our secret ingredient" and explained that good labor (shown in the photograph to be female) allows Del Monte to meet its high quality standards for produce. Similarly, illustrations in a promotional brochure meant to lure foreign agribusiness to Brazil's newly irrigated São Francisco Valley (CODEVASF n.d.) juxtapose pictures of sophisticated irrigation technology with images of women working side-by-side with their children in the fields. These instances reveal the corporate rationale for the trends that are visible in agricultural and employment records throughout Latin America. Like other labor-intensive export industries, the viability of export fruit and vegetable production is premised on women's labor.

The case studies recounted here show clearly, however, that it is not *simply* women's labor that is at issue. Women who have formerly been relatively excluded from waged work form a "reserve army of labor" that can be tapped by fruit and vegetable firms if there are no other vulnerable populations (such as migrants or non-citizens) available. They can be hired for the most skilled and responsible positions in the workforce in order to mark those positions as low status and low waged. Cultural constructions of gender lend a sense of "naturalness" and inevitability to these arrangements. These constructions also "naturalize" the social division of labor within firms, in which men hold positions of power, monitoring and control. They provide a rationale for a technical division of labor in which certain tasks are defined as women's work, and therefore are paid less. To say that women provide "cheaper" labor to these firms, is to miss the multiple ways in which firms make flexible and strategic use of gender to lower their wage bills in a highly competitive industry.

Any labor regime carries its own contradictions, and the mobilization of women within the fruit and vegetable sector, particularly in Chile, has begun to expose some of these. Chilean women have organized to demand child care. They have also established their own child care facilities through the *Casa del Temporero* (Valdés 1992:139–142). The contradiction addressed here is a simple one: if women are a "surplus" labor force by virtue of their location within the home, they cannot be extracted from the home without relieving them of some of the responsibilities they bear in that location. The *Casa del Temporero* in Chile has also organized communal kitchens during the "off" season to support workers who

have no alternative means of support during that period (Valdés 1992). This action speaks to the fact that firms can only employ workers on a temporary basis if other forms of work are available to assure their survival through the rest of the year. In most cases, Chilean fruit workers are no longer semi-proletarians who have their own land in other locations, but are fully dependent on the wage. Additionally, male unemployment has rendered women's income from their work in fruit production central to family income.

As the opening quote from Hall (1991:29) suggests, capital operates in and through the specificity/inequality it finds in local settings. Capitalist firms may lay hold of, use and deepen those inequalities (Fernández-Kelly 1983:101). An adequate analysis of labor force outcomes requires attention to those non-market processes and institutions that create the disadvantaged statuses on which workforce segmentation is based (Thomas 1985:20). The cases presented in this paper reveal the utility of a focus on local labor markets as a way of integrating concerns with the global imperatives that drive the employment practices of firms and the local social processes that make labor available. They reveal that firms rarely seek labor that is simply cheap; even within the agricultural sector, firms require workers with varying degrees of skills and experience. They are able to work within existing structures of inequality at the local level in order to expand the labor pool and reduce wages, to reduce the returns to skill, and to tap workers whose social characteristics render them especially vulnerable and subject to control. What this implies is that theories of labor market segmentation and the international division of labor, as currently constructed, can only provide part of the picture. The description of the needs of capital, or the needs of specific sectors and firms, must be combined with a description of those social institutions that operate at the local level to produce a differentiated workforce.

NOTES

1   These firms are Dole, Chiquita, Albert Fisher, Polly Peck and Del Monte. See Burbach and

Flynn (1980) and Friedland (1994) for an account of the history and functioning of these firms.

2 See Sanderson (1985, 1986) for a critique of broader trends toward new forms of agricultural export dependence.

3 See Safa (1990) for a discussion of the effect of male unemployment on women's employment in other sectors.

4 In fact as Garrett (1978) and Valdés (1992) have noted, women worked in Chilean agriculture in large numbers during the period of *inquilinaje*. Their rates of participation dropped sharply during the period of agricultural modernization (1960s and 1970s), only to rise again with the growth of the fruit sector in the 1980s and 1990s.

5 This account of grape production in Brazil's São Francisco Valley is based on research conducted by the author in the region in 1991 and 1993, in collaboration with Dr. Jose Ferreira Irmão and Andrea Melo of the Department of Economics of the Universidade Federal de Pernambuco. Research was funded by the National Science Foundation.

6 See Milkman (1983) for a similar point in industrial settings.

7 See Carter et al. (1993) and Collins (n.d.) for discussions of how a demand for highly interactive labor differentially affects the competitiveness of small and large firms.

8 This refers only to working class women employed in production. Women who were trained in agronomy or other technical specialties sometimes performed such tasks.

9 Thomas (1985) has described a similar situation in California lettuce production. Firms targeted the most vulnerable segment of the population – illegal immigrants – to fill the most "elite" positions in the lettuce fields. Thomas argues that firms appropriated a "difference" among workers that made little sense in terms of matching skill to task, but that allowed them to place controllable employees (who were subject to deportation, and had no legal rights) in jobs which would have ordinarily wielded the greatest bargaining power.

REFERENCES CITED

Appadurai, Arjun
1990   Disjuncture and Difference in the Global Cultural Economy. Public Culture 2(2): 1–24.

Arizpe, Lourdes, and Josefina Aranda
1981   The "Comparative Advantages" of Women's Disadvantages: Women Workers in the Strawberry Export Agribusiness in Mexico. Signs 7(2):453–473.

Baran, Barbara
1990   The New Economy: Female Labor and the Office of the Future. *In* Women, Class and the Feminist Imagination: A Socialist-Feminist Reader. Karen V. Hansen and Ilene J. Philipson, eds. Philadelphia: Temple University Press.

Barrón, Antonieta
1990   Jornaleras Agrícolas en Hidalgo, Guanajuato y Morelos. *En* Trabajo Femenino y Crisis en Mexico: Transformaciones y Tendencias Actuales. Elia Ramirez and Hilda Davila, eds. México: Universidad Autónoma Metropolitana.
1992   Características y Tendencias de los Salarios entre los Trabajadores de las Hortalizas. Problemas del Desarrollo 23(91):213–232.

Burbach, Roger, and Patricia Flynn
1980   Agribusiness in the Americas. New York: Monthly Review Press.

Carter, Michael R., Bradford B. Barham, Dina Mesbah, and Denise Stanley
1993   Agro-exports and the Rural Resource Poor in Latin America: Policy Options for Achieving Broadly-Based Growth. Agricultural Economics Staff Paper Series No. 364, University of Wisconsin, Madison.

Chapkis, Wendy, and Cynthia Enloe
1983   Of Common Cloth. Washington, D.C.: Transnational Institute.

Chinchilla, Norma
1977   Industrialization, Monopoly Capitalism and Women's Work in Guatemala. *In* Women and National Development. Wellesley Editorial Committee, ed. Pp. 38–56. Chicago: University of Chicago Press.

CODEVASF (Companhia de Desenvolvimento do Vale do São Francisco) Untitled and undated brochure.

Collins, Jane L.
1993   Gender, Contracts and Wage Work: Agricultural Restructuring in Brazil's São Francisco Valley. Development and Change 24: 53–82.
1995a   Gender and Cheap Labor in Agriculture. *In* Food and Agrarian Orders in the World Economy. Philip McMichael, ed. Westport: Praeger Press.
1995b   Tracing Social Relations in Commodity Chains: The Case of Grapes. Paper presented to

the Society for Economic Anthropology, Santa Fe, New Mexico.

n.d. Farm Size and Non-Traditional Exports: Determinants of Participation in World Markets. Forthcoming in World Development.

Cook, Roberta L.
1990 Challenges and Opportunities in the U.S. Fresh Produce Industry. Journal of Food Distribution Research. February: 31–45.

Crompton, Rosemary and Gareth Jones
1984 White Collar Proletariat: Deskilling and Gender in Clerical Work. Philadelphia: Temple University Press.

Dicken, Peter
1992 Global Shift: The Internationalization of Economic Activity, second edition. New York: Guilford Press.

Elson, Diane, and Ruth Pearson
1981 Nimble Fingers Make Cheap Workers: An Analysis of Women's Employment in Third World Export Manufacturing. Feminist Review 7:87–107.

FAO (Food and Agricultural Organization)
1985 Trade Yearbook, Vol. 39.
1989 Trade Yearbook, Vol. 43.

Feder, Ernst
1978 Strawberry Imperialism. Mexico City: Editorial Campesina.

Fernández-Kelly, Maria Patricia
1983 For We Are Sold, I and My People: Women and Industry in Mexico's Frontier. Albany: SUNY Press.

Friedland, William
1994 The Global Fresh Fruit and Vegetable System: An Industrial Organizational Analysis. In The Global Restructuring of Agro-Food Systems. Philip McMichael, ed. Pp. 173–189. Ithaca: Cornell University Press.

Fröbel, Folker, Jurgen Heinrichs, and Otto Kreye
1980 The New International Division of Labor. New York: Cambridge University Press.

Fuentes, Annette, and Barbara Ehrenreich
1983 Women in the Global Factory. Boston: South End Press.

Gana, Juanita, and Pilar Romaguera
1987 Desarrollo y Perspectivas del Sector Fruticola en Chile. Santiago: Centro de Estudios del Desarrollo, Materiales para Discusión no. 155.

Garrett, Patricia
1978 Growing Apart: The Experiences of Rural Men and Women in the Central Valley of Chile.

Ph.D. dissertation, University of Wisconsin, Madison.

Goldin, Ian
1990 Comparative Advantage: Theory and Application to Developing Country Agriculture. Paris: Organization of Economic Cooperation and Development, Development Centre Technical Papers 16.

Gómez, Sergio, and Jorge Echenique
1982 Trabajadores temporeros de la agricultura moderna de Chile Central. Santiago: FLACSO, Documento de Trabajo no. 3.

Hall, Stuart
1991 The Local and the Global: Globalization and Ethnicity. In Culture, Globalization and the World System, Anthony King, ed. Pp. 19–39. London: Macmillan.
1993 Culture, Community and Nation. Cultural Studies 7(3): 349–363.

Henderson, J., and M. Castells, eds.
1987 Global Restructuring and Territorial Development. London: Sage.

Islam, Nurul
1990 Horticultural Exports of Developing Countries: Past Performances, Future Prospects and Policy Issues. Washington, D.C.: International Food Policy Research Institute, Research Report no. 80.

Jaffee, Stephen
1992 Marketing Africa's Horticultural Exports: A Transaction Cost Perspective. Fresh Fruit and Vegetables Globalization Network (University of California, Santa Cruz), Working Paper #3.

Jenkins, Rhys
1984 Divisions Over the International Division of Labor. Capital and Class 22:28–57.

Krippner, Greta R.
n.d. Agricultural Restructuring and Changing Labor Recruitment Strategies in Mexico's Export Tomato Industry. Unpublished paper, Department of Sociology, University of Wisconsin, Madison.

Lago, Maria Soledad
1987 Rural Women and the Neo-Liberal Model in Chile. In Rural Women and State Policy: Feminist Perspectives on Latin American Agricultural Development. Carmen Diana Deere and Magdalena Leon, eds. Pp. 21–34. Boulder: Westview Press.

Lim, Linda
1978 Women Workers in Multinational Corporations: The Case of the Electronics Industry in

Malaysia and Singapore. Ann Arbor: University of Michigan, Michigan Occasional Paper no. 9.

Llambi, Luis
1994   Comparative Advantages and Disadvantages in Latin American Nontraditional Fruit and Vegetable Exports. *In* The Global Restructuring of Agro-Food Systems. Philip McMichael, ed. Pp. 190–213. Ithaca: Cornell University Press.

Lopez, Rigoberto A.
1989   Constraints and Opportunities in Vegetable Trade. Journal of Food Distribution Research. March: 63–74.

Medel, Julia, Olivos M. Soledad Olivos, and Veronica G. Riquelme
1989   Las Temporeras y Su Visión del Trabajo. Santiago: Centro de Estudios de la Mujer.

Milkman, Ruth
1983   Female Factory Labor and Industrial Structure: Control and Conflict over "Women's Place" in Auto and Electrical Manufacturing. Politics and Society 12(2).

Ong, Aihwa
1987   Spirits of Resistance and Capitalist Discipline: Factory Women in Malaysia. Albany: SUNY Press.

Oppenheimer, Valerie
1970   The Female Labor Force in the United States. Berkeley: Institute of International Studies, University of California.

The Packer
1991

Pugliese, Enrico
1991   Agriculture and the New Division of Labor. *In* Towards a New Political Economy of Agriculture. William H. Friedland, Lawrence Busch, Frederick H. Buttel, and Alan P. Rudy, eds. Pp. 137–150. Boulder: Westview.

Raynolds, Laura
1994   The Restructuring of Third World Agro-Exports: Changing Production Relations in the Dominican Republic. *In* The Global Restructuring of Agro-Food Systems. Philip McMichael, ed. Pp. 214–238. Ithaca: Cornell University Press.

Reich, Michael, David M. Gordon, and Richard C. Edwards
1973   A Theory of Labor Market Segmentation. American Economics Review 63(2):359–365.

Rodríguez, Daniel O.
1987   Agricultural Modernization and Labor Markets in Latin America: The Case of Fruit

Production in Central Chile. Ph.D. dissertation, University of Texas, Austin.

Rodríguez, Daniel O., and Sylvia L. Venegas
1989   De Praderas a Parronales: Un Estudio Sobre Estructura Agraria y Mercado Laboral en el Valle de Aconcagua. Santiago: Grupo de Estudios Agro-regionales.

Roldán, Marta
1982   Subordinación generica y proletarización rural: Un estudio de caso en el Noroeste Mexicano. *En* Debate sobre la mujer en América Latina y el Caribe: Las trabajadoras del agro, Magdalena León, ed. Pp. 75–102. Bogota: Asociación Colombiana para el Estudio de la Población.

Safa, Helen
1981   Runaway Shops and Female Employment: The Search for Cheap Labor. Signs 7(2):418–433.
1990   Women and Industrialization in the Caribbean. *In* Women, Employment and the Family in the International Division of Labor. Sharon Stichter and Jane L. Parpart, eds. Pp. 72–97. Philadelphia: Temple University Press.

Sanderson, Steven
1985   The "New" Internationalization of Agriculture in the Americas. *In* The Americas in the New International Division of Labor, Steven Sanderson, ed. Pp. 46–68. New York: Holmes and Meier.
1986   The Transformation of Mexican Agriculture. Princeton: Princeton University Press.

Sarris, Alexander H.
1984   World Trade in Fruits and Vegetables: Projections for an Enlarged European Community. U. S. Department of Agriculture, Foreign Agricultural Economics Report #202.

Scott, Alison
1990   Patterns of Patriarchy in the Peruvian Working Class. *In* Women, Employment and the Family in the International Division of Labor. Sharon Stichter and Jane L. Parpart, eds. Pp. 198–220. Philadelphia: Temple University Press.

Stichter, Sharon and Jane L. Parpart, eds.
1990   Women, Employment and the Family in the International Division of Labor. Philadelphia: Temple University Press.

Stolcke, Verena
1984   The Exploitation of Family Morality: Labor Systems and Family Structure on Sao Paulo Coffee Plantations, 1850–1979. *In* Kinship Ideology and Practice in Latin America. Raymond T. Smith, ed. Chapel Hill: University of North Carolina Press.

Thomas, Robert J.
1985 Citizenship, Gender and Work: Social Organization of Industrial Agriculture. Berkeley: University of California Press.

Thompson, Gary David
1987 International Commodity Trade and Illegal Migration: The U.S. Fresh Winter Vegetable Market and Undocumented Emigration from Mexico. Ph.D. Dissertation, University of California, Davis.

Valdés, Ximena
1987 Los Procesos de Incorporación y Exclusión de las Mujeres del Mercado de Trabajo Agrícola. *En* Sinopsis de Una Realidad Ocultada: Las Trabajadoras del Campo. Pp. 23–50. Santiago: Centro de Estudios de la Mujer.

1988 Feminización del Mercado de Trabajo Agrícola: Las Temporeras. *En* Mundo de Mujer: Continuidad y Cambio. Pp. 389–432. Santiago: Centro de Estudios de la Mujer.

1992 Mujer, Trabajo y Medio Ambiente: Los Nudos de la Modernización Agraria. Santiago: Centro de Estudios para el Desarrollo de la Mujer.

Venegas Leiva, Sylvia
1992 Una Gota al Día... Un Chorro al Año... El impacto Social de la Expansión Fruticola. Santiago: Grupo de Estudios Agro-regionales.

9

Inequality Near and Far: International Adoption as Seen from a Brazilian *Favela*

Claudia Fonseca

In a recent book on international adoption, the social worker responsible for describing the situation in Brazil underlines the superior quality of overseas adopters. Brazilian nationals, judging from the number of children returned to the court, "lack a serious attitude toward adoption." The author mentions factors such as poor financial conditions and unstable family structures which might explain this lack of seriousness, but, in her opinion, the real motive (and key to a solution?) lies in the fact that Brazilians don't pay anything for the adopted child: "In contrast, expenses for foreigners are huge, and the adoptive ties turn out to be strong and lasting" (Silva 1995: 126).

These comments serve as a springboard for the subject of my article: Brazilian adoption practices, placed within a globalized context. They speak of a problem which is central to my concerns – the so-called "gap" between law and actual behavior.[1] However, inverting the question which this social worker implicitly poses ("Why can't Brazilians measure up to international norms of adoption?"), I ask: How is it that Brazilian laws, often touted as being at the forefront of progressive international legislation, fail so utterly to take into account local values and social dynamics? In fact, in this article, I would hope to convince my reader that it is no surprise that foreign adopters conform more closely to Brazilian legal directives than national

candidates since the laws, rather than based on and adapted to an accurate assessment of local reality, derive directly from the abstract principles which dominate international debates.

The possibly reprehensible character of this fact derives from two hypotheses. First, that these abstract principles are not the neutral product of consensual humanitarian interests. They are, rather, the fruit of ideological power struggles, and are inevitably shaped by the hegemonic narratives which reflect above all First World contexts and values (Silbey 1997). Following this line of thought, the very popularity of legal adoption which seems to have recently swept the globe – from Clinton's speech in which Americans are urged to adopt the 500,000 children in foster care[2] to the Brazilian child welfare services' listing of adoptable children on Internet sites – may be considered part of a hegemonic narrative in which this particular form of child placement is presented as the "obvious" remedy for the ills of the world's children. The criticism of hegemonic narratives on adoption having been elaborated elsewhere (see, for example, Yngvesson 2000; Selman 2000; Fonseca 2000), I will dwell in this article on a second hypothesis: that, in many countries, distinct values and patterns of family organization, including non-mainstream forms of adoption, exist on a widespread basis. To illustrate, I rely on ethnographic research in Brazilian *favelas*, arguing that, to socialize and ensure the survival of younger generations, lower-income families have traditionally resorted to the informal placement of children in different substitute households, and that the dynamics of this "circulation of children"[3] have not only been ignored, but disavowed by legislators and social workers alike. Thus, I suggest, adoption laws have evolved in a way that simply does not make sense to a good many people – a supposition that not only would explain the "lack of seriousness" of local adopters, but which would also raise doubts about another fundamental issue in the adoption process: the treatment of birth parents in the legal procedures which render their child available for adoption. Having worked with the sort of poverty-stricken families from which most adoptable children are drawn, I shall concentrate my aim on this latter element: the understanding and possible misconceptions birth parents and, in particular, birth mothers have of the adoption process.

My approach is not entirely original. I have drawn inspiration from the abundant literature which points out discrepancies between state law and particular community practices concerning child welfare.[4] Judith Modell (1997), commenting on the tendency of Hawaiian state services to remove native children from their clan-like kinship networks to place them in non-Hawaiian (white and Japanese) families with a more mainstream way of life, furnishes a recent example of how official legislation, fashioned along historically specific family values, has been used to exploit and oppress minority groups. Her study reveals how Hawaiians, in the name of their distinct cultural heritage, seize upon the very weapons offered by the court – Western legal discourse – to protect their right to be different and raise their children in what might seem, according to official state criteria, substandard homes. Native Americans, Canadian Inuits, and Australian aborigines are among the many groups who have likewise proved competent in appropriating the political strategies of modern government to stem the flow of children extracted from their communities, whether by missionaries or adoptive parents, to be raised and educated in another way of life. Sally Merry would no doubt include many of these examples

in what she describes as "legal vernacularisation," a process whereby colonized minorities, in their bid for human rights, reinterpret and transform Western law according to their own legal conceptions (Merry 1997).

In our case, the matter is complicated by the fact that we are dealing with people whose mixed racial background (African, Native American, Polish, Portuguese) leaves them with no other identity than that of "poor." What are we to do with "uncool"[5] forms of social tradition such as the circulation of children when they do not benefit from the cover of a politically correct (for example, ethnic) movement?

Ever since the devastating critiques of the culture-of-poverty approach, anthropologists dealing with the urban poor have been skittish about framing their analysis in terms of "cultural difference."[6] This malaise has, if anything, been exacerbated by recent academic debates which, on the one hand, have placed increasing emphasis on globalization, and, on the other, have leveled severe criticisms against the notion of culture.[7] Today, analysts who speak of contextually specific value systems are all too easily judged to be romantics working with an outdated concept of (reified and overly coherent) culture, forged by people in complete geographic isolation.

Fortunately, certain researchers, taking a hard look at the analytical alternatives, have stood their ground, suggesting, as do Yanagisako and Delaney, that although the overemphasis on cultural differences may well have been instrumental in countless colonialist abuses, to ignore cultural specificities can also justify forms of social domination: "Assimilating 'them' to 'us', can do violence to what people cherish that is distinct about themselves" (1995: 16). In my study of adoption as seen from the Brazilian *favela*, such a stance seems not only analytically sound, but politically recommendable. Failing to consider certain forms of cultural specificity among the urban poor, state authorities have proceeded untroubled with the removal of children from what they consider problematic families. The consistent refusal to entertain the possibility of alternative family patterns leaves them no other option than to label many households "disorganized" – a diagnosis which can but contribute to the breakdown of existing dynamics. On the other hand, reframing the analysis in terms of cultural dynamics complicates this picture. Such an approach need not imply romantic pleas for traditional purity, not the idealization of practices such as child circulation, which, like any other social dynamic, can be fraught with conflict, internal contradictions, and, in some particular cases, may even justify energetic state intervention. This approach does, nonetheless, imply the existence of non-mainstream logics which, however foreign to the hegemonic narrative, make sense to certain sane and intelligent people, and – what's more – may actually work to their benefit in ways unimagined by convention-bound state authorities.

By emphasizing the specificity of family practices and values among Brazilian *favela* residents, I do not mean to produce the image of separate and isolated cultural spheres. On the contrary, I hope to demonstrate the interlinking processes which, from local practice to national legislation and global policy, influence family-related values. This perspective, inspired in the notion of "stratified reproduction" (Colen 1995), concentrates on how different cultural repertoires interweave, clash, or complement each other according to the particular historical circumstances. The scrutiny of cultural difference is, furthermore, inseparable from considerations of the political and social inequality which cause certain sets of values to be presented as superior to others.

To achieve my aim, I will first present the setting and a brief ethnographic account of child circulation among working-class families in Porto Alegre, Brazil. Having set the background, I zero in on those elements of the traditional system which most resemble legal adoption, drawing attention to *adoção à brasileira* (a sort of clandestine adoption) as a way in which the Brazilian poor bypass legal bureaucratic procedures in order to adjust the state apparatus to their needs. The active participation of birth mothers in the placement of their children is contrasted with prevalent national policy which, by its insistence on secrecy in the adoption process, leaves biological kin completely out of the picture. Finally, I suggest that, under the influence of international campaigns on children's rights, recent Brazilian policies of state intervention,

rather than becoming more sensitive to local-level "alternative" family practices, demonstrate increasing indifference. Altogether, by looking at the enchained processes of stratified reproduction, I hope to demonstrate how issues in the global arena pass through national legislators and local professionals to affect not only institutionalized children who might be given in adoption, but also those who remain in their lower-income families.

Continuity and Change in the Brazilian Context

When, in 1981, I began research in Porto Alegre,[8] I was singularly impressed by the lack of public agents in the city's working-class neighborhoods: no social workers, no nurses, and no domestic helpers. Poor people lived in informally segregated residential areas from which they made daily forays into middle- and upper-class neighborhoods, whether as workers or beggars; however, aside from an occasional nun doubling as a social worker, I seldom saw representatives of the state entering these zones. The particular *favela* I was then working in was known as "the lawless zone," since even the police were reputed to be afraid of penetrating the area. My estimate was that not more than a quarter of the adult couples with children were legally married. Most workers, being part of the informal economy, did not possess a social security number and a good many of the older people had no identity documents, much less the legally required voter's registration card. True, in less poverty-stricken zones, there were schools (offering a maximum of four hours' daily instruction to local children) and public dispensaries, but it was a rare day when the teachers or health officers entered anyone's home. In other words, unless they committed a serious crime, the urban poor had contact with the state authorities when and how they chose to – which was not all that often.

It was in just such a context that I first became aware of the circulation of children. In a first neighborhood of poverty-stricken squatters (ragpickers, beggars, and an occasional construction worker), approximately half the women had placed a child, whether on a short- or long-term basis, with a substitute family or at the state orphanage. Five years later (1986), I began a second phase of research in a less miserable working-class district – inhabited by artisans, janitors, maids, bus drivers, and other lower-income employees – where better-off families had an average income of around $200 a month. Here, I encountered a surprising number of women who had at some time taken in a child to raise. A fine line divided "foster" from adoptive offspring, as many children who had embarked on a short sojourn just "stayed on" in their new home. All in all, in more than 120 households which I canvassed during my field research, I discovered nearly 100 people who had, during their childhood, transited between the households of godmothers, grandmothers, and other sorts of mothers de *criação*.[9] Of these, not one had been legally adopted.[10]

Since the 1964 coup d'état, the military regime had manifested its concern for children and youth through a state-run service, the *Fundação Estadual de Bem-Estar do Menor* (FEBEM) which, aside from sponsoring a series of private and philanthropic institutions, basically limited its action to the institutionalization of poor, orphaned, and refractory children. Much to my surprise, the slum-dwellers I was studying neither feared nor resented this agency. Rather, they used it to their own advantage.[11] There were an infinite number of reasons a woman might want to institutionalize a child: for example, if she was going through a particularly bad financial period (which was often), if she had nowhere to live, or if she remarried and her new companion refused to support her children from previous unions. Parents might also use the threat of internment to keep their disobedient children in line.[12] If institutional authorities attempted to impose obstacles, alleging that the establishment was not meant to be a simple "boarding school," a woman could trump up more persuasive arguments, claiming, for example, that her child was in danger of rape by a new stepfather or menacing neighbor (see Fonseca 1986). At any rate, the mothers I knew who had institutionalized a son or daughter generally considered the arrangement temporary, and expected to bring the child home "as soon as things got better."

Those women who later showed up at the orphanage, ready to resume their motherhood, sometimes after years of absence, would thus be stupefied when told that their child had been declared "abandoned" and given up for adoption. Even those who had signed a paper consenting to their child's adoption did not seem to grasp the idea that they had been permanently stripped of their motherhood and that the child had disappeared forever. From their point of view, they had left their children in the care of the institution in the same spirit they would have resorted to a grandmother or neighbor. On occasion, these substitute mothers also insisted that the transfer of parental responsibilities should be permanent, but experience often proved them wrong. In the great majority of cases, the birth mother and child would eventually end up in contact, and the child would not be lost to its kin group. In the birth mother's confrontation with state authorities, the clash of different rationalities was glaringly evident.

During the 1980s, the Brazilian political scenario went through important changes. Emerging from 20 years of military dictatorship, the country witnessed with tolerance an effervescence of social movements: workers' strikes, invasions of housing projects, marches for land reform, and church-led neighborhood associations. With an increasing number of university-educated professionals, including social and community health workers, as well as a technologically more efficient state bureaucracy, there arose a demand for greater intervention in people's domestic affairs. The writing of a new constitution (completed in 1988) mobilized thousands of activists aiming at social reforms who then turned their attentions specifically to the subject of children. Spurred on by the international attention given to the theme (events such as the 1989 United Nations Convention on the Rights of the Child), as well as the Brazilian government's desire to avoid unflattering publicity on its "street children," the National Congress passed, in 1990, the *Estatuto da Criança e Adolescente* (hereafter referred to as the 1990 Children's Code).

Touted as a document "worthy of the First World," in some respects, "even more advanced than the United Nation's Declaration on the

Rights of the Child," the Code was seen by many activists as a hallmark in the history of Brazilian children. Aside from guaranteeing to all children the right to "life, health, food, education, sports, leisure, preparation for a future profession, culture, dignity, respect, and liberty," it declared radical changes in institutional policies. "Orphaned" children were to be separated from juvenile offenders, allowing for each category to be placed in specialized and decentralized institutions adapted to their particular needs. No child was to be institutionalized (whether because or despite of his parents' pleas) merely for reasons of poverty. The quality of a child's home environment was to be monitored through local-level "Children's Tutelary Councils," made up of commissioners whose sole concern would be to guarantee the rights and conditions of children within their families, school, and public space.

Brazil, however, has a long history of passing "symbolic legislation" which has very little effect on its citizens' concrete behavior (Vianna 1996). In 1993 and 1994, curious as to the extent to which changes in the political agenda had affected the lives of common citizens, I conducted a series of interviews in working-class families. The following accounts, used to convey ethnographic details of the circulation of children in Brazilian *favelas*, are drawn from this second phase of field research. Because so little time had passed since the enactment of the new Children's Code, my study did not ultimately reveal the new legislation's full impact on local populations. However, as we will see in the first example given below, it did demonstrate the presence of deep-rooted values linked to a sort of "fosterage culture" which, four years after the new law, still appeared to be highly relevant to people's lives. And, as we observe in the second example, it furnished insights into certain forms of legal consciousness linked to a baby's "clandestine" adoption. Through a birth mother's tale, we not only come to imagine why, to certain actors, such a procedure might appear to be more attractive than proper legal adoption, but we also begin to wonder about the political factors bearing on adoption laws which have left this sort of mother so few options.

Inez's Mothers: Survival, Conflict, and Blood Ties

Inez was 38 years old when I met her. At the time, her husband was distributing newspapers while she worked as an attendant at the neighborhood day-care center. As a preamble to her life story, she mentioned the odds she was up against during her early childhood: 9 of her 16 brothers and sisters had died in infancy: "My mother was very poor. She didn't get enough to eat so the babies would be born already undernourished." Inez was lucky enough to have been placed with her godmother, Dona Joana, early on. She explains: "They took me to visit my godmother and when it was time to go home, I grabbed on to a table leg, and nobody could pry me loose. So, they just let me stay on."

Dona Joana, despite being sterile, had always been surrounded by children, brought in by her activities as a midwife and foster mother.[13] Twenty years before Inez entered her life, she had acquired a son, an "abandoned" child whom she'd illegally registered as though he were her own flesh and blood. This son became, for a short period, Inez's stepfather, making the (then) little girl a sort of granddaughter in the three-generation household. However, for a good part of her childhood, Inez had called the elderly woman who cared for her neither "Godmother" nor "Grandmother," but rather "Mother." When, eventually, Inez's birth mother, long since separated from Dona Joana's son and living elsewhere, demanded her daughter's return, the conflict had to be settled in court.

Disputes, in fact, are not uncommon; the coexistence of different sets of parents is hardly pacific. Especially when a child transfer takes place because of a crisis situation in the mother's life, there is often a great deal of ambiguity about who is actually helping whom. Birth mothers will claim they have made a gift to another household, blessing it with the gracious presence of a child. Foster parents, for their part, often broadcast a different sort of discourse – insisting they have accepted the care-taking "burden" in order to help out, and implying that, in reward, they deserve to keep the child permanently. Considering the inadequacy (if not total lack) of old-age pensions among working-class individuals, the moral issue – to whom a grown child owes his or her loyalty – instead of waning, takes on increasing importance with time, and quibbling between different mothers is not uncommon.

Of course, a birth mother may clarify the ambiguous terms of informal child placements by paying the foster family for the child's upkeep, thus reaffirming her maternal status. However, the question then arises: if a woman cannot afford to support a son or a daughter in her own home, how is she to pay for its upkeep in someone else's? We may reasonably assume that Dona Joana – who earned her living as a foster mother paid either by the state or directly by her ward's parents – was expecting to be financially compensated for taking in Inez, and that it was precisely the non-payment of this debt which led Joana to claim maternal privileges. As in many other situations we observed, the child's caretaker saw maternal status – with its emotional and long-term material benefits – as compensation for the unpaid debt.[14]

It is no coincidence, on the other hand, that Inez's mother, when recounting her version of the story, underlined the fact that Dona Joana was an elderly widow. In an evident attempt to reverse the flow of obligations, she presented the gracious company of her little girl as a sort of gift to this solitary woman. Her stance is made credible by the fact that, in the neighborhoods where I worked, children appear to be indeed cherished. Young, unmarried mothers as well as widows and recently divorced women going through hard times will be bombarded with offers by people seeking to take babies and toddlers off their hands (see Fonseca 1985). Since, according to local values, both Inez's birth and foster mothers had valid claims over the child, they resorted to the court to resolve the question of the girl's legal custody.[15]

Notwithstanding the various conflicts that result from this "invented kinship," the bonds it forms appear to be more long-lasting than the grudges. Well into old age, Dona Joana – finding herself with no retirement benefits, no property, and incapable of making a living – was taken in by her former rival, Inez's mother – Maria. At the time of our interview, she was reigning as proud

"grandmother" over an extended household that included at least four nuclear families (those of Maria and three of Maria's married children). The fact that she had no blood connection to the other members of the family appeared to trouble no one, exactly because her tie to this family was as unquestionable and enduring as a biologic fact. "*Mãe é quem criou*" ("Mother is whoever brings you up"), her family members explained, using an adage known to all – one which states that to give food and lodging to another person carries with it all sorts of affective and symbolic consequences, creating in the case of child placement a bond not only between tutor and ward, but also between the different adult partners of exchange.

The example of Inez and her family demonstrates how a child's placement may be used to cement or even create new social networks. A woman, for example, may expect to receive periodic aid from her brother in exchange for raising his children. A grandmother will see her own married children far more often if she is raising one of their offspring. By taking in a poor cousin or an orphaned nephew, an upwardly mobile relative will demonstrate to his kin group that he is not getting "uppity," nor does he intend to sever ties. Finally, the circulation of children also serves to expand the kin group to neighbors and unrelated friends, such as Dona Joana, as momentary affinities are transformed into lifelong relationships through the sharing of parental responsibilities.

The placement of a child may well have a utilitarian aspect. Women are often driven by sheer necessity to find substitute families for their children, but poverty does not explain the willingness with which people take in unrelated youngsters. It never ceased to amaze me how many even very poor households open their doors to "help out" an extra child or young person.[16] As they say, "*Onde come um português, come dois, três*" ("Where there's food enough for one, there's food enough for two, three"). Amid so dynamic a play of household arrangements, the question arises: How do people view the subject of kinship and personal identity?

The story of Inez's family underlines the socially forged nature of kinship; it also serves to illustrate the enormous weight attributed to blood ties. Of Inez and her six siblings, only the last two were raised by their biological parents. Nonetheless, the Sunday I arrived unexpectedly to interview Maria (the mother of this family), I found her at a backyard barbecue, surrounded by six of her seven offspring. (The seventh, who had spent the night at Maria's, was having lunch with his parents-in-law). With no hesitation, they all chimed in to piece together their family romance. Two of them had been raised by Dona Joana. Another, carried off by his paternal grandparents, was tracked down 20 years later by his brothers and sisters who simply followed a tip on where his father worked. Still another recounts how, as a baby, he endured the mistreatment of a negligent wet nurse, before being brought back to live with his mother and stepfather. The oldest brother had simply run away from home at age eight, "never to be seen again." In fact, Maria's children eventually all found their way back, but the arrival of the oldest, after a ten-year silence, had become a sort of family saga. His sister recounts in vivid detail the day she ran into this 18-year-old youth, pushing his bike up the hill:

> He waved me over and asked, "Listen, you don't happen to know a Dona Maria living around here? A woman with a whole lot of kids?" I said, "I guess you're talking about my mother. She's the only Dona Maria around here and she has a pile of children. I don't know if it's her, but I'll take you to see." I didn't pay much attention; I just left him with Mom saying, "This boy says he wants to talk to you." But when I came back a couple of minutes later, my mother introduced us: "This is your brother."

Six years later, working as a night watchman, this particular son was still living (with his wife and two children) in a house he had built in his mother's backyard.

This story is far from exceptional. Innumerable times, I ran into a family ostensibly united – where the mother lived side by side with several married offspring with whom she interacted daily and celebrated the usual family rites – despite the fact that the children, spread out among different "mothers," had not grown up together. To ex-

plain this situation and reaffirm what, for this group, seems to be fundamental belief in the biological connection, people (who moments before were telling me "*Mãe é quem criou*") will now cite another proverb: "*Mãe é uma só*" ("Mother, there's but one"). It is as though the tie between blood relatives, going beyond individual acts of volition, could not be broken. Birth mothers and adoptive mothers alike appear to credit the belief voiced by one of our informants: "Even though that [6-year-old] boy doesn't know I'm his mother, I know I attract his attention every time he sees me. I feel it ... Because it's like my mom says, it's the blood – it's the drawing power of blood [*o sangue puxa*]." The symbolic nature of this bond dispenses with the necessity of a person's physical presence. Small children will be taught – through photos on the wall, or birthdays recalled – to remember their siblings who are living elsewhere. The bond also entitles apparent strangers to become sudden intimates. As Inez said, describing her reencounter with one of her long-lost brothers: "When we met, I knew right away he was my brother. We hugged with all the emotion of brother and sister, even though we'd spent all those years apart."

Despite the strong emotion of such reencounters, child circulation is often treated as a banal event by the various people concerned. In one example, a woman wanting to spend a weekend at the beach left her 6-day-old daughter in the care of a neighbor. The unpaid babysitter, whose two adolescent children were just becoming independent, called in her sister to wet-nurse the child. A triangular sort of arrangement ensued which had lasted, when I met them in 1994, for at least eight years. As the foster mother said, "She sleeps and eats in my house, and I'm the one she calls mother." Called momentarily away from her playmates to speak to me, the 8-year-old endorsed her foster mom's story with apparent delight. "I have three mothers," she beamed: "The mother who nursed me, the mother who raised me and the mother who gave birth to me."

A good number of children claim to have set up their own arrangements. It is not unusual to hear an 8-year-old explaining: "Auntie asked me to visit, I liked it, so I told my mom I was just going to stay on." Adults will include in their life histories a list of various households in which they lived during childhood – with a predictable variety of commentaries. Some foster parents are remembered as wicked slave-drivers, some as fairy godmothers, but most are described in quite matter-of-fact terms. A good many people will speak of two, three, and four "mothers" with no embarrassment or particular confusion.

Thus, as children scatter among different foster families, they acquire new parents and siblings. Such additions, however, do not necessarily imply a rupture or replacement of previous relationships. Rather, just as with ritual kin (which adds godparents to a child's list of relatives), so foster arrangements serve to enlarge the pool of significant others in a person's social universe. It is as though the child's social identity were "multilayered," revealing a perception of self that is inseparable from the various relationships which form a background sociality to his or her existence.

The case of Inez well illustrates the comings of goings of children within the deep-rooted fosterage culture prevalent in many Brazilian working-class neighborhoods. There are moments, however, when children are given away on a permanent and irrevocable basis, much as in the system of legal adoption. With the following case, we come to know a woman who, faced with intolerable conditions, actually surrendered her maternal status. The story of how she gave up her third-born child highlights how, working between local values and state mandates, the *favela* residents have fashioned a creative bricolage to insure the reproduction of future generations.

Eliane's Story: Clandestine Adoption in Context

Eliane, a tall, thin black woman, received me in the front room of the little wooden house where she was living with her husband and four of her children. Between chuckles and sighs of exasperation, she had chatted with me for well over an hour about the exploits of her various offspring when suddenly she fell silent. Taking a long puff on her cigarette, tears welling in her steady gaze, she let out an almost inaudible whisper: "I forgot to tell you. Now that you mentioned adopted kids... I gave one away [*pause*]. ... I gave one away."[17]

Eliane tells a story not much different from that of many other mothers from the outskirts of the city. Her extended kin group had been able to absorb her first two unprogrammed children, but, still unmarried and living with her mother when she got pregnant a third time, Eliane had reached the limits of her family's endurance. Her third child was simply banished from the kin group before he was even born: "They were saying things like, 'This child can't be my nephew, it can't be my grandson. It's a child of the night, of the partylife. It has no father.' They just kept after me. All that revolted me. When you're pregnant, it's easy to get upset."

The young woman had no hope of being able to pay a non-relative to keep her child. Even were she to work, for example, as a maid, she could not expect to receive more than one or two minimum salaries ($60–$120 a month), hardly enough to feed and pay for the day care of three children. (The government-allotted family allowance, available only to salaried workers, would add no more than a monthly $6 per child.) She knew that many families – recently married couples with no children of their own, sterile women, and simply older couples whose children were all grown – would be on the look-out for a precious bundle such as she had to offer. But, especially when coveting the infant of a non-relative, the prospective parents were reluctant to share parental responsibilities, and even less willing to consider their parenthood of only temporary standing. In these circumstances, Eliane had little choice but to give her newborn child away.

(We should remember that there is good reason to believe that, in Brazil, the great majority of children given up for adoption have identifiable parents.[18] There is also reason to presume that many of these parents "consent" to give up their children for adoption owing to sheer poverty.[19] In other words, they are not embarrassed adolescents trying to cover up a sexual faux pas so they can start life anew. It therefore makes sense that, no matter how poor or unprepared they are, many women, like Eliane, seek an active role in the decisions affecting their child's future – first and foremost of which is the choice of surrogate parents.)

Eliane thus went searching among relatives and acquaintances for her future child's adoptive parents and, shortly before giving birth, found what she was looking for. Her choice fell upon the baby's paternal aunt, a woman who, after years of trying for a pregnancy, had recently lost a stillborn child. Eliane recalls the circumstances of this encounter with amazing detail: the hesitation, the tears, and the respect with which the potential mother treated her: "[The adoptive mother] said, 'Look Eliane, we don't want to force you.' She gave me liberty to do what I wanted." But, after a week's soul-searching and mutual support, the decision was made. As our narrator tells it, she went to the would-be mother's house, and the two women sat there crying – the baby between them, in his crib – until Eliane summoned up the courage to say, "No, you keep him."[20]

Six years later, this birth mother is enjoying a new, more prosperous phase in life. Her present husband earns a good living collecting junk and transporting goods with his horse-drawn cart. Eliane has her own house now, and has brought all her children to live with her – all but the one she gave away. Living in the same neighborhood as the adoptive parents, she is able to see her third-born faring well, and even occasionally visit his home, but she categorically rejects the idea of reclaiming him:

> I always say, even if I won at the lottery, even if I was rich enough to pay back [the foster family], I wouldn't do that. What for? Sure, I could if I wanted. Wow! Just think of it, all my kids here together with me! But I wouldn't do that to them [the adoptive parents.] After six years! How could they avoid loving the child? For God's sake! It would be a crime.

Whereas, before, the lack of money had obliged Eliane to give her child away, now, the financial aspect of her maternal rights reappears in the idea of ransoming her son. Her ties to the child are inalienable (*o sangue puxa*), but, in order to activate these ties, she must have money to pay back

all those years of the adoptive mother's financial input. In other words, to reintegrate her child into her household, she must be able to provide much more than the bed, schooling, and regular meals she gives her other four children. At this point, only by cashing in on a winning lottery ticket could she hope to merit her "priceless child."[21]

Eliane, however, is insistent that there are other concerns which are more important than any financial calculation. She clearly pictures the transfer of her son as a gift made to a couple "who had always dreamed of having a child." She also respects the attachment formed between her child and his new family: "As far as he's concerned, I'm no one – at least not his mother. When I go by to visit, he calls me 'Auntie'." The value of the gift she made to the other couple is heightened by her feeling of sacrifice. These feelings are, nonetheless, contingent on her active participation in the adoption process.

We arrive now at the point, in Eliane's story, of central importance to our investigation. The adoptive parents of this woman's baby were not content with an informal, oral contract made with the birth mother. In order to ensure the binding nature of this transaction, they went to the proper public authorities and took out the child's birth certificate as though they had borne him. It was not, in fact, difficult for them to pose as the biological parents. Since hospitals do not require or even facilitate the issuing of birth certificates, parents are obliged to take the necessary measures, locating the appropriate registry office and normally paying a fee. In such circumstances, it is not then surprising that, according to 1998 statistics, nearly one-third of Brazilian births were not registered within the legal deadline. The fact that many children acquire a legal identity only when they enter first grade or even many years later (when, for example, boys embark on their military service) makes it relatively easy to manipulate information on their birth register.

By participating in this sort of procedure (often referred to in the literature as "clandestine adoption," but known locally as *adoção à brasileira*),[22] Eliane and the adoptive parents of her child have technically committed a crime. All three have been guilty of what the law labels "ideological falsity," punishable by up to six years in jail. However, the illegality of their act does not seem to intimidate most potential parents. According to some estimates, this form of adoption was, until recently, ten times more common than legal adoption[23] and, what's more, enjoyed the tacit support of a good many members of the judiciary. At the end of the 1980s, a T.V. debate was broadcast in which judges and lawyers spoke in favor of the "obvious nobility of spirit" which moved families to thus take in foundlings.[24] And, although an occasional newspaper story might connect clandestine adoption with baby-snatching, there are still today serious sources pointing out certain advantages to the system.[25]

Such tolerance of technically illegal practices horrifies the professionals working at the public adoption board in Rio Grande do Sul, and fuels criticisms from overseas on the purported corruption and possible commercialization linked to the adoption process. Nonetheless, a closer look at local dynamics suggest that *adoção à brasileira* is not necessarily an isolated practice. It fits into a long-standing behavior pattern of people who have traditionally lived on the margin of state bureaucracy, i.e, of a working class which deploys "weapons of the weak" (Scott 1985) in order to exert a certain control over its conditions of existence.

Historical Precedents

Students of Brazilian history point out how, since colonial times, the central government has had great difficulty in inciting even banal collaboration from its average citizens. From military conscription to jury service and vaccination campaigns, working-class groups have historically sidestepped state intervention in their daily affairs (Carvalho 1996). This independent spirit was, if anything, more pronounced in the sphere of family organization. Brazilians were proverbially averse to legal marriage (performed, until the 1889 Republic, by scarce and often corrupt church officials), and attempts to impose civil birth registration in the mid-nineteenth century provoked such a reaction that, in most parts of the country, the measure was revoked within a year (Carvalho 1996; Meznar 1994). Notwithstanding the tenacious myth, held by many social

workers, of a golden age of unified families,[26] female-headed households appear to have been extremely common since at least the beginning of the nineteenth century, accounting for as much as 40 percent of the population in certain urban neighborhoods (Ramos 1978). Out-of-wedlock births were relatively banal, and, in many day-to-day routines, stigma against unmarried mothers and bastards was hardly perceptible. In recognition of the number of people who fell between the cracks of the official norm, the law made official allowances for a man to exert paternal authority over, and leave his inheritance to, *illegitimate* sons and daughters (Kuznesof 1998; Venâncio 1986; Fonseca 1997).

In such a context, lower-rank Brazilians found ingenious ways if not always to get around, at least to stamp their own values onto, the existing structures of the legal system. Meznar (1994), for example, recounts how particular historical conditions in the northern state of Paraiba (the recent abolition of slavery and a spurt on the agricultural market due to the 1870s cotton boom) brought officials to judge certain single women unfit for motherhood, withdrawing their sons who were old enough to work and placing them as cheap farm labor with "respectable," land-owning tutors.[27] To preempt the system, a woman would negotiate the placement of her child with a suitable patron *before* the courts interfered. Some – widows in particular – would petition to foster their own child, agreeing to pay a monthly sum to be held in the youngster's name until he reached adulthood. (Whether or not payments were ever made is another matter.)

The extraordinary realism with which mothers would evaluate the prevailing mood of the courts is evident in other modes of behavior I registered while poring over the Porto Alegre Archives to examine child custody disputes of the early 1900s. Whereas, at the time, certain women were obliged to demonstrate utter chastity in order to maintain guardianship of their children, others would, on the contrary, underline their sexually promiscuous behavior, exactly to cast doubt on their ex-mate's paternal status. (One woman went so far as to bring in a policeman to testify she was a prostitute.) Since fathers, even of illegitimate offspring, had priority legal rights, a woman would frequently omit her companion's name on a child's birth certificate so as to guarantee her own authority. In at least one significant case, the child's paternal grandparents were registered on the birth certificate, while leaving the father's name blank (Fonseca 1993).[28]

In both Meznar's and my study, we see how the law produced unforeseen effects which may even have discouraged the formation of legally constituted family units. The conclusion to be drawn from such observations is not that working-class groups had some sort of pristine family patterns that were somehow corrupted by "external" laws. On the contrary, it is precisely that these family patterns have evolved in constant interaction with the various state laws. It is in this sense that we interpret more recent practices – such as clandestine adoption and even the way, during the 1980s, women would use the state orphanage as though it were a private boarding school – as part of a long-standing pattern of working-class family dynamics.

In each of these instances, those on a lower income resort to legal means to exert their authority, guarantee the survival of their offspring, or protect their interests. They do so, however, not necessarily in utter reverence for the rules but rather in the hope of finding loopholes in their favor. Whereas such maneuvers have been identified with the working classes elsewhere (see Merry 1990; Ewick and Silbey 1998), in Brazil there is evidence that people from all walks of life share a profound suspicion of the court system, counting on personal connections and individual cleverness rather than on the impersonal legal system to see justice done (Da Matta 1979). Furthermore, whereas in common-law regimes such as those found in Britain or the United States, some effort is made to adapt laws to local practices and values, in Brazil, legislators have consciously espoused the idea of "symbolic legislation" – laws which, by providing a sort of blueprint for the ideal society, point out the direction social change will hopefully take. In such circumstances, the "gap" between, on the one hand, the legal ideal and, on the other, the lived values held by a good number of lower-income Brazilians leaves many people little choice but to contrive strategies to adjust the laws to their reality.

The International Mood of National Laws

Whereas the social dynamics of lower-income families have indeed been influenced throughout history by national laws, the opposite does not seem to hold true. The evolution of national legislation on child placement, for example, appears to be oriented by anything but local realities. Briefly, the present national policy is to promote plenary adoption as the progressive option for extremely poor, mistreated, and otherwise institutionalized children. This option not only ignores traditional circuits of fosterage, but eliminates any possibility of the birth mother's active participation in her child's placement, much less that of shared parental responsibilities.

The Evolution of Adoption Law: Toward Equality and Exclusivity

Of course, the overriding principle of all legislation concerning children is today "the child's best interests." And it is undeniable that in many ways the adoption laws have gradually introduced important reforms mandated by universally accepted values. Up until recently, for example, adoption law condoned discrimination against adopted children, institutionalizing social inequality within the household.[29] During the nineteenth century, besides using their wards as cheap labor,[30] people could "adopt" a boy in order to send him to do military service in the stead of a biological son. The 1916 Civil Code, aimed at creating a certain uniformity throughout the national territory, reflected traditional biases. Adopted children, transferred from one adult to another by a simple notarized contract, could be returned to their parents (or public institution) with little fuss. They would have no inheritance rights whatsoever if their new parents had borne any "legitimate" children before the adoption, and only half the share of any brothers and sisters who might be born after the adoption. It was not until the 1979 Children's Code that it became possible for adopted children to become permanent members of their new family, with full inheritance rights, and only in 1990, with the elimination of "simple adoption," was this privilege extended to all adopted children.

Significantly, together with the equality of adopted children, the other major change in adoption legislation has been the gradual elimination of the child's birth family from the adoption process. Up until the middle of the twentieth century, an adopted individual maintained a sort of double filiation – sharing rights and obligations in his adoptive as well as biological family. The Law 4,655 of 1965 was the first to frame the child exclusively in terms of membership in his new, adoptive family. Following the sensitivities of the country's cosmopolitan elite, the law was inspired in the idea that adoptive families should "imitate nature" (Siqueira 1993). Since *naturally* a child had but one mother, adoption should signify a total rupture with the child's biological parents.

Since the 1965 law theoretically pertained only to children under seven years of age whose parents were dead or unknown, the erasure of a child's original genealogical ties provoked few reactions. However, with the enactment of the 1979 Children's Code, guidelines were laid down as to the treatment of living birth parents: children could be adopted only if these parents had been stripped of authority or else had expressly consented to the procedure. Plenary adoption (which now assumed this name) was extended to all children under seven years old who were found by the courts to be "in an irregular situation" – a condition which could include anything from children who were badly abused, abandoned, or being raised in a morally inadequate milieu to those who, because of parental omission, had been deprived of the essential conditions of subsistence, health, or schooling. The amplitude of this category soon fell under attack, explaining why, in the 1990 Children's Code, there is an explicit clause declaring that poverty alone should, under no circumstances, justify the loss of parental authority. However, as many researchers have demonstrated (Cardarello 1998; Ferreira 2000), despite ostensive safeguards, the near-totality of children withdrawn from their parents comes, still today, from homes in which parental neglect is barely distinguishable from the effects of dire poverty.

One cannot help but suspect that the consistently low socioeconomic status of birth parents has had a lot to do with the way, since the 1970s,

their role has been progressively supplanted (rather than complemented) by their child's adoptive parents. During the 1980s, in most regions in Brazil, the name of an adopted child's biological parents was removed from the birth certificate, thus rendering the state official guardian of the "secret of (the child's) origin." With the 1990 Children's Code, and the consolidation of plenary adoption, the secret of the adopted child's origins became a definitive part of the Brazilian adoption process,[31] and the notion of plenary adoption, based on a distinctly middle-class family ideal, was declared the sole legal means of adopting a child.[32]

The Influence of International Adoption

Much of the change introduced in Brazilian legislation has been inspired in international debates on child rights. This fact is hardly surprising considering that, in many ways, Brazilian legislators and policy-makers, as members of the elite, have been historically closer to European metropolitan ideas than to those of their rustic next-door neighbors. Furthermore, just as in numerous other donor countries, it was, to a great extent, the increasing presence of *foreign* adoptive parents which led Brazilian policy-makers to turn their attentions to the plight of the country's children and refine policies concerning in-country adoption (Yngvesson 2000; Abreu 2000).

During the first three-quarters of the twentieth century, it was quite possible for anyone, including a foreigner, to legally adopt a child without ever having seen a public authority. It was sufficient for a woman, after having first registered her baby, to sign a notarized document passing complete parental responsibility onto a second party. With this document, the new parents could obtain a birth certificate in their name, guaranteeing their child a passport (Brazilian or of the parents' nationality) for travel abroad. (See *O Globo*, 14 August 1980 for a report on several Americans who were able to adopt children in this way.)

As early as the 1970s, newspapers fueled the image of foreigners descending en masse to adopt Brazilian children, causing special clauses on intercountry adoption to be written into the 1979 Code. Henceforth, adoption by foreign nationals had to pass through the Juvenile Court. By the 1980s, Brazilian social planners were anxious to take measures which would not only check the "theft" of Brazilian children, but would also counteract negative images, dwelling on abandoned street children, in the foreign press. It was at this point that *adoção à brasileira* began to be singled out as a backward practice, and concerted efforts were made to bring all adoptions, both national and intercountry, under the control of the Juvenile Court.

After the enactment of the 1990 Children's Code, the flux of Brazilian adopted children toward foreign countries slowed down for a year or two, and there is some indication that, even with the renewed impetus of the mid-1990s, international adoption increasingly involves children who are too old, black, or handicapped to be accepted in local homes. These trends bear the mark not only of international directives (see, in particular, the 1993 Hague Convention on Adoption), but also of nationalists who see children as part of Brazil's national resources and resent the demeaning role of producing children to be "saved" by First World countries (see Abreu 1998). However, the impact of international influence should not be measured merely by the number of children sent overseas. Campaigns for *in-country* adoptions have never before been so vigorous. Recent nationwide movements for legal adoption have put posters on the walls of town halls and advertisements for available children on the Internet sites of state orphanages.

The important point here is that, in Brazil, not only has adoption become more centralized and rigidly defined, it is managing to expunge alternative state-sponsored as well as traditional forms of child placement. In Rio Grande do Sul, for example, state-coordinated fosterage, long considered a poor stepsister to adoption, is today practically nonexistent.[33] The previous system of foster care that placed children in lower-income families (at the cost of half a minimum salary – $30 – per child) is considered not up to present standards. To meet the standards laid out in the 1990 Children's Code, the state has replaced the old orphanages with a series of smaller

units which, at a monthly cost of over $1,000 per child, offer comforts approximating those of an upper middle-class home (complete with swimming classes and riding lessons). At this price, the state has a strong incentive to limit the number of state-financed children, and, thus, juvenile authorities – taking as a parameter the naturalized nuclear family – tend to frame their policies in terms of either/or. *Either* the child stays in its birth family (where, presumably, biology compensates for poverty) *or* he or she is given to a new family through plenary adoption. In the latter case, the fact that the great majority of children are under three years of age spells out inevitable rupture with the birth family.

Many of the poverty-stricken parents I dealt with evidently do not agree with either of these options. Like Dona Maria, they may feel that their children, at times, would be better off in another household, and so they seek, among relatives and neighbors or even in state-run programs, allies who might share in child-care responsibilities while not entirely usurping their identity as parents. Or, like Eliane, they may be willing to give their children *permanently* into the keeping of another family that they have helped to choose and which they can keep track of from afar. Certainly, these "traditional" practices are not without their hitches, and could invite state assistance and/or supervision. The possibility of abuse such as that documented in foster homes elsewhere must be taken into account.[34] However, there is every reason to believe that the less publicized accounts of relatively successful foster parenthood (Cadoret 1995; Hoelgaard 1998) could prove equally relevant to the Brazilian case. Despite this fact, debate over such issues is practically nonexistent. Foster, as well as birth parents, have been all too easily removed from the scene, leaving adoptive parenthood the single viable alternative for children in serious difficulty.

I would suggest that the violence of inequality which up until recently branded adopted children as inferior members of their new family has, today, been relocated in another relation written into the adoption procedure – that between birth and adoptive parents. Let us remember that child circulation in the *favela* traditionally involves adults of more or less equal status. In the working-class districts of Porto Alegre, it would be difficult to distinguish a class of child donors, separate from a class of child recipients. Many women who, as young mothers, placed their children in a substitute family, end up taking in somebody else's child to raise. The slight financial advantage enjoyed by foster and adoptive mothers is generally due to factors linked to the life cycle rather than to social stratification. Near-equal social status may explain why, in the local setting, birth mothers maintain a certain power of negotiation. Similarly, it is quite possible that the increasingly unequal status between birth and adoptive parents is a relevant factor in the progressive effacement of the former from the adoption process, and that the greater the inequality the stronger the tendency to do so. Considering this hypothesis, we would have reason to believe that, in intercountry adoption where socioeconomic and cultural differences are at their peak, birth mothers would have less power than ever.

In terms of political influence, *favela* residents appear to be at the bottom rung of the global system of adoption. We should remember, however, that, as Starr and Collier (1989) have pointed out, asymmetrical power relations are not always defined according to national borders. Ruling groups should be thought of in terms of a coalition of forces stretching through and beyond the nation. We know that the legal vulnerability of *favela* mothers' parental status has much in common with that of lower-income women in Western Europe and North America. In like fashion, there are many Third World adoption workers, such as the one cited in the opening paragraphs of this article, whose attitudes bear more in common with upper-income adoptive parents in the prosperous regions of the globe than with local birth mothers.[35] In this article, by bringing to bear the relevance of "localized" family dynamics to the issue of adoption, and by pointing out the way these dynamics have been consistently shunted aside by apparently progressive legal reforms, we hope to raise doubts about certain hegemonic narratives, undermine the alliances which support them, and help to redirect the debate in a way which might facilitate dialogue between the unequal partners concerned in today's globalized forms of adoption.

NOTES

1 For a critical overview of the "gap studies" of the 1970s, see Sarat and Silbey (1988).

2 I am referring to the 1997 speech made during the signing of the Adoption and Safe Families Act.

3 The "circulation of children" is a generic term which permits the comparative analysis of different forms of child placement found throughout the globe and at different moments in history (see, among others, Lallemand 1993).

4 See, for example, the special issue of the *International Journal of Law, Family, and Policy* on the principle of a "child's best interests" (vol. 8, 1994).

5 I borrow the term from Comaroff and Comaroff (1999) to refer to particular forms of social dynamics which deviate from the "modernist script."

6 For a critical assessment of this field of research, see Leeds 1971. Analogies with E. P. Thompson's English working class have furnished hopeful openings toward new forms of analysis (see, in particular, Scott 1985). However, in general, the present political climate appears to favor the category of "ethnicity" over "class," especially for the analysis of Third World situations.

7 For recent commentaries on this ongoing debate, see the special issue of *Current Anthropology* (vol. 40, supplement, February 1999): "Culture – a second chance."

8 Porto Alegre is the capital city (3 million inhabitants in the metropolitan area) of Rio Grande do Sul, the southernmost state in Brazil. With borders extending to Argentina and Uruguay, this region is known for its relatively high standard of living, sporting social indicators (infant mortality, literacy, etc.) closer to those of First World countries than to the Brazilian Northeast. This fact no doubt explains in part certain discrepancies between my observations and those of N. Scheper-Hughes (1992).

9 The verb *criar* in Portuguese means both "to raise" and "to create." Kin ties formed by caring for one

another are labeled *de criação*. I have loosely translated the term here as "foster" relatives.

10   According to a 1985 census taken in Brazil's major cities, 2.9 percent of the children under 18 were adopted, less than a third of them by legal means. Over half these children had left their birth parents before the age of 3 (see Campos 1991).

11   We should remember that in Rio Grande do Sul, the institution was minimally adequate – providing individual beds and regular meals to the interns, which was more than many children got in their homes. Furthermore, older children with no behavior problems could come home on weekends and holidays. See Blum (1998) for a similar use of state institutions by the poor in nineteenth-century Mexico.

12   See Merry (1990) for examples in contemporary America of a similar use of the Juvenile Court.

13   At times, the children were sent to her by the Juvenile Court, at other times, they were brought in by their own mothers. In any case, payment was highly irregular.

14   More than once, I saw babies held ransom by a doting foster mother for as little as one or two liters of milk. People claimed that this commodified aspect of child exchange was endorsed by the public courts which, in mediating disputes, would routinely establish a certain amount of financial compensation a biological mother had to pay in order to regain custody of her child.

15   In this particular dispute, which must have taken place in the late 1960s, the court followed the child (by then a pre-teen)'s preference, assigning her to her foster mother.

16   Donna Goldstein (1998) describes a Rio de Janeiro maid living in the *favela* who, besides raising her own children, took in four of her deceased sister's offspring as well as three of her ex-lover's children. Such a case would not be entirely uncommon in the neighborhoods where I worked.

17   Whereas most women, like Dona Maria, will say they simply "left" (*deixei*) a child with a certain caretaker, Eliane explicitly states that she "gave" (*dei*) her child to someone else.

18   Ferreira's study (2000) covering 12 years of adoption processes in Porto Alegre shows that the mother was located in approximately 90 percent of the cases.

19   In the 1985 study of over 150,000 Brazilian mothers who had separated from a child before its first birthday, the overwhelming majority said they had done so because of the "total absence of financial conditions" (Campos 1991).

20   It would be misleading to frame the analysis of this scene entirely in terms of individual maternal rights. A birth mother's decisions are enmeshed in a social fabric wherein other members of the extended family (particularly older women) are constantly giving opinions and exerting pressure to influence what many consider the collective rights and obligations over the group's offspring. Yet, in general, mothers occupy and, what's more, wish to occupy a central place in this process.

21   Zelizer's study (1985) on the priceless child will be further discussed below.

22   Evidently, the informal name given this illegal practice carries with it a connotation of widespread acceptance.

23   Interview with a state judge, quoted in *Isto É*, August 26, 1990.

24   "Nobility" here is an important legal point since according to article 242 of the Penal Code, in cases where people have acted for recognizably noble motives, the punishment for clandestine adoption may be diminished or waived altogether.

25   In her research on adoption in the state of Paraná, Weber, for example, found that, while Brazilians who consult legal adoption services show a persistent preference for light-skinned babies, *adoção à brasileira*, carried out in general by lower-income people, tends to concern older children of darker color (1998. "Famílias adotivas e mitos sobre laços de sangue," Páginas brasileiras de adoção – Netscape).

26   The seminal work of Gilberto Freyre on patriarchal, extended families among the ruling elite of colonial Pernambuco has been used and abused to support various (and often erroneous) theories on Brazilian families (see Corrêa 1993).

27   Girls who provided domestic service were not fought over in the same way, and did not receive a monthly stipend.

28 See Lazarus-Black (1994) for an extremely relevant analysis of law and paternal status in the Caribbean.

29 The logic of inequality was inscribed in the very vocabulary used in better-off families where the same word (*criado*) was used to signify servant and adopted child.

30 Historians have furnished ample evidence as to the association between pre-modern adoptions and domestic service (Meznar 1994; Neff 1996; Blum 1998; Kuznesof 1998).

31 According to its terms (art. 47, §4), an adopted child's original certificate, as well as the court proceedings, are to be sealed unless unusual circumstances lead a judicial authority to reveal them.

32 Yngvesson (2000), in her study of intercountry adoption in India, names some of the Western family values embedded in plenary adoption: the ideas of kinship relations based on choice and affection, the perception of children as separate individuals, detachable from their kin groups (see also Hecht 1998; Boyden 1990; Stephens 1995).

33 A 1994 study on child placement in the state of Rio Grande do Sul indicated that there were only 80 children in foster homes, against 350 in institutional care (not counting juvenile offenders), and 243 given in adoption (both national and international) that year (Cardarello 1996). Since 1990, the program of substitute families has been phased out, reducing the number of such homes to four in January 2000.

34 For just one of the frequent newspaper articles on the problems connected with abusive foster homes in the United States, see the *New York Times*, October 27, 2000, p. A18. Gailey (1998) offers an interesting study on abuse within foster as well as adoptive homes.

35 We may cite a certain Peruvian social worker advocating that, even if the foreign parents are not ideal, the adopted child "would still have a better chance for a decent life ... in a country where children are not condemned by conditions to suffering" (in Jaffe 1995: 187). We might also recall the opinion of a Colombian adoption worker who, turning down the petition of loving, foster families to adopt their wards, explains that Western couples "possess superior moral qualities and parenting abilities, besides being better off materially than local applicants" (cited in Hoelgaard 1998: 219).

BIBLIOGRAPHY

Abreu, Domingo
1998 Assim Falou "o Povo": Adoção Internacional no Dizer Jornalístico. *In* Tecidos do Cotidiano Brasileiro, ed. I. Barreira and S. Vieira. Special issue. Cultura e Política 2: 133–150. Fortaleza: Editora da Universidade Federal do Ceará.
——— 2000 No Bico da Cegonha: Por uma Sociologia da Adoção no Brasil. Doctoral thesis, Department of Sociology, Universidade Federal Do Ceará (Fortaleza).

Blum, Ann S.
1998 Public Welfare and Child Circulation, Mexico City, 1877 to 1925. Journal of Family History 23(3): 240–271.

Boyden, Jo
1990 Childhood and the Policy Makers: A Comparative Perspective on the Globalization of Childhood. *In* Construction and Reconstructing Childhood: Contemporary Issues in the Sociological Study of Childhood. A. James and A. Prout, eds. pp. 184–215. London: Falmer Press.

Cadoret, Anne
1995 Parenté Plurielle: Anthropologie du Placement Familial. Paris: Harmattan.

Campos, Maria M. M.
1991 Infância Abandonada – O Piedoso Disfarce do Trabalho Precoce. *In* O Massacre dos Inocentes: A Criança sem Infância no Brasil. J. S. Martins, ed. Pp. 117–153. São Paulo: Hucitec.

Cardarello, Andrea D. L.
1996 Implantando O Estatuto: Um Estudo sobre a Criação de um Sistema Próximo ao Familiar para Crianças Institucionalizadas na FEBEM-RS. M.A. Thesis in Anthropology, PPGAS-UFRGS (Porto Alegre).
———1998 A Transformação de Internamento "Assistencial" em Internamento por "Negligência": Tirando a Cidadania dos Pais para dá-la às Crianças. Ensaios FEE 19(2): 306–330.

Carroll, Vern, ed.
1970 Adoption in Eastern Oceania. Honolulu: University of Hawaii Press.

Carvalho, José Murilo De
1996 Cidadania: Tipos e Percursos. Estudos Históricos 9(18): 257–424.

Colen, Shellee
1995 "Like A Mother to Them": Stratified Reproduction and West Indian Childcare Workers and Employers in New York. *In* Conceiving the New World Order: the Global Politics of Reproduction. F. D. Ginsburg and R. Rapp, eds. (Pp. 78–102. Berkeley: University of California Press.

Comaroff, John L. and Jean Comaroff, eds.
1999 Civil Society and the Political Imagination in Africa: Critical Perspectives. Chicago and London: University of Chicago Press.

Corrêa, Mariza
1993 Repensando a Família Patriarcal Brasileira. *In* Colcha de Retalhos: Estudos sobre a Família no Brasil. Pp. 15–42 São Paulo: Brasiliense.

Da Matta, Roberto
1979 Carnavais, Malandros e Heróis: Para Uma Sociologia do Dilema Brasileiro. Rio De Janeiro: Zahar.

Ewick, Patricia and Susan S. Silbey
1998 The Common Place of Law: Stories From Everyday Life. Chicago: University of Chicago Press.

Ferreira, Kátia Maria Martins
2000 Os Reflexos do Estatuto da Criança e do Adolescente na Justiça da Infância e Juventude de Porto Alegre – Análise Sociológica dos Processos de Destituição do Pátrio Poder. MA thesis in Sociology, PPGS-UFRGS (Porto Alegre).

Fonseca, Claudia
1985 Amour Maternel, Valeur Marchande et Survie: Aspects de la Circulation d'Enfants dans un Bidonville Brésilien. Les Annales ESC 40(5): 991–1022.
——— 1986 Orphanages, Foundlings and Foster Mothers: The System of Child Circulation in a Brazilian Squatter Settlement. Anthropological Quarterly 59(1): 15–27.
——— 1993 Parents et Enfants dans les Couches Populaires Brésiliennes au Début du Siècle: Un autre Genre D'amour. Droit et Cultures 25: 41–62.
——— 1997 Ser Mulher, Mãe e Pobre. *In* História Das Mulheres no Brasil. M. Del Priore, ed. Pp. 510–553. São Paulo: Editora Contexto.

——— 1999 Circulation d'enfants ou Adoption?: Les Enjeux Internationaux de la Filiation Adoptive. Droit et Cultures 38: 136–167.
——— 2000 The Politics of Adoption. Paper presented at the CRN Meeting, "Hegemonies and Counter-Hegemonies", Annual Meeting of the Law and Society Association, Miami.

Gailey, Christine W.
1998 Making Kinship in the Wake of History: Gendered Violence and Older Child Adoption. Identities 5(2): 249–292.

Goldstein, Donna
1998 Nothing Bad intended: Child Discipline, Punishment, and Survival in a Shantytown in Rio De Janeiro, Brazil. *In* Small Wars: the Cutural Politics of Childhood. N. Scheper-Hughes and C. Sargent, eds. Pp. 389–415. Berkeley: University of California Press.

Hecht, Tobias
1998 At Home in the Street: Street Children of Northeast Brazil. Cambridge: Cambridge University Press.

Hoelgaard, Suzanne
1998 Cultural Determinants of Adoption Policy: A Colombian Case Study. International Journal of Law, Policy, and the Family 12(1): 202–401.

Jaffe, E., ed.
1995 Intercountry Adoptions: Laws and Perspectives of "Sending" Countries. London: Martinus Nijhoff Publishers.

Kuznesof, Elizabeth Anne
1998 The Puzzling Contradictions of Child Labor, Unemployment, and Education in Brazil. Journal of Family History 23(3): 225–239.

Lallemand, Suzanne
1993 La Circulation des Enfants en Société Traditionnelle. Prêt, Don, Échange. Paris: Editions Harmattan.

Lazarus-Black, Mindie
1994 Alternative Readings: the Status of the Status of Children Act in Antigua and Barbuda. Law & Society Review 28(5): 993–1007.

Leeds, Anthony
1971 The Concept of the "Culture of Poverty": Conceptual, Logical, and Empirical Problems, with Perspective From Brazil and Peru. *In* The Culture of Poverty: A Critique. E. Leacock, ed. Pp. 226–284. New York: Simon & Schuster.

Merry, Sally Engle
1990   Getting Justice and Getting Even: Legal Consciousness Among Working-Class Americans. Chicago: University of Chicago Press.
—— 1997 Legal Pluralism and Transnational Culture: the Ka Ho'okolokolonui Kanaka Maoli Tribunal, Hawai'i, 1993. *In* Human Rights, Culture & Context. R. Wilson, ed. Pp. 28–48. London: Pluto Press.

Meznar, Joan
1994   Orphans and the Transition from Slave to Free Labor in Northeast Brazil: The case of Campina Grande, 1850–1888. Journal of Social History 27(3): 499–516.

Modell, Judith
1997   Rights to the Children: Foster Care and Social Reproduction in Hawai'i. *In* Reproducing Reproduction: Kinship, Power, and Technological Innovation. S. Franklin and H. Ragoné, eds. Pp. 156–172. Philadelphia: University of Pennsylvania Press.

Neff, Charlotte
1996   Pauper Apprenticeship in Early 19th Century Ontario. Journal of Family History 21(2): 107–124.

Ramos, Donald
1978   City and Country: the Family in Minas Gerais, 1804–1836. Journal of Family History 3(4): 361–175.

Sarat, Austin, and Susan Silbey
1988   The Pull of the Policy Audience. Law and Policy 10 (2–3): 97.

Scheper-Hughes, Nancy
1992   Death Without Weeping: the Violence of Everyday Life in Brazil. Berkeley: University of California Press.

Scott, James C.
1985   Weapons of the Weak: Everyday Forms of Peasant Resistance. New Haven: Yale University Press.

Selman, Peter
2000   Adoption: A Cure for (too) many Ills? Paper presented at 6th Biennial EASA Conference, Krakow.

Silbey, Susan
1997   "Let Them Eat Cake": Globalization, Postmodern Colonialism, and the Possibilities of Justice. Law & Society Review 31(2): 207–235.

Silva, Daisy Carvalho
1995   The Legal Procedures for Adopting Children in Brazil by Citizens and Foreign Nationals. *In* Intercountry Adoptions: Laws and Perspectives of "Sending" Countries. E. Jaffe, ed. Pp. 121–138. London: Martinus Nijhoff.

Siqueira, Liborni
1993   Adoção no Tempo e no Espaço. Forense: Rio De Janeiro.

Starr, June and Jane F. Collier
1989   Introduction: Dialogues in Legal Anthropology. *In* History and Power in the Study of Law: New Directions in Legal Anthropology. J. Starr and F. Collier, eds. Pp. 1–28. Ithaca and London: Cornell University Press.

Stephens, Sharon, ed.
1995   Children and the Politics of Culture. New Haven: Princeton University Press.

Venâncio, Renato Pinto
1986   Nos limites da Sagrada Família: Ilegitimidade e casamento no Brasil colonial. *In* História e sexualidade no Brasil. Ronaldo Vainfas, ed. Rio de Janeiro: Graal.

Vianna, Luiz Werneck
1996   Poder Judiciário, "Positivação" do Direito Natural e História. Estudos Históricos 9(18): 257–424.

Weber, Ligia N. D., ed.
1998   Famílias adotivas e mitos sobre laços de sangue. *In* Laços de Ternura: persquisas e histórias de adoção. Ligia N. D. Weber, ed. Curitiba: Santa Mônica.

Yanagisako, Sylvia and Carol Delaney, eds.
1995   Naturalizing Power: Essays in Feminist Cultural Analysis. New York: Routledge.

Yngvesson, Barbara
2000   "Un Niño De Cualquier Color": Race and Nation in Intercountry Adoption. *In* Globalizing Institutions: Case Studies in Regulation and Innovation. J. Jensen and B. De Sousa Santos, eds. Pp. 247–305. Aldershot: Ashgate.

Zelizer, Viviana
1985   Pricing the Priceless Child: The Changing Social Values of Children. New York: Basic Books.

Part III

Identities, Practices, Hybridities

10

History, Culture, and Place-Making: 'Native' Status and Maya Identity in Belize

Laurie Kroshus Medina

Introduction

Over the last decade, pan-Maya organizing has had a dramatic impact in Guatemala and Mexico. Both the Maya movement in Guatemala and the Zapatistas and their civilian supporters in Mexico have mobilized Maya across traditional linguistic divisions (Fischer and Brown 1996; Stephen 1998; Warren 1998). In Guatemala, the Maya movement has focused most intensely on protecting and vindicating Maya cultural difference and Maya languages, asserting a right to cultural difference based on their indigenous status. In Mexico, Maya representing several linguistic categories have mobilized together to provide much of the momentum behind both military (Zapatista) and non-military organizing in Chiapas, making claims as indigenous peoples to cultural autonomy, political self-determination, and land (Stephen 1998).

Mobilization across Maya linguistic boundaries in Belize parallels these movements in some ways. In Belize, Mopan and Kekchi have begun mobilizing together as Maya over the last two decades to defend their cultural and linguistic distinctiveness and to demand expanded and more secure

access to land (Wilk 1991). However, while the Belizean movement parallels Guatemalan and Mexican mobilizations in its demands and its bridging of linguistic boundaries among Maya (albeit on a smaller scale), the Belizean movement is distinct in some important ways. For example, Mopan and Kekchi in Belize have neither been targets of military repression by the state nor organizers of military opposition to the state. Another distinction, which provides the focus for this paper, involves the contestation around Mopan and Kekchi claims to native status in Belize. Although Maya claims to 'native' or indigenous identity are not usually disputed in Mesoamerica, in Belize they have been challenged, as a number of groups compete to assert native status. The contestation around claims to native status in Belize has implications for the kinds of identities Mopan and Kekchi might most strategically claim: challenges to their nativeness provide additional impetus for Mopan and Kekchi to organize across linguistic boundaries as Maya.

The claim to 'native' identity connects people to place through bonds which are understood to be both intimate and ancient. At present, both aspects contribute to the legitimacy and moral imperative attributed to native claims to resources and autonomy by international organizations such as the United Nations and human rights or environmental NGOs. However, if 'native' status is generally ascribed to people who are understood to have inhabited a particular place – a 'here' – 'first,' histories of Belize have been contentious around issues of who was 'here' 'first.' One set of issues involves defining what constitutes the 'here' of Belize as a place. Should Belize be defined territorially? Or does Belize encompass more than a geographical space, being more precisely defined by a distinctive way of life which constitutes Belizean territory as a particular – *cultural* – place? Competing answers to these questions raise further questions: If Belize is defined territorially, who has lived 'here' longest and most continuously? If Belize is defined as a particular mode of living in this location, who has created the forms of thought and practice that are seen to constitute this Belizean mode of living? Another point of contention involves the question of whether Belize as a territory should represent the only legitimate land in which Belizean nativeness might be 'rooted,' or whether other, larger territories which encompass Belize might provide legitimate 'soils' for claims to nativeness.

As Malkki (1997) notes, links between territory and identity, peoples and places, have been deeply naturalized through the deployment of botanical metaphors: "people are often thought of, and think of themselves, as being rooted in place and as deriving their identity from that rootedness" (Malkki 1997:56). The unity of people and soil has become so taken for granted that the phrase 'the country' refers either to the citizens of a nation-state or its territorial expanse (Malkki 1997). Often, the identity of people with territory is reinforced through constructions of history which account for and produce both people and place simultaneously, demonstrating that the history of 'a people' is the history of 'their place.' One set of arguments about nativity in Belize participates in and follows from this conflation of people and territory and their intertwined histories.

However, Gupta and Ferguson (1997) remind us that notions of 'culture' are often integral to a people's project of creating a particular 'place' out of a given territorial space. Thus "place making" as a practice involves the "cultural territorialization" of space, not just its geographic circumscription (Gupta and Ferguson 1997:4, 6). Making a place out of geographical space often requires the attribution of particular cultural practices and perspectives to its inhabitants. Cultural territorialization as a mode of place making attends to the details of "dwelling," of how "culture" or cultural practices are produced in and through particular landscapes. This aspect of cultural production is one which anthropologists have only recently begun to explore in explicit terms. Contributors to the recent collection *Senses of Place* "explore in close detail cultural processes and practices through which places are rendered meaningful," how people *sense* place, attribute sense *to* place, and *derive* sense from place (Feld and Basso 1996a:7). Basso focuses on "dwelling" as the production of "lived relationships" which bind Apaches to their reservation lands (Basso 1996). In this context, people produce a sense of self and of historical continuity with ancestors by learning and associating particular meanings with features of the landscape through which they move daily. Volumes such as Feld and Basso (1996b) and Gupta and Ferguson (1997), which mark an emerging anthropological focus on the production of place, demonstrate that the practices through which people produce history and place are simultaneously the processes through which they produce themselves as 'a people' (Feld and Basso 1996a:11; see also Pred 1986:198).

In the situation which Basso describes, people and place are relatively isomorphic, and "sense of place" is a product of the practices of "dwelling." However, in contexts not characterized by such isomorphism, constructions of both people and place may be more contested, and narratives of belonging may be more explicitly and competitively elaborated. For example, Blu examines a "multicultural space" in North Carolina, and discovers "contestation over place – where it shall be, whose it shall be, what kind it should be" (Blu 1996:219). Such contests shift analysis away from the spatial practices of dwelling toward competition among conflicting constructions of place and belonging (Blu 1996; Borneman 1997; Clifford 1988). Accordingly, contestation over claims to 'native' status in Belize direct me to attend more to the competing constructions of people, history, culture, and place which confront one another in political arenas in Belize and less to the everyday experiences, enacted in and through place, through which people solidify self-identities. In this paper, I examine how efforts to assert 'native' status in Belize hinge on competing configurations of both territory and place. In concluding sections of the paper, I return to the distinction I have drawn between explicit narratives of belonging and more implicit practices of dwelling.

Contentious History

History provides a tool for fashioning peoples and places and the bonds between them which become inherent in their identities. In Belize, claims to nativeness draw heavily on history. Histories of particular ethnic groups are narrated in ways which cast these ethnic histories as intertwined with and definitive of *Belizean* history itself. The production of Belizean history has been fraught with tensions, although most histories include episodes which are not disputed as well as those which are. In what follows, I can only briefly sketch out 'Belizean history' and a few of the debates which have characterized its production and its use in making claims to nativeness. I will not attempt to adjudicate among competing constructions of Belizean history, but rather to identify some of the areas of controversy.[1]

Ancient Inhabitants

One aspect of Belizean history which is not much disputed is the ancient existence of Mayan settlements and cities in what is now Belizean territory; however, the boundaries, names, affiliations, and fates of the Mayan groups who inhabited this territory prior to colonization have been subject to debate, as has their "Belizeanness" in a cultural rather than geographic sense. Thompson (1988)

asserts that Belizean territory was inhabited by three major groupings of Maya just prior to and during the period of Spanish colonizing efforts: Yucatec Maya in the north, associated with Mayan polities of the Yucatan Peninsula; Chan Maya in the central region, which extended westward into present-day Guatemala; and Manche Chols in the far south. The second category, Chan Maya, is one proposed by Thompson himself. He argues that

> in vocabulary, promunciation, personal names, religion, and religious practices the Maya speakers of variant forms of Yucatec in the Petén and adjacent Belize, including the so-called Itza, as known to us from colonial sources and present-day observation, are closer to the Mopan Maya than to the Maya of Yucatan. Consequently it is proposed that those Petén Maya, the Mopan Maya, the Cehach, the Chinamita, and the Yucatec-speaking Lacandon should be constituted a subgroup, related rather closely to the Yucatec Maya.... For this subgroup the name Chan Maya, or Chan, is suggested on the grounds that it is short, it is easily remembered, and it was a common... surname in the area. Complete uniformity of culture within the subgroup is not implied (Thompson 1977:3).

Thompson asserts that the northern boundary between Chan and Yucatec Maya was not rigidly demarcated. Rather, the "Chan" Maya spoke "variants of Yucatec Maya," with those closest to Yucatecos being most similar to them and difference increasing with distance (Thompson 1977:40). The largest centers of political power in this region would have been at Lake Peten in Guatemala and Tipu in west-central Belize.

Already this abbreviated account raises questions about the determination of the identities of the aboriginal population of Belize. First, contemporary researchers and colonial-era archival sources do not all perceive the same groups, and they label the 'groups' they distinguish on a number of bases: name of their settlement, name of the local political leader or dynasty, name of the regional political center or its leader to whom allegiance was owed, linguistic similarity or difference, or convenience (being short and easy to remember). Second, the degree to which labeled categories represent 'groups' is called into question by accounts which indicate the permeability of their boundaries through migration and marriage, the existence of factionalism within labeled 'groups,' alliances formed and broken, the presence of people with different political and linguistic affiliations in the same communities, and the cultural variability to which Thompson alludes (Thompson 1977; Scholes and Thompson 1977). These factors undermine assumptions about the stability, boundedness, and 'purity' of the 'groups' we attempt to demarcate with labels.

"Content" at British Colonization

A more contentious issue is the 'content' of Belizean territory at the time of British settlement in the mid-17th century. Though Spanish colonial records indicate a Maya presence during this period, British colonizers "left no record of contact with Maya for the first century of their occupation" (Bolland 1977:70). While some have interpreted this as an indication that there *were* no Maya in Belize, others have noted that the British colonizers were primarily pirates-turned-woodcutters – probably mostly illiterate – who did not share the record-keeping zeal of Spanish missionaries. Moreover, British extraction of logwood was largely confined to coastal areas, while the Maya lived further inland. The lack of recorded contacts between British and Maya led early histories to portray Belize as 'empty' upon British arrival. One of the governors of the colony asserted that

> there is no record of any indigenous population and no reason to believe that any such existed except far in the interior. . . . There are traces of extensive Maya Indian Population . . . all over the Colony . . . but this occupation was long before British settlement (Burdon 1931; v.1, 4 quoted in Bolland 1988:91).

Stephen Caiger, author of a colonial-era history, echoed this assertion that the Maya

> had abandoned the Belize district long before the seventeenth century. Afterwards, however, hearing of the mild rule of the logwood-cutters as contrasted with Spanish

arrogance and cruelty, they percolated over the frontiers from Mexico and Guatemala, in such large numbers that today these Indians compose more than one sixth of the total population (Caiger 1951:126–127).

Colonial-era authors thus argued that British occupation did not displace an indigenous population; rather Maya from the domains of other colonial powers migrated to Belize relatively late in the colonial period, because they preferred the "mild rule" of the British over Spanish "arrogance and cruelty." Caiger's suggestion that "Indians" chose British rule refers to migrations of Yucatec-speakers from Mexico into northern and western Belize and Mopan- and Kekchi-speakers from Guatemala into western and southern Belize during the latter half of the 19th century (to which I return below).

Against this position, several post-colonial histories (Bolland 1988; Shoman 1994; Stone 1994) argue that a Maya presence was continuous in Belizean territory. In a book published in Belize, Bolland provides evidence which, he asserts, demonstrates that

> the territory now known as Belize was definitely occupied by Maya who were displaced and dispossessed by the British, that relations between the Maya and the British were generally antagonistic in nature, and that the rule of the British, neither mild nor chosen, was imposed upon the Maya in the nineteenth century by force of arms (Bolland 1988:92).

Many authors concur that southern Belize may have been largely depopulated as a result of the introduction of infectious diseases by the Spanish; slave-raiding by Waika, Miskitu, and Europeans; and, finally, the Spanish military's campaign to round up and forcibly remove the rebellious Chols from southern Belize to the Guatemalan highlands, in response to their rejection of Spanish missionizing efforts (Wilk 1991:54–55). However, there is also some evidence of a continued indigenous presence in the area (Wilk 1997, n.d.).

Maya populations of west-central Belize, usually labelled Chan or Mopan, like the Chols, repeatedly rebelled against Spanish efforts to Christianize and 'pacify' them. Their numbers were augmented during the 1630s, as Maya from the Bacalar region of what is now southern Mexico fled to Tipu in what is now Belize in the wake of Maya uprisings (Scholes and Thompson 1977). In the late 1600s, a substantial number of Maya from the area of central Belize succumbed to Spanish efforts and were resettled by the Spanish around the *reducción* town of San Luis in the Guatemalan Peten (Stone 1994:31). However, some histories present evidence that Maya continued to inhabit the upper Belize River valley. Indeed, after the 1770s, as British logging efforts shifted from logwood, which grew along the coast, to mahogany, which grew in inland forests, hostile encounters with "Indians" were increasingly recounted (Burdon 1934:58). Thompson suggests that references to confrontations with "Indians" in western Belize during the late 1700s and early 1800s "provide convincing proof of a continuity to the present day of an indigenous Maya population in western Belize" (Thompson 1977:10). Though Wilk and Chapin, in a Belizean publication, suggest that the British drove most of the remaining Mopan out of Belize and across into the Guatemalan Peten during the expansion of mahogany extraction during the 18th and 19th centuries (1990:14), Assad Shoman, the first Belizean to write a history of Belize, emphasizes British failure to permanently eradicate the Maya. Shoman asserts, "Contrary to what passes as conventional wisdom, the Maya did not just enter Belizean territory in the nineteenth century; they have been here, and in significant numbers, all along." Explicitly recognizing the contemporary political significance of claims to native status, Shoman links this assertion to the national present, suggesting, "Surely this has important implications for how they are perceived in the make-up of the modern nation state?" (Shoman 1994:16).

Migration to Belize

If the circumstances in which British woodcutters encountered or failed to encounter indigenous inhabitants as they colonized what is now Belizean territory have been disputed, the circumstances of arrival of many other categories of persons in Belizean territory have been less contested. Enslaved Africans were brought to work

in the settlement during the 18th century and soon outnumbered Europeans. While this is not disputed, the relations which obtained between master and slave in Belize represent another hotly contested historical topic. In response to abolitionist campaigns in England and racial tensions within the colony, slave holders elaborated arguments about the "kindness, liberality, and indulgent care" which they extended to their slaves, such that "slavery [could] hardly be said to exist in the colony" (Burdon 1934:187). To counter this portrayal, postcolonial histories have focused on slave rebellions as an avenue for reading the slaves' perspectives on their situation (Bolland 1988; Shoman 1994; Stone 1994).

The first of a sequence of immigrant 'groups' to arrive in Belize over the course of the 19th century were 'Black Caribs,' now known as Garifuna. On the island of St. Vincent in the eastern Caribbean, the Island Caribs, who had incorporated Africans into their society, mounted fierce and prolonged resistance to British incursions on the island. When the British finally defeated the Caribs, they classified them into two 'color' categories, returning lighter-skinned 'yellow' Caribs to St. Vincent and deporting darker-skinned 'black' Caribs to Roatan in the Bay of Honduras in 1797 (Gonzalez 1988:23). The 'Black Caribs' dispersed along the Caribbean coast of Central America, with small numbers settling along the southern coast of Belizean territory as early as 1802.

Later in the 19th century refugees from the Yucatan Peninsula of Mexico migrated into northern and western Belize. When the Caste War in Yucatan pitted more rebellious Maya against Spanish and *mestizos* (Reed 1964), groups of less rebellious Maya migrated to Belize to avoid pressure to participate in the war (Jones 1977). Spanish and *mestizos* also crossed into northern Belize seeking refuge during this lengthy conflict (Cal 1991).

During the latter half of the 19th century, migration into Belize from Guatemala was also recorded. As liberal reforms began to be implemented in earnest in Guatemala after 1871, Kekchi land in Verapaz was confiscated for the cultivation of coffee, and the Kekchi were coerced to provide labor for the new coffee plantations

(Wilk and Chapin 1990:20). In response, Kekchi began migrating into lowland areas in order to obtain land for cultivation and escape onerous labor regimes. Some migrated into the Toledo District of southern Belize, founding small villages; another large group of Kekchi were brought to Belize to labor on a large coffee estate in the southwestern corner of the colony, until that plantation went out of business during World War I (Wilk and Chapin 1990:20). In the 1880s, the determined liberal extension of government and commerce into the Guatemalan Peten brought increased logging and prompted Mopan from the community of San Luis to migrate to Belize to escape taxation and forced labor; a large group of migrants founded San Antonio in the Toledo District (Wilk and Chapin 1990: 14; Gregory 1984). Other Mopan settled into villages in western Cayo District, where they interacted closely with Yucatec Maya, Spanish-speaking *mestizos*, and perhaps Mopan already/ still there (Wilk and Chapin 1990: 14; Gregory 1984).[2]

This sequence of arrivals is standard in histories of Belize. The precision with which these arrivals tend to be recounted treats each of the largest ethnic categories recognized in present-day Belize as an already-formed, monolithic group, a kind of "collective individual" (Handler 1991) who arrived in Belize at a particular point in time (Medina 1997). For each ethnic category, this arrival date marks the point in time when their history as an ethnic group/people became intertwined with the history of Belize. As a result, histories of Belize seldom refer to continued border crossings by people from Mexico and Guatemala who largely came to be labeled *mestizo*, Afro-Caribbean migration from the West Indies, or on-going Garifuna migration among Belize, Guatemala, and Honduras. However, recent work always notes, with alarm, renewed immigration from Guatemala, El Salvador, and Honduras during the 1980s, the result of civil wars, political violence, and the intensification of poverty. The immigrants of the 1980s were primarily classified in Belize as *mestizo*, but not as Belizean; thus their presence undermined the Belizeanness of the *mestizo* category itself. A small proportion of these immigrants were also

thought to be Kekchi Maya joining kin in rural communities in the southern Toledo District (Palacio 1988:170).

Thus, some Belizean histories render all current Belizean ethnic categories immigrants to Belizean territory from elsewhere near and far. However, as we will see below, immigrant status does not preclude claims to nativeness, though it does complicate such claims. Other Belizean histories accord a continual – non-immigrant – presence to 'Maya' in Belize, providing a ground for Maya claims to native status which no other ethnic category enjoys.

Who Claims 'Native' Status?

'Native' identity accords its holders a certain moral priority with respect to political rights and economic resources, in Belize as well as internationally. A number of groups have self-identified as 'natives' in order to claim such rights and resources. The four ethnic categories I focus on here are often cast as core members of the Belizean nation, while membership in the nation is more contested for several smaller categories: East Indian, Chinese, the Mennonite, Lebanese or Arab, and White.[3] Among these core members of the Belizean nation, claims to 'native' status may be read as claims to priority in competition over access to resources, jobs, and land (competition which incorporates foreign investors as well). This competition occurs in the context of immigration, emigration, and related demographic shifts which favor the *mestizo* category. *Creoles*, Garifuna, and Maya have organized to press claims to priority access to resources and opportunities.

During the colonial period, the 'Baymen,' the British woodcutters who established the Belize settlement and their Belizean-born descendants (many of parentage described as 'mixed'), defined themselves as 'natives' as part of their efforts to circumscribe the power of British colonial administrators: as natives of the Belize settlement, they demanded a voice in administering it (Judd 1989). Indeed, the Baymen credited themselves with having won the territory away from Spain by force of arms. During the period in which British loggers began settling and working the coast, the

Spanish had continued their activities in the interior of what is now Belizean territory. Intermittent armed conflicts and subsequent negotiations between Spain and Britain resulted in the British loggers being granted use rights to cut timber on Belizean soil, while Spain retained its claim to ownership. However, the frequent breakdown of Anglo-Spanish relations resulted in numerous Spanish attacks on the British settlement in Belize, culminating in the 1798 Battle of St. George's Caye, just off the Belizean coast. In dispatches to London, the colonists described how they and their slaves had fought together to drive the Spanish navy from Belizean waters. They explained, " 'We have rendered the galling yoke of Slavery so light and easy as to animate our Negroes to a gallant defence of their Masters, by whose sides they fought with the most determined bravery and fidelity' " (Burdon 1931: 272). Their gallant defense of the settlement, they suggested, had delivered Belize to Britain by right of conquest.

In addition, the 'Baymen' believed they had established a way of life in the settlement which was distinct from and superior to that of the Spanish colonies which surrounded it, organized according to 'British values' of democracy and fairness. They cast Belize as a civilized – Anglo and Anglican – place which they had carved out of former Spanish territory: beginning from their base at Belize Town on the coast, they had gradually extended their logging work and lifestyle into the interior, expanding 'Belize' as they went until it came to fill the boundaries which now contained it. Thus, from the Baymen's perspective, they had both 'peopled' this territory and fashioned Belize as a distinctive *kind* of place in Central America.

Parts of these claims have devolved today to *creoles*, who are often defined as descendants of the African slaves and 'Baymen' who built the Belizean economy. As Judd (1989) points out, the term "*creole*" itself refers to native status and has been used as a self-identifier in Belize precisely to lay claim to native status. *Creoles* have legitimized these claims by invoking their participation in the establishment of the forestry-based economy which provided the rationale for Belizean existence. Adopting – sometimes adapting (Hyde

1995) – the legends associated with the Battle of St. George's Caye, some *creoles* have also cast themselves as founders of Belize on the basis of the actions of their forebears – both slave and free – who risked their lives in the battle. Indeed, self-identified *creoles* played a major role in celebrating and mythologizing the battle as a foundational event in 'Belizean history' one hundred years after it took place (Judd 1989), and a recent article in a local newspaper made oblique reference to the battle two hundred years later to assert priority for Belizeans of African descent: "Afro-Belizeans built Belize, slaved for it, bled for it, died for it" (Cohen 1998:11).

At the same time, *creole* claims to nativeness also rest heavily on assertions that Belize is more than a geographic territory wrested from the Spanish by their ancestors in 1798. They describe Belize as a culturally unique place in Central America: as a bastion of peace and 'democracy' on a generally violent and undemocratic isthmus (see Fernandez 1989; Medina 1998); as black and Anglo-Caribbean in orientation; as the place in Central American where blacks are least outnumbered and least oppressed (Editorial *Amandala* 1991). Thus, *creole* place making involves the imputation of cultural distinctiveness to Belize and involves claiming a significant role in the creation of the culture which makes Belize unique.

The Garifuna, clearly immigrants, also lay claim to 'native' status, but they use different kinds of arguments to buttress their claims. Although they have obtained national recognition for Settlement Day, a holiday which celebrates the early 19th-century arrival of Garifuna in Belize (Macklin 1986), their assertion of 'native' status is based more on their embrace of a dual ancestry which includes African and Carib forebears. Their Carib ancestry makes them *indigenous to the Caribbean*. Indeed, Belizean Garifuna belong to Caribbean Organization of Indigenous Peoples, which also includes the Caribs of St. Vincent. Forcibly deported by the British from their home in the eastern Caribbean to the shores of Central America, they claim nativity in Belize in terms of the larger Caribbean region to which they – and Belize – belong. In asserting 'native' status for themselves, they also emphasize their non-western (Arawakan) language and cultural practices (Kerns 1983; Gonzalez 1986, 1988). Further, although most Garifuna have embraced the arguments presented by anthropologists and historians that the Africans incorporated into Carib society were slaves who escaped, were shipwrecked, or were carried away during Carib raids on colonial settlements (Gonzalez 1988; Cayetano n.d.), some Garifuna have drawn upon Van Sertima's (1976) argument in *They Came Before Columbus* to extend the arrival of their African ancestors in the Americas further into antiquity (Kirby 1997).

Mestizos also at times make claims to 'native' status, though they have not done so collectively. In fact, *mestizos* are the least organized of the major ethnic categories in Belize. The implication of 'mixture' associated with the *mestizo* label imputes 'native' ancestry at some point in the past. While relations between *mestizo* and Maya in Belize have been hierarchically structured, the differences and hierarchical ordering at present appear to be less extreme in Belize than in neighboring countries. Recent decades have seen a great deal of boundary crossing in northern Belize as economic opportunities in commercial agriculture opened up for smallholders: as they shifted from *milpa* cultivation to sugar cane production many families shifted from Yucatec Maya to *mestizo* identities (Brockmann 1977, 1985; Birdwell-Pheasant 1985; Henderson 1990; Wilk 1986). Wilk and Chapin's designation of this population as "Spanish-speaking *mestizos* mostly of Maya Ancestry" reflects these shifts and the ambiguity they have produced (Wilk and Chapin 1990:7).

Belizean-born *mestizos* generally make claims to nativeness in response to challenges by *creoles* or Garifuna, who often confound them with the Central American immigrants who arrived in Belize in the 1980s. Notwithstanding the hierarchical ordering of *mestizo* and Maya categories, when challenged like this individual *mestizos* sometimes invoke their imputed Mayan ancestry to assert the legitimacy of their presence in Belize and the depth of their 'roots' there. For example, at a soccer match I attended in 1990, which pitted a Belizean team against a team from Guatemala, I was seated near a group of *mestizo* Belizeans, who were cheering for the Belizean team. During the

second half of the match, with the Belizean team trailing, an Afro-Belizean man – rather drunk – stopped in front of the bleachers and turned to shout at the *mestizo* fans, "Aliens! Go back where you came from!" One of the *mestizo* women shouted back, "I'm as Belizean as you are! We're from Benque! If you ever came out to Benque you would see that there are no blacks there, but it's still Belize, and we are Belizeans!" Benque is a town near the border with Guatemala, whose population is largely classified as *mestizo* (though it was earlier known as a Maya community (Jones 1977)). Her assertion that "there are no blacks there, but it's still Belize" indicated her understanding of the man's logic: blacks can be assumed to be Belizeans; others cannot (see Medina 1997). But she challenged his assumption by arguing that *mestizos* can be "as Belizean as" he is. "All of you just crossed the river!" the man retorted, asserting that the woman and her companions were Guatemalans who had recently crossed the border illegally, and that their presence in Belize was therefore illegitimate. Growing angry, the *mestizo* woman asserted the legitimacy of her presence in Belize on the basis of the 'native' origins implied by the *mestizo* label. She answered, "My people were here in Belize long before the white man brought you as a slave!" Her reply reversed their identities, casting herself as the 'native' and her adversary as the immigrant.

In similar fashion, even immigrants from Guatemala who see themselves as *ladino* (a label best defined as the *opposite* of "Indian") sometimes claim indigenous heritage when their presence in Belize is challenged by Belizeans. For example, a Guatemalan immigrant, who had been working in Belize for years, recounted this story of a confrontation he experienced as he was returning by bus from a visit to Guatemala. An Afro-Belizean man seated behind him on the bus asked him what he was doing "in a black country." The Guatemalan asserted on behalf of himself and a Guatemalan traveling companion, "We are Indians; we are from here. I am on my continent! The white people brought you here as a slave, but this continent is ours." ("*Nosotros somos indios; somos de aquí. Yo estoy en mi continente. Los blancos le trajeron a usted como un esclavo, pero este continente es de nosotros.*") These claims to nativeness by both

Belizean-born and immigrant *mestizos* locate themselves in a region larger than Belize itself; indeed, the last example claims a continental indigenousness. Further, *mestizos* tend not to refer to a particular indigenous identity, but rather to a *generic* one: "Indian." Its genericness suggests a great time depth for the 'mixture' in one's ancestry, such that specifics are no longer known (perhaps making them 'less' Indian while still allowing them to claim that ancestry.)

Although the Mopan and Kekchi can claim more specific identities, the history of 19th-century immigration from Guatemala has confounded their efforts to claim native identity in Belize *as* Mopan and Kekchi. If historical accounts of the early colonial period are disputed, and names applied to fluid socio-political groupings are contested, Belizean textbooks have been clear in their references to the 19th-century immigration of Mopan and Kekchi from Guatemala. Thus Mopan and Kekchi are widely understood to be immigrants to Belize like everyone else. As noted above, some ethnographers and historians have argued for a persistent Mopan presence in western Belize (Shoman 1994; Stone 1994), and others cite evidence for a continual indigenous presence in southern Belize, in spite of the Spanish removal of much of the population (Wilk 1997, n.d.). Further, Thompson has suggested that the Manche Chols, who the Spanish forcibly removed from southern Belize, were absorbed by the Kekchi, such that Kekchi migration to southern Belize represents a *return* (Thompson 1988:6). However, given the fact of Mopan and Kekchi immigration in the late 1800s, their most persuasive claims to 'native' status may be based on an identification as Maya rather than as Mopan or Kekchi. "Indian" or "Maya" labels and identities emerged during the 1960s and 1970s, as road construction in southern Belize led to intensified interactions with other categories of Belizeans (Gregory 1984; Howard 1975). Embracing a broad "Indian" or "Maya" label rather than narrower Mopan or Kekchi identities, Mopan and Kekchi leaders formed the Toledo Maya Cultural Council in 1978. The TMCC claims ancestry from the ancient Maya, to whose presence in Belizean territory 'Mayan ruins' attest.

The TMCC argues that Maya migration into Toledo in the 1800s involved "returning to our ancestral lands... Most of the Ke'kchi and Mopan Maya came in groups from neighboring Guatemala to find their roots here in Belize" (TMCC and TAA 1997:9). They ask,

> How can we, Mayas, be considered immigrants? We are the original inhabitants of Toledo Belize who know no boundaries.... The Mayas of Toledo are the direct descendants of the ancient Mayas whose civilization reached its peak around A.D. 900. The continuous use of the Maya temples for religious purposes is testimony to their connection with the past (TMCC and TAA 1997: 2–3).

As Maya, they can more convincingly claim a continual presence in Belizean territory. Thus, Mayan identity may confer indigenous status upon its holder in a way which Kekchi or Mopan identity cannot.

Mopan and Kekchi claims to 'native' status made as Mayas or Indians resonate strongly beyond Belize; the TMCC has found support in international organizations which represent or work on behalf of indigenous peoples. For example, the Toledo Maya Cultural Council is a member of the Central American Indigenous Council (CICA) and the *Coordinadora Regional de Pueblos Indígenas* (CORPI). The TMCC (as well as the National Garifuna Council) has also participated in the Indigenous Development Fund, and they have received support from the Indian Law Resource Center in the U.S. Indeed, a report produced for the Toledo Maya Cultural Council by the Indian Law Resource Center in the U.S. explicitly defines Mopan and Kekchi as Maya and counters arguments which label them immigrants to Belize:

> [I]t would be a mistake to make too much of the Spanish efforts to expel the Maya. The fact that some Maya may have been removed against their will across what was then an imaginary border, only to return 150 years later, does not mean that the Maya abandoned their homeland or relinquished their aboriginal rights to Toledo District. The aboriginal territory of the Maya encompassed southern Belize and the area across the border in Guatemala.

From the Maya point of view, their land was a single territory that could not be divided by an artificial border drawn by non-Indian colonial powers (Berkey 1994:3–4).

Ancient Nation, Developing Nation: Implications for Claims to 'Nativeness'

As a nationalist movement emerged in Belize during the 1950s, its leader sought to produce the Belizean nation by producing Belizean history. Drawing on the 'Mayan ruins' distributed across the Belizean landscape, he rooted the nation's origins in ancient Mayan civilization. His embrace of the ancient Maya in the name of the Belizean nation grounded that nation and its demand for sovereignty in a more distant and legitimate territorial past than that of disputed British woodcutting activities. Since Guatemala claimed to have inherited ownership of Belizean territory from Spain, this move was important in adding depth and legitimacy to Belizean history, which in turn bolstered demands for Belizean independence. With self-government and later independence, new textbooks began the narrative of Belizean history with the ancient Maya civilization and the traces it left in the Belizean landscape. In an unusual move which reinforced the connection between the emerging Belizean nation and the ancient Mayan polities of the same territory, the government buildings in the new capital built in the 1970s were designed and arranged to resemble an ancient Mayan plaza.

These moves were opposed by some *creole* leaders. As nationalist leaders extended Belizean history backwards in time by claiming and incorporating the ancient Maya, some *creoles* accused them of attempting to "Mayanize" Belize. They demanded that African history be included in the teaching of history in Belize as well. However, the principle of territoriality in national identity worked against their demands in the late 1960s and 1970s and continues to work against them in the present: the history of the Maya and the history of Belize can be understood as having happened in the same geographical space, and Belizean claims to this territory may be strengthened by its cooptation of the ancient Maya as early Belizeans. However, African his-

tory is intelligible as part of *creoles'* history as a *people*, but not as part of the history of Belize as a *place*, since it happened 'somewhere else' rather than 'here.' Further, it does not solidify Belizean ownership of the territory of Belize, an important goal for nationalist leaders, since Belizean sovereignty was and still is disputed by Guatemala.

The government's rooting of the Belizean nation in ancient Maya cities provided grounds for Mopan and Kekchi to identify and press claims as Maya. The marginalization of Mopan and Kekchi from agro-industrial development efforts and their inadequate and insecure land base provided motivations. The colonial government had allocated reserve lands to them, but the reserves were not clearly demarcated, tenure was not secure, and the reserve lands were insufficient to meet their needs. Thus, the Toledo Maya Cultural Council was formed to pursue the goals of developing a shared Maya identity and mobilizing cooperatively to protect Kekchi and Mopan culture and languages and expand their land base. In 1988 the TMCC petitioned the Belizean government for half a million acres of land in the southernmost Toledo District to create a Maya "homeland." This homeland would replace the smaller currently existing reserves; within the homeland, the TMCC proposed to allow each village to determine its own mixture of communal and privately owned lands (Wilk 1991:235). In arguing for a Maya homeland, the TMCC has emphasized "ancestry from the ancient Maya and identity with the people who built the ancient ruins of Toledo" (Wilk 1991:235).

The land which the TMCC has targeted is officially under government control, and the government has recently granted concessions for logging tracts of lands it controls in the Toledo District to a Malaysian corporation. This company's logging efforts have further galvanized Maya activism both inside Belize, where the TMCC has filed a suit against the Belizean government, and beyond Belizean borders, as the TMCC has established alliances with environmental NGOs, human rights organizations, and transnational organizations that support the claims of indigenous peoples. The government has countered the TMCC's claims in part by redefining its members more narrowly as

Mopan and Kekchi rather than as Maya. Government officials have argued that the Mopan and Kekchi are immigrants to Belize, just like everyone else; thus they have no ancestral rights to a homeland and should be treated like all other Belizeans with regard to land ownership (Wilk 1991:235).

An article recently published (under a "pen name") in the nation's largest newspaper echoed the government's argument in condemning Maya demands:

> They talk about their heritage, meaning that they have been occupants of Toledo lands from time immemorial. This is not true. Had both lots of them, Kek'chi and Mopan Mayas, lived for ages together in the relatively small geographical area of the Toledo District, their languages would not have evolved separately and be mutually unintelligible, as they are today.
>
> We conclude from this that at least one lot of them must be newcomers. In fact, both lots are.... In historical times, the only times that matter, the Toledo District was largely innocent of human habitation until the Garifuna came to Barranco in 1802. They, the Garifuna are the true pioneers of the settlement of this part of what is now the Belizean polity.... The Afro-Belizeans built Belize, slaved for it, bled for it, died for it. They should not now face exclusion from any part of it (Cohen 1998:11).

Responses from Maya leaders printed in the following week's edition of this newspaper sought to vindicate Mayan claims and refute the argument that the Maya are "newcomers" by citing "enlightened historians" and referring to Maya cultural practices and values which require access to land to ensure cultural survival:

> Enlightened historians have proven that Mayas were in Belize before the Europeans arrived. The noted historian O.N. Bolland in his book *Belize: A New Nation In Central America*, on pg. 11, wrote 'Contrary to the claims of colonially oriented historians, many Mayas were still present in Belize when the Europeans came in the sixteenth and seventeenth centuries'... The Mayas in essence are claiming their rights to land in Southern Belize based on two criteria: (1) the existence

of a culturally distinctive community or society with historical origins that predate the effective exercise of sovereignty by the country or its colonial precursor, and (2) customary or traditional land tenure or resource use that can be identified as part of the cultural life of the community or society (Coc 1998:23).

Here, contemporary activists claim continuity with Mayan ancestors and demand that the state recognize their cultural heritage and facilitate their continued practice of cultural traditions. Their arguments incorporate concerns with "dwelling" as spatial practice into discursive contests over intertwined constructions of people, history, culture, and place. In this context of struggle, the practices of dwelling, their production of "lived relationships" with the land, are being made explicit rather than taken for granted. Maya practices of dwelling are being articulated as aspects of an increasingly *conscious* practice of culture of the sort anthropologists have noted elsewhere (Handler 1988; Turner 1991). In the 1970s, Wagner argued that anthropologists imagined culture for people who did not imagine it for themselves; while the people anthropologists study see themselves as "doing life," he suggested, the anthropologist instead understands them to be "doing culture" (Wagner 1975:26–27). If this might have been true in the 1970s, over the space of two decades the culture concept has become popularized enough that people have increasingly begun to see themselves as "doing culture" on a routine basis.

Thus the Maya struggle for a homeland in Belize participates in a larger trend in which everyday cultural practices are becoming increasingly objectified *as* cultural practices. For example, a message on "Land, Value and Economic Development in Toledo (A Maya Perspective)" posted online by Gregory Ch'oc criticizes the "unfortunate 'Euro-American' attitude to land use [which] is gaining ground in Belize," which alienates land from man by commoditizing land. He contrasts this with a Maya attitude about land which "has evolved over a time scale of many centuries."

> Land that can grow corn is still important for the Mayas and they have evolved an

agronomic system using forest fallowing to ensure that the soils remain reasonably fertile. Their system provides the nearest thing to sustainable production of essential food crops in most of Central America. Despite years of agricultural use, the land is still largely clothed in forest. To turn loose Asiatic entrepreneurs to destroy the Mayan agricultural system (and the cultural values that go with it) is something about which all Belizeans should be ashamed.... [T]here is a battle in progress in Toledo between an Indigenous (to Central America) ethnic group who care about how they treat the land and have no wish to sell or buy land, and foreign ethnic invaders who think of land only as a means of making profit by acquisition and subsequent sale – something Mayas simply cannot understand, or approve of.

For the Mayas the 'value' of land and its' (sic) resources is life itself; something priceless. For centuries the Mayas derived their food, clothing and shelter from the land. The cultural identity is still tied to the land – therefore a land base is vital for the continuity of the Mayas.......

We are not against 'progress' or development per se, but there is the need to find a fair solution to the cultural orientations underlying the land conflict in Toledo. The ideological, spiritual and economic relation of the Mayas to the land has meant that land and its resources are perhaps the most decisive element to ensure successful economic development. It is critical if the Mayas are to successfully pursue traditional forms of economic life, since development programs supported by government continued to cause social and cultural stress to the Mayas.... All the Asiatic loggers are doing is creating an irreversible ecological nightmare for the Mayas. At the same time disorienting Mayas environmental concepts which centers on the preservation of the Maya Culture.

The Mayas are fighting back by strongly opposing the logging concessions. For now this is the only means by which the Mayas are defending their habitat against the drastic changes associated with commercial logging to ensure free access to the natural resources in Toledo upon which the Maya Culture

depends.... Their organizations are working hard, and in many ways to foster the survival of the Maya Culture. The Mayas are endangered by the exploitation of the resources of their land.

Can the Mayan people survive this attack or will they become part of the statistics as another victim of ethnocide in the world today? (Ch'oc 1996).

Ch'oc's argument for expanding and securing a land base for Maya in Toledo District asserts the absolute necessity of such a base for the continuation of Maya Culture, an objectification of the routine practices of dwelling. Significantly, Maya Culture entails relationships between people and land which are both intimate and ancient; the severing of those relationships, Ch'oc warns, could constitute ethnocide against the Maya of Toledo.

The articulation of the cultural practices of dwelling is also manifested in the recently completed *Maya Atlas: Struggle to Preserve Maya Lands in Southern Belize* (TMCC and TAA 1997). The atlas was a joint production of members of all Maya villages of Toledo and Stann Creek districts of Belize and geographers from the University of California, Berkeley. Its aim is to document Maya land use in its many aspects – farming, hunting, fishing, religious – as "the first step to secure land for all the Mayas of Toledo" (Cho 1996). The atlas extends the objectification of the cultural practices of dwelling by documenting their "emplacement" in great detail. As the authors explain,

> This atlas aims not only to show the boundaries of the Maya Homeland but to bring out the dynamic interactions of the various communities and their relationship to the environment.... In addition, the atlas gives us an opportunity to explain our links to the sacred Mayan temples dotting the country of Belize and tell you how we have preserved our tradition and culture (TMCC and TAA 1997:2).

This trend towards the articulation and objectification of culture is the primary means of seeking to change government policies for land use in Toledo District. At the same time that the government has resisted these pressures, it has been involved in actively promoting this trend as part of its ecotourism development strategy. While the government has rejected as illegitimate Mopan and Kekchi claims to a Maya homeland, arguing that they are immigrants like everyone else in Belize, its tourism development efforts have painted a different picture of the Maya. Mopan and Kekchi of far southern Belize were largely marginalized from the agro-export development strategy which has dominated Belizean policy for decades. However, as free trade undermines this strategy (Medina 1998), the government has begun to promote more aggressively an alternative development strategy based on ecotourism. This strategy does two things which actually contribute to Maya claims: 1) it associates contemporary Maya with ancient Maya ancestors, and 2) it articulates and objectifies the cultural practices of dwelling for the education and enjoyment of ecotourists.

The ecotourism strategy seeks to capitalize on the relatively 'unspoiled' Belizean environment, its Mayan ruins, and the cultural difference its population can offer to western travelers. In pursuit of this strategy, Belize joined with El Salvador, Guatemala, Honduras, and several states of southern Mexico in 1992 to launch the Mundo Maya or "Maya World" project. This joint public-private sector project discursively and practically constructs a *regional* 'Maya' space which reflects the expanse of 'Maya civilization' during the Maya Classic and Post-Classic periods and incorporates contemporary Maya groups as the continuing manifestation of that ancient culture. Within the regional space of Maya World – unlike the national space of Belize – the nativeness of Mopan and Kekchi as Maya is unquestioned. Further, the Maya World project constructs them as 'native' for an audience – tourists – to whom Maya culture and civilization have already been represented as monolithic and singular (Castañeda 1996). Thus, the economic and symbolic forces of tourism development may contribute to a reordering of nativeness and space which shifts the terms of discourse to the possible advantage of Maya claims to nativeness.

Ecotourism strategies have also focused increased attention on Maya practices of dwelling. For example, the Toledo Ecotourism Associa-

tion's Village Guest House Program enables ecotourists to travel to small, rural Maya villages to learn about Maya Culture and the interactions villagers sustain with their surrounding environment. The program involves thirteen Mopan and Kekchi villages (and one Garifuna village), which have constructed small guest quarters for tourists and developed tours of the village and surrounding ecological and archaeological attractions. Promotional materials for the TEA offer tourists "a colorful and breathtaking natural environment, exposure to ancient philosophies, rituals and medicines, as well as a profound understanding of the balance of nature." Local experts – 'natives' – will guide tourists through rainforest habitats, *milpas*, and Mayan ruins to provide a "unique cultural and ecological experience." Through such practices, the ecotourism development strategy contributes to the articulation and objectification of practices involved in dwelling: tourists are invited to observe and learn about Maya ways of conceptualizing, relating to, and living in the natural world from Maya who both explain and perform them.

While the promotion of an ecotourism development strategy may contribute to a shift in the relative strength of arguments with which different ethnic groups claim 'native' status in Belize, it is important to note that other groups may also take advantage of opportunities afforded by ecotourism to claim 'native' status by more fully articulating their practices of dwelling. For example, though the Garifuna have focused primarily on their cultural distinctiveness to attract tourists and attest to their non-western origins, the incorporation of one Garifuna village along with thirteen Mayan villages into the village guest house program of the Toledo Ecotourism Association Program may contribute to the objectification and articulation of the more mundane subsistence practices of the Garifuna in order to communicate them to tourists.

Further, Garifuna ritual and cosmology might be understood to enact a claim to 'native' status, binding them to Belizean soil in ways which parallel the interdependence of people, culture, and land articulated by Belizean Maya leaders. The Garifuna *dugu* ritual, which placates ancestors who have returned to trouble their living descendants, lays claim to place by locating ancestors in the soil. Ethnographer Byron Foster suggests that, in *dugu*,

> Myth and history are fused together in the ritual portrayal of the ancestral journey from the past to the present. Because of this fusion, the picture is initially confusing, for the ancestors arrive at the cult house both from St. Vincent and from the mud floor of the cult house itself. But it is from this ambiguity that the rite derives its meaning, for the journey from St. Vincent portrays the group's origin, while the emphasis on the mud floor of the cult house stresses that it is in Belizean soil that the dead are buried (Foster 1986:41).

Thus *dugu* ritual connects its participants to two homelands simultaneously – Belize and St. Vincent – by summoning ancestors from each.

> What *dugu*, then, 'says' is this: our St. Vincentian ancestors, who themselves searched for a homeland, travel thence to the shores of Belize to celebrate *dugu* with their descendants. But for almost two centuries we have buried our dead in the soil of our new homeland. Belizean soil contains the mortal remains of our dead, and in order for the ancestors to revitalize us and our society, their spirits must be transferred from the soil. In effecting this transition, the earth, from which the bodies of the unborn derive, is also revitalized (Foster 1986:44).

Foster's analysis suggests that *dugu* ritual goes beyond the arborescent metaphor of rootedness to link contemporary Garifuna to both ancestors and descendants, through ritual processes which unite people and soil, revitalizing both.[4]

In addition, ecotourism may provide new openings for *creole* or *mestizo* assertions of nativity as well, especially for those who live in rural areas. Ecotourism promotes the articulation and objectification of dwelling practices into discourses which make native status, local knowledge, and an intimate relationship with the environment valuable and visible. Indeed, ecotourism presumes necessary linkages among the three. Insofar as *creole* or *mestizo* residents of rural villages are successful in defining themselves as local experts on flora and fauna for ecotourists,

this expertise may provide another channel for their claims to native status.

Conclusion

As we have seen, 'native' identity is much contested in Belize, and a large part of this contestation involves the selection and imposition of the criteria by which nativeness will be judged. Though always linked to territoriality, claims to nativeness in Belize have been rooted in territories of many different scales – national, Caribbean, Mesoamerican (the expanse of the ancient Maya civilization), hemispheric. Place-making efforts to conflate identity with territory, history, and culture also produce conflicting and non-congruent arguments about the attachments of people and modes of life to territories confined to or including Belize. This contestation has placed Belizean Maya (or Mopan and Kekchi) in the unusual position of having to make an argument for their indigenousness in the face of skepticism from many fellow Belizeans. Thus, while pan-Maya mobilizing in Belize parallels larger-scale Maya movements in Guatemala and Mexico in terms of some of its goals and concerns, it confronts the additional liability of having the legitimacy of its claims to indigenousness questioned and challenged. Indeed, this vulnerability may contribute to the utility of mobilizing as Maya rather than as Mopan and Kekchi.

The economic and symbolic forces of ecotourism development may work to reorder relationships between peoples and places to the possible advantage of Mopan and Kekchi claims to Maya identity and native status in Belize. However, while the adoption by Belize of an ecotourism development strategy may work to the advantage of Maya claims to native status, by foregrounding a continuous Maya identity from ancient past to the present, this strategy provides opportunities for other Belizean ethnic groups to continue to elaborate bases for their claims to native status as well. Increasingly, both ethnic activism and ecotourism are tending toward the objectification of the practices of dwelling, which might previously have 'gone without saying,' and their articulation into discourses which link people to place through culture. Thus, 'culture' is becoming an increasingly important ingredient in claims to nativeness in Belize, alongside history, whose evidence proved inconclusive.

Arguments about generic and specific Maya identities in contests over indigenousness in Belize intersect with academic debates about Maya peoplehood and Maya culture. Castañeda (1996) has argued that 'The Maya' and 'Maya Culture' have been produced through interaction among anthropologists, tourists, those who claim a Maya identity, and the states in which Maya live. From this perspective, 'Maya Culture' is a relatively recent rather than an ancient artifact, a product of professionalizing strategies among anthropologists, nation-building strategies of states, and economic development strategies involving cultural tourism. Other scholars – both Maya and North American – have argued that an identifiable core of values and beliefs, a cosmology, was shared across the expanse of the ancient Mayan World and continues to orient Maya communities in the present (for example, Carlsen 1997; Freidel, et al. 1993; Raxche' 1996). This perspective posits both a spatial continuity across Maya polities in the past and a temporal continuity from past to present.[5] The significance of this academic debate is heightened, as some groups in Mesoamerica invoke an objectified Maya culture to legitimate their claims, while competing groups question the authenticity of 'Maya culture' or the right of those groups to claim it (see Warren 1998).

In Belize, as competing groups struggle to impute meanings to a broad Maya identity or to narrower Mopan and Kekchi identities, they are confronted with ambivalent 'data.' Historical accounts indicate that differences among Maya in Belizean territory were not clear-cut in the past, because of gradual rather than abrupt differentiation of language and practice across space, multiple migrations which often produced villages containing groups with multiple origins, and marriage across labeled categories. At present, differences between Mopan and Kekchi are not always clear-cut either: many live in ethnically 'mixed' villages; marriage across linguistic boundaries continues; and cooperative activism is enlarging a shared Maya identity (Wilk 1986). Recent shifts by significant numbers of Belizeans from Maya to *mestizo* identity further complicate efforts to draw firm boundaries differentiating Maya and non-Maya or specific Maya identities from one another. The simultaneous openness and differentiation across specific Maya identities cannot be accommodated easily in conceptualizations which produce bounded peoples, each linked to its own place through its own distinct culture, whether peoplehood is defined in generic (Maya) or specific (Kekchi, Mopan) terms. As a result, culture will also likely prove inconclusive as a basis for Maya claims to 'native' status in Belize.[6]

NOTES

1   I draw primarily (though not exclusively) on sources available in Belize, since these are most easily and most often deployed in struggles among Belizeans.

2   Wilk and Chapin use the conflation "Maya/ *mestizo*" to label these *mestizos*, suggesting that their ancestry was Mayan, though they had adopted the Spanish language and a "*mestizo*" identity (Wilk and Chapin 1990: 14).

3   The 1991 census counted 43.6% of the population *mestizo*, 29.8% *creole*, 6.6% Garifuna, 4.3% Kekchi Maya, 3.7% Mopan Maya, and 3.1% Other Maya (including Yucatecs), for a total of 11.1% Maya. Among the smallest categories, East Indians accounted for 3.5% of the population, Mennonites 3.1%, Whites 0.8%, Chinese 0.4%, and Syrians 0.1%.

4   Garifuna claims to native status have also been institutionalized, with Maya support, through the recent formation of the Belize National Indigenous Peoples Council (BENIC) in April, 1997. BENIC was formed by delegates from the Toledo Maya Cultural Council, the Toledo Alcalde Association, the Xunantunich Association (representing Mopan from Cayo District), the Masewalt Institute (representing Yucatecs from Cayo District and northern Belize), the National Garifuna Council (*TMCC News* 1997); all are Maya organizations with the exception of the National Garifuna Council. BENIC is linked to the Central American Indigenous Council (CICA), headquartered in Panama.

5 My framing of this debate focuses on only a small portion of the larger debate. For discussions of the larger debate, see Watanabe (1990), Smith (1991), Warren (1992, 1998), and Fischer and Brown (1996).

6 Indeed, Wilk (n.d.) argues that "culture" cannot be conclusive. Whether argued in terms of older, static, bounded conceptions of culture or contemporary conceptions which portray culture as open and 'in motion,' "[a]ll cultural claims to resources can be argued and contested, but they can rarely be conclusively proven" (Wilk n.d.:7). Consequently, Wilk argues in favor of distributing control over resources through a system of "stakeholding," which has the advantage of being "openly political," rather than hiding politics behind the concepts of social science.

REFERENCES CITED

Periodicals

Amandala
TMCCNews

Other Published Sources

Basso, Keith
1996 Wisdom Sits in Places: Notes on a Western Apache Landscape. *In* Senses of Place. Steven Feld and Keith H. Basso, eds. Pp. 53–90. Santa Fe: School of American Research.

Berkey, Curtis
1994 Maya Land Rights in Belize and the History of Indian Reservations. Report to the Toledo Maya Cultural Council. Washington, DC: Indian Law Resource Center.

Birdwell-Pheasant, Donna
1985 Language Change and Ethnic Identity in Eastern Corozal. Belizean Studies 13(5–6): 1–12.

Blu, Karen
1996 'Where Do You Stay At?' Home Place and Community among the Lumbee. *In* Senses of Place. Steven Feld and Keith H. Basso, eds. Pp. 197–228. Santa Fe: School of American Research.

Bolland, O. Nigel
1977 The Maya and the Colonization of Belize in the Nineteenth Century. *In* Anthropology and History in Yucatán. Grant Jones, ed. Pp. 69–102. Austin: University of Texas Press.
1988 Colonialism and Resistance in Belize: Essays in Historical Sociology. Belize: Cubola/SPEAR/ ISER

Borneman, John
1997 State, Territory, and National Identity Formation in the Two Berlins, 1945–1995. *In* Culture, Power, Place: Explorations in Critical Anthropology. Akhil Gupta and James Ferguson, eds. Pp. 93–117. Durham: Duke University Press.

Brockmann, Thomas C.
1977 Ethnic and Racial Relations in Northern Belize. Ethnicity 4:246–262.
1985 Ethnic Participation in Orange Walk Economic Development. Ethnic Groups 6:187–208.

Burdon, John
1931 The Archives of British Honduras, Vol. 1. London: Sifton Praed.
1934 The Archives of British Honduras, Vol. 2. London: Sifton Praed.

Caiger, Stephen
1951 British Honduras Past and Present. London: George Allen and Unwin.

Cal, Angel
1991 Rural Society and Economic Development: British Mercantile Capital in Nineteenth-Century Belize. Ph.D. dissertation. University of Arizona.

Carlsen, Robert
1997 The Struggle for the Heart and Soul of a Highland Maya Town. Austin: University of Texas Press.

Castañeda, Quetzil
1996 In the Museum of Maya Culture: Touring Chichen Itzá. Minneapolis: University of Minnesota.

Cayetano, Sebastian R.
n.d. Garifuna History, Language and Culture of Belize, Central America, and the Caribbean.

Cho, Julian
1996 Message from Julian Cho, Executive Chairman of the Toledo Maya Cultural Council, May 31, 1996. www.belize.com/toledo/chol.html

Ch'oc, Gregory
1996 Land, Value and Economic Development in Belize. www.belize.com/toledo/chocl.html

Clifford, James
1988 The Predicament of Culture. Cambridge: Harvard University Press.

Coc, Pio
1998   Letter to the Editor, Amandala 1477:23
Cohen, Richard
1998   Turmoil in Toledo. Amandala 1476:11
Editorial
1991   A Message to the Garinagu Amandala 1153:2
Feld, Steven and Keith H. Basso
1996a Introduction. *In* Senses of Place. Steven Feld and Keith H. Basso, eds. Pp. 3–11. Santa Fe: School of American Research.
Feld, Steven and Keith H. Basso, eds.
1996b Senses of Place. Santa Fe: School of American Research.
Fernandez, Julio A.
1989   Belize: Case Study for Democracy in Central America. Brookfield, VT: Avebury.
Fischer, Edward F. and R. McKenna Brown, eds.
1996   Maya Cultural Activism in Guatemala. Austin: University of Texas Press.
Foster, Byron
1986   Heart Drum. Benque Viejo, Belize: Cubola Press.
Freidel, David, Linda Schele, and Joy Parker
1993   Maya Cosmos: Three Thousand Years on the Shaman's Path. New York: William Morrow.
Gonzalez, Nancie
1986   Garifuna Traditions in Historical Perspectives. Belizean Studies 14(2):11–26.
1988   Sojourners of the Caribbean: Ethnogenesis and Ethnohistory of the Garifuna, Chicago: University of Illinois Press.
Gregory, James
1984   The Mopan: Culture and Ethnicity in a Changing Belizean Community. University of Missouri Monographs in Anthropology #7, Columbia: Department of Anthropology, University of Missouri.
Gupta, Akhil and James Ferguson
1997   Culture, Power, Place: Ethnography at the End of an Era. *In* Culture, Power, Place: Explorations in Critical Anthropology. Akhil Gupta and James Ferguson, eds. Pp. 1–29. Durham: Duke University Press.
Handler, Richard
1988   Nationalism and the Politics of Culture in Quebec. Madison: University of Wisconsin Press.
1991   Who Owns the Past? History, Cultural Property, and the Logic of Possessive Individualism. *In* The Politics of Culture. Brett Williams, ed. Pp. 63–74. Washington, DC: Smithsonian Institution Press.

Henderson, Peta
1990   Development and Dependency in a Belizean Village. Second Annual Studies on Belize Conference, SPEA Reports 4. Belize: SPEAR.
Howard, Michael C.
1975   Ethnicity in Southern Belize: The Kekchi and the Mopan. Museum Brief #21, Museum of Anthropology, University of Missouri, Columbia.
Hyde, Evan X
1995   [1969] Knocking Our Own Ting. *In* X-Communication: selected writings. Pp. 1–20. Belize City: The Angelus Press.
Jones, Grant
1977   Levels of Settlement Alliance among the San Pedro Maya of Western Belize and Eastern Petén, 1857–1936. *In* Anthropology and History in Yucatan. Grant Jones, ed. Pp. 139–190. Austin: University of Texas Press.
Judd, Karen
1989   Cultural Synthesis or Ethnic Struggle? Creolization in Belize. Cimarron 2(1): 103–118.
Kerns, Virginia
1983   Women and the Ancestors: Black Carib Kinship and Ritual. Chicago: University of Illinois Press.
Kirby, I. A. Earle
1997   The origin of Black Caribs. Amandala 1153:2
Macklin, Catherine
1986   Crucibles of Identity: Ritual and Symbolic Dimensions of Garifuna Identity. Ph.D. dissertation, Department of Anthropology, University of California, Berkeley.
Malkki, Liisa
1997   National Geographic: The Rooting of Peoples and the Territorialization of National Identity Among Scholars and Refugees. *In* Culture, Power, Place: Explorations in Critical Anthropology. Akhil Gupta and James Ferguson, eds. Pp. 52–74. Durham: Duke University Press.
Medina, Laurie Kroshus
1997   Defining Difference, Forging Unity: the co-construction of race, ethnicity, and nation in Belize. Ethnic and Racial Studies 20(4):757–780.
1998   The Impact of Free Trade Initiatives on the Caribbean Basin: from 'Democracy' to 'Efficiency' in Belize. Latin American Perspectives 25(5):27–49.
Palacio, Joseph
1988   Illegal Aliens in Belize: Findings From the 1984 Amnesty. *In* When Borders Don't Divide.

Patricia Pessar, ed. Pp. 156–177. New York: Center for Migration Studies.

Pred, Allen
1986 Place, Practice and Structure. Cambridge: Polity Press.

Raxche'
1996 Maya Culture and the Politics of Development. *In* Maya Cultural Activism in Guatemala. Edward Fischer and R. McKenna Brown, eds. Pp. 74–88. Austin: University of Texas Press.

Reed, Nelson
1964 The Caste War of Yucatan. Stanford: Stanford University Press.

Scholes, France V. and Sir Eric Thompson
1977 The Francisco Pérez Probanza of 1654–1656 and the Matricula of Tipu (Belize). *In* Anthropology and History in Yucatán. Grant Jones, ed. Pp. 43–68. Austin: University of Texas Press.

Shoman, Assad
1994 Thirteen Chapters of a History of Belize. Belize: The Angelus Press.

Smith, Carol
1991 Maya Nationalism. Report on the Americas 25: 193–228.

Stephen, Lynn
1998 The Zapatista Opening: the movement for indigenous autonomy and state discourses on indigenous rights in Mexico, 1970–1996. Journal of Latin American Anthropology 2(2):2–41.

Stone, Michael
1994 Caribbean Nation, Central American State: Ethnicity, Race, and National Formation in Belize, 1798–1990, Ph.D. dissertation, University of Texas at Austin.

Thompson, J. Eric S.
1977 A Proposal for Constituting a Maya Subgroup, Cultural and Linguistic, in the Petén and Adjacent Regions. *In* Anthropology and History in Yucatán. Grant Jones, ed. Pp. 3–42. Austin: University of Texas Press.
1988 The Maya of Belize: Historical Chapters Since Columbus. Belize: Cubola Productions.

Toledo Maya Cultural Council (TMCC) and Toledo Alcaldes Association (TAA)
1997 Maya Atlas: The Struggle to Preserve Maya Land in Southern Belize. Berkeley: North Atlantic Books.

Turner, Terrence
1991 Representing, Resisting, Rethinking: Historical Transformations of Kayapo Culture and Anthropological Consciousness. *In* Colonial Situations. George Stocking, Jr., ed. Pp. 285–313. Madison: University of Wisconsin Press.

Van Sertima, Ivan
1976 They Came Before Columbus. New York: Random House.

Wagner, Roy
1975 The Invention of Culture. Chicago: University of Chicago Press.

Warren, Kay
1992 Transforming memories and histories: the meaning of ethnic resurgence for Maya Indians. *In* Americas: New Interpretive Essays. Alfred Stephan, ed. Pp. 189–219. New York: Oxford University Press.
1998 Indigenous Movements and Their Critics: Pan-Maya Activism in Guatemala. Princeton: Princeton University Press.

Watanabe, John
1990 Enduring yet Ineffable Community in the Western Periphery of Guatemala. *In* Guatemalan Indians and the State: 1540 to 1988. Carol A. Smith, ed. Pp. 183–204. Austin: University of Texas Press.

Wilk, Richard
1986 Mayan Ethnicity in Belize. Cultural Survival Quarterly 10(2):73–77.
1991 Household Ecology. Tucson: University of Arizona Press.
1997 Mayan People of Toledo: Recent and Historical Land Use. Expert witness testimony prepared at the request of the Indian Law Resource Center and the University of Iowa Legal Clinic, Feb. 16, 1997.
n.d. Whose Forests? Whose Land? Whose Rivers? Ethics and Conservation. Science and Engineering Ethics (in press).

Wilk, Richard and Mac Chapin
1990 Ethnic Minorities in Belize: Mopan, Kekchi, and Garifuna. Benque Viejo del Carmen, Belize: SPEAR and Cubola Productions.

11

The Carnivalization of the World

Richard Parker

Sin, the saying goes, does not exist beneath the equator. It is an idea that has been traced as far back as the writings of the austere Dutch historian Gaspar von Barlaeus, in his seventeenth-century chronicle *Rerum per Octennium in Brasilien* (Barlaeus 1980). First published in 1660, Barlaeus's work would become a classic document of the Dutch occupation of northeast Brazil (see Freyre 1956, Boxer 1957).

> All wickedness was amusement and play, making known among the worst the epiphany: "– On the other side of the equinoctial line there is no sinning" –, as if morality did not pertain to all places and peoples, but only to the northerners, and as if the line that divides the world separated as well virtue from vice. (Barlaeus 1980, 49)

Barlaeus's chronicle seems to have marked Brazil out as somehow unique and problematic: hardly, in this instance, a tropical Eden, but rather a land of sin and wickedness, whose inhabitants seemed to believe that the universal laws of morality and virtue did not apply to them. With his northern severity, Barlaeus, of course, could only scoff at such a misguided notion before going on to outline the renewed sense of order that Dutch rule had gradually been able to enforce upon the chaotic existence of the tropics. Surely he could not

have imagined the impact that his own words would later have in shaping a very different understanding of the world.

In the early 1970s, at the height of the military dictatorship that lasted from 1964 until the return to civilian rule in 1984, the poet and novelist Ledo Ivo published his prize-winning political allegory *Ninho de Cobras* (Snakes' Nest), set in the provincial port city of Maceió, in the northeastern state of Alagoas, during World War II (see Ivo 1981). Exploring the underside of social and political life in Maceió, Ivo focused on the often conflicting perceptions of reality that result as much from political as from psychological repression. The almost mythical power of the past in the present reappears throughout his text. It is most evident, however, in a chapter entitled *A Festa* (the Portuguese term for both "party" and "festival"), following the description of a night-long party held by members of the local elite at Dina's, one of Maceió's leading houses of prostitution, when Ivo echoes the words of Barlaeus for his own purposes:

> "Beyond the Equator sin does not exist," Barlaeus had noted when writing the chronicle of the Dutch period. Then that landscape had been part of New Holland and through the rows of crooked streets and warehouses bursting with sugar passed the worst scum of

the earth. Besides the Portuguese, there were
Dutch, French, Scots, Englishmen, Jews, and
Germans who, sought after or hunted by the
Inquisition and other tribunals which fore-
shadowed the eve of the stake or the gallows,
had arrived there with their dreams and vices.
... "Beyond the Equator, sin does not exist,"
they alleged in word or in thought; and they
killed Indians and Blacks and their own white
companions. They sacked plantations, robbed
warehouses and ravaged women, depositing
in them, in their burning or Negro cunts, the
seeds of the green or blue eyes of those red-
haired and white-featured Northeasterners of
today. This permissive code has crossed the
centuries. And today, in Maceió's turbulent
brothels, when somebody shouts "everybody
naked," or wild orgies splash creek or ocean
waters awakened by man's lasciviousness, a
hidden tradition surfaces once again. It is a
tradition of creatures faithful to the life of the
flesh and the senses and suffocated by the
Church and the State.... It is as if the Alago-
ans momentarily remembered those remote
times when everything was permitted. (Ivo
1981, 113–15)

In the face of centuries of social development
and repression, the vision of a past in which, as
Ivo puts it, "everything was permitted" continues
to interrupt the flow of social action. What Ivo
describes as a "hidden tradition" surfaces to give
meaning to contemporary life.

Here, in the present, however, what is most
striking about this "hidden tradition" is the
degree to which it has been re-created in positive,
rather than negative, terms. A vision of evil and
wickedness has given way to a kind of playful
celebration of the most fundamental possibilities
of life. This quality has been captured by Chico
Buarque de Hollanda in *Não Existe Pecado ao Sul
do Equador* ("Sin Doesn't Exist to the South of
the Equator"), his reinvention of Barlaeus, and
one of the most successful songs of the past two
decades of Brazilian popular music:

Sin doesn't exist
on the side beneath the equator.
Let us commit a sin
spread open, sweaty, all steamy.
Let me be your depraved doormat,

your devilish bouquet, stream of love.
When it's a lesson of disorder,
look out, get out from under, I'm the professor.
Leave sadness aside,
Come to eat, dine on me,
sarapatel, caruru, tucupi tacacá,
See if you can use me, abuse me, soil me,
Because your mixed-blooded woman can't wait.
Leave sadness aside,
Come to eat, dine on me,
sarapatel, caruru, tucupi tacacá,
See if you can exhaust me, put me on your table,
Because your Dutchwoman can't wait.

Playing on the double-entendre of the human
body as a world unto itself, and the waist as an
equatorial line dividing north from south, *Não
Existe Pecado ao Sul do Equador* takes Ledo Ivo's
text one step further, suggesting that if sin exists,
it is only in the mind. True to the transgressive
logic of erotic ideology, beneath the waist is a
world of pleasures and passions, of tastes and
flavors, that would be unimaginable in Barlaeus's
northern reality.

Once again, then, what emerges from these
various texts, fragmentary as they are, is a vision
of a world divided, split into two sharply opposed
modes of being or forms of experience. The seriousness and severity of daily life, which is made
possible only through the repression of desires
and the prohibition of pleasures, is contrasted
with a rebellious world of sensuality and satisfaction in which the pleasures of the body can escape
the restrictions imposed by an oppressive social
order. It is a vision of a world free from sin and
given over to the sensuality of the body, and it is
most fully realized today in the experience of
carnaval, the annual pre-Lenten festival that has
existed in the West since the early days of Christianity but that has taken its most elaborate form
in contemporary Brazilian culture.

Like the myths of origin that tell of the formation of a uniquely sexual people in an exotic land,
the carnivalesque tradition has taken on new
meaning, beneath the equator, as somehow definitive of the peculiar character of Brazilian reality (see Da Matta 1978). For Brazilians and
foreigners alike, the *carnaval* has become almost
synonymous with Brazil itself. Yet even if it were
nothing else, *carnaval* would still be the clearest

example in contemporary Brazilian life of those peculiar moments when a hidden tradition comes out of hiding and an entire society discovers and reinvents itself – when, for a few brief days, myths of origin take shape in cultural performance, the past invades the present, and the sensuality of the body defies sin. It is a time when everything is permitted, when anything is possible.

Celebrating the Flesh

The carnivalesque tradition has, of course, already been described and analyzed extensively by any number of writers (see, for example, Bakhtin 1968; Baroja 1979; Burke 1978; Gaignebet and Florentin 1974; Ladurie 1979). It has been interpreted, through its essential opposition to the world of daily life, as a kind of ritual of reversal or rebellion in which social life is turned on its head and time played back to front (Davis 1975, Leach 1961, Turner 1969). It has been seen as a world of laughter, of madness and play, in which the established order of daily life dissolves in the face of an almost utopian anarchy, in which all hierarchical structures are overturned and the fundamental equality of all human beings is proclaimed. Above all else, it has been understood as a celebration of the flesh in which the repressions and prohibitions of normal life cease to exist and every form of pleasure is suddenly possible (Bakhtin 1968). Indeed, even the name of the festival itself has been interpreted as meaning "a farewell to flesh" (from the Latin *carnis* or "flesh" and *vale* or "farewell") – a kind of final triumph of sensuality before Lent (Leach 1972).

The sensuality of the carnivalesque tradition is nowhere more evident than in Brazilian *carnaval*, which is arguably the most elaborate, widespread recreation of the logic of the festival anywhere in the contemporary world. No less than the traditional carnival of medieval Europe, the modern Brazilian *carnaval* embodies a single, overriding ethic: the conviction that in spite of all the evidence to the contrary, there still exists a time and place where complete freedom is possible. If the carnivalesque tradition has taken root in Brazil, however, it has hardly remained stagnant. On the contrary, it has clearly continued to change and

grow in response to the specific circumstances of Brazilian life, merging with the "hidden tradition" of the Brazilian past that is essential to the understandings that Brazilians have built up of themselves as a people. In other words, the *carnaval* itself has been "Brazilianized" and has itself become a kind of metaphor with its own highly complicated set of meanings.

Once again, some sense of what all of this means on the ground, of how it is experienced and understood by the people who participate in it, can best be approached through the language that they use to make sense of it. The world of *carnaval* is a world of diverse pleasures. As Nancy Scheper-Hughes has noted, one of the key metaphors structuring the Brazilian perception of reality is the notion of normal daily life (as opposed to the world created by the *carnaval*) as a kind of *luta*, "struggle" (Scheper-Hughes 1988). This *luta* takes many forms and is played out on a number of different levels, but it clearly characterizes the nature of day-to-day existence, filled, as it is, with *trabalho* (work) and *sofrimento* (suffering):

> The meaning of this is that life, survival, is an eternal war. The struggle for our daily bread . . . The struggle for a miserable salary . . . The struggle because of a lack of hope . . . In itself, everything in order to arrive at the end is simply a total struggle to the death. (Antônio)

This linear (and ultimately tragic) trajectory of one's life is interrupted each year by the cyclical rhythm of the seasons, by the time outside of time, during *carnaval*, when the work and suffering of daily life give way to a world of *risos* (laughter). Here, in this world of laughter, the normal conditions of human existence, marked as they are by an almost overwhelming *tristeza* (sadness), are transformed in the *felicidade* (happiness) and *alegria* (joy or elation) of the festival:

> It's like in that song from the film Black Orpheus: *Tristeza nao tem fim, felicidade sim* (Sadness has no end, but happiness ends). Leaving sadness, the struggle of day-to-day life, forgotten inside an imaginary drawer, the people allow themselves to be carried away by the reality of fantasy (*uma fantasia real*) in the

three days of *carnaval*. They are three days of merrymaking, sweat, and beer, but everything comes to an end on Shrove Tuesday. (João)

In these fleeting moments of happiness, the daily struggle of life is reinvented, transformed into *brincadeira* (play, fun, amusement, joking, etc.). No longer the deadly serious battle for existence, the playful struggles of the *carnaval* take on an altogether different form in the chaotic battles of the traditional *entrudo* (a ritualized street fighting in which the participants pelt one another with filth, garbage, mud, excrement, or urine); the somewhat tamer jests and jokes of *foliões* (literally, "merrymakers" or "revellers," but derived from the French terms for madness and madmen); the *brincando* (playing) with water pistols, clubs, or similar weapons in the street; or even the playful *campeonatos* (championships) of the great *escolas de samba* (samba schools) that are a focus today for the *carnaval* of Rio de Janeiro.

The use of the verb *brincar* (to play) is instructive, for it is especially here, in this notion, that the sexual meanings in the symbolic structure of the festival are most evident. *Brincando* (playing) can take shape on any number of different levels. On the one hand, it refers to the apparently innocent play of children, the *brinquedos* (toys) and *brincadeiras* (fun and games) that everyone remembers from their childhood:

> In the life of a child, the word *brincar* is perhaps one of the most frequently used, not to mention "to eat" and "to drink." This word is heard all the time in the life of the child, not only from the child himself, but from everyone around him. (Rose)

At the same time, however, there is less innocent play of early adolescence and even adulthood – the *brincadeiras sexuais* (sexual play) that has such an important place in the formation of the erotic universe:

> The *brincadeiras sexuais* in the life of a child around the age of puberty pass from the material toys (*brinquedos*) to the playthings (*brinquedos*) of the sexual organs. . . . The doll and the toy car are left aside, or almost totally forgotten, in order to give room for the so-

called *brincadeiras* of discovery of the body in transition to adulthood. (Rose)

It is this notion of play as not only pleasurable, but also profoundly sexual in nature, that shapes the fully adult use of *brincar* as a synonym for both sexual intercourse itself and erotic play more generally:

> The verb *brincar* is also used. "I want to play (*brincar*) with you" or "I want to play (*brincar*) in your cunt (or your ass, or your mouth)." "Let's play a good game (*brincadeira*). "I have a toy (*brinquedo*) here that you will like." "Can I put my toy (*brinquedo*) in your garage?" (João)

Linking the play of children to that of adults, then, and true to the totalizing and transgressive logic of erotic ideology, the use of *brincar* breaks down the kinds of hierarchical categories and distinctions that normally order daily life. It builds up another, very different, understanding of human experience, in which enjoyment and pleasure become the focus of attention, the most important reason for being.

It is hardly surprising, then, that *brincar* should be used as well as the verb for "doing *carnaval*":

> *Brincar* is used also for the *carnaval*. You say that you are going "to play" (*brincar*) the *carnaval*. "Let's play (*brincar*) the *carnaval*." This verb was chosen because of giving adults the liberty to let everything out during these three days of merrymaking and paganism for the Christians. To play (*brincar*) the *carnaval* is to dance, to drink, to fuck, to get high, to kill, and to die. They are days to let out your emotions like a child – but the adult, when he plays (*brinca*) the *carnaval*, these are perhaps the only days of the year that he can really be himself and not some jester from everyday life. (João)

The past that is re-created in the carnivalesque present is at once social and individual: the hidden tradition of an unruly and sensual historical past and the repressed freedom of childhood. For young and old alike, the oversized *chupeta* (pacifier) is among the most common *brinquedos* used during the *carnaval*, and since its original recording in 1937, *Mamae Eu Quero* ("Mommy I

Want"), with all of its possible meanings, has continued as perhaps the most popular of all *carnaval* songs:

> Mommy I want,
> Mommy I want,
> Mommy I want to suckle.
> Give me the pacifier,
> Give me the pacifier,
> Give me the pacifier,
> So that the baby won't cry.

Re-creating a world outside of time, a world where wishes and desires can always be satisfied, this emphasis on sucking and suckling breaks down the lines that separate children from adults and the divisions that separate one individual body from another.

This emphasis on union, on the fundamentally erotic merging of the body with other bodies, is especially evident in the experience of the carnivalesque crowd – the *massa* (mass) of revelers playing *carnaval* (see Bakhtin 1968).

> During the *carnaval* you stop being the master of your own body. The mass becomes master . . . (Alexandre)

Losing control, losing mastery, over one's body and merging with the bodies of others, the individual finds himself integrated into the masses, or perhaps more accurately, the *povo* (people). The *povo* in turn is offered a new and different awareness of its sensuality, its material unity and community. For a few brief moments, hierarchy and patronage collapse, and the masses rule the streets.

Within this unruly crowd, bodies not only rub up against one another and, at least in symbolic terms, merge into one: they can be exchanged and transformed. The *carnaval* proposes that fantasy should become reality, and *fantasia*, the very term used to describe the mental images of psychic fantasy, is also used for the costumes of *carnaval*. Through *fantasias* and masks, individual reality is transformed and the fantastic reality of *carnaval* is created. The diversity and complexity of the *carnaval* costumes defies description, ranging from clownlike fools and Chaplinesque tramps to grotesque monsters, anthropomorphic animals, skeletons, and ghostlike representations of death. While many of these fantastic disguises might just as likely be found today in the carnivals of Europe or the Caribbean, and obviously draw on a carnivalesque tradition that subsumes the Brazilian *carnaval*, it is not surprising that just as many have taken a particularly Brazilian turn. The characters of a number of imaginary figures, such as Zé Pereira, from carnivals of the past, are re-created and become popular motifs in the present. *Pretos-Velhos* (Old Blacks, who are among the principal *guias*, or "guides," in ecstatic trance religions such as *Umbanda*), and any number of other figures from the world of the Afro-Brazilian religious cults, are common in the world of *carnaval*. And while indigenous peoples have been driven further and further into decay and extinction, costumed *grupos de indios* (groups of Indians) have become a special focus in carnival celebrations throughout Brazil.

Marginalized and oppressed in contemporary life, in the world of *carnaval* these figures come to the center of attention. They call up a violent Brazilian past, yet they integrate it into a form derived originally from Europe. Indeed, in properly cannibalistic fashion, they almost devour that form: they ingest it, digest it, and spit it out again in what is somehow a distinctly Brazilian shape. They create a present that is clearly part of a broader carnivalesque tradition, while at the same time uniquely Brazilian – the quintessential expression of the Brazilian spirit.

The playful manipulation of sexual images dominates this world of masks and costumes. Joking clowns adopt enormous, clublike phalluses that can be used to beat upon the bodies of other merrymakers. Grotesque, diabolical, or monstrous figures combine the body parts of male and female in order to create ambiguous *andróginos* (androgynes). Men transform themselves into women, and women (though somewhat less commonly) into men. Indeed, no symbolic form dominates the symbolism of the festival as completely as transvestism.

The transvestism of the festival is anything but a single, structural phenomenon. On the contrary, it is multiple and varied. There are the comic *blocos de sujos* (groups of filthy ones), for example, whose gender-crossing is relatively balanced between male and female, and whose tone is largely comic or absurd:

In the 1950s, 1960s, and even the 1970s, it was common for children to cross-dress and go out asking for coins.... The girls would put on, and put on even today, large asses, and with their faces hidden they can play (*brincar*) and say improper things to people or flirt with the guys that they are after. They liberate themselves a little more than normal. The boys put on large false breasts and let people play with their boobs and with asses made out of pillows. This transvestism starts very early. Parents help to make the costumes, and sometimes the whole family goes out together cross-dressed, or in large groups called *blocos de sujos* – which may or may not use masks, but with heavy makeup and extravagant feminine clothes. (João)

While the *blocos de sujos* often seem to focus on the mundane and ordinary – maids, housewives, and the like – in building up their comic transformations, there are also far more stylized and serious performances. Young adolescent males from the lower sectors dress as high-class whores and call themselves *piranhas*. Homosexually identified males from the more modern middle sectors choose low-cut gowns exposing their masculine chests, make use of an exaggerated makeup, and sprinkle glitter in their beards or mustaches in a carnivalesque version of what has been described in English as "gender-fuck" (Read 1980, 17–18). And most ubiquitous, the *travestis* (transvestites) who usually work the shadowy streets of almost all major Brazilian cities during daily life become absolute centers of attention with their elaborate gowns and stylized performances. What at first glance appears to be a unified symbolic inversion takes shape, upon closer inspection, then, as a set of transformations as diverse as the sexual universe more generally. Celebrating the confusion and ambiguity, but building up subjective meanings as varied as their subjects, these multiple transvestisms push and pull at the seams of any system of meanings that would seek to separate the world into two distinct, opposed, and hierarchically related categories, in order to organize the better part of collective life around this separation.

As the emphasis on transvestism obviously suggests, the sexual universe that the *carnaval*

opens up is altogether different from the world of daily life. The festival creates a special time and space, opposed to this everyday life, when the silent, and sometimes perverse, pleasures that occur "within four walls" escape their boundaries and create a fully public world in which, like the private world of erotic ideology, anything is possible. The two seem to reinforce one another, each providing a kind of model for the other, and even in the cyclical passage of time, they are intimately tied together:

> The sexual rhythm of the year gets faster during the summer, principally with the arrival of *carnaval*. With the heat of the summer, people have more energy for everything.... Everyone tries to find the sun, and the beaches become super-full with sweaty and golden bodies. Clothes become a key for the exhibitionism and display of the body, of the gifts of nature. Everything is very semi-nude, especially in cities where there are beaches. The nights are exhilarating, and there is no place where there aren't people. They are hot nights, propitious for love, sex, freedom of the body. In the summer, nothing is a sin (*nada é pecado*), principally with the arrival of *carnaval* mixing with the summer and tropicalism of this country. Everything comes to a climax in the *carnaval*.... This is the key that closes the psychological summer of the Brazilians. After the *carnaval*, the sun is still there for a few months, but the interior heat and the hope don't generate so much excitement as in the summer that comes before *carnaval*. (Antônio)

Linking notions about the sensuality of *sol* (sun), *suar* (sweat), *praia* (beach), and *verão* (summer) to the practice of *sacanagem* (transgressive sexual interaction), then, the *carnaval* embodies a "tropical" vision of the world. Like the carnivals of the northern hemisphere, this *carnaval*, too, offers a vision of the future: a utopian vision of the possibilities of life in a tropical paradise, somewhere south of the equator, where the struggles, suffering, and sadness of normal human existence have been destroyed by pleasure and passion. In the *carnaval*, everything is permitted, as it would be in the best of all possible worlds. The polymorphous pleasures of erotic ideology become the norm, rather than the transgression of the established order, and the fullest possibilities of sexual life take concrete form in the play of human bodies:

> During the *carnaval* everything is permitted in terms of sex or drugs. The *carnaval* balls are, in certain places, a true orgy. Everything is permitted. You understand? There is no censorship, and the unrestrained exhibitionism and the desire to expose oneself are very common in the carnivalesque atmosphere. During this period, sex is present everywhere, and bodies, souls, and semen are left at their will, giving to everyone the freedom to do what they really desire. It is a good period for prostitution and the buyers of pleasure. Everything is sold, everything is bought, everything is given, everything is received with a lewd and inviting smile on the face. Beaches, corners, bars, bathrooms, parks, buses, trains, and other places are stages for sensuality and sex. The streets become completely given over to the beat of *samba* and the frenzy of sweaty bodies having sex. (João)

Impersonal sex between strangers who may never see one another again, sex in groups, sex in the streets or on the beach, sex in public, in full view rather than hidden within four walls – all become part and parcel of the play of *carnaval*. Sexual transactions that cross the lines of class, age, and race, lesbian and homosexual interactions, exhibitionism, and any number of other marginal pleasures become possible in a world where repression and oppression cease to exist. Playing, pressing up against other bodies (and ultimately losing one's own) in the crowd, entering the bodies of unknown partners, their faces hidden behind masks or beneath makeup – anything is possible in a world where sin ceases to exist. Freeing the imagination from the seemingly interminable struggles that are inevitably one's lot in life, it offers a better world, a world of pleasure and satisfaction, of joy and happiness. Even if these few moments of pleasure and joy must always come to an end on the morning of *Quarta-Feira de Cinzas* (Ash Wednesday), they nonetheless hold out the possibility of something better than the endless sadness of daily life. They offer *esperança* (hope), and they root it in pleasures and passions of the people as a whole.

In the Wheel of Samba

Carnaval in Rio de Janeiro, Recife, or Salvador is not just a somewhat more contemporary version of the traditional carnivals of Venice, Madrid, or Lisbon. It has not merely responded to, but has in fact fully integrated, a distinctly Brazilian reality into its symbolic structure. Through a kind of cannibalism that modernists of the 1920s and 1930s could not help but admire, the contemporary Brazilian *carnaval* seems to have fed upon a traditional European form in order to invest it with a particularly Brazilian content. Just as sexuality has been seen as the concrete mechanism of the racial mixture that is understood as fundamental to the formation of the Brazilian people, the *carnaval*, with its symbolism of sexuality, and its own mixture of European, Amerindian, and African cultural traits, has increasingly been offered up as the most authentic expression of the underlying ethos of Brazilian life.

That the *carnaval* should have provided fertile ground for the elaboration of both indigenous and African cultural traditions is hardly surprising. Because the festival creates a space outside of the normal social order, outside of the structures necessary for *civilização* (civilization), it takes shape as something somehow *primitivo* (primitive) and *selvagem* (savage). It is understood as a time when the most "primitive" and "savage" urges of the individual unconscious rise up and play themselves out on an elaborate stage. To many early observers, there was really little difference between the pagan excesses of *carnaval* and the excessive ceremonies of the pagans. The grotesque anthropophagous ceremonies of the native Brazilians and the orgiastic dances of the African slaves seemed to flow into and merge with the obscene celebration of the flesh during *carnaval*, and it is not unexpected that the symbolism of these "savage" performances should have been incorporated into the festival (Sebe 1986).

The symbolism of anthropophagy is especially well suited to the semantic structure of the *carnaval*. The transgression of a food taboo can easily be linked to the transgression of sexual taboos in a symbolic construct focused on

devouring the flesh of another human body in
order to incorporate it within one's own. As a
symbol of incorporation, then, anthropophagy
can be invested with layers of meaning ranging
from cannibalism itself, to the act of sexual intercourse, to the mixture of races and cultures that is
taken as definitive of Brazilian reality. In the
persons of the *blocos de índios*, the use of masks
and costumes harking back to the totemism of the
native Brazilian tribes, and the altogether unruly
and chaotic incorporation of "savage" imagery
(ranging from the use of colored feathers and
headdresses to bows and arrows), the symbolism
of the *carnaval* not only overturns the order of
daily life, but offers an interpretation of Brazilian
reality as less modern and civilized than savage
and primitive (see Sebe 1986, 48–53).

As important as this configuration focused on
indigenous culture has obviously been, however,
the distinctly Brazilian character of *carnaval* has
been most clearly asserted in the music and dance
derived from the African cultures of a slave-holding society. The *batucadas* (the rhythmic beating
of percussion instruments) and *sambas* (both a
style of dance and a specific type of music) that
dominate the contemporary *carnaval* are interpreted in terms of their African roots, and their
perceived sensuality is linked to the milieu from
which they emerged. African music and dance
have been seen, in turn, as closely associated
secular expressions of African culture that were
originally derived from the context of religious
ritual, but that took on new meaning, at least in
part, because of the encouragement of the slave-
owners themselves, who viewed them in erotic
terms and saw them as useful in increasing the
size of their herds:

> The *samba* dance was introduced in Brazil by
> the Africans. In the slave quarters, and in
> their rituals, the dance began to take on
> great force. It was seen, even by the masters,
> as an erotic dance – a kind of aphrodisiac.
> You understand? The slaves spent their days
> at forced labor on the plantations. At night,
> they got together in circles, and with the
> palms of their hands and a few primitive
> drums began to sing and dance *samba*. The
> ritualization of the *mulata* woman's walk and
> the agile grace of the feet of the *mulato* man

began to spread in Brazilian culture. From
the most remote and marginalized places, it
was gradually introduced into the general
culture, and now it is not known as just a
part of black culture, but is generalized and
known worldwide. (Sérgio)

Following the freed slaves from the rural plantations to the cities, and up into the hills and *favelas*
of Rio de Janeiro and Salvador, *rodas de samba*
(wheels or circles of *samba*) sung and danced to
the beating rhythms of the *batucada* situated
themselves at the margins of Brazilian society –
in the shantytowns where even the police were
unwilling to venture, in the Afro-Brazilian religious cults with their perceived emphasis on
witchcraft and sorcery, in the bohemian bars associated with crime and prostitution. Yet like the
sambistas (*samba* composers or dancers) who
invented them, they come down from the hills
each year for *carnaval*, when the most marginal
elements of Brazilian society come to the center
of the social universe and create a world of fantasy
and happiness.

Like the symbolism of anthropophagy, the
symbolic associations of the *samba* are particularly
well fitted to the world of *carnaval*. Re-creating
the festival in Brazilian terms, *samba* simultaneously reproduces the erotic focus of carnivalesque symbolism. In its rhythms and
movements, as much as in its lyrics, it reinvents
the body, freeing it (as on the plantations) from
the discipline of work and opening it up to the
experience of pleasure:

> The first thing that is important for the *samba*,
> in order for you to really dance the *samba*, is
> that you have to let your body go free. You
> have to be light, to have free movements. The
> second thing is to make it charming. And to
> get across the grace of the *samba*, you have to
> smile, to let out energy with your face. It's the
> happiness (*felicidade*) of *carnaval*. The third
> thing is to place the *samba* principally in
> the arms, in the belly, in this part here....
> The *samba* is divided between the head,
> the torso, and the limbs. With the head,
> it's the movement that announces the *samba*.
> With the smile, with singing, with the music
> ...You understand? With the torso, you give
> lascivious movements, sexual movements.

With the feet, you give the rhythm and the movement of the *samba*. If you have a good foot, if you know how to move with your feet, your body will go along in the swaying movement also.... The rhythm, the movement that comes from the feet, fills the whole body with the shake-shake (*mexe-mexe*) of the *samba*. The belly, the ass, the thighs, the belly-button.... These are the most important parts of the body for the lasciviousness of the *samba*.... The movements are well defined with the movements of sex. (João)

Rising up from the feet and filling the entire body with life, the movement of the *samba* opens out, like the outstretched arms that are among the most characteristic gestures of the *carnaval*, to *abraçar* (embrace) the world. Reproducing the strangely controlled madness that has always been associated with the *carnaval*, but giving it a specifically Brazilian cast, *samba* frees the body from the daily constraints imposed upon it, defying sadness and suffering within the space of the festival. Like the symbolism of *carnaval* more generally, it celebrates the flesh. It focuses on the sensuality of the body. It offers a vision of the world given over to the pleasure and passion, joy and ecstasy.

The role of *samba* in the *carnaval* also plays into the wider system of inversions that bring the most marginalized sectors of Brazilian society to the center of the festive world. Just as *samba* descends from the *favelas*, so too do the *sambistas* – the poorest (and darkest) segments of urban society, whose struggles and suffering in an oppressive economic and social system cannot be stated strongly enough, become the focus of the *carnaval*:

> In the *carnaval*, the poorest *sambista* goes out to play (*brincar*) costumed (*fantasiado*) as a king of France or Portugal. In daily life he has no importance within the society. But on the avenue, he's the professor. (Sérgio)

If the poor and the powerless can become kings and queens, however, this carnivalesque inversion is hardly the only way in which the *sambista* comes down from the hills in order to take center stage during the festival. The symbolism of *car-naval* works as much through intensification as through inversion, and it is perhaps in the figures of the *malandro* (translated, at best, as a "rogue" or a "scoundrel") and the *mulata* (a dark-skinned, mulatto woman) that the marginalized reality of the *favela* is most clearly enacted in carnivalesque performance.

Treated normally as a "bad element," a dangerous good-for-nothing who is likely to be a criminal, a racketeer, or a thief, in the carnivalization of the world the *malandro* becomes a kind of culture hero – a trickster, really, known for his ability to circumvent the rules and regulations of the established order:

> The *malandro* always likes to "put something over on" or "rob" other people. He's a man who is looking for freedom – freedom of expression and financial freedom...Society labels him as an assailant or a thief. It treats being a *malandro* as if it were like being a bum, an easy and dangerous life.... (Jorge)

If it is the mark of the *malandro* that he is able to find a way around the structures of authority, it is no less clear that he lives not for hard work or struggle, but for pleasure and sensuality:

> The *malandro* is a poet, an artist of life. Most times, he doesn't like to work. He waits for everything to fall from the sky. He lives for pleasure, for *sacanagem, carnaval*, all these things. (José)

Like the *malandro*, the *mulata* is given a key role in the symbolic universe of the *carnaval*. Defined, ever since the days of slavery (as the writings of Gilberto Freyre made so evident), as an erotic ideal in Brazilian culture, the *mulata* is perceived as the perfect embodiment of the heat and sensuality of the tropics (see Sant' Anna 1984).

> The *mulata* is the black goddess of Brazilian culture. She is a symbol of sexuality and fertility, and is known as one of the most beautiful women in the world. She possesses movements and gestures that no other kind of woman possesses. Like the way she walks, talks, smiles, makes love.... Her voluptuous way of moving her body is imitated by many, but only the *mulata* has such grace in moving her behind. (João)

Yet if the *mulata* appears as an ideal of female attraction, it is an ideal that exists within the paradoxes of Brazilian life, within the double standard of a patriarchal tradition developed in a slaveholding society. Perhaps best captured in a proverb cited by Freyre, the *mulata* has been held up as a sexual, rather than social ideal: *Branca para casar, mulata para foder, negra para trabalhar* (White woman for marrying, *mulata* woman for fucking, black woman for working) (Freyre 1956). In the most sensual of celebrations, however, the *mulata*, perhaps even more forcefully than the *malandro*, comes to the center of attention:

> The *mulata* is known as a sexual symbol of the *carnaval*. It's the *mulata* who knows how to stir things up, who knows how to *samba* and play. She is the symbol of the attractive woman, the Brazilian woman. (Wilson)

In the elaborate theater of the *carnaval*, the *mulata* thus emerges as the most concrete symbol of a much broader ethos. Embodying an entire ideology, she becomes a representation of Brazil itself – of the Brazilian people, formed from the mixture of three races and cultures, somehow marginal and distant (beneath the equator) from the world's great centers of wealth and power, yet possessing a seductive charm that sets them apart from any other people anywhere on the face of the earth.

If much of the sexual symbolism of *carnaval* seems to undercut the certainty of established classifications, relativizing and destroying them through grotesque combinations or elaborate transvestisms, then in a strange way this world of *samba* that has been integrated into the structure of Brazilian *carnaval* seems to display them in an intensified or exaggerated form. *Samba* itself, at least in its most popular manifestations, is created within a fundamentally male space: the popular bars where the predominantly male composers spend their free time, and where women who wish to avoid being labeled as *putas* or *piranhas* are unlikely to venture. Even the language, the poetry, of *samba* is a kind of male discourse, which often focuses on the suffering and injustice imposed, it is claimed, upon men by women.

Even here, however, as everywhere in the world of *carnaval*, things are not always all that

they seem to be – or, perhaps more accurately, things are often *more* than they seem to be. If the symbolism of the *samba* displays the hierarchy of gender in particularly stark form, it simultaneously calls into question the neatly ordered structures of bourgeois sexual morality. It offers up a sexuality that is at once primitive, savage, and tropical. Situating itself within a structure of fantasies that is perhaps as old as the first European contact with the non-European world, it plays on a whole set of white images about black sexuality and sensuality. Transforming these images into a vision of a uniquely Brazilian sexuality – a vision built up in the rhythms and movements of *samba*, the trickery and cunning of *malandragem*, and the voluptuous pleasures of the *mulata* – this configuration identifies itself as somehow more "authentic" or "true" to the tropical nature of Brazilian reality, and certainly as more "alive," than the pale conformity of the bourgeois order could ever be. If it reproduces in exaggerated form certain oppressive structures from the world of normal daily life, it simultaneously uses these structures to overthrow others in the kind of constant, playful, sarcastic movement characteristic of a world that has been *carnavalizado* (carnivalized). From the point of view of the elite, it is here that both its fascination and danger lie.

The Greatest Show on Earth

For as long as there has been a historical record of the festival, it has been marked by discord and debate. At the same time that the transgressive values of the *carnaval* have been loudly proclaimed in the streets, they have been constantly criticized by the voices of restraint and order. Like the myths of origin that tell of a licentious past, an atmosphere of "sexual intoxication" resulting in the mixture of distinct races, and ultimately, the formation of the Brazilian people, the sometimes violent and always sensual performances of the *carnaval* have been met with a profound ambivalence (see Turner 1983). It has been the object of extensive criticism as well as outright repression. Over the course of more than a century, there has been an ongoing effort (particularly in Rio de Janeiro, where the festival has been most visible to the wider world) to domesticate the most savage expressions of the carnivalesque tradition, to find a way of organizing its disorder. Ironically, this process has contributed to the attention that has been focused on the festival, to its gradual development as a symbol for an even larger reality.

From the early colonial period on, the celebration of *carnaval* in Brazil was marked by a sharp dichotomy that has continued on up to the present: a distinction between the *carnaval da rua* (*carnaval* in the street) and the *carnaval do salão* (*carnaval* in the large hall or ballroom). This opposition between *rua* and *salão*, in turn, has been translated into any number of other oppositions between the popular classes and the elite, between the influences of African or Amerindian cultures and the predominance of European patterns, and so on. The *carnaval da rua*, perhaps most frequently described as the *entrudo*, was characterized by its unruly and rebellious nature, its violence and dirtiness, as the *foliõs* pushed, shoved, and pelted one another with water, mud, urine, and other unidentified substances. It was the *carnaval* of the poor, which meant that its participants were overwhelmingly black – the so-called savage, primitive, African elements in Brazilian society. The *carnaval do salão*, by contrast, was a celebration of the white elite, regulated by invitations or paid admission. Held most often in large theaters, the elaborate *bailes* (balls) were modeled on Portuguese and Italian celebrations and characterized by their elaborate costumes and disguises (see Da Matta 1978; Eneida 1958; Sebe 1986).

By the middle of the nineteenth century, the celebration of the *entrudo* had become the object of considerable concern on the part of the elite, and by 1853, an edict had been issued banning the *entrudo* as a carnivalesque game. While a succession of similar mandates issued over the course of the next fifty years would never completely succeed in doing away with the *entrudo*, the battle lines had clearly been drawn, and an attempt to civilize the *carnaval* had begun. Gradually, this process took shape through the formation of somewhat more organized groups, derived from different classes and communities that came together to celebrate the festival. Beginning in the

1850s, for example, members of the rising middle classes came together to form what were known as *Grandes Sociedades* (Great Societies) which paraded through the streets of the city in elaborate costumes, marching to the music of brass bands and pulling floats that often focused on political issues of the day, as well as organizing balls for the participation of their members. The poorer sectors, in turn, adapted this notion to the more scattered reality of the traditional *entrudo*, joining in somewhat less ordered groups known as *cordões* (cordons), *ranchos* (literally, "strolling persons"), and *blocos* (blocks). Composed largely of members of the working class or the petit-bourgeoisie, the *cordões* and the *ranchos*, like the Great Societies, paraded in costume throughout the city, marching to the music of bands and choruses. The *blocos* were made up of the poorest segments of the population, and had little formal structure aside from the spontaneous grouping of the festival, when participants would dress up in old clothes and comic hats in order to parade about as Zé Pereiras or comic clowns (Eneida 1958; Sebe 1986).

Given the significant presence of poor blacks and mulattos, it was principally in the *blocos* that the influence of *samba* was first felt during the 1920s and 1930s. The earliest samba schools arose out of a number of the larger, better organized *blocos* during the twenties and were closely linked to specific neighborhoods, principally *favelas*, that existed on the margins of Brazilian society. As highly visible organizations of poor blacks – and, hence, in the eyes of the elite, of *malandros, vagabundos* (vagrants or vagabonds), and *marginais* (marginals) – the same schools were subject, especially during this early period, to more than a small amount of harassment on the part of the police, and were themselves extremely concerned with projecting an image that would be respected and accepted by the elite sectors of the society. Their marginal position within society as a whole led to an ongoing struggle over just how they would be incorporated not only within the festival, but within the world of normal daily life.

The position of the samba schools changed radically, however, in the 1930s, with the rise of populist politics and the emergence of Getulio Vargas as president of Brazil. In seeking to recruit support among the lower sectors – and thus to incorporate them into the existing political structure – populist politicians began to turn significant attention to the schools and to offer public funding for their activities. By 1934, the *União Geral de Escolas de Samba* (General Union of Samba Schools) had been formed and had begun, with the blessing of the government of Rio de Janeiro, to sponsor a *carnaval* parade of up to thirty different schools. City authorities, newspapers, and the police had all become involved in planning and organizing the *desfile* (parade or review), and an increasingly elaborate set of rules and regulations had been invented in order to organize a competition between the schools. The most notable requirement was the stipulation that the *enredos* (plots) of the *sambas* presented by the schools were to be based upon "national motifs" – on the events or personalities of Brazilian history. At the same point that elite writers such as Gilberto Freyre were turning to history in order to create myths of origin, the participants in *carnaval* were being pushed to turn to history in order to create ritual, in order to present a reading of the Brazilian past to the Brazilians in the present. The elaborate performances of the samba schools would become a way of representing the past – again, not necessarily in terms of any kind of empirical, historical understanding, but along the lines of a particular ideology, a cultural construction.

By the 1950s and 1960s, the samba schools had achieved a remarkable degree of legitimacy within the wider society. The *sambistas* had come down from the hills to perform at the very heart of the *carnaval* in Rio de Janeiro – and like the *carnaval* in Rio more generally, had been held up to Brazil as a whole as a kind of model for the performance of the festival. Indeed, even the membership of the schools had been transformed. While they continued to be based in predominantly poor black neighborhoods, they had been subject to what has been described as an "invasion" on the part of the predominantly white middle and upper classes:

> From the 1960s on, the samba schools became fashionable for every type of social class. They weren't just made up of only

blacks and poor people anymore, but of everyone who was attracted by the *batuques* of *agogos* (a percussion instrument consisting of two different sized bells that are hit with a stick), *tambores chocalhos* (rattling gourd percussion instruments), and every type of instrument that awakens in the hearts and minds of the Brazilian the contagious rhythm of the carnivalesque plots. (José)

This invasion of the schools by the middle and upper classes has been interpreted in different ways. It has been seen as a sign of the incorporation of the marginal *sambista* into the structure of the global society, as evidence of the hegemonic appropriation of a popular form of black expression by the white elite, and as a product of the inclusion and *communitas* of the *carnaval* itself. Whatever else it may be, however (and it is all of these things), it is vivid evidence of the extent to which the world of *samba* has come to the center of the carnivalesque world while the festival itself has become a massive spectacle – what by 1965 could be described, without exaggeration, as *o maior espetáculo popular do mundo* (the largest popular spectacle in the world) or *o maior show da terra* (the greatest show on earth) (see Sebe 1986, 72–73).

As befits the greatest show on earth, the parade of the samba schools has moved to the central avenues of downtown Rio – indeed, since the early 1980s, a whole avenue has been set aside for it, and a huge concrete structure known popularly as the *Sambódromo* (Sambadrome) has been constructed as a permanent replacement for the temporary bleachers of the past. The competition between the schools has been divided into three levels: *Grupo I*, the *superdesfile* (superparade) of the largest schools, parading with anywhere from 2,000 to 3,500 members, *Grupo II*, of slightly smaller, intermediate schools; and *Grupo II*, made up of the smallest schools.

Placing thousands of performers on the avenue, each school arranges its component parts in slightly different ways, depending upon the demands of its particular theme. Yet even this variation takes place within an overall structure that has itself become an accepted tradition throughout Brazil. The parade of the samba schools has not only become central to the shape of the festival in Rio but has also become largely synonymous with Brazilian *carnaval* more generally – a quintessential expression of everything that the *carnaval* involves and, certainly, among the most widely popular parts of the festival. Ordered and controlled by the state, it has also replaced the frightening chaos of carnivalesque play with what is, in its own way, a highly disciplined alternative. However, it has hardly succeeded in silencing the all-encompassing sensuality that is so fundamental to the whole meaning of the festival. It would be more accurate to suggest that the parade, as well as the samba schools more generally, has managed to incorporate the whole carnivalesque system of meanings into its own structure at the same time that it has incorporated itself into the wider structure of the *carnaval*.

Focusing on the world of *samba*, with all of its connotations of savagery, poverty, and marginality, yet re-creating this world as a fantastic spectacle of color and movement, the parade creates a kind of utopian illusion:

> The parade of the samba schools is called the greatest show on earth. The beauty of the colors of the costumes, accompanied by the steps of the *samba* as well as the plot, gives an incredible beauty. The sequins, precious and semi-precious stones, satins, silks, and purpurins fluttering in plumes.... It is a parade of great happiness and incredible energy. It is one of the marvels of the world. (Oscar)

This world is as far from the abject poverty of the *favelas* as is imaginable. And without ever losing sight of the often oppressive, exploitative bureaucratization and commercialization of the festival, it is still a world in which the experience of oppression and exploitation is swept away in a sense of freedom – a world in which the masses are healthy and energetic, well fed and well informed.

Linking the passion of the carnivalesque present to the dream of liberty in the future, this utopian vision incorporates, as well, the whole sexual symbolism of the *carnaval*. The sexual imagery of the festival is most vividly displayed in the world of plumes and papier-mâché. As in

less organized forms of carnivalesque play – in fact, all the more forcefully because of its highly organized nature – the schools focus on sexuality and sensuality as intimately linked to the deepest meaning of the festival:

> The parade has become a type of stage for sensuality, with its floats and its different sections in their tropical, sensual frenzy.... The bodies are for the most part semi-nude, showing the energy of hot, happy, virile bodies.... The couples of *passistas* or *sambistas* intertwine with their legs and with movements of their buttocks in a totally sensual form. The in and out movements of their legs, bellies, sexes, and buttocks give the connotation of an eternal sexual climax. (José)

The symbolism of *carnaval* has responded most clearly (even if in a particularly stylized way) to the changing shape of the Brazilian sexual universe through the parade of the schools. Over the course of the past decade, for example, the increasingly open expression of female sexuality has been pushed, each year, to an extreme in the performances of the schools:

> Nowadays, there are enormous floats with dozens of beautiful women partially or, many times, totally naked. Wearing only plumes on their heads to cover up from what the most extreme might say, they would otherwise be totally nude. Strong, young, muscular men, with small loincloths, are placed on these floats also. The demonstration of their sexual attributes, as much of the man as of the woman, has been one of the great attractions of the parade of the samba schools. (Francisco)

As well as women, the most marginalized groups of transvestites and homosexuals have come more to the center of carnivalesque performance in the samba schools, and they can customarily be found not only in the *alas* but also among the most important *destaques* ("eminences," specific individuals who stand out from the crowd because of their elaborate costumes) in even the most traditional schools:

> Transvestism and homosexuality have been important parts of the samba schools. There

are special floats for male homosexual *destaques* with their luxurious and extremely feminine costumes. They dress up as Gal Costa or Maria Bethania, or other famous figures from pop music or television. The number of gay groups in the parade has increased every year. They develop all sorts of different types, from the most sophisticated to the most grotesque. They stuff their costumes with large asses, hips, breasts, and bellies. Fruits and vegetables are used often as well.... Squash, pears, oranges, watermelons, cucumbers, or the traditional manioc root as a phallic symbol . . . the manioc root is used a lot for the joke of the carnivalesque prick. The carrot and the banana also. You're going to see this a lot with the *destaques* on the floats during *carnaval*. (João)

Sexual meanings have been fundamental to the highly ordered pageantry of the schools. Indeed, in the drama and spectacle of the parade, as much as in other forms of carnivalesque play, sexual imagery has not only responded to changes taking place in the everyday world but has also pushed the structures and meanings of daily life beyond their limits, incorporating even the most marginal elements of the Brazilian sexual universe into the heart of the carnivalized world.

The impact of this presentation of the sexual universe has been magnified by the attention the schools have received. Broadcast live to every region of the nation, the parade characterizes the festival for the widest possible public. Marketed, both at home and abroad, as the greatest show on earth, the parade has become synonymous with the *carnaval* as a whole. Undercutting the sobriety of daily life in a world of motion, music, and color, this remarkable pageant is the greatest illusion of all. Yet in the reality of fantasy that it creates, it pushes up against the repressive limits that structure the world of convention. It plays with them and stretches them. Like every form of carnivalesque play, it offers an alternative vision of life as it might be rather than as it is. As much as the more haphazard chaos that it was originally designed to replace, the organized chaos of the parade shapes and defines the nature of sexual life in contemporary Brazil. Ironically, in so doing, it has shaped and defined the nature of Brazil itself.

Carnaval as Metaphor

The vision of *carnaval* is quite clearly utopian – a model of the world as it might be rather than as it is. It is also, of course, an illusion, and no matter how fully they throw themselves into its peculiar reality, its participants never completely lose sight of its fleeting quality:

> Everyone knows that *carnaval* is an illusion created to forget about day-to-day life in such difficult times. There are songs that refer to the *carnaval* as "smoke," "wind," "light," or "heat." There is a song that says "for everything comes to an end on Ash Wednesday." Another highlights love: "Love that takes place in the *carnaval* disappears in smoke." They are three days of fun and madness, until Wednesday, when everything begins again. (Maria)

Yet if the ephemeral, imaginary character of the *carnaval* is not lost on the men and women who live it each year, neither is its power to transform experience, and even, perhaps, to change the world around it:

> In spite of being an illusion, the *carnaval* still possesses great psychological power for the Brazilian. They say that liberty went to live in some other place. . . . So *carnaval* tries to search for liberty. It is a utopia that in reality is real and not just a dream. Within this surrealism of the *carnaval*, it is possible to imagine a better world, a world that is really made up of true fantasies and freedom. (Antonio)

Within the space of the festival, it becomes possible not only to transgress the restrictions of daily life, but to push the limits, to reinvent the possibilities, of that wider social and cultural universe. Built, perhaps, on shifting sand, but rebuilt each year again, this often contradictory capacity for transformation, for the continued search for freedom and happiness, lies at the heart of the whole carnivalesque fantasy. It is central to the meaning of the *carnaval* within Brazilian culture.

Because of its internal contradictions, one can read this symbolic configuration in any number of different ways. For example, it is impossible to ignore the extent to which the symbolic structures of the festival exaggerate the most oppressive structures of the real world – male fantasies and desires continue to define a particular vision of female sexuality, and, for that matter, bourgeois morality continues to organize the expression of what is perceived to be a more "savage" or "primitive" sensuality:

> There are various interpretations – from sexism to the sin of the flesh. Because everything is permitted in these days, there are controversial ideas about what is called "morality" and "proper conduct." There are certain intellectuals, or false-intellectuals, that talk about the "opium of the people." Others deplore the worship of high luxury or of carnality. But, in reality, these people are a pretentious minority. For the majority of Brazilians, playing (*brincar*) the *carnaval* is an authentic expression of the people (*povo*). Playing the *carnaval* is to feel free. It is to feel extremely Brazilian. (Jorge)

Thus it is also impossible to ignore the degree to which carnivalesque imagery destroys conventional assumptions, offering women as well as men, the *povo* as well as the bourgeoisie, the opportunity to manipulate the webs of meaning and the systems of power in which they find themselves enmeshed, to create a sense of themselves as a whole, an identity as a people. What is most striking about the *carnaval* is its ability to encode and articulate so many different, often contradictory, meanings and thus to open itself up to so many divergent interpretations.

Because of this ability to incorporate contradictory interpretations within a single whole, the *carnaval* has offered a fundamentally popular counterpart to the myths of origin of elite writers such as Paulo Prado and Gilberto Freyre, with their emphasis on the formation of the Brazilian people through the process of racial mixture. With all of its chaos and confusion, its contradictions and its juxtapositions, its exaggerated sexuality and its transgressive laughter, the *carnaval* stands as an ironic answer to the search for a sense of identity that has troubled Brazilian thinking for more than a century. As much as the stories that Brazilians have told themselves about their

own formation as a people, it has offered its own reading of Brazilian reality – a reading focused, like the myths of origin, on the sensual nature of Brazilian life, on the chaotic mixture of races and cultures that has given rise to a new world in the tropics. While the elite myths of origin have focused on the past as a way of giving meaning to the present, however, the more popular performances of the *carnaval* have themselves cannibalized this past not simply as a way of reinventing the present, but as a means of inventing a future. The symbolic system that they create is ultimately less closed than open, and the identity that they suggest, less singular than plural – like the *carnaval* itself, diverse and multiple, based not so much on the fusion of opposites as on the juxtaposition of differences.

In its invention of another (more fundamentally popular) reading of Brazilian reality as still in the process of becoming, the *carnaval* has emerged as far more than a secular ritual marking out the cycle of the year. It has become a metaphor for Brazil itself – or at the very least, for those qualities that are taken as most essentially Brazilian, as the truest expression of Brazilianness. No less than the myths of origin, it has become a story that Brazilians tell themselves about themselves (about their past, certainly, but also about their future). It is a story that they use as yet another frame of reference that allows them to manipulate, rearrange, and even reinvent the contours of their own sexual universe. It suggests, to Brazilians and outsiders alike, that here beneath the equator life might best be understood and appreciated as a work in progress, that reality is complex and multiple, and that nothing is ever quite what it appears to be. Even what appears the most absolute can always be transformed, it would seem, in a world where sin ceases to exist and anything is possible.

NOTE

For a complete and fully-annotated version of this essay, see chapter six of the author's *Bodies, Pleasures, and Passions: Sexual Culture in Contemporary*

Brazil (Boston: Beacon, 1991), 136–164. Copyright and permissions are held by the author.

BIBLIOGRAPHY

Bakhtin, Mikhail
1968. *Rabelais and His World*. Cambridge, Mass.: MIT Press.
Barlaeus, Gaspar
1980. *História dos Feitos Recentemente Praticados durante Oito Anos no Brasil*. Recife: Fundação de Cultura Cidade do Recife.
Baroja, Julio Caro
1979. *El Carnaval: Analisis Historico-Cultural*. Madrid: Taurus Ediciones.
Boxer, C. R.
1957. *The Dutch in Brazil, 1624–1654*. Oxford: Clarendon Press.
Burke, Peter
1978. *Popular Culture in Early Modern Europe*. New York: Harper and Row.
Da Matta, Roberto
1978. *Carnavais, Malandros, e Heróis: Para uma Sociologia do Dilema Brasileiro*. Rio de Janerio: Zahar Editores.
Davis, Natalie Zemon
1975. *Society and Culture in Early Modern France*. Stanford, CA: Stanford University Press.
Eneida
1958. *História do Carnaval Caroica*. Rio de Janeiro: Editora Civilização Brasileria.
Freyre, Gilberto
1956. *The Masters and the Slaves: A Study in the Development of Brazilian Civilization*. New York: Alfred A. Knopf.

Gaignebet, Claude, and Marie-Claude Florentin
1974. *Le Carnaval: Essais de Mythologie Populaire*. Paris: Payot.
Ivo, Lêdo
1981. *Snakes' Nest*. New York: New Directions Books.
Ladurie, Emmanuel Le Roy
1979. *Carnival in Romans*. New York: Braziller.
Leach, Edmund
1961. *Rethinking Anthropology*. London: Athlone.
Leach, Maria, ed.
1972. *Funk and Wagnall's Standard Dictionary of Folklore, Mythology, and Legend*. New York: Funk and Wagnall's.
Read, Kenneth E.
1980. *Other Voices: The Style of a Male Homosexual Tavern*. Novato, CA: Chandler and Sharp.
Sant'Anna, Affonso Romano
1984. *O Canibalismo Amoroso*. São Paulo: Editora Brasiliense.
Scheper-Hughes, Nancy
1988. "The Madness of Hunger: Sickness, Delirium, and Human Needs." *Culture, Medicine, and Psychiatry* 12(4): 1–30.
Sebe, José Carlos
1986. *Carnaval, Carnavais*. São Paulo: Editora Ática.
Turner, Victor
1969. *The Ritual Process: Structure and Anti-Structure*. Chicago: University of Chicago Press.
——. 1983. "*Carnaval* in Rio: Dioniysian Drama in an Industrializing Society." In *The Celebration of Society: Perspectives on Contemporary Cultural Performance*, ed. Frank E. Manning, 103–24. Bowling Green, OH: Bowling Green University Popular Press.

12

"Playing with Fire": The Gendered Construction of Chicana/Mexicana Sexuality

Patricia Zavella

Mexican sexual/gender discourse grafts a particular twist onto the Catholic Mediterranean "honor and shame" cultural configuration.[1] Rooted in dislocations generated by a history of Spanish conquest, colonization of indigenous peoples, and a war of independence, sexuality, gender, and nationalism are deeply intertwined in Mexican society.[2] According to this Mexican cultural "master narrative," women should submit to sexual repression embedded in Catholic-based discourse, institutions, and everyday practices in part because of the mythologized actions of one of their sex. The "national allegory," classically articulated by Octavio Paz, posits the betrayal of her people by Malinche, Cortés' translator and concubine, as instituting a cultural configuration in which the act of sexual intercourse (*chingar*) is seen as conquest, violation, and devaluation of women by men who are shamed for being mestizos – sons of Spanish fathers and socially denigrated Indian mothers.[3] The Virgin of Guadalupe (the "brown virgin") symbolizes proper servility and modesty for Mexican women, as well as the subversive spiritual power of the indigenous who conformed to Catholicism in form if not in faith. Male dominance and the double standard are integral in the cultural polemics of macho/chingon and virgin/

whore. Feminist scholars have contested this misogynist interpretative framework on its own allegorical terms, arguing that doña Marina or Malintzin (as she was originally named) can be seen as having acted strategically in the horrific circumstances of Spanish conquest.[4]

The research on Chicana/*Mexicano*[5] sexuality in contemporary times confirms the continuing importance of Catholic repression and the double standard.[6] This research, however, often ignores the regional variations in this cultural configuration in Mexico, and it is unclear how Mexicans reared in the United States construe its meaning.[7] Moreover, Mexican residents in the U.S. – like others – do not simply follow church doctrines when it comes to decisions about contraception, abortion, or submitting to sexual violence.[8] Beyond the Church, cultural constructions in Mexico and the United States are influenced by other forces – popular culture, state policies regarding the body, or increased incidents of sexually transmitted diseases. Many Chicano gay men and lesbians openly contest this interpretive framework and transgress these gendered scripts, struggling to dismantle Mexican heterosexism and homophobia by creating discourse and social spaces (what Emma Pérez calls *lengua y sitio*) for acknowledging homoerotic sexuality.[9]

Lesbian theorists also claim *La Virgen de Guadalupe* as their icon, reconfiguring her as symbol of indigenous liberation and women's empowerment.

How do individuals in general construct their sense of sexual pleasure or identity in conformity and/or resistance to cultural discourse? How is power coded into sexual behavior and relationships? And how do heterosexuals and lesbians differ from one another in defining a sense of sexual subjectivity? This piece contributes to an understanding of Chicana/*Mexicana* sexuality through the use of ethnographic interviews to engage critically these questions.[10]

Using interviews to understand sexuality is problematic, as knowledge about sexuality is often "nondiscursive," that is, knowledge that is assumed rather than made explicit.[11] The people I interviewed in the course of a larger, multiraced study of poverty in Santa Cruz County, struggled to convey their ambivalent feelings or to describe experiences that they had previously repressed. I heard a common refrain: "We just *knew*. There were certain things you did not talk about, and sex was one of them" or, more pointedly, "Talking about sex meant I was a bad person. So I didn't talk about it." The interviews themselves, then, were transgressions of the silencing in which women had been trained.

The problematics of discussing sex with an interviewer are compounded by memory lapses, where the experience of childhood is, in some ways, irretrievable.[12] Some of the people I interviewed sometimes had difficulty recalling what they were taught and by whom; this in itself was telling. In these instances, I culled from their recollections of childhood experiences and admonitions to understand their enculturation regarding gender and sexuality. For others, memories were what Penelope Lively calls "brilliant frozen moments," because of their significance; yet they too were "distorted by the wisdom of maturity"[13] and influenced by the social context of the interview setting. These narratives are thus representations, "situated knowledge" at multiple levels, and should be read critically.[14] They are also, though, our only means – absent autobiography – to gain access to the self-construction of sexuality among the poor.

My purpose is to explicate the political economy of gender and sexuality among impoverished and working-class Chicanas and Mexicanas, to show how social meaning regarding sexual practices is culturally constructed. This analysis begins with two women's narratives of sexual practices and meaning, individual narratives that take place in an arena of plural, competing, and often conflicting social narratives about sexual practices and meanings. Roger Lancaster suggests that each of these spheres is "traversed by various degrees of autonomy, control, freedom and determinism, rebellion and conformity, power and love."[15] To understand the meaning of sexual practices or identity, I will examine these women's "cultural poetics" of sexual desire.

The metaphors "playing" and "fire" recurred in the cultural poetics of sexual desire among all my Chicana and Mexicana interviewees, metaphors rendered banal in popular culture.[16] Heterosexuals and lesbians indicated that in seeking sexual desire they were "playing" – flirting, teasing, or testing potential lovers. Fire contained dual meanings, signifying both the repressive forces of culturally sanctioned silence regarding Eros in Mexican society; and simultaneously, in seeking the "powers of desire,"[17] women imagined sexual pleasure as fire – "hot," "passionate," "boiling," "explosive" – and difficult to stop. They envisioned seeking out potential sexual partners as a "game" played within the limits imposed by cultural authority of church doctrines, family practices, and the sanctions of conventional society. While women did not always "win" the game, and indeed sometimes "got burned," playing was pleasurable, often because the game was taboo in some sense. Seeking a mate, then, often pushed societal parameters and made these women feel a sense of power and the ability to pursue that which they desired. During interviews, women recalled even failed loves occasionally with tears of pain, but more often with smiles and joy.

Two women speak below – a heterosexual Chicana, Mirella Hernández (a pseudonym), and a *lesbiana* Mexicana – María Pérez.[18] In presenting these particular narratives, I do not mean to impose binary oppositions – cultural vs. essential self, heterosexual and homosexual, feelings and logic. Rather, following Jean Franco, I here write women into the plot of sexuality, showing their historical agency in contesting traditional expectations. I argue that these women's cultural poetics of sexuality entailed struggling with the contradictions of repressive discourses and social practices that were often violent towards women and their own desires. I chose these women among my many informants because their narratives particularly represent, as Franco has described certain literary texts, "incandescent moments when different configurations of gender and knowledge are briefly illuminated."[19]

Mirella Hernández

Her mother immigrated from a rural Mexican village with virtually no education; her father was from New Mexico and had a high school education. Born in California and twenty-one years old, Mirella identified herself ethnically as "Mexican."

Mirella had vivid memories of experiences related to sex and family. "I've always been curious about sex," she said. She told me about an incident that occurred when she was about eight. She and a neighbor boy were in a swimming pool and they began playing by exposing their bodies. Her brother discovered them and "blackmailed me." When the brother did tattle to their mother, Mirella was forced to go apologize to the boy's parents about the incident. She recalled with embarrassment: "That was the worst." Mirella also recalled that sex itself – or anything even alluding to sex – was not to be discussed openly:

> I remember this really clearly. This lady came over when my mom was pregnant, and she told me "when your Mom buys the baby" and I thought, "You're so stupid, I know where they come from." My Mom gave me the eye, like, "don't you dare say a word," you know. Later I asked her, "Why can't I tell them where they come from?" And she just told me, "Out of respect."

Clearly, respect – for herself or for elders – meant that discussion of anything related to sex was to be avoided.

Mirella's mother was a battered woman whose alcoholic spouse would beat and rape her, sometimes in front of the children. "When I was old enough my Mom told me about it [the rape]. And sometimes we would run into their room when it was happening and catch him and I saw." Witnessing the abuse and rape was a traumatic experience for Mirella: "I felt really sick. I remember looking at my mom the next day and thinking, you know, how dirty a person could feel. I hated my father when that happened. I didn't want him to touch me. I just couldn't stand him, and even my Mom, I wouldn't let my Mom touch me; I wanted her to but I didn't want her to." Mirella's mother would occasionally call the police to stop the battering, but then would not press charges. Mirella managed to keep any knowledge about the violence at home from her friends and teachers: "I kept it a secret from everybody. I wanted everybody to think that my family was just fine." When other children talked about their families, Mirella became a master at deception: "I wouldn't say anything and pretended like everything was okay."

As Mirella became an adolescent and began to receive more explicit knowledge about her body, adults gave her mixed messages. When she began menstruating, her mother and aunts offered congratulations for her new status as a woman, which she found to be embarrassing but pleasing. Mirella also experienced a new reticence towards men:

> I knew that I could have kids now, so that was really scary. Yet it was also exciting because I thought, "I could be a mom," you know? Then after that I hated men [she laughed nervously]. I mean, I didn't want them to get too close to me, for a period of about half a year. I don't know if it was because of my Dad, or it was just me; it was a weird feeling I got. My Mom would always say, "All men are alike, *que son cabrones*" (they're bastards). So I thought maybe they really are.

Mirella was also encouraged more to be "ladylike," foregoing her usual attire of pants for dresses, curling her hair and being allowed to wear makeup. Her father warned her about impregnation in clinical terms: "My Dad told me it took two people, you have to be in love, you know. He also said usually when you marry. And 'intercourse' was the word, it wasn't sex, it was intercourse. He explained that certain times of the month you could get pregnant, or you couldn't, which was really confusing for me." Her mother was more direct: "She'd tell me not to throw myself at boys: 'Have respect,' and 'I was never with anybody until I got married.' I always told myself, because of my mother's values, that I would not have sex until I was married." The strategy of saving her virginity for marriage and eventual motherhood would provide her with the expectation of economic stability, for the assumption was that a young man would support her in exchange for her unsullied reputation.

Mirella never received any sense that having a homosexual relationship was a possibility: "Well I heard the word 'fag,' but I didn't know what it meant. I just laughed along with everybody else." Thus she was encouraged to be feminine and celebrate her apparent fecundity, but only to a limited degree. Becoming a woman meant the possible threat of pregnancy, distasteful intimacy with men, the importance of self-respect, and the prospect of economic support.

At age fifteen, Mirella's family celebrated her *quinceañera*, a religious coming-of-age debut that indicates a young woman's availability for courtship and marriage:

> At first I didn't want one because I didn't know what it meant and I thought it was just to have a big bash. When I started going to catechism, I knew the real meaning of a *quinceañera* and why my Mom wanted me to have one. It represents purity, your virginity, which was neat, of course. But I thought I was one of the only virgins at 15 [she laughed]. I had so much fun!

Over three hundred people attended, including relatives who came up from southern California. She worked part time to save enough to purchase all the food and the dresses for the attendants. Her mother ordered food from a caterer, at discount, since her brother worked there. Mirella's parents had separated just prior to the *quinceañera*. "It was a real turning point for us, as a family, to be able to do this on our own." This celebration of virginity and family, then, was meaningful at several levels.

Although Mirella had permission to date, her mother applied different standards of behavior to her and her brother, who was free to come and go as he pleased. Mirella always had to report where she was going, with whom, and to obey a strict curfew. She also had to leave a phone number if she changed her plans. Perhaps because she was parenting by herself (supporting her family on her wages as a cook), Mirella's mother seemed particularly vigilant: "My Mom would tell me to have fun, but be careful, you know, '*cuídate*.' I know what that means now."

Mirella's mother let her know she would be able to tell if a woman has lost her virginity:

> My Mom says she can tell under the eyes, I guess you get bags under your eyes. And she can tell when someone's pregnant, even if they're not showing just by their face, if they look drained or pale. It's weird: Our neighbor came over once and Mom asked her. And she'd be, "No, I'm not planning on having any kids," and then she turned out pregnant. I think that my Mom was trying to scare me to think, "Well if I have sex, she is going to know right off."[20]

Her mother advised Mirella to date a lot of different men so she would not end up "tied down" as she had been: "She loves the guys that I've gone out with, but she never wanted me to have a serious relationship with anybody and she doesn't know about what I've done with them. She was always open to birth control and I can talk to her about sex if I wanted to." Again, the message was mixed, with the apparent openness about discussing sex with her mother tempered by the caution: "She said, 'don't have sex until you get married, then you don't have to worry about birth control.'"

Clearly Mirella was expected to remain a virgin until marriage. She was trained and closely watched – primarily by her mother, but with strong reinforcement from Catholic catechism and with support from her brother and father – to guard her body from male abuse and to repress her own sexual desires. She came of age in northern California during the late 1980s, however, a time when Madonna was the popular cultural icon and the seductive Kenny G. was her favorite musician. Mirella received very different messages from the dominant culture and her friends than she received at home and at church. As Olaiz finds, "Among friends, women allow themselves to explore different forms of sexual expression, like dress, make-up, the way they talk, the music they listen to and how they dance to it, and how these different forms convey that a woman is attractive and available for romantic relationships."[21]

Mirella started dating her first boyfriend at sixteen, after years of flirting and "playing hard to get." Michael was four years older, white – of Portuguese ethnicity in a community that was predominantly Mexican – and from an upper-middle-class family. Mirella found him attractive because, "I think it was his body, which is odd because I always had the image of going out with someone who was tall and built, with green eyes and black hair [implying a Mexican]. Where he was short, with a nice body, and his eyes, his eyes talked. They were sending out these messages, like he always got what he wanted type of thing. And I wasn't the girl who gave what you wanted, which I think was a big challenge for him and it was a challenge for me." With her long, black hair and "olive" skin, Mirella's beauty was classically Mexican. Michael's mother did not approve of the relationship, was blatantly rude towards Mirella whenever she called or visited, and would not deliver messages that she had called. Mirella's brother did not approve either:

> He always told me Michael was bad news, 'cause he did drugs in high school and he was a rebel. He would always tell me that "this guy just wants one thing, to get you in the sack." I knew if I went out with him I couldn't talk to my brother about it. At first it was hush-hush; only Mom knew. When I finally told him, he said, "Well you gotta do what you have to do," and "Be careful." But that's not what I saw, because it took a long time for me to even sleep with this guy. Michael was very respectful. He was my first real love, even though then I really didn't know what love was.

Mirella, then, was playing with fire, drawn to this man but wanting to preserve her reputation as a "good girl." His membership in the local powerful white community added to the sense of taboo and enhanced the challenge. Proving her brother wrong was an added enticement. Mirella was asserting her own independence within the confines of her family's control. As has been found with other Chicanas/Mexicanas, the fact that she was in love with the man provided a rationale in which a young woman was considered respectable despite the loss of her virginity.[22]

The relationship with Michael only lasted about nine months before Mirella discovered that he had dated another young woman and was seen kissing her at a local movie theater.

> When I found out he had cheated on me, it broke my heart. And I didn't give him any chances either. It was over. I said "fuck you, that's it." It grossed me out to think that I was sleeping with him and he went out with someone else and I remember hating him. I said to myself, "Why am I so stupid, I should have listened to my Mom, I shouldn't have had sex until I get married." I was so afraid that if anyone found out, they're going to think that I'm a tramp or something. Especially if my Mom found out, she would kill me. I was the worst person.

Since neither her mother nor brother found out she had lost her virginity, her reputation remained unscathed.

It was another year and a half before Mirella felt she could trust a man enough to go out with him. During this period she reflected upon how she would conduct herself in relationships and made a profound change from her previous thinking: "I thought maybe I shouldn't fall in love, you know. It's okay just to date someone and sleep with them, that type of thing." Mirella was beginning to reconfigure her own sense of pleasure despite the confines of her life.

Her next relationship was with another white boy, Jim, a Slovenian – an ethnic group whose members owned much land in the area – but he was of working-class background. Even though he was very handsome, and had an "even better body" than Michael, Mirella was attracted to his personality rather than by the challenge of dating a wealthy man: "I wasn't looking for a boyfriend, I was just bummed and not wanting to do anything. But he was really sweet and fun. I thought 'okay, not all guys are the same.'" Still, Mirella would not have sex with Jim for quite some time. Then an opportunity for privacy presented itself:

> My grandmother went away for vacation and I was taking care of her house [she laughed]. But it was really weird because my grandma's fairly religious, and everywhere you turn there's a crucifix or *santos*. I remember being in her room and there's this cross looking at me, and I thought, "Oh my God, how evil I am." But then things happened, and I could care less about what was up on the walls.

Their relationship lasted three years and the couple discussed getting married. Jim had drinking problems, however, and Mirella asserted her independence from him: "I'm not going to put up with that, not after what my mom went through. She says, 'you give him one chance and they expect more from you.' And I was giving too much and not receiving enough back." Despite "still being in love with him," Mirella ended the relationship. Meanwhile she had enrolled in a community college, working towards a nursing degree, and took a part-time job as a lab technician, moving towards economic self-sufficiency.

At the time of the interview, Mirella had just started dating another young man, a Chicano university student who was a friend of her brother's. This was the first "Hispanic" she had ever dated, and she found that their same ethnic background "really makes a difference" and was a powerful attraction of a different type:

> Now that I've dated Ray, I realize that they can understand your culture. With Ray, I don't have to teach him anything, and he knows what I'm saying when I talk to my mom in Spanish. And he's got this little saying, he calls me "*mija*" (my little daughter), which I think is the cutest thing. It gives me the neatest feeling. And I could see my mom's face light up, the first time I took him to a *quinceañera*. Ray can dance and everything. I'm happy when I go out with him.

Mirella was attracted to Ray because of his good looks, but this time she appreciated something more: "He's so smart, and that's a turn-on for me. He's going to school and he's got goals and he's going for it. And that's what I'm doing too. I can talk to him about school and he understands." Even though they did not have a commitment to one another, the couple spent time together almost every night, and she had met his family. She was the first Chicana that Ray had dated also, and his mother was delighted.

The couple delayed initiating sex. Mirella was taking the pill to regulate her menstrual periods, and made it clear to him that nevertheless she was not "easy": "I explained it wasn't because I was sleeping around or anything. He said, 'that's fine.'" An educated man himself, Ray was not judgmental about Mirella's sexual past. The couple was making plans to solidify their relationship:

> We were talking the other night. I haven't told Ray "I love you" straight out and he hasn't told me either. But I think I'm getting there. He asked me, "Are you falling in love?" And I told him how I felt about him and he told me. He says that he can see himself marrying me.

Mirella's ideal relationship would "work 50–50," where each was committed to the relationship, and they spent as much time on their relationship as on their careers.

I asked her directly, "What gives you sexual pleasure, or what would you desire in a sexual relationship," Mirella got flustered, stammered a bit, and then responded: "I don't think I'm turned on by just the thought of having sex. I do have to care for the person. I don't think if I wanted it, I just could have it. Because I have wanted to have sex but that hasn't happened. I don't know. If something could work out between us." Later she clarified, "I just think its a turn-on to think that he's got so much going for him. He can make a life out of what he's doing, and I know that I definitely can too." In talking about meeting the rest of Ray's family, and developing their relationship, Mirella admitted, "I'm excited. I'm really excited."

A maturing young woman, Mirella Hernández now realizes that sexual relationships are not inherently dangerous and that all men are not stupid, abusive, or mistrustful. She has incorporated some of the teachings of her mother and the Catholic Church as guides for her behavior so that she would not be considered "easy"; this is one source of her self respect. But she also resisted her family's preoccupation with virginity and her mother's model of a traditional role within marriage. Now closer to economic stability herself, Mirella prefers a relationship with a man working towards a career, and she claims the right to her own sexual pleasure outside of marriage.

María Pérez

In contrast to Mirella, thirty-five year old María Pérez had more experiences and more reflections about them. María was reared in a small town in the state of Puebla. The daughter of mestizo campesinos, María attended all-girls schools in Mexico on scholarships and completed some college classes. Highly intelligent and precocious – as a child she won prizes during school competitions for her literary performances and superior essays – her "biggest dream" was to receive her doctorate at the Sorbonne, in Paris. While she was raised Catholic, she no longer attends church regularly, and considers herself to be "very eclectic religiously," combining a sardonic devotion to La Virgen de Guadalupe, Buddhism, and the Goddess. Formerly a bilingual community educator at a social service agency, at the time of the interview María was unemployed and the couple was experiencing dire financial difficulties, with the threat of losing their home. Initially she interrogated me about my motives, theoretical perspective, and methodological approach, and even took note of my publications. I apparently passed her test, for María was delighted to be interviewed and gave me over ten hours of her time. This moved her lover to observe, "Sure she's writing a book, but it's not just about *you*."

Like Mirella, María received traditional gender socialization as a child:

> I was taught that it is very important to have a family, and sacrifice for your family. You should get married because the husband will take care of you; he has to be the provider.

> You need to learn how to cook, sew, clean up the house and do all the chores, and especially make good food because that will give happiness to your husband. You've got to have children because that's your role in life, as a woman, is to have children. If you don't have children, nothing in life that you may do will be meaningful.

Her family assumed that heterosexuality would be the norm.

María received clear messages that sex was sinful and sexual pleasure was to be avoided. She recalled that as a five-year-old child, she and a male cousin of the same age engaged in exploration of their bodies: "Oh, you have a penis and I don't. What do you use that for?" When her caretaker found them, she reported the incident to María's mother, who became very angry and slapped María, saying "I don't want you doing this." There was some discussion about whether her cousin had raped her, and if so her mother threatened to kill him. María was forbidden to play with her cousin again. Regarding sexual self-exploration, María recalled,

> One time my mother found me exploring myself, and she was pretty pissed off. She brought me by the hand and she slapped me and she says "those things you don't do, you can get infected." Later I learned about masturbation, the concept, but it was like, "don't do it," right? Don't give yourself pleasure, that's a sin, you're being in temptation, and then God will punish you. The Ten Commandments were kind of mandatory.

María recalled that during childhood games of playing house, she usually took the male role:

> There were no boys in the school, so I became the male figure in our games. So I had a girlfriend instead of a boyfriend. Not only one, but I had two or three. We used to play movies, and because my name is María Luisa, I became Luis. I chose this: "I want to be the head general; I want to be Batman instead of Bat Girl." I remember that we played to kiss each other, but it wasn't on the mouth, it was more pretend, or we held hands. But it was the characters in the movies that we used to express those feelings.

Despite having few male companions to learn from, María was drawn to the male gender and sexual script. Through Mexican romantic cinematic images, she already had a view of men as having more than one lover, and through play was able to assert authority and power by assuming male roles.

When María became adolescent, she gained the rudimentary knowledge about conception and male–female sexual differences in a sixth-grade course at school. Her mother had been reared in a convent, yet unlike many women, was relatively open to discussing menstruation and sex: "I learned that you should be a virgin when you get married, and then you should be sexually available for your husband." Other than warning her to preserve her virginity, however, María's kin offered no information about sexual relationships.

At twelve, María realized that females could have relationships with other females through the discovery of two girls at school who were in love: "Everyone said '*jotas!*' (dykes) with a horrible contempt, and I was scared." Age twelve was also when María fell in love for the first time with a young woman, a fellow classmate. But she was afraid of her desires:

> I didn't want to accept that she was it. I passed through a denial stage, you know, "How can I be in love with a girl?" Later, at secondary school I would see popular guys in the group of girls, and I would say "I wish I could *be* that boy." I pretended, "He's very handsome, and I would be honored to be his girlfriend," but I was lying all the time. I thought, "I can't let them say dyke to me. I have too much to lose, all of my prestige." So I covered up [my sexuality].

Even though María was afraid of others finding out, she persevered in a context where there were implicit mixed messages. Girls were not allowed to spend time alone together, although it was acceptable for them to sleep in the same bed in the large dormitory room. María and her friend would casually sleep together without arousing suspicion about their interest in one another: "We began to play sexually, but no more than kissing, and we never ever talked about this."

María then began a period where she perceived herself as "the most popular boy," when she had "a heap of admiring girls." She began a process of sexual exploration and play (*juego sexual*), only with women and usually with more than one. In a classic Mexican sense, María was solidifying her sense of herself as male and predator.

She then met a younger woman and the relationship became serious: "She was so young, and she had such beauty. Her body was just beginning to become defined, and it was the first time that I paid attention to the body of a woman." They were open with each other about the sexual nature of their relationship and, since they had no money, would court by writing love notes or bringing each other gifts of flowers or leaves. María composed love poems to win over her lover. Their relationship was cast in a heterosexist mold, in the sense that María played the male and her lover the female when they made a commitment. María would tell her lover "you cannot go out with other boys," and her lover responded,

> "All this time you have been with so and so and no more, you can't go out with other girls." And I would say, "well, I didn't seek them out" [she laughed sheepishly]. I was copying *los patrones machistas* (the male bosses) because I didn't have anyone else to copy. It was not easy for a girl to play the role of a boy. The role of a woman is defined. But I was a girl who desired to be a boy, and with no one to learn from. Also there was much about boys that I did not like. I didn't know much in this interior struggle. Anyway, at that time I was *muy macha, muy marimacha* (very male, very butch).

Talking about her behavior over two decades later, María was embarrassed about her past mimicry of what to her were the negative male qualities of jealousy, infidelity, and possessiveness towards her girlfriend. Reflecting upon her behavior, she said "I was a *macho* Mexican *cabrón*." María's experience parallels that of Cherríe Moraga, who noted: "In the effort to avoid embodying *la chingada*, I became the *chingón*. In the effort not to feel fucked, I became the fucker, even with women."[23]

Because they were openly lovers among themselves, the two women felt an even stronger sense that they must remain secretive about their relationship in public. They could sleep in the same bed in the large dormitory, but their sexual exploration became stifled:

> No one knew so we were careful that only we would know what was going on. And this is very important: it became an *adventure*. It had to be in a manner that was so quiet – we couldn't make any noise or movements to be able to do this. It was like the night clouds, like a smooth breeze that barely moved. We couldn't do anything else because if everyone knew, there would be a scandal. We began exploring our lips, exploring what does it feel like to be kissed, the power of a kiss. She was playing with fire.

This relationship ended when the young woman entered another school. Her lover next pursued a sexual relationship with a young man, so her "playing with fire" was temporary. María, however, was drawn to the "power of a kiss" with women.

At fifteen, María became involved with another Mexicana, Josefina, who eventually became "the love of my life," her *compañera* or wife.[24] In the initial stages of their relationship, María used the subterfuge of innuendo to communicate with her love object. "I'd say, 'Well you must love your boyfriend a lot since you won't leave him.' What I was saying is 'I want you to leave your boyfriend.' We could not really clarify what was happening." Once they did get involved, María recalled that Josefina "had the most beautiful eyes and beautiful hair. She was all woman, in the sense that she was *the* woman, *la madre abnegada, la mujer sufrida* (the self-denying mother, the suffering woman) and all that. It was very appropriate for me to get in that relationship because I was the macho prototype, a macho man in the tradition of values." As the prototypical female, Josefina was protective and nurtured María:

> She believes that no one would love me like her. She's right. She was mother, even in the sense of nurturing me. I became a baby sometimes in her arms. Sometimes when she embraced me, she made me feel like I had regained something, completed something that I missed when I was a child. I became

mature with her. And I taught her how to be independent, how to be less preoccupied and focus on the qualification, to get an A. You had to fight for it.

María's vision of gender roles for women, then, was "defined" and restricting, complementing those for men which were assertive and strong.

The lovers suffered through an initial period of denial, then admitted their feelings for one another.

> It was really a Romeo and Juliet thing; it was very passionate, very intense and we were running from it, like it can't be. I had my first real sexual relationship with her. She was the woman who taught me how to kiss. Not like before. With Josefina, it was the giving part and the exchanging part of the kiss, where you lose yourself in the pleasure of kissing somebody.

The lovers would be together for nine years, and experienced the full panoply of romantic feelings:

> We did it all. We had passion, we had confrontations, we had growing, we had turbulence, we had the caring. It was a struggle against everything. We were claiming our right to be in love. We couldn't avoid touching each other in front of everybody. It was like water boiling over, you know, when you're boiling water and it gets out of control? It was not possible for us to deny we loved each other. We would hold hands and walk in front of everybody, we said, "We don't care, fuck you, our love is meant to be and we are gonna defend it no matter what."

The school officials suspected the girls were lovers and sent them to a psychologist, who was sympathetic: "She would smile. She knew exactly what was happening, and she wanted us to be careful. She didn't want us to sleep together. But that was our daily sanctuary, even though it was in the middle of a large building." The other girls began protecting them with "*la ley del hielo*," an unwritten code of honor in which no one would "break the ice" and tell the authorities. María and Josefina knew they were in love, but did not understand exactly what was happening to them. María began to investigate through books and found a term for her desires – lesbianism.

During this period María and Josefina dated several boys, "to play the role that I had a boyfriend. But the boyfriends were only a mask to cover up that there was more between Josefina and I. It was just because I was general secretary, and so forth, so I needed to do that. I had to be normal." The boyfriends did not interest María – "not even a kiss. They asked me why, and I said 'no, I take care of my honor,' something like that. And they believed in that and I manipulated that." Although María knew she preferred intimate relationships with women, she used the subterfuge of virgin honor to mask her blossoming homosexuality.

The lovers' relationship was made public inadvertently. María's mother discovered they were lovers by opening a letter from Josefina. María's father beat her and her mother was upset, raised a big scandal and eventually went to the police, but then dropped any charges. The discovery only pushed the two lovers together: "We would say, 'If the world doesn't want us we will leave this world – I will die for you and you will die for me.' We wanted to do it [commit suicide] if it became necessary." María moved out and the breach with her mother has never fully healed. María, then, was pushed out of the closet, suffering the humiliation of Mexican homophobia.

Josefina's parents were more accepting, although they did not fully approve. Eventually María became like an adopted daughter in Josefina's parents' home. Ironically, María's "father-in-law" provided her with a role model for how to be an honorable man. It would be some time, however, before María fully learned the lesson.

Despite Josefina's parents' good will, María and Josefina were not open about their lesbianism:

> It was a big *secreto a voz* (unspoken secret). That is a big concept in the Latino family in Mexico, whenever some sin is going on, we have a social psychology happening here protecting the victim and the victimizer. And it has come here [to the U.S.] somehow. They say, "Don't say anything about your aunt,

poor thing, she has a big problem." And it's like [groans] now I'm guilty too. You break the guilty feeling in pieces and distribute it among the whole family, but over a long period of time. Whenever someone gets pissed with somebody, they will yell it and say, "Enough is enough, I'm going to tell the secret!"

María and Josefina's relationship was a huge *secreto a voz*: "Everyone pretended that we were great friends."

María and Josefina's relationship was premised on three vows they made to one another: One was that during sex they would not engage in vaginal penetration, so they would preserve their virginity:[25] "Sex was a lot of mutual masturbation and other things, but no penetration." They waited two years before agreeing to vaginal penetration. María explained the significance of giving up one's virginity: "The social oppression to marry as a virgin, all of that, was so strong that it really was a sacrifice to lose one's virginity. It was protection for each other, until we got to the point where we could walk out on the street and say 'fuck your mother, I'm not a virgin and so what!'" Like Mirella, María was told that one could tell if a woman lost her virginity – the backs of her knees would change. A related promise was that their relationship took priority: "If we wanted to give it [virginity] to anyone, it would be among ourselves first, or it wouldn't happen." The third agreement was that "if we found a man who became the love of our life, we would end our relationship." In some ways this was a quixotic promise for, as María noted, "That was very crazy, very far from happening after nine years." Implicit in their agreement was that having a sexual relationship with a man was acceptable, because it would not seriously threaten their relationship, and that for either of them to have a relationship with another woman was considered an infidelity since it would betray their more important love as women.

María did have sexual relations with other women, and even though she described herself as "promiscuous," she made it clear that "I'm not the type of person to make out on the first date. I needed something more from the person." In one of these relationships, her lover pressured her for sex with penetration. Like the macha that she was, María cleverly asked the lover to wait: "I told her, 'I'm not ready, let me think about it.' I directed the thing with Jóse emotionally so that we got to the point of where we complied with my promise to have that experience with her and not another woman. In the end it happened and it was a good experience, very satisfying." Later María had vaginal penetration with the other woman but she had honored her and Josefina's commitment.

María was successful with other women because of the clarity of the boundaries she established with them: "I couldn't promise those women the heavens and the stars. I would say, 'I have this relationship with another woman but I can play with you sexually.'" She found sexual pleasure in her identification with the sexual prowess of men:

> I was very fortunate because I've had the experience of receiving that gift [a woman's virginity] not from one woman, from many, like six, seven. A true man, whoever, if he heard this, would envy me enormously. He would say, "How did you do that, that you had all these virgins and you didn't have to marry any of them?" And I did not have to violate them either. I guess I was charming, I don't know [smiles winningly].

María still viewed herself as male – in control, guiding the relationship with Josefina, playing the field with many lovers at the same time, and gaining the ultimate male conquest, a woman's virginity. Her vision of men was that they had more power and freedom than women, and would stop at nothing to satisfy their pleasures. María sought the entitlements of Mexican masculinity even as she constructed a lesbian identity that was in opposition to patriarchal authority.

After nine years, the relationship between María and Josefina soured. The primary reason was that Josefina, the "self-denying mother," wanted children, and María could not sire children. Her voice broke as she explained the crisis:

> The last three years, our relationship was very very bad. We would make love at night and fight during the day. It was more painful to

make love because we knew that we couldn't have children, that was clear. But we wanted a consummation of our relationship. When we made love, she usually ended up crying. And I was so guilty, like, "I can't!" I felt so impotent, without reason. I was not at fault for that.

Desperate, María investigated having a sex change operation and becoming a "transsexual," even though it would have been very painful. Of course she still would have been "impotent." At a cost of "a million pesos," she could not afford it.

For reasons that are not entirely clear, María decided to be faithful but Josefina had her own affair with a man, became pregnant, and fell in love with him. María was jealous and initially had doubts that Josefina was actually pregnant, fearing it was some sort of ruse. Josefina then got an abortion, and that created an irreparable rift in their relationship.

> The abortion is what hurt me, more than her being in love with somebody else. I didn't understand, why did she do that? She said, "I knew that you were jealous, and feeling sad." But it was more sad at that point in our relationship to not have it. I said, "Let's have it, it will be our child. It's good that you are pregnant. Yes, I am jealous but when you have the child, those jealousies will be gone. But let me work on it, let me process this." No. That was a very strong breach.

María's own Catholicism and desire for a child that consummated their love made Josefina's rationale for the abortion unfathomable: "When I asked her why, she said 'because I love you and I don't want you to be resentful of this. I'm gonna have it when you and I are better.' The guilt, the pressure of the guilt was too large. I couldn't believe that it happened." Unable to control Josefina on something so important, María reacted with her idea of a male response. Anticipating the *dénouement* of their relationship, María resumed her macha ways: "And then I started being unfaithful again, with two more women at the same time. I started being promiscuous." Ironically, Josefina "came out of the closet" several years after their relationship ended.

María had a number of different lovers after that, from each one learning something new.

Despite promises of fidelity, she was often unfaithful. She kept track, with great respect, of the number of women who gave her the gift of their virginity. She even had a sexual relationship with a man, just as an experiment. Given his inattention to her sexual pleasure, María found straight sex boring.

In 1978, María moved to Mexico City, where she became involved in a network of other *lesbianas*. But without public safe spaces such as the lesbian bars in the United States[26] and a nascent gay and lesbian rights movement centered in Guadalajara (a day's bus ride away),[27] coming out as a lesbian was not particularly appealing to her: "We didn't say 'we're *lesbianas*,' but we would just be together. Whenever people would say something about it, we would just look at them like, 'You better shut up.'" Looking for adventure and still grieving the loss of her relationship with Josefina, María moved to the United States in 1986, about the time that Mirella was coming of age.

Here María experienced a new awareness of racism and found more openness regarding sexuality.[28] Economically her life took a tailspin; despite her middle-class credentials, she could not find a job and worked as a farm worker for about a year until she found work as a bilingual staff person in a social service agency. Her social life was a different story: She met a number of lesbians and bisexual women who were out of the closet. Indeed, a national magazine dubbed Santa Cruz as the new "lesbian utopia" (displacing Amherst, Massachusetts) and there are regular features in the local press indicating the presence of many lesbians. In this context, María began dating Latinas and white women, and with their encouragement she underwent a profound transformation. With the active support of one lover, María came out of the closet herself and began accepting herself as female: "She's very beautiful and she made me realize that if women were with me, it wasn't because I appeared to be a man or I was pretending to be a man. No, it was because I was a *woman*. So I confronted that. Now I say, 'Yeah I'm a woman and I love women.'" This reconciliation with herself even had a dramatic effect on her body. "Before, I was less femme, I didn't have large breasts. I looked like a boy." She

gained weight and became more curvaceous, and changed from androgynous-looking to having a more female body type: "Because of the comfort of being accepted, I have learned to cope. And my body changed after I accepted that I was a woman. I think it was psychosomatic." With her self-described more feminine body, María now wears pants, oxford shirts, and short hair; from a distance she appears gender-neutral. María also experienced a new sense of the importance of masturbation in her life, incorporating self-pleasure as an explicit political stance, in part to counter any possible threat of AIDS, but also as part of her self-conscious attempt to redefine herself.

María is currently living with her lover (who during her interview chose the pseudonym Frida) in an open lesbian relationship. She is proud that their relationship is based on fidelity and honesty. María characterized Frida as "more femme" than herself, because of Frida's appreciation of a feminine self-presentation of her body through dress and hair styles. The couple experienced economic difficulties, as the defunding of social services in California often meant that one or both of them was temporarily unemployed. Their financial vicissitudes provided the base of the couple's desire for flexible gender expectations: "In the beginning I was the provider for a few months, and then I became the housewife. And I'm the mom sometimes, because she's younger than me, and I'm the teacher most of the time. She's a very good student." María described their love: "I'm very lucky to be with Frida. When I am in love with a woman, I'm very passionate. I'm a Scorpio so it's extreme: It's like a big explosion – *boom*."

María's coming-out story, however, is not just a process of self-actualization as she struggles with contradictions in a heterosexist society. Frida occasionally bullies María by throwing furniture or hitting walls with her fists during arguments, although according to both women Frida does not actually hit María. Despite her happiness with Frida, because of these outbursts, María considers herself a battered woman. Ironically, even as María has accepted her own womanhood, she views herself as not in control and relatively powerless to stop the violence – as *la mujer abnegada*, a suffering woman. The couple has sought help with a social service agency that provides lesbian-sensitive services for battered women so María does not see herself as a victim but as a survivor. She laments that those services are not offered in Spanish, the language of their intimacy. María hopes to establish an organization of *lesbianas Mexicanas* that could provide culturally sensitive, bilingual services for lesbians experiencing domestic violence of all types. María seeks a new kind of power – collective mutual aid with other women.

Conclusion

Despite being of different generations, nationalities, and sexual orientations, these two women articulated strikingly similar cultural poetics regarding gender and sexuality. They were both expected to conform to traditional Catholic expectations that women forgo sexual exploration or pleasure, guard their virginity and reputations for marriage and children, and denigrate homosexuality. This powerful cultural message created a virtual cult of virginity – not unlike that in other cultures – that was being undermined by the end of the twentieth century. Both women learned that their own bodies would alter to reveal their deviation from "purity" and a loss of status, confirming findings in other research on the importance of virginity for Mexican women. When these women did "give up" their virginity, they heard their lovers use the language of play, referring to them as little daughters. Both heard echoes of honor and respect for their conformity to these ideals of proper womanhood, or experienced shame, anguish, and scandal for the transgressions – confirming notions Gutiérrez found much earlier in Mexican society. This cultural message contained a deep pragmatism, promising life-long economic support by a man in exchange for playing the part. Despite having more education than most Latinas, they learned few culturally sanctioned messages that confirmed their yearning and faced contending ideas about sexuality in the United States, particularly in popular culture.

These women, however, are not the subjugated, essentialized category of woman in the Mexican allegory of virgin/whore. As historical

actors, they both regarded Catholic ideology as a template to be contested. Their own volition and support of other women shaped how they came to know their bodies, whom they found attractive, and the pleasure they found in sexual relationships with others. Each struggled to create a discourse about the power of love in this culturally mediated world where the female gender was subject to male dominance.

Mirella's "plot" involved coming to desire a man of her own racial background, despite the deep emotional scarring of male violence and Catholic-inspired control over her body, and having been "singed" through her social transgressions with white men. Despite the cadences of "valley girl" speech with inferences of nonchalance, her dreams carry serious economic consequences. The potential stable life together with Ray, with their combined income as a professional couple, would provide definite prospects of economic and social mobility much beyond what she could provide for herself. Mirella links the vision of a companionate ideal family – one sanctioned by institutionalized heterosexuality – with sexual pleasure.

María also recoiled from the crucible of patriarchy and Catholicism even as she was drawn to the entitlements of masculinity. She, too, was "scorched," this time because of her desire for women and for flaunting the conventions of virginity and femininity. Her choice of lesbianism means that she would not have the economic support afforded to women who marry well. María's position in marginally funded social services brings the challenge of building on her human capital and becoming economically stable with a partner in the same situation.

These women's narratives illustrate structures of gender, of sexuality, and of racialized bodies in Mexican culture that profoundly affect decisions that appear to be individualistic. While the boundaries proscribed for women seem rigid and limiting, they were certainly malleable enough for these women to create space for themselves. In following her desires, each woman subverted male dominance and reconstructed power, claiming an autonomous life and subjectivity. Each maneuvered through the fires of control to embrace the body enflamed.

NOTES

Thanks to Tomás Almaguer, Gloria Cuádraz, Micaela di Leonardo, Barbara García, Ramón Gutiérrez, Mirella Hernández, Aída Hurtado, Francisca Angulo Olaiz, María Pérez, Carter Wilson, and the graduate students in my Latino Ethnographies graduate seminar at the University of Michigan for their helpful comments on various versions of this paper.

1 David D. Gilmore, ed. *Honor and Shame and the Unity of the Mediterranean* No. 22 (Washington: American Anthropological Association, 1987); J. Peristiany, ed. *Honour and Shame: The Values of Mediterranean Society* (Chicago: University of Chicago Press, 1965); Julian Pitt-Rivers, "Honor," *International Encyclopedia of the Social Sciences* (New York, 1968), pp. 131–51.

2 Jean Franco, *Plotting Women: Gender and Representation in Mexico* (New York: Columbia University Press, 1989). This cultural configuration is specific to Mexican society; Roger Lancaster asserts that " 'sexual purity' in the sense of virginity is not and never has been an important element of the Nicaraguan ideal of proper womanhood." See Roger N. Lancaster, *Life is Hard: Machismo, Danger, and The Intimacy of Power in Nicaragua* (Berkeley: University of California Press, 1992), p. 310.

3 There is a long intertextual tradition of reflection on the Mexican national character ("*lo mexicano*"). Two key texts are: Octavio Paz, *The Labyrinth of Solitude, Life and Thought in Mexico* (New York: Grove Press, 1961) and Samuel Ramos, *Profile of Man and Culture in Mexico* (Austin: University of Texas Press, 1962). Anthropologist Claudio Lomnitz-Adler calls instead for the study of regional and intimate ideologies. See Claudio Lomnitz-Adler, *Exits from the Labyrinth: Culture and Ideology in the Mexican National Space* (Berkeley: University of California Press, 1992).

4 Adelaida R. del Castillo, "Malintzin Tenepal: A Preliminary Look into a New Perspective," in *Essays on La Mujer*, eds. Rosaura Sánchez and Rosa Martínez Cruz (UCLA: Chicano Studies Center Publications, 1977); Norma Alarcón, Chicana Feminist Literature: A Re-Vision Through Malintzin/or Malintzin: Putting flesh Back on the Object", in *This Bridge Called My Back,*

Writings by Radical Women of Color, eds. Cherríe Moraga and Gloria Anzaldúa (Watertown, MA: Persephone Press, 1981); Cherríe Moraga, *Loving in the War Years: lo que nunca pasó por sus labios* (Boston: South End Press, 1983). Ramón Gutiérrez argues that in Spanish colonial society there were prescribed gender-specific rules of proper social comportment, where honor was a male attribute while shame was intrinsic to females because of their "natural weakness" and association with nature. Men were encouraged to be sexually active even through coercion or deception. "Decent" women, unless given in Church-sanctified matrimony, were shamed and dishonored through illicit sexual behavior. Thus women were to be "militantly protected" by family members and the church, their honor-virtue "fiercely contested and rather scandalously lost," and the seduction of a virgin of high status subject to legal sanctions during the eighteenth century. Low-status women – who had lost institutional ties to men and/or were members of inferior racial categories – were considered sport for the prowess of men. Thus conflicts over maintaining honor – how norms and values were imposed or contested – or the repercussions of lost honor and inevitable shame, illuminate the social construction of sexuality in colonial Mexican society. See Ramón A. Gutiérrez, *When Jesus Came the Corn Mothers Went Away: Marriage, Sexuality and Power in New Mexico, 1500–1846* (Stanford: Stanford University Press, 1991).

5 The terms Chicano/o or Mexicana/o, designed to get away from the use of the generic "he" in the word Chicano or Mexicano, are cumbersome. I use Chicana/Mexicano to designate people of Mexican origin in the United States of both sexes.

6 Olivia M. Espín, "Cultural and Historical Influences on Sexuality in Hispanic/Latin Women: Implications for Psychotherapy," in *Pleasure and Danger: Exploring Female Sexuality*, Carol Vance, ed. (Boston: Routledge and Kegan Paul, 1984), pp. 149–64; Emma Guerrero Pavich, "A Chicana Perspective on Mexican Culture and Sexuality," *Journal of Social Work and Human Sexuality* 3 (Spring, 1986), pp. 47–65; Ana Maria Alonso and Maria Alonso and Maria Teresa Koreck, "Silences: 'Hispanics,' AIDS, and Sexual Practices," *Differences: A Journal of*

Feminist Cultural Studies 1 (1989), pp. 101–24; Amado M. Padilla and Traci L. Baird, "Mexican-American Adolescent Sexuality and Sexual Knowledge: An Exploratory Study," *Hispanic Journal of Behavioral Sciences* 13 (1, 1991), pp. 95–104.

7 Alonso and Korek, "Silences: 'Hispanics,' AIDS, and Sexual Practices." Also see James M. Taggart, "Gender Segregation and Cultural Constructions of Sexuality in Two Hispanic Societies," *American Ethnologist* 19 (1, 1992), pp. 75–96; Carter Wilson, *Hidden in the Blood: AIDS in Yucatan* (New York: Columbia University Press 1995).

8 David Alvirez, "The Effects of Formal Church Affiliation and Religiosity on the Fertility Patterns of Mexican American Catholics," *Demography* 10 (1973), pp. 19–36. Hispanic teenagers are just as likely to have an abortion as black and white teenagers. See Katherine F. Darabi, Joy Dryfoos and Dana Schwartz, "Hispanic Adolescent Fertility," *Hispanic Journal of Behavioral Sciences* 8 no. 2 (1986), pp. 157–71. For a discussion of women's escape from sexual violence, see Lourdes Argüelles and Anne Rivero, "Violence, Migration, and Compassionate Practice: Conversations with Some Women We Think We Know," *Urban Anthropology*, special issue on Latino Ethnography 22 no. 3–4 (1993), pp. 259–76.

9 Literally "tongue and place": Pérez is calling for a discourse and social space "that rejects colonial ideology and the by-products of colonialism and capitalist patriarchy – sexism, racism, homophobia." See Emma Pérez, "Sexuality and Discourse: Notes From a Chicana Survivor," in Carla Trujillo, ed. *Chicana Lesbians: The Girls Our Mothers Warned Us About* (Berkeley: Third Woman Press, 1991), pp. 159–84. See also Moraga, *Loving in the War Years*; Gloria Anzaldúa, *Borderlands/La Frontera: The New Mestiza* (San Francisco: Spinsters/Aunt Lute, 1987); Juanita Ramos, ed. *Compañera: Latina Lesbians (an Anthology* (New York: Latina Lesbian History Project, 1987); Norma Alarcón, Ana Castillo and Cherríe Moraga, "The Sexuality of Latinas." Special Issue of *Third Woman* 4 (1989); Tomás Almaguer, "Chicano Men: A Cartography of Homosexual Identity and Behavior," *Differences: A Journal of Feminist Cultural Studies* 3 no. 2 (1991), pp. 75–100; Trujillo, ed. *Chicana Lesbians*; Emma Pérez, "Speaking From the

Margin: Uninvited Discourse on Sexuality and Power," in *Building with Our Hands: New Directions in Chicana Studies*, Adela de la Torre and Beatriz M. Pesquera (Berkeley: University of California Press, 1993), pp. 57–74.

10 I am currently doing historical and ethnographic research on the construction of family and household among the poor in Santa Cruz County, California, thus far interviewing mainly women – Mexicanas, Chicanas and whites, heterosexual and queer. I query how people were socialized regarding sex, family and marriage; inquiring about early experiences with sexual experimentation; messages they received about their bodies, experiences regarding starting to menstruate (for women); sexual histories; notions of sexual pleasure; and current experiences and values regarding family and sex.

11 For a discussion of nondiscursive knowledge, see Michael Burawoy, et al., eds., *Ethnography Unbound: Power and Resistance in the Modern Metropolis* (Berkeley: University of California Press, 1991), p. 5. Roger M. Keesing argues that women's "muteness" or the richness of their narratives "must always be historically and contextually situated, and bracketed with doubt." See "Kwaio Women Speak: The Micropolitics of Autobiography in a Solomon Island Society," *American Anthropologist*, vol. 87 (March 1985), pp. 27–39, p. 27.

12 In autobiographical written narratives, writers often struggle with the blurring of "memory" and "reality." See Penelope Lively, *Oleander, Jacaranda: A Childhood Perceived* (New York: HarperCollins, 1994); and Judith Ortiz Cofer, *Silent Dancing: A Partial Remembrance of a Puerto Rican Childhood* (Houston: Arte Publico Press, 1990).

13 Lively, *Oleander, Jacaranda*, vii.

14 Donna Haraway, *Primate Visions: Gender, Race, and Nature in the World of Modern Science* (New York: Routledge, 1989).

15 Lancaster, *Life is Hard*, p. 318.

16 Although this trope emerged with white women as well, that analysis is beyond the scope of this paper.

17 Ann Snitow, Christine Stansell and Sharon Thompson, eds. *Powers of Desire: The Politics of Sexuality* (New York: Monthly Review Press, 1983).

18 María went over my narrative about her, making corrections regarding dates and names, and clarifying her views. She preferred that I use her real name, and viewed this disclosure as part of her process of coming out as a lesbian: "I know its a tremendous risk but this is reality, this is not fiction. They cannot deny me."

19 Franco, *Plotting Women*, p. xxiii.

20 Other Chicanas and Mexicanas reported changes that occur in women's bodies after losing their virginity, including that women's hips get wider, that they walk differently, or that their faces become more "knowing."

21 Francisca Angulo Olaiz, "Struggling to Have a Say: How Latino Adolescents Construct Themselves as Sexual Adults and What this Means for HIV Prevention Programs," Masters' thesis, Anthropology Department, University of California, Los Angeles, 1995, p. 54.

22 Based on participant observation in a southern California high school and in-depth interviews with Chicana/Latino high school students (women and men), Francisca Angulo Olaiz finds that virginity is socially constructed. Women especially do not denigrate a woman who lost her virginity if she was in love with the man and expected permanence in the relationship. See Olaiz, "Struggling to Have a Say," chapter 3.

23 Moraga, *Loving in the War Years*, p. 125.

24 While *compañera* literally means companion or sexual partner, María explicitly characterized Josefina as her "wife."

25 Alonso and Koreck argue that it is acceptable for a heterosexual couple to have anal intercourse prior to marriage for it does not negate a woman's vaginal virginity and is a form of birth control. See Alonso and Koreck, "Silences: 'Hispanics,' AIDS, and Sexual Practices."

26 Elizabeth Kennedy Lapovsky and Madeline D. Davis, *Boots of Leather, Slippers of Gold: The History of a Lesbian Community* (New York: Routledge, 1993).

27 Ian Lumsden, *Homosexuality: Society and the State in Mexico* (México, D.F.: Solediciones Colectivo Sol, 1991).

28 Immigrant lesbian women from various countries report experiencing shock from the differences between their home countries and the United States. See Olivia M. Espin, "Crossing Borders and Boundaries: The Life Narratives of Immigrant Lesbians," *Division* 44 (1995), pp. 18–27.

13

Returned Migration, Language, and Identity: Puerto Rican Bilinguals in Dos Worlds/Two Mundos[1]

Ana Celia Zentella

The poem 'Dos Worlds/Two Mundos' was written by a Rochesterican, Henry Padrón, in 1982 (an excerpt is given in the Appendix). It portrays a bilingual's struggle with the two worlds represented by the two languages he/she knows, a struggle which can cause cultural conflict and 'un tremendo strain en tu brain'. In this regard, the Puerto Rican experience is no different from that of every other poor immigrant with a foreign-language background. The linguistic literature is full of examples of the we–they dichotomy experienced by members of language minorities when they attempt to participate in the dominant society (Gumperz 1964, 1976; Fishman 1966). The 'we' language, that spoken at home, the mother tongue, is endowed with many positive affective variables such as intimacy and solidarity, but it is considered low in prestige. The 'they' language, in contrast, enjoys high status because it is linked with the outside world of power and money (Lambert 1972). In some communities, the high and low linguistic codes are kept strictly apart (Ferguson 1964; Fishman 1967), but in others, such as the Chicano and Puerto Rican communities in the US, the pervasiveness of the close cultural contact and the resulting lack of functional differentiation are reflected in code switching, as in Padrón's poem. Often, code switching is misinterpreted as evidence only of lack of linguistic knowledge. But a spate of recent research has proved that switching serves many significant social and discourse functions beyond that of filling in forgotten phrases or words (Gumperz 1976; McClure 1977; Valdés 1981; LPTF 1980; Zentella 1985). Nor does code switching signal the deterioration of one or both of the languages involved; in fact, switchers display formidable syntactic knowledge by switching at points that maintain the grammatical integrity of both languages at the same time (Poplack 1979; Sankoff and Poplack 1980). Thus code switching allows us to make a graphic statement about the way we live with a foot in each of 'dos worlds/two mundos'.

In the United States, code switching helps us to hold onto some of our Spanish, in the face of ever-mounting pressures to become English monolinguals. Strong community support for bilingual education reflects our commitment to retain Spanish while learning English. But even with, and mostly without, bilingual education, our children do become English-dominant as they go through the educational process. If they remain in the community as adults, however, increased contact with recent immigrants and the assumption of adult roles renew their fluency in Spanish (Flores et al. 1981; Zentella 1987).

This is the scenario which seems to be challenging the traditional pattern of immigrant language loss by the third generation in the USA (Pedraza et al. 1980). For many Puerto Ricans, however, there is an added wrinkle, and that is that the polarity that constitutes the two worlds of the community can suddenly reverse itself, and people who were once struggling to hold onto their Puerto Ricanness and Spanish in the US can suddenly find themselves struggling to hold onto their 'Nuyorican-' or 'Rochestericanness' and English in Puerto Rico.

The Puerto Rican experience is unique because the US has controlled both homeland and new-land political, economic, and educational systems since 1898, when Puerto Rico became a colony of the United States, and it continues to play a key role in the push-pull of the migration flow (Bonilla 1983). The revolving-door migration of Puerto Ricans, which represents a distinct departure from the usual immigrant pattern, challenges the prevalent model of assimilation and demands a reevaluation of the objectives and impact of many governmental policies, such as the proposed English language amendment, and of some educational approaches, particularly transitional bilingual education.

Returned Migrants

Just as the earlier waves of Puerto Rican immigration to the US had repercussions for the educational system and all the social services here, the return of approximately 35,000 people per year to Puerto Rico since 1973 has caused widespread reaction there (Underhill 1981). Almost 20 percent of Puerto Rico's entire population of nearly three million are Puerto Ricans who have returned to the island after living in the US, and their offspring. They amount to approximately 10 percent of the total public-school enrollment, or close to 70,000 pupils. Approximately two-thirds of the children of returnees in the school system were born in the US and spent more than five years here before going to the island. Many of them learned to function primarily or only in English, whether they were born in Puerto Rico or not, and could not adjust to monolingual Spanish classes in Puerto Rico. Some 14,000 attend

remedial classes in basic skills as part of the Migrant Child Education Program (Freidman 1982). Another 45,000 are enrolled in bilingual education programs in 17 municipalities across the island, predominately concentrated in the metropolitan area (Junta de Planificación 1980).

The introduction of bilingual instruction in Puerto Rico for the children of returnees, who had initially been pushed out of the island because of economic problems and now were not welcomed back because of the same worsening problem, fanned the flames of the language debate. This debate has polarized the island's political and intellectual leadership ever since the US troops landed in 1898 and imposed 'English-only', i.e., as the medium of instruction and in all legal proceedings, leading to educational failure for thousands and resulting in great socio-political unrest (Zentella 1981).

As a result, the language behavior, attitudes, and even dress of these youngsters are topics of island-wide concern. A government publication devoted to the Immigrant Population of Puerto Rico reflects this concern forthrightly:

> Por otro lado la inmigración tiene otras implicaciones a nivel social. Los puertorriqueños que regresan y sus descendientes, los cuales estuvieron expuestos a una cultura y modo de vida completamente distintos al nuestro, traen consigo una serie de patrones de vida, valores morales y actitudes hacia la autoridad que pueden entrar en conflictos con los de la población no migrante. (Junta de Planificación 1980: 45).
>
> [On the other hand the immigration has other implications at the social level. The Puerto Ricans who return and their descendants, who were exposed to a culture and a lifestyle completely different from ours, bring with them a series of behaviors, moral values, and attitudes toward authority which can come into conflict with those of the nonmigrant population.]

This quote should have a familiar ring for anyone acquainted with the literature on immigrants to the US; with the elimination of the words 'Puerto Ricans who return', the statement is a classic warning about the cultural conflict caused by foreigners, reappearing today in the propaganda of the proponents of the English language amendment, especially English First and U.S. English (Zentella 1988).

The Planning Board clearly assumes that Puerto Ricans in the US are exposed to a culture with which island Puerto Ricans have no contact, and that the differences between them may cause conflict. My interest in the cultural and linguistic issues raised by these assumptions, and in the returnees' perceptions of their experience, led me to undertake this research with teenagers in Puerto Rico.[2]

This paper presents the results of observations of, and individually taped interviews with, 43 junior and senior high school students (23 females, 20 males) in bilingual programs in Bayamon and Levittown, conducted in 1983.[3] The students ranged in ages from 12–20, with 81 percent (35) in the 16–18-year-old bracket. Sixteen percent were born in Puerto Rico and 26 percent had lived there before their most recent migration, but most had never lived in Puerto Rico before moving there from one to three years previously. They came from working-class backgrounds in New York, Chicago, Philadelphia, and Hartford and were living in lower-middle-class urbanizations just outside the capital in Puerto Rico. Nearly the entire group were English-dominant bilinguals (41/43). They were interviewed in both English and Spanish, except for two newcomers who were unable to speak or understand Spanish, and they were observed during their free periods on the school grounds.

We shall report on three aspects of the study here:

1. the link between Puerto Rican cultural identity and language;
2. attitudes toward bilingualism and biculturalism;
3. the future of Spanish and English in Puerto Rico.

Puerto Rican Cultural Identity and Language

The language debate in Puerto Rico is not an intellectual exercise in the pros and cons of linguistic purity. It brings Puerto Ricans face to face with a basic cultural issue which has significant political ramifications. That issue is, does language change/loss necessarily spell cultural loss? More pointedly, are returnees who cannot speak Spanish Puerto Ricans? Given the influence of 400 years of Spanish rule, the history of struggle vs. the US's imposition of English, and the lack of other national identifiers, the survival of Spanish has become inextricably linked for many with the survival of Puerto Rican identity and that of the Puerto Rican nation itself. The depth of feeling for Spanish is frequently communicated in emotional newspaper articles, such as 'En la esencia del ser puertorriqueño nuestro idioma español posee una fuerza singular de identidad irrefutable' [In the essence of the Puerto Rican being, our Spanish language possesses a singular strength of irrefutable identity] (Casillas Alvares 1983). Even when some scholars attempt to broaden the definition of Puerto Rican to include features other than language, they do not dispense with language. When philologist Rubén del Rosario maintains that 'Es evidente que lo que hace al puertorriqueño no es sólo la lengua (su entonación, sus palabras, su fraseología particular)' [It is evident that what makes a Puerto Rican is not only the language (its intonation, its words, its particular phraseology)] (Rosario 1983), he nevertheless starts from the premise that 'el ser puertorriqueño envuelve el conservar vivo del idioma corriente de nuestra pueblo' [being Puerto Rican entails the live conservation of the common language of our people]. Then, in what I interpret as a veiled reference to the returnees, he advises, 'Mientras Ud. esté en Puerto Rico y se considere boricua, hablará igual que nosotros y preferirá el español para expresarse por escrito' [While you are in Puerto Rico and consider yourself Puerto Rican, you will speak like us and prefer Spanish when expressing yourself in writing] (Rosario, 1983, p. 16). United States Puerto Rican scholars generally heed this advice, and they pass it on to their students because they fear the negative reactions that can be stirred up if it is ignored. On a visit to the island, one US PR sociologist was quoted in a newspaper as saying, 'To be Puerto Rican is to be inseparable from your language, so it is particularly offensive to any Puerto Rican to listen to anyone who claims to be Puerto Rican and does not know the language' (Betances, quoted in Ghigliotty 1983).

Parallel with the consistent identification of Puerto Rican identity with the Spanish language is a concern for the repercussions of extended contact with English. Many of the island's intellectuals and others believe that English has had a continuously deteriorating effect on the Spanish of Puerto Rico and that, as a result, Puerto Rico's national identity itself is being threatened. Well-known writers are reluctant, however, to link publicly their constant railing against the mutilation of Spanish and 'la crisis cada vez más acentuada que vive el español en Puerto Rico' (González 1982) [the ever more accentuated crisis of Spanish in Puerto Rico] to the presence of the returnees. Consider the following newspaper article by the well-known writer, Salvador Tió, who claims to have coined the term 'Spanglish' decades ago, in which he catalogs the deterioration of Spanish and English and predicts that both will be buried in Puerto Rico:

> La confusión del sentido de las palabras; los calcos que llegan hasta la calcomanía; los préstamos tan crecidos que exponen a muchos individuos a la quiebra total de la expresión, están contribuyendo a desfigurar la lengua propria. Pero si es grave lo que le está sucediendo al español, mucho más grave es lo que le está sucediendo al inglés. A este paso la isla de Puerto Rico puede llegar a ser, en pocas generaciones, el cementerio de las dos grandes lenguas de América (Tió 1982: 24).

> [The confusion in the meaning of words, calques to the extreme of calcomania, borrowings so numerous that they make many individuals susceptible to a total breakdown in communication, are contributing to a disfiguring of the language itself. But if what is happening to Spanish is serious, what is happening to English is much more serious. At this rate, the island of Puerto Rico may come to be, in a few generations, the cemetery of the two great languages of America.]

Although Tió lays the blame for this situation at the door of US experimentation with school language policy during the first half of the twentieth century, many of his readers may understandably

conclude that the largest group of bilinguals in their midst, the return migrants, share some of the blame.

Although most intellectuals are loath to attack the returnees directly, at least one prominent anthropologist, Eduardo Seda Bonilla, has openly questioned the right of a group that does not speak Spanish to consider itself Puerto Rican, labelling it 'pseudo-ethnicity' (Seda 1975). The writer of a letter to the editor of a major Spanish daily expressed herself much more categorically:

> ...ni los 500,000 nacidos, criados y educados en Nueva York son puertorriqueños aunque vayan a cien mil desfiles puertorriqueños, vivan 100 años en Puerto Rico o sus padres hayan tenido la dicha de haber nacido en esta encantadora isla. Acepte la realidad: si usted nació se crió y educó en Estados Unidos, es americano y no puertorriqueño. Es tambien neoyorquino (Vélez 1983).

> [...nor are the 500,000 born, raised, and educated in New York, Puerto Ricans even if they go to 100,000 Puerto Rican parades, live 100 years in Puerto Rico, or if their parents were lucky enough to have been born on this enchanted island. Accept reality: if you were born, raised, and educated in the US, you are American and not Puerto Rican. You are also a New Yorker.]

Support for the Nuyoricans against charges such as these comes from unexpected quarters, the pen of Puerto Rico's renowned literary figure and *independentista* 'independence supporter' in exile, José Luís González. González is one of the most vociferous critics of the effect of English on Spanish; he believes it is replacing Spanish vocabulary and syntax (1982). One would expect him to be equally critical of the group that has these language characteristics, but, when he is confronted with the reality that some who identify as Puerto Ricans cannot speak Spanish well or at all, he prefers to attack those who dare to judge them:

> ¿Tienen derecho a sentirse declararse puertorriqueños los 'niuyoricans' cuya lengua materna es el inglés o en muchos casos el todavía poco analizado 'espanglish'? De

entrada hago constar que la pregunta misma me parece ociosa, porque los únicos que tienen derecho histórico y moral al responder a ella son los propios 'niuyoricans' cuya lengua materna no es el español que se habla en Puerto Rico. Si ellos se consideran puertorriqueños y como tales exigen que se les reconozca, ¿quién es el juez llamado a dictaminar sobre la legitimidad de su pretensión? Alguien, acaso, cuyos antepasados no fueron obligados por la necesidad de abondonar la isla? Me consta que esos jueces autodesignados abundan en la isla, pero lo cierto es que su autoridad moral no me convence del todo (González 1983: 8). [Do niuyoricans whose mother tongue is English or in many cases the still little analyzed 'Spanglish' have the right to feel and declare themselves Puerto Rican? From the outset I want to make clear that the question itself seems idle, because the only ones who have the historic and moral right to answer it are the niuyoricans themselves whose mother tongue is not the Spanish of Puerto Rico. If they consider themselves Puerto Ricans and ask to be recognized as such, who is the judge called upon to decide on the legitimacy of their claim? Someone, perhaps, whose forbears were not obliged by necessity to leave the island? I am aware that self-appointed judges abound on the island, but the truth is that their moral authority does not completely convince me.]

González's backhanded defense of the returnees is not totally convincing either, particularly since comments about the differences between the returnees and the rest of Puerto Rico's population are not limited to a few critics with questionable motives. That these differences are frequently commented on in their schools and communities is attested to by the students themselves, and it is to their own experience and attitudes, rarely reported on in the press, that we must turn for a more accurate and complete picture of these issues.

The widespread interest in the returned-migrant 'problem' and the increased intensity of the attacks on Spanish and English do not appear to be disconnected, and this is not lost on the returnees. They too have strong views on the matter. For one, they definitely do not believe that they are deteriorating the island's Spanish: 87 percent rejected this, and 76 percent of them said they were not damaging the English language. Those who agree that they were having a deleterious effect on the languages could mention only slang words as evidence. Most important is their position on the link between language and culture.

We asked the bilingual teens in Puerto Rico whether it is possible for someone who speaks only English to be Puerto Rican. There was more agreement among them on this issue than on any other: 91 percent of the students believe that it is possible for someone who speaks only English to be Puerto Rican. This attitude had been probed earlier in the New York Puerto Rican community by Joshua Fishman's groundbreaking study (Fishman et al. 1971) and more recently by John Attinasi and members of the Language Policy Task Force of the Centro de Estudios Puertorriqueños (Attinasi 1979; LPTF 1980). The Centro found that 100 percent of the 91 East Harlem residents, mainly adults, and all 62 bilingual teachers they interviewed in New York agreed that 'you can speak English and be part of Puerto Rican culture'. In our study, we referred only to English monolinguals, specifically excluding people who know English in addition to Spanish, and this may account for the 9 percent difference in our results.

In both the Puerto Rico and New York studies, there was less agreement about the inverse situation, that is, whether Spanish speakers could be part of North American culture. In Puerto Rico, where I limited the example to Spanish monolinguals, only 63 percent of the students believed that Spanish monolinguals could be part of North American culture, whereas 94 percent of the El Barrio sample agreed with the Centro's less limiting question that 'people who spoke Spanish could be Americans'. For both groups, Puerto Rican national identity apparently allows for more flexibility in terms of language than does North American identity, an attitude which directly reflects their experiences in Puerto Rican and North American communities.

When the question was put more directly, 'Is Spanish necessary for Puerto Rican identity?' (Centro research in NYC) and 'Is Spanish indispensable for Puerto Rican identity?' (my research in Puerto Rico), the results were less overwhelming, particularly in the Puerto Rico sample, but they still included the majority of both groups: 83 percent of the East Harlem residents and 61 percent of the bilingual students in Puerto Rico thought that Spanish was not necessary/indispensable for Puerto Rican identity. The response of the bilingual teens on the island fell between that of the East Harlem residents and the NYC bilingual teachers; 62.5 percent of the teachers judged Spanish as necessary to our cultural identity, and 37.5 percent found it unnecessary.

The teens in Puerto Rico were asked the same question in still another way, in terms of their response to the widely advertised slogan of Puerto Rico's English language daily, the *San Juan Star*. Hourly on the radio in Puerto Rico, the *Star* announced, 'Porque ser puertorriqueño no es una (sic) cuestión de idioma' [Because being Puerto Rican is not a question of language]. The teens clearly aligned themselves with the newspaper's position, which had been widely repudiated in the local press: 81 percent of them agreed with the slogan, reaffirming that these youngsters feel quite comfortable with the notion of Puerto Rican identity without a language requirement. Needless to say, this attitude does not endear them to the island's intellectuals.

But comments about the differences between the returnees and the rest of Puerto Rico's population are more widespread than those of a few writers or academics. Evidence that it is a more generalized phenomenon is found in the terms of address that their neighbors and family used with them: 74 percent have been called 'gringo', 58 percent 'nuyorican', and 51 percent 'american'. Of these, 'nuyorican' is the one they are most likely to use among themselves.[4] The 'americano' and 'gringo' labels are of particular interest because they indicate that native islanders are incorporating the returnees into national groupings formerly limited to Anglos. Some returnees have been quite hurt by these labels, others say they are used in jest, and still others react defensively.

Seventeen-year-old Harry's response to them is typical of those who accept the fact that their bicultural identity exposes them to attack in both of their worlds:

H: A mi me llega to' igual. Soy 'bilingue', 'gringo', 'blanco', 'white boy'.

ACZ: Cuando lo dicen, ¿qué quieren decir con eso? ¿Es un insulto?

H: If they say it *insulto*, they say 'dirty gringo' and all this bull crap, pero que a mi – I was in New York and I was called SPIC about one hundred fifty times. I didn't do nothin' to them in New York, why am I going to say something here just because they call me a gringo. In New York, you defend yourself because they call you a Puerto Rican; here you defend yourself because they call you a gringo.

[H: I take it all the same. I am 'bilingual', 'gringo', 'white', 'white boy'.

ACZ: When they say it, what do they mean by it? Is it an insult?

H: If they say it *as an insult*, they say 'dirty gringo' and all this bull crap, but to me . . .]

Whatever their reaction to the terms, one result is that these youngsters are being defined as distinct from the native population. They, in turn, participate in this redefinition of their identity by referring to themselves as 'we/us, the bilinguals' or 'nosotros, los bilingües', and to their fellow students who are native-born Puerto Ricans as 'they/them, the regulars', 'ellos, los regulares'. These terms mimic the school's division into *programa regular* with all classes in Spanish and *programa bilingüe* with math, social studies, and science in English, but that does not explain the more telling distinction they make between 'us, the bilinguals' or 'nuyoricans', and 'them, the Puerto Ricans'. When challenged with, 'What do you mean? Aren't you Puerto Rican?' their response is 'Yeah, but you know, the *real* Puerto Ricans, from here.' This is, of course, the other side of the 'americano/gringo' coin; both groups have adopted labels for the differences they perceive between them.

Attitudes Towards Bilingualism and Biculturalism

Before we arrive at the conclusion that these differences represent irreparable cleavages in the Puerto Rican fabric, it is important to consider other data and to look beyond answers to questions, or poems, at actual behavior. It is not hard to find evidence of the 'nuyoricans' positive attitudes toward Spanish and Puerto Rico. We found that all of them speak Spanish or are trying to learn it, they are all committed to raising their children bilingually, and nearly one-half of the group plans to remain in Puerto Rico when they are on their own. They like the climate, the beaches, the relative calm, and the hospitality of Puerto Rico, and they do not have found memories of the dirt, the crime, and the danger that they left behind in the working-class ghettoes of the United States. These attitudes are as characteristic of them as their longing for the transportation, activities, and jobs of the States and their acceptance of an English-speaking Puerto Rican identity.

There is less conflict in this behavior and attitudes than some might think. Bilinguals in Puerto Rico seem to be saying that they want to be counted as Puerto Ricans and want the same for their children but they do not want it to depend on their knowledge of Spanish. This is a realistic response to their go–come relationship with the island. Less than a year after this study, five of the group had moved back to the States. We must also consider the effect of the criticisms made against their Spanish in view of a study by Ramos Perea (1972) which found that fluency in Spanish was crucial in the successful adjustment of junior-high-school returnees. In the group I studied, everyone had less confidence in their Spanish ability than in their English ability; most rated it as fair.[5] Many had been told by teachers, family, and neighbors that they talked *mata'o* 'killed' or 'Spanglish'. Nuyorican Spanish is generally stigmatized on the island. In a study which asked Puerto Rican college students to judge various speech styles, a bilingual Nuyorican speaking Spanish was judged most negatively on all scales. Island born/raised and US born/raised

students alike evaluated the Nuyorican speaker as the most unfriendly, the most passive, and the laziest of all (Irizarry 1981). These results are similar to those of the matched guise experiments made famous by Lambert et al. (1960) where the standard dialect or high language is consistently rated superior to the nonstandard or low code.

When the returnees speak the language they know best, they sometimes encounter ridicule and hostility from working-class island teens. They attribute the negative reaction to their speaking English to envy; that is, they believe they are resented because they can speak it and the 'Puerto Ricans cannot, but would love to'. This is probably an accurate estimation of the well-documented power of the metropolis's language in every colonial setting.[6] In Puerto Rico it is certainly true that in the competition for scarce jobs, the applicant who knows English has an advantage. The returnees and their children also have an educational edge of two and four years respectively over the permanent residents, which helped them fare better in the 1975 crisis (Junta de Planificación 1980). The harsh economic realities of an island plagued by a 50 percent unemployment rate, with 70 percent of its population on food stamps, in no small measure contribute to the islander vs. migrant misunderstandings.

Any analysis of the returnee vs. islander conflict must be viewed in the context of the political and economic forces that have resulted in the massive displacement and replacement of Puerto Rican people from their island. A people's language attitudes and behavior are shaped by the nature of their experiences with the social structure around them. Adolescents caught in the middle of the transfer of people and payments can be expected to reflect this conflict in their notions of identity and language. They attempt to resolve the conflict via their commitment to bilingualism and biculturalism, only to encounter hostility to this solution in the US and Puerto Rico. Nor are they without concern about the repercussions of biculturalism. Although 81 percent asserted that it was possible to be bicultural, 50 percent doubted that it was healthy, citing confusion as a problem. Given their situation, caught between the idealized dreams of their parents and the worsening economic crisis in

Puerto Rico, we cannot expect these youngsters to be free of conflict or to refrain from transforming traditional values.

On the other hand, many of these same youngsters, particularly the *salseros*, as lovers of latin dance music – mainly from the lower class – are called, were surprised to find the accelerated pace of Americanization on the island; in some ways they feel that they are more Puerto Rican than their *roquero*, that is, rock-music-loving, more middle-class cousins who never left. Their experience belies the island government's claim cited above, that 'The Puerto Ricans who return and their descendants . . . were exposed to a culture and life style completely different from ours' (Junta de Planificación 1980). *Salseros* often complain that it is easier to find rock-music radio stations and discothèques in Puerto Rico than any that feature latin *salsa*. It seems easier for the government to blame the island's cultural upheaval on the returnees than on the unfettered US penetration of island media and markets. The adolescents make a convenient scapegoat, and they suffer for it. In Tato La Viera's play *Am-e-Ricam* (1985), his poem 'nuyorican' accurately captures their feelings:

> . . .
> ahora regreso, con un corazón
> boricua, y tú, me desprecias,
> me miras mal,
> me atacas mi hablar,
> mientras comes mcdonalds en
> discotecas americanas,
> y no pude bailar la salsa
> en san juan, la que yo
> bailo en mis barrios
> lleno de tus costumbres,
> así que, si tú no me quieres,
> pues yo tengo un puerto rico
> sabrosísimo para buscar
> refugio en Nueva York,
> y en muchos otros callejones
> que honran tu presencia,
> preservando todas tus
> costumbres, así que,
> por favor, no me hagas
> sufrir, sabes.
>
> . . .
>
> [now I return, with a Puerto

me, you look at me funny,
you attack the way I talk,
while you eat McDonalds in
american discotheques,
and I couldn't dance salsa
in San Juan, the one that I
dance in my ghettoes
full of your customs,
so, if you don't want me,
well I have a super delicious
Puerto Rico to find
refuge in New York,
and in many other alleyways
that honor your presence,
preserving all your
customs, so,
please, don't make me
suffer, you know.]

The Future of Spanish and English in Puerto Rico

Nothing represents the transformation that the migrants represent better than the teens' opinions about the future of Spanish in Puerto Rico. A commentator's prediction that Spanish will not be spoken on the island in 50 years found support among the bilinguals in Puerto Rico; approximately 40 percent either agreed with the prediction, thought it possible, or did not know. Even though most of the group were of the opinion that Spanish *will* be spoken in Puerto Rico in 50 years, it is more significant that the majority were not distressed by the prospect of a non-Spanish-speaking Puerto Rico in the future: 56 percent stated that it would not bother them if the prediction were to come true. This differs radically from the response of the East Harlem residents, 96 percent of whom believed 'Spanish should be maintained in Puerto Rico'. The difference between the 'should' and 'will' wordings may account for most of the 50 percent difference, but there is the possibility that the young bilinguals in Puerto Rico have extended their acceptance of a Puerto Rican identity without Spanish to include a Puerto Rico without Spanish. Why should this occur in Puerto Rico and not New York? Undoubtedly the differences in the groups offer a partial explanation; for example, only English-dominant teenagers constituted the Puerto Rican sample, whereas the East Harlem residents covered a wide range of age groups, mainly Spanish-dominant. Furthermore, it is not difficult to understand why cultural issues tend to be idealized in New York's alienating ghettos. This phenomenon has been noted often in Nuyorican poetry which abounds in lush, warm images of a 'tropical paradise' Puerto Rico (Algarín and Piñero 1975). Perhaps the teens we interviewed in Puerto Rico believed that Puerto Rico should remain Spanish-speaking before they migrated to the island; they may have changed their opinion after confronting the reality of the impressive economic power of English on the island.

Since almost half of the Puerto Rico sample *did* care if Spanish were not spoken in Puerto Rico, we were intrigued by the variables that might account for the intragroup difference in attitude. Despite the fact that the most opposing attitudes toward Puerto Rico vs. the US and Spanish vs. English were held by two females (that is, one female was the most pro-US and English but another was the most pro–Puerto Rico and Spanish), gender is the variable that promises to provide the most rewarding explanations of the difference within a group. Although the majority of the males and females agreed on most questions, there were several indicators of greater female conservatism in matters of language loyalty. For example, the only students who stated that English monolinguals could *not* be considered Puerto Rican were women. Also, females supported the notion that Spanish is indispensable to Puerto Rican identity 18 percent more than the males (48 percent vs. 30 percent). In addition, whereas the women were equally divided as to whether or not they would care if Spanish were spoken in Puerto Rico in 50 years, the men showed less ambivalence: 67 percent of them would not care. Although our sample was too limited to allow us to assert that language loyalty is stronger among Puerto Rican bilingual females than males, there is enough sociolinguistic evidence of female concern for maintaining appropriate linguistic norms in this and other communities to suggest that further investigation will corroborate our initial findings (Labov 1972; Trudgill 1974; Zentella 1987). The appropriate norms may be the most conservative in the community, or they may be the ones on the cutting edge of change. In either case, women seem to take the language pulse of the community, perhaps to guide their children accordingly.

In our study of growing up bilingual in New York City (1981), we found that older migrant women were the most likely to speak Spanish in their social networks and the least likely to be bilingual. In contrast, although younger women tended to become English-dominant as rapidly as their brothers, their passive knowledge of Spanish surpassed that of their male siblings, as did their code-switching skill. The language proficiency and attitudes of each age-and gender-related network reflected the totality of their cultural experience in the US. Males, who were more likely to go beyond the confines of their buildings and blocks, acquired the English fluency and skills, particularly in Black English Vernacular, necessary for their participation in other networks. Older women and their female charges were more limited to house and childcare responsibilities and were responsible for contacts with the family in Puerto Rico; these activities maintained their links to Spanish. In addition to being socialized in the norms for appropriate Spanish usage, the younger women became keenly aware of the survival value of English in the world of education, housing, social services, and employment. They demonstrate and reflect their ability to maneuver in public and private domains, both of which require Spanish and English, by becoming fluent bilinguals and excellent code switchers. When they move to Puerto Rico, the latter style is still their badge of in-group membership with other Nuyoricans, but, in addition, they adopt the norms that stress the link between Puerto Rican identity and fluent Spanish for communication in the wider community. Undoubtedly, other factors, particularly age of arrival in Puerto Rico, combine with gender (those who arrive during their preteens or pre-'hang-out' years generally seem to experience less conflict with the language and customs than those who arrive between 15 and 18 years old) to provide a better picture of the differences among the returnees. Most important, until longitudinal studies are conducted, we do not know if these students, male and female alike, will change their minds about the role of Spanish in Puerto Rican culture in a few years, after they try to enter the work force in Puerto Rico and take on other adult roles.[7]

Language-Policy Issues

As the data stand now, we can imagine the reaction to what we have presented of those whose every fiber cries out against the vision of a non-Spanish-speaking Puerto Rico. Those in Puerto Rico who can exert some influence on policy must be able to move beyond the initial reaction of shock without rushing to support policies that represent the values of a well-educated and prosperous class who may posture about the inviolability of Puerto Rico's Spanish identity while they cultivate and cherish their own bilinguality. The clash between what some preach and what they practice came to the public's attention during the March 1982 polemic over Senator Peña Clos's legislation in favor of outlawing instruction carried out in English in all the public and private schools in Puerto Rico (Morales 1982). Although many applauded the Senator's efforts to bring the private schools back into the Spanish fold, others questioned his sincerity when they learned that he and his children were educated in English in Puerto Rico. The legislation was doomed from the beginning because most leaders of all political persuasions send their children to private schools where instruction is in English. Furthermore, the last 45 years of educational policy in Puerto Rico prove that the elimination of teaching in English does not necessarily bring about an improvement in the teaching of Spanish.

The truth is that Puerto Rican youngsters on both sides of the ocean are trapped in educational systems that produce failure (Santiago 1984). The bilingual programs that only some of them get to attend are, on the whole, neither well funded nor well supported and are limited to a deficit model, although many are successful despite these limitations. If the returnees I met in Puerto Rico had been able to learn to read and write in Spanish in the US, they would not have needed bilingual education in Puerto Rico. If Puerto Ricans on

the island learned English in the English classes that are required of all students in every grade, they would not have to fall behind when they transfer to the mainland. Students in the US and Puerto Rico want to learn English as well as Spanish, and too many feel that they are not learning either well enough.

Conclusion: Towards an Adequate Policy

What, then, is a viable language policy for Puerto Ricans? I have tried to convey some of the unique features of the situation which force us to discard traditional models and to question vested ideologies. Instead, we start from the premise that the Puerto Rican community differs from the more stable European immigrant communities of the late nineteenth and early twentieth centuries. In addition, there are different classes in the Puerto Rican community and different social realities for each class, not to mention for each racial and gender grouping within each class, both here and in Puerto Rico. Up to now the positions that have enjoyed the most favor have been articulated by the most organized and powerful group, but we have not heard from the majority. For that majority of Puerto Ricans – who are lower working class – migration and reverse migration in response to the vagaries of a fluctuating interlocking economy are a fact of life and a matter of survival. Their pursuit of English, Spanish, and a dual cultural identity may be anathema to secure professional politicos, but it is essential to their survival and should not be judged apart from that sobering truth. Educational policy makers in particular must grapple with this complexity and reject inadequate objectives and methodologies, including that of limiting bilingual education to a transitional model. As much as it hurts their vision of what they wish were true, they must acknowledge the impact of repeated migration. This requires acceptance of a dual US–Puerto Rican identity and of what Attinasi has called 'interpenetrating bilingualism'.

The fluid and creative use of all the environmental language resources at hand without purist separation of languages and without wholesale condemnation of the varieties spoken either by uneducated Spanish speakers or English speakers, including Black English vernacular (Attinasi 1983: 10).

That is what some support in the US as the only successful avenue to oral and literate proficiency in Standard Spanish as well as Standard English, but can we expect Puerto Rico to embrace it? The political stakes in Puerto Rico are so high that that which unaffected linguists can view dispassionately, that is, language change, shift, even extinction, cannot be divorced from the historical struggle against colonial domination. Given the highly charged status issue and the assumption that bilingualism paves the road for statehood, it should not surprise us to find fervent supporters of bilingual education in the US who question the concept in Puerto Rico. Leading members of the recently (1985) organized 'Comité pro Defensa del Vernáculo' [committee for the Defense of the Vernacular] have published numerous articles and sponsored various conferences in which they rail against cultural schizophrenia, impoverishment of the language, and what they view as the dangerous repercussions of biculturalism. Among their solutions is, on the one hand, strong support for maintenance bilingual education for all Puerto Ricans in the US, but on the other hand, a limited transitional approach in Puerto Rico that emphasizes Spanish in bilingual programs for migrants. Is this a hypocritical stance, or one that accurately reflects the different realities? An adequate answer must be based on future comparative ethnographic and attitudinal studies, now sorely lacking.

Appendix: Excerpt from 'Dos Worlds – Two Mundos', by Henry I. Padron

Cuántos tendrán que
    pasar
until we realize
lo que está pasando
people moving
to and fro
todos siempre
llamándonos 'bro'
    qué pasa

raza
Qué pasa
con mi raza
lots of party
lots of laughter
Always somethin
    hapnin
Porqué sera
que nuestro futuro
ya preparado esta
without us having
    a say
on what affects
us from day to day
Quizás you don't
understand lo que
está pasando
    porqué es que nuestra
lengua
is slowly disappearing
Es la programación
que le han dado
a nuestra nación
Nuestra juventud en tremendo
    lío estan
they don't know from
where they vienen
y no saben to where they van
Aunque muchos
listos y muy bien preparados
    están
Trying to understand this system
mejor dicho cistern
can cause you mucho pain.
Puede causar un tremendo
strain en tu brain.....

English translation:
How many will have to
    pass by
until we realize
what is happening
people moving
to and fro
everybody always
calling us 'bro'.
what's happening
    race
What's going on
with my race
lots of party
lots of laughter

Always somethin
  hapnin
Why is it
that our future
is prepared already
without us having
  a say
on what affects
us from day to day
Maybe you don't
understand what
is happening
why is it that our
language
is slowly disappearing
It's the programming
that they have done
to our nation
Our youth are in a
  big mess
they don't know from
where they come
and they don't know where
  they're going
Although many are ready
and very well prepared
Trying to understand this system
better yet cistern
can cause you a lot of pain
It can cause a tremendous.
  strain in your brain . . . .

NOTES

1 This article is a revised and expanded version of a paper delivered at the Conference on Perspectives in Bilingual Education, Yeshiva University, 4 June, 1984.

2 The cooperation of the principal of Papa Juan XXIII, Sr. Jesús Sánchez, and that of the bilingual students at Papa Juan and Pedro Albízu Campos secondary schools was invaluable; I owe them a debt of gratitude. Thanks are also due to Jazmin Rivera for her preliminary transcription of the interviews.

3 Initial support for the research was provided by the Hunter College George N. Shuster Fund and an American Psychological Association Short Term Study Grant. It was carried out with the help of a National Endowment for the Humanities Summer Stipend and a research grant from the Professional Staff Congress of the City University of New York.

4 Although Puerto Rican teachers, journalists, and researchers consistently speak/write about 'neoricans', interpreted to mean 'new Puerto Ricans' (Irizarry 1981), that term was unknown to the students.

5 Lack of Spanish fluency may account for some of the returned migrants' reported dissatisfaction with school in Puerto Rico; 'Not only do most of the children of returned migrants hate school but a whopping 62.9% actively dislike their teachers (as compared to 13.3% of children of non-migrants)' (Underhill 1981).

6 Evidence in support of this view appeared in the comments of some 'regulares'. When asked if he would mind if Puerto Rico spoke English only in 50 years, one monolingual Spanish speaking student responded, 'Me encantaría' [I'd love it].

7 A 1981 study of 282 returned migrants (adults) conducted by the University of Puerto Rico's School of Public Health found that it took them six years to get settled (Underhill 1981).

REFERENCES

Algarín, Miguel, and Piñero, Miguel (eds.) (1975). *Nuyorican Poetry: An Anthology of Puerto Rican Words and Feelings*. New York: Morrow.

Attinasi, John (1979). Language attitudes in a New York Puerto Rican community. In *Bilingualism and Public Policy: Puerto Rican Perspectives*. New York: Centro de Estudios Puertorriqueños, City University of New York.

——(1983). Language attitudes and working class ideology in a Puerto Rican barrio of New York. Unpublished manuscript.

Bonilla, Frank (1983). Manos que sobran: work, migration and the Puerto Rican in the 1980s. Paper prepared for the National Puerto Rican Coalition, December.

Casillas Alvarez, Juan (1983). Nuestro espanol es irremplazable. *Claridad*, 24–30 junio: 40.

Ferguson, Charles
(1964). Diglossia. In *Language in Culture and Society*, D. Hymes (ed.). New York: Harper and Row.

Fishman, Joshua
(1966). *Language Loyalty in the United States: The Maintenance and Perpetuating of Non-English Mother Tongues by American Ethnic and Religious Groups*. The Hague: Mouton.

—— (1967). Bilingualism with and without diglossia: diglossia with and without bilingualism. *Journal of Social Issues* 23, 29–38.

——, Cooper R., Ma, R., et al. (1971). *Bilingualism in the Barrio*. Bloomington: Indiana University Press.

Flores, Juan, Attinasi, J., and Pedraza, P., Jr.
(1981). *La Carreta* made a U-turn: Puerto Rican language and culture in the United States. *Daedalus* (Spring), 193–218.

Friedman, Robert
(1982). In Puerto Rico or States, some kids are nowhere. *New York Daily News*, Sunday, May 2.

Ghigliotty, Julio
(1983). Bilingual education said not a matter of language. *San Juan Star*, April 3.

González, José Luís
(1982). Los problemas del idioma en Puerto Rico. *El Nueva Dia*, I de agosto, 6–9.

—— (1983). Identidad y diáspora en nuestra realidad. *El Nueva día*, 21 de agosto, 6–9.

Gumperz, John J.
(1964). Linguistic and social interaction in two communities. In *The Ethnography of Communication*, J. Gumperz and D. Hymes (eds.). *American Anthropologist* 66 (6, pt. II), 137–154.

—— (1976). The sociolinguistic significance of conversational code-switching. Papers on Language and Context. University of California, Berkeley.

Irizarry, María Antonia
(1981). The attitudes of permanent and migrant Puerto Ricans determined by language use. Unpublished manuscript.

Junta de Planificatión de Puerto Rico
(1980). *La Población Inmigrante en Puerto Rico*. Santurce, P.R.: Junta de Planificación.

Labov, William
(1972). *Sociolinguistic Patterns*. Philadelphia: University of Pennsylvania Press.

Lambert, W.E.
(1972). *Language, Psychology, and Culture*. Stanford: Stanford University Press.

Lambert, Wallace, Hodgson, R. C., Gardner, R. C., and Fillenbaum, S.
(1960). Evaluational reactions to spoken languages. *Journal of Abnormal and Social Psychology* 60, 44–51.

Language Policy Task Force
(1980). Social dimensions of language use in East Harlem. Working Paper 7. New York: Centro de Estudios Puertorriqueños, City University of New York.

La Viera, Tato
(1985). *Am-e-Rican*. Houston, Texas: Arte Público.

McClure, Erica
(1977). Aspects of code switching in the discourse of bilingual Mexican-American children. In *Linguistics and Anthropology*, Muriel Saville Troike (ed.), 93–117. Washington, D.C.: Georgetown University Press.

Morales, Carlos M.
(1982). El Idioma y el Supremo Federal. *El Nueva Dia*, 27 enero, 25.

Pedraza, Pedro, Attinasi, J., and Hoffman, G.
(1980). Rethinking diglossia. Language Policy Task Force Working Paper 9. New York: Centro de Estudios Puertorriqueños.

Poplack, Shana
(1979). 'Sometimes I'll start a sentence in Spanish Y TERMINO EN ESPANOL': towards a typology of code switching. Working Paper 4. New York: Centro de Estudios Puertorriqueños, City University of New York.

Ramos Perea, Israel
(1972). The school, adjustment of return migrant students in Puerto Rican junior high schools. Unpublished Doctoral dissertation, University of Missouri at Columbia.

Rosario, Rubén Del
(1983). Ser Puertorriqueño. *Claridad*, Suplemento En Rojo, 5–11 agosto, 16–17.

Sankoff, D., and Poplack, S.
(1980). A formal grammar of code switching. Technical Report No. 495. Montréal: Centre de Recherches Mathématiques, Université de Montréal.

Santiago Santiago, Isaura
(1984). Language policy and education in Puerto Rico and the continent. *International Education Journal* 1 (1), 39–61.

Seda Bonilla, Eduardo
(1975). Qué Somos: ¿puertorriqueños, neorriqueños or niuyorriqueños? *The Rican: Journal of*

Contemporary Puerto Rican Thought 2 (2–3), 81–107.

Tió, Salvador
(1982). *Sobre la lengua*. El Nueva Dia, 26 enero, 24.

Trudgill, Peter
(1974). *Sociolinguistics: An Introduction*. New York: Penguin.

Underhill, Connie
(1981). Impact of the returned migrant. *San Juan Star Magazine*, September 20, 1–5, 15.

Valdés, Guadalupe
(1981). Code-switching as deliberate verbal strategy. In *Latino Language and Communicative Behavior*, R.P. Durán (ed.), pp. 95–108. Norwood, NJ: Ablex.

Vélez, Adelina
(1983). No es puertorriqueno. *El Mundo*, 24 junio.

Zentella, Ana Celia
(1981). Language variety among Puerto Ricans. In *Language in the U.S.A.*, Charles Ferguson and S. Heath (eds.). London: Cambridge University Press.

——(1985). The value of bilingualism: code switching in the Puerto Rican community. In *The Language of Inequality*, Joan Manes and Nessa Wolfson (eds.). Berlin: Mouton.

——(1986). Language minorities and the national commitment to foreign language competency: resolving the contradiction. *ADFL Bulletin* 17 (3), April.

——(1987). Language and female identity in the Puerto Rican community. In *Women and Language in Transition*, Joyce Penfield (ed.). Albany: S.U.N.Y. Press.

——(1988). Language Politics in the U.S.A.: the English-Only movement. In *Literature, Language and Politics in the 80's*, Betty J. Craige (ed.). Athens: University of Georgia Press.

14

A Place Called Home: A Queer Political Economy of Mexican Immigrant Men's Family Experiences

Lionel Cantú

Driving the Interstate 5 Freeway, near San Diego and the San Onofre border checkpoint, there are large yellow signs graphically depicting a fleeing family (father leading, mother, and child – legs flailing behind). The almost surreal signs are meant to warn motorists of the danger of "illegal" immigrant families trying to cross the busy lanes. This image reveals not only the extreme risks that many immigrants are willing to take to get to the United States but also the way in which we imagine these immigrants. While most motorists probably do not think of a sexual message when they see the warning sign, it's there for us to see; if we only really look. The sign is symbolic at multiple levels: a nuclear family unit, heteronormative in definition, a threat to the racial social order by virtue of its reproductive potential. The sign is also symbolic of the current state of international migration studies: sexuality is an implicit part of migration that has been overlooked – ignored.

In this chapter I examine some of the ways in which sexuality, understood as a dimension of power, has shaped the lives, intimate relationships, and migratory processes of Mexican men who immigrate to the United States.[1] More specifically, I utilize ethnographic data to examine how traditional family relations and alternative support systems such as "chosen families" (Weston 1991) influence migration among Mexican immigrant men who have sex with men (MSMs). The men whom I interviewed and introduce in this essay had a variety of sexual identities both prior to and after migration. An important part of my research, therefore, is to examine from a queer materialist perspective dimensions that shape the social relations of families of origin and families of choice and thus, the intimate context by which identity itself is shaped. I argue for a theoretical move toward a *queer political economy* in order to understand the dynamics that shape "the sexuality of migration" and the fluidity of identities in a global context. In the first section of this chapter I briefly discuss how I conceptualize this theoretical framework (specific to the issues discussed here). I then discuss the ways in which these theoretical concepts are grounded in the everyday experiences of Mexican immigrant men.

Queering the Political Economy of Family and Migration

Queer theory, a conceptual framework that by its very logic resists definition and stability (Jagose 1996), has become both an area of growing influence and an entrenched resistance in the social sciences. These tensions and contradictions are due in part to an increased focus on issues of identity (including that of nation, race/ethnicity, gender, and sexuality) among scholars from a variety of disciplines with different theoretical perspectives and empirical concerns. Yet these tensions are rooted in queer theory itself, descended from the more modernist concerns of early gay- and lesbian-studies scholars and the postmodern influence of semiotics and the work of Foucault.

Queer theorists more closely aligned with the semiotic tradition have built upon Foucault's assertion that sexualities and identities can only be understood through discursive strategies and an "analytics of power" that examines the multiple sites where normalization occurs through discourse and knowledge production. (Cousins and Hussain 1984; Foucault 1990 [1978]; Martin 1988). However, an analytics of power restricted purely to an examination of textual discourse, void of a material context, is obviously limited. There are, of course, numerous normalizing sites, including the body (which has received particular attention as an inscribed "text"), but my concern here lies with that of the family. As I demonstrate in the following discussion, the family and the home (or household) is a site where normalizing rules of gender and sexual conduct and performance are taught on a daily basis.

More recently there has been a move toward a queer materialist paradigm that asserts that "all meanings have a material base" from which cultural symbols and identities are constructed (Morton 1996; see also Gluckman and Reed 1997 and Seidman 1996). Furthermore, it is "the examination of the complex social conditions (division of labor, production, distribution, consumption, class) through which sexual preference/orientation, hierarchy, domination, and protest develop dialectically at a particular time and place" (Bennett 1996). Thus, in this section I briefly outline a queer materialist paradigm for analyzing the social relations between family, migration, and sexual identity.

The link between "gay" identity and socioeconomic forces[2] has been asserted by gay- and lesbian-studies scholars since at least the late

1960s with the work of Mary McIntosh (1968) and Jeffrey Weeks (1977). In his seminal article "Capitalism and Gay Identity," John D'Emilio (1993) asserts that the modern construction of a gay identity is the result of capitalist development and the migration of homosexuals to urban gay communities in San Francisco, Los Angeles, Chicago, and New York after World War II. In a similar vein, Gayle Rubin argues that gay identity is a result of the rural to urban migration of "homosexually inclined" men and women where communities and economic niches (which Rubin calls a "gay economy") were formed based on a shared identity as an "erotic minority" (1993 [1984]).

Key to these arguments is an understanding of how capitalist development has shaped and transformed *family* relations and structure. D'Emilio argues, "Only when *individuals* began to make their living through wage labor, instead of parts of an interdependent family unit, was it possible for homosexual desire to coalesce into a personal identity – an identity based on the ability to remain outside the heterosexual family and to construct a personal life based on one's attraction to one's own sex" (1993:470).

D'Emilio's argument thus expanded the historical materialist understanding of the patriarchal heterosexual-family structure long argued by feminists (cf. Donovan 1992; Hennessy and Ingraham 1997) and even Engels (1993 [1942]) and made more evident the relationship between the political economy of the modern family and sexual identity. This argument asserted that the economic interdependence of family members constrained gay identity formation and that these bonds were loosened by capitalist development.

Yet, the "capitalism/gay identity" argument is limited in several important ways. First, it fails to capture the complexity of stratified-power relations beyond a simple class argument even if held to the Western-industrial experience. Racial/ethnic dimensions are notably absent and must also be considered especially when family-economic interdependence plays so central a role in the paradigm. In the case of international migration, family-economic interdependence may continue to play an important role in relations and identity even while reconfigured through migratory processes and when new systems of support are created. Second, while most social constructionists agree that gay identity is linked with capitalist development, this body of literature fails to capture the multiplicity and fluidity of sexual identity and fails to conceptualize capitalist development as a global phenomenon with implications for sexuality and migratory patterns on a global scale. Unfortunately, migration-studies scholars have in turn ignored this literature marked as "gay studies" and have not examined how sexuality may shape migratory processes.

There are a number of theoretical-migration models that postulate the reasons why migration begins or the conditions that perpetuate it.[3] Traditionally, microlevel theories focus either on the rational choice of the individual or on the household;[4] while macrolevel theories examine the structural forces of capitalist societies such as the labor market, trade relations, or economic intervention by nations.[5]

In the 1980s other "social" factors also began to receive analytical attention, but not until Sylvia Pedraza's 1991 article, "Women and Migration: The Social Consequences of Gender," were feminist concerns taken seriously by migration scholars. Part of the reason for the delay (and continued resistance) in recognizing gender as an important dimension of analysis within migration studies has been the limited scope through which migration scholars have viewed the "economic" realm. For many, gender was perceived as a social factor subsumed by the economic or considered to be a variable of analysis, like age or education, that simply needed to be added to migration studies.

Feminist scholars, however, assert that gender is a much more complex dimension. For instance, while migration scholars argue that social networks and modes of incorporation such as ethnic communities and economies are an important aspect of personal transition linking migrants to social, cultural, familial, and economic resources, most studies have conceptualized social networks either in terms of familial relationships or in terms of men's labor networks, without theorizing how gender itself might shape these relations. As Pierrette Hondagneu-Sotelo demonstrates in

her book *Gendered Transitions* (1994), gender is more than a variable of migration; rather, it is a dimension of power relations that shapes and organizes migration. Similarly, sexuality is a dimension of power that I contend also shapes and organizes processes of migration and modes of incorporation.

In this chapter I examine the relations between materialist forces, family, migration, and sexual identity. A queer materialist or political economy paradigm is central to my analysis, for such a paradigm allows identity to be understood not only as a social construction but also as being fluid – that is, constructed and reconstructed depending upon social location and political economic context. Furthermore, my analysis is informed by what Anzaldúa (1987) refers to as "mestiza consciousness" (also sometimes referred to as border theory), in which the incongruities of binary systems are made visible as are the intersections of multiple marginal positions and relations of power. My analysis is thus centered on "the borders" in its conscious effort to incorporate structural dimensions of "the borderlands" into an identity that is constructed and draws meaning from marginality.

Border Crossers: Family, Migration, Identity

The immigrant men I interviewed for my research ranged in age from their early twenties to early forties and lived in the greater Los Angeles area. I met these men during my dissertation research fieldwork from 1997 through December 1999 by making initial contacts through organizations, fliers, and friends and then using a snowball sampling technique to meet others. While each of these men's stories was in its own way unique, there were also similarities that became more evident as my research progressed.

Most of the men came from the Pacific states of Mexico, and approximately two-thirds came from the state of Jalisco. About half described their communities of origin as small cities or towns, with only a couple describing their origins as rural; migration to larger cities (such as Guadalajara or border cities such as Tijuana) prior to migrating to the United States was also a common experience.[6] All the men included here were sixteen years old or older when they immigrated. Most came from lower middle-class Mexican backgrounds[7] and had at least a high-school education. Like many of their straight counterparts, many were undocumented. Only two of the men I met were not working at the time of their interview; one man was unable to work due to health reasons related to AIDS/HIV, and the other was looking for work. Several of the men were actually holding down more than one job; one full-time and one part-time. The average annual income of the men was between twenty and twenty-five thousand dollars. Their fluency in English was relative to their time in the United States, but none of the men were completely fluent.[8] Due in part to this, the men interviewed reported daily lives that were for the most part Spanish speaking. In addition, nearly all estimated that more than 75 percent of their social circles were Latino.

In the following paragraphs I introduce seven of the twenty men I interviewed formally.[9] I selected these particular interviews as representative of the range of experiences related to me. However, the interview excerpts I have included should not be considered representative of all Mexican-immigrant men to the United States who have sex with men – the diversity of experiences is far greater than can be captured here. The men I have included identified as either bisexual or homosexual (gay) at the time of the interviews. In addition, I do not include the voice of transgendered Mexican immigrants, although some of the men do have experience with cross-dressing.[10] Yet the voices represented here do reveal the complexity of the sexuality of migration and the importance of including sexuality in our analysis. I will first provide a general description of these men and then discuss their experiences as they relate to family, migration, and sexual identity.

Lalo is a thirty-three-year-old immigrant from Guadalajara, Jalisco. The fifth of nine children, Lalo comes from what he describes as a "very poor" class background. He migrated to the United States in 1983 and is a legal resident who currently lives in Fountain Valley.

Armando is a thirty-two-year-old Mexican national born in the state of Jalisco where he spent eight years in a seminary studying to be a priest. He is the oldest of eight children (four boys and four girls). He moved to the United States in 1995 and is an undocumented immigrant. He currently lives in Santa Ana but was living in Los Angeles with his brother when we met.

Gabriel is a twenty-three-year-old undocumented immigrant who has lived in the Orange County area for the past five years. He works as a medical assistant. The fourth of six children, Gabriel moved to the United States from Nayarit, Mexico in 1993 when he was eighteen. Gabriel is now living in Fullerton.

Paco is the youngest of six children, four sisters and a brother. His father died three months after he was born and Paco was raised by his mother and older siblings. Paco is a legal resident of the United States although he immigrated illegally in 1990.

Roberto is in his early forties and has lived in the United States since migrating from Mexico in 1994. The fourth of five children, he comes from a prestigious and well-to-do family in Nayarit, Mexico. Although never married, Roberto has a teenaged son who lives in Mexico with the son's mother. Roberto now lives in the San Fernando Valley and works as an AIDS educator for a Latino community organization.

Manuel is thirty years old, identifies as bisexual, and currently is unemployed although he worked as a registered nurse in Guadalajara, Mexico. He is the third of eight children (seven boys and one girl) and grew up in Tlaquepaque, a town famous for its artisans and now considered part of the Guadalajara metro area. A Jehovah's Witness, he considers himself to be very religious. Due to his HIV status, he moved to the United States in 1996 to be with his family and is an undocumented immigrant. He lives with his family in Santa Ana, who know of his condition but are not aware of his sexual identity.

Carlos migrated from Guadalajara in 1990 and is currently seeking political asylum in the United States based on his sexual orientation. Because

Carlos was an active member of the Democratic Revolutionary Party (PRD), an opposition party to Mexico's ruling Institutional Revolutionary Party (PRI), Carlos fears that he may be imprisoned or murdered if he returns to Mexico. He now lives in Los Angeles.

Family Life in Mexico

Social scientists have historically given great attention to the role of *la familia* in Latino culture. Scholarship often points to Latino "familism" – defined as the value and preservation of the family over individual concerns (Moore and Pachon 1985; Williams 1990) – as the contentious source of both material and emotional support and patriarchal oppression. The stereotype is problematic for a number of reasons, not the least of which is the fact that the same argument could be made of most families regardless of their cultural context.[11] Thus, in this section, while I discuss how the early family lives of Mexican immigrant MSMs influenced migratory processes, my aim is not to reproduce a cultural pathology of *la familia* but, rather, to examine the family as a site where normative constructions of gender and sexuality are reproduced and in which the dynamics of migration are materially embedded.

During my interviews, most of the men remembered their lives as children in Mexico fondly.[12] Yet, even when memories of early family life were positive, the daily lessons of normative masculinity learned by these men often resulted in emotional conflicts. I asked them to share with me their memories of family life and educational experiences in order to understand more fully the processes by which normative gender roles and sexuality are learned. Most early childhood memories were shared with smiles and consisted of generally carefree days: playing typical games and going to school. Most of the men also reported that they were good students who received awards for their scholarship and genuinely seemed to have enjoyed school. However, even men such as Paco, who reported that his childhood was "a great time ... a very beautiful stage of my life," expressed a sense of inner conflict rooted in normative definitions of masculinity.

These conflicts were even more pronounced for men such as Lalo, whose memories of early life in Mexico were not good ones. Recounting his childhood Lalo told me,

> As I child I was very mischievous. I was sexually abused when I was seven by the neighbor, a man of forty. It was a childhood experience that affected me greatly. This person continued to abuse me, he would give me money, later I would go looking for him myself and I was like his "boyfriend" until I was nine. I knew what he was doing was wrong so I never told anyone.

Paternostro (1998) reports that child sexual abuse by a family member is a common phenomenon in Latin America (whether it is more prevalent than other countries is debatable). In fact Lalo was not the only man I interviewed who was sexually abused as a child, but he was the most forthcoming about the experience.[13] Later in the interview he explained that he had also been abused by two older male cousins and that when he told his father about the abuse, his father's response was to rape him for being a "*maricón*."

None of the sexually abused men, including Lalo, remember connecting these experiences to homosexuality at the time of their occurrence; in part because they didn't really know what homosexuality was. Lalo explained that although he had never heard the word "homosexual," words such as "*maricón*" and "*joto*" were commonly heard in his home. However, Lalo related these terms to effeminate men or *vestidas* like the man in his neighborhood who dressed like a woman. Many informants related similar experiences. Carlos explained, for example, "Across from us lived the town *maricón*. In every town there is the drunk and the *maricón*, and the *maricón* lived across the street." As children the question of what a *maricón* was remained somewhat of a mystery; although they knew it wasn't anything "good." For instance, it wasn't until later that Lalo started to understand what "homosexual" meant. He explained,

> After about the age of twelve or thirteen there was a lot of sexual play among the boys of the *colonia*. We would masturbate one another. There were about twelve of us in the group and we would form a circle and masturbate

one another. Later, couples would form and we would penetrate one another. Now they are all grown up and married but there was a lot of sexual play when we were kids. . . . There were some boys who would refuse to join us, saying, "that's for *maricones*" or "you're going to be a *joto* or a woman." It was then that I started to understand but I never thought that I was going to be like a woman.

Masculine discourse that devalues the feminine and equates homosexuality to the feminine, is of course, not particular to Mexican culture (cf. Fellows 1996 and Murray and Roscoe 1998). However, as Lalo explained, homosexuality and femininity are not popularly understood as synonymous.[14] "Being a *joto* is to not be man. Neither a man nor a woman, it is to be an abomination, a curse." Prieur's (1998) recent work on male-to-female transgendered residents of Mexico City supports Lalo's analysis and suggests that class perspectives are an important dimension of its construction. Thus the relationship of homosexuality to the feminine is more complex than a synonymous equation implies. Homosexuality is not only the opposite of masculinity, it is a corruption of it, an unnatural form that by virtue of its transgression of the binary male/female order poses a threat that must be contained or controlled.

The liminal/marginal location of homosexuality, perhaps best understood as shaped by what Almaguer (1993) refers to as a sex/gender/power axis, is reproduced through messages in everyday life. Discussing his daily chores at home, Paco explained,

> My duties at home in particular, well, they were almost never designated to us. I liked very much to sweep, mop, wash the dishes, and when [my mother and sisters] would make cake I always liked to be there when they were preparing it. But, only when my mom and my sisters were there, because my brother would often be in the United States. I always liked to help my mom and my sisters, but when my brother would get there, I always had to hide or not do it because he would tell me "You are not a woman to be doing that, that's for the *maricones*." Then, since I was scared of him, I wouldn't do it anymore. But it was what I liked to do, up till

now; I like cleaning very much and chores like that. I like to cook very much, I like to have everything clean – I've always liked that.

When I asked Paco to discuss the issue of "women's work" in more detail, he explained,

> In Mexico they say "Oh, a homosexual person or a *maricón* or a *joto* are those persons that are dressed like women." They always have a little of that mentality. For example, there were times that a guy named Luis would pass by and he always left his nails long and his hair long like a woman. He had a bag, and he would put on women's pants or a woman's blouse, and he might have put on make-up but not a lot, but obviously he would go around like a woman. Then all the people, well, they said things, but in my family one time I heard my mother call him, she would call them *frescos* (fresh), there goes this *fresco*, there goes that *fresco*, I would hear my mom say that. Then, I would get angry when I would hear that, because I would say "Well, I am not like that, but I am attracted to young men."

Armando expressed learning the same type of sex/gender message through child's play. Armando explained that he liked to play with paper dolls and more than anything liked to cut out the clothes, yet he hid when he did so. When I asked him why, Armando replied, "It's the only game I remember playing secretly. I knew my parents wouldn't like it. I thought it was perfectly normal, it was only bad because it was something that little girls do."

The struggle that Paco and Armando relate in attempting to negotiate the perceived contradictions of sex, gender, and sexual identities was a common theme of many of my interviews. Participants expressed a certain sense of isolation or "not belonging" and not wanting to disappoint their families. Even learning to emulate normative gender and sexual performances was not, in itself, sufficient to resolve these conflicts. For some men, these tensions were a catalyst for migration itself.

Leaving Home

One of the questions that I asked immigrant interviewees was what their top three reasons for immigrating were. After analyzing the answers given, it became clear that sexuality was indeed an influencing reason for migration and that "family" dynamics were often linked to these reasons. However, understanding how sexuality actually influenced these decisions was not always as clear-cut as having people respond, "it was my sexuality" – although that sometimes happened. For example, Lalo told me, "Ninety percent of the reason I migrated was because of my sexuality." Such reasons obviously resonate with D'Emilio's (1993) and Rubin's (1993 [1984]) models of rural to urban migration by gay men and women seeking greater anonymity and gay life in the cities. Yet, in order to understand more fully how sexuality is linked to other socioeconomic dimensions, one must attempt to connect the micro with the meta and macro dimensions of life. That is to say, one cannot separate individual reasons for migration from the larger processes that shape people's everyday lives and perceived choices. Several themes did arise from the interviews, sometimes from the same source, and these themes are implicated in a queer political economy in different ways.

For example, all of the men I interviewed, in one form or another, gave financial reasons for migrating to the United States. And indeed, immigration scholars have traditionally placed a great deal of emphasis on economic reasons for migration, yet to a great degree their vision of the economic realm is extremely limited. The social inequalities of sexuality, like race and gender, are integrally linked to the economic structures of society. Groups that are marginalized as sexual minorities are constrained by the limits of discrimination and prejudice that may limit their socioeconomic opportunities. Thus, when immigrants, who are a sexual minority, say that they immigrated for financial reasons, part of the analysis must include sexuality. For instance, even the person I interviewed in Mexico who owned his own pesticide and fertilizer business felt the constraints of heterosexism. Business networks, he explained, depend upon having the right image, which means a wife, children, and social events tied to church and school. Clearly, as a gay man he was outside this world. His class privilege and the fact the he is his own boss, however,

permit him to remain in Mexico relatively free from some of the pressures that drive others to migrate.[15]

Thus, while men such as Lalo clearly migrate to escape a sense of sexual oppression, for others the decision to migrate to the United States is influenced by a combination of sexual liberation and economic opportunities. For example, Gabriel moved to the United States from Nayarit, Mexico, when he was eighteen but explained that he had begun to prepare himself for immigrating at sixteen. When I asked him why, he explained that he had two major reasons for coming to the United States:

> First, I wanted to get a better level of education. And the second reason was sexuality. I wanted to be able to define myself and have more freedom with respect to that. I wanted to come here to live, not to distance myself from my family but to hide what I already knew I had. I knew I was gay but I thought I might be able to change it. I needed to come here and speak to people, to learn more about it, because in Mexico it's still very taboo. There isn't so much liberation.

Gabriel's experience reveals how the tension of sexual desire versus "not wanting to distance" oneself from family may serve as a migratory "push." Yet while he clearly moved to the United States seeking a more liberal sexual environment, it was not just a personal matter, it was also because he felt he had limited economic opportunities as a gay man in Mexico. Staying in Mexico might very well have meant either attempting to create a heteronormative family or dealing with social and economic discrimination as a gay man.

Sometimes homosexual relationships might have subtle influences such as serving to establish or expand social networks or they might have a more direct influence driving migration itself. For instance, Roberto explained to me that he was quite happy with his life in Mexico as a civil servant but that people had begun to gossip about his sexual orientation and he feared for his job security, especially since he had recently learned that he was HIV positive. Roberto had met a man from the United States who was vacationing in Mexico and had maintained a friendly relationship with the man. When the American suggested to Roberto that he move to the United States to live with him, Roberto took advantage of the opportunity and moved to Los Angeles. Although he is no longer in a relationship with the American, they continue to be friends. In such a case, new (transnational) social bonds are created similar to the kinship networks that migration scholars argue facilitate migration, yet these are not blood-based but, rather, based on affiliation-transnational gay networks.

Finding Their Way Home

Adapting to life in the United States is difficult for any migrant, but for immigrants like Lalo, who migrate to the United States expecting a gay utopia, the reality of life in the United States can be quite a blow. Indeed Lalo had returned to Mexico for two years after first migrating to the United States because of his disillusionment, returning only when he realized that his prospects as a gay man were limited in Mexico. Thus, for Lalo, home was no longer Jalisco. While there are a number of important aspects of an immigrant's experiences adapting to their new home, in this section I focus on how sexuality might be related to a migrant's adaptation and incorporation. Specifically, I am concerned here with both kin networks and the home as mechanisms for adaptation.

In her discussion of gay and lesbian kin relations Weston (1991) demonstrates how gays and lesbians construct "chosen" families based on shared affinities and relationships of both material and emotional support. Kinship (biological) plays a central role in migration as a means through which immigrants receive support and acquire important knowledge for survival and adaptation (cf. Chavez 1992). While the Mexican men I interviewed often utilized kinship networks to these ends, they also depended upon networks that were similar to those described by Weston. About half of the immigrants I spoke with utilized preexisting gay networks to migrate to the United States. They were like Lalo, who migrated with the help of a gay compatriot already living in Los Angeles, and like Roberto, who came with

the help of a gay American. But even some of those who utilized kin networks for initial migration also used gay networks for meeting other gay Latino men, finding gay roommates, making job contacts, and acquiring other types of information. The existence and use of these alternative networks depended to a large extent on how the men identified sexually, to what extent they were "out of the closet," and, to some extent, on their ability to speak English (and thus expand their networks into the mainstream gay world).

For instance, although Paco migrated and found his first job using kinship networks, he was soon able to develop a gay network as well.

> My second job was in a company where they made pools. I obtained that job through a [gay] friend, an American, who is the person, the third person that I have to thank about my legal status here in this country. He helped me get the job because it was the company of a friend of his. In the morning I would clean the offices and then I would go to the warehouse and take inventory or I would clean the warehouse or cut fiberglass, or things like that. And they paid me well at that time but I worked only a few hours. So after that, since they said "Oh, you clean so well," and they had some very beautiful houses, over in Laguna Beach. Sometimes I would stay over because I could not finish in the weekend. The owners of the company were gay. They would go to San Francisco, or wherever there were going, they always traveled on the weekend, they left me the key, "Here is the stereo and here is the television," and everything like that because I had to sleep over. Then I would go home when they returned on Sundays.

Ironically, Paco is one of the people who assured me that sexuality had not influenced his migratory experiences in the least. This excerpt, however, reveals that gay-social networks were an aid in his finding work. In addition, Paco shares a home with a lesbian niece and has allowed other gay immigrants to stay with him temporarily until they are able to move on.

Carlos also made use of gay networks in a similar manner. When he migrated to the United

States, he first lived for two months in Watsonville, California, with a brother and then went to live in Milwaukee for two years with his two sisters, who are lesbians. He then moved to Los Angeles after meeting and starting a relationship with a gay man. Like Paco, Carlos revealed that his gay friends had helped him find work and even helped him out financially. "Because of my gay friends, I have never gone without," he said.

Both Paco's and Carlos's experiences also point to the fact that sexuality is an important dimension of immigrant-household arrangements. While recent immigration literature has discussed the importance of household arrangements as "landing pads" for migrant adaptation (cf. Chavez 1992, 1994), the sexual dimensions of these arrangements are missing from the analyses. For an individual who has migrated to the United States seeking a more liberal sexual environment, it makes little sense to live in a home constrained by heteronormative relations. While about half of the Mexican men I interviewed originally lived with family members when they migrated, most had formed alternative living arrangements as soon as they were able to. Lalo's home exemplifies this alternative type of arrangement.

When I first met Lalo he was living in Santa Ana in an apartment he shared with three other immigrant men, all gay. Since our first meeting, Lalo has moved twice and has had a number of different roommates, always gay Latino immigrant men. Sometimes the men, especially if they were recent immigrants, would stay only a short time until they found another place to live. It was clear that Lalo's home was a landing pad, but it was one where Latino men could be openly gay, support one another and share information that was essential for adaptation. Although the men did not explicitly define these relations as "family," they did sometimes refer to each other affectionately as siblings (sometimes as "sisters" and sometimes as "brothers"). Regardless of how these relationships were labeled, it was clear that an alternative support system had been created. It is precisely in this type of living arrangement that many men discover the space that transforms the way they think about themselves and their sexual identities.

Migrating Identities

One of the contributions of postmodern (including queer theory) and postcolonial literature is that identity is no longer understood as something inherently fixed and stable. Rather, identity is understood as mutable and plural – that is, the subject is the intersection of multiple identities (race/ethnicity, gender, sexuality, and so forth) that change and have salience at different moments in time and place. Given the dramatic sociospatial changes that immigrants experience, their sexual identities cannot therefore be assumed stable. As Iain Chambers puts it, "identity is formed on the move" (1994:25). The effects of migration upon the sexual identities of Mexican immigrant MSMs are ultimately linked to their emotional and material relationships to their biological families and the degree to which they have been able to resolve the normative sexuality and gender conflicts that fed their desire to migrate.

I asked the men I interviewed if they felt that they had changed at all since migrating to the United States. Nearly all of the men responded with a resounding yes. The changes they described generally centered around racial, gender, sexual, and class identities. Most of the men inevitably referred to a more liberal sexual environment as a reason for their transformation. Migrating to the United States was for many men one step in a series toward what might be called "a journey to the self."[16] For Gabriel, the desire to live in a place where he could develop his human potential as a gay man was a driving force in his decision to immigrate. He added,

> I have two names, Gabriel Luis, and my family calls me Luis. I've always said that Luis is the person who stayed in Mexico. Once I came here, Gabriel was born. Because, like I've told you, once I was here I defined myself sexually and I've changed a lot emotionally, more than anything emotionally, because I found myself.

This journey of self-discovery is intimately linked to resistance to the normative gender and sex regimes I have described earlier. While earlier scholarship asserted that Mexican male sexual identities were based on the active or passive (*activo/pasivo*) role of the participant (where only the passive was deemed homosexual) more recent research, including my own, finds that Mexican sexual identities are more complex.

Most interviewees remembered first being aware of their attraction to boys or men in early childhood. Some remembered being attracted to the same sex as young as age four, but the majority of recollections were a bit later. Carlos remembered, "I was around eight years old. I could recognize the beauty of men. But from then on it was an issue of denial." The pressure to conform, or as Lalo described, "*la lucha de no querer ser gay*" (the struggle of not wanting to be gay) took a toll on most of the men I interviewed but perhaps was most eloquently described by Armando. He explained that he had been tormented by schoolmates after around the fourth grade who would call him *joto* and *maricón*. He stated,

> But I learned how to hide it better, so it wasn't noticeable. I no longer isolated myself, instead I would mix with the troublemakers at school so that their reputation would rub off on me and so no one would tell me anything anymore. A new student arrived who was even more obvious than me and to a certain extent he was my salvation. Everyone focused their attention on him and it was a load off of me. It gave me the opportunity to get closer to the other students and do everything that they did, to act like them, have girlfriends, and not be the "good boy" anymore – to take on the heterosexual role.

Armando would later join a seminary in an attempt to escape his sexual feelings and began to lift weights so that his appearance was more masculine. Eventually, however, he realized he needed to face who he "really" was.

> I feel that I lost a lot of my essence as a homosexual during that time. I see it like that now. At that time I only wanted to be part of a group, to be accepted. It's horrible to feel marginalized, in a corner, abnormal. In my attempts to be like everyone else wanted me to be I lost much of my self.

Two months after migrating to the United States, seeking the freedom to be a gay man, he confessed to a cousin, with whom he was staying, that he was gay. She told him that she accepted and loved him as he was but that he needed to talk to his brothers. Armando told his brothers one by one and they all accepted his homosexuality (although it was by no means easy). He then decided to tell his widowed mother. At the time of our interview it had been five months since he had written his mother a five-page letter explaining his struggle to accept himself. A month later Armando's mother wrote him back asking forgiveness and assuring him that he would have her support and unconditional love. Armando has been able successfully to integrate his calling to service with his desire to be true to himself. He now works as an AIDS educator and program coordinator for an organization that serves gay Latino men.

Like Armando, other men who migrated to the United States also came out to their families and some found acceptance as well. In some of these men's cases it seems that the acceptance is in part tied to a reversal in family roles. Where once they were dependent upon their families for support, now their families are dependent upon them. Thus, while Almaguer (1993) has argued that economic interdependence stifles a gay identity from forming among Latino MSMs, my research reveals that it may actually facilitate familial acceptance. For instance, since migrating to the United States Lalo has also gained acceptance from the family who threw him out of the house. He explained to me that he has sent money to Mexico to have his mother's house repaired and to pay for his brother's tuition and that his family now respects him. Lalo related, "I'm much more secure now. I'm not afraid to say I'm a homosexual. I'm content being gay and I can help others. I'm stronger and have achieved a lot of things."

Thus the transformation in economic roles and physical separation has allowed Lalo the opportunity to be both gay and accepted by his family.

There were, however, a couple of men I interviewed who were openly gay prior to migrating to the United States. In both cases these men had upper-class backgrounds. The difference that class makes in mitigating the effects of homophobia is significant and needs to be studied more closely. For example, when I asked Roberto about his son he laughed out loud and said.

> Oh my son! My son was the product of an agreement. His mother knew that I was gay. My partner of ten years and I lived together [in Tepic, Nayarit] and she lived in front of us. She knew of my relationship with Alejo and the three of us would go out to dance. In a small town, well, it was known that she was the friend of "the boys." We would go out to dance, she would come to our home to watch television, listen to music, or have a drink. Then one day she told me flat out that she wanted to have my baby. Then between the jokes I began to understand and between the jokes we ended up in bed. We had sex for two or three months and one day she called me and told me she was pregnant. I was twenty-three or twenty-four and was completely out of the closet with my family and I didn't care about anything.

Without a doubt, Roberto's class privilege allowed him to not "care about anything" as an openly gay man. In all probability it also shaped his gay-social networks that allowed him to migrate to the United States.

To be clear, for those men who do not have such privileges in Mexico, migrating to the United States does not necessarily afford them these privileges either. While there may be more space to be gay in the United States, migrating has its costs. For example, as Carlos lamented,

> Being away from Mexico creates a strong nationalistic feeling with a lot of nostalgia. You begin to notice how different the system is here than in Mexico, an economic system that changes your life completely – a system where one forgets about other things that in Mexico were a priority. Here one lives life from the perspective of money. Working and making enough money to pay your bills is more important than having friends and doing what you like. In Mexico it's very different. It's more important to have friends. One lives less a slave to the clock. One forgets these things and becoming aware of that has made me very sad.

Discovering the virulence of racism in the United States seems to counterbalance any feelings of sexual liberation. I asked the men, in an open-ended manner, if they had ever experienced discrimination (without defining the type). Nearly all of the men responded in ways similar to Carlos: "For being Latino, for not speaking English perfectly, for the color of my skin." The irony, of course, is that in their attempts to escape one form of bigotry, most of the Mexican men I interviewed discovered that not only had they not entirely escaped it but they now faced another. As Lalo said, "It wasn't true that homosexuals are free, that they can hold hands or that Americans like Mexicans." Under these circumstances the role of a support system becomes all the more important and for queer Latino-immigrant men this often means that new families must be created.

Building Family

I was naively surprised by the responses I received when I asked immigrant men about their future plans. I suppose that I had allowed myself to become so immersed in the migration literature that I was expecting to hear something more along the lines of "return to Mexico and start my own business." More common, however, were responses such as Paco's:

> I want to be anywhere close to the person I love, to support me. If it's in Mexico, a lot better because I would have my family and that person near me. But, more than anything, right now I worry a lot for my own person and for the partner who I think will be what I wait for in my life. And I see myself in a relationship with a lot of affection, and maybe by then, living with that person, together. And maybe even to get married.

In response to my next question, "So your plans for the future are to have a partner?" Paco answered:

> A stable partner, be happy, and give them all my support, and I would help that person shine, succeed in anything I could help. I will try to do it all the time. If he accomplishes more than I have it will make me very happy because in that aspect I am not egotistical. And still more things that are positive;

get more involved in helping people that need me, in every aspect. Be happy, make my partner happy, above all make myself happy, and my family, my friends, all the people that like me, and I like.

This type of response does not exclude dreams of material wealth and entrepreneurship, but it centers and gives priority to affective dimensions – to building new families. The desires for stable relationships reflect not only the difficulty for maintaining such relationships in Mexico but also the isolation that these men feel in the United States. This isolation that gay Mexican immigrant men feel is due in some measure to language difficulties, but racial and class issues also play into it. For instance, Carlos explained to me that although he was in a relationship at the time of our interview he didn't see much of a future in it.

I don't have many expectations for my relationship because my partner is not Latino. I think that, ideally, for a stable relationship I need to be with a Latino...someone who identifies as Latino. Someone intelligent and a little more cultured. Someone who has the capacity to go to an art or photography exhibit and enjoy it. Someone open-minded, open to learning from other cultures and who is financially independent.

The problem, of course, is that the social location of Mexican immigrant MSMs in the United States is a marginal one. Stability is not easily established and financial independence may take years to accomplish, if at all. The problem is exacerbated by the fact that there are few public spaces where Latino gay men can openly meet one another. Thus, creating family or even a sense of community depends in no small part upon the ability of queer Latinos to build a new home with limited resources and external support.

"Who do you turn to for support?" I asked the men I interviewed. The standard response was: "family and friends." Yet it is clear from my discussions with these men, and the data presented here, that these relationships (whether biological or chosen) were sometimes strained, always evolving, and ultimately negotiated. A queer materialist analysis of the experiences of Mexican-immigrant men who have sex with men reveals the ways in which dimensions of family, migration, and sexual identity intersect and are embedded within a political economy. Many of the men interviewed felt marginalized by heteronormative definitions of masculinity reproduced through and embodied in the traditional family. These norms, reproduced in daily activities since childhood, marginalize not only men with "feminine" characteristics but also those able to pass, who were instilled with a fear of discovery. Associations of femininity with homosexuality created a sense of confusion in some men who, although attracted to men, did not identify as feminine. The economic liability that derived from not creating a heteronormative family unit as an adult also influenced the immigration process. These strict gender/sex regimes were powerful enough to drive many men to migrate to the United States in search of a more liberal environment.

A queer political-economy perspective of migration also aids in unveiling how sexuality has shaped processes and strategies for adaptation such as social networks and household arrangements. Alternative relations to biological families, which serve as systems of support, are created based on sexual orientation. The members of these "chosen families" assist one another through the trials and tribulations of being a queer Mexican-immigrant man. Such assistance takes a variety of forms, including helping with migration itself, sharing knowledge and resources such as job information, and even sharing households.

New economic arrangements mean that some men find that they are empowered to come out to their biological families as gay men and maintain a level of acceptance and respect from their loved ones. Shared space is also an important dimension linked to the futures of these gay men. Faced with a sense of isolation and a deep desire to form the stable relationships – which they were prevented from having in Mexico – space becomes the base for adaptation, community, and shared futures. Thus, for many men who have come to identify as gay, new family structures become a means by which dreams may be realized.

Although my focus has been on Mexican-immigrant men, there are larger implications that need to be explored. When we understand sexuality as a dimension of power (that intersects with other dimensions such as race, gender, and class) in which certain groups are privileged over others, then these implications become more visible. For instance, Argüelles and Rivero (1993) argue that some immigrant women have migrated in order to flee violent and/or oppressive sexual relationships or marriage arrangements, which they contest. Little research has been conducted on Latinas in general, far less exists on the intersections of migration and sexuality (regardless of sexual orientation). While it is clear that biological families reproduce normative constructions of gender and sexuality, the ways in which these norms and power relations influence different groups of people in terms of migration and identity is not understood. I hope the research presented here will be a step toward the development of a queer materialist paradigm by which the sexual dimensions of migration can be understood and by which further research may be conducted.

NOTES

1   This chapter represents part of a larger dissertation research project entitled *Border Crossings: Mexican Men and the Sexuality of Migration*. The author gratefully acknowledges the comments and suggestions of the editors and Nancy Naples, as well as the funding support of the Social Science Research Council's Sexuality Fellowship Program and the Ford Foundation, which made this research possible. In addition, the author wishes to express his gratitude to the men who participated in this project.

2   While recent debates between social constructionists and what are sometimes belittlingly called essentialists have heated up with genetic research, I assume that sexuality is more complex than the either/or debates allow for. I therefore focus on the social aspects of sexuality, i.e., the social constructionist perspective. The constructionist argument has also been made

from a cultural perspective. In his classic study of the Sambia of New Guinea, anthropologist Gilbert Herdt (1994 [1981]) examined the cultural meanings of homosexuality and masculinity in a nonindustrial society and demonstrated, through his examination of "boy-inseminating rituals," that meanings of homosexuality and norms of gender are not universal but, rather, are culturally constructed.

3   This section of my discussion is meant to highlight and illustrate only part of the theoretical framework of my research and my ideas for "queering" it.

4   C.M. Wood (1982) attempts to reconcile these differences by focusing on the household as a unit of analysis that bridges micro- and macroeconomic concerns, but the household analysis also has its limitations, including a bias toward the individual actor that obscures some of the macrolevel dimensions of migration such as the role of the state and sociocultural influences. In addition, a focus on the household *exclusively*, tends to conceal dimensions of the transnational or binational household and other adaptive strategies by assuming (in at least some of the literature) a nuclear household configuration with one head and fully shared resources – that a household has a choice is a problem of reification as well.

5   Douglas Massey and his coauthors (Massey, Arango, Hugo, Kouaouci, Pellegrino, and Taylor 1993; Massey and Espinosa 1995) categorize various theories of international migration into five conceptual frames, which I highlight: neoclassical economics, the new economics of labor migration, segmented labor market theory, social capital theory, and world systems theory.

6   This urban migration generally occurred during the participants' childhood and was not a common experience of their adult life.

7   Distinguishing social class was a difficult task in large part because the Mexican middle class is quickly disappearing from the country's socioeconomic landscape and also because of the international relativity of social class definitions. My measure of class is, therefore, informant defined and takes into account the men's educational and career backgrounds as well as that of their parents.

8   Interviews were conducted in Spanish and translated by the author.

9   The names of research participants are pseudo-
    nyms.
10 I do not mean to suggest that cross-dressing
    and transgender are the same.
11 For further elaboration of the ways in which
    stereotypical cultural arguments pathologize
    Latino culture see Cantú (2000).
12 All the men came from households with more
    than one child.
13 For ethical reasons, I did not pressure any of
    my interviewees to discuss traumatic experi-
    ences in more detail than they were comfortable
    with. I had informed all of them prior to the
    interview that if there were questions with
    which they felt uncomfortable, they could
    choose not to answer them and/or end the
    interview at anytime they so wished.
14 While earlier research on Mexican homosexu-
    ality found that the homosexual label was ap-
    plied to only passive (anally receptive) men –
    pasivos – this view seems to be changing (see
    Carrier 1995).
15 See Cantú (1999) for more on the queer life in
    Mexico as it relates to migration.
16 I do not mean to imply that there is some
    essential or "true" sexual nature that awaits
    "discovery"; rather, I utilize the term as a
    means to convey informants' expressed under-
    standing of their sexual journeys.

REFERENCES

Almaguer, Tomás
1993. "Chicano Men: A Cartography of Homosex-
    ual Identity and Behavior." In Henry Abelove,
    Michèle Aina Barale, and David M. Halperin,
    eds., *The Lesbian and Gay Studies Reader*. New
    York: Routledge.
Anzaldúa, Gloria
1987. *Borderlands/La Frontera: The New Mestiza*.
    San Francisco: Spinsters/Aunt Lute.
Argüelles, Lourdes and Anne M. Rivero
1993. "Gender/Sexual Orientation Violence and
    Transnational Migration: Conversations with
    Some Latinas We Think We Know." *Urban An-
    thropology* 22 (3/4): 259–76.
Bennett, James R.
1996. Introduction to "Materialist Queer Theory: A
    Working Bibliography." In Donald Morton, ed.,

*The Material Queer: A LesBiGay Cultural Studies
    Reader*. Boulder, Col.: Westview Press.
Cantú, Lionel
1999. "Border Crossings: Mexican Men and the
    Sexuality of Migration." Ph.D. diss., University
    of California, Irvine, 1999.
——. 2000. "Entre Hombres/Between Men:
    Latino Masculinities and Homosexualities." In
    Peter Nardi, ed., *Gay Masculinities*, pp. 224–46.
    Thousand Oaks, Cal.: Sage.
Carrier, Joseph
1995. *De Los Otros: Intimacy and Homosexuality
    Among Mexican Men*. New York: Columbia Uni-
    versity Press.
Chambers, Iain
1994. *Migrancy, Culture, Identity*. London: Routle-
    dge.
Chavez, Leo
1992 *Shadowed Lives: Undocumented Immigrants in
    American Society*. San Diego, Cal.: Harcourt
    Brace Jovanovich.
——. 1994. "The Power of the Imagined Commu-
    nity: The Settlement of Undocumented Mex-
    icans and Central Americans in the United
    States." *American Anthropologist* 96 (1): 52–73.
Cousins, Mark and Athar Hussain
1984 *Michel Foucault*. New York: Macmillan.
D'Emilio, John
1993. "Capitalism and Gay Identity." In William B.
    Rubenstein, ed., *Lesbians, Gay Men, and the Law*.
    New York: New Press.
Donovan, Josephine
1992. *Feminist Theory*. New York: Continuum.
Engels, Frederick
1993 [1942]. *The Origin of the Family, Private Prop-
    erty and the State, in the Light of the Researches of
    Lewis H. Morgan*. New York: International.
Fellows, Will, ed.
1996. *Farm Boys: Lives of Gay Men from the Rural
    Midwest*. Madison: University of Wisconsin
    Press.
Foucault, Michel
1990 [1978]. *The History of Sexuality*. Trans. Robert
    Hurley. New York: Pantheon.
Gluckman, Amy and Betsy Reed, eds.
1997. *HomoEconomics: Capitalism, Community, and
    Lesbian and Gay Life*. New York: Routledge.
Gutmann, Matthew C.
1996. *The Meanings of Macho: Being a Man in
    Mexico City*. Berkeley: University of California
    Press.

Hennessy, Rosemary and Chrys Ingraham, eds.
1997. *Materialist Feminism: A Reader in Class, Difference, and Women's Lives*. New York: Routledge.

Herdt, Gilbert H.
1994 [1981]. *Guardians of the Flutes: Idioms of Masculinity*. New York: McGraw-Hill.

Hondagneu-Sotelo, Pierrette
1994. *Gendered Transitions: Mexican Experiences of Immigration*. Los Angeles: University of California Press.

Hondagneu-Sotelo, Pierrette and Michael Messner
1994. "Gender Displays and Men's Power: 'The New Man' and the Mexican Immigrant Man." In Harry Brod and Michael Kaufman, eds., *Theorizing Masculinities*. Thousand Oaks, Cal.: Sage.

Ingram, Gordon Brent, Anne-Marie Bouthillette, and Yolanda Retter
1997. *Queers in Space: Communities, Public Places, Sites of Resistance*. Seattle, Wash.: Bay Press.

Jagose, Annamarie
1996. *Queer Theory: An Introduction*. New York: New York University Press.

Martin, Biddy
1988. "Feminism, Criticism, and Foucault." In Irene Diamond and Lee Quinby, eds., *Feminism and Foucault: Reflections on Resistance*. Boston: Northeastern University Press.

Massey, Douglas S., Joaquin Arango, Graeme Hugo, Ali Kouaouci, Adela Pellegrino, and J. Edward Taylor
1993. "Theories of International Migration: Review and Appraisal." *Population and Development Review* 19(3): 431–67.

Massey, Douglas S. and Kristin Espinosa
1995. "What's Driving Mexico–U.S. Migration? A Theoretical, Empirical, and Policy Analysis." Unpublished paper.

McIntosh, Mary
1968. "The Homosexual Role." *Social Problems* 16(69): 182–92.

Moore, Joan and Harry Pachon
1985. *Hispanics in the United States*. Englewood Cliffs, N.J.: Prentice-Hall.

Morton, Donald, ed.
1996. *The Material Queer*. Boulder, Col.: Westview Press.

Murray, Stephen O.
1995. *Latin American Male Homosexualities*. Albuquerque: University of New Mexico Press.

Murray, Stephen O. and Will Roscoe, ed.
1998. *Boy-Wives and Female Husbands: Studies in African Homosexualities*. New York: St. Martin's Press.

Paternostro, Silvana
1998 *In the Land of God and Man: Confronting Our Sexual Culture*. New York: Dutton.

Pedraza, Silvia
1991. "Women and Migration: The Social Consequences of Gender." *Annual Review of Sociology* 17: 303–25.

Prieur, Annick
1998. *Mema's House, Mexico City: On Transvestites, Queens, and Machos*. Chicago: University of Chicago Press.

Rubin, Gayle
1993 [1984]. "Thinking Sex: Notes for a Radical Theory of the Politics of Sexuality." In Henry Abelove, Michèle Aina Barale, and David M. Halperin, eds., *The Lesbian and Gay Studies Reader*, pp. 3–44. New York: Routledge.

Seidman, Steven, ed.
1996. *Queer Theory/Sociology*. Cambridge, Mass.: Blackwell.

Weeks, Jeffrey
1977. *Coming Out: Homosexual Politics in Britain from the Nineteenth Century to the Present*. London: Quarter.

Weston, Kath
1991. *Families We Choose: Lesbians, Gays, Kinship*. New York: Columbia University Press.

Williams, Norma
1990. *The Mexican American Family: Tradition and Change*. Dix Hills, N.Y.: General Hall.

Wood, Charles, H.
1982. "Equilibrium and Historical Structural Perspectives on Migration." *International Migration Review* 16(2): 298–319.

15

Dominican Blackness and the Modern World

Silvio Torres-Saillant

The Dominican Republic, a place in the midst of the Caribbean sharing the island of Hispaniola (also known as Santo Domingo) with the Republic of Haiti, has an intercourse with blackness and African roots that would seem uncontestably to qualify it as an ideal candidate for induction into the watery corridors of the "transcultural, international formation" of "the black Atlantic" (Gilroy 1993:4). Yet specialists in social dynamics in Latin America and the Caribbean do not know the place. Only in Peter Winn's *Americas: The Changing Face of Latin America and the Caribbean* (1999) do Dominicans get center stage in the hemispheric discussion of blackness and racial identity but not without caricature.

The recent literature on blackness in the Americas has dealt with the Dominican case, then, in either of two ways: omission or trivialization. This might seem a strange lot indeed for a people whose land is called "the cradle of blackness in the Americas" (Torres-Saillant 1995:110). Hispaniola received the first blacks ever to arrive in the Western Hemisphere. It inaugurated the colonial plantation and New World African slavery, twin institutions that gave blackness its modern significance. On this island in 1503, black maroons first rose their subversive heads and the hemisphere's first black slave insurrection took place on December 27, 1522. The island eventually bifurcated into two contiguous colonial sites, a Spanish domain in the east and a French one in the west. The Dominican Republic, which came into being as an independent nation-state in 1844 by delinking from Haiti, which had unified the island under its rule 22 years earlier, broke the pattern of the typical independence movements in the region. Unlike them, which usually achieved independence by separating from European colonial powers, the Dominican Republic attained selfhood by dissolving its ties to a former colony, a nation founded by ex-slaves.

The Dominican case broke with the normal regional pattern in other ways as well. Black Dominicans interrogated the ideology of the independence movement and succeeded in shaping the way the "founding fathers" imagined the nation. Juan Pablo Duarte, the intellectual architect of the new republic, distinguished himself from the creole elites that championed independence projects in nineteenth-century Latin America in forging a nation-building doctrine that was devoid of racist formulations. He posited the vision of a multiracial society united by a common purpose: "white, black,/ copper-skinned, cross-bred,/ Marching together,/ United and daring,/ Let us flaunt to the world/ Our brotherhood/ And save the fatherland/ From hideous tyrants" (cited in Torres-Saillant 1998:126). On the surface these lines point to a racial ideology akin to the pluralism favored by the celebrants of Latin American *mestizaje*, a good many of whom pay lip service to diversity while adhering to white supremacist social practices. However, Duarte went beyond the conundrum of *mestizaje*. He radically proclaimed an end to the "aristocracy of blood." He also stayed clear of racial othering when articulating the need for the separation from Haitian rule (Duarte 1994:31). Once the independence was declared, the nascent government quickly passed a resolution to reassure Haitians who wished to stay on the Dominican side of the island that there were no plans to expel them and that the authorities would guarantee their personal safety and their possessions, thus fulfilling Duarte's anti-racist legacy (Campillo Perez 1994:45).

Further, the country wrestled with slavery and emancipation, culminating in anti-slavery policies of unprecedented radicalism. First, in 1801, the liberator Toussaint L'Ouverture came from Saint Domingue in western Hispaniola to Spanish Santo Domingo in the east and, having unified the island under the French banner he still represented, proceeded to abolish the "peculiar institution." Then in 1802, during the French invasion sent by Napoleon, a French commander took over the Spanish-speaking side of the island and immediately reinstated it. Slavery would remain in effect – a couple of anti-slavery uprisings having failed – until 1822, when Haitian President Jean Pierre Boyer, effectuating another unification of the island, abolished it.

With the birth of the new country, the independence movement having triumphed in 1844, the black and mulatto population pressed to have their freedom guaranteed. As a result, on March 1, 1844 – two days after the founding of the nation – the newly formed government declared that slavery had disappeared "for ever" from the land. When the resolution was ratified as a law on July 17, 1844, it carried an article that penalized the slave traffic with capital punishment. Another stated emphatically that slaves coming from overseas would become automatically free upon setting foot on Dominican soil (Alfau Durán 1994:373). This law becomes more radical if one

remembers that slavery still existed in the neighboring Spanish colonies of Puerto Rico (until 1878) and Cuba (until 1886), and that enacting it constituted a provocation to Spanish imperial authority in the region. For it created a lure that attracted runaway slaves whose masters had no hope of reclaiming them once they entered Dominican territory. Indeed, black slaves escaped regularly from Puerto Rico to Santo Domingo from 1822 through 1878 (Alfau Durán 1994:379). In declaring the immediate change of status of the servile population from abject slavery to unqualified freedom, the policy surpassed any other emancipation declaration in the region with its human rights logic. Clearly, the Dominican case is one that merits attention by anyone seriously interested in exploring the complexity of race relations and the black experience in the modern world.

The Genesis of Blackness

Blacks and mulattos make up nearly 90 per cent of the contemporary Dominican population. Yet no other country in the hemisphere exhibits greater indeterminacy regarding the population's sense of racial identity. To the bewilderment of outside observers, Afro-Dominicans have traditionally failed to flaunt their blackness as a collective banner to advance economic, cultural, or political causes. Some commentators would contend, in effect, that Dominicans have for the most part denied their blackness. Faced with the population's tolerance of official claims asserting the moral and intellectual superiority of Caucasians by white supremacist ideologues, analysts of racial identity in Dominican society have often imputed to Dominicans heavy doses of "backwardness," ignorance, or "confusion" regarding their race and ethnicity (Fennema and Loewenthal 1989:209; Sagás 1993). In the pages that follow, I invite reflection on the complexity of racial thinking and racial discourse among Dominicans with the purpose of urging the adoption of indigenous paradigms to explicate the place of black consciousness in Dominican society and culture.

The Dominican Republic came into being as a sovereign state on February 27, 1844, when the political leaders of eastern Hispaniola proclaimed their juridical separation from the Republic of Haiti, putting an end to 22 years of unification under a black-controlled government with its seat in Port-au-Prince. The Haitian leadership originally resisted the idea of relinquishing authority over the whole island and made successive attempts to regain the eastern territory, which resulted in sporadic armed clashes between Haitian and Dominican forces until 1855. As the newly created Caribbean republic sought to insert itself into an economic order dominated by Western powers, among which "the racial imagination" had long taken a firm hold, the race of Dominicans quickly became an issue of concern (Torres-Saillant 1993:33–37). In December 1844, near the end of President John Tyler's administration, U.S. Secretary of State John C. Calhoun spoke of the need for the fledging Dominican state to receive formal recognition from the United States, France, and Spain in order to prevent "the further spread of negro influence in the West Indies" (Welles 1966 [1928]: 76). Calhoun, as would many other American statesmen and journalists throughout the nineteenth century, conceived of Dominicans as other than black.

When in 1845 American Agent John Hogan arrived in Santo Domingo with the mandate of assessing the country for an eventual recognition of its independence, he sided with Dominicans in their conflicts with Haitians. As such, he became weary of the predominance of people of African descent in the country. Addressing the Dominican Minister of Foreign Relations Tomás Bobadilla, Hogan wondered whether "the presence in the Republic of so large a proportion of the colored race" would weaken the government's efforts to fend off Haitian aggression, but Bobadilla assuaged his fears by stating "that among the Dominicans preoccupations regarding color have never held much sway" and that even former "slaves have fought and would again fight against the Haitians" if need be, on account of the oppressiveness of the latter's past regime (Welles 1966 [1928]:77–78). In a despatch addressed to U.S. Secretary of State John M. Clayton, dated October 24, 1849, American Commissioner in Santo Domingo Jonathan E. Green reported that Haitian violence had given "force and uni-

versality to the feeling in favor of the whites in the Dominican Republic" to the point that a black "when taunted with his color" could conceivably remark: "Soy negro, pero negro blanco" (cited in Welles 1966 [1928]:103–104).

Nineteenth-century foreign observers of the Dominican scene had ample occasion to note the reticence of Dominicans to brandish their black identity. But the observers themselves remained ambivalent about the racial and ethnic characteristics of the new republic's population. For instance, the New York *Evening Post* on September 2, 1854 published a "genealogy" of Dominican political leaders with the intention of frustrating Secretary of State William Marcy's plan to secure the granting of official U.S. recognition to the Dominican Republic. The newspaper meant to show that "the Dominican leaders were all either negroes or mulattoes, and that the pure white population of the Dominican Republic was almost a negative quantity," thereby warning "Southern statesmen" about the danger of extending privileges to a "government based upon negro or mulatto supremacy" (Tansill 1938:181). The *Evening Post* highlighted the blackness of Dominicans in order to spark antipathy against them in public-opinion sectors of the United States. Six years later a book was published with the opposite intent, underestimating the black element of the Dominican population. The author represented the Dominican people as "made up of Spaniards, Spanish Creoles and *some* Africans and people of color" (Courtney 1860:132).

Two strains appear to stand out in the observations of Americans commenting on racial matters in the Dominican Republic at the time. One is the sense that "no austere prejudice against color prevails" in the country, or that "distinction of color, in social life, is entirely unknown" (*Santo Domingo* 1863:10; Keim 1870:168). The other strain is the insistence on magnifying the white component of the Dominican population. Thus, the U.S. Senate Commission of Inquiry that went to the Dominican Republic in early 1871 to assess whether the country was ripe for annexation to the U.S. territory found people there to be "generally of mixed blood," with the great majority being "neither pure black nor pure white," but showing areas inhabited by "considerable numbers of pure white" people, and noting that "generally in the mixed race the white blood predominates" (*Report* 1871:13). Still in the twentieth century, during the government of Theodore Roosevelt one could find American voices attesting to the presumed whiteness of Dominicans. One contended unambiguously that the inhabitants of the small Caribbean republic "with very few exceptions" were white and cited racial hostility, that is, "the refusal of the white Dominican to be governed by the black Haitian," as the cause of the partition of Hispaniola into two countries (Hancock 1905:50). In the same vein, an anonymous author affirmed that "white blood preponderates" in the Dominican Republic by contrast to neighboring Haiti, where "the black race is in complete ascendancy (Anon. 1906:18–19).

With these fluctuating pronouncements on Dominicans and race, the mixed testimony in the late 1920s of another American commentator, Envoy Extraordinary and Minister Plenipotentiary Sumner Welles, should come as no surprise. While affirming that "race discrimination in the Dominican Republic is unknown," he deemed it "one of the most noteworthy peculiarities of the Dominican people that among all shades, there is a universal desire that the black be obliterated by the white. The stimulation of white immigration has become a general demand," just as an interest in curtailing or regulating black immigration carried "similar force" (Welles 1966 [1928]: 909). Welles described what proponents of structural causes for attitudes about race would characterize as a contradiction since his scenario insinuates that negrophobia exists independently of racial oppression. This baffling possibility serves as a starting point for an inquiry into the concept of race as it has developed historically in Dominican society.

Nor is it insignificant that this inquiry should spring from the statements of Welles and the other North American voices. For I would contend that Dominican identity consists not only of how Dominicans see themselves but also of how they are seen by the powerful nations with which the Dominican Republic has been linked in a relationship of political and economic dependence. The texture of negrophobic and anti-Haitian nationalist discourse sponsored by official

spokespersons in the Dominican state has drawn significantly from North American sources dating back to the first years of the republic. I propose that as we proceed with this inquiry we avert the pitfalls of investigating Dominican attitudes about race exclusively through the utterings put forward by the scribes of the ruling class. I will assemble instances of active participation of Afro-Dominicans in building and defining their history. Those instances, compiled from the field of social action, offer an invaluable living text, an indispensable document that is hardly detectable through archival research.

Blacks and Cultural Production

People of African descent have excelled in the realm of cultural production in Dominican society. The country's history registers the achievements of many singular black and mulatto thinkers or artists. The Dominican feminist movement, for instance, owes a great deal to three black women: Petronila Gómez, Altagracia Domínguez, and Evangelina Rodríguez, who in the 1920s promoted a revolutionary creed of social, economic, and political equity between males and females (Zaglul 1980:80). Rodríguez distinguished herself also for being the first Dominican woman physician with considerable attainments in her field. Two male physicians, the mulatto Francisco Eugenio Moscoso Puello and the black Heriberto Pieter Bennet, left remarkable contributions as practitioners, educators, and scholars in the medical sciences during the first half of the present century.

In the field of literature, Dominican artistic writing began to exhibit a distinct voice with the compositions of the mulatto, Meso Mónica, in the eighteenth century. Another mulatto, the Jesuit priest Antonio Sánchez Valverde, wrote the seminal *La idea del valor de la Isla Española* (1785) (Sánchez valverde 1988), the most important work to appear in eighteenth-century Santo Domingo. In the latter half of the nineteenth century, the mulatto poet Gastón Fernando Deligne achieved great prestige as a literary artist. Scholars normally group him with the mulatto Salomé Ureña and José Joaquín Pérez among the founders of modern Dominican poetry. In fact, the internationally renowned scholar Pedro Henríquez Ureña, himself a mulatto, lavished more passionate praise on him than on any other Dominican literary figure (Henríquez Ureña 1978:315–325).

The literary visibility of black and mulatto Dominicans has been no less impressive in twentieth-century writing. Suffice it to mention the black author Ramón Marrero Aristy, who wrote the novel *Over*, easily the most frequently read and highly regarded Dominican fiction work from the first half of the century, or Aída Cartagena Portalatín (1918–94), a black woman poet who is the most revered twentieth-century Dominican female writer. Cartagena Portalatín, unlike many of the literary artists of her generation, openly asserted "her own racially mixed background" (Cocco de Filippis 1988:15–16). Her discussion, for instance, of the two sixteenth-century female slaves from Santo Domingo, Teodora and Micaela Ginés, who managed to travel across to the neighboring island of Cuba and there contributed their talent to the development of popular music, and whom she calls "Dominican black women," shows a clear sense of identification with her subject, especially in her presenting the topic as a way to "look for our roots" (Cartagena Portalatín 1986:124–125).

Blacks and Dominican Folk Culture

The African presence in Dominican culture transcends, of course, the creative contributions of talented individuals. Traces of African heritage appear in the language Dominicans speak, the "ethnolinguistic modalities" that characterize the people's handling of Spanish, showing peculiarities in the "lexical structure" as well as in the "phonetics, morphosyntax, and intonation" that suggest retentions from the languages of African slaves in colonial times (Megenney 1990:233). There was a significant presence of Haitian Creole in Afro-Dominican Spanish as a result of the intercultural contacts that "were firmly cemented" during the unification period from 1822 through 1884 (Lipski 1994:13). The original culture of the slaves has probably found its way also into the oral tradition of the Dominican people. Some scholarly research suggests the existence of "a type of tale of African origins... among us which forms part of the oral literary heritage of Dominicans" (Julián 1982:10). Blacks contributed to Dominican cuisine in the cultural transmissions brought by the slaves from Africa and as creole innovations traceable to the "plantation regime" (Deive 1990:133–135).

African cultural forms manifest themselves strongly in Dominican society in spiritual expression. Carlos Esteban Deive has convincingly posited the existence of a Dominican vodou with an indigenous pantheon and other characteristics of its own that distinguish it from Haitian vodou (Deive 1992:171–174, 182–183). He argues that people of diverse class extractions in Dominican society normally have recourse to the services and rituals of this folk religion, which has as much currency in the urban areas as in the rural ones (Deive 1992:17). The syncretic nature of Dominican culture, which allows for their coexistence with religious expressions of European origin, contributes to the spread and persistence of this and other African-descended forms of worship. In fact, the majority of vodou practitioners consider themselves "officially Catholic," having received their baptism and remaining active in the worship of that faith (Deive 1992:211).

Further research supports the existence of vodou as "part of Dominican folk religious expression" and identifies its utility as a crucial resource for popular medicine (Davis 1987:423, 221–223). Anthropologist Martha Ellen Davis has highlighted certain kinds of folk spiritual expressions with "strong African influences" that provide aid to the Dominican people in many of the social functions of their daily lives (Davis 1987: 194–195). Following the insight of such scholars as Deive and Davis, a team combining mental health and social science specialists has stressed the importance of vodou and other folk spiritual manifestations "to understand the Dominican people" from the "perspective of psychiatry and psychology" (Tejeda Ortiz et al. 1993:54).

The Gaga cult is a religious expression with strong links to the African past, but emerging on Dominican soil in connection with the modern sugar industry. Reflecting a profound religious sense, the Dominicanized Gaga cult, born of the vibrant interaction of Haitian and Dominican folk traditions in the vicinity of sugar plantations, constitutes the coming together of two spiritual sources that are differentiated expressions of the transculturation between African and European cultures (Rosenberg 1979:17, 31). In her pioneering monograph on this spiritual folk form, the anthropologist June Rosenberg insisted that "the celebration of the Gaga is part of the cultural richness of the Dominican people" (Rosenberg 1979:17).

Naturally, the state-funded guardians of the official culture, intent on stressing the exclusive predominance of the Hispanic heritage among Dominicans, have vigorously rejected the trace of any "pagan" forms of worship in Dominican society. Unable to deny that Dominicans do engage in African-descended spirituality, they have proceeded to ascribe that predilection to an unwelcome foreign influence, a logic that often has justified the persecution of folk religious practices as a threat to morality and Christian values. In the nineteenth century the poet Félix Maña Del Monte construed vodou as a savage, anthropophagous ritual, and an 1862 police ordinance proscribed a series of dances and festivities that involved expressions of African origins (Del Monte 1979:246; Deive 1992:163). During the Trujillo dictatorship, the period when the Dominican state became most emphatically committed to promoting Eurocentric and white supremacist views of Dominicanness, the official daily *El Listín Diario* on August 16, 1939 reported the arrest of two men for commemorating the War of Restoration by engaging in vodou practices along with other men and women who managed to escape. They had surrendered themselves "frantically," as the column says, to a "ritual that the police has so tenaciously persecuted" (cited in Deive 1992:164).

The Trujillo regime found it necessary to pass Law 391 on September 20, 1943 prohibiting participation in vodou ceremonies. The decree imposed a penalty of up to one year in prison plus a fine of 500 pesos to anyone found guilty of the crime either by direct commission or indirect collusion (Deive 1992:186). That the government's campaign to eradicate African spiritual expressions in Dominican society would not

relent is clear from an article published in the newspaper *La Nación* on October 5, 1945 by Emilio Rodríguez Demorizi, a scribe of the Trujillo regime. He denounced "cucaya dance, cannibalism, vodou, witchcraft, and other evil arts and customs" as rituals coming from "the land of Louverture and Christophe" that have occasionally tarnished "the simple habits of Dominicans," although he reassured his readers that the "dark roots" of those influences left no perceptible vestiges in the people. But, of course, in such affirmations Rodríguez Demorizi was merely indulging in wishful thinking. For even he, a consummate negrophobe, could ascertain that if his claim were true, the regime's police persecution, legislative actions, and his own article, which he militantly entitled "Against Vodou," would have been unnecessary.

But despite the aberrant negrophobia of the scribes of the ruling class from colonial times to the present, with a population that is predominatly of African descent, it is inevitable to find the omnipresence of black contribution to Dominican culture. That contribution began in 1502 and since then, "it has remained constant and decisive" (Alfau Durán 1994: 342). In addition to the areas of endeavor surveyed above, one could speak of the glorification and celebrity enjoyed by Dominicans of African descent in the fields of sports and popular music. Clearly, blacks have not lacked representation in the public sphere nor in the regard of the Dominican people. The overwhelming popular victory during the 1994 election of black presidential candidate José Francisco Peña Gómez of the *Partido Revolucionario Dominicano*, against the two white elders Bosch (of the *Partido de la Liberación Dominicana*) and Balaguer (of the *Partido Reformista Social Cristiano*), speaks eloquently. The fraudulent maneuvers of Balaguer's government did not permit the people's choice to materialize, and the octogenarian politician stayed in power. Nevertheless, the opposition's documentation of the fraud and the indignation of the international community caused the ruling party to agree to reduce its administration by two years and convene new elections for 1996, thereby admitting to the illegality of Balaguer's "reelection" (Peña Gómez and Alvarez Bogaert 1994).

That Peña Gómez did not become the President of the Republic matters less for the present discussion than the fact that the majority of the Dominican population went to the polls and cast their ballot in favor of a black man who, in addition, reputedly comes from Haitian parents. In voting for him massively, the Dominican people disregarded an elaborate, insistent, and virulent campaign orchestrated by the government and the conservative elite that aimed to cast doubt on the Dominicanness of the candidate on account of his race and presumed Haitian ancestry. The campaign, which employed the resources of the state and all the available media on a daily basis, insidiously sought to render it unpatriotic for voters to elect the black Peña Gómez. But the majority of Dominicans showed through their action that they have a mind of their own.

Racial Awareness: The Paradox of Language versus Action

At the core of the unchallenged deprecation of blackness by the ruling elite and the quiet but real ethnic self-affirmation by the masses of the people lies the complexity of racial dynamics in the Dominican Republic. For while one can discern the development of a racial discourse and the existence of racial attitudes, one cannot so easily fathom the dynamics of race relations. In fact, one can hardly speak meaningfully about the socioeconomic and political situation of blacks as a differentiated ethnic group in the country. To measure the living conditions of Dominican blacks and mulattos would mean no more than to assess the social status of the masses of the people, which would correspond more fittingly to an analysis of class inequalities and the social injustices bred by dependent capitalism than to a discussion of ethnic oppression. This by no means implies that there are no racial tensions or instances of racism in Dominican society. I do not mean to espouse the myth that presents Latin American countries as a region free of racial inequities (Burdick 1992:44). My contention is that only an interpretative examination of the historical background can help us provide the context for understanding existing racial attitudes in Dominican society.

There is a peaceful coexistence of the Dominican population's self-awareness as a people of African descent and the negrophobia contained in prevalent definitions of Dominicanness. The vicissitudes of the concept of race in Dominican society mean that Dominican blacks and mulattos seem to accept passively the rigid Eurocentrism of the official cultural discourse. In the Dominican Republic, where blacks and mulattos predominate, Balaguer can publicly proclaim the mental and moral superiority of whites and dreadfully warn about the country's "Africanization" without ever needing to recant his racist statements. Fradique Lizardo has indignantly charged that "Dominicans have generally and voluntarily lived with their backs turned to their culture" (Rosenberg 1979:13). However, I find it difficult to accept that a people should willfully choose alienation and confusion as a way of life. Nor does affirming that Dominicans who have voted for Balaguer "live in the past" suffice to explain their toleration of his views (Fennema and Loewenthal 1989:209). I prefer to believe that Dominicans possess the ability to discern the phenotypical characteristics that distinguish one racial group from another, and they recognize the traces of Africa in their ethnicity despite the insistent efforts of the conservative intellectual elite to define them as part of a Western, Caucasian community.

I propose that the mystery lies in the elusiveness of the concept of race itself and its tribulations in the peculiar historical experience of the Dominican people. Observers will note the lesser place African-descended Dominicans accord to racial traits in articulating their social identity as opposed to the centrality assigned to it by societies where ethnic groups are sharply differentiated and rigidly stratified. Black Dominicans do not see blackness as the central component of their identity but tend to privilege their nationality instead, which implies participation in a culture, a language community, and the sharing of a lived experience. Consistent with the racially mixed ancestry of the population, the ethnic vocabulary of Dominicans is rich in words describing gradations of skin color. A scholar looking at the city of Santiago de los Caballeros alone arrived at an elaborate classification of 21 terms used by the people there to denote racial traits (Gúzman 1974:37–40). Generally devoid of the language of racial polarity current in the United States, Dominicans have little familiarity with a discourse of black affirmation. Nothing in their history indicates to the masses of the Dominican people that their precarious material conditions or the overall indignities they suffer constitute a strictly racial form of oppression. As a result, they have not developed a discourse of black affirmation among their strategies of social resistance.

A close look at the particularities of the historical experience of Dominicans reveals the clues to explain the elasticity of their concept of race. The specific history Dominicans have lived simply did not beget the rigid racial codes found in North America. Thus, they have no difficulty recognizing a valid identity in their racial fusion, and, for the most part, would not experience the troubling perplexity of the speaker in Langston Hughes's short poem "Cross," who struggles with the dilemma of having a white father and a black mother: "My old man died in a fine big house/My ma died in a shack./I wonder where I'm gonna die,/Being neither white nor black" (Hughes 1974:158). Familiarity with the concrete historical background that explains the tendency of Dominicans to configure their racial identity in an intermediate conceptual space between the black and white polarities enables scholars to overcome the temptation to denormalize the way this community speaks of race. Since the Dominican people's racial language defies the paradigms prevalent in countries like the United States, well-intentioned observers from such countries would wish this community adopted the racial vocabulary generated by the historical experiences of *their* societies. But, apart from safeguarding us all from such ethnocentric compulsions, paying heed to the specificity of the Dominican case can incite reflection on the elusiveness of race as an analytical category both in the Dominican Republic and elsewhere.

Toward Recovering a Black Dominican Tradition

Dominicans of African descent have found ingenious ways to cope with the vociferous onslaught of the colonial ruling class and their contemporary descendants. In general, though, they have lacked an empowering discourse of retaliation and have settled for non-verbal modes of self-assertion. A retaliatory discourse now exists that gradually emerged from the pens of a new wave of progressive intellectuals who, since the late 1960s, have vigorously reproached the conservative power structure's white supremacist and Eurocentric views on Dominican history and culture. Starting from milestone publications that appeared in 1969 and the momentum incited by a memorable seminar on the "African presence" held in mid-1973 at the Autonomous University of Santo Domingo, an impressive body of writings has accrued in response to retrograde theories of Dominicanness. In surveying that scholarly production, Pablo Maríñez has pointed out "two currents" that predominate among the sociologists, anthropologists, and historians who have championed the debate: "the reinterpretation of Haitian–Dominican relations and the search for the African roots in the nation's historico-cultural experience" (Maríñez 1986:12).

The vindicatory scholarship of the new wave of Dominican intellectuals has rendered a valuable service to the society, but all seems to indicate that the longevous discourse of the plantocratic, Eurocentric ruling elite still weighs heavier in the schooling of the citizenry. Indeed, we now witness the unsavory resurgence of Hispanophile and racist declarations of Dominican identity that invoke the teachings of negrophobous intellectuals from the first half of the present century. Curiously, that trend often features the devout participation of black Dominicans such as the essayist Manuel Núñez and the older academician Jorge Tena Reyes. The mulatto Juan Daniel Balcácer, concurring with Balaguer on the "extraordinary relevance" of the thought of Manuel Arturo Peña Batlle concerning the centrality of "Christian and classical culture" as well as the Dominican people's age-old struggle against "Haitian ambition," has taken it upon himself to help Peña Batlle's living relatives mount an ambitious publicity scheme that would help remove the "mysterious black curtain" that "has lately enveloped" the late thinker's life and work (Balcácer 1989:v, xi). Balcácer would wish to restore the former currency enjoyed by the prose of one of the most caustic of Trujillo's scribes on account of his "important" ideas on "the ethno-anthropological composition of the Dominican people," (Balcácer 1989:xii). This is undue cordiality, given Peña Batlle's opinion of Balcácer's own African ancestors as a hideous mass of mongrels. Peña Batlle described the black slaves who rose against colonial oppression in eighteenth-century Saint Domingue as a people "without historical tradition, without cultural lineaments of any kind, without a spiritual structure, without an idea of either public or private law, without an established family order, without a sense of property organization, without collective norms" (Peña Batlle 1989:164).

At least until the late 1990s, the power structure in Dominican society and, consequently, the material resources as well as the ultimate authority on how to teach Dominicanness to the population, remained in the hands of cultural policy makers who were hesitant to promote changes that would ruffle the feathers of the old Trujillo guard and their ideological offspring. As a result, the truth about the ethnic and historical origins of the Dominican people persists as an unsettled, contested issue, with the proponents of definitions stemming from privileged portrayals of the old colony's ruling minority retaining the upper hand. Nor do the intellectual paladins of conservative views of Dominicanness show any sign of slackening, filled as their spirits are with the defiant self-assurance that power confers. We have here an obdurate ruling sector whose adamant commitment to a particular worldview knows no boundaries. For example, Moya Pons's *Manual de historia dominicana* (1992), whose ninth edition brings the chronicle of Dominican history up to 1990, lost its status as a textbook approved by the Ministry of Education due to the added chapters' critical appraisal of oppression and corruption during Balaguer's presidential terms.

Similarly, the Secretary of Education bluntly revoked the National Book Award given by a panel of literary experts in April 1993 to Viriato Sención's *Los que falsificaron la firma de Dios* because of the novel's unfavorable depiction of Dr. Mario Ramos, a character patterned after Balaguer. The conservative sector, in other words, has had the power to name reality and to render the opposition mute, which has put serious limits on what the new generation of Dominican scholars has been able to do for their people. Indeed, the Dominican government in 1994 found it politically expedient to make a gesture of ideological inclusiveness by hiring the services of progressive historians and sociologists such as Emilio Cordero Michel, Raymundo González, Walter Cordero, and Roberto Cassá. They worked with the Ministry of Education on drafting modernized social studies textbooks for the public school classroom. When the time came to publish the eighth-grade volume, the Ministry took the chapter on the period 1961–65, which spoke of "President Joaquín Balaguer and Donald Reid Cabral, critically narrating their political participation following the death of Trujillo," and deleted it from the manuscript before sending it to the printer (Rosario Adames 1994:6). This clearly suggests that while the conservative power structure may occasionally make courteous concessions to progressive intellectuals, only material that the regime finds ideologically inoffensive will in the end receive the stamp of approval.

I contend that intellectuals of the new wave cannot do much more than they have already done to denounce the falsified presentation of Dominican history and culture perpetrated by the ruling class. We can expect the negrophobia and Eurocentric notions of Dominicanness to live on for as long as those who are in power remain there, controlling the official tools of cultural definition and the institutions that shape public perceptions. We can rest assured that they will persevere in their effort to coerce the Dominican people into embracing their entrenched notion of national identity. They will do so either by overt censorship, as the above examples suggest, or by insidious conditioning, as illustrated by the conservative newspaper *El Listín Diario*, whose "society" pages are filled almost exclusively with photographs of white-looking people. In a country populated overwhelmingly by African-descended citizens such exclusivity entails a painfully methodical program of discrimination. The progressive scholarship since the 1970s has done an admirable job of intellectual refutation. What ought to follow now is a strategy to empower the population with the analytical tools with which, on their own, to dismantle state-funded racism. This will only come about when black and mulatto Dominicans have access to a liberatory legacy that they can wield against plantocratic discourse. The coming to light of the black experience on its own terms in Dominican society holds the clue to eradicating negrophobia in the cradle of blackness in the Americas.

Blackness in the Dominican Diaspora

Nearly seventy years after Summer Welles wrote his perplexed remarks about the attitudes of Dominicans toward blackness and whiteness, another American commentator, Loyola University Professor James Gaffney, traveled to Santo Domingo and returned to the United States in favorable awe at the racial scenario he encountered there. He marveled at the tendency of Dominicans to think of themselves as a *sancocho*, "the popular dish that owes its delicious flavor to a lavish multiplicity of ingredients," which persuaded him that "It would be hard to imagine a national culture more inherently resistant to racism" (Gaffney 1994:11). He read the "faceless dolls" that one finds in tourist markets as a symbol of "the ethnic indefinability of the country's population" and noted with sadness the political currency of a campaign promoted by the government of Joaquín Balaguer that, in keeping with the dogma of the old Trujillista guard, equates exultation of Dominicanness with deprecation of Haitians. Gaffney believes that contemporary anti-Haitianism in Dominican society can have dreadful consequences. He posits that it might engender "a nationalistic animosity" that might evolve "into a downright US-style racism in a country . . . whose cheerful acceptance [of racial diversity] is reflected in its typically and beautifully polychromatic families" (Gaffney 1994:12).

We have no way of knowing the extent to which future Dominican governments would be willing to embrace educational and social agendas aimed at repairing the cultural damage perpetrated by the scribes of the conservative power structure. Nor would it be advisable to place the nation's cultural future in the hands of the State

(Díaz Quiñones 1993:174). But we can be certain of the pivotal role that the Dominican diaspora in the United States will play, with or without the assistance of any government, in the configuration of a humanely inclusive conceptualization of racial identity in Dominican society. This is so because Dominicans cannot help but realize that in the United States race matters tremendously, ours as well as that of others. In this country Dominicans join the cast of an inescapable social drama wherein whites set the normative standard and "black people are viewed as a 'them'" (West 1993:3). Thus, race has implications that impinge on one's survival.

Dominican immigrants realize that American society does not distinguish between them and Haitians as the offspring of the two nations of Quisqueya. Along with other ethnic communities of immigrants from the Third World, Dominicans grapple for access to jobs, education, housing, and health services in an atmosphere of ever-scarcer resources and anti-immigrant feeling. In the diaspora, necessity allies Dominicans with Haitians. Anti-Haitianism, in other words, becomes impractical. Nor can Dominicans in the United States afford the embarrassment of seeming to detract a community with which, in the eyes of others, they visibly share racial kinship. For despite their particular manner of racial self-representation, Dominicans come into a society that "knows only black and white" (Bonilla 1980: 464). A personal anecdote may come in handy here. At a New York college where I taught, I was approached by a colleague who was working with a group in the creation of a Black Faculty Caucus. In truth, some members of the group had proposed my inclusion on account of my color, but others had second thoughts in light of my coming from a Spanish-speaking nation. Giving me the benefit of the doubt, the group agreed to let me decide whether or not I belonged in the caucus. My African American colleague put the question thus: "Do you consider yourself more black than Hispanic or more Hispanic than black?" Finding the question disarming, I was unable to quantify the immaterial. I was too fearful of saying the wrong thing and merely spent sentences galore in aimless circumlocution. My indecision made me suspect in the eyes of my colleague, with the predictable result that I never heard about the black caucus again.

In the United States, countless Dominicans, particularly dark-skinned ones, find themselves having to choose among options that their historical experience has not prepared them to recognize. Such is the predicament, for instance, of the Dominican characters in *Do Platanos Go Wit' Collard Greens?*, a recent work of fiction by a young African American author, David Lamb. The narrative features the romance of two Hunter College students, a young, African American man, Freeman, and his Dominican sweetheart Angelita, against a background of racial tension and local politics in New York City at the time of Mayor David N. Dinkins. To persist in courting Angelita, Freeman needs to go beyond the disgust of hearing her speak of her father's "sort of bad hair," which at first made him suspect "she had nothing in her head but air" (Lamb 1994:17). At first he takes her racially self-deprecating language as evidence of an intentional denial of African roots, but later he concludes, with the help of his father, who is a learned man, that Angelita and her family are just ignorant, and it would be a question of time before they recognized "their connections with us, and all of our connections with Africa" (Lamb 1994:28, 58). Moved by Angelita's rare beauty, Freeman undertakes her reeducation in racial matters, and at one point he congratulates himself on his "having a positive influence over her after all" (p. 66). Through the contact with Freeman not only Angelita has her mind straightened but so does her brother Ralph, a police officer who had married a Russian woman through a mail order catalogue as part of an existential quest for whiteness. In the end Ralph awakes from his cultural slumber and lifts the "political cataracts" that blurred his vision, and after a series of eye-opening events he starts dating, lo and behold, a Haitian woman (pp. 116, 119). In his gallant dedication to enable Angelita and her family to accept and cherish their African heritage, Lamb's Freeman embodies the mindset of many African Americans who construe the reticence of Dominicans and other dark-skinned Latinos to make blackness their primary identity as a form of alienation that requires urgent corrective treatment.

Many Dominicans have already assumed a discourse of identity that emanates from the particular struggles of the black liberation movement in the United States. A small contingent already exists in New York made up of individuals of various hues who think of themselves not as "Dominicans" but as "Africans born in the Dominican Republic." Similarly Dominican youngsters who are brought up in this country, where bipolar racial categories reign supreme, are likely to adopt the racial classifications administered by their environment. Sociologist Ramona Hernández looked at the 1990 U.S. Census with an eye on how Dominicans identify themselves ethnically and detected a pattern showing that the longer Dominican youngsters have resided in the United States the greater their chances of classifying themselves as black. Sociologist Ginetta Candelario has unearthed an invaluable sixty-year-long story of Dominicans in Washington, D.C., highlighting, among other things, that they choose black for their self-definition in the overwhelming majority of the cases (Candelario 2000).

Despite the inherent value of overcoming the vestiges of a negrophobic education, the question remains as to whether upholding a sense of racial identity that stems from the imposition of one's environment can in the end be considered liberating. For Dominicans to submit to the logic of North American racial polarities, to internalize extraneous paradigms of identity, would be to disregard the complexity of their own national experience regarding interracial relations. What Bonilla has said of Puerto Ricans applies equally well to Dominicans: our "complacency and equivocation with respect to race and even our more genuine accommodation of racial difference have little place here... We cannot continue to pretend to be an island of civility and racial harmony untouched by the storm of racial conflict that surrounds us" (Bonilla 1980:464). Like the Puerto Ricans and all other peoples dominated by the West, we come from a background that "taught us to experience blackness as misfortune," and to pass the test of our moral strength it behooves us individually and collectively to stand up for what is black in us as proudly as we do for our Dominicanness (Bonilla 1980:464).

We can point to instances of proud assertion of blackness within Dominicanness in the diaspora as many members of the community have come to terms with the unsung portion of their ethnic and cultural heritage. The often quoted phrase "Until I came to New York, I didn't know I was black," by the U.S.-educated Dominican woman poet Chiqui Vicioso, describes the state of mind of many Dominicans in this country (Shorris 1992:146). The historian Moya Pons argued in 1981 that Dominicans discovered their "black roots" in the United States and that they have in turn influenced their native land by returning home with their discovery. He viewed "returning migrants" as "new social agents of modernity, capitalism, and racial emancipation" that had contributed to the overall transformation of "Dominican society and the Dominican mind." Moya Pons illustrated this claim by pointing to the vogue enjoyed in the Dominican Republic by hairstyles, dress, popular music, and other expressions associated with American blacks, as well as the popularity of dark-skinned artists and politicians (Moya Pons 1981:32–33).

Judged from the vantage point of the present, when we witness a virtual consensus among public opinion sectors of the Dominican Republic regarding the image of return migrants as a menace to the health of Dominican society, we sadly fear that Moya Pons may have overstated his case. A point in his favor, though, could be that the antipathy and rejection that the Dominican diaspora is met with in the homeland may actually conceal a timorous acknowledgment of the diaspora's power to influence mainstream Dominican society. But the spirit of Moya's claims continues to find apt corroboration. The Cuban scholar Jorge Duany of the University of Puerto Rico attests to the transformation that Dominicans undergo as they experience international migration. Duany concurs that "migration has transformed the cultural conceptions of racial identity among Dominicans in the United States and Puerto Rico," arguing that for many of them "coming to America has meant coming to terms with their own, partially suppressed, sometimes painful, but always liberating sense of *negritud*" (Duany 1996:38).

A people doesn't ask to become a diaspora. There are normally unfortunate circumstances that render us so. And if we are permitted to invoke dialectical processes, we can speak of a good side to every bad thing. Whatever suffering Dominicans have endured in the foreign shores where despair has expelled them they have also learned to see themselves more fully, more fairly, particularly in matters of race. The long struggles for equality and social justice by people of color in the United States have yielded invaluable lessons from which Dominican people in the diaspora and in the native land have drawn and may continue to draw empowerment. The diaspora will render an inestimable service to the Dominican people if it can help to rid the country of white supremacist thought and negrophobic discourse, in whatever quantity those aberrations may survive in Dominican society. Then we shall be able to celebrate our rich African heritage as well as the social and cultural legacies bequeathed by Afro-Dominicans from their first arrival in 1502, to the Monte Grande rebellion in 1844, to the struggle for human dignity waged daily by the diaspora in places not always hospitable. Ultimately, this celebratory retrospective will bring our black consciousness into focus on the national arena but in a way that defies racial extremism. On the international arena, one hopes that this black awareness with a Dominican difference might become apparent to the scholars and thinkers who concur with Gilroy in viewing the discourse on racial and ethnic difference as crucial to the idea of culture in the modern West. If one accepts "the year Columbus crosses the Atlantic Ocean" as marking "the beginning of the modern era," it would seem odd to have a conversation about the sociohistorical processes and the cultural dynamics that ensued – with blackness at its core – without the least reference to the site where the paradigms of modernity triggered by the conquest of America were first rehearsed (Todorov 1984:5).

REFERENCES

Alfau Durán, Vetilio, ed.
1994 Escritos en Clio, vol. 2. Publicaciones del Sequicentenario de la Independencia Nacional. Santo Domingo: Gobierno Dominicano.

Anon.
1906 Santo Domingo. A Brief Sketch of the Island, Its Resources, and Commercial Possibilities with Special Reference to the Treaty Now Pending in the United States Senate. New York: New York Commercial.

Balcácer, Juan Daniel
1989 Peña Batlle y su marco histórico. Introduction to Ensayos históricos, by Manuel Arturo Peña Batlle. Juan Daniel Balcácer, ed. Pp. v–xix. Santo Domingo: Fundación Peña Batlle.

Bonilla, Frank
1980 Beyond Survival: Por qué seguiremos siendo puertorriqueños. In The Puerto Ricans: Their History, Culture, Society. Adalberto López, ed. Pp. 453–464. VT: Schenkman.

Burdick, John
1992 The Myth of Racial Democracy. NACLA's Report on the Americas 24.4: 40–44.

Campillo Perez, Julio Genaro ed.
1994 Documentos del primer gobierno dominicano: Junta Central Gubernativa, febrero–noviembre 1844. Santo Domingo: Colección del Sesquicentenario de la Independencia Nacional.

Candelario, Ginetta E. B.
2000 Situating Ambiguity: Dominican Identity Formations. Ph.D. dissertation, City University of New York.

Cartagena Portalatín, Aída
1986 Culturas africanas: Rebeldes con causa. Coleción Montesinos. Santo Domingo: Biblioteca Nacional.

Cocco de Filippis, Daisy ed.
1988 From Desolation to Compromise: Bilingual Anthology of the Poetry of Aída Cartagena Portalatín. Emma Jane Robinett, trans. Santo Domingo: Taller.

Courtney, W. S.
1860 The Gold Fields of Santo Domingo. New York: Anson P. Norton.

Davis, Martha Ellen
1987 La otra ciencia: El vodú dominicano como religión y medicina populares. Santo Domingo: Editora Universitaria UASD.

Deive, Carlos Esteban
1992 Vodu y magia en Santo Domingo. 3rd edition. Santo Domingo: Fundación Cultural Dominicana.
—— 1990 La herencia africana en la cultura dominicana actual. Ensayos sobre cultura dominicana. 2nd edition. Bernardo Vega, ed. Pp. 105–141. Santo Domingo: Fundación Cultural Dominicana/Museo del Hombre Dominicano.

Del Monte, Félix María
1979 Cantos dominicanos. Poesía popular dominicana. 3rd edition. Emilio Rodríguez Demorizi, ed. Pp. 244–246. Santiago: UCMM.

Díaz Quiñones, Arcadio
1994 Pedro Henríquez Ureña: Modernidad, diáspora y construcción de identidades. Modernización e identidades sociales. Gilberto Giménez and Ricardo Pozas H., eds. Pp. 59–117. México D.F.: Universidad Nacional Autónoma de México.
—— 1993 La memoria rota. San Juan, Puerto Rico: Ediciones Huracán.

Duany, Jorge
1996 Transnational Migration from the Dominican Republic: The Redefinition of Racial Identity. Paper presented at the Center for Latin American Studies 45th Annual Conference, Race, Culture and National Identity in the Afro-American Diaspora, University of Florida, Gainesville, February 21–24.

Duarte, Juan Pablo
1994 Simientes de la gloria: Ideario de Duarte. In Escritos en Clio, Vol. 2. Vetilio Alfau Durán, ed. Pp. 23–31. Publicaciones del Sequicentenario de la Independencia Nacional. Santo Domingo: Gobierno Dominicano.

Fennema, Meinder, and Troetje Loewenthal
1989 La Construcción de Raza y Nación en la República Dominicana. Anales del Caribe 9: 191–227.

Gaffney, James
1994 Race and Politics Where America Began. America 170(18): 10–12.

Gilroy, Paul
1993 The Black Atlantic: Modernity and Double Consciousness. Cambridge, MA: Harvard University Press.

Gúzman, Daisy Josefina
1974 Raza y lenguage en el Cibao. Eme-Eme: Estudios Dominicanos 11: 3–45.

Hancock, Henry J.
1905 The Situation in Santo Domingo. Annals of the American Academy of Political and Social Science 463: 47–52.

Henríquez Ureña, Pedro
1978 La utopía de América. Angel Rama and Rafael Gutiérrez Girardot, eds. Caracas: Biblioteca Ayacucho.

Hughes, Langston
1974   Selected Poems. New York: Vintage Books.
Julián, Rafael ed.
1982   Cuentos orales de origen africanos. Cuadernos del CENDIA, 312(10). Santo Domingo: Editora de la UASD.
Keim, Deb. Randolph
1870   San Domingo. Philadelphia: Clayton, Remsen, & Haffelfinger.
Lamb, David
1994   Do Platanos Go Wit' Collard Greens? New York: I Write What I Like, Inc.
"Liborio-Liborismo"
1986   Enciclopedia Dominicana. 3rd edition. Vol. 4: 248–265.
Lipski, John M.
1994   A New Perspective on Afro-Dominican Spanish. Research Paper Series No. 26. Albuquerque, New Mexico: University of New Mexico.
Mariñez, Pablo
1986   Relaciones domínico-haitianas y raíces histórico-culturales africanas en la República Dominicana: Bibliografía básica. Santo Domingo: Editora Universitaria UASD.
Megenney, William
1990   Africa en Santo Domingo: Su herencia lingüística. Santo Domingo: Museo del Hombre Dominicano/Academia de Ciencias de la República Dominicana.
Moya Pons, Frank
1992   Manual de historia dominicana. 9th edition. Santo Domingo: Caribbean Publishers.
——— 1981 Dominican National Identity and Return Migration. Occasional Paper #1, Gainesville: Center for Latin American Studies, University of Florida at Gainesville.
Peña Batlle, Manuel Arturo
1989   Ensayos históricos. Juan Daniel Balcácer, ed. Santo Domingo: Fundación Peña Batlle.
Peña Gómez, José Francisco, and Fernando Alvarez Bogaert
1994   Anatomía del fraude electoral: Testimonio preliminar. Santo Domingo: Acuerdo de Santo Domingo.
Report of the Commission of Inquiry to Santo Domingo
1871   Commissioners B. F. Wade, A. D. White, and S. G. Howe. Washington, D.C.: Government Printing Office.

Rosario Adames, Fausto
1994   Censura contra la historia contemporánea. Rumbo (October 17): 6–14.
Rosenberg, June
1979   El Gagá: Religión y sociedad de un culto dominicano. Santo Domingo: Editora Universitaria UASD.
Sagás, Ernesto
1993   A Case of Mistaken Identity: Antihaitianismo in Dominican Culture. Latinoamericanist 29(1): 1–5.
Sanchez Valverde, Antonio
1988   Ensayos. Biblioteca de Clásicos Dominicanos, 5. Santo Domingo: Ediciones de la Fundación Corripio.
Santo Domingo: A Paper from the Knickerbocker Magazine
1863   New York: American West India Co.
Shorris, Earl
1992   Latinos: A Biography of a People. New York: Avon Books.
Tansill, Charles Callan
1938   The United States and Santo Domingo: 1793–1873. Baltimore: Johns Hopkins University Press.
Tejeda Ortiz, Dagoberto, Fernando Sánchez Martínez, and César Mella Mejía
1993   Religiosidad popular dominicana y psiquiatría. Santo Domingo: Editora Corripio.
Todorov, Tsvetan
1984   The Conquest of America: The Question of the Other. Richard Howard, trans. New York: Harper & Row.
Torres-Saillant, Silvio
1998   The Tribulations of Blackness: Stages in Dominican Racial Identity. Latin American Perspectives: 25.3: 126–146.
——— 1995 The Dominican Republic. In No Longer Invisible: Afro-Latin Americans Today. Minority Rights Group, ed. Pp. 109–138. London: Minority Rights Group.
——— 1993 Western Discourse and the Curriculum (The Uniting of Multicultural America). Impart: Journal of OpenMind 1: 7–64.
Welles, Sumner
1966 [1928] Naboth's Vineyard: The Dominican Republic (1844–1924). Mamaroneck, NY: Paul P. Appel.

West, Cornel
1993   Race Matters. Boston: Beacon Press.
Winn, Peter
1999   Americas: The Changing Face of Latin
       America and the Caribbean. Updated edition.
       Berkeley: University of California Press.

Zaglul, Antonio
1980   Despreciada en la vida y olvidada en la
       muerte: Biografia de Evangelina Rodríguez.
       Santo Domingo: Taller.

Part IV

Popular Cultures

16

Jennifer's Butt

Frances Negrón-Muntaner

The materiality of the body is not to be taken for granted, for it is acquired, constituted, through the development of morphology.
Judith Butler, *Bodies That Matter*

True wealth and abundance are not on the highest or on the medium level, but only in the lower stratum.
Mikhail Bakhtin, *Rabelais and His World*

I went to see the recent Gregory Nava movie *Selena* (1997), in a half-empty suburban theater in Philadelphia with about a dozen other solemn, mostly Puerto Rican families dressed up in their Sunday best; parents scolding *los niños* in a low voice, so they would eat popcorn, sit down, and shut up. The sight was unusual, even extraordinary, since one rarely sees Phila-Ricans outside of a few segregated neighborhoods, and much less in the bizarrely named middle-class suburb of Andorra. Once the movie began, unsure about what mystical forces had dragged me to that cushioned seat on a Sunday afternoon, I wondered why *los otros puertorriqueños* had also trekked so far from the streets of *el norte*, where people are more likely to follow La India, Olga Tañón, and Thalía than Selena, and bootleg video copies can be obtained easily from your neighborhood corner store at a cost of only $9.00.

There is the possibility that we – as many others – were swept away by an intense necrophilia, momentarily followed by spasms of melancholia and sadness for the loss of a young

life, a frequent occurrence in inner-city Latino-America. Unlike most Latino youths, who get killed after a drug deal has gone sour or a bullet surprisingly arrives with their name on it, Selena has passed on to sainthood: not only for dying young, but for dying on the way to another, better place; the immigrant fantasies of the seamless plot known as the American Dream. But, even for those of us who no longer believed in a dream that slips away faster than welfare reform is enacted, Puerto Rican viewers were spared any psychic anxiety. On the one hand, the film affirmed that with hard work, talent, and a strong family, "we" can make it, too. On the other, the possible trepidation over not belonging to an ambitious, close-knit clan, over having raised ordinary kids or lacking the strength to push hard, was pacified by how Selena died: *los ricos también lloran.*

Yet, twenty minutes into *Selena*, a queer sense of dread began to overtake me. Like Quintanilla's big bus, the mimetic pact that generally binds spectator and biopic inexplicably broke down.

Regardless of how hard I tried, I did not see Selena. I either saw Jennifer Lopez and Selena, phantasmagorically juxtaposed as if on a glass surface, or *simplemente* Jennifer. This mystifying state of mind seemed to have occurred not only in Selena's parents and producers while filming the reenactment of the Houston Astrodome concert, but in Selena's fans as well. " 'When I came into the stadium, the fans started screaming,' recalls Lopez. 'They were saying "Selena!" But they were saying "Jennifer," too.' "[1] This holy ghost effect was not, of course, an accident. Mark Sanchez, makeup artist for both Selena and Jennifer Lopez, takes the credit for altering Lopez's features to match Selena's: "Jennifer has a wider, flatter nose than Selena, almost like a boxer's. I had to contour Jennifer's to make it look narrower and larger.... As the makeup progressed, I was taken aback, and had to stop what I was doing. It was almost as if I had Selena in my makeup chair again."[2] Despite Mark's efforts, however, "Jennifer" continued to ring louder in my ears than "Selena." From the heavens above me, I heard voices ordering my removal to the lower depths of cultural criticism; away from the American dream, and into the flesh of unjustly denied discursive pleasures. Possessed, I began to write deliriously in the darkness.

Rear Endings: Jennifer Is the Medium

In contrast with the other U.S.-born Puerto Rican actresses of the last four decades, Jennifer Lopez can play on the hyphen and come out *al otro lado*. Embodying ideal "Latin" beauty (which Rosie Péres seemingly "fails" to do) – that is, neither too dark nor too light – the Puerto Rican label doesn't seem to stick to her even in the white media. For example, a *People* magazine columnist referred to her ethnic background as "being of Puerto Rican . . . *descent*" (italics mine).[3] In a handful of other popular newspapers and magazine articles, she is simply a New York "native" and/or raised in the Bronx. While the "Bronx" is a loud enough cue for those in the know, it certainly doesn't ring the same bell in Texas – or perhaps it does. Ironically, the only time during the *Selena* pre-release hype Lopez unequivocally became a *puertorriqueña* was when

some Mexican-Americans protested her being cast as a Chicana: "While many of her fans of Mexican descent anxiously awaited the opening of the movie, some are angry that a Puerto Rican was cast as Selena."[4]

The epic scale of *Selena*'s casting call has been compared to that of *Gone with the Wind*. The ironies of such a comparison aside, much was at stake in the making of *Selena*. No interested parties – Warner Brothers, the Quintanillas, or the Chicano producer and director – were going to chance blowing the movie's possibilities of becoming the "official" celluloid story on Selena, the biggest Latino movie hit since *La Bamba*, and a moneymaker that would finally (once and for all) prove that the soon-to-be-largest minority in "America" will pay to see "themselves" on the big screen. The bottom line was that, as the hottest Latina actress in Hollywood at the time, Lopez was picked so she could deliver in the language every backer understood best: *dinero, mucho dinero*. (That she had performance experience and dance training probably helped, too).

Constantly quizzed by the media on the disapproval that met her being cast for the part, Lopez argued that she was well-suited to play Selena because they shared an ethnic identity as Latinas beyond their "national" identities. "I don't think the actress who played her had to be Mexican-American because Selena was," Lopez said. "Selena and I are both Latinas and both had the common experience of growing up Latina in this country. This was good enough."[5]

Lopez's defense points to interesting dystopias. While it is arguable that a Latino identity "exists" as a cultural formation across the United States, and that this identity has erased or displaced nationalist investments, it is also undeniable that for those born and raised in major urban spaces with significant and diverse "Latino" communities, the construct, although not exhausting our complexity, has constitutive materiality. Selena's career, for instance, is a good case study. In order to go beyond the *tejano* niche market, Selena expanded her repertoire to include Caribbean, South American, and pan-Latin American genres such as boleros, and later went on to record in English, incorporating New York Caribbean influences. In this marketing and audience-building trajectory, Selena went from being a Tejana (a territorialized "regional" identity) to being a Latina (an "ethnic minority"). "Latino," in this case, does not refer to a cultural identity, but to a specifically American national currency for economic and political deal making; a technology to demand and deliver emotions, votes, markets, and resources on the same level as other racialized minorities.

Simultaneously, given the actual political economy of representation in Hollywood, Puerto Ricans, with less institutional clout, general population, and numbers on Hollywood's home turf, need "Latino" a lot more than other "Latinos" (i.e., Chicanos and Cubans) need us. Consider that if Puerto Rican actors could only play Puerto Ricans, and not other "Latino" roles, Puerto Ricans would only be seen on the screen in secondary roles as criminals, prostitutes, and maids. Hence, Jennifer Lopez's argument is both strategic and ironic. As a strategy, "Latino" are delivered and talked about as a cohesive identity and as a market, the groups so alluded to know that communities, alliances, and power structures are usually not "Latino," but specifically Mexican-American, Cuban, and/or Puerto Rican.

Although the controversy did not go any deeper than these territorial *dime y directes*, and many who were disgruntled by the casting choice later admitted that "once we saw the trailers, we were happy,"[6] there was one site of Latina identification that Jennifer Lopez relentlessly pursued as overriding all other instances. "I'm all in favor of Latinos playing Latinos," Lopez said, "but saying a Puerto Rican couldn't play Selena, a Texas girl, is taking it a bit far. Selena looked like me. She was dark and she was, well, *curvy*"[7] (italics mine).

Jennifer Lopez's close identification with Selena seemed not only based on their parallel crossover successes, but on a common experience of having a similar build, a body generally considered abject by American standards of beauty and propriety. In fact, some writers have compared Selena's popularity among Mexican-Americans to the Virgin of Guadalupe's. "With her simple clothes and cinnamon skin, [Selena] looked exactly like the people. . . . She showed us just how beautiful we could be and she did it without dying her hair Fanta orange or wearing those oppressive

blue contacts that make so many of us look like fallen angels – she was the gorgeous *chola morena* who never forgot her pueblo and we feel under her protection."[8] This pious site of identification between fan and star was not lost on director Gregory Nava, who had a significant part in casting Lopez. "If you're raised in this country, since childhood, you're given this image of beauty. And if you're *pocha* – Mexican-American – it's not you. So you're made to feel bad about the way you look or the way your body is, having big hips or whatever, from when you're a kid."[9]

"Latino" cultural practices tend to be managed discursively by "serious" concepts such as class, language, religion, and family – the stuff of sociology and political activism. It was precisely the body, however, particularly the curves (or in less poetic Puerto Rican street language, the *culo*), that proved to be the most compelling way that Lopez and others found to speak about how "Latinas" are constituted as racialized bodies, what kind of cultural capital is associated with these bodies, and how the body surfaces as a site of pleasure, produced by intersections of power, but not entirely under its own control.

Although race was hardly mentioned in this debate over curves and rear ends, for any Caribbean interlocutor, references to this part of the human anatomy are often a way of speaking about Africa in(side) America. Not coincidentally, the major work on racism by a Puerto Rican author, Isabelo Zenón Cruz, is titled *Narciso descubre su trasero* (Narcissus discovers his rear end). And despite the fact that Selena was Chicana, an ethnicity not associated in the Caribbean popular imagination with big butts, she was definitely curvy. "Jennifer has the same measurements Selena had," said Julie Ramirez, Selena's seamstress.[10] In fact, Selena's butt was, from a Puerto Rican perspective, one of the elements that made her not specifically Chicana, but "Latina," and hence more easily embraced as one of our own.

An Epistemology of the Butt

Marketing Selena to "Latino" audiences required that the cast, director, and producers be available to the Spanish-speaking media, which mostly caters to Spanish-dominant immigrants. This inevitably created the context for each key player to show their fluency in Spanish, and hence their "realness" in relation to national culture. During a special episode on *Cristina*, a popular Univisión talk show, the audience had a chance to discern whether these "Latinos" were "one of us" (Puerto Ricans or Mexicans), secondhand copies (Niuyoricans or Chicanos), or downright impostors (Americanos). Thus, while Jon Seda (also of Puerto Rican "descent") could only begin his sentences in Spanish and then quickly had to switch to English, and Moctesuma Esparza spoke *bien mejicano*, Jennifer Lopez's Spanish was classic Niuyorican. She spoke a second-generation, Bronx-inflected Spanish, with its distinctive twang, occasional English vocabulary and Spanish syntax. But, whatever the qualms any Puerto Rican language purist entertained while Jennifer spoke Spanish, these must have quickly withered away when the main question of the night finally arrived. As in other talk shows during the promotion of Selena, there came a moment during the interview when the question had to be posed to Jennifer Lopez: "¿Todo eso es tuyo?" (Is that body for real?) In other words, is that big butt yours or is it prosthetic? Although a fair question for many Hollywood actresses' faces and breasts, Jennifer Lopez smiled as if she had been waiting a long time for this moment. She stood up, gave a 360-degree turn, patted her butt, and triumphantly sat down: "Todo es mío." It's all mine. But, like the Puerto Rican rapper Lisa M. warns the inexperienced suitor or ligón, "No invente, papito/que no va'a tocar" (Don't even think you're going to have a piece of this!)

Jennifer Lopez's need to speak about her own butt in interview after interview – before and after the movie's release – can only constitute a keen awareness of her historical role as the next big bottom in the Puerto Rican cultural imaginary and our great avenger of Anglo analphobia. In the context of American popular magazines and "entertainment" sections of daily newspapers, however, Jennifer's affirmation of her body simply read as a defense of another sensuality and alter/native standards of beauty. "Rita Hayworth (who was actually Rita Cansino) and Raquel Welch could only become stars after they disguised themselves. Selena could be who

she was and, as for me, for once, I could be proud of my big bottom. . . . In my movies, I've always had costume people looking at me a little weary and immediately fitting me out with things to hide my bottom. I know it. They didn't say, but I know it. With this film, it was different."[11]

As just and noble as the claim of diversifying the concept of beauty may be, I would take Jennifer's praise of the ass further, and propose it as a way of popularizing an "attitude" in relation to dominant culture, more like "kiss my ass" after having one's "ass kicked" for being Puerto Rican and/or Latino. As Freud put it, an invitation to view or (visually) caress the rear end expresses "defiance or defiant scorn, and this is in reality an act of tenderness that has been overtaken by repression."[12] As Bakhtin argued in his study on Rabelais, showing ass is also a sign of getting even. "The rump is the 'back of the face,' the 'face turned inside out.' The grotesque gesture of displaying the buttocks is still used in our day."[13] Jennifer's display was (at least) a triple sign: "showing ass" as a sign of identity and pride, "kiss my ass" as a form of revenge against a hostile cultural gaze, and "I'm going to kick your ass" vis-à-vis the economic exploitation implicated in racism. In Lopez's case, this third rear victory is evident in her current status as Hollywood's highest-paid Latina actress. No wonder she says, "I have a curvaceous Latin body . . . . I like to accentuate that."[14] So would I, all the way to the bank.

Constantly speaking about big rumps in the American media is also a way to "lower" the discussion away from the self-importance granted to celebritydo(o)m and the upper stratum of breasts, straight noses, blonde hair, and (white) faces. Despite Jennifer's relative victory and the Latino community's growing demographics, the big Latin behind is far from sitting easy. Dominant culture still obsessively prohibits its display and punishes transgressors. In one of Selena's last music videos, for example, included in a sixty-minute tape titled *Selena Remembered* (1996, produced by Abraham Quintanilla and José Behar of EMI Latino), she sings her number three hit single, "No me queda más," in a tight white sequined dress. Within the documentary, the actual music video is intercut with scenes from its making, including some "spontaneous" sequences of the production process. The viewer can see an awkward Selena walking under archways wearing what seems to be a white, see-through veil – or better still, tail – cascading from her waist. A few minutes after the enigmatic garment makes its entrance, Selena speaks to the camera in a candid moment between takes, while several attendants undo her dress's hem. The mystery of the tail is revealed: "This is what happens when you gain weight before a video." Selena breaks down laughing and one might fancy her making fun of people who think a big butt is something to hide. Unfortunately, that was probably not the case.

According to journalist María Celeste Arrarás (but denied by Abraham Quintanilla), had Selena lived the dream, she would have done so with a surgically intervened body. Selena had already been caught in the crossover fire. As her success increasingly placed her in a mainstream – white – stage, Selena's insecurities about her body mounted. "She started watching her diet and keeping herself looking svelte. . . . She drank gallons of water with lemon juice and she herself would massage her thighs in a circular pattern, believing this could help her to combat cellulite. She also saw herself as having a more than abundant derriere, not realizing that her voluptuousness was one of the characteristics her fans most adored about her."[15] Indeed. Yet, sometime after September of 1994, Arrarás adds that Selena actually did have liposuction surgery. The spanking gaze of puritan culture was breaking Selena down. Her growing attachment to the doctor that performed the surgery, Doctor Ricardo Martínez, also proved to be doubly treacherous. Not only did it represent Selena's flight from her voluptuous body, but a turning point in her relationship with Yolanda Saldívar. "Yolanda had to settle with tending to her friend and taking care of her after the [liposuction] operation, giving her massages to prevent air bubbles from forming under the skin. Yolanda was not at all happy that her friend was coming to depend more on Martínez and less on her. She was quite perceptive and immediately knew she was losing control of the situation."[16] While it is impossible to speculate whether Selena's destiny would have been different had she not met the doctor, narratively speaking, the operation was a fateful turning point.

Perhaps Jennifer Lopez was aware of this story's seductiveness, and as a talisman against death repeated a litany of complaints aimed at American bottomphobic attitudes. She loudly and publicly complained that costume fitters and producers suspiciously looked at her behind and mentally rehearsed different ways to hide it. "All the other movies I've done [besides *Selena*], it always seemed like they're trying to hide it or they think I look fat. Or I'm not in the American tradition of beauty."[17] Given all the bad blood about this state of affairs, it seems fitting to ask: Why is a big butt so upsetting to American image gatekeepers?

A big culo does not only upset hegemonic (white) notions of beauty and good taste, it is a sign for the dark, incomprehensible excess of "Latino" and other African diaspora cultures. Excess of food (unrestrained), excess of shitting (dirty), and excess of sex (heathen) are its three vital signs. Like hegemonic white perceptions of Latinos, big butts are impractical and dangerous. A big Latin rear end is an invitation to pleasures construed as illicit by puritan ideologies, heteronormativity, and the medical establishment through the three deadly vectors of miscegenation, sodomy, and a high-fat diet. Unlike the functionality of breasts, big bottoms have no morals, no symbolic family function, and no use in reproduction. Or, in Simone de Beauvoir's classic words, "the buttocks are that part of the body with the fewest nerves, where the flesh seems an aimless fact."[18]

Of course, feminists and politically correct activists will complain that the exaltation of the big rear end is but another way of enslaving women to their bodies and linking Latinos to stereotypes of hypersexuality. In addition, there are *puertorriqueñas chumbas*, Latino men with the sex appeal of dirty dishes, and other erotogenic zones that should not be subsumed and ignored under the weight of the big butt. But what makes the ass a seductive trope is that nobody can quite take a culo seriously, and even when its deployment is meant to be offensive or political, its lowliness allows all implicated sides to ease out of the situation with a smile. Like the camel hump, the Puerto Rican butt suggests that bodies are made of something else besides language, even when we can only speak about them discursively, and that the gap between the materiality of language and flesh can never be totally bridged. Island-based writer Magali García Ramis, for instance, claims that Puerto Rican "identity" is not based on politics nor an exaggerated love for the *mono-estrellada* flag, but in the amount of excess fat we consume. "Un tun tun de grasa y fritanguería recorre las venas borincanas, nos une, nos aúna, nos hermana por encima de la política y los políticos, los cultos y las religiones, la salsa y el rock, el matriarcado y el patriarcado."[19] In other words, the rear end is where our Puerto Ricanness is safely stored.

Still, while starch and grease may bind some of us, Jennifer, who as we may recall grew up in the Bronx, has likely seen the effects of too much *arroz y habichuelas* on her fundamental commodity, and has found a distinctive American way of putting a stop to its overflowing traffic. "Unlike the real Selena, who jokes that she kept her curvy shape by eating pepperoni pizza, Lopez watches her diet and works out four times a week."[20]

Moderation is not unwarranted. Times have changed from the golden years of Puerto Rico's most notorious big butt, dancer and singer Iris Chacón. Ambiguity about the "rightness" of a woman being able to build a career on such a "low" attribute as her bottom even invaded one of the most celebratory genres of rump worship: salsa. In "Talento de televisión," a parody of Iris Chacón's rise to stardom due to the unanimous acceptance of her having a fabulous butt, Willie Colón – do I dare say Culón? – attempted to trivialize La Chacón's achievements by moralizing against her strategy: "No tiene talento pero es muy buenamosa" (She has no talent, but looks good). This moralization was premised on several other high/low dichotomies that include television as the site for unsophisticated pleasures, the trasero or rear end as a politically incorrect seduction, and a heterosexual universe in which men have "gran simpatía por su esplendor" (great sympathy for her splendor) and women "antipatía por la razón/de que su palanca fuera su cuerpo y no su valor" (antipathy because/she used her body and not her merit to climb up). Yet, even

Willie had to concede that in the realm of television, or indeed any spectacle (including cinema), "talent" and "seduction" are difficult-to-sustain dichotomies, and that *un buen cuerpo* (a good-looking body) is not only *otra cosa* (something else) but also a *razón poderosa* (powerful reason) for making it. Furthermore, it is doubtful that talent is not needed to become a legend on the basis of your accumulated fatty tissue. How many big rear ends become songs, novels, popular wisdom, and the paradigm for a whole country's wet dreams and cultural self-representation? I say that it takes at least some "talent" to make the talented – Willie himself included? – pay attention to such a thing as your humble little culo.

The prominence of the Puerto Rican butt rests not only on popular musical genres but on several noted literary epistemological texts, including Edgardo Rodríguez Juliá's essays in *Una noche con Iris Chacón*[21] and Luis Rafael Sánchez's well-known novel *La Guaracha del Macho Camacho*,[22] with its refrain of "La vida es una cosa fenomenal/lo mismo pal de alante que pal de atrás" (Life is a fabulous thing/regardless if you're on top or bottom). In each case, sexuality is the discursive flow where the butt acquires its meaning and raison d'être. This framing is, however, limiting. Even in Puerto Rico, references to the butt have many other discursive uses. For example, when a social situation turns chaotic or out of control, we say that it became an *arroz con culo* (rice and butt) or that *se formó un culo* (it became an ass). If we are *groseros* with our mothers or helplessly ask what to do about any displaced object, we will be smilingly told to stick (blank) in our ass.

In the diaspora, the sexual epistemology of the butt gets even more complicated. Gay men may carry the bottom's fetishism to bed as a nostalgia for Condado fucks; nationalistic lesbians use their *culómetros* to distinguish the *boricuas* from other too-close-to-call ethnicities; and many Puerto Rican women, who have and admire their Chacón bodies for their power over men and circumstances, roar as they are subjected to the everyday indignities of being told that they are fat, should get on a diet, or should sign up for the gym. Migrant life, with its characteristic economic and emotional instability, ultimately becomes a struggle to avoid ending up with *el culo al aire* (our butts exposed).

Enter Jennifer Lopez

Enter Jennifer Lopez playing Selena and at last the Puerto Rican diaspora has a big culo to call our own, ending a long stretch of second-class citizenship in both the United States and Puerto Rico. Which doesn't mean that we have forgotten La Chacón. The myth of La Chacón lives on, specially in the Latino drag repertoire, but it is no secret that younger generations are growing up without anyone to fill her *tanga*. Perhaps no one can really replace La Chacón, a queen for a different era. And certainly not Jennifer Lopez, who is a "serious" actress and won't be seen flipping her rear end on Saturday nights in a cheesy television show. More to Willie Colón's liking, Jennifer is not on television, but on the big screen; she is not "vulgar" and her claim to Latino fame is through a "modern-day saint in Spandex."[23] Yet, Jennifer's butt commands respect in its own right and style. A gay journalist and friend based in Miami confirmed my flickering appreciation – only based on images – with the following eyewitness account. "I saw Jennifer at a party with her husband, and I could not help but to stare at her butt. Her dress was so tight you needed a can opener to get it out. She looked glorious."

In gendered terms, the big rear end acts both as an identification site for Latinas to reclaim their beauty and a "compensatory fantasy"[24] for a whole community. Insisting to write or talk about big butts is ultimately a response to the pain of being ignored, thought of as ugly, treated as low, yet surviving – even thriving – through a belly-down epistemology. The pain alluded to by Selena's operation and Jennifer's narcissism (in the Freudian sense) can be re-signified not as an "icono de la inclinación erótica del varón puertorriqueño"[25] (as an icon of the erotic inclinations of the Puerto Rican male) or as an exotic (racist) entertainment for American men, but as an inscription of a different sexual and cultural energy in *gringolandia*. Through Jennifer's butt, the rear end becomes a more ample trope for cultural belonging, as one of the last bastions of Island-Puerto Rican specificity is re-defined, and more elitist signs such as language and place of birth are effectively challenged. In this second sense, Jennifer's popularity among Puerto Ricans – including Islanders – underscores that our intimate relationship with "American" culture and capital is also a domestic affair. Different from La Chacón, Jennifer's butt reaches our Puerto Rican living rooms through Blockbuster Video, funded by a Hollywood studio, speaking English, and playing a Tejana.

In defending his choice to sidestep the circumstances around Selena's death, Gregory Nava said that *Selena* is about "celebrating the American dream."[26] Ilan Stavans optimistically wrote that Latinos are confident that sooner or later "gringos will make room for Latino extroversion and sentimentality."[27] Removed from the prophets' words, and the chimeras of identity discourse and upward mobility, I joyously watched Jennifer's Lopez's quintessential Puerto Rican butt splashed on a suburban (white) screen, and humbly offer my testimony.

Thank you, Saint Selena, for allowing us the grace to see it.

NOTES

I would like to thank Steve Huang, Larry LaFountain, Yolanda Martinez, and Chon Noriega for their useful suggestions and support in writing this essay.

1   Bob Strauss, "Putting an Icon in Film," *The Daily News of Los Angeles* (March 16, 1997): L3.

2   Leila Cobo-Hanlon, "Jennifer Becomes Selena," *Latina* (April–May 1997): 48–53, 52–53.

3   Pam Lambert and Betty Cortina, "Viva Selena," *People Magazine* (March 24, 1997): 160–61.

4   Lynn Carey, "Selena's Posthumous Celebrity Is Taking a Life of Its Own," *The Tampa Tribune* (March 25, 1997): 5.

5   Barry Koltnow, "Jennifer Lopez Plays Selena with Joy and Sorrow," *Dayton Daily News* (March 23, 1997): 5C.

6   Luz Villareal, "New Film Has Selena Fans Singing Star's Praises," *The Daily News of Los Angeles* (March 21, 1997): N3.

7   Mal Vincent, "Lopez is Bursting into Hollywood Spotlight," *The Virginian-Pilot* (March 22, 1997): E8.

8   Barbara Renaud-González, "Santa Selena," *Latina* (April–May 1997): 83.

9   Joe Leydon, "Keeping Dreams Alive," *Los Angeles Times*, December 8, 1996: 6.

10 Pam Lambert and Betty Cortina, "Viva Selena," 160.

11 Mal Vincet, "López Is Bursting," E8.

12 Sigmund Freud, "Character and Anal Eroticism," in *The Freud Reader*, ed. Peter Gay (New York: Norton, 1989): 296.

13 Mikhail Bakhtin, *Rabelais and His World* (Bloomington: Indiana University Press, 1984): 373.

14 "50 Most Beautiful People in the World," *People* (May 12, 1997), 124.

15 María Celeste Arrarás, *Selena's Secret* (New York: Simon and Schuster, 1997), 59–60.

16 Ibid., 81.

17 Leydon, "Keeping Dreams Alive," 6.

18 Simone de Beauvoir, *The Second Sex* (New York: Vintage Books, 1989), 158.

19 Magali García Ramis, "La manteca que nos une," in *La ciudad que nos habita* (Río Piedras: Ediciones Huracán, 1993), 83.

20 "50 Most Beautiful People in the World," 124.

21 Edgardo Rodriguez Juliá, *Una noche con Iris Chacón* (Río Piedras: Editorial Antillana, 1986).

22 Luis Rafael Sánchez, *La Guaracha del Macho Camacho* (Barcelona: Argos Vergara, 1982).

23 Richard Corliss, "ÀViva Selena!" *Time Magazine* (March 24, 1997): 86–87.

24 Judith Butler, *Bodies That Matter* (New York: Routledge, 1993).

25 Rodríguez Juliá, *Una Noche*, 117.

26 Vincent, "Lopéz Is Bursting," E8.

27 Ilan Stavans, "Santa Selena," *Transition* 70 (1997): 36–43.

17

La Quinceañera: Making Gender and Ethnic Identities

Karen Mary Davalos

The church looked empty, but I could hear a man talking to someone about how late it was getting. He complained that the girl and her family had not yet arrived, and he was scheduled to perform a wedding in less than an hour. He sounded angry, so I glanced only briefly at the plastic and natural flowers decorating the pews and the statue of the *Virgen de Guadalupe* before heading outside. Those guests who had arrived stood on the church steps and showed no interest in entering the Byzantine building.

The guests, some dressed in blue jeans and others in formal clothes, greeted each other and talked about the girl of honor. They didn't stand, hushed and quiet, in circles and whisper amongst themselves. No, there was a feeling of familiarity and confidence as the guests mingled around greeting and kissing each other on the cheek. This was not an idle or impatient wait, but a moment for friends and family to catch up on family news, especially news about the girl of honor. However, even when the greetings slowed down to a trickle, no one made a move to go inside. People remained waiting on the steps.

After several minutes, the family began to arrive in small groups. The mother of the girl, bringing a bouquet of flowers, looked tired but happy. Next, the eldest sister arrived with her husband. The girl's brothers brought more flowers and gifts. One brother ran from his car to find the pastor. He called out to me, saying that his sister's limousine had not shown up at the house. Finally, the girl whose fifteenth year we were celebrating and her oldest brother drove up in a dark blue Lincoln Continental. This was the moment for which we had been waiting.

Making Gender and Ethnic Identities Through Cultural Practices

The above story, which comes from my field notes made during dissertation research in Chicago (1990–1992) among *mexicanas* and their families, deliberately leaves the reader at the door of the church waiting for the special celebration to begin.[1] Although the special celebration, called *la quinceañera*, is the concern of this paper, I avoid writing my own representation of this public and familial event because I want to examine how others describe and experience *la quinceañera*.[2] The strategy to highlight the *mexicana* voices of my "field notes" is influenced by fieldwork experiences, university training, and indirect schooling from Chicano ethnographers.

As a self-identified *mexicana* (when in the Midwest) and Chicana (when in the Southwest),

I have often been told that my dissertation research was auto-ethnographic or that I am an "insider." In my years as a student, I felt that this rhetorical comment was an attack or a defense. However, from fieldwork I have found that the everyday dance of getting to know someone, finding one's way through a city, and making mistakes demonstrates how anthropology mystifies the landscape by imposing a cartography of "outsiders" and "insiders" onto a world that is described as "cultural."[3] Patricia Zavella's fieldwork experiences and candid reflection on them encourage us to reexamine the cartography. Zavella, a self-identified Chicana feminist, eloquently writes of her experience as an "insider" conducting fieldwork among women cannery workers in the Santa Clara Valley of California and how she makes the mistake of assuming her identity will "provide ready access to this community of informants." She tells how her "privileges as an educated woman" and her feminism made her an "outsider," creating "some awkward moments."[4]

Not only did I experience awkward moments, *mexicanas* explicitly made me an insider or outsider. *Mexicanas* told me at various times that I was "too dark," that my Spanish was "too perfect," or that "I should have known better." They reversed the color line with which I was familiar (brown skin as the sign of the authentic Chicano), they exploded the rule I had learned in college (fluency in the "native" language promotes rapport with one's informants), and they scolded me for not being what I appeared to be (someone like themselves). Comments such as these blurred the boundaries between "insider" and "outsider" and forced me to realize that I could never speak for these *mexicanas*, only find partial representations of them in my "field notes."

From university-based experiences, I was inspired by the work of James Clifford and Renato Rosaldo, who encourage readers to examine how ethnographies are made and how ethnographers authenticate their work.[5] Clifford writes convincingly about writing styles and strategies used by ethnographers to project a false image of an objective, detached social scientist. Rosaldo advises his contemporaries to imagine themselves as "positioned subjects" who "grasp certain human phenomena better than others" over their lifetime.[6] He tells how his own experience with death made him better able to examine Ilongot emotions. In fact, Rosaldo reminds us, ethnographers usually begin rethinking and revising their project (or perspective) while in the field.[7] The changing perspectives that I anticipated, along with an awareness about writing for academic authority, led me to recognize that this ethnography cannot pretend to be a "unified master summation" about the *quinceañera* and the *mexicanas* who engage in one.[8]

University-based experiences also encouraged me to examine how writing strategies echo larger theoretical perspectives and agendas. The work of third world feminists, such as Chandra T. Mohanty and Gloria Anzaldúa, argues that western feminists who imagine that they are "speaking for" third world women rely on the perspective that dominated women cannot speak for themselves.[9] They each suggest that the process of decolonizing feminist anthropology requires that we study women as active agents, not just exploited and oppressed victims. Therefore, I avoid a general description of the *quinceañera* because I have a third world feminist concern with how *mexicanas*, as social analysts, construct the event and "have a critical perspective on their own situation."[10] I argue that what *mexicanas* have to say about the *quinceañera* can tell us how they construct themselves as historical and oppositional subjects. In addition to paying attention to human agency, I follow Anzaldúa's argument that in the context of domination *mexicanas* invent new meanings and knowledges for their lives that are both creative and contradictory. That is, their agency is not a heroic response to oppression but a negotiation between various, often conflicting, views about women, family, and *mexicano* culture.

My focus on the negotiation and contestation surrounding the event encourages a rethinking of "tradition." The arguments over the *quinceañera* do not spring from misinformation or miscommunication but are indicative of the thing itself. Instead of searching for the "real" or "traditional" *quinceañera*, I seek to discuss "tradition" as an open, and sometimes chaotic, terrain that is constantly reconfigured in everyday experience. The text tries to reflect this fluidity by not taking too seriously (or reifying) the descriptions and categories that invoke the "traditional." For example, during the period of my field research (May 25, 1990 to November 8, 1992), Catholic clergy and laity entered into a heated argument about the most "traditional" meanings and practices that constitute the *quinceañera*. I do not try to settle the argument, but interpret the debate as the on-going construction of "tradition" by the people who are attributed with traditionality.

Indirect, though consistent, training by Chicano ethnographers also influenced my writing and field strategy. This training was not a formal part of my university instruction but resulted from happenstance encounters in the hallway or classroom with Chicano professors who would recommend a book or an article. Like many students of Chicano culture, I read Octavio Romano and Américo Paredes who taught me to distrust anthropological accounts of Mexican Americans that rely on a cultural determinism model.[11] After the smoke cleared and the cultural determinism model was found dead, a more lasting lesson encouraged us to attack anthropology's tendency to abuse its informants by not offering an exchange for information and intrusion. Because of this legacy of abuse, many Chicano ethnographers are determined to "give something back" to the community in which they study. Maxine Baca Zinn identifies non-exploitative reciprocity and exchange as a particular concern of Chicano ethnographers doing research among Chicanos.[12] My approach in the field was to offer my friendship, assistance with employment and employment training, educational counsel, the use of my computer, printer, and typewriter (especially to make résumés), and photographic services at family events (including *quinceañera*) in exchange for a place in people's lives. Post-fieldwork commitments include continued friendship, educational counsel, translation, and writing. *Mexicanas* encouraged me to expand the notion of "giving something back" to include the documentation of their experiences. They repeatedly told me and each other that they were eager to read "my book" about their lives. During my first return to Chicago (July 2 through August 10, 1994), we

spent most of our time together reading my dissertation. For them, the dissertation (and subsequent writing) is a kind of reclaiming of cultural memory, a witness to their past and for their future.[13]

Point of Reference

In what follows, I examine the ways in which people regard the *quinceañera*. For ease of illustration, my analysis is divided into two parts. When read together, the two parts of this paper bring to light how particular explanations, descriptions, and forms of the *quinceañera* are embedded within people's ideas about appropriate gender roles, ethnic identity, traditional culture, sexuality, class position, and anticipated results of culture contact. The first part examines how Catholic priests and journalists regard the event. The popular discussion by Catholic officials and the media enjoys wider circulation and authority than the discussions I heard among *mexicanas* and their families, taken up in the second part of the paper. However, these two parts should not be made to stand for distinct or homogeneous communities that are inherently opposed to each other.

Let me briefly explain. First, there was considerable disagreement among Catholic worshippers, particularly *mexicanas* and their daughters, over the form of the *quinceañera*. They argued over the format, aesthetics, and design of the event. Second, complicated life experiences of members of this group make it difficult to describe them as "immigrants" or to categorize them by "generation." Although the more than forty *mexicanas* that I met in Chicago all have legal standing in the United States and have been raised in Chicago, they have various ties to Mexico and the United States as a homeplace. Half of the women consistently travel to Mexico, spending their summer or winter vacations there. Between the ages of fifteen and twenty-one, *mexicanas* might spend up to six months in Mexico. *Mexicanas* with children told me that they deliberately traveled to Mexico during a child's first few years so that the infant could learn to speak Spanish. Family members from Mexico also "vacation" in Chicago. The length of the visit often depends on the job market, upcoming family celebrations, and emotional ties. At any given time, I could visit households composed of both Mexican and United States citizens, the former often becoming a significant part of my research. In addition, I found several households in which United States citizenship did not indicate someone's place of birth or their homeplace. In one family the first and third child were born in Mexico, while the second and last in the United States. The parents, one born in the United States and the other a naturalized U.S. citizen, had "returned" to Mexico after retirement. Dispersion, travel, and reterritorialization better describe their experiences.

In the same light, we must recognize that Catholic officials do not come from discrete communities. Many of Chicago's Spanish-speaking clergy are from Spain and Poland. The Chicago Archdiocese requires that those who minister to *mexicano* neighborhoods such as Pilsen, Little Village, Back of the Yards, and South Chicago have a functional understanding of Spanish. Language ability, however, reveals nothing about one's multicultural sensibilities, so that even the *mexicano* parishes with origins in the 1920s find little support from the Archdiocese of Chicago.[14] Multicultural insensitivity is the result of a history of Americanization efforts within the Archdiocese of Chicago and a legacy of national parishes that promoted xenophobia rather than interethnic tolerance. Nonetheless, the Hispanic Caucus, composed of clergy who minister to Spanish-speaking neighborhoods, attempts to hold the Archdiocese accountable to the needs of *mexicano* and Puerto Rican worshippers. The Hispanic Caucus does not, however, have a united perspective on the *quinceañera*.

Although I am not willing to generalize about the *quinceañera* in an attempt to encourage readers to focus on different voices and discourses, other ethnographers and journalists have been willing to do so. I include their accounts of the *quinceañera* to provide the reader with a point of reference. The following accounts compare a *quinceañera* to a bar mitzvah, to a Southern debutante coming-out party, and to a wedding.

In one of two Chicago ethnographic accounts,[15] anthropologist Gwen Stern had this to say about a "traditional" *quinceañera*:

[It] can be an elaborate event, equal to a wedding, in both time and expense.[16]

The first part of the quinceañera involves a mass in church where the girl gives thanks for guidance and makes a promise before the altar of the Virgin of Guadalupe. There is a procession up the aisle, with the girl on her father's arm, preceded by her attendants. During the mass, the religious medal is presented to the girl by her padrinos, and blessed by the priest.[17]

Less affluent families, and less traditional ones, may simply give a birthday party on a daughter's fifteenth birthday, since a full-fledged quinceañera is an expensive affair.[18]

Although Stern's dissertation rejects the acculturation and assimilation models popular in the 1960s and early 1970s, her account of the *quinceañera* assumes that the contents of people's lives can be reduced to "more or less" traditional. Stern produces a code for behavior instead of her goal to take a "process-oriented approach" sensitive to how actors "manipulate symbols."[19]

Journalist David Beard also focused on the movement of the girl and her attendants, making it easy to compare the event to a wedding. His lengthy article for *Lifestyle*, a Sunday supplement in the *Chicago Tribune*, was accompanied by photographs of the girl dancing, her father and mother, and the reception.

A court of 14 couples slowly strolled down the center aisle as the organist played the processional. At the altar each couple parted, the girls turning left and the boys turning right. Only the girl in white satin remained; her head tilted downward in a show of respectful deference; heavy breaths moved her shoulders up and down, betraying feelings of expectation and fear. Her father walked to her left; her mother to her right.

There was only one person missing – the groom. In a *quinceañera* (keen-sa-an-YAIR-uh), a Mexican celebration of a girl's 15th birthday that dates back to the Aztecs, there is no groom. It is hard for non-Mexicans to understand the *fiesta quinceañera* (Spanish for "15th party"), although hundreds are performed each year in Chicago, especially in later summer and early autumn. Think of it as a social debut. Or as a Catholic bar mitzvah for girls.[20]

Ten years later, Constanza Montaña, the *Chicago Tribune*'s specialist on Latino events, also described the procession.

Fourteen young women in long pink gowns, escorted by 14 young men wearing high school ROTC uniforms, walked down the aisle at St. Philomena's Catholic Church in the North Side neighborhood of Hermosa recently. They were followed by a little boy in tails and a little girl in a formal dress, each carrying a white satin pillow.

As they filed into the pews, the young people turned to watch the slow steps of Candy Marroquin as she approached the altar.

The flower-decked church had all the trappings of a wedding. But the guests were not there to witness Candy's marriage vows. Rather, they had come to celebrate her 15th birthday, a tradition known in Latin America as *quinceañera*.[21]

Let me remind the reader that these brief accounts should not serve as general descriptions, codes for behavior, or predictions. By themselves they tell little about the quality and politics of the event, and perhaps they reveal more about the writers than about the practice itself. The descriptive narrative and the focus on material features of the event places the accounts in the genres of journalism and classic ethnography. (Both genres proclaim to report "the truth.") Constanza Montaña even borrows the now-classic trope from ethnography and uses shock and surprise to allow readers to imagine Candy Marroquin and her family as exotic foreigners whose confusing behavior requires translation. Nevertheless, the accounts provide a point of reference for the reader.

Explaining the *Quinceañera*

Catholic officials, journalists, and social scientists in Chicago have shown striking similarity in their description of the *quinceañera*. Between 1971 and 1991 there are repeatedly uniform descriptions and explanations of the event in daily newspapers, dissertations, research reports, parish bulletins, diocesan guidelines for a *quinceañera* service, and internal Catholic periodicals written by and for church officials.[22] I refer to these manuscripts as the public discourse on the *quinceañera*. Although not the Archdiocese's spokesperson for popular religiosity or the Spanish-speaking ministry, Rev. Peter Rodriguez is the most prolific and most cited author on the *quinceañera*. Perhaps due to his exposure from serving at Chicago's historically important Mexican parishes (the Northside's St. Francis of Assisi and the Southside's Immaculate Heart of Mary), Rev. Rodriguez has gained a reputation as the local authority on the event. The other Catholic officials participating in the public discourse are members of the Hispanic Caucus, including Rev. Arturo Pérez, pastor of former St. Casmir, Rev. Charles Dahm, pastor of St. Pius V, and Rev. Juan Huitrado, pastor of former St. Vitus Parish.[23] Each ministers in predominantly *mexicano* neighborhoods.

Within the public discourse, the *quinceañera* is regarded in three ways: as an extension of particular Catholic sacraments, as a rite of passage, and as a practice that has historical continuity or "tradition." Similar descriptions, however, are not based on similar projects. Some journalists and clergy write about the *quinceañera* to convince other Catholic officials of its significance. They imply that priests who refuse to celebrate the *quinceañera* are not acting in a Christian way. More critically, a few priests refer to papal decrees that promote popular religiosity and cultural diversity within the Catholic Church. Writing for a clerical audience, Rev. Arturo Bañuelas reminds clergy of their duty to "support the religious expressions of the common people."[24] Rev. William Conway, in a series of articles on the importance of the *quinceañera*, refers to a papal sermon in which clergy are encouraged to "respect the integrity of the culture in which they are working."[25] Turning to necessity and not papal authority, Rev. Pérez argues that the *quinceañera* is an "opportunity for evangelization," or a "teachable moment," that clergy should not refuse.[26] The opportunity to evangelize, he claims, is important because most youth do not attend church services.

Other clergy and journalists attempt to convince the reader that worshippers who celebrate the *quinceañera* are misguided. This literature reflects a national trend to regulate popular forms of religiosity among *mexicano* worshippers.[27] Clergy argue that worshippers can be misguided in two ways: first, they are overly concerned with money and social prestige, and second, with sex. *Mexicano* worshippers, Catholic officials claim, have made the event into a farce because they spend too much money or because they encourage sexual activity among youth. In 1990, Rev. David Pavlic, the pastor of Providence of God parish in the predominantly *mexicano* neighborhood of Pilsen, argued that "the families that throw these often go into tremendous debt...[and] I have a problem with the message of the ceremony: 'Here's the girl and she's ripe for the picking.'"[28] Rev. Pavlic was adamant that not only is it against Catholic principles to encourage sexual activity among unmarried youth, but it is unethical "when you have a situation, not just among Hispanics but among all youth today, where you see so much teen pregnancy."[29]

Journalists Lisa Holton, Constanza Montaña, and Jorge Casuso each report what Casuso identifies as a "rift between the church hierarchy and the many in the Hispanic [Mexican] community" over the cost of the event.[30] However, Holton's article did not appear in the municipal or religious section but in the business section. In this cover page article complete with a table detailing the "Hispanic Market," Holton describes how "Hispanic consumers" spend thousands of dollars on a *quinceañera*. She quotes owners and managers of bridal shops and department stores who attest to the rapidly growing business in dresses for the *quinceañera*. Holton claims that despite the various forms for a *quinceañera*, retailers can count on one mainstay – the dress – which she reassures them costs from $100 to $500. Ed Kubicki, manager of a department store, calculates for the reader that this can add up since "there may be as many as 14 attendants" in the celebration.[31]

Despite their differing justifications for the event, Catholic priests and journalists describe the "most genuine" *quinceañera* in similar ways. The following attributes are repeatedly found in

the public discourse on the *quinceañera*. The ceremony begins with a procession to the church in which the parents accompany their daughter. During the ceremony the girl prays to God in order to renew her baptismal commitment, to strengthen her faith, to ask for a blessing as she enters a new stage in life, to give thanks for arriving at the age of fifteen, and to honor her parents. The ceremony focuses on the relationships between the parents and their daughter and between God and the family. Local guidelines recommend that the *quinceañera* "should be celebrated in the spirit of prayer, solemnity, simplicity and festivity."[32]

Many clergy are explicit about the number of attendants, the kinds of objects allowed in the ceremony, and who may sponsor the girl. Increasingly, family sponsors [*padrinos*/godparents] are limited to baptismal godparents or members of the nuclear family. In the late 1970s, Rev. Peter Rodriguez, while at Immaculate Heart of Mary in the Back of the Yards, argued that the use of *padrinos*, attendants, an escort for the girl, rings, medals, pillows, and a bouquet of flowers are "totally strange to the festivity" and were "impurities recently adopted in cities such as Guadalajara."[33] According to Rev. Rodriguez, objects are attributed with authenticity if they can be "traced" to Mexico or if they do not resemble the objects used in Catholic weddings. He implied that the *quinceañera* should not resemble a wedding precisely because of what a wedding ceremony permits: sexual activity and expression.

As early as 1971 Rodriguez had begun to restrict the participation of young men in an effort to limit heterosexual expression. The *chambelan*[34] who escorted the girl was naturalized as the catalyst for heterosexual encounters. In that year, church officials and lay leaders of St. Francis of Assisi, under the guidance of Peter Rodriguez, issued the following statement:

> The *quinceañera* is profoundly a religious and Christian celebration...[I]t is contradictory and with negative effects that the *quinceañera* [the girl] arrive at the church accompanied by chamberlains: in little pairs as if they are engaged to each other. *In our Parish, we will not admit quinceañeras accompanied by young*

men. Young men should be invited to the celebration of the Mass and the fiesta, but they are NOT allowed in the procession entering the church.[35]

Ignoring other types of sexual activity (such as father–daughter incest), by 1980 several parishes in the Chicago Archdiocese codified the practice of having both parents or the father escort the daughter into and out of the church. When I arrived in Chicago a decade later, Catholic officials referred to the parental escort as a traditional practice.

Quinceañera as Rite of Passage

Invariably, Catholic officials and journalists describe and legitimate the *quinceañera* as a traditional religious ceremony that marks a rite of passage into adulthood. Several clergy and journalists specifically define adulthood as a movement from an irresponsible to a responsible member of society and church.[36] Adulthood, however, is not a generic stage of the life cycle, but one that is embedded in Catholic expectations of a woman.

According to Rev. Bañuelas, the ancient "initiation rite" on which the *quinceañera* is based taught girls "to be virtuous and to care for the poor and the handicapped."[37] His claim to "tradition" legitimated his argument that a contemporary "young woman could work on a project with the poor. She could participate in several community programs: visits to the elderly, [serve] meals on wheels, or help the handicapped."[38] During an interview, Rev. Arturo Pérez claimed that "adulthood" was a time when "you start saying, 'I give'... and not thinking of yourself." Childhood, he explained, was a time when girls are allowed to "think only about themselves," but adulthood is a time that they should "think of others first." His ideas echo a statement made in 1980 by Rev. Peter Rodriguez. At that time, Rev. Rodriguez argued that at the age of fifteen "the girl is not a child anymore. She cannot blame her parents for her faults. She is now entering the responsibility of womanhood."[39] In one of his most explicit instructions for womanhood, Rodriguez argued that after the event, "The responsi-

bility lies with the girl to preserve her [sexual] purity until her wedding day."[40]

However, as Rodriguez admits, the church cannot trust that girls will understand or accept this responsibility without proper instruction.[41] Therefore, several clergy require that girls attend special classes prior to the event. In 1980 Rodriguez required that girls in his parish "give a confession and discuss personal values."[42] In a manuscript he shared with me, Rev. Pérez outlined a three-month program in which young girls develop specific plans to help their family, their friends, and their parish.[43] At St. Casmir, Pérez initiated a mandatory weekend program for all youth who wished to participate in the procession and the ceremony. After a year of refusing to celebrate the event at St. Pius V, Rev. Dahm decided that mandatory classes for the girl, her family, and her *padrinos* taught over four weekends would allow him to instruct the entire family about Catholic views on womanhood, service, and the family. At St. Vitus, Rev. Huitrado required the girl and her escorts to meet four times to reflect on the family, hope, and dignity. Interviews revealed that Pérez, Dahm, and Huitrado were ultimately concerned with the girl's virginity, but they employed code words such as "family" and "dignity" to disguise this focus.

According to Catholic officials and journalists, the *quinceañera* is an extension of baptism, an opportunity for conversion, and a chance to encourage young girls to begin a life of service. Church officials emphasize the role the *quinceañera* plays in bringing people to the church and in teaching gender roles and cultural traditions. Through the *quinceañera*, Catholic priests provide instruction to parents on how to educate their daughters about gender roles, "female" behavior, and sexuality. The regulation on family sponsors codifies the nuclear family as the legitimate participants in a *quinceañera* and as legitimate participants in the structuring of a girl's sexual and ethnic identity. *Mexicanas* and their families who refuse to follow Church requirements or who practice the *quinceañera* in ways not approved by their pastor are referred to as untraditional, pagan, amoral, unfit parents, or "lacking [cultural] identity."[44]

Quinceañera as Continuity: History and Tradition

Catholic officials, social scientists, and journalists claim that the *quinceañera* is a tradition or custom that has historical origins or roots. People who regard the *quinceañera* as historical or traditional are usually attempting to convince other clergy to celebrate the event. That is, they view the *quinceañera* as a legitimate "tradition" from Mexico and part of a legitimate popular faith. Catholic officials who want to defend the *quinceañera* as a form of popular religiosity do so by using history.

Most claim that the *quinceañera* has roots in or comes from indigenous cultures of Latin America, but different times and places are credited. In the last twenty years, the *quinceañera* is said to have "come from Mexico,"[45] from an "ancient European social custom" that was later "adopted in Latin America,"[46] and from the "Aztec Empire in Mexico."[47] By 1990, journalists and church officials narrowed their claims to Aztec and Mayan cultures. The following are some accounts of the origins of the *quinceañera*.

In 1975 Rev. Peter Rodriguez claimed that the *quinceañera* has European origins. In his Spanish-language weekly column in the archdiocesan newspaper, Rev. Rodriguez suggested that the contemporary practice can be attributed to Latin Americans who "changed the meaning" of the event.

> The *quinceañera* celebration has its origins in an ancient European social custom that had been the last part of a public presentation of young girls when they arrived at the age of taking part in society. In Europe the age for this ceremony was eighteen years old, or that age at which a woman becomes an adult according to civil and religious law. When this ceremony was adopted in the Latin American countries, the age of the ceremony was reduced to fifteen... They added new elements that at the time enriched the ceremony and they significantly changed the meaning.[48]

Five years later, the agents of historical change were different. In 1980 journalist David Beard imagined that Spaniards transformed the event, not the people of the New World:

> It began in the 15th Century with the rise of the Aztec Empire in Mexico. With a life expectancy rate of 30 years, the *quinceañera* marked the midway point of an Aztec girl's life, the time when she would become a woman and marry. She was officially presented to the tribe, an event that kept the fathers of pretty young girls busy sorting and selecting marriage offers. When the Spaniards arrived in the 16th Century, traces of Catholicism and the traditional Spanish 18th birthday debut appeared in the ceremony.[49]

At the height of the debate in 1990, Rev. William Conway, writing for a Catholic Spanish-language audience, emphasized the actions of both Spanish missionaries and Mayans. In his article, Conway encouraged other Catholic clergy and laity to celebrate the event because it is the result of religious syncretism:

> The *quinceañera* tradition has its roots in the cultural and religious practices of the Maya. Perhaps the great wisdom of the first missionaries that came from Spain to evangelize in the Americas was based on the ability to respect the culture and religious traditions of the indigenous population. Therefore, today we find a mixture of indigenous and Christian traditions. One example of this mixing is the celebration of the Day of the Dead.[50]

Instead of one civilization transforming another, he focuses on the syncretism of Catholicism and Mayan theology. Nevertheless, he constructs a romantic mixing between Spaniards and indigenous populations, mystifying the way colonialism devastated most of the New World. In the end, Conway imagines *mexicano* culture in the same light as other clergy and journalists by placing the original (and therefore the presumed authentic) *quinceañera* in the ancient past. Ironically, these versions of the past include a model that views culture as porous and flexible, but they do not extend this model to the present and instead imagine that *mexicano* and "American" cultures are distinct, independent, and coherent.

Making a *Quinceañera*/Making the Self

My dissertation research was not designed as an exclusive study of the *quinceañera* but rather an investigation of the multiple displays of ethnic identity. In many ways, I stumbled upon this form of expression in my field notes. As I prepared to write the dissertation, I found page after page detailing dozens of conversations about the *quinceañera*. In fact, one of my first field note entries describes a conversation with Victoria and several other *mexicanas* about her sister's *quinceañera*.[51] During a lunch break at the Spanish Coalition for Jobs (a federally-funded job-training center and my field site for the first eight months), Victoria described the details of each photograph to an interested group. A smaller group stood a few feet away and spoke under their breath about the old-fashioned celebration that had little meaning for women who want to have an "office job."

Taking the notes back into the field, I conducted structured interviews with twelve *mexicanas* and their mothers.[52] Those twelve were the *mexicanas* who consistently returned my phone calls and welcomed me into their homes; in other words, they were my closest friends. The group included *mexicanas* between the ages of eighteen and twenty-nine and their mothers (ages fifty to sixty-five, approximately); *mexicanas* who prefer Spanish and *mexicanas* who are monolingual English-speakers; and *mexicanas* with a G.E.D. and *mexicanas*, like Victoria, with some college education. The interviews were supplemented by participation in three *quinceañeras* and by an examination of photographs.[53] In fact, photographs became a point of entry for the discussions, as I would often begin by asking if they could show me their pictures of the latest *quinceañera*.

The field notes and transcriptions from the interviews include aspects of the *quinceañera* that are rarely mentioned in the public discourse. For example, young *mexicanas* spoke about the arguments they had with their parents over things such as the color of the dress, number of guests, or the location of the reception. This kind of parent–child conflict was missing in the public discourse. *Mexicanas* talked about the choreographed dance that might occur during the party. Older *mexicanas* spoke at length about the problems a family might face with particular clergy when trying to organize and coordinate a *quinceañera*. Most *mexicanas* spoke about the focus on the *Virgen de Guadalupe* during the service. A few mothers and daughters even discussed the option of taking a trip to Mexico or buying a car instead of celebrating one's fifteenth year. In general, *mexicanas* discuss a wider range of issues surrounding the *quinceañera* than clergy and journalists.

Although the *quinceañera* is described and practiced in several ways, mothers and daughters spoke most often about the *quinceañera* as "something that has to be done because of who we are" and as a way of "holding onto your roots." I interpret these expressions as an imperative to practice one's ethnic culture in an event that *makes* a girl into a woman, but more importantly *makes* her into a Mexican woman. However, the making of a *mexicana* is not an overnight transformation but an ongoing process and negotiation. Their own expression – becoming *conocido* – conveys the passage of time and relational process. The expression has at least two translations: becoming recognized as a woman and becoming known as a *mexicana*. "Becoming *conocido*" is a concept that focuses on the self, but it is not a compartmentalization of the self. It is an event that leads girls to discover and experience themselves as women, Mexicans, Catholics, and adults.

For one woman, whom I call Gloria, the *quinceañera* is an imperative because she believes that Chicago offers very few role models and even fewer opportunities to learn about Mexican culture. The event gave her daughter a sense of pride and self-worth as a *mexicana* in the face of local forms of discrimination and "assimilation." Gloria grew up in a parish that practiced segregation in the church and the classroom until the early 1970s. She experienced a history of institutional neglect that left many in her Back of the Yards neighborhood bitter and angry toward the Catholic church. During a long interview at her home, she explained it to me this way:

Gloria: Because of who we are and because of who I wanted my daughter to be ... my daughter's life has always been Americanized. We live here [in Chicago]. She went to school here. English is her first language, Spanish her second. So, how do you hold on to your roots? How do you put a value to it [if] you can't see it? ... [It is] something that has to be done.[54]

In subsequent interviews, Gloria spoke about the *quinceañera* as an important time for a mother to encourage her daughter to become an independent woman. When I pressed her to clarify what she meant by an independent woman, she referred to her oldest daughter who had gone to college and was seeking a steady job. Gloria was proud that her daughter aspired to work in the media and did not pursue work outside of the Chicagoland area.

Although some *mexicanas* would agree with Gloria's reasons to celebrate the *quinceañera*, others would point instead to "our right" *[tenemos derechos]* to celebrate a girl's fifteenth year. Ruth, a mother who raised her ten children in Indiana, Illinois, and Mexico, argued that the Catholic church has no right to stop these celebrations, and it was her "right" to perform aspects of her cultural heritage. Only one of Ruth's daughters, however, celebrated the *quinceañera*. According to her oldest daughter, Ruth refused this "right" for her daughters when money was tight, when daughters did not live up to her expectations, or when too many things were pulling the family apart.

Recalling her own *quinceañera*, Alicia, a young woman born and raised in Chicago, focused on the transformative powers of the event. Over lunch, Alicia described how she experienced her sexuality and cultural identity through the *quinceañera*.

Alicia: I just knew that a *quinceañera* was something that was very important to us. ... It's something that a young lady should look forward to. I believe wholeheartedly that it's a step forward. Because I think that culture just makes you, not realizing that you are a woman. You have to make decisions as a woman, you know. When you are fifteen and younger you can be a kid ... it's a step

forward. It's saying it's okay to be a woman, it's okay to see those changes in any way it should be, mentally, physically, spiritually. It's kind of a jolt reaction ... but it's good for you ... 'cause otherwise I wouldn't know how or where the dividing point was in my life. I think the dividing point was there only because I actually thought and saw everyone together. After that I started losing weight like I said. When I look back I see that my life started at that point. After that. I am not saying right away when I turned fifteen, I am saying a couple of months later I started seeing that I like guys. For a long time I couldn't wear makeup ... [Before that] I don't remember much except studying and school.

For Alicia, the event is experienced through a physical placement of one's body and begins the process of sexual awareness. Alicia's photographs from her *quinceañera* confirm her construction of a processual sexuality and cultural identity. For her first dance, Alicia danced with her uncle, not a boyfriend.

Victoria, a resident of the United States who never expects to return to Mexico, explained it to me this way: *niñas* become *jovenes*, but not *mujeres* [little girls become young women, but not adult women]. Using the combination of Spanish and English, the point is subtle but clear. The girl comes to experience herself as a sexual being, but not as a person who engages in sexual intercourse (or becomes pregnant).

Finally, a girl's heterosexual and religious identity is reinforced and constructed through the *quinceañera*. Many girls spoke about the *quinceañera* as the beginning of a personal relationship with the *Virgen de Guadalupe:* woman to woman, mother to mother, or woman to intercessor. According to Felicita, she, like many young women in her family, prayed everyday to the *Virgen*, a practice initiated after her *quinceañera*. The act of praying to the *Virgen* can be seen as a private moment in which *mexicanas* find their own voice. As Felicita once told me, "I talk to her about being a woman." Felicita and others not only found that women in their families developed a deep relationship with the *Virgen* after their *quinceañera*, but they also noted that most *mexicanas* wore a gold medal with the image of the *Virgen*. It stayed with them constantly, hidden under their clothes, but nonetheless physically near – an immediate reminder of their relationship with the *Virgen*.

The simultaneous creation and re-creation of their multiple identities through the *quinceañera* allows women to invent their own images of the *mexicana*. However, their construction of themselves is not based on carefree choices that produce harmonious images of whole *mexicanas* but instead leads to contradictory presentations of the self. For example, the event may be constructed as their entrance into womanhood and their desire to "improve" but the categories clash in unanticipated ways. Girls describe improvement as getting an education, an office job, or at least getting out of the factory. Improvement is future-oriented and illustrates a movement away from patriarchial gender roles. However, other future-oriented talk also includes a desire to find a boyfriend who won't beat you, who will support you, and who will not go to jail. Contradiction surfaces in their claim to the event as well. The argument that *mexicanas* have a right to celebrate their ethnic identity challenges local concepts of culture contact that encourage *mexicanas* to erase, hide, or forget their cultural identity and history. Nevertheless, *mexicanas* remake themselves through an event that is imagined as highly "traditional" within a patriarchal institution.

"Just a Tradition": Cultural Meaning and Affirmation

Though the *quinceañera* is framed as a "tradition," the category takes different meaning than the one constructed in the public discourse. *Mexicanas* do not value the *quinceañera* because they can locate its origins in a specific ancient civilization. Rather, they claim that the *quinceañera* is important because it transforms and physically connects a person to "Mexican culture" – a time and space that has particular meaning for each individual. Furthermore, mothers and daughters construct their version of the authentic *quinceañera* not by the form or practice of the event, but by the meaning behind or within the event. Since authenticity is located in meaning, it

is not surprising that various forms and practices are referred to as a *quinceañera*.

Women spoke of "tradition" as a living practice in which innovation and continuity are not mutually exclusive. Objects, language, music, practices, and tastes need not have a traceable and unchanged precedent from the past. (This, of course, can infuriate scholars who devote careers to tracing the origins of cultural practices that they assume are passed down intact from generation to generation.) Adult *mexicanas* explain that the "*quinceañera* is just a tradition" that they locate in specific memories and family experiences. Following more than a temporal connection, most women link the *quinceañera* to a specific person, to a specific memory, or to a specific place – that is, to a sister, to *una quinceañera en el año pasado* [a *quinceañera* last year], or to the *rancho* of their childhood. Tradition can mean "What did sister do?" "What did *tía* [aunt] do?" The experiences of *padrinos* – members of the family either by marriage, birth, or sentiment – often play a significant role in tradition-making. In this way, "tradition" is a bodily experience authenticated by memory and practice.

When I asked women to describe the "most traditional" way to celebrate a *quinceañera*, they usually smiled tolerantly but disappointedly. Several contexts could produce their smiles. First, the facial expression can be understood as mutual positioning between researcher and participant. I was known to people as the Mexican whose research on "Mexican Culture" made me both an expert and a novice. Among women who attributed me with expertise, my questions about the *quinceañera* may have been perceived as a challenge to their own status. Or, they may have simply wished to defer to another person.

Second, some women might have smiled disappointedly because my question was too familiar. Many clergy who refuse to celebrate the *quinceañera* justify their actions by claiming that people do not know the "most traditional" way to celebrate the event. Therefore, my questions about the "most traditional" *quinceañera* could have led some women to believe that I agreed with their clergy. I suggest that underlying this kind of disappointed smile is a criticism of the Catholic church.

Third, women were uncomfortable with a scale of "more or less traditional" because they saw the various forms of the event as an indicator of people's economic position. *Mexicanas* would not refer to a person as "less traditional" because she could not afford a fancy dress, a large reception, or a gold medallion. The forms of the *quinceañera* are directly related to one's economic position or the ability to solicit support from *padrinos*, who might pay for the cake, the photographer, the food, or any item that parents cannot afford. No one would describe the *quinceañera* of a family with fewer resources as "less traditional." As Nancy's mother told me, "It's just a tradition, but there was no money [for us to have one]." This view contrasts to that commonly held by anthropologists, journalists, and Catholic priests who routinely describe people as "more traditional" or "less traditional" by measuring attributes, characteristics, and behaviors. In this contexts, the smiling implies a challenge to the dominant narrative about traditionality, and it demonstrates a sophisticated analysis of the intersection between poverty and culture.

Fourth, nearly all women and girls would not allow me to generalize about the practice and form of the *quinceañera*. During interviews, *mexicanas* would not offer a definitive account of the *quinceañera*. They tended to disagree with my general description of the event, and sometimes there was considerable disagreement among family members. A daughter might claim that the dance was the important moment and her mother might claim that the church service was the important moment. They seemed to view the *quinceañera* as undefinable or beyond definition. I suggest that in their contestation, women and girls practice the negotiation of themselves, and they make negotiation an important aspect of the *quinceañera*.

This particular smiling and contestation, therefore, is based on the women's notion that culture can vary within one ethnic community. Their view of multiple identities is different from the dominant perspective of distinct "either/or" identities and nations. The popular narrative imagines people as members of homogeneous and mutually exclusive communities. *Mexicanas* signaled through their smiles and contestation that people are never either Mexican or United States Americans but a hybrid form. Furthermore, this understanding of ethnic communities is itself a challenge to popular ideas about culture contact that assume that people are absorbed into the (imaginary) mainstream American experience. Finally, their ability to contest gender roles subverts the dominant view of a passive Mexican woman.

Another interpretation of this facial expression is illustrated in the following interview with Victoria, who despite the fact that she had organized her sister's *quinceañera* six months prior to our conversation claimed that she did not "know much" about the event.

Karen: I want to ask you . . . what do you know about *quinceañeras*?

Victoria: Well, I don't know much. The only thing I know is . . . it's that it's more like a tradition, it's just a tradition. . . . I don't know much about it. I wish I could help you. But I don't, I don't know 'cause it was just like a tradition.

Karen: Tell me about your experience.

Victoria: Okay . . . Well in church they do give you some kind of history about that, because they want you know what it's all about. I read my sister's [booklet] and what I understood was that it came, it started with French people. Funny too, French people . . . ? [W]hat it means is that a girl is turning from a little girl, a little girl is turning to a teenager, I guess. Not a teenager, like a . . .

Karen: A young woman?

Victoria: Older woman . . . what I remember from what I read, it said that it's like a girl is ready to get married. Once they do the cotillion [*quinceañera*] she's already like a woman.

Karen: Do you think that it's an important thing to do?

Victoria: My opinion, not really. I used to think so but then, I was talking to one priest and he made me change my mind . . . And I was talking about this one time and he said . . . "I think it would be just nice just to make a ceremony for her. And that's it. But why make all that party and those people?" He goes, "That's like saying, here's my daughter, like take her, like showing her off . . . Well, you're making a big party just because she's turning fifteen, like saying she's ready to get married. You know, here she is, take her." You know, that's how he put it... Then I started thinking, "Yeah, why make a big party when you turn fifteen...?" [H]e says that the thought it was good to just make a ceremony for her. You know, and maybe like, not a big party, but I guess like a family reunion and all that, but he didn't believe in cotillions. Something about the dresses too. He goes, "Why just waste all that money on that dress. Just put her in a nice dress." He was picky too... Well I guess they are blessing you and... See I know why I don't know, 'cause I'll ask my mom and she won't know what to answer me. I tell her. 'Cause I asked her, what does it mean...? She says she doesn't know. But I have thought about it. And I cannot come up with an answer either... [E]verybody turns fifteen and they make a big party, that's the way I do see it. They make a big party. And it's like a tradition, you do it because other people do it, I guess. And because they, well, you know. I don't know...

Victoria expresses two important aspects of the *quinceañera* – gender and ethnic identity. First, people have different kinds of information about their own culture, in this case the *quinceañera*, that can seem incomplete and confusing (as with Victoria and her mother). "She says she doesn't know." Second, people's ideas about the event and their own gender and ethnic identity are dramatically shaped by the views of Catholic officials. I suggest that Victoria's expression, "I don't know," illustrates that ethnic identity is sometimes re-invented, confusing, and often imposed. Furthermore, Victoria's ability to plan, organize, and celebrate a *quinceañera* illustrates that she is not decultured, assimilated, or passive. Victoria, like many women, is able to create new ways of expressing and displaying herself when faced with uncertainty, unequal (but not determined) social relationships, or negative views of Mexicans.

Discussion

This paper begins with my field notes about the events that took place before one *quinceañera* and

explains to the reader that a general description is not forthcoming. It claims that a general description obscures diversity and an increasing contestation. More important, the paper argues that different explanations of the *quinceañera* are social analysis; that is, theories for experience. It then examines a wide range of ideas about the *quinceañera* and suggests that individuals have particular meanings of the *quinceañera* that are embedded in their understanding of ethnic identity, gender roles, sexuality, faith, and culture. The talk about the *quinceañera* is a discursive practice on the making of "*mexicana*."

For Catholic officials, the event, and therefore the construction of "mexicana," is grounded in *another* culture and *another* time, or perhaps *beyond* culture and *outside* of time. Catholic officials do not need to determine the place or time from which the event originates because they derive meaning from Catholic doctrine. They consistently claim that the event should be an expression of religious devotion and commitment to the church. The girl is encouraged to be subservient and to subordinate her wants and needs to those of her family and the church. Embedded within their image of a selfless mother/daughter is the codification of Catholicism's heterosexuality – delayed until marriage but nonetheless compulsory.

It is not surprising that the Catholic church encourages this for women, but it is interesting that some clergy view alternate forms and practices – cultural sensibilities, if you will – as impurities from which they must "rescue" the *quinceañera* and their parishioners. Catholic officials who regulate the celebration claim they are saving *mexicanas* and their families from frivolously spending money or from focusing on social prestige and beauty. In 1990 Rev. Dahm publicly condemned the practice because he believed that the *quinceañera* is "just one big bash that costs an enormous amount of money, creates great indebtedness and brings no one to the churches." Dahm felt torn between maintaining a custom and promoting "materialism."[55] Rev. Raniero Alessandrini of St. Anthony Parish felt that the event was "a farce" because youth are "focusing on their appearance and the dinner that follows."[56] It is ironic that clergy in the Chicago Archdiocese, an archdiocese that between 1916 and 1929 organized one of the nation's most intensive Americanization programs for immigrants, currently discourage practices usually associated with assimilation. Why do Catholic clergy believe that extravagance dilutes a traditional practice? Why are they trying to save the *quinceañera*?

Perhaps their actions echo a classic motif of colonialism identified by Renato Rosaldo as imperialist nostalgia. Rosaldo argues that colonial administrators have a nostalgia for the culture they dominate and attempt to "rescue" traits of "the precious culture before it disappears forever."[57] Rosaldo's patronizing tone is deliberate because the "rescuer" rarely recognizes his own role in the destruction of the culture he longs to save.

Rosaldo does not acknowledge, however, that the liberal anthropological agenda of the late 1800s and early 1900s took a similar tone with Native Americans. American anthropologists, such as Franz Boas and Alfred Kroeber, saw their work among Native Americans as a "rescue mission" in the face of increasing culture contact and westernization. A fear of the end of traditional society and the vanishing primitive motivated Kroeber's work on Ishi, the last surviving Yahi Indian in California.[58] Despite cultural anthropology's rethinking of "the primitive" and rejection of nineteenth-century evolutionary models, the rescue motif persists. In fact, anthropology's attention to global capitalism often implies a prophetic warning of a disappearing object of study.[59]

It is important to clarify that I am not denying that aspects of culture (i.e., language) disappear as the result of particular encounters. The encounter between the New and Old World contributed to the disappearance of millions of people and their languages, practices, and customs. However, as James Clifford points out in his analysis of the rescue motif in anthropology, the problem with this framework is "the assumption that with rapid change something essential ('culture'), a coherent differential identity, vanishes."[60] Catholic officials and journalists have imagined particular practices and forms of the *quinceañera* as essential aspects of *mexicano* culture. By identifying "something essential,"

they appear as advocates in the fight to save a vanishing tradition, a position that makes counterclaims appear ignoble.

"Rescue missions" in Chicago depend upon another anthropological convention. Catholic officials imagine *mexicano* culture as a self-contained and homogeneous unit that is distinct from the nation and culture of the United States. As Akhil Gupta and James Ferguson explain, anthropology tends to imagine distinct societies, nations, and cultures that correspond to divisions of space (i.e., national boundaries and political territories).[61] The assumption that space is discontinuous encourages anthropology students to specialize in geographic regions (i.e., Africa, Latin America, Asia) and not the spaces between them. When employed by Catholic officials and others in Chicago, this perspective allows people and practices to appear as if they originate from a single, independent culture.

Reclaiming and recreating ethnic culture, gender, faith, and heterosexuality in a cultural practice is a very different project than institutionalizing a ritual in the image of Catholic doctrine. *Mexicanas'* explanations for the *quinceañera* are grounded in an experience of dispersal that can produce ambiguous and conflicting meanings and practices. In Chicago, *mexicanas* encounter political and social institutions that promote, organize, and normalize assimilation through the erasure of their history or appropriation of their experience. Again Renato Rosaldo's work is helpful for understanding the process of cultural encounters. Rosaldo argues that all cultural encounters resemble a border-crossing experience because they can produce chaotic, confusing, and creative results. He borrows much of his argument from Chicana creative writers Gloria Anzaldúa and Sandra Cisneros, whose semiautobiographical works tell stories about crossing cultural, sexual, and other borders.[62] He argues that when two cultures collide, as they do in Chicago, people can find themselves in a "zone between stable places" – on unstable ground.[63] Instability can result from institutions that promote normalized identities (i.e., American and heterosexual) and informal processes that restrict historical memory. As social critics of assimilation, *mexicanas* "cluster around remembered or imagined homelands, places or communities in a world that seems increasingly to deny such territorialized anchors in their actuality."[64]

The *quinceñera* is an anchor between two cultures. It is a space in which *mexicanas* position themselves outside of and within dominant narratives about Mexican woman and the United States. First, the event publicly enacts and celebrates a culturally specific identity, a space in which *mexicanas* are positioned as social critics of the "melting pot" – that is, the event challenges the myth that immigration begins the inevitable process of shedding one's former culture.[65] They have avoided the inevitable by celebrating, defending, and contesting a "traditional" cultural practice. Second, the *quinceañera* borrows from practices and meanings found within the dominant culture. The two most obvious dominant narratives are roots and rights, motifs that have developed within "American" culture. Therefore, *mexicanas* create and participate in an event that contributes to their own assimilation.

Nonetheless, as Gloria Anzaldúa points out, *mexicanas* move through the uncomfortable territory, "this place of contradictions" between their Mexico and their United States, between patriarchy and equality in order to make sense of their lives.[66] It is a territory that permits two or more cultures, multiple meanings, and complicated constructions of a *mexicana*. It is a site of negotiation in which people and cultural practices are not coherent, whole, or distinct. The discourse and practice of the *quinceañera* encourage us to examine the paradoxical and ambiguous nature of "tradition." The discourse and practice suggest that what we intend as "cultural" is fluid, slippery, contradictory, spontaneous, and chaotic.

ACKNOWLEDGEMENTS

The field research for this article was conducted from May 1990 to October 1992 among approximately forty *mexicanas* and their families. This work could not have been done without them. This paper benefitted from the comments of the anonymous reviewers at *Frontiers*. I would also like to thank Tamara Hamlish and the symposium participants at the American Anthropological Association 1992 Annual Meeting in San Francisco for their helpful comments on an earlier version of this paper. The research was funded by the Cushwa Center for the Study of American Catholicism at Notre Dame University, the Enders and Williams Fellowships from Yale University, and the Institute for Intercultural Studies.

NOTES

1 The term *mexicana* is the self-referent most commonly used by the women I met in Chicago. It should not be mistaken for an indicator of a person's nationality, length of time in the United States, or citizenship. Later in the paper, I more fully describe the *mexicanas* and their families.

2 *Quince años* [fifteenth birthday] is another, but less popular, term for the event. "*Quinceañera*" can refer to a person and to a thing (event). According to some Catholic leaders and a few *mexicanas*, "*quinceañera*" is Spanish for "cotillion," a formal ball or group dance. However, the Cordi-Marion Sisters and their Woman's Auxiliary distinguish between their own community-wide Annual Cotillion and the family-centered *quinceañera*.

3 For further reading on anthropology's cartography of insider and outsider see Elizabeth Enslin, "Beyond Writing: Feminist Practice and the Limitations of Ethnography," *Cultural Anthropology* 9:4 (Nov. 1994): 537–568; Akhil Gupta and James Ferguson, "'Beyond Culture': Space, Identity, and the Politics of Difference," *Cultural Anthropology* 7:1 (Feb. 1992): 6–23; and Stephen Tylor, "Post-Modern Ethnography: From Document of the Occult to Occult Document," in *Writing Culture*, ed. James Clifford and George Marcus (Berkeley: University of California Press, 1986).

4 Patricia Zavella, "Feminist Insider Dilemmas Constructing Ethnic Identity with 'Chicana' Informants," *Frontiers* 14:3 (1993): 58.

5 James Clifford, *The Predicament of Culture: Twentieth-Century Ethnography, Literature, and Art* (Cambridge: Harvard University Press, 1988); Renato Rosaldo, *Culture and Truth: The Remaking of Social Analysis* (Boston: Beacon Press, 1989).

6   Rosaldo, 19.

7   Rosaldo, 7.

8   Rosaldo, 147.

9   Gloria Anzaldúa, *Borderlands/La Frontera: The New Mestiza* (San Francisco: Spinsters/ Aunt Lute Book Company, 1987); Gloria Anzaldúa, ed., *Making Face, Making Soul/ Haciendo Caras: Creative and Critical Perspectives by Women of Color* (San Francisco: Aunt Lute Books, 1990); and Chandra Talpade Mohanty, "Introduction" and "Under Western Eyes," in *Third World Women and the Politics of Feminism*, ed. Chandra Talpade Mohanty, Ann Russo, and Lourdes Torres (Bloomington, Ind.: Indiana University Press, 1991), especially pages 66–74.

10 Mohanty, "Introduction," 29.

11 Octavio Romano-V., "Minorities, History and the Cultural Mystique," *El Grito* 1:1 (Fall 1967): 5–11; "The Anthropology and Sociology of the Mexican American," *El Grito* 2:1 (Fall 1968): 13–26; and Américo Paredes, "On ethnographic work among minority groups," in *New Directions in Chicano Scholarship*, ed. R. Romo and R. Paredes (La Jolla: University of California at San Diego, Chicano Studies Program, Chicano Studies Monograph Series, 1978).

12 Maxine Baca Zinn, "Field Research in Minority Communities: Political, Ethical and Methodological Observations by an Insider," *Social Problems* 27:2 (Dec. 1979): 216.

13 I do not intend to produce a romantic image of our reading together. As I expected, they did not agree with all of my interpretations of their words or ideas, and a few women did not respond to my phone calls and letters announcing that I would be in town for the summer. Nonetheless, each woman who received a copy of my dissertation (twelve in all) wanted to see and read her own words first. I eventually created an index for each woman so she could find herself/my representation of herself in my writing.

14 The most recent example of the Archdiocese's limited sensibility is their closing of St. Francis of Assisi, one of two *mexicano* national parishes established in the late 1920s. *Mexicanos* from the greater Chicago metropolitan area had been making St. Francis of Assisi the destination of pilgrimages since the mid-1960s.

15 See also Ruth Horowitz, *Honor and the American Dream*: (New Brunswick: Rutgers University Press, 1983), 52–54, 243, n. 1.

16 Gwen Louise Stern, "Ethnic Identity and Community Action in El Barrio" (Ph.D. Dissertation, Northwestern University, 1976), 42.

17 Stern, 43.

18 Stern, 44.

19 Stern, 5–6.

20 David Beard, "The Quinceañera: A Mexican Girl's Day as Cinderella," *Chicago Tribune*, 17 August 1980, section 12, p. 1ff. (italics in original). This article received wide circulation and was recommended to me by several Catholic priests.

21 Constanza Montaña, "Some Latinos Spare No Expense When Their Daughters Come of Age," *Chicago Tribune*, 19 June 1990, Metropolitan Section, p. 1ff.

22 The time under review (1971–1991) does not imply rigid periodization. Before the 1970s the Archdiocese of Chicago showed sporadic interest in the Mexican population. The analysis is based on an inventory of descriptions and explanations that surfaced several times and in different kinds of publications. Formal and informal interviews with Catholic priests, deacons, and nuns supplied additional information about the *quinceañera*.

23 In 1990 and 1991, the Archdiocese closed and consolidated over fity-two parishes and schools. St. Casmir was consolidated with nearby St. Ludmilla in 1991 and renamed Our Lady of Tepeyac, a name that signifies the identity of its *mexicano* parishioners. St. Vitus was closed in 1990 but later purchased by a community coalition that is converting the building into a day care, arts, and neighborhood center for Pilsen.

24 Arturo Bañuelas, "La Tradicion de la Quinceañera," *Liturgy 80: Special Edition* 12:7 (Oct. 1981): 5.

25 Guillermo (William) Conway, "La Quinceañera: Segundo Artículo en una Serie," *New Catholic Explorer*, 5 October 1990, 20. Trans. by author.

26 Quoted in Lisa Holton, "Church Divided Over Quinceañera," *Chicago Sun-Times*, 18 July 1990, Business Section, p. 51; see also Arturo Pérez, "15 años Celebration" (unpublished manuscript, Chicago, Ill., 1990).

27 The Archdioceses of Los Angeles and San Antonio regulate the celebration of the *quinceañera*. Clergy in those cities are allowed to
prohibit the event if worshippers do not fulfill
certain prerequisites. Several parishes in the
Archdiocese of Chicago have developed their
own regulations based on the Los Angeles
guidelines. Other Catholic officials in Chicago
simply refuse to celebrate the event.

28 Holton, 51.

29 Holton, 51.

30 Jorge Casuso, "Coming-out Parties Split Hispanics, Church," *Chicago Tribune*, 24 June
1990, 4C. See also Montaña, "Some Latinos
Spare No Expense," p. 1ff.

31 Lisa Holton, "Tradition a Key to Hispanic
Market," *Chicago Sun-Times*, 18 July 1990,
Business Section, p. 47ff.

32 Bañuelas, 6.

33 Pedro [Peter] Rodriguez, "Los 15 Años: Rito
Sagrado o Pura Pachanga...," *El Puertorriqueño*, 21 August 1978[?], p. 10.

34 I suspect that the word comes from the British
title for a male servant (chamberlain) and in
Chicago it refers to male escorts. The female
attendants are *damas*.

35 *Boletín, San Francisco de Asís* (Oak Park, Ill.:
Claretian Missionaries Archives, March 21,
1971). Emphasis in the original. Trans. by
author. From 1969 to 1976, Rev. Peter Rodriguez served as Pastor of St. Francis of Assisi
parish.

36 See Bañuelas; Laurie Hansen, "Hispanic Rite
of Passage Seen as 'Teachable Moment' for
Church," *New Catholic Explorer* 12 (Oct.
1990): 23; Pérez manuscript; and Pedro
[Peter] Rodriguez, "Reflexiones," *New World*,
28 February 1975, p. 6.

37 Bañuelas, 5.

38 Bañuelas, 6.

39 Quoted in Beard, 4.

40 Rodriguez, "Reflexiones," 6. Trans. by author.

41 Rodriguez, "Reflexiones," 6.

42 Quoted in Beard, 4.

43 Pérez manuscript.

44 Rodriguez, "Los 15 Años," 10. Trans. by
author.

45 Bañuelas, 5.

46 Rodriguez, "Reflexiones," 6. Trans. by author.

47 Beard, 1. Ironically, a reference to Toltec civilization is rare, even though Chicago clergy

extensively use Sister Angela Everia's guide
for the *quinceañera*. Angela Everia, *Quinceañera*
(San Antonio, Texas: Mexican American Cultural Center, 1980). In her guide she claims
that the event originated in either the Aztec
or the Toltec civilization.

48 Rodriguez, "Reflexiones," 6. Trans. by author.

49 Beard, 1.

50 Conway, 20.

51 The names of *mexicana* informants are fictitious in order to protect their privacy.

52 It was not my original intention to interview everyone's mother, but since several of
my visits took place in the presence of
mothers, I decided to include their comments
as well.

53 This is probably faulty methodology for some
anthropologists who emphasize observation
over talk but I simply could not get myself
invited to more than three celebrations.
Though *quinceañeras* were celebrated three or
four times every weekend throughout the
spring and summer and at nearly every *mexicano* parish in the city, ethical guidelines prevented me from observing these officially
public events without a personal invitation.
Instead, I take the words of *mexicanas* seriously
and call for continued research.

54 Though Spanish is her first language, Gloria
spoke to me in English during this interview.

55 Quoted in Montaña, "Some Latinos Spare No
Expense," p. 1ff.

56 Quoted in Hansen, 23.

57 Rosaldo, 81.

58 Theodora Kroeber, *Ishi in Two Worlds* (Berkeley: University of California Press, 1963).

59 See for example, Susan Skomal's "Whither
Our Subjects – And Ourselves?" *Anthropology
Newsletter* 35:7 (Oct. 1994): 1ff. Skomal introduces the newsletter's annual theme for the
1994–1995 academic year. Her article opens
with questions about what will happen to the
Lakalai of Melanesia by the year 2034. Skomal
asks, "... will the sociocultural underpinnings
that held the Lakalia have loosened beyond
recognition?"

60 James Clifford, "On Ethnographic Allegory,"
in *Writing Culture*, ed. James Clifford and
George Marcus (Berkeley: University of California Press, 1986), 113.

61 Gupta and Ferguson, 6.

62 Anzaldúa, *Borderlands/ La Frontera*; Sandra
    Cisneros, *House on Mango Street* (Houston:
    Arte Publico Press, 1985).

63 Rosaldo, 85.

64 Gupta and Ferguson, 11.

65 Rosaldo, 81.

66 Anzaldúa, *Borderlands/ La Frontera*, Preface.

18

Two Sides of the Same Coin: Modern *Gaúcho* Identity in Brazil

Ruben George Oliven

I

Rio Grande do Sul, the southernmost state in Brazil, has always had special characteristics because of its location, colonization, and history. In the past, the state was an area of intense dispute between Portugal and Spain. Throughout its history, the state has had a long tradition of wars and conflicts that continued well after Brazil's independence in 1822. One of these conflicts, the Farroupilha Revolution, which began in 1835, resulted from dissatisfaction with the excessive political and economic centralization imposed by the Brazilian Empire. The revolutionaries, who fought for ten years, succeeded in proclaiming an independent republic in 1836 and, only after assuring amnesty for themselves, signed a peace treaty with the imperial government. But the republic proclaimed by the revolutionaries continues as a figurative presence even today in the flag of Rio Grande do Sul. In this flag, one finds featured not only the republic's name, Rio Grandian Republic, and the date of the deflagration of the Farroupilha Revolution, September 20, 1835, but also its motto, "Liberty, Equality and Humanity," assuring a place for the episode in the collective memory of the inhabitants of the state.

The inhabitants of Rio Grande do Sul consider themselves Brazilian by choice, and they like to emphasize their individuality with regard to the rest of Brazil. In the social construction of their identity, they use elements that refer to a glorious past, one dominated by the figure of the *gaúcho*, a word that initially meant a vagabond and cattle thief but later came to mean the farmhand and warrior always associated with the figure of the horseman. Today, the word is a patronymic for the citizen of the state of Rio Grande do Sul.

Since the 1930s, Brazil has experienced a growing economic, political, and administrative centralization that has brought about a weakening of regional and state powers. This process became accentuated after 1964, when the military took over power, promoted a greater integration of the national market, and established networks of roads, telecommunications, mass communication, and so on.

However, in spite of – or perhaps because of – this growing centralization, one can observe today in Brazil certain opposing tendencies manifested through needs such as those for a true federalism, the affirmation of the advantages of administrative decentralization, a tributary reform that would give more resources to states and municipalities, and the affirmation of regional and state identities that highlight the issue of Brazilian diversity. Among these regional identities is that of Rio Grande do Sul, a state in which one finds a strong revival of gaúcho culture.

At the end of the 1970s, it was common to hear that gaúcho tradition was an endangered species or that it was reduced to pockets of tradition and folklore. After all, Brazil was taking huge steps toward national integration. The military government that took power in 1964 promoted conservative modernization, expressed through gradual political and economic centralization. This meant, among other things, that Brazilian television, with its prime-time soap operas watched by millions of people, began to reach a growing number of homes and began to promote a culture that increasingly seemed to be national in nature. Considering that Rio Grande do Sul was becoming an industrialized state in which a large majority of the population was urban, it was thought that there was no space within its culture for the rural and equestrian figure of the gaúcho.

The end of the 1970s and the beginning of the 1980s were marked by the process of *abertura* (political opening) whereby Brazilian civil society organized itself and began to pressure the government for the democratization of the regime. As new political spaces were conquered, different political actors appeared and new social identities were created. It came as a surprise to many that the organization of civil society occurred not only at the level of political parties and labor unions but also at the level of social movements, of groups that fought for specific issues and, up until then, had not played an important role in Brazilian politics. Such voices came from feminist groups, homosexuals, "green" movements, consumer movements concerned with price increases, religious movements, and so on.

II

It is in this context of clamoring for a voice that we find the revival of "Gauchism." When one observes the cultural manifestations that were evident during the 1980s and 1990s, the number of activities linked to traditions is impressive. The revival of gaúcho memorabilia is responsible for approximately two thousand Centers for Gaúcho Traditions (CTGs) throughout Rio Grande do Sul, as well as other states and countries where Rio Grandians have migrated (Oliven 1996); more than forty gaúcho music festivals involving a population of approximately one million people (Araújo 1987); and several rodeos. This growing interest also helps to explain the consumption of cultural products surrounding

gaúcho themes: television and radio programs (there is even an FM radio station in the metropolitan region of Porto Alegre that plays gaúcho music exclusively); newspaper columns, magazines, and specialized newspapers; publishing houses, books, bookstores, and regional book fairs; publicity that refers directly to gaúcho values (Jacks 1998); folk dance halls (Maciel 1984); music groups, singers, and records; typical restaurants featuring music and dance shows; stores that specialize in gaúcho clothing; and so on. It all adds up to a significant and expanding market, for material and symbolic goods that move a great number of people and resources.

Although there always was consumer demand for gaúcho cultural products, it was previously much smaller and was concentrated in the countryside or in the suburban and urban layers of society that had rural origins. The novelty is that young people in the cities, a good number of them from the middle class, have recently begun to drink mate tea, wear *bombachas* (baggy pants traditionally worn by the gaúcho), and enjoy regional music – all habits that have lost their stigma of inferiority. Considering that approximately 80 percent of the state's population lives in urban settings, this market is concentrated in the cities and is formed, for the most part, by people who have had no experience in rural areas. It is also interesting that a new field of intellectual debate has developed and that, within it, different actors have appeared wishing to speak on behalf of gaúcho tradition.

III

The image that readily emerges when one hears of gaúcho things is based on a past that existed in the pastoral region of the Campanha in southwest Rio Grande do Sul and on the real or idealized figure of the gaúcho. This is the center around which the debates about gaúcho identity turn. Today, the construction of this representation posits the question in a new light, for we are in an era during which Rio Grande do Sul has become urbanized and modern. At the same time, Brazil itself has developed a greater integration in politics, economics, transportation, and communication that effectively articulates its regions.

During the 1980s gaúcho identity was the subject of an intense and heated debate. Although trying to position themselves in opposite camps, the contenders were revolving around the same semantic field: the figure of the gaúcho, the means of constructing it, the criteria for defining its authenticity, the instances of its legitimacy and consecration, and so on. Basically two groups were involved in this dispute: the *traditionalists* and the *nativists*. Although they frequently proclaim themselves the antitheses of one another, they follow essentially the same model, varying merely in outward appearances.

The first and oldest actors in Gauchism are the traditionalists. They currently maintain an organized movement, Movimento Tradicionalista Gaúcho (Gaúcho Traditionalist Movement), are attentive to all that is related to symbolic goods of the state, and try to exercise control and orientation over these goods. They are joined by intellectuals who write about the movement and occupy strategic positions. For them it is fundamental to demarcate what the "true" gaúcho values are; hence, they need to make themselves the guardians of tradition. The maintenance of the distinction between Rio Grande do Sul and Brazil is a way to preserve the state's cultural identity. Therefore, a recurring theme in the traditionalist discourse is the threat hovering over gaúcho integrity.

Threats to gaúcho integrity come from the outside, from the introduction of "alien" customs spread by mass communication. They also arise from the inside, through the misrepresentations of "bad" traditionalists, inadequate use of artistic groups, and aberrations in the choreography of gaúcho dances. From there springs the need to define what is right and wrong or, even more precisely, what is authentic and spurious. Therefore, the traditionalists are constantly preoccupied with establishing parameters, separating the pure from the impure, in a process analogous to that described by Mary Douglas in *Purity and Danger* (1966). Thus, no amount of care is too great to stop the "unbridled decharacterization of culture and customs" (Tradição 1981:4).

This preoccupation translates into a search for norms and the elaboration of documents that attempt to design directives. One of the most important examples is the *Manual do Tradicionalista (Traditionalist Manual)* by Glaucus Saraiva (1968), one of the creators and theoreticians of the movement and the author of *Carta de Princípios do Movimento Tradicionalista (Charter of Principles of the Traditionalist Movement)*.

It is interesting that the *Manual* begins by affirming that "a large segment of traditionalists do not know what traditionalism is!" (Saravia 1968:7). Therefore, the book warns, "demonstrations, parades, expositions, contests, everything in fact that has a didactic character for popular consumption and that can be assimilated must loyally follow folkloric criteria, so that we do not distort or leave out characteristics of what exists or existed in our traditions and customs" (1968:30). However, when one interviews traditionalists, despite their preoccupation with delimiting concepts and parameters, one observes a great difficulty in defining and distinguishing such terms as *tradition, folklore, regionalism, nativism, gaúcho culture*, and so on.

True, we are facing a group of intellectuals who wield a certain amount of knowledge as a form of power. In the final analysis, it is a matter of who monopolizes the right to affirm what is and what is not gaúcho tradition and culture as well as who exercises influence over the marketing of symbolic goods.

One of the questions traditionalists struggled with when they established their movement was precisely how to establish what gaúcho tradition actually was. Thus, scholars began to study legends, songs, dances, poetry, and clothing. They came to the conclusion, however, that the existing material was scarce:

> When one goes to the Northeast, one finds folklore exemplified in every movement of daily life. This does not happen here. If one analyzes the Rio Grandian folklore[, one verifies that it is] very weak in popular manifestations. It is rich in the cult of tradition. Proof of this is that one values things the most at the time one begins to lose them. [Paixão Côrtes 1981:23]

The supposed poverty of gaúcho folklore does not exactly correspond to reality, but it creates one more way for the intellectuals to legitimize

their need to invent traditions – an activity that
may be easier than researching already existing
traditions. Likewise, one must point out that
many traditionalists view as folklore only that
which has been cataloged, thus ignoring popular
manifestations that have always existed spontan-
eously in the state. These traditionalists have
constructed a figure that is frequently outside
reality, one that they "defend" and consider the
legitimate representative of Rio Grandian values.
The social construction of the identity of this
crystallized gaúcho comes from the past and is
not subject to great modification.

After participating in the group of Brazilian
representatives who attended Tradition Day in
Montevideo, Uruguay, in 1949, two of the founders of the 35 CTG, which was the first modern
center for gaúcho tradition, Paixão Côrtes and
Barbosa Lessa, came back "disillusioned with our
poverty in musical and choreographic themes with
a clear traditional stamp. When we arrived here,
we conducted a preliminary survey and we verified
that – in contrast to lively northeastern folklore,
for example – little or nothing was left to us, in
dance." Because no record was left of several of
these cultural manifestations, they thought it necessary to invent them. Thus, when the 35 CTG
was invited to make a presentation at the Third
National Week of Folklore in Porto Alegre in 1950,
sponsored by the Brazilian branch of UNESCO,
the group's imagination gave way:

> Hurriedly we sent for chintz dresses for
> our sisters and cousins; we tried to reconstruct
> a *media-canha* [a historical popular dance per-
> formed to polka music; today it is one of the
> versions of the fandango] that we had seen in
> Montevideo, and on the night of the festivities
> we presented to the public, for the first time,
> pieces of the choreography that we had
> gathered here and there: the *Caranguejo* [an
> old Rio Grandian dance probably of Azorian
> origin], the *Pezinho* [literally, "little foot" –
> another typical Rio Grande dance that re-
> quires intricate footwork on the part of the
> dancers]. The "Little Foot" was a total novel-
> ty.... Nevertheless, the public accepted it.
> What's more, they applauded enthusiastically.
> Confirming what we would read thirty
> years later in Eric Hobsbawm: The dance of

the "Little Foot" was responding to a need felt
not only by our group of young men but also
by the spectator public. Having discovered
that night the communicative force of popular
dance, Paixão Côrtes and I faced a dilemma.
Either we would run back to Montevideo to
learn instantly with our "eastern brothers" the
"*Gaúcho* dances of the Great Pampas
fatherland" or else roll up our sleeves and
search Rio Grande do Sul in an attempt to
discover melodic and choreographic shards
that, conveniently gathered and glued, might
approximate our Luso-Brazilian heritage.
[Barbosa Lessa 1985:71–72]

Of interest in this quote is the reference to
Hobsbawm, an author who criticizes the invention of traditions as an a posteriori legitimizer of
the Gaúcho Traditionalist Movement. This demonstrates the kind of knowledge the movement's
intellectuals have in present-day bibliography.

Upon analyzing the folkloric manifestations in
the state, Augusto Meyer (1952) criticized the
romantic vision that presumed folklore would
originate within the popular levels of the population. He also pointed out that "the contribution of
the 'people' is relatively *circumspect* in contrast to
the creative initiative of the educated minorities"
(1952:23). This becomes clear in the case of the
old gaúcho fandango dances, which moved from
the rancher's great room to the peons' bunkhouse
as the new European dances began to be adopted
by the ruling classes. In the words of João Cezimbra Jacques,

> Among the ruling classes, the *fandango*,
> which up until 1839 and 1840 was still popu-
> lar, began to be replaced by the dances that
> originated in Europe such as the *ril*, the
> *gavota*, the *sorongo*, the *montenegro*, the
> waltz, and later the polka, the *chotes*, the *con-
> tradanças*, the mazurkas, and finally the beau-
> tiful Spanish *havaneiras*. [1979:75]

This process brings to mind the phenomenon
of circularity in the relationship between the culture of the popular classes and that of the ruling
classes first described by Bakhtin (1984) and
again examined in the work of Carlo Ginzburg.
These authors show that in preindustrial Europe
there was, between the culture of the upper

classes and that of the subaltern classes, a circular relationship formed by reciprocal influences that traveled from top to bottom as well as from bottom to top. In a similar manner, studying the modifications that the Catholic saints went through in Afro-Brazilian religions, Bastide (1978) developed the concept of *reinterpretation*, showing how a group may attribute new meaning to a cultural expression in terms of its own symbolic system.

The gaúcho traditionalists began inventing and appropriating a series of traditions, some of which became so popular that they were frequently considered to have folk origins in spite of their originators' claims that they were indeed their own creations. Thus, one of the most popular songs composed by Barbosa Lessa and based on the homonymous legend is generally considered part of the state's folklore, to its author's surprise:

"The Little Black Boy Who Tended the Pasture" was a song I wrote when the 35 CTG was just beginning, when we had no music; there was no traditionalist music, no regionalist music, nothing. You could count on one hand [what was available,] so we had to compose our own songs, and one of the songs I wrote was "The Little Black Boy Who Tended the Pasture." Later the Farroupilha Group adopted it as a theme song in their television programs and it was heard everywhere and became well known. Today it practically belongs to the heritage of Rio Grande do Sul and that has given me much satisfaction, since I have made friends through "The Little Black Boy Who Tended the Pasture" and other songs as well. I resent it that Rio Grande do Sul is so backward when it comes to culture. There is no respect for intellectual endeavors, no respect for the artist, and a malicious overtone whenever someone mentions that a writer or a composer has stupidly decided to speak of things from his homeland ... so that becomes folklore. The Symphonic Orchestra of Porto Alegre presented "The Little Black Boy Who Tended the Pasture" as having no known composer. One day, they performed on the anniversary of the Anne Frank School at the end of 1978. They rented the Leopoldina

Theater for the Anne Frank performance (my daughter studied there), and the announcer said: "And now, by an unknown composer, 'The Little Black Boy Who Tended the Pasture.'" My wife was in the audience and [she thought that] it could have been another "Little Black Boy Who Tended the Pasture," but it was mine. When they finished the performance, she stood up from the audience and said: "Hey ... the author is not unknown; I sleep with him every night and his name is Barbosa Lessa." [Barbosa Lessa 1983]

Another area in which much tradition was invented is that of dress, a theme of endless discussions about authenticity. It seems that the bombacha (baggy pants) – the key item in masculine dress – has an interesting trajectory. Glaucus Saraiva, one of the founders of the '35 CTG and author of the *Traditionalist Manual*, argues the following:

[Gaúcho clothing] is characterized as the most precious typical Brazilian clothing, since, symbolized by the *bombacha*, it is made from cloth of various weights, adaptable to the several different climates in our state. It is the most popular clothing because it is worn in the fields as well as the city, at fiestas and at formal ceremonies; it is the most democratic garment because it is worn by the peon in the humble farms and by the boss in the mansions in the city; it is the most glorious because, wearing it, the *Gaúcho* wrote a large part of the history of Rio Grande do Sul and Brazil. [1968:51]

Franco, however, makes this argument:

[The *pilchas* were] work clothes worn generally by the peons and not by ranchers. The higher levels of rural society always tried to identify with city dwellers, wearing suits with straight pants, ties, short boots, or shoes. There exists, therefore, a component that is not duly underscored in the traditionalist movement: the movement searched for a valorization of the lower levels of rural society; it looked for models of authenticity not in the bosses but in the horsemen, the tamers, the herd peons, the farm hands, and the rodeo hands. The elite did not serve as a model for tradition. [1985:2]

If we can generalize from this, the adoption of clothing would have originated among the popular classes – a debatable issue – even though today the bombacha is worn by middle-class urban youth.

Tau Golin has a another opinion. He argues that the bombacha originated with English mercantilism:

> Rare are the registers about the *bombacha* before the Paraguay War. The *bombacha* entered the Prata region thanks to the Crimean War, when English manufacturers produced thousands of uniforms for the Turkish army. However, the conflict ended earlier than expected, and so many "Turkish pants" were left over. The Prata River market became the salvation for the great losses by selling the pants to the troops in the Triple Alliance. As a demonstration that traditionalism never lives in isolation, the *Gaúcho* only began wearing the honorable *bombachas* of today because the English mercantilist did not admit a negative balance in their books. [1983:93]

Leaving aside the discussion about the authenticity of the bombacha or about British imposition thereof, it is interesting to verify that after taking care of their own clothing, traditionalists went on to decide what to do with the clothing of women. The traditionalists decided to call the men *peons* as a way of designating the activities that the gaúcho carried out on the ranches. They decided to call the women *prendas*, a word that does not refer to any activity but means adornment, jewelry, or an object that may be given as a gift. Thus, women were reduced to the status of adornments in a process in which men were essentially active and women were passive. The traditionalists decided that the male garment should reproduce that worn in the fields by the gaúcho. But the question remained about what to do with the female garment:

> From 1865 until today, there are numerous illustrations of female clothing: in paintings, Daguerreotypes, and photographs. But when

the Traditionalist Movement founded the '35 CTG in Porto Alegre on April 24, 1948, the young men (only sometime later did the first young women join) felt the need to create a feminine set of clothing that matched the brilliant masculine garment. Thus they consulted photographs of their own families and were inspired by the simple clothing worn by women who worked in the fields as well as by the Uruguayan traditionalists, and even – although this hard to believe – by the "redneck" dress of those they had fought against, and, as a result of all this, they created the famous "*prenda* dress," using as a guideline the simplest feminine dress in Rio Grande do Sul – the printed calico or chintz – of the end of the nineteenth century and beginning of the twentieth. In spite of it being a traditionalist creation, the *prenda* dress conserved the pattern and seriousness of the model of the *Gaúcho* woman. [Fagundes 1977:24]

Some, however, are of another belief:

> The *Gaúcho* woman did not and does not have typical clothing. With the development of the Traditionalist Movement and the first young women joining the CTGs, two things were created: the term *prenda* to symbolically classify women as female associates and, based on old photographs and other research sources, the "*prenda* dress." It was circumspect and simple, so that the young women might be able to follow the dress of the "peons" and distinguish themselves as associates of a Center for Traditions. All of this is nothing more than convention to give the *prendas* a typical dress that they did not know how to maintain throughout our sociological formation, and this was done for a very simple reason: women's universal vanity, always trying to follow the "fashion," no matter where it comes from. And this very feminine impulse has already transformed that circumspect and simple "suit" into a thousand and one different dresses with different accessories. We are not going to be the ones who will convince or unravel the universal force of feminine coquettish behavior. We merely plead that our dear traditionalists, attending to the virtues of circumspection,

simplicity, and reserve which the *Gaúcho* has attributed to them, will not transform the "*prenda* dress" and their accessories into costumes that tempt the moral sense of austerity of our Traditionalist Movement. . . . The function of the feminine dress is to serve as a frame for women's grace and beauty, not to make them look grotesque or ridiculous. [Saraiva 1968:57–58]

One can perceive in this an attempt not only to place women in a subaltern position but to control their femininity and sexuality as well. The Traditionalist Movement's emphasis on circumspection and moral austerity reveals a fear of the power women might have, through their behavior, to shame men and therefore blemish what the men considered to be their most precious possession: their honor. Therefore, as occurs in other societies, an obsessive preoccupation with the need to control women emerged.

However, in spite of all the regulations about the feminine garment, when women dress in gaúcho style, they frequently prefer to wear the masculine clothing rather than the prenda. For example, Miss Brazil, Ieda Maria Vargas, a woman from Rio Grande do Sul, upon becoming Miss Universe in 1963, presented herself abroad in a *chiripá*, a gaúcho garment made up of a strip of material that goes between the legs and is attached to the waist by a leather belt. This was always a male, not female, garment. It is not difficult to understand this preference if we recall that when the traditionalists speak about Rio Grande do Sul, it is always the male figure that is exalted. Women are left with the subaltern role of the prenda. When they dress in the male garment, women are appropriating the symbols of prestige that are reserved for the gaúcho, the representative social figure in a society in which women hold a secondary position.

IV

Frequently the revival of gaúcho culture is seen as a victory for traditionalism. Of course this "victory" falters on the fact that new artists are re-elaborating Rio Grandian themes without adhering to any kind of dogma and at times are even

parodying the traditional figure of the gaúcho. The Gaúcho Traditionalist Movement cannot control all cultural expressions in the state, nor can it hegemonically disseminate its messages. These are different times, engendering different notions of what it means to be a gaúcho, notions that do not necessarily correspond to the beliefs of the Center for Gaúcho Traditions. The market for symbolic goods has increased, and new actors have begun to claim positions in it.

Music festivals are arenas where much of the debate about what it means to be gaúcho takes place. The California of Rio Grandian Native Song is an example of this. It takes place annually in December in Uruguaiana, a city in the Campanha that is on the Argentine border. Sponsored by the Sinuelo do Pago Center for *Gaúcho* Traditions, the California was the first of the gaúcho music festivals, and it has served as a model for dozens of festivals that take place in the state.

The growth of the California from the time of its creation in 1971 is impressive. Today, it brings together hundreds of composers who compete for prizes and for the possibility of having their compositions included in a recording of all the finalists' compositions. Thousands of people go to Uruguaiana to attend the festival, and most of them camp in a "Tent City," a large campground where the campers take part in barbecues, drink mate tea, tell "tall tales," and listen to the music of the festival.

As participation in the event increased, its organizers found themselves impelled to define what gaúcho music is. Thus, the rules of the 11th California, which took place in December 1981, state, "We understand the meaning of music from Rio Grande do Sul to be that which evinces the theme of the *Gaúcho* homeland, based on its folkloric rhythms" (Regulamento da 11a Califórnia da Canção Nativa do Rio Grande do Sul 1981:2). The rules state that the competing compositions are evaluated by the judging committee

in three different verses, all obligatory and necessarily based on folk rhythms from Rio Grande do Sul. These areas are defined as (a) *country verse* – that which identifies itself with the man, the environment, and the customs of the countryside in Rio Grande do Sul, (b) *Rio Grandian manifestation verse* – that which focuses on other sociocultural and geographical aspects of Rio Grande do Sul not strictly limited to the countryside; and (c) *verse of folkloric representation* – that which stems from the verses defined in items (a) and (b) above and projects itself universally as an art in terms of its poetic and musical treatment. [1981:3]

Among the objectives of the California is "discovering new paths for the true music of Rio Grande do Sul, through the present-day language of *Gaúcho* origins and constants" (Regulamento da 11a Califórnia da Canção Nativa do Rio Grande do Sul 1981:1). The problem, of course, is how to define what the state's "true" music is. This issue has generated heated polemics that culminated in the episode of the *Uruguaiana Charter* on the occasion of the 11th California. The Triage Committee of that California, meeting before the festival, introduced a document entitled *Uruguaiana Charter* "with no other motive than that of attempting to collaborate on the improvement of Rio Grandian music of native extraction" (Rillo et al. 1982:1). Among other salient points in the *Charter* with regard to the compositions of the most recent Californias, we find

> the repetition of themes linked to *Gaúcho* tradition and folklore; exhaustive and generally inadequate usage of certain *Gaúcho* themes; compulsion with the past and with infancy as a background for the lyrics; scarce focus on the contemporary human and socioeconomic realities in Rio Grande do Sul; repetitive use of clichés; rare utilization of certain rhythms, and utilization of foreign rhythms. [Rillo et al. 1982:1–2]

One of the disqualified composers (of the 297 compositions entered in the contest, 36 were chosen) decided to present *The Uruguaiana Anti-Charter*, in which he contests the arguments of the *Uruguaiana Charter*. After refuting the *Charter*'s arguments one by one, the author concludes, "As one reads in the objective 'C' of the regulation of the California of the Rio Grandian Native Song, they are trying to 'discover new

paths for the true music in RS.' What is the path? Does anyone know it? It seems there must be someone who knows it . . . or is there not?" (Lopes 1982:2).

The regulations of the California also point out that

> the Organizing Committee of the Eleventh California of Native Song, with the intention of preserving the seriousness with which one searches for and revitalizes the values and characters of *Gaúcho* culture will not permit the participation of persons or groups wearing an incomplete *Gaúcho* garment or those with features that render it uncharacteristic. [Regulamento da 11a Califórnia da Canção Nativa do Rio Grande do Sul 1981:6]

Every year, certain musicians are invited to participate in evening presentations, although they do not compete for the awards. During the 11th California, one of the invited groups was Os Tapes, which had won the Second California but subsequently had developed a rather critical vision of the festival and a musical project quite distant from the vision of the Gaúcho Traditionalist Movement. Because they were not competing, and therefore not subject to the regulations, the group members decided deliberately not to wear gaúcho garments. When I had the occasion of interviewing them, they assured me that they saw no reason to present themselves "in costume" as gaúchos from the frontier because they were from Tapes, a small city 100 kilometers from Porto Alegre (the capital of Rio Grande do Sul) at Lagoa dos Patos, a region where there is rice cultivation.

It is significant that such polemics almost always surround music festivals. It is in this arena that the actors of Gauchism come to battle, with music as the instrument of dispute. Music festivals have become privileged arenas where one can study the conflicts that surround the construction of gaúcho identity inasmuch as they are the outlet for antagonistic positions struggling against one another. It is there that we witness controversies about music styles, regional accents, garments, and so on. In the final analysis, all these polemics deal with what gaúcho culture is and who has the competence to define it. During my fieldwork, there were even occasions when I was asked to intervene to give the "word of the university" in the several disputes being waged by different groups.

V

The other group of contenders in this polemic is formed basically by artists and journalists who call themselves *nativists* and who do not accept the control and patronage imposed by the Gaúcho Traditionalist Movement. A constant dispute rages between these two groups, which can be illustrated by a quasi-manifesto article entitled "Ayatollahs of Tradition" written by two journalists who cover musical movements in the state. For these journalists,

> The ayatollahs of tradition...are already risking resurrecting dogmas and reliving authoritarian forms of thinking, and little by little they come to judge themselves as proprietors of the manifestations that have something to do with *Gaúcho* singing. They occupy posts of influence in the festival organizations and in their judging committees, are active within the systems of communication, and in official institutions of all kinds. And most of the time they are always prohibiting, limiting, and dictating rules and forms of behavior, at times aggressively attacking those who did not learn how to read with their primer. [Fonseca and Eitelvein 1986:8]

They go on:

> It cannot be said that a Nativist Movement exists by right, but it is undeniable that it exists in fact. The nativist is not dogmatic, he is not linked to preestablished criteria, and he knows that besides Rio Grande do Sul, other Brazilian states exist, and that beyond Brazil, another world. In music, he wants to experiment, invent, create, without someone permanently telling him that such and such a thing is all right and another is not. The nativist believes that guitars and synthesizers are merely musical instruments, neither diabolical nor corrupting. He also wants the freedom to be influenced by other musical ideas in peace, as occurred with his ancestors in the nineteenth century. These ancestors enlivened the musical field with rhythms

that came from European centers and these rhythms were transformed by other personalities who were regional and unique. The nativists want to dress however they wish, not according to canons and traditionalist figurines. The nativists have before them today's reality and they know that the very exalted (and ironically also ostracized) peons, of whom the ayatollahs of tradition speak, are not happily roaming the fields. These peons work very hard wearing *bombachas* or mended pants, not wearing shiny boots but mundane thongs. Or else they walk the roads or stay in camps for the landless. The nativists are in favor of agrarian reform, of a more just social order, and are against the latifundia and the almost slavelike system that still persists. The nativists do not agree with the hierarchy that is fed and defended by the traditionalists, as if the world were a large barracks. The nativists know they have a past, but they do not worship this past as a way to distance themselves from the present, nor do they worship mystifying heroes who are already fossilized, as if Rio Grande do Sul were parked in the beginning of the century . . . Certain traditions need to be preserved, and in this the Centers for *Gaúcho* Traditions fulfill their role. But to encamp the Rio Grandian festivals as the property of the Traditionalist Movement is an aberration. To encircle *Gaúcho* music and artistic manifestations with a barbed-wire fence is something we cannot understand or permit. The agropastoral world has weakened with the inevitable industrial growth. Urban centers have swelled with the uncontrollable avalanche of the rural exodus. Meanwhile, the ayatollahs of tradition, all well placed in cities, want to revive and maintain the music of the countryside, under the fleeting argument that it was there that the peons had a home, food, and happiness – a mystical ideal fed by ranchers who lost a stable and disciplined labor force. But why did these people leave the country to become, today, unqualified workers in civil construction, office workers, washer women, domestic maids, and prostitutes, bringing forth abandoned children and assailants, illiterates without roots, guerrilla fighters of the lower class? Those who fled the countryside imagined they would find better days. And of course they did not find them. The ayatollahs want to sing of the ideal past, not of their drama. Evidently it will not be with sweet words nor with metaphors that one will achieve that. However, it needs to be done, in a rhythm that most closely approaches the reality of the mud in the marginal villages. At no time does this stop them from singing of their passion, sex, love, and whatever else may stimulate daily life. [Fonseca and Eitelvein 1986:8]

The document had strong repercussions, and several people supported it. As a comeback, one of those who wore the cap of "ayatollah of tradition" called the journalists cowbirds in an interview:

I believe they are tradition's cowbirds. A cowbird does not make a nest but lays eggs in other birds' nests and waits until they hatch. They have no ideological or affective commitment to Gauchism. When they saw that nativism was a phenomenon that was opening and enlarging its space, they entered and took their piece of cake. My dream is to hear the criticism of those who are identified ideologically with Gauchism; people who know the cause, not outsiders or foreigners who are riding the wave of success and who will promptly abandon nativism if it begins to wane. [Fagundes 1986:6]

During the music festivals, a constant dispute brews between the traditionalists and the nativists. The latter believe that their style is just the opposite of the former, which is labeled "nheconheco culture" (this is the onomatopoetic depiction of a musical rhythm that is very poor — therefore, when referring to culture, this means a musical culture that does not introduce innovations such as the electric guitar), meaning one that is poor in resources, founded only on the accordion, without making use of any electronic resources, and tied to well-beaten themes from the past. The traditionalists, on the other hand, invoke their authority from their having been the creators of the first festivals and the processors of the revival of all things gaúcho. These differences, besides generating heated debates, do not run deep, however, for the traditionalists and the

nativists both deal with the same theme. In the words of Rosângela Araújo, who conducted indepth research about the music festivals.

The "nativists" songs present themselves as more innovative than those of the "traditionalists" in the aspect of their contemporary themes and style of rhythm. However, in essence they follow the same "pattern," the design changing only in the details. Thus both factions have as a base images of the "countryside" as a habitat par excellence of the typical regional human figure. For a child of traditionalism, nativism does not seem to be its antithesis, as some would like it to be, nor is it traditionalism itself as others would like it to be, but merely an offshoot dressed in new clothing, under the influence of some ideas from its time. [1987:76]

That this debate is taking place among urban, middle-class intellectuals is clear in the research carried out by Araújo. When she analyzed, from a sample, the social origins of the composers in the most important state music festivals, she found out that only 20 percent of them lived the daily country life of their youths or adolescences. The majority were born and reared in cities. These cities were predominantly in the interior and frequently in the Campanha region — a fact used to justify knowledge of country life. As for family origins, most of the composers came from groups with some economic and cultural capital, which is reflected in the fact that 85 percent of them had attended university and only 15 percent made a living from their music alone (Araújo 1987:65–69).

If one weighs the polemics, the differences between traditionalists and nativists are a matter of style. The former almost deliberately assume a more conservative and less developed position, whereas the latter appear more progressive and innovative, intending to bridge the state's past and present. What they have in common, besides the preoccupation with gaúcho roots, is that they fight for the same market of symbolic goods and access to recognition, such as the music festivals, journalistic debates, and so on. In a certain way, they could be characterized as intellectuals who are on the periphery of the established circles of intellectual legitimization, insofar as they do not have access to the classic institutions, such as universities, academic journals, and scientific congresses.

VI

At first sight, it may seem strange to find this revival of Gauchism at the turn of the century, when Brazil is well integrated politically, economically, culturally, and in its transportation and mass communication networks. A growing economic, political, and administrative centralization and the development of sophisticated communication networks are frequently considered responsible for the weakening of regional power, the deepening of homogeneity, and standardizing of habits and attitudes in the population. Today in Brazil one observes tendencies, in opposition to – or perhaps as a result of – this growing centralization, that are contrary to this process – tendencies that manifest themselves through the affirmation of regional identities, with Rio Grande do Sul serving as an expressive example. Significantly, Gauchism gained strength again when Rio Grande do Sul, a state with a firm rural past whose population is now mainly urban, felt it was increasingly losing its importance in Brazil, a country that has accentuated its centralizing tendencies at the political and economic levels as well as at the cultural level.

If Gauchism rewrites rural tradition and life, it does so in an urbanized state that wishes to be modern. It may seem curious that this movement should take hold of rural and past values when Rio Grande do Sul is predominantly urban and quite industrialized. This fact has made some consider the phenomenon as a mere passing fashion or an anachronistic ideology, albeit curiously efficacious, something like the concept of *cultural survivals* (Tylor 1913:16). However, because of the breadth and duration of the phenomenon, it is difficult to label it as a fashion or an ideology that has passed its time. With regard to the aspect of fashion that publicity can attribute to any phenomenon, this has lasted far longer than other waves. Although a considerable number of intellectuals point to the ideological and reactionary aspect of the return to an idyllic time that either never

existed or no longer exists, this denouncement does not resolve the question either. In this sense, for example, it is difficult to explain why a state in which a conservative ideology would be hegemonic has an oppositionist political tradition.[1]

It happens that the movement is far from losing energy, a fact that coincides with a tendency that has lately been occurring in Brazil. With the political opening that began at the end of the 1970s, an intense process of establishing new political actors and building new social identities emerged. Inasmuch as identities are representations formulated in opposition or in contrast to other identities, what is sought is precisely the differences. Thus, the construction of these identities goes through the development of traits in Brazilian culture that are appropriated and used as diacritical marks, that is, as signals that confer a mark of distinction on different social groups.

What is happening in Rio Grande do Sul seems to indicate that today, for the gaúcho, the national is realized through the regional. That is, the people of Rio Grande do Sul can only be Brazilian if they are gaúcho first. Currently, gaúcho identity is no longer formulated in terms of the Farroupilha tradition but, rather, through the expression of cultural distinction in a country where the means of mass communication tend to homogenize society culturally through standards that often originate on the beaches of Rio de Janeiro. When one attempts to compare Rio Grande do Sul with the rest of the country, pointing to differences and constructing a social identity, it is almost inevitable that this process will reach out to the state's rural past. And it will reach to the figure of the gaúcho, the distinguishing emblem of the state.

NOTE

This article was translated from the Portuguese by Carmen Chaves Tesser.

1 The progressive Workers' Party has a strong presence in the political system of the State of Rio Grande do Sul.

REFERENCES CITED

Araújo, Rosângela
1987   Sob o Signo da Canção: Uma análise de festivais nativistas do Rio Grande do Sul. M. A. thesis, Department of Social Anthropology, Federal University of Rio Grande do Sul, Porto Alegre.

Bakhtin, Mikhail
1984   Rabelais and His World. Bloomington: Indiana University Press.

Barbosa Lessa, Luiz Carlos
1983   Interview with Luiz Carlos Barbosa Lessa. October 4.
1985   Nativismo: Um Fenômeno Social Gaúcho. Porto Alegre, Brazil: L&PM.

Bastide, Roger
1978   The African Religions of Brazil: Toward a Sociology of the Interpretation of Civilization. Baltimore: Johns Hopkins University Press.

Douglas, Mary
1966   Purity and Danger: An Analysis of the Concepts of Pollution and Taboo. New York: Praeger.

Fagundes, Antônio Augusto
1977   Indumentária Gaúcha. Porto Alegre: Fundação Instituto Gaúcho de Tradição e Folclore.
1986   De Coronel a Silva Rillo. Zero Hora, June 7: 6.

Fonseca, Juarez, and Gilmar Eitelvein
1986   Aiatolás da Tradição: Apontamentos para uma história natural. Zero Hora, June 14: 8.

Franco, Sérgio da Costa
1985   Pilchas. Zero Hora, October 8: 2.

Golin, Tau
1983   A Ideologia do Gauchismo. Porto Alegre, Brazil: Tchê.

Jacks, Nilda Aparecida
1998   Indústria Cultural e Cultura Regional. Porto Alegre, Brazil: Editora da Universidade Federal do Rio Grande do Sul.

Jacques, João Cezimbra
1979   Ensaio sobre os Costumes do Rio Grande do Sul. Porto Alegre, Brazil: ERUS.

Lopes, Cícero Galeno
1982   A Anticarta de Uruguaiana. Uruguaiana.

Maciel, Maria Eunice de Souza
1984   Bailões, é disto que o povo gosta. M.A. thesis, Department of Social Anthropology, Federal University of Rio Grande do Sul, Porto Alegre.

Meyer, Augusto
1952   Cancioneiro Gaúcho. Porto Alegre, Brazil: Globo.

Oliven, Ruben
1996   Tradition Matters: Modern Gaúcho Identity in Brazil. New York: Columbia University Press.

Paixão Côrtes, J. C.
1981   Falando em Tradição e Folclore Gaúcho: Excertos jornalísticos. Porto Alegre, Brazil: Sultepa.

Regulamento da 11a Califórnia da Canção Nativa do Rio Grande do Sul
1981   Regulamento da 11a Califórnia da Canção Nativa do Rio Grande do Sul. Uruguaiana.

Rillo, Aparício Silva, Diogo Madruga Duarte, Juarez Fonseca, Luiz Carlos Borges, and Mauro Dante Aymone Lopes
1982   Carta de Uruguaiana. Uruguaiana.

Saraiva, Glaucus
1968   Manual do Tradicionalista. Orientação Geral para Tradicionalistas e Centros de Tradições Gaúchas. Porto Alegre, Brazil: Sulina.

Tradição
1981   Introdução à Carta do Seival. No. 1.

Tylor, Edward Burnett
1913 [1871] Primitive Culture. London: Murray.

19

The United States, Mexico, and *Machismo*

Américo Paredes

One of the most widely discussed Mexican national types is the *macho*, the superman of the multitude. He has preoccupied psychologists, sociologists, philosophers, historians, poets, and even folklorists. Some, like folklorist Vicente T. Mendoza, have explained him as a phenomenon caused by the climate, or as a result of tendencies inherited by the Mexicans from the people of Andalusia.[1] On the other hand, many others have explained *machismo* in terms of Freudian theories. *Machismo* – so they tell us – has its origins in the conquest, when Hernán Cortés and his conquistadors arrived in Mexico and raped the women of the Aztecs. From this act of violence is born the *mestizo*, who hates and envies his Spanish father and despises his Indian mother – in both cases as a result of his Oedipal complexes. Various Mexican writers have taken this line, but Samuel Ramos may be singled out as the initiator and Octavio Paz as one of the most eloquent defenders of this theory. In Argentina, too, Ezequiel Martínez Estrada applied a similar point of view to the *gaucho*.[2] The characteristic traits of *machismo* are quite well known: the outrageous boast, a distinct phallic symbolism, the identification of the man with the male animal, and the ambivalence toward women – varying from an abject and tearful posture to brutal disdain. The Mexican *macho*, Santiago Ramírez tells us, "is terribly fond of all articles of clothing

symbolizing masculinity: the hat (either the fancy *sombrero* or the wide-brimmed Borsalino), the pistol, the horse or automobile are his pleasure and his pride."[3] *Machismo* finds expression in Mexican folklore, especially in the folksong. As Felipe Montemayor states, "The folksongs of Mexico are openly tearful and addressed to the woman who has gone away with another man 'who is no doubt more of a man than I am,'... in which he openly admits his frustration and failure; as for the rest, they are strings of phrases typical of one rejected, who tries to conceal his humiliation or the scorn directed at him by resorting to aggressive or compensatory forms."[4]

If all this has resulted from the rape of some Indian women by the soldiers of Cortés, then Mexican *machismo* is very ancient indeed. It has existed some four centuries at least, if one is to suppose that effects follow soon after causes. It should be possible, then, to make an interesting study of the folkloric expressions of Mexican *machismo*, from the time of the first *mestizo* up to the present. Such a work cannot be expected from either psychologists or poets, to whom we owe but superficial references to Mexican folksong and other folkloric genres. We would expect it from a folklorist, a Vicente Mendoza for example. And in truth, there is at least one study by Vicente T. Mendoza on this subject,

"El machismo en México al través de las canciones, corridos y cantares," published in Buenos Aires in 1962.[5] In this essay, one of the last left us by the late Mexican folklorist, we are told that "there are two kinds of *machismo:* one that we could call authentic, characterized by true courage, presence of mind, generosity, stoicism, heroism, bravery," and so forth, and "the other, nothing but a front, false at bottom, hiding cowardice and fear covered up by exclamations, shouts, presumptuous boasts, bravado, double-talk, bombast.... Supermanliness that conceals an inferiority complex."[6] Mendoza goes on to cite more than thirty Mexican folksongs as examples of what he calls "authentic" and "false" *machismo.*

There are at least three points of interest in this study of Mendoza's. The first is his definition of the two kinds of *machismo.* Mendoza's false *machismo* – with its "presumptuous boasts, bravado, [and] double-talk" – is what all other writers on the subject would call the real *machismo,* that configuration of attitudes which has so preoccupied writers as divergent as Samuel Ramos and Octavio Paz. What Mendoza calls authentic *machismo* is no such thing. It is simply courage, and it is celebrated in the folksongs of all countries. Admiration for the brave man who dies for the fatherland, for an ideal, or simply because he does not want to live without honor or without fame is found among all peoples. It is the heroic ideal in any time and in any country. Furthermore, the examples of boastful songs that Mendoza gives us date from the last third of the nineteenth and the first third of the twentieth centuries. That is to say, they belong to the period of the Revolution or to the times of Porfirio Díaz, immediately preceding the revolutionary period. Finally – and this is the most surprising thing of all – in all the examples Mendoza gives us of folksongs illustrative of Mexican *machismo,* not once does there occur the word *macho* or any of its derivatives. The heroes of the folksongs cited by Mendoza "die like men"; they are said to be "real men," and they are "valiant" or "brave." But they are never *machos.* The words *macho* and *machismo* occur repeatedly in the essay, but only in Mendoza's discussion of this supposedly Mexican phenomenon.

If the reader believes that the examples given by Mendoza are not representative, he can consult the major collections – those of Vázquez Santa Ana, Rubén Campos, and others including Mendoza himself.[7] The reader will find no traces of *machismo* in the songs of the colonial period, the war of independence, or even the Reform. He will encounter many brave men in those songs, but rarely will he find the bully. The Mexican bully as a folkloric type begins to appear in the *décimas* printed in the last two decades of the nineteenth century, in leaflets from presses like that of Antonio Vanegas Arroyo and with titles like "El guanajuateño," "El valiente de Guadalajara." Let us emphasize that these boastful *décimas* of the last part of the nineteenth century are of a decidedly comic character. They abound in humorous sayings and proverbial phrases. A *décima* from "El guanajuateño" (The Man from Guanajuato) may serve as an example for the whole genre:

> No se arruguen, valentones,
> traigan dispuestos sus fierros
> que aquí está "El Guanajuateño"
> para darles sus lecciones.
> Acérquense los matones
> que yo no les tengo miedo,
> firme y parado me quedo
> esperando cuchilladas;
> me parecen enchiladas
> que me trago las que puedo.[8]

> Don't back down on me, you bravos,
> and carry your blades at ready;
> here's a man from Guanajuato,
> to teach you a thing or two.
> Come a bit closer, you bullies;
> I am not afraid of you.
> Here I stand, firm and erect,
> awaiting your thrusts to parry;
> to me they're like enchiladas,
> and I'll guzzle all I can.

One must be extremely ingenuous to think that we have here a faithful picture of the Mexican bravo in real life. The man who is convinced that life is not worth living does not waste time on well-turned phrases and colorful words. Artistic boasting is found among Mexican males, but almost always it is the buffoon of the group who cultivates this genre. Usually he is the drunkest and least courageous member of the group, whose lack of valor and manliness gives him a certain minstrel-like license. It is this type, and not the bravo, who is described in the *décimas de valientes*. And let us also keep in mind: the boastful protagonist of these *décimas* says he is "a real man," "valiant," and "brave." He may compare himself with the tiger and the panther, or he will say that he is "a fever on stilts." But he never calls himself a *macho*.

The Mexican boast turns serious once the Revolution begins, and then it passes from the *décima* to the *corrido*. The idea of manliness existed in the Mexican *corrido* before the Revolution, as Mendoza shows in his study, for example in the *corrido* of "Demetrio Jáuregui":

> Le contestó don Demetrio:
> – Yo no me vine a rajar,
> yo vine como los hombres
> aquí a perder o ganar. –[9]

> Don Demetrio replied,
> "I didn't come to back out of a fight;
> I came here like a man,
> either to win or to lose."

Now the *corrido* picks up the kind of boast seen earlier in the *décima*, no longer in jest, however, but with all the seriousness of spirits inflamed by the Revolution. For example, in the *corrido* "De la persecución de Villa," the singer pokes fun at the efforts made by Pershing's forces to capture Pancho Villa:

> Qué pensarán los "bolillos" tan patones
> que con cañones nos iban a asustar;
> si ellos tienen aviones de a montones
> aquí tenemos lo mero principal.[10]

> What did these bigfooted *gringos* think,
> that they scare us with cannon.
> They may have piles of airplanes,
> but we have the thing that really counts.

"The thing that really counts" is, of course, courage – concentrated in the testicles of the Mexicans – what will give them the advantage over all the cannon and airplanes of the United States. Here we come much closer to what is usually meant by *machismo*. Another *corrido* of the same era presents the same attitudes even more explicitly, this one being "Los ambiciosos patones":

> Se va a mirar muy bonito de gringos el tenderete,
> después no quedrán la gorda; les sudará hasta el copete.

> La verdad, yo les suplico que traigan a sus gringuitas,
> porque estamos enfadados de querer a las inditas,
> sé que las tienen bonitas, gordas y bien coloradas,
> ahora es tiempo, camaradas, de pelear con muchas ganas,
> que les vamos a "avanzar" hasta las americanas.[11]

> It will be a pretty sight, to see all those *gringo* corpses;
> they will flinch from the tortilla, and they will sweat up to here.

> In truth, I hope they will bring their *gringo* women along,
> because we are getting tired of loving our Indian girls.
> I know that they have some nice ones, plump and with red faces.
> Now is the time, my comrades, to fight with a will; there will be lots of plunder, even American women.

This last song has the melody of a *corrido*, but the text is composed in *décimas*. Moreover, the influence of the braggart type of *décima* may be seen in the number of proverbial phrases it contains, such as "they want to scare us with the dead man's pallet," "they are going to stake out their hides," and "go slow in reaching in there, or you'll get your hand full of thorns." It must be noted it is in the *corridos* about United States intervention in the affairs of Mexico where we find these examples of what could be called the "boast taken seriously." Nevertheless, the word *macho* does not occur in these *corridos* either. Not until the 1940s, during World War II, do we begin to run across it. Mendoza published a *corrido* entitled "De pistoleros y moronistas" (About Gunmen and Partisans of Morones), collected in 1949 but dating from the period between 1940 and 1946, the administration of President Manuel Ávila Camacho. The last stanza goes like this:

¡Viva el pueblo siempre macho! ¡*Agustín el general*!
y ¡Viva Ávila Camacho y la vida sindical!¹²

Long live the people, always *machos!* Long live
  Agustín, the general!
Long live Ávila Camacho and the labor unions!

In another *corrido*, very popular in the 1940s, the protagonist brags about Mexican courage, and how the Mexicans are going to wreak havoc on the Axis once Mexico decides to join in the war, adding that their president is "Ca...macho!" In still another song of the same period, threats are hurled at the Axis nations, as the singer says:

Yo soy puro mexicano
y me he echado el compromiso con la tierra en que
  nací
de ser macho entre los machos,
y por eso muy ufano yo le canto a mi país.

I am a true-blue Mexican,
and I have an obligation to the land where I was
  born,
to be a *macho* among *machos;*
and that is why I proudly sing
  to my country.

In these *corridos* of the 1940s, where we do find the word *macho*, we almost always see it in association with other well-defined factors. One of these is the grim figure of the *pistolero*, one of the most dismal products of the postrevolutionary period. This is the man of the Revolution projected into peacetime, and therefore out of his element: the pistol-toting bully who sates his brutal impulses by trampling on the common citizen, and who can do it with impunity because he has money or political influence or simply because he is the bodyguard of some congressman or governor. Another factor is World War II, in which Mexicans took almost no part, in which they were not threatened by danger, desolation, or death – as they were during the Revolution. This is why the boasts ring so false in the *corridos* of the 1940s as compared to those of the Revolu-

tion. The revolutionary boasts directed against the United States arose from a situation both dangerous and real, and they expressed the sentiments of a majority of Mexicans. The boasts against the Axis during the 1940s sound like those of a little man who hurls threats while hiding behind a protector much larger than he. And let us remember that in this case, the "protector" was the traditional enemy, the United States. A third factor is the accident that in this period the last name of the Mexican president included the sound "macho." I am not suggesting that the word *macho* was not used in Mexico prior to the 1940s, or that *machismo* would not have appeared in Mexico if Ávila Camacho had not been president. But we must remember that names lend reality to things. The name of Camacho – because it rhymes with *macho* and because it was well known when other factors favored *machismo* – gave to both word and concept a popularity they did not have before. Before that time *macho* had been almost an obscenity, and consequently a word less used than *hombre* or *valiente*. Now it became correct, acceptable. After all, wasn't it in the name of the president himself?

Then appear the *corridos* for which Mexico is known abroad, the same ones cited repeatedly by those who deplore *machismo*. The following stanzas exemplify the style:

¡Traigo mi cuarenta y cinco
con sus cuatro cargadores!
¡Y traigo cincuenta balas,
las traigo pa' los traidores!

I'm wearing my forty-five
with its four cartridge clips!
And I carry fifty bullets;
they are for renegades!

And another one, even more foolish:

¡Caramba, yo soy su rey
y mi caballo el segundo!
¡Ora se hacen a mi ley
o los aparto del mundo!

Caramba, I am your king,
and my horse is second only to me!

Now you will bow to my law,
or I'll send you from this world!

Such *corridos* were disseminated in Mexico and abroad by the voice of popular singers like Pedro Infante and Jorge Negrete. That is to say, these were moving-picture *corridos*. And when one says moving-pictures, one says middle class. These have been the songs of the man from an emergent middle class, a man who goes to the movies, has enough money to buy a car, and enough political influence to go around carrying a gun. During World War II, it was this middle class that became emotional hearing Pedro Infante sing:

¡Viva México! ¡Viva América!
¡Oh pueblos benditos de Dios!

Long live Mexico! Long live America!
Oh, nations blessed by God!

The feelings of the common man are revealed in a well-known anecdote. The news that Mexico has just declared war against the Axis reaches a little Mexican village. The authorities lead the people in the execution of various "vivas" to Mexico. In a pause a voice is heard yelling, "Viva México, and death to the *gringos!*" "Shut up, stupid!" they tell him. "The *gringos* are our allies." "But how?" he says. "If it isn't the *gringos*, then who are we fighting?"

It seems, then, that Mexican *machismo* is not exactly as it has been painted for us by people who like to let their imaginations dwell on the rape of Indian women. *Machismo* does not appear in Mexican folklore until very recent times. In a more-or-less comic form, it was characteristic of the lower classes in prerevolutionary times. In a more sentimental and meretricious style, it is identified today with the Mexican middle class. We note, furthermore, a certain influence of the United States. All this makes us ask: How Mexican is *machismo* and to what degree is it a Hispanic, a New World, or a universal manifestation?

We know that courage and virility have always been identified as the ideal traits of the male, and that both primitive and modern man often have equated the coward with the homosexual. Among some groups it has been the custom to dress in woman's clothes any man who did not show sufficient courage in battle. There is no lack of examples making direct identification between courage and manliness. In an Eskimoan song published by C. M. Bowra, an old man remembers his youth, when he was a great hunter. And he sings:

I remember the white bear,
With its back-body raised high;
It thought it was the only male here,
And came towards me at full speed.
Again and again it threw me down,
But it did not lie over me,
But quickly went from me again.
It had not thought
Of meeting other males here,
And by the edge of an ice-floe
It lay down calmly.[13]

Let us take a second example from the Nordic peoples, of times past but not very remote, from the *Volsunga Saga*. Two heroes, Sinfjotli and Granmar, prepare to duel to the death; and as a preamble Sinfjotli says to his opponent:

Dim belike is grown thy memory now of how thou wert a witch wife on Varinsey, and wouldst fain have a man to thee, and chose me to that same office of all the world; and how thereafter thou wert a Valkyrie in Asgarth, and it wellnigh came to this, that for thy sweet sake should all men fight; and nine wolf-whelps I begat on thy body in Lowness, and was the father to them all.[14]

Except for the archaic English, this might be a *pelado* doing the Mexican equivalent of the "dozens" with another of his type. But let us move to the eighteenth century, to the classical English poet John Dryden and his famous ode on Alexander the Great, which includes a kind of refrain that has become proverbial: "None but the brave, None but the brave, None but the brave deserve the fair." That is to say, the most valiant and vigorous *macho* wins the coveted female, a poetizing of the natural selection of the species before Darwin was even born. Yet, this is also the theme of many *Märchen*, and of numberless plots in our popular literature, movies, and television.

The ingredients of *machismo*, then, are found in many cultures; however, what has been observed in Mexico is a whole pattern of behavior, a popular philosophy, so to speak. Is Mexico unique in this respect? Martínez Estrada would have said no, since he thought he had found the same thing in the Argentine *gaucho*. But let us look in the opposite direction, and we will find a country – the United States – where something very similar to Mexican *machismo* took place, with lasting influences on folklore, literature, and even politics.

The North American *macho* first appears in the 1820s and 1830s. This was for the United States a time of revolution, the age of Andrew Jackson. Earlier the country had been dominated by the aristocrats of the Atlantic Coast, the big landholders of Virginia and the rich merchants of New England. They talked, dressed, and lived in the English manner: their poets and fiction writers were mediocre imitators of the Europeans. The age of Jackson brings radical changes; the country openly enters its nationalistic period. The man of the forest – the frontiersman dressed in animal skins – becomes a political force, and the aristocrats on the coast look with horror at the vulgarity of the new leaders. In letters we have the dawning of a truly North American literature, which goes from the humorists of the 1820s to the novelist Mark Twain, and from him to the modern North American writers.[15] In folklore, the North American nationalistic movement is expressed in the tradition of the man from the backwoods, dressed in animal skins and armed with knife and long rifle. This figure – at the same time hero and buffoon – is expressed folkloristically in the tall tale, the humorous anecdote in which the stranger or Anglicized aristocrat from the coast is ridiculed, and the boast. Above all in the boast. The North American bully boasts of his vulgarity – the one thing the European and the easterner held most against him. He thinks of himself as the bravest and most ferocious man in the world; he can fight more men, love more women, and drink more whiskey than any other man alive. He compares himself to the bear and the tiger, to the alligator and the hurricane. He challenges the whole world with rowdy yelling; he leaps in the air and then struts around. In short, he is the spitting image of the Mexican *pelado* making out as the bravo from Guadalajara or the panther from Guanajuato.

We need not stress that the North American *macho* expressed feelings of inferiority in respect to European culture. The North American was trying to attain a true independence within his own country, to fashion a culture of his own. In order to reach his goal, he would boast even of his weaknesses. On the other hand, he could not completely ignore the technological superiority of Europe and his own East. He could laugh at English literature, at Italian music, and at French dancing masters; but he knew that the English navy ruled the seas, and that his rifle had been made by eastern craftsmen. Technology enabled him to conquer the West, although he always tried to deny it, giving the credit to his own manliness. Then came the Civil War, after which the United States began its march toward industrial and military world power. On the national level, Anglophobia gave way to Anglo-Saxonism, the glorification of a supposed Anglo-Saxon type.[16] During the period from 1870 to 1914, North American *machismo* undergoes some interesting changes. The *macho* becomes civilized, at least part of him. In folklore the frontiersman remains a comic character. The tall tales and the jokes in which the frontiersman appears as a boor continue to be told. That is to say, as a historical figure the *macho* persists in his role of buffoon. But the hero takes on new types (or stereotypes). In movies and dime novels, the *macho* becomes the cowboy. In serious literature he reappears as protagonist in the novels of Frank Norris, Jack London, and other writers of the naturalist school.[17]

In passing from folklore to the naturalistic novel, the North American *macho* loses not only his comic character but also his sexuality; that is to say, he becomes a Puritan *macho*, adjusting to the novelistic tradition of the times. He is all muscle and virility, but he releases his energy in orgies of violence against his enemies. The female still is the reward of his exploits, but all he does is show off in front of her – seriously now, and not in jest as the frontiersman had done. When he is not committing acts of barbarism against other men, he is a model of sobriety, filial love, and courtesy. In sum, he bears a surprising resemblance to the *charro* of recent Mexican movies, who – after shooting down half a dozen men – goes into church all loaded down with his guns, to sing a pious song to the Virgin of Guadalupe.

Aside from his asexual character, the *macho* of the naturalistic novel differs from the frontier *macho* in another respect: his nationalism turns into racism. The protagonist is always Anglo-Saxon, of course, and the cowardly, bad types are men darker than he – Italians, Portuguese, Spaniards, Mexicans, or Indians. The plot shows us that the blond *macho* is more of a *macho* than the dark ones; and therefore, he is Nature's chosen, according to the law of the jungle and the struggle for existence. This is nothing less than the superman as "blond beast," some forty years before Hitler. Furthermore, only the Anglo-Saxon blond is superior; the German, the Scandinavian, and the Irishman appear in the role of comedians or well-intentioned simpletons. This is a result, on the one hand, of Darwin's theories and, on the other, of the North American impulse toward empire and world power during this time. The pattern has its parallels in politics, and it is here that we find a historical figure, one single man, who symbolizes this second stage of North American *machismo*. This is Theodore Roosevelt – politician, cowboy, cavalry colonel, undersecretary of the navy, president, and a devotee par excellence of novelistic *machismo*. Not only in politics but in his personal life, Roosevelt made a determined effort to present before the public the figure of the *macho*, with all its strengths and weaknesses. Sickly as a child, myopic as to be almost blind, Roosevelt made it his business to show the world that, in spite of his physical deficiencies, he was just as good as any other man. It was this preoccupation that led him to try the most dangerous tasks of the hunter, the cowboy, and the soldier.

After World War I, a decided shift from *machismo* to feminism occurs in the United States, but it is not immediately apparent in literature. On the contrary, it is at this time that a figure analogous to Roosevelt appears in North American literature, this being the novelist Ernest Hemingway – the most hallowed interpreter of the *macho*. The popularity of Hemingway's works in the period between the two world wars – as much among the critics as with the general public – shows us the attraction the *macho* still had for the North American, although in real life the man of the United States made less and less of a show over his masculinity. Hemingway himself understood this, and almost all his novels and short stories develop the theme of *machismo* in Spain, Mexico, or Cuba. Today Hemingway is scorned by the critics. This is not surprising, since the protagonist of the novels now acclaimed by the critics no longer is the *macho* but the homosexual – the other extreme, or perhaps the same thing seen from another point of view. And although Hemingway has not been rejected by the general public, his works no longer are as popular as are novels of the type begun by Mickey Spillane. These are an exaggeration of the Hemingwayesque theme: the *macho* heroes are fierce, sexual, and brutally sadistic with the female. They do not stop with a simple beating, as might the "primitive" man. They riddle their women with bullets, a favorite target being the woman's belly. In North American folklore also, *machismo* is not completely a thing of the past. The boast and the tall tale still are cultivated among white folk groups. In the cities, meanwhile, the North American Negro has developed a genuinely *macho* folklore, with heroes that are bad men of insatiable sexual appetites. Their feats are narrated in folk poems and stories of an exaggerated obscenity. In the poetry are many boasts such as the following, taken from Roger Abrahams's book about the Philadelphia Negro:

I live on Shotgun Avenue, Tommygun Drive, Pistol Apartment, and Room 45.[18]

This brings to mind what Santiago Ramírez has to say about the Mexican's fondness for pistols, big hats, and automobiles – above all for the pistol, symbol par excellence of *machismo*. A sexual symbol, the disciples of Freud would tell us; and in truth, *pistola* is one of the many terms that the Mexican uses for "penis." But the pistol has other meanings for the Mexican, historical meanings related to the clash of cultures in the West, especially in the region of the Great Plains. The Spaniards arrived at the borders of the Great Plains centuries before the North Americans appeared, but they never occupied these areas.

One of the obstacles they encountered were mounted Indians like the Comanches, who gave a lot of trouble to the Spanish garrisons on the edge of the plains. Then come the North Americans; and in less than fifty years they totally subdue the Indians, occupy the Great Plains, and civilize the whole area. To what did the North American owe the ability to do in half a century what the Spaniard did not even begin in three? In a work on the subject, entitled precisely *The Great Plains*, the well-known Texas historian Walter Prescott Webb has explained it very simply: the North Americans were racially superior to the Spaniards. The Spaniards, being Europeans, were able to conquer inferior races like the Mexican Indians, in whose veins – Webb tells us – flowed ditchwater instead of blood. But the Comanche was too fierce to be overcome by Spaniard or Mexican. Only the Anglo-Saxon could be a manlier man than the Comanche; and in subduing the Comanche the Anglo-Saxon proved his superiority over other Europeans like the German, the Scandinavian, and the Italian. As Webb tells it, the men who conquered the Great Plains all had English or Scottish names.[19]

No better examples exist of the influence of *machismo* in the academic world than the books of Walter Prescott Webb, in which we find an almost infantile admiration for the man who totes a gun and wears boots and a big hat. The explanation by this distinguished historian of the conquest of the Great Plains in terms of manliness – and exclusively of Anglo-Saxon manliness – ignores well-known facts: all classes of men participated in the conquest of the West, including Negroes, and the technology of the eastern United States was a decisive factor in the superiority the North American of the West gained over Indians and Mexicans.[20] The surprising thing is that these facts were well known to Webb himself, since he discusses them with erudition and insight in other chapters (especially 5, 7, and 8) of *The Great Plains*. It seems to have been necessary for Webb, the man of the West, to reveal his personal feelings, boasting of the manliness of his region and its independence with respect to the East. Then Webb the historian gives us a careful study of the role played by the technology of the East in the conquering of the

Great Plains: the importance of the repeating rifle, barbed wire, windmills, the revolver, and machines for large-scale agriculture. What he says about the revolver is of special interest for us.

The old long rifle was the North American's ideal weapon while he conquered the forests east of the Mississippi, where he fought in the woods on foot. But when he emerged on the plains, the North American found himself at a great disadvantage. His rifle, which he had to load through the muzzle with a ramrod, was an ineffective weapon against Indians and Mexicans, who were men on horseback. Once he fired his rifle, the North American had only his knife to defend himself with, and in the use of this weapon he found the Mexican a dangerous adversary.[21] The Indian was even more formidable, since he could discharge twenty arrows in the time necessary to load a rifle.[22] Furthermore, both Mexicans and Indians used the lance as well. Confronted with this problem, the North Americans in the West seriously considered two solutions that were not at all heroic. One was to build a series of forts on the borders of the Great Plains to contain the Indians – that is to say, precisely what the Spaniards had done. The other was the settling of French colonists in these same areas, to serve as a buffer between the Indians and the North Americans.[23] But it did not become necessary to carry out these projects, and the reason was the technology of the East. In New Jersey an artisan from Connecticut, Samuel Colt, began to produce the first revolvers in 1838. The North American army showed little interest in them, but the Texans and other men of the West received them with enthusiasm.[24] In 1844 the revolver was put to the test for the first time in a battle between Texans and Comanches; each Texan was armed with two revolvers and a rifle. The Indians fled in disorder; the revolver had changed the balance of power on the Great Plains in favor of the man with the two pistols.[25] A quarter of a century later, the Winchester rifle replaced the revolver as the preferred weapon in the Great West, but the revolver – as a result of its initial impact – remained the symbolic weapon as much in folklore as in popular literature, and later in the movies and on television.

The revolver not only changed the character of conflict with the nomadic Indian, but it also revolutionized the North American concept of manliness. Let us not forget that, before the arrival of the North American in the Great West, the Mexican had faced the Indian armed only with lance and knife, as did the Argentine *gaucho* against the Indian of the pampas. The North American, Webb tells us, recognized the Mexican as an "artist with a knife."[26] Webb says it not in admiration but in a contemptuous tone, since it is part of the tradition of *machismo* in the United States to scorn the man with the knife, who is always given the role of coward and traitor.[27] It was not always this way, for there was a time when the North American boasted of his skill with the knife and held it in such high esteem that he gave personal names to his favorite blades, as did the medieval knights to their swords. This was, naturally, before the revolver, in the days of the backwoodsman, typified by Davy Crockett, who died in the defense of the Alamo against the troops of Santa Anna. Another of the defenders of the Alamo was James Bowie, whose name became a synonym for knife, because Bowie was a virtuoso in what Martínez Estrada calls "the art of cutting throats."[28] Considering the derogatory associations later given the knife in the folklore of the United States, it is truly ironic that legend should picture Bowie at the Alamo, knife in hand against the Mexican muskets. And in truth, if we imagine a confrontation between two men – one armed with a rifle or revolver and the other with a knife – which of the two would we say is taking the greater risk? Let the Knight of the Sad Countenance give us the answer, in the celebrated disquisition on arms and letters that Don Quijote makes in the chapters dealing with the Captive of Algiers.

Happy the blest ages that knew not the dread fury of those devilish engines of artillery, whose inventor I am persuaded is in hell receiving the reward of his diabolical invention, by which he made it easy for a base and cowardly arm to take the life of a gallant gentleman; and that, when he knows not how or whence, in the height of the ardour and enthusiasm that fire and animate

brave hearts, there should come some random bullet, discharged perhaps by one who fled in terror at the flash when he fired off his accursed machine, which in an instant puts an end to the projects and cuts off the life of one who deserved to live for ages to come.[29]

Cervantes reveals his own sentiments, no doubt, since he was maimed as a result of one of those "accursed machines." But he also expresses the feelings of most soldiers of his time. This is also the point of view in *Martín Fierro*, where we see the valiant *gaucho*, with "the one that never misfires" in his hand, facing cowards and scoundrels armed with revolvers and muskets.[30] But if we are gun-toters ourselves, we cannot accept such a judgment. We must change the situation, and thus it was in the North American tradition. The knife was made the weapon of the renegade, of the coward; the pistol became the weapon of the *macho*, the brave man. A paradox? It is, in truth, but it agrees with the tendency to change an unpleasant reality by inverting it, the very thing that is at the base of *machismo*.

Understandably, the Mexican did not immediately accept the North American's point of view. In much of Mexican folklore the steel blade retained its character as a suitable instrument for admirable deeds, and it was considered a very Mexican weapon as well. In a *corrido* from central Mexico of the 1930s, "Conversation between Two *Rancheros*," we hear of a migrant worker who returns to Mexico from the United States, full of *gringo* ways and saying insulting things about Mexico. His *compadre*, who had stayed home on the farm, takes out his huge knife to punish him. Seeing the knife, the Americanized migrant falls on his knees and begs forgiveness for having offended the fatherland.[31] By this time, however, the Mexican had learned to use the revolver. The *norteño*, the Mexican from the border, recognized its worth at an early date by having been on the receiving end of more than one revolver. It is through the Border *corrido* – in *norteño* folklore – that the revolver enters the folklore of Mexico, as the Mexican folk hero first abandons the knife for the gun. This corresponds with actual fact, for the border Mexican was a man with a pistol in his hand by the end of the 1850s. In 1859, when Juan Nepomuceno Cortina rebelled against North American authority in Texas, he did so after a shootout with a North American city marshal who had beaten one of his mother's farmhands. From Cortina on, the protagonists of the Border *corrido* are men "pistol in hand." That is to say, they fight "American style," as we are told in a *corrido* from Sonora, "De Cananea":

> Me agarraron los cherifes
> al estilo americano –
> como al hombre de delito –
> todos con pistola en mano.

> The deputies arrested me,
> in the American style –
> as they would arrest a criminal –
> all with pistols in their hands.

"With a pistol in his hand" or "with his pistol in his hand" becomes a conventional phrase in the *corrido* of the border between Mexico and the United States, distinguishing it from the *corrido* of southern Mexico, where this formula rarely appears before the 1930s. The man with pistol in hand is rarely a bully in the *corridos*. He pursues other goals, as did Cortina, defending himself against the abuses of an oppressive authority.

In a *corrido* from Coahuila, as late as the 1930s, a young man named Arnulfo and a state policeman gun each other down after the policeman slaps Arnulfo, simply because Arnulfo did not lower his eyes when the policeman looked at him. After the two are dead, the singer tells us in a fit of enthusiasm:

> ¡Qué bonitos son los hombres
> que se matan pecho a pecho,
> cada uno con su pistola,
> defendiendo su derecho!

> How beautiful it is to see two men
> gun each other down, standing face to face!
> Each with his pistol,
> each defending his right!

Something remains of the *corridos* on the clash-of-cultures theme, but this also sounds like *machismo* – presented in a situation like that of a Wild West movie. And there is good reason for the resemblance, since there is a very close relationship between Hollywood and the gun-toting *macho*, the *pistolero*. Let us return to the North American *macho* with his pistol in hand, and we will find him converted into the cowboy. Why the cowboy became the type chosen to synthesize the *macho* is another question, but let us look at these two figures – the *macho* and the cowboy – in relation to that great North American *macho*, Theodore Roosevelt. Roosevelt's admiration for cowboys was excessive, almost childish. He lived with them, working at their tasks, in order to prove his manliness. Later, during the Cuban war, he formed a regiment of cowboys, putting into practice his conviction that the cowboy was the best soldier possible because he was the epitome of all the austere, manly virtues. Nothing speaks more emphatically – Mody C. Boatright tells us in a study entitled "Theodore Roosevelt, Social Darwinism, and the Cowboy" – of Roosevelt's delight in the life of the cowboy than the fancy and expensive clothes he wore. Boatright quotes from a letter written by Roosevelt to his sister:

> I wear a sombrero, silk neckerchief, fringed buckskin shirt, sealskin chaparajos, or riding trousers, alligator hide boots, and with my pearl-hilted revolver and my beautifully finished Winchester rifle, I shall be able to face anything.[32]

The cowboy was taken almost totally from the Mexican tradition, but the North American made some important contributions, among them the pistol, the Stetson hat (an adaptation of the Mexican *sombrero*), and in our days the substitution of the horse with the Cadillac of the rancher-turned-millionaire. The pistol, above all – first the revolver and then the .45 automatic with its four cartridge clips. A phallic symbol perhaps, but in a much more direct sense a symbol of power – and of the abuse of power as well. A symbol of the manliness of the bully, the *macho* of the movies, who guns his rival down in the middle of the street, lifts the girl to his saddle, and rides into the sunset on his faithful horse. Or on his Cadillac, heading for Houston, or Austin, or Washington. The pistol above all – symbol of the overbearing bully. The

Mexican knew this well enough, from the day the first Colts arrived on the border. Harassed, dispossessed by the man with the gun, the Mexican lost no time in wishing to be a man with a gun also. And so it was that the Mexican took back from the North American something he had lent him, the figure of the *vaquero*; but he received his loan with interest, since the *vaquero* returned as cowboy – a *pistolero* and a *macho* among *machos*.

It would be an overstatement to say that the Mexican *macho* is merely a mirror image of the North American cowboy (although it is not much more extravagant to claim that he originates in Oedipal complexes caused by the conquest). But any evaluation of Mexican *machismo* will not be complete if the following point is ignored: The fundamental attitudes on which *machismo* is based (and which have caused so much distress to those wishing to psychoanalyze the Mexican) are almost universal. What might distinguish Mexican *machismo* is not the presence of those attitudes but their undeniable exaggeration; yet, this is not peculiar to the Mexican, since something very similar has occurred in a modern and neighboring country, the United States. There is no evidence that *machismo* (in the exaggerated forms that have been studied and condemned in Mexicans) even existed in Mexico before the Revolution. Available evidence suggests that it is a phenomenon dating from the 1930s to the present, that is to say, from the period after the Revolution. There is an intriguing parallel between North American and Mexican *machismo*. In the United States the sense of manliness is exaggerated during the 1820s and 1830s, because of a growing sense of nationalism, resulting in greater participation by the common man in the democratic process of the country, as well as in a marked feeling of hostility and inferiority toward Europe, especially toward England. During this period the idea of North American manliness is mainly unconscious and expresses itself generally in folkloric forms, especially in the boast and the tall tale. Nor is this supermanliness completely divorced from reality, since it occurs at a time when the North American male becomes an explorer and conqueror, extending the borders of his country farther and farther to the west.

An analogous period in Mexico is the Revolution and the years immediately preceding it. The boundaries extended by the Mexican during this time are not geographic but of the spirit. Nevertheless, the attitudes are more or less the same: a growing feeling of nationalism accompanied by sentiments of distrust and inferiority toward outsiders, particularly toward the United States; and a movement toward democracy and equality. As with the North American during the 1820s and 1830s, such sentiments in the Mexican were for the most part unconscious; and they were expressed in folkloric forms – in the artistic boast during the final years of the Díaz regime and in the *corrido* during the Revolution. Again, it may be said that the Mexican sense of manliness had a firm basis in reality during the Revolution, when struggle and death were accepted as daily occurrences.

North American *machismo* becomes artificial and grotesque when the frontier ends, when the Wild West disappears and men no longer live in the midst of conflict and danger. Then comes on scene the cowboy, fabricated by the cheap popular writers, the *macho* of Theodore Roosevelt's type, with the fancy cowboy suit, the pearl-handled revolver, and the enormous spectacles of the myopic scholar. Close after him comes the cowboy of the cities, the "professional Texan" with his white Stetson, his embroidered boots, and his Cadillac. The sense of manliness passes from folklore to the movies and popular literature, where we have the scorned woman abused by the man, at times physically tortured by the *macho* in forms of undoubtedly sexual symbolism. North American *machismo* in this late and exaggerated form goes even further than does Mexican *machismo*, since the North American type is dignified in serious literature, in the novels of Frank Norris, Jack London, Ernest Hemingway, and many other lesser writers. In Mexico, too, the sense of manliness typical of the Revolution is converted into exaggerated *machismo* once the period of armed conflict has ended, more or less by 1930. This is also the date, by the way, that Vicente Mendoza singles out as marking the end of the truly folk *corrido*.[33] The *corrido* after 1930, according to Mendoza, passes from folklore to the movies and other mass media.

Both in Mexico and in the United States, *machismo* betrays a certain element of nostalgia; it is cultivated by those who feel they have been born too late. The North American *macho* acts as if the Wild West had never come to an end; the Mexican *macho* behaves as if he is still living in the times of Pancho Villa. But we must make an important distinction. The United States began with feelings of inferiority toward England; today it is perhaps England that may feel inferior in respect to its former colony. Such is not the case with Mexico, since despite its undeniable progress it still lives under the shadow of the old Colossus of the North, today more colossal than ever. And here, at least, Samuel Ramos may have been right. But he also remarked that to feel inferior is not the same as being so.[34] We might add that to feel poor and to be poor are not exactly the same thing; and even more, that often the first is a necessary condition in doing away with the second. Upward-moving groups and peoples on the go are among those most disposed to feelings of inferiority. Both in the United States and in Mexico, *machismo*, despite all its faults, has been part of a whole complex of impulses leading toward a more perfect realization of the potentialities of man.

NOTES

This article is translated from Américo Paredes, "Estados Unidos, México y el machismo," *Journal of Inter-American Studies* 9 (1967): 65–84, by Marcy Steen. The current version was originally published in *Journal of the Folklore Institute* 8 (1971): 17–37. Reprinted by permission.

1   Vicente T. Mendoza, *Lírica narrativa de México: El corrido*, Estudios de Folklore, no. 2 (Mexico City: Instituto de Investigaciones Estéticas, Universidad Nacional Autónoma de México, 1964), 34; and Vicente T. Mendoza, "El machismo en México al través de las canciones, corridos y cantares," *Cuadernos del Instituto Nacional de Antropología* 3 (1962): 75.

2   Ezequiel Martínez Estrada, *Radiografía de la Pampa*, 2 vols. (Buenos Aires: Editorial Losada, 1942).

3   Santiago Ramírez, *El mexicano: Psicología de sus motivaciones* (Mexico City: Editorial Pax-México, 1959), 63.

4   Felipe Montemayor, "Postemio antropológico," in *Picardía mexicana*, ed. A. Jiménez (Mexico City: Libro Mex, 1960), 229–230.

5   Mendoza, "El machismo en México," 75–86.

6   Mendoza, "El machismo en México," 75–76.

7   It is necessary to include the collections of *décimas* as well as those of *corridos, canciones,* and *cantares.*

8   Vicente T. Mendoza, *La décima en México* (Buenos Aires: Instituto Nacional de la Tradición, 1947), 611.

9   Mendoza, "El machismo en México," 82.

10 Mendoza, *Lírica narrativa*, 95.

11 Mendoza, *Lírica narrativa*, 82.

12 Mendoza, *Lírica narrativa*, 146.

13 C. M. Bowra, *Primitive Song* (New York: New American Library, 1962), 122.

14 William Morris, trans., *Volsunga Saga: The Story of the Volsungs and Niblungs*, with a new introduction by Robert W. Gutman (New York: Crowell-Collier, 1962), 113.

15 We must remember that there is another literary tradition, oriented toward Europe, that of Henry James.

16 Locally, especially in the center of the country, where there are many people of Germanic and Scandinavian ancestry, Anglophobia persists even today.

17 See Maxwell Geismar's *Rebels and Ancestors: The American Novel 1890–1915* (New York: Hill and Wang, 1963) concerning *machismo* in these authors.

18 Roger D. Abrahams, *Deep Down in the Jungle: Negro Narrative Folklore from the Streets of Philadelphia* (Hatboro, Pa.: Folklore Associates, 1964), 147.

19 Walter Prescott Webb, *The Great Plains* (Boston: Ginn, 1931), 114–138, 509.

20 See Walter Prescott Webb, *The Great Plains* (Boston: Ginn, 1931), vi, where the author considers the conquest of the Great Plains as "a new phase of Aryan civilization."

21 Webb, *The Great Plains*, 168.

22 Webb, *The Great Plains*, 169.

23 Webb, *The Great Plains*, 180–184.

24 Webb, *The Great Plains*, 167–179.

25 Webb, *The Great Plains*, 173–175.

26 Webb, *The Great Plains*, 168.

27 Note, for example, this passage from a so-called history book. The famous bandit Billy the Kid has captured several Mexicans and taken their weapons:

> The Kid examined the knives, lying on the ground beside the fire. They were of the finest steel and workmanship. He admired the knives and had an impulse to keep them, but he gave another order. "Throw these on the coals. Only renegades use knives" (William Lee Hamlin, *The True Story of Billy the Kid* [Caldwell, Idaho: Caxton Printers, 1959], 209–210).

28 Martínez Estrada, *Radiografía de la Pampa*, vol. 1, 64.

29 Miguel de Cervantes Saavedra, *Don Quixote of the Mancha*, vol. 1, trans. John Ormsby (Barcelona: Limited Editions Club, 1933), 374.

30 José Hernández, *Martín Fierro* (Buenos Aires: Espasa-Calpe Argentina, 1938), 51, 54, 89.

31 Paul S. Taylor, "Songs of the Mexican Migration," in *Puro Mexicano*, ed. J. Frank Dobie, Publications of the Texas Folkore Society, no. 12 (Austin: Texas Folklore Society, 1935), 241–245.

32 Mody C. Boatright, "Theodore Roosevelt, Social Darwinism, and the Cowboy," *Texas Quarterly* 7.4 (1964): 17.

33 Mendoza, *Lírica narrativa*, 14.

34 Samuel Ramos, *El perfil del hombre y la cultura en México* (Mexico City: Espasa-Calpe Mexicana, 1951), 52.

20

Spectacular Bodies: Folklorization and the Politics of Identity in Ecuadorian Beauty Pageants

Mark Rogers

Her name is Verónica, but now the papers call her "the Flower of the Awakening Valley". The daughter of college-educated parents and a self-described *indígena* (indigenous woman),[1] she had gone from the rural community of Peguche in Ecuador's Otavalo valley to the capital city of Quito to study marketing at an elite private college. But it wasn't until she attempted to enter Otavalo's 1996 Queen of *Yamor* (*Reina de Yamor*) pageant that she became the darling of the Ecuadorian and international press.[2] Her notoriety derived from the fact that she was the first *indígena* to eschew the pageant intended for young indigenous women and instead try to enter the municipal pageant in a historically white-dominated town. Her bid was promptly rejected by the president of the Municipality of Otavalo, leading to press and popular charges of racism and heated protests in her home town of Peguche. Verónica became a standard-bearer for ethnic pride in the local communities at the same time that she was held up in the press as a paragon of the ideal post-ethnic Ecuadorian society in which even *indígenas* should be allowed full participation. Indeed, the controversy over her candidacy, and her subsequent notoriety, led to public reconsideration of the municipal ordinances barring *indígenas* from taking part in the contest, caused the collapse of the indigenous Corn Princess (*Sara Ñusta*) pageant,[3] and landed her a job in the national government's Office of Indigenous Affairs.

Verónica's story attests to the role of public performance in constituting and challenging ethnic, national, local, gender, and other identities.[4] The controversy over her participation has given new vitality to ongoing ideological struggles over the meaning of indigenous culture and "tradition" and the relationship of these problematic constructions to ideologies of white superiority, racial/ethnic mixture (*mestizaje*), progress, and Ecuadorian nationhood. It also demonstrates the relevance of such apparently trivial contexts as beauty pageants for processes of identity-construction. Hence, this article is ostensibly an account of beauty pageants, as the title suggests, but it is also about both more and less than that. More, in the sense that it speaks to larger issues about representation, performance, and identity applicable to discussions of theater, spectacle, and public festival. Less, in that the implicit suggestion that the very performance genre category "beauty pageant" is applicable to the ethnographic material treated here is only vaguely correct. While the phenomena I will discuss are identifiably appropriations and transformations of a recognizable genre of public performance principally mediated by television coverage of such events as the Miss America, Miss World, and Miss Universe competitions, they are not necessarily concerned with "beauty" in the same way as are their mass-mediated models. Instead, they place culturally specific and context-bound dimensions of gendered models of personhood, which may or may not include familiar notions of sexualized physical beauty (facial features, physique, hairstyle), on display as objects of competitive aesthetic evaluation. What remains is the use of the genre-derived performance framework as a vehicle for clarifying and embodying cultural ideals through the women who participate. Yet even on the local level, these ideals are rarely consistent, either with one another or with the lived reality of the pageants' audiences.[5] Instead, pageants become sites of struggle in which notions of personhood, gender, ethnicity, citizenship and nationality are reworked (cf. Wilk 1996).

In order to illustrate such processes of struggle, this article will address two sets of pageant events that take place as integral parts of discrete public festival complexes in two regions of Ecuador.[6] In the northern highland town of Otavalo, during the municipally-sponsored *Yamor* festival, the *Reina de Yamor*[7] and *Sara Ñusta* (Corn Princess) competitions select from the "white" and "indigenous" populations female representatives who stand metonymically for their respective "communities." In the lowland Amazonian town of Archidona, during the municipally-sponsored *Chonta* festival, the *Reina de Archidona* (Queen of Archidona) and *Chonta Huarmi* (*Chonta* Palm Woman) competitions serve similar functions.[8]

Both festivals appear to be appropriations of celebrations previously associated solely with the indigenous populations of the two regions. Each of the original celebrations took place in rural indigenous communities and centered on the harvest and consumption of locally favored foods (corn and corn beer in Otavalo, palm fruit and palm fruit beer in Archidona). Prior to the development of the municipal folkloric festivals, these local indigenous celebrations were either ignored or decried as primitive, pagan, and unruly by municipal white elites. In the latter part of the twentieth century, these celebrations of the

annual agricultural cycle have been harnessed to enactments of municipal (historically, implicitly white) community identity by municipal governments in search of local distinction and tourist income.[9] That is, the historic polarity between the ethnically white municipal center, focused around prominent political and religious institutions, and the ethnically indigenous rural agricultural communities, was transcended by the effort to incorporate elements of indigenous culture into celebrations of municipal identity in folkloric festivals. In the process, these local celebrations were incorporated into the municipal festival complexes as markers of local authenticity and sources of folkloric attraction, and the dual pageant system came to reflect this relationship.

This process of folklorization has produced a situation in which the white festival as a whole, as well as the white beauty pageant and its chosen queen are said (primarily by the organizers of the festivals and representatives of the municipal governments) to stand in an unmarked way for the entire population, supposedly transcending ethnic division. The white pageant constitutes a totalizing municipal identity, while the indigenous pageant constitutes a special identity for a marked segment of the total municipal population.[10] The totalizing function of the white pageant is marked in performance by the fact that the white contestants don versions of "traditional" indigenous dress during one segment of the pageant. During an early phase of the competition, structurally equivalent to the talent segment in the canonical beauty pageant, the participants dance in some approximation of traditional indigenous clothing, to traditional musical themes, using traditional dance steps.[11] Yet this apparent assumption of indigenous identity is immediately shed, never to be revisited over the course of the pageant. Thus, while actual indigenous people are not present at the performance, indigenousness is acknowledged as playing some role in the constitution of a generalizable municipal identity. But this identity is discarded in favor of a transcendent whiteness that incorporates indigenousness as a constitutive but not characterizing element.[12]

The indigenous pageant, on the other hand, is executed as part of a larger effort on the part of indigenous political organizations to "seize control of and separate out of the larger society" cultural elements that can be used to create an ideology of "ethnic worth" (Hendrickson 1991: 300). It attempts to demarcate and lay claim to indigenousness in the face of such efforts at incorporation, and it establishes notions of a uniquely indigenous culture and tradition distinct from, but in peaceful coexistence with, white society. As in the white pageant, the semiotic work is achieved through the operations of the female body, in this case through the constitution of an ideal of indigenous womanhood whose relevant dimensions are highlighted by the competition.[13] Curiously, the "talent" segment of the competition is similar to that of the white pageant, in that the dress, music, and dance steps are marked as "traditional" and differentiated from the already distinctive indigenous woman's *traje* (clothing). Here, however, the intent is not to incorporate the white other in order to constitute the indigenous self as a higher-order, incorporative identity, but rather to resist such processes by retrospectively constituting and fortifying a separate, uniquely indigenous identity. But in doing this, the indigenous pageant reproduces and draws upon a historical prototype of indigenous authenticity, and in that respect it is similar to the white pageant.

Here I will be concerned principally with the meaning of the indigenous pageant within the larger festival context. What are the ideological and social consequences of the performance of indigenous pageants, considered in relationship both to the white pageants and to the largely indigenous audiences for which they are performed? In order to answer this question, I will treat not only the white but also the indigenous pageants as examples of folklorization, considered here as a process in which a social group fixes a part of itself in a timeless manner as an anchor for its own distinctiveness: what Néstor García Canclini has called "a melancholic attempt at subtracting the popular from the massive reorganization of society . . . and guarding it as an imaginary reserve of nationalist political discourses" (1995:151, cf. McAllister 1996). Just as beauty pageants in general partially constrain the range of female expression by attempting to forge consensus on beauty and proper behavior (Cohen et al. 1996:7), the

indigenous pageant attempts to shape indigenous womanhood, and implicitly indigenous identity writ large, in ways that are not necessarily accepted by the audience. Thus, the festival complex as a whole (*Yamor* or *Chonta*) incorporates multiple lines of tension both within the respective pageants as well as between them and other aspects of the festival complex (including their alter pageants). Although it would be fruitful to examine the full range of intertextual relations between the pageants and their festival and even extrafestival contexts, within the scope of this paper I must limit my analysis to the intra- and interpageant levels. Nevertheless, some background on the festival context is necessary in order to understand the pageants themselves.

Pageants and Festivals

The two festival complexes – the *Yamor* festival in Otavalo and the *Chonta* festival in Archidona – establish a first level of context for the pageants. That is, in each case the official, public recognition of these festivals spatially and temporally demarcates a special realm of behavior with a different set of constitutive norms than those applicable to everyday life. Thus, to differing degress, residents suspend normal work activities and everyday behavioral strictures. The festival frame is understood by many as one of increased danger, due to the higher incidence of drunkenness and nighttime activities such as public dances, as well as the attraction such events are thought to provide for thieves and other malcontents. The fears brought on by relaxation of normal behavioral controls are often expressed in racial or ethnic terms: whites may be especially wary of "drunken Indians,"[14] *indígenas* may fear assaults from "Colombian thieves," etc.

In both regions, the festivals are sponsored and organized by committees supported by municipal revenues as well as private companies. Thus, the activities spread over the four to ten days of the festivals (depending primarily on availability of funds) may be sponsored by beer or cigarette companies (cf. Crain 1990: 50, Guss 1996), or by such organizations as transportation cooperatives or merchants' associations. The festivals cobble together a wide range of activities, from soccer and volleyball tournaments, to car races, equestrian displays, religious services, parades, and, of course, the obligatory elections of the beauty queens. The nighttime public dances, which present live bands (*orquestas*) or sound systems (*discomóviles*) along with copious amounts of liquor, are popular elements of the festivals, and they occur almost every night.

Since the early 1970s in Archidona and the early 1980s in Otavalo, these festivals also incorporate activities sponsored by the indigenous political and cultural organizations. These include competition in traditional sports, indigenous food exhibitions, roundtable discussions about the history and meaning of indigenous culture, indigenous film and video exhibitions, and public ritual events specially choreographed for inclusion in the festivals. In contrast to the other festival activities, these events rarely receive corporate sponsorship.[15] As long as they are carried out within the time-space demarcated by the municipal festival, they are considered by most to be part of the total event, though perceptions of their relative importance vary according to ethnic, social, and political background. While the generally accepted association with the larger festival has certain benefits in terms of attracting an audience and making claims to equal participation in the municipal collectivity, however, it also places indigenous organizations in a difficult position. They must implicitly acknowledge the higher-order totality that is constituted by the festival, and their participation contributes to the reproduction of the part-whole relationship between indigenous and municipal identity mentioned previously with respect to the white beauty pageant. Thus, participation allows indigenous groups to achieve at least some control over the symbolic constitution of indigenousness – a process that can easily occur without them, as the white pageant shows – but it does so at the price of contributing to the totalization of an identity that transcends them.

The perception of this predicament is especially acute in the Otavalo area, where the issue of participation has been explicitly politicized for over a decade. The rise of *Yamor* as Otavalo's municipal festival appears to have been related to efforts to attract the tourist trade to the town.

Yamor began to be promoted explicitly as a tourist attraction in 1967, and in 1968 the planning of the festival was formally placed in the hands of the municipal government, which coined the town's slogan – "the happiest festival in the country's most likable city" – that same year (KIPU 1983:9). By 1983, however, the region's emergent ethnic political federation, the *Federación de Indígenas y Campesinos de Imbabura* (FICI), had decided to boycott the festivities, declaring that indigenous festivals were "sacred religious rituals that cannot be manipulated for utilitarian, touristic, and folkloric interests" (KIPU 1986: 10–11). In lieu of participation in the municipally-sponsored festival, FICI proposed a separate indigenous "cultural encounter" whose intent was the "recuperation, defense and unity of indigenous culture" (KIPU 1986: 10–11).

In 1992, however, FICI surprisingly decided to rejoin the official *Yamor* celebration, and the festival's official administrative committee incorporated the participation of indigenous groups into the festival's official programming, under the subsidiary direction of FICI. From 1992 to 1994, FICI-sponsored events were simultaneously incorporated into the official *Yamor* program and described as forming a semiautonomous celebration of "*Colla Raymi*," identified as the indigenous festival of the autumnal equinox. The election of the *Sara Ñusta* was described in promotional materials as symbolic of the ancient "*acllas, ñustas y coyas*"[16] who themselves were identified with *Allpa Mama*, or the female representation of the earth's powers. *Colla Raymi* was described as a "fertility ritual" in preparation for the sowing of corn, in which female reproductive capacity was associated with the renewal of the agricultural cycle.

The uneasy alliance between FICI and the municipal commission charged with the planning of the *Yamor* festival was short-lived, however. The 1995 *Colla Raymi* celebration, while substantially similar in content and organization to those of recent years, was extricated from the festival frame of *Yamor* and temporally displaced to a date approximately two weeks after *Yamor* had ended. The *Colla Raymi* was thereby isolated from *Yamor* and elevated to the level of an autonomous indigenous festival. The celebration was also spatially displaced. In previous years some events had been carried out in Otavalo proper, whereas others were realized in the surrounding indigenous communities. In 1995, that balance was shifted more strongly toward the communities and away from the parks and other public spaces of the town. The reasons for these changes were twofold: on the one hand, FICI and its followers continued to perceive association with *Yamor* as asymmetrical and exploitative, a relationship in which the municipal festival appropriated and "whitened" their cultural contributions. As one indigenous activist asked rhetorically, "Whom does participation [in *Yamor*] benefit?" On the other, there was an intensification of the focus on the constitution of an autonomous realm of indigenous tradition, free of supposed contaminations by white society. Whereas in previous years FICI had stressed the reaffirmation of the "original" or "true" meaning of the *Yamor/Colla Raymi* festival through participation within the contested framework of *Yamor*, in 1995 the decision was made to redirect that effort toward a stronger degree of autonomy for the "true" indigenous festival.

Verónica's attempt to enter the Queen of Otavalo pageant represented a new kind of challenge to the perceived inequities and exploitative tendencies of the *Yamor* festival. Rather than continue to develop a discrete, competing festival framework to contest the appropriation of the "authentic" indigenous harvest festival, she chose (with significant backing from Peguche and other indigenous communities) to challenge the internal logic of the white pageant itself. This was in essence a bid for inclusion rather than separateness, a more conservative attempt to undermine the ethnic grounding of the festival in order to challenge its inherent asymmetry without vitiating the underlying idea of a transcendent municipal identity. The rejection of this gambit by the president of the municipality preserved the original logic of the *Yamor* pageant, but it did so at the cost of overt accusations of racism both locally and in the national press. As a result, there is some possibility that the rules may be reconsidered for future pageants, though some *indígenas* have expressed doubts about whether "suitable" indigenous candidates can be marshalled in the future.[17]

At the same time, Verónica's strategy and the response to it seem to have caused at least the temporary demise of the *Sara Ñusta* pageant. This may be a result of the overwhelming popularity of this alternative approach to ethnic stratification in the region, which does not question the articulation of the indigenous population with the state (cf. Wright 1995:247) or favor strict, separatist constraints on the appropriate forms of expression of ethnic identity such as those described below for the *Sara Ñusta* pageant. Verónica's gambit appears to have exposed the fragility of the federation's attempts to construct a prescriptive indigenous identity through activities such as the indigenous beauty pageant.

The case of the Archidona *Chonta* Festival appears somewhat less contentious. It would seem to have been formed as an appropriation of a harvest festival that previously had been enacted in a dispersed fashion in the surrounding indigenous communities. Such celebrations, which could last up to a month, were carried out under the sponsorship of a *prioste* (ritual sponsor), and were devoted to the celebration of the abundance of *chonta* fruits through dancing, drinking, and hunting of the animals who would feed on the ripe *chonta* (cf. Ponce 1993:274). The municipal festival was devised in 1972 with the active participation of local indigenous leaders. It was later combined with celebrations of the anniversary of the founding of Archidona in 1510 and its elevation to the status of *cantón* (county) seat in 1981. Indigenous participation in the festival appears to be much less problematic in Archidona than in Otavalo, perhaps due to the less radical culturalism of the provincial indigenous political federation, *Federación de Organizaciones Indígenas del Napo* (FOIN) and the absence of an abstract, Inca-derived standard that can be employed as a yardstick for cultural normalization. Nevertheless, the *Chonta* festival, like *Yamor*, is ethnically riven and serves largely to reproduce the ethnic dividing line, despite an overt commitment to municipal unity.

Womanhood and Collective Identity in the Pageant

Due to their symmetry, the beauty pageant components of these festivals provide perhaps the clearest and strongest illustration of how the *Yamor* and *Chonta* festivals contribute to the reification and separation of discrete indigenous and white identities. Attendance at all of the pageants is strongly correlated with ethnic identity, and the events themselves are concerned with electing representatives of larger-scale social units, thereby reinforcing certain aspects of local social structure. In the case of indigenous pageants, the candidates are ideally drawn from and said to represent the different outlying communities.[18] Thus, in the 1993 *Chonta Huarmi* competition, the spectators were roughly divided along community lines in their support of the various competitors, and the crowd's cheers explicitly invoked the community affiliation of the respective candidates.[19]

In addition, there is at least a vague notion of the nesting character of such competitions – akin to the city-county-state-national structure of the U.S. beauty pageant process – in which the winner at a lower structural level will go on to compete as the representative of that entire level in a future competition. This principle is extremely tenuous, however. It appears to be more fully elaborated in the case of Archidona, where, at least occasionally, a community-level pageant will choose the representative who will compete in the municipal pageant, and the winner of that level will compete in a province-wide pageant. In such a case, the same candidate serially indexes the local, the municipal, and, potentially, the provincial indigenous population, such that the structural levels are organically tied to one another through their common expression in her body. The contestants in the white pageants, on the other hand, tend to represent factions within urban elite society and are sponsored by financial backers such as bus cooperatives or prominent local businesses.

In this respect, the candidates metonymically stand for the factions that support them. They are the residents of their communities, the daughters of prominent merchants, or the members of cultural revival organizations. This use of women as emblems of various kinds of social groupings is not limited to the beauty queens, but is extended as well to arenas such as sports competitions, in which teams are represented by female figures

known as *madrinas*.[20] Whereas the teams compete with one another on the field with an eye toward the tournament championship, their *madrina* representatives take part in a separate competition to choose the best *madrina*. In both cases, victory contributes to the glory of the team as a whole. *Madrinas* may also be chosen to represent other kinds of social groupings, such as the classes within a school.[21] These examples illustrate one dimension of the beauty queen phenomenon, namely their capacity to serve as emblems of all manner of social groupings. The composition of the field of competitors and the election of a queen is thus a statement about social structure, in which collectivities are indexed by their representatives, and the hierarchical relationship of candidates produced by the competition mode of the pageant is, at least to some degree, an indexical rearrangement of the relationships among the corresponding collectivities.

This structural dimension of the pageant shapes, but does not fully specify, the content of the performance. The event is a competition in which the candidates are evaluated and ranked by the judges, in accordance with relatively implicit aesthetic criteria. As far as I know, there is no standardized guideline that instructs judges on how to evaluate candidates. Hence the division of the event into stages, each of which is a micro-competition that highlights a different dimension of the candidates in relationship to their total evaluation by the judges. The division into stages creates a modular structure that can be manipulated by pageant organizers, who have the option of including some, discarding others, and arranging them in the order they see fit. This structure is borrowed, in varying degrees, from the canonical beauty pageants such as Miss America and Miss World, which divide competitions into permutations of dress (swimsuit, evening gown, semiformal) and behavior (talent, interview, silent walking) and intersperse them with musical and dance performance numbers. Thus, the various competitions include events in which candidates present themselves in "traditional" or "typical" indigenous dress, evening gowns, casual fashion ensembles, or even swimsuits, and either dance, walk in a stylized manner, or speak while doing so, as well as performances by dance troupes, musical groups, or the contestants themselves (as a group). The actual combinations are highly variable, although white pageants always involve presentation in indigenous costume and indigenous pageants always include a presentation in traditional costume. Both pageants also always include some kind of interview or public speaking component.

Given that the pageants explicitly and redundantly mark themselves for gender, from their titles to their promotional materials to their actual content, the stages of any individual pageant can be seen as permutations of an idealized image of femaleness. Each permutation is designed to foreground some component of an idealized image of womanhood on which judging is based. Since the judges are not responsible for the design of the competitions, they must attempt to gauge the intent of the organizers in formulating their evaluative criteria, though there is much leeway for individual variation among judges. That is, the composition to some degree sets the ground rules for evaluation by delimiting those aspects of womanhood considered relevant. This general level of composition also sets the boundaries within which contestants negotiate the judges' attention. The choreography of the events, and sometimes even the contents of the interview questions, are communicated to the participants beforehand, and this allows them to develop aesthetic strategies relative to each stage. Of course, all of these parties formulate their contributions with an historically informed image of their intended audience in mind. They are aware of the composition of past pageants, the strategies chosen by past participants, the decisions made by past judges, and the reception of the event by past audiences. The resulting performance can thus be seen as a negotiated product of the contributions of organizers, sponsors, judges, contestants, and audience. This negotiation occurs in the broader context of the past history of the pageants as well as the intertextual field of television transmissions of canonical pageants.

This last influence shapes the composition to a high degree in most (but certainly not all) pageants. The presentation by the master(s) of ceremonies, the use of male escorts during certain phases of the pageant, the use of musical and dance performances to break up the sequence of events, and even the fetishization of voting through conspicuous mention of computer technology and mathematical computation of scores, are drawn from televised images. One principal organizer of a pageant preliminary to the *Chonta Huarmi* competition explicitly pointed out that he had recently viewed the Miss America competition on television and had sought to reproduce it as faithfully as possible, which might help explain why this was the only pageant I have witnessed that contained a swimsuit competition. In a similar vein, the organizers of that year's *Chonta Huarmi* competition borrowed a computer from the municipal offices – one of the organizers was an employee, as well as co-organizer of the preliminary contest – and set it up at stage right, though it was not actually used to compute the scores. The white pageants are much more elaborate and faithful to the model, as a result of their superior financing and greater familiarity with the genre.

Yet none of the pageants is a completely faithful rendering of Miss America or Miss Universe. Rather, the genre is adapted according to the interests and financial capacities of the organizers, as well as the cultural content and political aims of the performance. With reference to the interview component of the competitions, for example, white pageants tend more strongly to incorporate elements that have to do with romance (boyfriends), motherhood, and careers, whereas, on the whole, indigenous pageants tend to be much more strongly political in the content of their questions. Thus, an indigenous contestant might be asked to describe the importance of indigenous federations to Ecuadorian society, whereas a white contestant might be asked what dish she likes most to cook, or how many children she hopes to have. Similarly, a larger portion of indigenous pageants is devoted to presentation in traditional dress, whereas white pageants tend to foreground a focus on contemporary fashion, poise, and style. These compositional concerns in turn influence the contestants' presentations, in that indigenous contestants are aware that political dimensions of their performance will become the focus of the audience and the judges, whereas white contestants assume a more detachedly aesthetic orientation.

It is the presentation in typical or traditional dress that constitutes the most striking divergence in content from the genre archetypes seen on television, as well as the locus of much of the ideological import of the pageants with respect to ethnic identity. While contestants in both types of pageant utilize many of the same costume components in arranging their presentations for this segment of the competitions, there are significant differences, both in content and in contextualization within the pageant as a whole, that influence their semiotic import. In the *Reina de Archidona* and *Chonta Huarmi* competitions, for example, contestants make extensive use of such "traditional" implements as *tigrillo* (ocelot) skins, feather headdresses, grass skirts, bead necklaces, and woven baskets, all of which are strong markers of indigenous authenticity for both white and indigenous populations.[22] Yet the white contestants are more likely to intersperse such costume elements with incongruous items such as colored ribbons, rhinestones, and brightly colored synthetic fabrics (though indigenous contestants will occasionally do this as well). White contestants are also more likely to develop their costumes along the lines of a bikini swimsuit, whereas indigenous contestants are more likely to adopt an alternative version of traditional dress consisting of a light blue bordered blouse and navy skirt tied with a woven belt. The former is an imagined version of a pre-conquest costume that concedes to modesty by the fashioning of some form of brassiere-style top from animal skin or banana leaves (or fabric, for white contestants). The latter is drawn from the relatively recent past and is based on the costume employed by indigenous women within living memory. While white contestants may be more likely to adopt the bikini and indigenous contestants the blouse/skirt, this division is by no means strict. In fact, the winner of the 1993 *Chonta Huarmi* competition was the only contestant to employ the bikini style.

The success of an incongruously bikini-clad indigenous contestant attests to the importance of the details of the way the style is realized, and especially to the ideological marking of the materials used in the elaboration of a costume. In both white and indigenous pageants, the use of animal skins is highly valued, as they confer an aura of authenticity and rarity to the costume. In addition, the bikini-clad indigenous candidate sported a live monkey riding on her shoulder, an embellishment which curried favor among the judges.[23] Other candidates took the stage accompanied by young men dressed in grass skirts and feather headdresses, presented traditional foods to the judges, or enacted stylized versions of the preparation of *chonta asua*, a drink prepared by mixing a paste of cooked *chonta* fruit with water and sometimes allowed to ferment. *Chonta asua* is a staple of the indigenous diet during the *chonta* season, as are other kinds of *asua* at other times of the year. The presentation of food or *chonta asua* to judges is often a very effective strategy, for it breaks the performance frame which separates performer from audience and it iconically indexes that most characteristic of feminine activities: the distribution of food to family or guests.[24]

Stylistic elements such as these contribute to the communication of an image of traditional, authentic indigenous culture, which is ideally the basis for evaluation of this component of the indigenous pageant. This message is reinforced by the high degree of redundancy that characterizes the *Chonta Huarmi* pageant. Thus, the contestants perform the interview segment of the competition in traditional dress, and overall spend a much greater amount of time in this costume than in others, such as evening gowns. This is combined with the generally politicized content of the interview questions, the use of bands playing traditional music for the entertainment interludes, and the use of Quichua, to produce an image of ideal womanhood as an ethnically marked womanhood. This message is reinforced outside the strict pageant frame as well, as contestants wear their traditional dress in parades or other events. Even the floats carrying the indigenous contestants in the principal parade of the festival may reinforce the image of tradition by portraying jungle scenes or old-style bamboo and straw houses.

The white *Reina de Yamor* contestants, by contrast, produced much more accurate replicas of indigenous dress than their lowland white (*Reina de Archidona*) counterparts, although their costumes were, on the whole, still identifiable as distinct from the everyday dress of indigenous *Otavaleñas*. Some contestants embellished their costumes with old-style long earrings or hard, felt, wide-brimmed hats, whereas others chose to mimic contemporary costume. The indigenous *Sara Ñusta* competition in Otavalo contrasts with Archidona's indigenous *Chonta Huarmi* in that contestants largely employ a fancy version of their own everyday dress, akin to their "Sunday best," rather than archaized costumes. This may be due to the greater ethnic markedness of contemporary *Otavaleña* dress in comparison to their lowland indigenous counterparts. The *Otavaleñas'* costumes may be embellished with one of the felt hats mentioned above. On the whole they tend to resemble, e.g., a dress worn to the Saturday market rather than a replica of past women's costume.[25] Again, the presentation in traditional dress is correlated in the *Sara Ñusta* pageant with other components that reinforce the image of an ethnically marked womanhood, such as political speeches and musical and theatrical productions based on traditional themes.[26] Indeed, the *Sara Ñusta* pageant eschews the evening gown competition found in the *Chonta Huarmi*, in favor of maintaining ethnically marked dress throughout. In both cases, however, the "traditional dress" component – which almost always involves dancing to traditional music – is singled out as the most important, with respect to dress, in constituting ideal womanhood, whereas it takes on the role of a rather trivial, albeit entertaining, component of the white pageants. In the white pageants, indigenous dress is donned as costume and shed immediately after the "number," with virtually no other components of the event reinforcing it as a central component of identity. In the indigenous pageants, by contrast, the constitutiveness of traditional dress is reinforced by many other components of the event, one of the most important of which is the interview component.

Cultural Competence in Spoken Performance

Performance in the interview segment is crucial to success in both white and indigenous pageants. It is often the case that the person who spoke the "best" in the interview competition is elected queen, even when spectators judge her performance in other segments as less compelling.[27] This may be because this segment requires not only the poise and fluidity of bodily movement demanded by the other phases of the competition, but involves as well the additional skills of memorization (of possible answers) and improvisation (of actual answers). Speaking competence requires not only command over the grammatical and stylistic dimensions of language use, but also over the physical faculty of speech production, such that the utterance is produced with adequate projection, timbre, intonation and fluidity. Thus, if we accept Bauman's (1977, 1992) definition of performance as the assumption of responsibility for a display of communicative competence, the degree of competence required is greatest during this phase of the competition. In addition, the semantic content of a contestant's self-expression adds another layer of interpretation for both judges and audience.

This component of the pageant poses a serious challenge to all pageant contestants, white or indigenous, though the latter may be especially burdened by virtue of the special requirements of bilingualism. As some analysts of gender in the Andes have attested, indigenous women are often excluded from use of a register of public speech most commonly associated with men's participation in certain political events (e.g., Harris 1980, Harvey 1994). Harvey identifies some components of this register, used for speechmaking in Spanish: long, complex utterances; special vocabulary; increased use of proverbs and clichés, citing of names and dates, and distinctive intonation (1994:46). The interview component of the indigenous beauty pageant requires mastery of a related, derivative register, whose principal feature is a formulaic opening sequence of greetings addressed to the assembled authorities and the audience. In the 1993 *Chonta Huarmi* competition, for example, this opening segment was marked grammatically and lexically, as well as with a distinct pause, which allowed for the insertion of audience applause upon its successful completion. Those contestants who were able to devise innovations without diverging from the parameters of the formula were especially well received, whereas those with inconsistencies or inordinate hesitation were occasionally jeered.

Although many of the contestants are able to master the formulaic opening with some degree of proficiency, on the whole their uneasiness with the interview component is patently visible. This is due in part to their unfamiliarity with public, performance-oriented speaking and in part to their lack of command of the formulaic register of speech associated with it, but it is at times also a product of their relationships to the language(s) required by the performance. In the *Chonta Huarmi* competition, contestants are required to be fluent in Quichua, and they are expected to answer the questions twice, once in Spanish and once in Quichua. Differing degrees of bilingualism can thus affect their performance in one or the other answer. In other competitions, either Spanish or Quichua may be privileged. In the competition for the Queen of Porotoyacu (an Archidona-area indigenous community), for example, the contestants were questioned in Spanish and expected to answer in Spanish. This plan broke down, however, when it turned out that all but one of the contestants were incapable of answering the questions that had been posed to them in Spanish. The master of ceremonies thus resorted to translating the questions into Quichua, though it was not specified whether contestants were to respond in Quichua or Spanish. In the event, the one contestant who was able to answer in Spanish did not win the competition. Rather, it was the contestant who had by far the most compelling presentation in traditional costume who eventually triumphed.

The composition of this pageant, as well as its outcome, attest to the variability of the organizer-contestant-judge-audience negotiation that informs the pageant. The conflictedness of this event was due to an incongruity in its organization whereby the Spanish interview component, which was also carried out in formal evening gowns, conflicted with the ethnic markedness of other stages of the competition (as did the swimsuit competition, in which the Spanish-speaking candidate also performed strongly), effectively isolating the traditional dress phase from the phase associated with Spanish proficiency and white dress. This incongruity was exacerbated

by the fact that the judges were all indigenous politicians. In this case, the judges selected the winner of the component that was most strongly ethnically marked and chose her as the overall winner, a decision which provoked angered dissension from the backers of the Spanish-speaking candidate, who represented the local bilingual high school. The redundancy of bilingual or monolingual Quichua interviews in traditional dress, especially in the presence of politicized judges, forestalls such dissension to a greater degree and produces a more coherent idealized image. This particular pageant was the most strongly ideologically conflicted of any that I have seen, and as a rule, the lowland pageants are more conflicted than those that take place in Otavalo.

In Otavalo, the pageants are on the whole much more strongly oriented toward Quichua, and the challenge becomes mastery of that language in a public performance mode. In some cases, command of Quichua, and especially of a particular politicized, revivalist register of Quichua, can become a stumbling block for contestants. Such was the case for one contestant in a competition among the communities of the Otavalo-area indigenous community of Quichinche that was sponsored by the political organization known as the *Unión de Communidades Indígenas de Quichinche* (UCINQUI). In order to understand her difficulty, it should be pointed out that the Quichua required in the interview segment of this pageant was of a special kind, namely a version characterized by an avoidance (to the degree possible) of Spanish vocabulary and constructions, and the use of Quichua grammatical constructions and archaic or invented Quichua vocabulary in their stead. This register in its strongest versions is easily distinguishable from everyday Quichua, and the movement between the two implies a more elaborated communicative competence indicative of participation in the speech community of cultural revitalization activists (cf. Dorian 1994, Hill and Hill 1986, Roseman 1995). The following excerpt from this pageant represents a case in which lack of command of this register leads to a withdrawal from complete performance or "hedged performance" indicated by an explicit "disclaimer" in Bauman's (1992) terms:[28]

Bueno, ñuka saludapani, este, compañero, pres....F. M., a nombre de todos nos.... mmm... Bueno, perdon, voy a hablar en castellano porque no puedo hablar muy bien en Quichua. Espero que me disculpen.

[Well, I greet, um, comrade, pres(ident)...F. M., in the name of all of u(s)... mmm... Ok, pardon me, I'm going to speak Spanish because I don't speak Quichua very well. I hope you'll excuse me.]

Contrast this example with the following excerpts from two other candidates, who achieve performance with lesser degrees of Spanish intrusion:

Ñuka primer lugar saludapani compañero F. M., y **ñuka shutimi kapan** M. P. **Wata kapan** trece años, y representapani comunidad Achupallas. Gracias.

[First of all, I greet comrade[29] F. M., and my name is M. P. I'm thirteen, and I represent the community of Achupallas. Thank you.]

Ñukami kay...**kaymandaman shamupashkani, tukuylla** unión Quichinchiku-**nata rikuchingapaj**, y **ñuka shutimi kapan** M. T., y **watata charipanimi** trece añota. Imasht.... comunidad Larkakun-gamanda. Diusulpagui.
[I have....I have come here to present myself to the entire Union of Quichinche, and my name is M. T. and I'm thirteen years old. Umm...I'm from the community of Larkakunga. Thank you.]

Not surprisingly, the third candidate was the eventual winner, based almost exclusively on her linguistic performance, which was delivered in a clear, strong voice, almost shouted.

In keeping with the more highly consistent culturally purist nature of the Otavalo-area pageants, the expectation of competence in this revitalized register of Quichua serves a didactic or normative purpose. The message conveyed is not only one of ethnic autonomy, but also a kind of "ethnic correctness" in which the contamination of white society is kept at bay through the standardization of Quichua language and culture along purist lines. The task of the pageant, as other public political events, is to re-create the standard

performatively as a way of teaching it to a public which does not necessarily have command of it. Ironically, the very public to which this message is addressed is responsible for the maintenance of the "vernacular" indigenous language and culture on which the standard is based (cf. Roseman 1995).[30] In this sense, the pageant is an effort to normalize and officialize an identity that is supposedly compatible with the quotidian reality of the populace which the sponsoring indigenous political organizations claim to represent. As Friedman observes in the case of the Hawaiian nativist movement, such organizations "search for an adequate sociocultural framework for institutionalizing the collective experience that is already present in ... everyday existence" (1992:355). Actual everyday existence is not adequate to the semiotic and political demands of an objectified identity in a world where authenticity and radical otherness are the prerequisites for effective ethnic political action. On the other hand, as Friedman points out, an overly ideologized representation runs the risk of failure as well, for it may diverge too strongly from everyday practice to find a widely receptive audience.

Conclusion: Folklorization and Identity

Broadly considered, the white and indigenous pageants represent two conflicting uses of folklorization in support of divergent identity projects. The white pageant seems to conform to received notions of folklorization as a means of constituting the legitimacy of elites or the state, in that it objectifies indigenous culture and inserts it in a subordinate position within the national totality (cf. Crain 1990, Poole 1990:118, Rowe and Schelling 1991:4). The indigenous pageant, on the other hand, challenges the notion that the process of folklorization must necessarily be associated with the imposition of external forms of domination. Instead, the indigenous pageant demonstrates a process of reactive self-objectification that recuperates a more authentic past identity as a form of defense against cultural domination.[31] I have suggested that the indigenous pageant folklorizes the everyday culture of those whom the ethnic political movement claims to represent. In this respect, the indigenous political movement, especially the highly culturalist strain active in the Otavalo area, is similar to European nationalisms of the nineteenth century, in which the "discovery" of popular culture occurred within the context of "movements to revive traditional culture, often in societies which were under foreign domination, or domination which was perceived as foreign by at least some of the dominated" (Burke 1992:295; cf. Gal 1991). Folk culture became a symbolic resource for the constitution of autochthony in the face of a perceived external threat, and it was consequently reified through processes of folklorization. This suggests the possibility that similar processes characterize, for example, nineteenth-century European nationalisms, nineteenth-century creole Latin American nationalisms, and twentieth-century white (Abercrombie 1992) and indigenous (Rogers 1996) varieties. Thus, caught between the racist folklorization of the white pageant and the "ethno-Orientalism" (Carrier 1992: 198)[32] of the indigenous pageant, *indígenas* are subject to a kind of double folklorization. In order to understand this process, we must clarify how processes of self- and other-objectification are deployed to specific ends in these various instances.

In the case of the white pageant, it would appear that the objectification of indigenousness is a component of a larger act of self-objectification similar to that described by Abercrombie for the Oruro carnival celebration (1992). He suggests that such participation, in which white elites not only join in the celebration, but do so by dancing costumed as Indians, allows these revelers simultaneously to assume and reject indigenous identities as part of a process of transcendent incorporation necessary to the constitution of the ideal Bolivian national subject.[33] In the Oruro carnival celebration, the appropriation of images of indigenousness serves to establish the autochthony and legitimacy of a dominant white population ultimately capable of transcending those images in pursuit of civilization. In a similar fashion, the white beauty queen dressed as Indian effects the incorporation of indigenousness as constitutive of municipal, regional, or national specificity as against other units of the same structural level in a way that does not compromise the privileged position of

civilized whiteness within the sphere so constituted.[34] Like the performance of carnival, then, the white pageant allows the participants, and indirectly the audience, "to be their own Indians and at the same time transcend them" (Abercrombie 1992:285). In contrast to the carnival celebration, however, in the white beauty pageant it is specifically women's bodies that facilitate this mediation of identity.

The use of the indigenous woman as semiotic operator in the construction of collective identities predates the republican period, stretching from images of America as a beautiful woman during the earliest phases of contact and conquest (Amodio 1993, Platt 1993) through the various manipulations of female imagery in Republican attempts at national self-constitution (Muratorio 1994, Platt 1993). Stephen Greenblatt has pointed to the role of Cortez's interpreter Doña Marina, known colloquially as *La Malinche*, as a "go-between" or mediator whose body is "the site of the strategic symbolic oscillation between self and other" (Greenblatt 1991:143, cf. Kidwell 1992). Of course, *La Malinche* was not only interpreter but also mistress to Cortez, and this eroticization of the bodily mediation between Spanish and Indian is characteristic of the dominant imagination of the indigenous woman as mediator (Abercrombie 1992, Amodio 1993, Burton 1994, Muratorio 1994). In the case of the white beauty pageant, this image is incorporated by a more encompassing white female identity that appropriates its mediatory capacity in the service of a statement about ethnic unity. This apparent unity, however, is in reality a hierarchical arrangement of discrete parts, in which the white category is established as unmarked and able to stand for the inclusive totality.[35]

In contrast to the white pageant, whose overt message is one of unity and transcendence of ethnic differentiation, the indigenous pageant is overtly concerned with the separation and objectification of an authentically Indian identity. In this case, the mediatory capacity of the indigenous woman is nullified, and she is instead used to constitute an autonomous realm of indigenous tradition. How, then, are we to understand the image of the indigenous woman elaborated from within this ideology? One suggestion that appears compatible with the materials is the idea that women are "more Indian" (de la Cadena 1991) and therefore apt vehicles for the projection of an already constituted ethnic identity that finds its purest expression in them. In this view, women are "the guardians of indigenous culture" (Harvey 1994:55) because they are associated with "insider" status exemplified by the domestic realm of the household and family: "women are the core while men are the periphery" (Spedding 1994:40).

An interpretation of the pageant from this perspective might suggest that it is logical that a statement about the value of indigenous culture would be made through women, who are its reproducers. And it is true that, on the whole, indigenous women are more strongly ethnically marked in their appearance than men. Yet the images presented in the context of the pageant go beyond this everyday markedness to project an intensified version of indigenous otherness that largely appeals to the past for its persuasiveness. That is, in both regions, but especially in Archidona, an integral component of the pageant involves the assumption of "traditional" dress and behavior, which is thought by organizers, contestants, judges, and audience to be a more authentic or truer expression of essential indigenousness than the still ethnically marked costume and behavior of contemporary indigenous women.[36] This temporal displacement of essential ethnic identity is similar in function to geographic displacements described by Rappaport (1994) for the Pastos of southern Colombia. It is an outgrowth of the general idea that "who we are depends on who 'we' were" (Burke 1992:297), an idea given great force by the reliance of indigenous political legitimacy upon the image of historical continuity with past populations whose sovereignty was violated by the Spanish.

The assumption of past identities by participants in the pageant moves them from the everyday realm of existence to one in which "to be is to be performed" (Bouissac 1977:151; cf. McAllister 1996: 108–109). Rather than a simple exhibition of indigenous women's everyday, unreflective reproduction of practices and ideas seen as especially ethnic, the pageant is a reflexively constituted representation of an ideal of indigenous womanhood consistent with the overt polit-

ical aims of the event as a whole. It is in this sense that the pageant is a form of spectacle, for it is characterized by a separation between "the 'show' and external reality" in which the participants assume identities noticeably distinct from those of everyday life (Beeman 1993:379). Of course, quotidian and performance realities are not unrelated to one another; the former provides the latter with much of its raw material and, perhaps more importantly, the latter feeds back upon the former, helping to define and shape everyday cultural reality by "creating specific interpretations and modes of consciousness" (Turner 1991a:310). Yet the difference between the mundane and the performed (Bauman 1977, 1993), between those practices that simply occur and those that are made objects of reflection and manipulation (Thomas 1992:64), between self-expression and self-objectification (Friedman 1992:354) is important for understanding the nature of the meanings generated by the pageant. The objectification inherent in the very act of representation sets it apart from other kinds of practice in ways that are crucial to understanding the ideological potential of the pageants as well as their place in celebrations of communal identities.

Deborah Poole has insightfully argued that the totalizing, objectifying function of representation is inherently normative, and she has associated state-supported folklore with "the cultural surveillance of dance" in the Inca empire, in which ethnic identity was totalized in order to facilitate its subordination to the state (1990:120). Indeed, the folklorized representation of indigenousness presented in the white beauty pageant could easily be read in these terms. Yet, similar acts of totalization occur in the context of the indigenous pageant, a fact which seems to contradict Poole's claim that Andean dance (of which the pageant is an instance) is not concerned with representing a "collective 'ethnic' identity" because "representation as a totalizing practice remains a privilege of the dominant culture" (1990:118). Part of the confusion seems to rest with Poole's assumptions that if an identity is being represented, it must be for the benefit of an external audience, and that the "possessors" of the represented identity have no need for such acts of objectification (1990:120). Yet the political and cultural particularities of the

Ecuadorian beauty pageants suggest otherwise. As was noted above, the indigenous pageant is part of a larger effort to "recuperate" and give positive value to a unique ethnic tradition. The very fact that such an effort is perceived to be necessary, however, indicates some degree of slippage between the everyday realities of indigenous life and the ideal of identity held by the organizers of events such as the pageant. The idea that there is "a culture" which can be, "recuperated," "possessed," and "demonstrated" and the use of representational media such as theater, radio, writing, and video toward these ends are in fact intrinsically related (Turner 1991a, 1991b).

The re-presentation of indigenous culture and tradition in the pageant is thus made not only for consumption by an external audience, but also to make normative claims about the practices of those whose identity is supposedly represented. This process can be described as an instance of semiotic regimentation, which Michael Silverstein defines as the "formulation of standards bespeaking adherence to various larger social and political values" (1985:221, cf. Parmentier 1994). In the case of the indigenous pageant, the regimentation process primarily affects directly the participants' bodily hexis, those durable ways of walking, talking, speaking and thinking that Bourdieu calls "political mythology realized" (1990:69–70). In this instance, certain arenas of bodily hexis are foregrounded and subjected to explicit evaluation, thereby exposing the standards by which extra-performance behavior, speech, and thought are to be regimented. This "scheme transfer," in which the foregrounded bodily technique becomes a "kind of *pars totalis*, predisposed to function in accordance with the fallacy of *pars pro toto*, and hence to recall the whole system to which it belongs" (Bourdieu 1990:69), is the mechanism by which the female body becomes the semiotic operator for a larger ideology of indigenous authenticity and autonomy. This process is reinforced by redundancy, in which the phases of the pageant (potentially including even the musical interludes) reinforce one another (cf. McAllister 1996:117), and stylization, which increases the coherence of meaning by selecting out and formalizing aspects of everyday indigenous life.[37]

The construction of a regimented and stylized version of indigenous identity in the pageant, while it may serve the purpose of presenting "culture" in a tangible form for political ends (as a kind of counter-folklorization to that perpetrated by the white pageant), also tends to render some persons, activities, and social relations invisible, a process that Gal and Irvine refer to as "erasure" (1995:974).[38] Elements that do not fit the interpretive structure are discarded, as the indeterminacy and dissemination characteristic of the flow of identity in everyday life is fixed. Wright has noted that such pageants create models of womanhood that refer to but do not include aspects of the "traditional" cultures on which they draw, as well as introduce new performance genres that call on new skills (e.g., individual performance dancing and question-answer public speaking) which must be specifically learned by contestants (1995:255). The visible discomfort of the participants during the course of the performance attests to the difficulty of this shift in habitus.

I suggest that this process helps explain the tepid response of Otavalo-area *indígenas* to the *Sara Ñusta* pageants of years past, as well as their reaction to Verónica's attempt to enter the 1996 *Yamor* pageant. They saw little promise that alternative festival activities such as the *Sara Ñusta* would effectively challenge their own marginalization from municipal society, and they saw little of themselves reflected in the *Sara Ñusta* pageant itself. The acquisition of individual performance skills such as those required by the beauty pageant represents a process of cultural alienation largely similar to that characteristic of the process of *mestizaje*. As a result, a candidate such as Verónica, who clearly already possesses the requisite skills to compete effectively in a pageant framework, might as well participate in the *Yamor* pageant. In attempting to do so, she constituted herself as the quintessential *Otavaleña* success story, competing on an equal footing within the ideological framework established by the Ecuadorian nation-state while at the same time challenging the inequality of access to the dream of progress based on ethnic identity and enforced by the local white oligarchy. The *Chonta Huarmi* pageant, on the other hand, appears to be less fully regimented and more ideologically hybrid than its highland counterpart, at the same time that its prototype of authenticity is more fully located in a socially remote past. The image constructed by the pageant appears less as an erasure than as an amplification of the boundaries of local indigenous identity. Thus it would appear that, paradoxically, ethnic political movements' attempts to establish their legitimacy through the construction of unifying images of indigenousness are more successful precisely where the everyday elaboration of a coherent ethnic identity is weakest.

NOTES

Acknowledgements

The research on which this article is based was conducted from September 1991 to June 1993 in Otavalo and Archidona, Ecuador. The fieldwork was supported by grants from the Social Science Research Council, the Wenner-Gren Foundation for Anthropological Research, the Fulbright Institute for International Education, and the American Institute for the History of Pharmacy. I gratefully acknowledge the support of these institutions. I would also like to thank Rosemary Lévy-Zumwalt, Blenda Femenías, and Elizabeth Rogers for valuable critical commentary on earlier drafts of the paper.

1   This is the local term for an ethnic category of "indigenous" or native persons. That category is conceptually opposed to those with "European" content, indexed by the terms *blanco* or *mestizo*. I use both the Spanish terms and their English translations "indigenous" and "white." These terms should be read as category labels rather than as transparently objective modifiers that denote essential characteristics. While accounts may vary as to who is or is not white, and individuals may shift from one category to the other depending upon the context, his intentions, and the identity of those who make the assessment, the categories themselves are discrete and enduring, and they have great ideological potency when applied. Hence

the facility in identifying the white and indigenous pageants; these events are at least partially concerned with reproducing the categorial distinction and are therefore strongly ethnically marked.

2   This article is based on fieldwork conducted in Otavalo and Archidona, Ecuador, from September 1991 to June 1993, as well as occasional follow-up visits in 1995. The events surrounding Verónica's candidacy occurred after I left the field and are reconstructed from articles in the popular press and secondhand accounts. As a result, I have been unable to pursue her particular story in greater depth.

3   This event, sponsored from 1992–95 by regional and national indigenous political organizations as an overt challenge to the white-controlled *Yamor* pageant, historically would have been the "proper" arena for Verónica's participation.

4   The beauty pageant genre itself has recently come under anthropological scrutiny as a particularly fruitful arena for exploring such processes (e.g., Behrman 1995; Cohen et al. 1996; Hendrickson 1991; Wright 1995). Cf. Lentz (1995) on the use of dress among migrant laborers from Chimborazo to redefine indigenous culture and restructure interethnic relations.

5   This conflicted nature of pageants has been pointed out by recent commentators. Drawing on Bakhtin (1981), Lavenda (1996:31) refers to a Minnesota pageant explicitly disavowed as such (i.e., labeled "not a beauty pageant") as an "ideologically hybrid" production, and Wilk (1996:228) refers to the corresponding "aesthetic diglossia" characteristic of many pageants.

6   The research on which this paper is based was conducted during dissertation fieldwork on shamanism, ethnicity, and politics in Ecuador. During the course of my principal research I had occasion to attend several pageants in both Otavalo and Archidona, as well as to speak informally with residents of both regions and occasionally with pageant organizers about the pageants. I had much less occasion to speak with either pageant

contestants or judges. The paper clearly reflects these research biases in its concentration on the performances themselves and their broader social and political contexts. Further research on all dimensions of the complete process of performance production and reception (Schechner 1985) is needed to build fruitfully on what is admittedly only a first step toward understanding these complex events.

7 *Yamor* is the name of a special variety of *chicha* (Quichua: *asua*), a fermented corn beverage often translated as "beer." Due to its arduous production process, *yamor* is considered a special, festive beverage. The municipal festival of Otavalo has adopted *yamor* as its core image, such that the beverage, the festival, and the municipality are indexically interconnected. In this sense, the queen of *Yamor* is also the queen of Otavalo.

8 Borland (1996) discusses a similar festival complex composed of Beautiful Indian and Festival Queen components, though in this case, both are organized by the official Patronal Festivals Committee. Other examples include the National Indigenous Queen and Miss Guatemala competitions discussed by McAllister (1996) as well as the Queen of the Settlement and Queen of the Bay contests in Belize (Wright 1995, Wilk 1996).

9 This adhesion of white elites to celebrations they had previously reviled as base and uncivilized has been explored recently by Tom Abercrombie (1992) in his discussion of *carnaval* in Oruro. Tristan Platt anchors this process, which he calls a "metaphorical internalisation of the 'savage indian' by 'civilised whites'" in an "organic assimilation of the envied aboriginal right to the national territory" (1993:171).

10 Thus, for example, the theme of the 1994 *Reina de Yamor* competition was "confraternity," and the contest's masters of ceremonies made a concerted effort to establish that all of Otavalo was represented there in unity and harmony, despite the fact that, as far as I could see, only one indigenous couple was present in a crowd of well over a thousand people.

11 I have chosen not to place the term "tradition" in quotation at every usage, though that is essentially the approach taken here. My use of the term indicates instances in which participants view some practice or object as representative of a tradition, though the existence, time depth, or "authenticity" of such traditions may be contested by other participants or by outside observers.

12 Wilk notes that pageants often serve the state's goals of "domesticating difference" by displacing social divisions into the realm of taste (1996:218). In some instances, such as the Guatemalan "*Rabin Ahau*" pageant described by McAllister (1996), the core of indigenousness is accorded an autonomous semiotic/performative elaboration that is nonetheless part of the larger nationalist project of self-identification, rather than a counterhegemonic elaboration of an ideally autonomous indigenous political movement. In the case of the Belizean pageants, Wright (1995) contends that the sponsorship of pageants and other public activities by a Garifuna "medial class" of teachers and public sector workers helps articulate local Garifuna groups with the state through the elaboration of "Garifunaness" as an ethnic category.

13 Whereas in most cases the contestants in indigenous pageants are not asked to mimic white women in the same way that they themselves are mimicked by participants in the white pageants, the presence of evening gown and even swimsuit competitions in some lowland pageants might serve as the basis for an interpretation that parallels my reading of the white pageant. Of course, the ideological implications of mimicry are different when the imitators are at the bottom rather than the top of the ethnic/power hierarchy. The mimetic appropriation of elements of whiteness in lowland pageants seems to indicate a less consistent, internally conflicted indigenous identity that corresponds to the generally less ethnically contentious nature of the Archidona-area pageants.

14 I employ this term in order to index the ideological dimension of the choice of label. While *indigena* is the label of choice for indigenous self-designation, "Indian" (*indio*) is more likely to be used by *mestizos* when they speak pejoratively about *indigenas*.

15 This appears to be changing in Otavalo, however. As the tourism and export economy continues to boom, the number of Indian-run businesses willing to sponsor activities is increasing. And in some cases, companies do in fact sponsor indigenous festival activities, even outside of the municipal celebrations. In 1983, the "Full Speed" tobacco company sponsored a revival of a harvest festival near Cotacachi, at which free cigarettes were distributed (KIPU 1983:18).

16 These terms refer to female roles in Inca society and are drawn (directly or indirectly) from colonial accounts of the Inca empire. Such anachronistic Peruvianisms illustrate a broader process of appropriation of an Incaic cultural model that is arguably intended to lend cultural credence to the model of indigenous culture constructed by the dominant Ecuadorian indigenous political movement.

17 Such doubts stem from the extent to which an indigenous candidate must control cultural capital associated with whiteness, especially skills associated with the interview component of the competition, which is described in detail below.

18 In the 1995 version of the *Sara Ñusta* competition, however, the majority of candidates represented various indigenous political and cultural organizations rather than actual communities. I believe that this indicates FICI's inability to insert itself as an appropriate representative of the majority of indigenous communities in the Otavalo area. Rather, a proportion of each community associates with FICI and this dispersed population is more easily represented via FICI-affiliated organizations than by communities as totalities.

19 I employ the term "community" in a somewhat loose way here in order to cover the variety of actual situations. In the 1993 *Chonta Huarmi* competition, for example, the contestants represented rural parishes or other supra-community units (such as the *Rucullacta* Cooperative) and in some cases had been elected in preliminary competitions among smaller units more akin to individual "communities." My use of the term should not be understood as strictly referring to these minimal units, but rather to social collectivities at varying levels of complexity.

20 This term literally means "Godmother" and is a metaphorical play on the idea of godparents' ritual "sponsorship" of their godchild. In this case the godmother of a team is expected to provide refreshments for team members or perhaps even to subsidize the purchase of their uniforms, although such obligations are not vigorously upheld. Though they themselves are always female, *madrinas* may represent either male or female sports teams.

21 Interestingly, however, *madrinas* are often not segregated by ethnicity, as *mestizas, indigenas*, and even the occasional *gringa* (foreigner) may compete against one another. This is due to the less overtly politicized and often interethnic nature of the events in which they participate.

22 Indeed, the current dress of Archidona-area *indigenas* – brightly colored polyester dresses and plastic shoes for women and slacks and T-shirts or button-down shirts and leather shoes or rubber work boots for men – occasionally draws criticism from both whites and *indigenas* who view it as an inauthentic departure from "true" indigenous dress. *Indigenas* often incorporate some traditional elements for specific purposes such as political rallies, while whites sometimes argue that contemporary indigenous dress is grounds for disqualifying them as truly indigenous, as did the sheriff of Archidona in a conversation about what he perceived to be the undue "favors" given by the national government and NGOs to local indigenous populations.

23 The ideological import of the bikini style may have been mitigated by the fact that

two of the judges in this case were the provincial queen and runner up in the white contest system. As far as I can tell, other kinds of judges, usually indigenous male politicians, do not favor the bikini style because it violates normal strictures of modesty. The fact that these judges were chosen for this pageant, as well as the fact that an evening gown competition was included, may be related to the generally less politically contentious character of the *Chonta Huarmi* pageant in comparison to the *Sara Ñusta* competition. Both may also be related to the fact that one of the principal organizers was an extremely moderate indigenous politician who at the time was employed by the municipal government.

24 In one preliminary competition, the elaborate lengths to which candidates had gone in past competitions caused pageant organizers to place limitations on such activities.

25 To the extent that emblems of traditionality are employed, this would appear to be a strategy for grounding the contestant's indigenousness in what is perceived to be a more authentic past.

26 The 1994 *Sara Ñusta* pageant included theatrical dance productions by a Quito dance troupe which liberally interpreted "indigenous" themes such as the phases of the agricultural cycle.

27 In the 1992 *Reina de Archidona* competition, the election of the woman who performed best in the interview segment prompted a violent reaction from some crowd members and a show of protest from the third-place winner, who refused to wear her sash (Ponce 1993:269).

28 Spanish is indicated in normal type, Quichua is denoted by bold type. Note the increased preponderance of Quichua from the first to the third example.

29 The use of "comrade" to translate *compañero* is intended to capture the term's overtones of task- or institution-focused solidarity, but it should not be read as an implication of any explicit association with communism.

30 Dorian (1994:479–480) has argued that this disjuncture between the prescriptivism of purist reform movements and the consciousness of vernacular users may in fact threaten the success of language standardization efforts.

31 Gewertz and Errington (1994) describe a similar process of performative self-objectification that takes the opposite tack of establishing a disjuncture between present and past identities, distancing the Duke of York Islanders from their "savage" past in order to distance themselves from the negative associations that such an identity incurs.

32 Carrier identifies this as "essentialist renderings of alien societies by the members of those societies themselves" (1992:198).

33 The role of such practices in reproducing relations of domination could also be viewed from the perspective of the pseudo-magical power of mimesis (in which the ability to copy implies a degree of control or mastery over the original) whose role in some forms of resistance has recently been discussed by, among others, Stoller (1994) and Taussig (1993).

34 Cf. Muratorio (1994:188) on Expo '92 and Hendrickson (1991:290) on the Miss Universe contest.

35 The volubility of this process is illustrated by conflicting uses of the term "*Otavaleño/a.*" This name is used to designate denizens (ideally of any race or ethnicity) of the town of Otavalo, but it is also employed as an ethnic label for the circum-Otavalo indigenous population. The white pageant reappropriates this term in its municipal sense through repeated reference to Otavalo and *Otavaleños* in the context of the larger statement of community "unity." The term is thus at least temporarily shifted away from its marked designation of a specific ethnic group and toward an unmarked municipal identity. Yet, as feminists have observed for the psychological implications of markedness in English gendered pronouns, the "unmarked" is more marked than it would seem on the surface. Just as "man" in English arguably carries psychological overtones of maleness, so too the municipal sense of "*Otavaleño*" as used in the white pageant to refer to all denizens of the Otavalo area

carries an implicit connotation of whiteness, a connotation that is reinforced by the fact that it is virtually unheard of for *indigenas* to attend the white pageant.

36 Interestingly, the contestants in the white pageants also adopt older styles during the "traditional dress" component of their competitions.

37 Bouissac (1977:148) refers to this process as "iconization," meaning the augmentation of the conventional aspect of the icon at the expense of its "natural" aspect (cf. Ricoeur's [1994] concept of "iconic increase").

38 Conklin (1997:713) discusses a similar process of erasure in the Amazon. Cervone (1998:110–111) describes a case from the central highlands of Ecuador in which a Church-sponsored festival was appropriated by an indigenous political organization, which used the festival as a means of consolidating its own power with respect to its constituency by creating and promoting a folklorized version of indigenous identity.

REFERENCES CITED

Abercrombie, Thomas
1991   To Be Indian, to Be Bolivian: "Ethnic" and "National" Discourses of Identity. *In* Nation-States and Indians in Latin America. Greg Urban and Joel Sherzer, eds. Pp. 95–130. Austin: University of Texas Press.
1992   La fiesta del carnaval postcolonial en Oruro: Clase, etnicidad y nacionalismo en la danza folklórica. Revista Andina 10(2):279–325.

Amodio, Emanuele
1993   Formas de la alteridad: Construcción y difusión de la imagen del indio americano en Europa durante el primer siglo de la conquista de América. Quito: Abya Yala.

Bakhtin, Mikhail
1981   The Dialogic Imagination: Four Essays. Michael Holquist, ed. Caryl Emerson and Michael Holquist, trans. Austin: University of Texas Press.

Bauman, Richard
1977   Verbal Art as Performance. Prospect Heights, IL: Waveland.
1993   Disclaimers of Performance. *In* Responsibility and Evidence in Oral Discourse. Jane Hill and Judith Irvine, eds. Pp. 182–196. Cambridge: Cambridge University Press.

Beeman, William
1993   The Anthropology of Theater and Spectacle. Annual Review of Anthropology 22:369–393.

Behrman, Carolyn
1995   "The Fairest of them All": Gender, Ethnicity and a Beauty Pageant in the Kingdom of Swaziland. *In* Dress and Ethnicity. Joanne Eicher, ed. Pp. 195–206. Oxford: Berg.

Borland, Katherine
1996   The Indian Bonita of Monimbó: The Politics of Ethnic Identity in the New Nicaragua. *In* Beauty Queens on the Global Stage. Colleen Ballerino Cohen, Richard Wilk, and Beverly Stoeltje, eds. Pp. 217–232. New York: Routledge.

Bouissac, Paul
1977   Semiotics and Spectacles: The Circus Institution and Representations. *In* A Perfusion of Signs. Thomas Sebeok, ed. Pp. 143–152. Bloomington: Indiana University Press.

Bourdieu, Pierre
1990   The Logic of Practice. Stanford: Stanford University Press.

Burke, Peter
1992   We, the People: Popular Culture and Popular Identity in Modern Europe. *In* Modernity and Identity. Scott Lash and Jonathan Friedman, eds. Pp. 293–308. Oxford: Blackwell.

Burton, Pauline
1994   Women and Second-Language Use: An Introduction. *In* Bilingual Women: Anthropological Approaches to Second-Language Use. Pauline Burton, Ketaki Dyson and Shirley Ardener, eds. Pp. 1–29. Oxford: Berg.

Carrier, James
1992   Occidentalism: The World Turned Upside Down. American Ethnologist 19(2):195–212.

Cervone, Emma
1998   Festival Time, Long Live the Festival: Ethnic Conflict and Ritual in the Andes. Anthropos 93:101–113.

Cohen, Colleen Ballerino, Richard Wilk, and Beverly Stoeltje, eds.

1996 Beauty Queens on the Global Stage: Gender, Contests and Power. New York: Routledge.

Conklin, Beth
1997 Body Paint, Feathers, and VCRs: Aesthetics and Authenticity in Amazonian Activism. American Ethnologist 24(4):711–737.

Crain, Mary
1990 The Social Construction of National Identity in Highland Ecuador. Anthropological Quarterly 63(1):43–59.

de la Cadena, Marisol
1991 Las mujeres son más indias: Etnicidad y género en una comunidad del Cusco. Revista Andina 9(1):7–47.

Dorian, Nancy
1994 Purism vs. Compromise in Language Revitalization and Language Revival. Language in Society 23:479–494.

Friedman, Jonathan
1992 Narcissism, Roots and Postmodernity: The Constitution of Selfhood in the Global Crisis. In Modernity and Identity. Scott Lash and Jonathan Friedman, eds. Pp. 331–366. Oxford: Blackwell.

Gal, Susan
1991 Bartók's Funeral: Representations of Europe in Hungarian Political Rhetoric. American Ethnologist 18(3):440–458.

Gal, Susan and Judith Irvine
1995 Disciplining Boundaries and Language Ideology: The Semiotics of Differentiation. Social Research 62(4):967–1002.

García Canclini, Nestor
1995 Hybrid Cultures: Strategies for Entering and Leaving Modernity. Minneapolis: University of Minnesota Press.

Gewertz, Frederick and Deborah Errington
1994 From Darkness to Light in the George Brown Jubilee: The Invention of Nontradition and the Inscription of a National History in East New Britain. American Ethnologist 21(1):104–122.

Greenblatt, Stephen
1991 Marvelous Possessions: The Wonder of the New World. Chicago: University of Chicago Press.

Guss, David
1996 "Full Speed Ahead with Venezuela": The Tobacco Industry, Nationalism and the Business of Popular Culture. Public Culture 9:33–54.

Harris, Olivia
1980 The Power of Signs: Gender, Culture and the Wild in the Bolivian Andes. In Nature, Culture and Gender. Carol MacCormack and Marilyn Strathern, eds. Pp. 70–94. Cambridge: Cambridge University Press.

Harvey, Penelope
1994 The Presence and Absence of Speech in the Communication of Gender. In Bilingual Women: Anthropological Approaches to Second-Language Use. Pauline Burton, Ketaki Dyson and Shirley Ardener, eds. Pp. 44–64. Oxford: Berg.

Hendrickson, Carol
1991 Images of the Indian in Guatemala: The Role of Indigenous Dress in Indian and Ladino Constructions. In Nation-States and Indians in Latin America. Greg Urban and Joel Sherzer, eds. Pp. 286–306. Austin: University of Texas Press.

Hill, Jane and Kenneth Hill
1986 Speaking Mexicano: Dynamics of Syncretic Language in Central Mexico. Tucson: University of Arizona Press.

Iser, Wolfgang
1993 Representation: A Performative Act. In The Aims of Representation: Subject/Text/History. Murray Krieger, ed. Pp. 217–232. Stanford: Stanford University Press.

Kidwell, Clara
1992 Indian Women as Cultural Mediators. Ethnohistory 39(2):97–107.

KIPU
1983 KIPU: El mundo indígena en la prensa ecuatoriana. Quito: CDIPI.
1986 KIPU: El mundo indígena en la prensa ecuatoriana. Quito: CDIPI.

Lavenda, Robert
1996 "It's Not a Beauty Pageant!": Hybrid Ideology in Minnesota Community Queen Pageants. In Beauty Queens on the Global Stage. Colleen Ballerino Cohen, Richard Wilk, and Beverly Stoeltje, eds. Pp. 31–46. New York: Routledge.

Lentz, Carola
1995 Ethnic Conflict and Changing Dress Codes: A Case Study of an Indian Migrant Village in Highland Ecuador. In Dress and Ethnicity. Joanne Eicher, ed. Pp. 269–293. Oxford: Berg.

McAllister, Carlota
1996   Authenticity and Guatemala's Maya Queen. *In* Beauty Queens on the Global Stage. Colleen Ballerino Cohen, Richard Wilk, and Beverly Stoeltje, eds. Pp. 105–124. New York: Routledge.

Muratorio, Blanca
1994   Nación, identidad y etnicidad: Imágenes de los indios ecuatorianos y sus imagineros a fines del siglo XIX. *In* Imágenes e imagineros: Representaciones de los indígenas ecuatorianos, Siglos XIX y XX. Blanca Muratorio, ed. Pp. 109–196. Quito: FLACSO.

Parmentier, Richard
1994   Signs in Society: Studies in Semiotic Anthropology. Bloomington: Indiana University Press.

Platt, Tristan
1993   Simón Bolívar, the Sun of Justice and the Amerindian Virgin: Andean Conceptions of the *Patria* in Nineteenth-Century Potosí. Journal of Latin American Studies 25:159–185.

Ponce, Magdalena
1993   La fiesta de la *Chonta* en Archidona. MARKA 3:267–274.

Poole, Deborah
1990   Accommodation and Resistance in Andean Ritual Dance. Drama Review 34(2):98–126.

Rappaport, Joanne
1994   Cumbe Reborn: An Andean Ethnography of History. Chicago: University of Chicago Press.

Ricoeur, Paul
1994   Imagination in Discourse and Action. *In* Rethinking Imagination: Culture and Creativity. Gillian Robinson and John Rundell, eds. Pp. 118–135. New York: Routledge.

Rogers, Mark
1996   Beyond Authenticity: Conservation, Tourism, and the Politics of Representation in the Ecuadorian Amazon. Identities 3(1–2):73–125.

Roseman, Sharon
1995   "Falamos como Falamos": Linguistic Revitalization and the Maintenance of Local Vernaculars in Galicia. Journal of Linguistic Anthropology 5(1):3–32.

Rowe, William and Vivian Schelling
1991   Memory and Modernity: Popular Culture in Latin America. London: Verso.

Schechner, Richard
1985   Between Theater and Anthropology. Philadelphia: University of Pennsylvania Press.

Silverstein, Michael
1985   Language and the Culture of Gender: At the Intersection of Structure, Usage, and Ideology. *In* Semiotic Mediation: Sociocultural and Psychological Perspectives. Elizabeth Mertz and Richard Parmentier, eds. Pp. 219–259. Orlando, FL: Academic Press.

Spedding, Alison
1994   Open Castilian, Closed Aymara? Bilingual Women in the Yungas of La Paz (Bolivia). *In* Bilingual Women: Anthropological Approaches to Second-Language Use. Pauline Burton, Ketaki Dyson and Shirley Ardener, eds. Pp. 30–43. Oxford: Berg.

Stoller, Paul
1994   Embodying Colonial Memories. American Anthropologist 96(3):634–648.

Taussig, Michael
1993   Mimesis and Alterity. London: Routledge.

Thomas, Nicholas
1992   Substantivization and Anthropological Discourse: The Transformation of Practices into Institutions in Neotraditional Pacific Societies. *In* History and Tradition in Melanesian Anthropology. James Carrier, ed. Pp. 64–85. Berkeley: University of California Press.

Turner, Terence
1991a   Representing, Resisting, Rethinking: Historical Transformations of Kayapo Culture and Anthropological Consciousness. *In* Colonial Situations: Essays on the Contextualization of Anthropological Knowledge. George Stocking, ed. Pp. 285–313. Madison: University of Wisconsin Press.
1991b   The Social Dynamics of Video Media in an Indigenous Society: The Cultural Meaning and Personal Politics of Video-Making in a Kayapo Community. Visual Anthropology Review 7(2):68–76.

Wilk, Richard
1996   Connections and Contradictions: From the Crooked Tree Cashew Queen to Miss World Belize. *In* Beauty Queens on the Global Stage. Colleen Ballerino Cohen, Richard Wilk, and Beverly Stoeltje, eds. Pp. 217–232. New York: Routledge.

Wright, Pamela
1995   The Timely Significance of Supernatural Mothers or Exemplary Daughters: The Metonymy of Identity in History. *In* Articulating Hidden Histories. Jane Schneider and Rayna Rapp, eds. Pp. 243–261. Berkeley: University of California Press.

Part V

Regional, National, and Transnational Political Cultures

21

Gender, Politics, and the Triumph of *Mestizaje* in Early 20th-Century Nicaragua

Jeffrey Gould

In 1942, a National Guard detachment marched into the indigenous villages of Matagalpa, Nicaragua and uprooted cotton bushes used in the manufacture of traditional clothing. The soldiers arrested and burned the huts of those who protested. In 1954, an Indian in Camoapa, Boaco assassinated a former mayor who had been stealing the lands of his family and the indigenous community. Following the incident, the National Guard unleashed a wave of vicious, anti-Indian repression. According to one indigenous survivor, "the *ladinos* let out all their hatred on us."[1] Unfortunately, politicians, scholars, and revolutionaries have failed to mention, let alone take seriously, events such as those of Matagalpa and Camoapa.

This article will analyze the creation of a discursive field, in and through which such acts of racist repression could be enveloped in silence. For, by the 1950s, official discourse had categorized Nicaragua as an ethnically homogenous, *mestizo* society whose indigenous population had disappeared by the turn of the century. My research suggests that, as late as 1950 the indigenous population[2] still formed over 10 percent of the total population outside of the Atlantic Coast and a substantial majority of some areas in the Central Highlands (Gould n.d.).

The "myth of *Nicaragua mestiza*," i.e., the common sense notion that Nicaragua had long been an ethnically homogenous society, is one of the elite's most enduring hegemonic achievements (Gould 1993). The creation of this nationalistic discourse in Nicaragua depended upon the increasing disarticulation of the *Comunidades Indigenas*. This was realized in the highlands departments of Matagalpa, Jinotega, and Boaco through *ladino* pressures on indigenous labor and land, which contributed to the weakening of the *Comunidades* (Gould 1993). The incessant questioning of indigenous authenticity that coincided with the *ladino* advance, contributed both to the consolidation of *ladino* power and to the erosion of indigenous communal identity. Moreover, that delegitimization of indigenous authenticity, in turn, was related to the development of a democratic discourse of equal rights and citizenship that effectively suppressed specific indigenous rights to communal land and political autonomy (Gould 1993).

It is important to understand that political context. On the one hand, politics provided an important avenue of resistance to the above tendencies. During the 1910s and 1920s, the indigenous communities of the Central Highlands represented the most important social base of the Conservative party. A 1932 State Department report commented that a "large majority of the Indians who vote are located in the Departments of Chontales and Matagalpa, which have been controlled in the past by Emiliano Chamorro."[3] In the contested elections from 1920–1934, the Indians arguably formed the single most important block of voters.[4]

On the other hand, political conflict at once perpetuated and weakened the indigenous communities. The eclipse of the Conservative party, with its heavy indigenous base, also contributed to the rise of *mestizaje*. There were several reasons for this. The power struggle that led to the decline of Conservatism seriously debilitated the coherence of the community, as distinct factions came to ideologically banish each other from the indigenous community. Similarly, the extreme identification of Indians with the Conservative leader Emiliano Chamorro led to a kind of disenfranchisement through his loss of power. Partisan conflict among the highlands Indians also contributed to the imagery of the evolving discourse of *mestizaje*, in particular through the portrayal of the frightened indigenous male.

The first part of this article will discuss the search for an anti-imperial symbol that involved the suppression of the ethnic category "ladino" and the creation of a hybrid symbol, "*nuestra raza*." The second section discusses Sandino's contribution to the discourse of the "*raza indohispana*" and the indigenous struggles that coincided with his own. The next section reflects on gender and hybridity; I will suggest that the imagery of *mestizaje* suppressed Indian male and the female transmission of heroic pre-Columbian blood into the "virile" Indo-Hispanic race. The final section of the article points to some of the political consequences of the centrality of *mestizaje* in Central America.

The article questions a trend in contemporary ethnography and political discourse that celebrates cultural hybridity, while assuming that the notion of cultural loss is but a vestige of colonialist anthropology.[5] Just as the notion of "Indian" has to be historicized and stripped of essentialism, so too should we deconstruct the notion of *mestizaje* or hybridity. This article will attempt to portray the intimate relationship between the construction of *mestizaje* in Nicaragua and the nationally unacknowledged assault on its indigenous communities. Klor de Alva (1995:257) has expressed this point well:

> . . . [M]estizaje . . . is the nation-building myth that has helped link dark to light-skinned hybrids and Euro-Americans, often in opposition to both foreigners and the indigenous "others" in their midst. And it has been effectively used to promote national amnesia about or to salve the national conscience in what concerns the dismal past and still colonized condition of most indigenous peoples of Latin America.

The Search for an Anti-Imperial Symbol

The triumph of the Liberal Revolutions in Central America along with the growing impact of United States cultural, political and economic imperialism had important consequence. Both exacerbated and displaced ethnic divisions, and they created a need for national symbols that would respond to imperial arrogance, essentialized as the Anglo-Saxon race.

The term *ladino* could not serve as an effective symbolic vehicle for nationalism in the era of U.S. intervention.[6] The existence of a substantial and embattled minority of Indians, often located within the coffee-based areas of El Salvador, Honduras, and Nicaragua (the middle isthmus), proved a stumbling block toward the emergence of an anti-imperial symbol. Despite their demographic weight – they represented between 20 and 35 percent of the population at the turn of the century – elites situated Indians, in the words of Lomnitz-Adler (1992:276), as "standing on the margins of progress, on the margins of nationality and outside history."

Ladino had multiple meanings in the middle isthmus, which emerged through a complex set of historical pressures. By the end of the colonial period we can discern at least three meanings for the term, and they continued to circulate throughout the region. In the Americas, Spaniards first employed "*ladino*" to describe native peoples who had adopted Spanish dress and customs in addition to language, as in "*es un indio muy ladino*" or "*es un indio ladino.*" (Meaning I). By the mid-18th century, however, *ladino* no longer referred exclusively to "Hispanicized" Indians but rather was used to refer to *castas*, all intermediate strata between Spaniard and Indian, including *mestizos* and *mulattos*, as well as to "former" Indians (Meaning II). As a mixed race category, *ladino* served remarkably well as a symbol that facilitated the smoothing over of colonial racial categories and therefore impeded a conflation of class and race that might have proved devastating to the Central American elites.[7] Finally, in regions with large indigenous population, such as Matagalpa, the term *ladino* was used on baptismals as synonymous with all non-Indians. The emergence of *ladino* in binary opposition to Indians, in lieu of other available racial categories (*mestizo, mulatto,* or white), further extended the repertoire of its meanings, as it could now include "white" (Meaning III).[8]

By the end of the 19th century, under the stratifying impact of coffee and liberalism, the meaning of *ladino* as Hispanicized Indian (I) had ceased to circulate. At a national level, people continued to employ the mixed-race meaning (II) of *ladino*.[9] But *ladino*'s dominant meaning emerged in the coffee zones of El Salvador, Nicaragua and in western Honduras as the binary opposite of Indian (III). Indeed the locally salient meaning of *ladino* was implicitly referred to in the existence of a "*ladino* race." Thus, for example, the civil and ecclesiastical birth records in the Central Highlands of Nicaragua at the turn of the century list members of the "*casta indígena*" and the "*casta ladina.*" Moreover, the birth records treated "*ladino*" as a racial category (roughly equivalent to white) when they employed the word *mestizo* to describe the off-spring of an *indigena* and a *ladino*.[10]

Thus, by the early 20th century, the multi-vocality of *ladino*, with meanings ranging from "white" to "non-white," reflected and conditioned elite and opposition intellectual's incapacity to produce hegemonic forms and the active consent of the majority of the population to their rule.[11] Anti-imperialists could not use "*ladino*" as a national symbol since one of its powerful racial resonances communicated an unacceptable, blatant exclusion of Indians. Although their imagined nation promised to extend citizenship and rights (to males), it was impossible to envision an alliance with Indians while operating within the discursive field of the *ladino* (thinking with and through that symbol); because in each of its contemporary meanings *ladino* implied superiority over Indians.

The contradictory meanings of *ladino* in middle isthmian, anti-imperial discourse can be glimpsed in the writings of Salvador Mendieta and Juan Mendoza. In 1919, both men wrote studies that diagnosed the ills of Central America and proposed similar solutions that involved overcoming existing political and economic hierarchies. They both shared a vision of *mestizaje* at the core of Central American nationalism. Indeed, both were militants of the Central American Unity Party (Mendieta was the founder and leader). Moreover, they were natives of the same town, Diriamba, Nicaragua, of the same generation and similar class background (provincial petit-bourgeois). We would assume that they shared a common language. Mendieta (1919:56) wrote the following definition of *ladino*:

> Ladino in Central America refers to the type that emerges from the mixture of our three mother races and does not present the distinctive characteristics of any one of them: he is not white like the Spaniard; nor copper-colored like the Indian, nor black like the African.

Yet Mendieta's *compañero* Juan Mendoza (1920:78), used the term to mean, in effect, white: "All of the talent, riches, and honors belonged within the patrimony of the *ladino*. For the *ladino*, miscegenation with Indians was unacceptable. (*El cruzamiento con indigena era inaceptable.*)" Thus two intellectuals in 1919 with early identical backgrounds and politics could not communicate using the term *ladino*. Such radically contradictory meanings of *ladino* did not allow for the creation of national symbols that would mean something to everybody and that would allow for some kind of conversation about the new nation, even one based on some degree of misunderstanding.

I do not mean to suggest that the multi-vocality of the term *ladino* led to its demise; rather, I think that those incompatible meanings revealed an extraordinarily fractured political cultural terrain. In part, the local terrain of coffee plantations helped to produce the sharp bifurcation between Indian and *ladino* throughout the middle isthmus and of course in Guatemala. Moreover, the importance of the coffee cultures, where the non-Indian meaning (Meaning III) circulated, would have made it extraordinarily difficult for the alternative mixed-race meaning of *ladino* (Meaning II) to include the indigenous population. Since the two dominant meanings excluded Indians, "*ladino*" was indeed a doubtful vehicle for anti-imperialist unity. But no substitute national symbol for the people emerged – only Honduran, Nicaraguan, or the even vaguer "*nuestra raza.*"

As early as 1898, the *Guía Ilustrada* gave voice to the idea of Nicaragua as a heroic product of *mestizaje* in opposition to the cold, technical Anglo-Saxon race: "*De la fusión de la antigua raza americana con la sangre española resultó este tipo característico que en si contiene las energías del soldado, la tenacidad del agricultor y los ensueños del poeta*" (Falcinelli Graziozi 1989:210).[12] Modesto Armijo, who by the 1930s had become one of that country's leading intellectuals, penned the following denunciation of annexationism in 1908:

> Comprendiendo, pues, el antagonismo que existe entre las dos razas que pueblan el continente americano, comprendiendo que el dominio de la una acarreará necesariamente el desaparecimiento de la otra, sólo puede explicarse el sentimiento anexionista en un estado de corrupción, que posponga la dignidad nacional ante la brutal satisfacción de nuestros apetitos. [Armijo 1908/09:73][13]

In these declarations, the writers discovered a method of challenging nascent United States imperialism by creating a fictitious racial opposition. Although the racial definition of the United States as Anglo-Saxon was easy enough at the time, the imagined racial unity of Central and South America could only be based on some kind of hybrid, *mestizo* race.

By the late 1910s and early 1920s, intellectuals began to present an increasingly positive valorization of the hybrid nature of "*nuestra raza.*" Thus, for example, Mendoza (1920:78) looked to the

mestizo as the new harbinger of progress and national cohesion:

> ... Ignoraban los ladinos lo que hoy está resuelto por los sociólogos más avanzados ... no así los elementos originados por virtual del cruzamiento de las razas que hoy sobrepujan con la fuerza imperiosa del capital unido a la experta dirección que imprime la inteligencia en el seno de los progresos.

Mendoza invented a scientific underpinning for *mestizaje* as he counterposed a technologically progressive, mixed-race class to a backward, seigneurial, racially pure, white *ladino* domination.

Although in Mendoza's version of *mestizaje* the indigenous element was still subordinate, by the early 1920s under the influence (we can assume) of the Mexican Revolution, the Indian blood within the race was becoming increasingly valued. Thus, by 1923, Manuel Quintana, a Catholic intellectual, found the Spanish contribution, "*la raza híbrida de nuestros conquistadores,*" far less impressive than the indigenous. He wrote: "*Nuestra raza es, pues, el punto de intersección de esas grandes corrientes ... ojalá de esta conjunción de fuerza y de luz, de romanticismo y heroísmo, surja el bloque diamantino que nos amuralle contra el nuevo invasor!*" (Quintana 1923). Here Quintana drew out the logical consequences of the growth of the developing anti-imperial symbol of "*nuestra raza,*" strongly emphasizing the heroic (pre-Columbian), indigenous, component.

Sandino and the Making of the Indo-Hispanic Race

The unfurling of the banner of the hybrid "*nuestra raza*" coincided with the outbreak of several popular, nationalistic struggles. The most important of these urban-based struggles – virtually the only popular social movements in the country during this period – involved the Indians of Monimbó, Sutiava and Nindirí. The Monimboseños, artisans, *vivanderas* (female market vendors), and smallholders led demonstrations and riots against the United States-owned railroad in 1919 and 1922. They were protesting against accidents and company measures that adversely affected the *vivanderas*.[14]

Similarly, in 1919, the Indians of Nindirí (five miles away) rioted against the rate hikes of the oligarchic-owned water company.[15] Near León, in 1922 and 1923, the Indians of Sutiava staged several armed demonstrations against the construction of a highway on their territory and in defense of their cultural autonomy.[16]

At a key moment in the struggle against US intervention, non-indigenous Nicaraguans recognized (at least informally) the leadership role of the Indians, in the case of the Masayan movements. (In 1978, the Sutiavas and Monimboseños would play similar, if far more important, roles in the insurrections.) In 1919 and 1922, these struggles condensed a variety of aspirations, resentments, and concrete demands of the three indigenous communities. Yet in Nindirí and Masaya, the struggles in 1919 and 1922 did not appear to outsiders to have an indigenous content, for the protagonists framed their actions as aggrieved Nicaraguan citizens.[17] Similarly, throughout this period at least one faction of the Sutiavan leadership forged an alliance with anti-imperialist artisans in León. In other words, these movements were about the defense of indigenous communities without involving the politics of ethnic identity.

The Indians' role in these nationalistic, but communally-rooted struggles might well have facilitated their ideological incorporation into the emerging *mestizo* nation by stretching the meaning of "Indo-Hispanic." The inclusion of these indigenous groups would strengthen "*nuestra raza*" as an antagonistic pole against the United States and its oligarchic allies. Ironically, the integration of Indians as citizens at the same time marginalized them as ethnic groups: they were incorporated as equal citizens without special rights to cultural or political autonomy.[18] This promise of integration and practice of exclusion had even more profound consequences for the rural indigenous population of the Central Highlands whose contemporary struggles received virtually no support nor recognition from the nationalist movement. On the contrary, the nationalists viewed the highlands Indians as servile followers of anti-democratic and anti-patriotic forces embodied in the Conservative party.

Urban indigenous participation in the popular, nationalistic struggles set the stage for a major linguistic and conceptual shift. During Augusto Sandino's war of national liberation the Indo-Hispanic race was discursively enshrined and the categories of *ladino* and Indian were suppressed. Indeed, Sandino himself played an important role in that process as he placed the Indo-Hispanic race as the core symbol of popular nationalism.

Sandino's war of resistance against U.S. intervention, between 1927 and 1933, coincided with, and provoked a variety of forms of rural class conflict. Although the majority of the highlands Indian population did not actively participate in Sandino's army, most indigenous groups *did* attempt to use the changing war-time political conjuncture to their advantage. In particular, they took advantage of the breakdown in the normal repressive operations of the state as the Marines and the *Guardia* devoted most of their resources to the war effort.

For example, some indigenous leaders in Matagalpa apparently operated as bandits with no clear political agenda or affiliation.[19] Others pursued specific collective goals. Consider the example of indigenous resistance against the English *cafetalero*, Fred W. Fley. He was the owner of a relatively small plantation (valued at US $2,500) situated near the village of San Marcos in the western part of the territory of the *Comunidad Indígena de Matagalpa*.[20] Since 1924, he had been involved in a land conflict with his neighbors. In 1927, after the US intervention had ended the civil war, the Conservative government named Pedro López and Benacio Méndez as *capitán de cañada* (specifically indigenous police officer) and *juez de mesta* of San Marcos. Much to Fley's chagrin they were his principal antagonists in the land dispute. The *cafetalero* thus complained to the Marines:

> They have shown me their enmity by robbing my cattle, by cutting my cows' tails and by inciting the other Indians against me and my family ... now that they are representatives of law and order they are the only people who are armed with government rifles. Their duty is to disarm everybody but they only disarm

Liberals. . . . Here there are brutish, armed Indians (usually more drunk than sober) and the foreign element has nothing to defend themselves.[21]

At several points over the next six months, Fley attempted to gain the support of the Marines in his battle with his indigenous neighbors. Colonel Berry sympathized with Fley but, as he explained, given the growing conflict with Sandino he needed to keep the *capitanes de cañada* armed until he was able to obtain more recruits for the *Guardia Nacional*. Fley responded that the situation was

> going very badly outside of the city Matagalpa . . . armed Indians have occupied my land as squatters . . . they use my plantation as pasture. I have no legal protection. I ask the Marines for the protection that they promised – the intervention was to protect the property of foreigners – and I want to know when are they going to keep their promise. . . . I am rapidly losing the little cattle that I held onto following the revolution and I am sure that the thieves are these Indians who have squatted on my land, armed with government-issued Springfields . . . we are unarmed.[22]

A reading of Fley's racist complaint reveals something of how Sandino's resistance caused a shift in the local balance of power. Although Sandino did not gain significant indigenous support in the region, his presence in the nearby Segovias created conditions that aided indigenous struggles against *cafetaleros*. To cite another example, the indigenous inhabitants of Uluse, Matagalpa were able to claim and work 350 hectares of "La Escocia" plantation.[23]

Just as Matagalpan Indians managed to advance in their agrarian struggles thanks to Sandino's battle with the Marines, so too they were able to press their labor demands. Thus, indigenous coffee pickers thwarted coffee planter efforts to enforce debt obligations and pressures to increase their wages.[24] By 1934, following years of varied forms indigenous resistance, the Nicaraguan legislature enacted measures that effectively ended the seasonal debt peonage system (illegal since 1923).[25]

Although Sandino did not receive direct support from the Matagalpan Indians, they gave none to the Marines or the *Guardia*, at least during the first three years of the struggle. In 1930 when a Matagalpan Indian helped the Marines capture a Sandinista who had kidnapped his wife, Major Cruse reported: "This incident is very important since it is virtually the first time during the three years of the campaign that the Marines or the *Guardia Nacional* have received any effective aid from these inhabitants."[26] Thus, despite the militarization of their local leaders (the *capitanes*), the Matagalpan Indians did not collaborate with the Marines or the *Guardia Nacional*. It is indeed possible that the lack of collaboration reflected their awareness of Sandino's role in shifting the balance of power in favor of their land and labor demands.

There were also highlands Indians who *did* join Sandino and his army, in particular among the *Comunidades Indígenas* of Jinotega and San Lucas. Consider the testimony of Ramón Martínez, a Jinotegan *ladino* peasant who spent part of his adolescence in the Indian village of San Esteban. Martínez, who worked in the village store, arrived there in 1932 at the end of the conflict. He recalled, "*Habían muchos indígenas que andaban con Sandino . . . todos los indígenas de allí . . . Se fueron porque Sandino peleaba contra el Yanqui. . . .*"[27] The Jinoteganos, according to Martínez, resented the US presence specifically because they had evacuated an area that included many indigenous villages in order to carry out a scorched earth policy. Although the policy was suspended after one month, there is little doubt that it earned the enmity of the indigenous inhabitants.[28] Ramón Martínez claimed that agrarian issues had little to do with indigenous support, and Sandino himself also discounted an "agrarian problem" in the zone. Yet, the political framework of the agrarian battles that flared up in the Jinotegan countryside from 1915–1921 (Conservative Indians versus Liberal *terratenientes*) might provide an important clue to how Sandino garnered Jinotegan Indian support. For example, in the electoral campaign of 1928, six Liberal leaders were assassinated near the Indian village of Mancotal, and according to one report, "a patrol of 40 to 50 men was responsible . . ."[29]

Similarly large groups of armed men had their base of operations in the Indian villages of El Roble y Paso Real.[30] It seems likely that during the 1928 campaign the partisan warfare created political opportunities for Sandino in the zone, in that his enemies were the class/ethnic antagonists of the Indians.

Despite such indigenous participation in Sandino's ranks, their numerically significant presence in the highlands and the pervasiveness of collective resistance against the *ladino* elites, Sandino's writings are *silent* on the *Comunidades Indígenas*. His most important statement about Indians was made in an interview with a Basque journalist in 1933: "... [T]here is a refrain that goes: 'God will speak for the Indian of the Segovias.' And he certainly has spoken! They are the ones who have done a great part of all this. The Indian here is timid, but cordial, sentimental and intelligent" (de Belausteguigoitia 1985: 192).[31] Sandino then called over two Indians to introduce to the journalist. In order to show off their intelligence he had them converse in Miskito, Spanish and then English. Sandino continued:

Well now you see that they are intelligent. But they have been entirely abandoned. There are some hundred thousand of them without education, without schools, without anything of government. This is what I want to do with the colony, to lift them up and make true men out of them. [de Belausteguigoitia 1985:193]

It is indeed striking that Sandino uttered the phrase about the "Segovian Indians" and then, as it were, illustrated it with Indians from the Atlantic Coast. This confusion is remarkable, given the significant differences between the two groups, including language and dress and the Segovian Indians' roots in the Segovian mountains, a fact of much military importance to Sandino.

How are we to understand the Segovia's hero's apparent ignorance about the people of the Segovias?[32] The interview also includes a statement that denied the importance of the agrarian question in the Segovias despite recent expropriations of indigenous communal land, betraying a similar distortion in his view of the local social landscape. And yet in other parts of the interview, he describes with a great degree of complexity different aspects of Nicaraguan reality. The textual evidence suggests that Sandino either knew relatively little about the local cultures of the Segovias or simply found such matters unimportant.

Sandino's silence with respect to the *Comunidades* was derived, I would argue, from his nationalist project. As other scholars have suggested, Sandino was weaving a popular-nationalistic discourse, in effect reinventing a nation that had become the "patrimony of oligarchs and traitors" (Ramírez 1981:151,168). Sandino's nationalism was in turn rooted in a Central Americanist liberalism that was deeply enmeshed in Western notions of progress and civilization.[33] However sincere his commitment to aiding the indigenous peoples of the Atlantic Coast, Sandino could not break free from the discourse of assimilation: he sought to "make true men out of them." Sandino's few statements about Nicaraguan Indians did not waver from this civilizing mission, "to do whatever necessary to civilize these Indians who are the marrow of our race" (Román 1983:104). That civilizing process, it is worth emphasizing, included Sandino's suppression of the role and practices of *suquias*, charismatic shamans, vital to the reproduction of Miskitú culture (Román 1983:102).

Sandino's nationalism and liberalism impeded his understanding of the *Comunidades Indígenas* of the Segovias or Matagalpa on a more practical level as well. Creating a nation out of the divided and dominated political cultures of Nicaragua was a daunting task. Sandino thus stressed that which unified people: language and a shared colonial heritage. The fact that Segovian and Matagalpan Indians spoke Spanish and in some cases were willing to support his army confirmed his belief that Nicaraguans in fact formed one Indo-Hispanic race. In fairness to Sandino, it should also be stressed that a strong recognition of ethnic identity might well have damaged the cause of national liberation.

From the dawn of his struggle in 1927, Sandino called for the defense of the Indo-Hispanic race and reiterated that call until the end.[34] Thus, for example in 1933, following the departure of the Marines, he returned to the theme of Central American unity issuing a proclamation signed by "the Indo-Hispanic citizen General Augusto C. Sandino: The spiritual vibration of *la Raza Indo-Hispana* at this time revolves around the Autonomist Army of Central America in order to save its racial dignity. . . ."[35]

Alejandro Bendaña has argued in his recent study *La Mística de Sandino* that Sandino's *indohispanismo*,

> . . . nace de un reconocimiento de la hermandad y solidaridad impuestas por la historia, y por los estragos del colonialismo presente y pasado; es un llamado a la fraternidad humana . . . fue parte de la sustentación cultural de la lucha política . . . [Bendaña 1994:98–99]

Bendaña further argues in defense of *indohispanismo* and against my interpretation of Sandino's lack of understanding of the *Comunidades Indígenas* that "*El compromiso de Sandino con la auto-gestión comunitaria y carácter social de la propiedad . . . abarca valores y formas organizativas compatibles con la afirmación y defensa de la identidad étnica*" (Bendaña 1994:99).[36]

It is important not to confuse Sandino's heroic efforts on behalf of national liberation with the putative emancipatory nature of Sandino's *indohispanismo*. Sandino's *indohispanismo* was elastic enough to include Spaniards and Indians and any questioning of the primordial value of *mestizaje* threatened that racial unity in the face of Anglo-Saxon imperialism. Moreover, this discourse surely did help combat some of the racist opprobrium against darker-skinned Central American artisans and peasants. Similarly, the blurring of ethnic boundaries among Sandino's social bases of support undoubtedly prevented in 1934 the kind of anti-indigenous repression that had scorched the Salvadoran countryside two years earlier.

Nevertheless, it is important to recognize the political and cultural cost of his project. One part of the cost was surely unintended: the political disenfranchisement of the *Comunidades* that accompanied the crippling of the Conservative party. Although Sandino's struggle against the US intervention momentarily dealt a powerful blow against the bipolar world of Nicaraguan politics, it mainly undermined the Conservative party. In so doing he helped to produce the political eclipse of the Conservative *caudillo* Emiliano Chamorro, who by 1934 would lose a senatorial election in Matagalpa, the Conservative's impenetrable bastion. The degree to which the Indians had identified with Chamorro can be glimpsed in a Marine report in 1928 that claimed that the Jinotegan Indians " . . . worship only one God and that one is Chamorro. . . ."[37] And this *Chamorrista* identification, in turn, was keyed to manipulation of the political system in defense of indigenous communal objectives.[38] Along with Chamorro's defeat those "*indios emilianistas*" lost their position as a key fixture of the Nicaraguan political landscape, consequently losing their only available means of defense. Although Sandino was not directly responsible for that outcome, he made no effort to recast the disintegrating Indian-Chamorro alliance.

Sandino's lack of interest in the *Comunidades* derived, in part, from their traditional identification with Emiliano Chamorro, a classic *vendepatria* in his eyes. Regardless of the political context, Sandino did not recognize the independent existence and rights of the *Comunidades Indígenas* in the very mountains where he battled against the Marines. Moreover his failure to support the *Comunidades* was particularly grievous in that unique conjuncture where indigenous groups were in a position to rebound from decades of political, cultural, and economic losses.

Sandino provided a brilliant, dramatic symbol of anti-imperialist valor to the Central American Left and to the people it strove to represent. Yet his refusal to engage the indigenous communities also formed part of Sandino's legacy and a failure to recognize that area of silence in his discourse only covers up yet another land mine on the road to emancipatory politics in Central America.

Gender and *Mestizaje*

Sandino's *indohispanismo* represented, in part, the culmination of the Central Americanist search for an anti-imperial symbol. That symbol, the "*raza indohispana*," emerged not only as an aspect of the anti-imperialist struggle but also as a product of the disintegration and neglect of the indigenous communities. Thus, for example in response to European scientific racism, the unionist leader Salvador Mendieta developed a method for "constructive miscegenation" that effectively excluded indigenous males.[39]

Mendieta (1919) prescribed to "Central American parents" the proper physical characteristics for a prospective "pure Indian" daughter-in-law: "should have a straight and wide back, prominent breasts and well formed hips as a vital receptacle for future healthy and strong men and women, full of intense vitality." Less radical strands of Liberalism shared Mendieta's concern with the biological aspects of the Indo-Hispanic race. Thus, for example in 1943, a Liberal *Somocista* senator argued against Chinese immigration on the grounds that "Nicaraguan women by procreating children with the Chinese will degenerate the *indolatino* race of which we Nicaraguans are very, very proud."[40] Mendieta's focus on constructive miscegenation was significant in that the discourse of *mestizaje* built directly upon contradictory gendered images of Indians. Within the anti-imperial resistance, the Indo-Hispanic race was painted in virile images of prehispanic Indian warriors. Yet simultaneously, the new race evolved out of the "feminization" of indigenous males.

The feminization of indigenous males was a direct consequence of the violent subjection of the Indians – land evictions, military recruitment and forced labor on the coffee plantations – that intensified during the 1910s and 1920s. Moreover partisan violence and the authoritarian structure of village government and politics contributed greatly toward creating and projecting this frightened, effeminate image of the Indians. Consider the anti-*Chamorrista* gloss on the 1924 campaign and electoral violence:

La fuerza del chamorrismo descansa aquí en la masa indígena y analfabeta que con muy poco tiene para amiedarse. No obstante, con esa clase de elementos ganó en Matagalpa la elección el chamorrismo, lo cual prueba hasta la evidencia que no ha existido la imposición gubernativa que se quiere hacer aparecer a toda trance.[41]

The text points to the place of the Indian in *ladino* political logic: given that the Indian was, by nature, fearful and since Indians voted overwhelmingly for Chamorro, therefore the government could not have used force to swing the Indian vote. The highlands Indians were caught at the heart of this vicious logical construction. *Ladinos* possessed an essentialized view of the Indians as "naturally timid of authority" (the *ladinos* harped on the effeminate characteristics of contemporary as opposed to pre-Columbian Indians). Even Bartolomé Martínez, one of the few politicians who had close relations with the Matagalpan Indians, commented in a letter in 1912 to Emiliano Chamorro: "*todo el mundo sabe que esa casta es muy pusilánime. ... *"[42] Similarly, the collective yet hierarchical nature of indigenous organization (to control the *capitanes de cañada* appeared to control the indigenous vote) fostered a view of the Indians as major impediments to effective electoral democracy.

The violent subjection of the Indians during the first decades of the century had solidified an effeminate image that contrasted with the masculine *mestizos*, inheritors of virile pre-Columbian indigenous blood, genetically apt for a democratic society. Poets and intellectuals expressed such an image frequently during the 1930s and 1940s.[43] Albino Román, in 1937, for example issued the following patriotic appeal:

... estamos unidos por el lazo de la sangre resuelta y valerosa, la española; reacia, indómita, y dispuesta a sacrificarlo todo para la patria, esa es la [sangre] india, compañeros, la raza sin mas escudo que sus pechos no cedía un palmo de tierra sin una tumba española; una sangre heróica corre por nuestras venas. [Román 1938:44][44]

In this vision, indigenous women transmitted the heroic, pre-Columbian blood into the Indo-Hispanic race. Indigenous women in Nicaragua, as elsewhere, were also bearers of ethnic emblems and endogamy was key to ethnic reproduction. Strict indigenous patriarchal limitations on indigenous female sexuality – including arranged marriages until the 1950s in Matagalpa – would, to some degree, thwart the biological *mestizaje* that Mendieta advocated as the foundation for Central American nationhood.

Mendieta's plan for constructive miscegenation thus went to the heart of the problem of how to create the ethnic homogeneity that would unify a Central America capable of withstanding North American imperialism. The Indian communities would have to be merged into the nation through an attack on indigenous patriarchy (an attack involving the feminization of indigenous males) and the appropriation of indigenous female sexuality by the makers of the new Central American race.

The wall of indigenous patriarchy not only had contributed to internal tensions but also had blocked the vision of sympathetic outsiders. Thus, for example, a peasant leader from western Honduras claimed that her Lenca Indian neighbors in the 1940s practiced incest with the father exercising "his patriarchal right by deflowering his daughters." Similarly, a progressive Nicaraguan journalist visiting Sandino's camp in the Miskitú zone of Bocay, claimed that the practice of incest among the local Indians was "very common." Finally, *ladino* concerns about indigenous sexuality at times struck very close to home. To cite a graphic example: during the 1932 rebellion in the Indian areas of western El Salvador, *ladinos* feared a "*noche de bodas*" in which the rebels would "seize all the pretty young girls of town...and parcel them out among the revolutionary forces" (Anderson 1992:138). It is tempting to speculate – while awaiting further research – about the role that such sexual roots had on the peculiar Central American construction of the *mestizo* nation in the 1930s and 1940s. At the very least, the above examples suggest two points: first, the drama of civilization versus barbarism played itself out vividly in the minds of non-indigenous actors (including those of the left) where the images of barbarity were deeply sexual. Second, the examples suggest that the structures of indigenous patriarchy presented an extraordinarily powerful symbol to even sympathetic outsiders.[45]

Some evidence implies that indigenous groups were not immune to the sexual ideology that formed part of the discourse of *mestizaje*. For example, in the 1850s, according to Wilhelm Mahr (a German scholar and founder of Anti-Semitic philosophy), in the Indian town of Masaya, local indigenous families "rented" their daughters for ten pesos to "whites," (but specifically not to people of African descent) on the condition that the off-spring be returned to the communities to participate in the family labor force (Mahr 1864:264). The racial connotations in Mahr's account are striking: some Indians apparently were committed to a policy of whitening their population.

There is some circumstantial evidence to support Mahr's narrative. First there are evident ambivalences in Monimboseño racial attitudes. In particular, until quite recently, *barrio* residents referred scornfully and ironically to *ladinos* of all complexions as "*mulatos.*" Second, several interviews express negative views of indigenous phenotypes. Third, the practice of renting daughters fits within the general contours of 20th-century practices whereby impoverished rural Nicaraguans gave away, lent, or even sold their children to wealthier families (preferably but not exclusively to kin and not primarily for sexual favors).[46]

Moreover, according to Augustín Gamboa, a local intellectual in Monimbó, this practice had a special, degrading twist among the indigenous families of Masaya during the depression years. José María Moncada, president from 1928 to 1932, built a mansion near Lake Masaya, to which some Monimboseños out of desperation sent their daughters:

> ...Monimbó comenzó a sentir hambre...los inviernos fueron secos y sembraron la aridez dentro de sus tierras, algunos jefes de familia vendieron lo poco que tenían otros no tenían nada que vender mas que la virginidad de sus hijas y muchas niñas de delicados cuerpos fueron acariciadas por las asquerosas manos del inmoral Presidente de Nicaragua, José María Moncada....[47]

Augustín Gamboa's recounting of Moncada's depravity receives some backing from oral testimony. There seems little doubt that the practice of renting daughters to non-Indians for sex was not uncommon. Moreover, in Gamboa's narrative and interviews with other Monimboseños, the image of the coerced, deflowered virgins directly signalled the repetition of conquest relations and symbolized the emergence of *mestizaje* in the indigenous *barrio*. Although it is difficult to evaluate either how widespread the practice of prostituting daughters was or the degree of Moncada's involvement, there is no doubt that the discussion of biological *mestizaje* does touch a communal nerve in Monimbó.

The reproduction of the discourse of the Indo-Hispanic race in an indigenous community like Monimbó has posed thorny questions. We have Mahr's report that the Indians actually sought to whiten their race. Similarly, elements of contemporary scholarly and political discourse suggest that the forging of the Indo-Hispanic race has been a natural, voluntary process. Thus the anthropologist, Claudio Esteva Fabregat (1988:185), wrote of the colonial period,

> ...dada una fácil relación sexual no era extraño que dichas indias preferirían en muchos casos a quienes vencían en estas batallas aparte de la pura satisfacción sexual la compensación simbólica de unirse con un vencedor.[48]

Esteva Fabregat's analysis, at the least, does suggest how felicitous is the notion of *mestizaje* for reading indigenous males, coercion, violence and resistance out of the historical record.

The local intellectual Gamboa also makes reference to this particular form of racial ideological domination. He recalls how a beautiful woman during his youth spurned all Monimboseño suitors. Indeed, she made it clear that she sought to better her "race." With great vulgarity she turned away the Indian suitors: "*este cusuco no es para ningún indio.*" She actively sought liaisons with light-skinned *ladinos* (*mulatos* in Monimboseño parlance). The tale, however, has a moralistic ending: the woman, rejected by her lovers, returned to the *barrio*. When she attempted to find a relationship, the Monimboseños scorned her, throwing back in her face her original, vulgar declaration.

The above anecdote, substantiated in interviews, reflects the relative success of the discourse of *mestizaje*.[49] Earlier we saw how the violence exercised against indigenous males helped create a portrait of their feminization. In a sense, these tales from Monimbó form a counterpart of that emasculinization in that they make female sexuality a principal site of anxiety and contention. Whether or not the anecdote is an accurate reflection of historical reality, its plausibility for a Monimboseño audience signals the depths of male anxiety about miscegenation and the pervasiveness of the kind of internalization of dominant racial norms that Mahr reported in the 1850s. While awaiting further research, we can tentatively conclude that the construction of the Indo-Hispanic race had some gnarled sexual roots and that it was far from a harmonious affair.

Mestizaje after Sandino

A discourse of *mestizaje* became widely accepted in Central America shortly after it had become the official ideology of post-revolutionary Mexico. Alan Knight's analysis of *indigenismo* and *mestizaje* reveals the degree to which that discourse valorized the indigenous contribution to "*lo indigena*" in Mexican culture and recognized the existence and legitimacy of indigenous cultures. Knight (1990) outlines its fundamentally racist assumptions, but at the same time underscores how *indigenismo* has helped to break down pre-existing caste-like barriers. During the immediate post-revolutionary period, contemporary indigenous peoples were thus celebrated at an ideological level, despite the persistence of prejudice and social inequality. Knight cogently summarized the paradox in the following terms: "Official ideology proclaims their worth, even their superiority...but sociopolitical circumstances repeatedly display the reality of prejudice" (1990:101).

Although formally similar to the Mexican discourse in its praise of the historic contribution of Indians to the nation, the middle isthmus version of *mestizaje* effaced indigenous communities from modern history with the violent bursts and silent fumes of ethnocide. Unlike in Mexico, by 1940 official and popular discourse in El Salvador, Honduras, and Nicaragua not only described their societies as *mestizo*, but moreover posited that Indians had ceased to exist at some time lost in the deepest recesses of historical memory. Virtually identical statements about Honduras and El Salvador were penned in the 1940s as the following example: "The Nicaraguan people, formed during colonial times, was a product of *mestizaje*. In reality, there is no other Central American country where this process has been realized to the same degree. Practically speaking, the Indian element has ceased to exist" (Editorial 1968:1).[50]

This reactionary texture of *mestizaje* derived, in large part, from the defeats suffered by the Central American popular movements. The Guatemalan popular uprising in 1920–21, Sandino in 1927–34, El Salvador in 1932, the Honduran labor movement of the 1920s, and a 1925 Lenca uprising tied to a *caudillo* all went down to bitter defeat.

I would suggest, however, that the radically distinct development of the discourses of *mestizaje* in Central America and in Mexico also had much to do with their different political cultures, and not only the difference that a successful revolution could make. In particular, Florencia Mallon and Peter Guardino's work on Mexico points to a vibrant 19th-century political tradition of popular liberalism whose relative strength and geographical diversity marked it off dramatically from an analogous current in Central American liberalism. Moreover, Mexican popular liberalism blurred the lines between municipal and indigenous lands and political autonomy in ways that at times favored the latter. In Central America, the lack of a rural variant of popular liberalism allowed the state to drive a wedge between notions of citizenship and local, indigenous rights. These broad ideological and political contours, in turn, affected the way in which political actors understood the local cultures within which they operated. In this sense, a comparison between the levels of local knowledge of Farabundo Martí, Sandino and Zapata would be interesting. Zapata worked and fought with the peasants of his native Morelos, whereas Martí and Sandino had to organize and fight on unfamiliar ground.

Sandino left a legacy in Nicaragua where progressives sought to extend equal citizenship to all, but without recognizing how problematic that concept had been to the indigenous communities of the isthmus. Yet even the most authoritarian regimes that arose following the defeat of the region's popular movements would have to address the workers and peasants in the language of citizenship and equal rights. At the same time, however, the progressives who survived the years of reaction or those who emerged in subsequent generations could not resolve a fundamental dilemma of Latin American liberalism: the democratic demand for equal rights for citizens versus the recognition of special rights and autonomy for indigenous peoples.[51]

The Central American left has recognized neither the complexity of indigenous memory nor the 20th-century pain caused by the birth of the Indo-Hispanic race. Thus, the left has failed in its efforts to forge popular alliances across both visible ethnic divides and across those that have been camouflaged by the discourse of *mestizaje*.

Politics and Memories: Concluding Notes

Some insight into the left's failure to resolve the dilemmas of liberalism can be gleaned from an analysis of the Sandinistas' attempts to understand the local culture and social memories of those rural subjects they sought to represent. At one extreme, the Sandinistas have had great political success in the formerly indigenous villages of Yúcul and Uluse in the department of Matagalpa. Both of those communities experienced a radical process of primitive accumulation in the early part of the century that effectively enclosed the villages within coffee plantations. In the case of Yúcul, the generations that grew up following the expropriation of 1916 as *colonos* on the plantation of José Vita forgot about the indigenous identity of those who had lost the battle for the land. Between 1963 and 1965, descendants of those Indians who had lost the land organized a union and fought successfully for decent labor conditions and for land.

The labor struggle resuscitated the *memory of primitive accumulation*, but was cut off from its indigenous roots, and thus placed in the remote past: "*antes de que la cogiera Vita toda la tierra era libre para todos los indios*."[52] By using "primitive accumulation" I am suggesting that a social memory can only be understood with reference to real historical processes. More importantly the term is useful because it may refer to several processes of proletarianization ranging from land exporpriation to other forms of extra-market coercion. In Yúcul, in particular, the memory of accumulation formed a key aspect of the mobilization process in the 1960s precisely because it could be condensed into one moment, or one story, far more easily than other forms of economic, political, or cultural domination. That memory provided not only a dramatic reference point, but moreover a diaphanous vision of good and evil, so powerful that whoever shared the memory had to recognize the justice of the cause.

The memory of accumulation in Yúcul and Uluse has been interwoven with a memory of *mestizaje* that refers directly to indigenous ancestors, but recognizes a fundamental cultural transformation that occurred between the distant past and the present. Yuculeños could recognize the indigenous character of their grandparents' generation, while attributing to themselves a distinct identity.

Along with the creation of a memory of primitive accumulation there developed an ambiguous identity of the Yuculeños, as autochthonous, but not Indians. It is that ambiguous identity in Yúcul and Uluse that favored their incorporation into union and revolutionary movements: rebels of indigenous ancestry but Nicaraguans like everyone else. One union leader alluded to the historical roots of current political practice: "*Yúcul siempre ha sido revolucionario. Durante la gran rebelión indígena de 1881, Yúcul desempeñó un papel importantísimo, la baluarte de la rebelión. Aquí el Frente siempre tuvo un gran apoyo.*"[53]

In Yúcul, then, the ambiguous identity that emerged from the narrative of primitive accumulation and *mestizaje* could be easily assimilated into the discourse of revolutionary nationalism. However, in indigenous communities such as Samulalí, less than twenty kilometers away from Yúcul, the *Frente Sandinista* never obtained significant political support. That failure derived in part from the fact that the local social memory of primitive accumulation and the local, related identities were not easily assimilated into the narrative of revolutionary nationalism. An important reason why the local memory did not fit well was its level of complexity.

We glimpsed in the opening paragraph of this article the Indians' principal memory of primitive accumulation: the *Guardia Nacional*'s march into the *cañadas* to uproot the Indians' cotton bushes which coincided with the demise of indigenous weaving. The destruction of a subsistence economy was the strongest social memory in Matagalpa in part because the elite expropriation of communal land, such as its loss of Yúcul, had been partial and largely terminated by the late 1920s. Moreover, the Indian *caciques* were largely responsible for the continued loss of land through the privatization of the "*mejoras*" (improvements such as coffee bushes, fruit trees, and dwellings).

Unlike the Yuculeño memory of accumulation, the destruction of the cotton bushes offered an ambiguous, rather than a clear-cut moral. The *Guardia*'s action pushed the Indians further into the clutches of the cash economy and away from the subsistence bases (however tenuous and partial) of their previous economic existence. Yet, at the same time, another message was captured in the words of a *Guardia* officer who made the statement "*eso de andar mantiado es cosa de indios,*" as if they must move beyond Indian-ness. Although the *Guardia* forced them further into the cash economy it also "helped" to push them into a "non-Indian" category. In other words, the key memory of primitive accumulation, at the same time a memory of *mestizaje*, had both negative and vaguely positive consequences for the survivors.

Taken together with similar assaults on their culture during the same period, the memory of these events also demonstrated the bankruptcy of the indigenous leadership. The memories of the loss of *mantiado* dress, the impotent leadership, and the endless moments of humility before the *ladinos* incorporated an important element of shame. Ann Norton (1993:458–9) argues that shame, that is a sense of complicity with one's own oppressors, must be absent from local memory for it to be absorbed into a nationalist narrative. In Matagalpa such memories have been conditioned by those political compromises necessary for the limited reproduction of cultural autonomy and indigenous identity. And it is the element of complicity and shame interwoven into the narrative of indigenous resistance that has proved incompatible with the discourse of *mestizaje* and revolutionary nationalism. To the nationalists, the stench of colonial complicity relegates that indigenous memory to a recycling bin marked "artifacts of the past."

This tension between national narrative and local memory has much to do with the cultural gulf between revolutionary militants and indigenous peasants.[54] The militants' lack of access to local, ethnically-salient memories of complicity with oppression thwarted *Sandinista* efforts to bring revolutionary change to the indigenous *cañadas*. Yet the Revolution of 1979 did bring about a radical change in peasant consciousness in Matagalpa. Thus, for example, an indigenous leader, who had been an anti-*Sandinista* since he had learned of their existence commented: "*En 1979 nos despertamos y nunca mas nos va a engañar ningún rico!*"[55] Remarkably he did not attribute any significant role to the *Frente Sandinista* in the awakening of the indigenous peasantry in 1979. He could marginalize the *Frente* from the revolutionary process because they had such difficulty in recognizing indigenous identity in Matagalpa. At the same time, the revolutionary vanguard could not imagine a radical change in peasant consciousness without being able to assume responsibility and represent the subjects of that transformation. The *Frente Sandinista* was thus incapable of understanding both the limitations and extent of their great achievement: the creation of conditions for radical change in the countryside through the destruction of the Somoza regime. The short statement by the indigenous leader reveals the tension between nationalist discourse and local memory. At the national level, July 19, 1979 represented liberation from a dictatorial regime and United States imperialism, the victory of all who supported the *Frente Sandinista*. Yet in a dirt-poor indigenous village, people could experience a sense of liberation without any of its national references. The historic antagonists of both the Indians of Matagalpa and the *Frente Sandinista* have artfully exploited that deep misunderstanding with tragic consequences for all Nicaraguans.

NOTES

1   Interview with Doña Carmelina Lopez, Salinas, Boaco, January 1992.

2   The term "Indian" used here is, to some degree, locally specific; it is employed in those areas where the population divides itself up into *ladinos* and Indians. That division, in turn, typically has been based upon fictive common descent and upon membership in *Comunidades Indigenas*. Those corporate organizations, enjoying varying degrees of rights to land and to political autonomy, have been under constant legal, political, and economic attack since the 1870s.

3   Beaulac to the Secretary of State, March 18, 1932, National Archives, US State Department, RG 57, 817.00/7373.

4   In the 1928 elections won by the Liberals with 57.4% of the national vote, over 80% of the indigenous vote in Matagalpa went Conservative. Electoral percentages were calculated based on returns published by the Consejo Nacional de Elecciones, Managua, 1929, and by the American Electoral Mission in the U.S. State Department, 817.00/6298. The Conservatives received 65% of the Matagalpa departmental vote. They also received 59.3% of their total votes from the six departments with significant indigenous populations, which accounted for only 43% of the registered voters.

5   Les Field (1994) provides a very able discussion of such trends. The political discourse of *mestizaje* was particularly apparent in the May 1995 "*Encuentro Interdisciplinario Sobre la Identidad y la Nación*," in Managua, in which the majority of the talks glorified *mestizaje* as the core of the Nicaraguan nation. The Instituto de Historia de Nicaragua will soon publish a volume of the conference proceedings.

6   At a national level, without at all discarding its late colonial mixed-race meaning, *ladino* continued to mean non-Indian, very broadly defined. Under the impact of coffee and liberalism, the use of *ladino* in opposition to Indian became a dominant meaning in coffee zones of Salvador, Nicaragua and in western Honduras. This sharpened the locally salient meaning of ladino implicitly referred to in the existence of a "*ladino race*." Indeed the civil and ecclesiastical birth records in the Central Highlands of Nicaragua at the turn of the century list members of the "*casta indígena*" and the "*casta ladina*." Moreover, the birth records treated "*ladino*" as a racial category (roughly equivalent to white) when

they employed the word *"mestizo"* to describe the offspring of an *indígena* and a *ladino*.

7 For an excellent discussion of colonial racial categories see Lutz (1994).

8 Another meaning, albeit minor and subsidiary, also emerged during the mid-18th century when *ladino* at times was used interchangeably with *mulatto*, which in turn ceased to refer exclusively to the offspring of blacks and whites. Although the conflation of *criollo/ladino/mulatto* might have been congruent with peninsular Spanish prejudices that viewed the *criollos* as people of dubious origin, it is also possible that this subsidiary meaning of *ladino* – especially its interchangeability with *mulatto* – emerged and circulated among the indigenous population as when the Indians of Monimbó referred to the mayor of Masaya as the *"alcalde mulato."*

9 Thus, for example, the census instructions for Honduras in 1887 suggested the exclusive use of *ladino*, *"a fin de avatar confusión está dividida en ladinos, bajo cuya denominación se comprende a todos los individuos de cualquier raza y en indígenas del pais."* Special thanks to Darío Euraque for this reference.

10 Based on a revision of the municipal records of Boaco and Camoapa in the department of Boaco for the 1890s.

11 Thus, for example, in *Historia de Diriamba* (1920:78) the Nicaraguan Juan M. Mendoza uses *ladino* as synonymous with white oligarch. Simultaneously Salvador Mendieta from the same town and class as Mendoza used the term to indicate the racial mixture of Indians, blacks, and Spaniards in *La Enfermedad de Centroamérica* (1919:56).

12 Although written by an Italian, there is little doubt that President Zelaya or at least his immediate subordinates approved its contents. The author wrote in a note to the reader: *"Este libro está puesto bajo la protección del Exmo Señor General Don J. Santos Zelaya, Presidente del Estado de Nicaragua."*

13 On Armijo's acquisition of cultural capital as an Indian expert, see Gould (n.d.).

14 *El Comercio* 9 April 1919; 9 May 1922; *La República* 26 January, 1919; *El Eco Nacional* 29 January 1919; *El Figaro* 22 January 1919; Charles Curtis to the Secretary of State, 28 January 1919, USNA, RG 57, 817.00/78.

15 *El Comercio* 9 April, 1919; Interview with Panflio Narváez, Nindirí 1990.

16 Two other protests were against a non-Sutiavan priest running a school and against the Church's removal of a sacred image. For a more detailed discussion, see Gould (1990a).

17 For a detailed account of these struggles, see Gould (n.d.) *El Mito de Nicaragua Mestiza y la Resistencia Indigena*, Editorial de la Universidad de Costa Rica, Chapter 4, "Los Indígenas de Masaya, Las Luchas Populares, y el Discurso Ladino, 1919–1922." (forthcoming).

18 Curiously, from this period onward Monimbó is identified as the *"cuna del folklor nacional,"* a key symbol of national *mestizaje*. Some Monimboseños today identify themselves as *"mestizos"* in contradistinction to other Nicaraguans.

19 See for example the following USMC report, National Archives, RG 127, Entry 209, Box 2, Informe de 24 de junio 1928, Jinotega: "Unverified information that the Captain Pablo Muñoz has organized a group of bandits in the Valley of Samulalí, jurisdiction of Matagalpa. He has four officers and about 12 men and they have a total of about 30 rifles."

20 See the list of foreign coffee plantation owners in, National Archives, USMC, RG 127, E198, Box 7. The plantations were considered to be worth an average of nine thousand dollars.

21 Letter from Fred Fley to Major Erskine, 6 September 1927, USMC, National Archives, RG 127, E220, Box 6.

22 Letter from Fley to the British Consul, 16 May 1928, in National Archives, USMC, RG 127, E 220, #6.

23 *Proceso Legal*, *"Neil Hawkins demanda a Catarino Lopez otros por desocupación de terreno de 'La Escocia.'"* 1925–1935. Juzgado Civil, Matagalpa. The protest of the leaders of the *Comunidad* of Muy Muy was published in *El Eco Nacional*, 20 June 1929. Neil Hawkins, a U.S. citizen attempted to evict twenty-nine families, who belonged to the *Comunidad Indígena* of Muy Muy. He sued the "squatters" who received the legal backing of the *Comunidad Indígena*. For four years, Hawkins attempted unsuccessfully to evict the indigenous families. It is probable that the combination of Sandinista incursions and the public protest of the *Comunidad* in 1929 convinced Hawkins to

accept a tactical defeat. In 1935, Hawkins would emerge victorious thanks to the weakness of the Conservative *Comunidad* operating in a conjuncture dominated by Liberals, with no balance provided by a Sandino.

24 See Gould (n.d.), Chapter 5, "Los Indígenas del norte y la Lucha de Sandino," 1926–1933.

25 See *Nueva Prensa* and *La Noticia*, 28 June 1934.

26 Report by Major Fred Cruse, 1 July 1930, ULNA, US State Department, 817.00/6736.

27 Interview with Ramón Martínez, Matagalpa, February 1990.

28 Mathew Hanna to the Secretary of State Managua, 6 June 1930, US State, 817.00/6673.

29 Report from Rigoberto Reyes to the President of the Republic. 30 September 1928, National Archives, RG 127, E 220 Caja 7. The armed groups attempted to thwart the elections. It is unclear whether they were pro-Sandinista groups or Conservatives who had lost their ties with the national party, which did not call for abstention.

30 23 February 1928, Commanding Officer, Fifth Regiment to the Brigade Commander, USMC, National Archives, RG 127, E 220, Box 2. On the numerous military contacts in the indigenous zone, see Michael Schroeder (1993).

31 Interview with Sandino, in 1933, in de Belausteguigoitia (1985:192).

32 Perhaps Sandino merely wanted to simplify the definition of "Indian" for a foreign journalist. But Belausteguigoitia did recognize that the two Indians were from the Atlantic Coast.

33 Haya de la Torre's indo-american vision as translated through Esteban Pavletich arguably influenced Sandino's thought more than did the Unionists.

34 Letter to Froylán Turcios, 20 September 1927, in "*El Pensamiento Vivo*," T. I, p. 151.

35 "*Suprema Proclama de Union Centroamerica*," 16 August 1933, in "*El Pensamiento Vivo*," T. II, P. 349.

36 Bendaña also defends Sandino from my charge of silence on the indigenous question and attacks this author with the same arguments with which I contextualized Sandino's position in a paper entitled "*Nicaragua: la nación indohispana*," presented at the *Semanario Balance Histórico del Estado-Nación en Centroamérica*, FLACSO, San Salvador, 22–24 November, 1993.

37 Julian Frisbie to Major H. Schmidt, Jinotega, July 13, 1928. National Archives, U.S. Marine Corps, RA 127 E220, box 11. Copy kindly provided by Michael Schroeder.

38 Thus, for example, the Portillo group attempted to spread the notion that Chamorro and B. Martínez "*son los principales que venden terreno y todavía quieren volver a la presidencia.*" Although some Matagalpan indigenous land had been lost to lawyers during the administrations of Emiliano and Diego Chamorro (1917–1923), the government also granted 3600 hectares of land to the *Comunidad*. Thus the propaganda about land was less than successful.

39 Stepan (1991:137) writes:

> *Especially damaging to Latin American self-images was the scientific view of racial hybridization, universally condemned by biologists abroad as a cause of Latin American degeneration... They (intellectuals) asked whether racial mixture was always a sign of inferiority... whether hybridization could not have more positive biological-social meanings, whether it should be encouraged as a biological process of nation formation, allowing the emergence of a national homogenous type through a process of racial fusion.*

40 26 August, 1943, *La Prensa*. On Mexico, see Alan Knight (1990). On El Salvadoran Sinophobia see Hector Perez-Brignoli (1932).

41 *Cultura Setentrional* III:43, October 1924, p. 11.

42 Bartolomé Martínez to Emiliano Chamorro, 23 February 1912 in "*Correspondencia Privada Escrita y Recebida por el Gral. Emiliano Chamorro, 1904–1929*" (*Biblioteca del Banco Central in Managua*). Miguel Gobat facilitated this letter.

43 According to Pagden (1989) this elite use of the pre-Columbian past was quite common even during the colonial period. He explains, however, that such a use of the past did not aid the indigenous peoples: "Their culture destroyed by the conquerors, both lay and ecclesiastical and their identity all but erased by Spanish efforts to 'civilize' them, the living Indians were ill-suited to play the role of the heirs to the Aztec Empire" (1989:75).

44 In the same publication, D. René Vivas (1938:46) wrote, "*...los descendientes de Nicarao*

y Dirangen que llevan en su venas la sangre . . . in-dómita del nativo. . ."

45   On *mestizaje* and sexuality see Smith's (n.d.) pioneering article, "The Symbolics of Blood" and Kutzinski's (1993) book. She writes that *mestizaje* at once "celebrates racial diversity while disavowing troubling social reali-ties . . . this evasiveness (about race) which im-plicitly extends to issues of gender and sexuality . . . is constitutive of what I term the discourse of *mestizaje* that nourishes Cuban nationalism . . ." In analyzing a poem by Guil-lén, she remarks that *"mestizaje* is a trope for racial mixing without female participation." (p. 172)

46   See for example Elizabeth Dore, "Property, Marriage, and Sexuality in Rural Nicaragua."

47   Augustín Gamboa, "Monimbó." Unedited manuscript graciously provided by his son, Flavio Gamboa. The manuscript was written during the 1980s, although based on notes taken down earlier. The Gamboa family was one of the wealthier families of Monimbó.

48   Similarly he wrote (1988:129) *"las indias que no se les resistían y que se ofrecian libremente y con gusto a sus requerimientos."*

49   Interviews with Isabela Pérez, Pedro Namendi and Humberto Ortiz, Monimbó, Masaya (April–May 1995).

50   Carlos Pereyra (1940:10) wrote about El Salva-dor: *"Su composición étnica se basa en un mesti-zaje muy avanzado de elementos indígenas y españoles."* On Honduras, see the fascinating paper by Darío Euraque (1994) in which he suggests that the discourse of *mestizaje* evolved in opposition to the Caribbean and Garífuna presence on the North Coast in the context of U.S. intervention.

51   The dilemma is not limited to Latin American liberalism. On the roots of the problem in lib-eral thought and its relation to contemporary issues of multi-culturalism, see Charles Taylor (n.d.).

52   Interview with Urbano Pérez, Yúcul, Mata-galpa, 1990.

53   Interview with union leader who asked for ano-nymity, Yúcul, 1990.

54   I discuss this gulf (Gould 1990b) at some length in connection with the struggles of *mes-tizo* peasants in Chinandega. See in particular chapters eight and nine.

55   Interview with Santos Pérez (Susulí, Mata-galpa, 1990).

REFERENCES CITED

Anderson, Thomas
1992   Matanza. Wllimantic Court: Curbstone Press
Armijo, Modesto
1908/09 Redención. 2(5). León.
Bendaña, Alejandro
1994   La Mística de Sandino. Managua: Centro de Estudios Internacionales
de Belausteguigoitia, Ramón
1985   Con Sandino en Nicaragua. Managua: Edi-torial Nueva Nicaragua.
Editorial
1968   Revista Conservadora del Pensamiento Cen-tramericano. 98.
Esteva Fabregat, Claudio
1988   El Mestizaje en Iberoamérica. Alhambra: Barcelona.
Euraque, Darío
1994   Labor Recruitment and Class Formation on the Banana Plantations of the United Fruit Co. and the Standard Fruit Co. in Honduras, 1910s–1930s. Paper presented at AHA, San Francisco, CA.
Falcinelli Graziozi, H.
1898   Guía Ilustrada del Estado de Nicaragua. Rome.
Field, Les
1994   Who are the Indians? Reconceptualizing In-digenous Identity, Resistance, and the Role of Social Science in Latin America. Latin American Research Review 29(3):237–248.
Gamboa, Augustín
n.d. Monimbó. Unedited manuscript.
Gould, Jeffrey
1990a   La Raza Rebelde: Las luchas de la comuni-dad indígena de Sutiava. Revista de Historia (Costa Rica) 21–22: 69–117.
1990b   To Lead as Equals: Rural Protest and Pol-itical Consciousness in Chinandega, Nicaragua, 1912–1979. Chapel Hill: University of North Carolina Press.
1993   Vana Ilusión: The Highlands Indians and the Myth of Nicaragua Mestiza, 1880–1925. Hispa-nica American Historical Review 73:3.

1995   Y El Buitre Respondío: La Cuestión Indí-gena en Nicaragua Occidental, 1920–1960. Mesoamérica 30:327–354.

n.d. El Mito de Nicaragua Mestiza y la Resistencia Indígena. Editorial de la Universidad de Costa Rica.

Klor de Alva, J. Jorge

1995   The Postcolonization of the (Latin) American Experience: A Reconsideration of 'Colonialism,' 'Postcolonialism,' and 'Mestizaje.' *In* After Colonialism: Imperial Histories and Postcolonial Displacements. Gyan Prakash, ed. Princeton: Princeton University Press.

Knight, Alan

1990   Racism, Revolution and Indigenismo: Mexico 1910–1940. *In* The Idea of Race in Latin America, Richard Graham, ed. Austin: University of Texas Press.

Kutzinski, Vera

1993   Sugar's Secrets: Race and the Erotics of Cuban Nationalism. Charlottesville: University of Virginia Press.

Lomnitz-Adler, Claudio

1992   Exits from the Labyrinth: Culture and Ideology in Mexican National Space. Berkeley: University of California Press.

Lutz, Christopher

1994   Santiago de Guatemala, 1541–1773: City, Caste, and the Colonial Experience. Norman: Oklahoma University Press.

Mahr, Wilhelm

1864   Reise Nach Central-Amerika. Hamburg: Otto Meisner.

Mendieta, Salvador

1919   La Enfermedad de Centro-América, Tomo II. Barcelona: Tipografia Maucci.

Mendoza, Juan M.

1920   Historia de Diriamba. Staebler: Guatemala.

Norton, Ann

1993   Ruling Memory. Political Theory 21(3).

Pagden, Anthony

1989   Identity Formation in Spanish America. *In* Colonial Identity in the Atlantic World 1500–1800. Nicholas Canny and Anthony Pagden, eds. Princeton: Princeton University Press.

Pereyra, Carlos

1940   Prologue to Rodolfo Baron Castro, La Población de El Salvador. San Salvador.

Perez-Brignoli, Hector

1932   Indios, Comunistas y Campesinos: La Rebelión de 1932 en El Salva dor. Cuadernos Agrarios 5.

Quintana, Manuel

1923   Nuestra Raza. Paz y Bien. 29 July (León).

Ramírez, Sergio, ed.

1981   Augusto C. Sandino: el Pensamiento Vivo. T. I. Managua: Editorial Nueva Nicaragua.

Román, Albino

1938   Arenga a la Juventud de Nicaragua. *In* Academia de Sociología e Historia de San Pedro Canisio. Granada: Colegio-América.

Román, José

1983   Maldito País. Managua: Ediciones la Pez y la Serpiente.

Schroeder, Michael

1993   To Defend Our Nation's Honor: Toward a Social and Cultural History of the Sandino Rebellion in Nicaragua, 1927–1934. Ph.D. dissertation, University of Michigan.

Smith, Carol

n.d. The Symbolics of Blood. Unpublished ms.

Stepan, Nancy Leys

1991   'The Hour of Eugenics': Race, Gender and Nation in Latin America. Ithaca: Cornell University Press.

Taylor, Charles

n.d. The Politics of Recognition. Working Papers of the Center of Psychosocial Studies, 51, Center for Psychosocial Studies, University of Chicago.

22

The Construction of Indigenous Suspects: Militarization and the Gendered and Ethnic Dynamics of Human Rights Abuses in Southern Mexico

Lynn Stephen

Many recent analyses of political change in Mexico offer an enthusiastic assessment of the country's transition to democracy through permitting political opposition and through the strength and variety of social movements that have come to be known as civil society. My own research reveals a fundamental contradiction in Mexico's transition to democracy: a political opening accompanied by increased militarization of Mexican society and accompanying human rights abuses. I use the tools of ethnography to analyze the gendered and ethnic patterns of militarization and torture in southern Mexico. Such patterns replay gendered and sexual stereotypes of indigenous men and women as captured in national myth and vision.

While such an analysis is useful for Mexico, it draws from and is applicable to other situations of political violence such as Northern Ireland (Aretxaga 1997; Feldman 1991), El Salvador (Binford 1996), Guatemala (Warren 1993), Sri Lanka (Daniel 1996), and the case of Hutu refugees in Tanzania (Malkki 1995). Such an analysis also provides a way of understanding the underlying

culture wars being waged to redefine nations. In Mexico, the targeting of specific indigenous populations by militaries and paramilitaries signals a crisis of representation at the state's margins in the south. Military presence in indigenous regions in Oaxaca and Chiapas (as well as in Guerrero, Hidalgo, and elsewhere) underlines the importance of local and regional movements for indigenous autonomy and rights that are at the heart of the fight to redefine Mexico as a multi-ethnic nation. The insights of anthropological analysis – particularly historical and cultural analysis – are key in clarifying the rationales that may be provided for treating some people differently than others and thus constructing them as suspects who become victims of political violence and human rights abuses. Anthropologists have a responsibility to put their analytical tools to use in telling the stories that are difficult to hear, but must be told.

If torture is unimaginable in unmediated form, unpresentable for what it is, its representation must be fit into existing, acceptable discourses: patriotism, retaliation for real or imagined past injustices, separatism, terror-

Dedicated to Dr. Martin Diskin

ism, communism, subversion, anarchy, the need to preserve the state's territorial integrity, the need to protect the nation from subversion through ethnic cleansing, the fight against crime, the war on drugs. (Nagengast 1994:120)

No state or its agencies will endorse decontextualized violence as an explicit policy tool. The cultural packaging of violence and its acceptable victims is a key ingredient in how human rights abuses come to be committed and how they are justified by states. The use of justified physical and symbolic violence by states is a time-honored cross-cultural tradition. Symbolic violence includes aggressive behavior, vehement conduct, infringement of property or dignity, the use of physical force, and the threat or dramatic portrayal of any of the above.[1] State-sponsored political violence may involve direct physical violence but may also include "actions taken or not by the state or its agents with the express intent of realizing certain social, ethnic, economic, and political goals in the realm of public affairs, especially affairs of the state or even of social life in general" (Nagengast 1994:114).

Many discussions of human rights in anthropology have focused on whether or not it is appropriate for anthropologists to impose universal definitions of human rights on particular cultures and what the consequences are of accepting culturally relevant criteria as a basis for defining human rights (Howard 1992; Messer 1993, 1995; Renteln 1990; Thompson 1997). A more relevant concern here is how dominant representations of the dangerous, the subversive, the worthless, the marginal, and the unimportant become linked to making particular groups of people susceptible to violent abuses that allow them to be treated with less than human respect and dignity (see Binford 1996; Muller-Hill 1988; Nagengast 1994:122; Taussig 1984). People who are both powerful and powerless can be viewed as dangerous and worthless, creating a range of political suspects. In each situation of human rights abuses, the key to what actually happens lies not so much in a deliberate neglect of universal human rights declarations but in particular ideological interpretations that permit and justify the use of violence

for particular ends, often political. In the case of the indigenous suspects discussed here, those groups of people who are gauged as the most vulnerable and least likely to be able to defend themselves are often the first and most intensive targets of political violence. Victims of political violence can also include leading cultural figures who are targeted for silencing and retribution. There is a range of political suspects in contemporary Mexico, from well-known politicians, journalists, and indigenous leaders to anonymous men and women. Gender and ethnicity are important aspects of the ideological justifications used to legitimate political violence. Often, such justifications have deep historical roots.

In the low-intensity war being carried on in southern Mexico, the militarization of communities and the arrest and torture of indigenous people and their construction as guerrilla suspects operate through figurations of gender and indigenous ethnicity. The scripts of current militarization indirectly replay crucial colonial and postcolonial tropes such as that of La Malinche and the Virgen of Guadalupe. Since the arrival in 1519 of Cortés and his troops in what is now Mexico, the subjugation of indigenous identity, the feminization of indigenous men through domination by other men, and the conquest of indigenous women and men through sexual assault and coercion have been standard practices of militarization (see Trexler 1995). Such practices have always been fused to military practices and are found not just in Latin America. Begoña Aretxaga, for example, describes the colonization of the female body by British soldiers and Royal Ulster Constabulary (RUC) officers in West Belfast (1997:131–136). In part, her book could easily be about southern Mexico: women required to submit to searches at military checkpoints and endure sexual comments, strip searches during interrogation, and continual threats of sexual assault.[2] The empowerment and accompanying masculinization of military and paramilitary men through feminization and sexualization of their victims is, unfortunately, a common colonial and postcolonial theme. What makes such continuing practices in Mexico interesting in the 1990s is not only their perseverance through the last 500 years, but their continued existence in a modern state that publicly maintains it is struggling to make a transition to democracy and become a multi-cultural nation. Anthropology can have a key role in lifting the veil from the cultural processes that are taken for granted within militarization.[3]

While the violation of basic rights abuses can be read in relation to conflicting ideologies and larger political and economic structures, an equally important dimension of militarization and its accompanying abuses is the pain and suffering on the part of those who are living in situations of political violence. Engaging in fieldwork during a war (an increasingly common occurrence; see Bourgois 1991) requires that anthropologists provide cultural, political, and economic explanations of what they see. It also requires that they communicate the human dimensions of daily fear, insecurity, horror, pain, and suffering – as well as the periodic hope and optimism that are a part of the everyday experiences of political violence (see Scheper-Hughes 1992 for such a perspective outside of war). In their volume on social suffering, Arthur Kleinman, Veena Das, and Margaret Lock propose that anthropologists collapse old dichotomies such as those that "separate individual from social levels of analysis, health from social problems, representation from experience, suffering from intervention" (1997:x). In their search for ways to connect social structural violence with language and pain, image and suffering, they suggest that anthropologists use a "language of dismay, disappointment, bereavement, and alarm" to get at the human experience of social suffering (1997:xi). The work represented in this article is very much in the spirit of the call issued by Kleinman, Das, and Lock.

While I was in Oaxaca doing fieldwork for this article, I learned that Martin Diskin, my close friend, mentor, and colleague, had died in Boston. I dedicate this article to the memory of Martin and to his vision of the key role that anthropologists can and should play in international human rights work and in interpreting government policy. It seemed appropriate that I was grappling with the kinds of questions we often discussed: what is the location of anthropology in relation to human rights work? What are

the boundaries and grounds of this field science? What are our obligations in terms of commenting on policy both at home and abroad? What are our ethical and moral responsibilities as anthropologists in relation to issues of social and economic justice? How do we represent the suffering and pain of others? These questions remain at this article's close.

I conducted the fieldwork for this article between 1994 and 1997, for a total of seven months. In many cases, my identity in this work was not that of a solo anthropologist, but a member of a human rights team, an international observer, or a member of a team delivering humanitarian aid. On other occasions, it was as a concerned person trying to understand the complexity of indigenous rights and the difficulties of living under militarization. These multiple identities "in the field" begged me to ask larger questions about the relationship between anthropology and human rights work. The conditions of war in Chiapas and parts of Oaxaca made it impossible to carry out long-term, continuous fieldwork in some areas. A community that was safe to work in one week became completely inaccessible the next because of a new military encampment, paramilitary activity, or a request for outsiders to stay away. My fieldwork was carried out through repeated trips that had to be undertaken as conditions permitted for the collection of testimonies, detailed observations, and discussions with humanitarian aid workers, human rights workers, doctors, and the staff of non-governmental organizations who worked in areas of political violence and conflict.

Defining the Mexican Nation: Winners and Losers

Few people would dispute that in Mexico, the indigenous population has a sustained legacy of marginalization and invisibility in the nation. While Mexico is often distinguished by having a national culture that praises the historical contributions of Indians to the country, the accompanying hegemonic discourse of *mestizaje* (mestizoness – a nationalist ideology promoting mixed Indian and Spanish blood as superior to pure Indian origins) that became official ideology in post-revolutionary

Mexico effectively marginalized indigenous peoples as political subjects (see Gould 1996:22–23; Klor de Alva 1995; Knight 1990). While mestizaje was projected by the state as the blending of Spanish and indigenous cultures, indigenous peoples increasingly read it as the erasure of indigenous culture and identity in the Mexican nation. The emergence of *indigenismo* (indigenism) as official state policy (meant to assist indigenous ethnic groups, this administrative policy consistently views indigenous peoples as objects of study and not subjects of their own history) and the creation of the National Indigenous Institute (INI) in 1948 resulted in contradictory initiatives that vacillated between legitimizing and romanticizing indigenous culture and pushing for assimilation (Hernández Castillo 1997; Hindley 1995; Stephen 1997a, 1997c). The rise of independent indigenous and peasant organizations in the 1970s began to put indigenous peoples on the map as regional and national political actors (Harvey 1998; Mejía Piñero and Sarmiento Silva 1987).

In the 1990s, the emergence of the armed rebellion of the Zapatista Army of National Liberation (EZLN) in Chiapas helped move indigenous peoples and the question of their rights to center stage in Mexican political discourse (see Collier 1994; Díaz Polanco 1997; Esteva 1996; Harvey 1994, 1998; Hernández Navarro 1997, López y Rivas 1995; Mattiace 1997; Stephen 1997a, 1997c, in press). Apart from the rebellion itself, which brought national and international attention to the plight of the indigenous peoples in the eastern part of Chiapas, the political opening created by the EZLN helped to forge a national indigenous movement.

Those currently in power in various agencies of the government and often affiliated with the PRI (the Institutional Revolutionary Party, which has been in power since the late 1920s) are struggling for their political lives. The strategy used by those currently holding political power to extend their political lives involves permitting wider electoral opposition, encouraging rhetoric that acknowledges Mexico as a multi-cultural nation, yet maintaining economic and military control over those parts of the country that question fundamental economic and political power arrangements. The Mexican state is attempting to ensure conformity to unitary national images through limiting the range of acceptable "social, political, ethnic, and national identities" (Nagengast 1994:109).

National marches, meetings, congresses, and networks have emerged and brought together for the first time a broad coalition of indigenous peoples from many parts of Mexico. Using the platform of the peace accords on indigenous rights and culture negotiated between the Mexican government and the EZLN as a launching pad, groups such as the National Indigenous Congress (CNI) have set forth an alternative vision of the Mexican nation that would grant indigenous people the right to self-determination and control over their territories and natural resources. At the same time, other sectors of Mexican society such as labor, students, farmers, and housewives unable to pay off their loans, as well as the urban poor, have also severely questioned the PRI's legitimacy.

Competing visions of Mexican nationalism that challenge the state come from indigenous movements that have recently unified to build a common identity around being Mexican and indigenous within a multi-ethnic state. The centerpiece of this indigenous nationalism is the tenet that national territorial boundaries should defend plural, self-autonomous cultural entities with roles in regional and local economic, political, and social decision making (Stephen 1997a, 1997c, in press). In their analysis, indigenous leaders sever the nation from the state, liberating the concept of *nation* for reappropriation defined from below in relation to particular regional and historical circumstances. Such a reinterpretation also allows for the simultaneous existence of a larger nation tied both to a state political structure and multiple local and regional nations with unique historical constructions. Such a multidimensional understanding of the meaning of *nation* is what confounds and frightens some representatives of the Mexican government. Mexican president Ernesto Zedillo and others accused advocates of indigenous autonomy of Balkanizing the country and of promoting a secessionist movement.

The possibility of indigenous movements (and others) mounting successful political challenges is an important part of the ongoing political transition in Mexico. Political and economic turmoil in recent years met increasing militarization of many sectors of Mexican society. The so-called war on drugs has provided the justification for the militarization of the countryside and surprise raids on urban neighborhoods with soldiers outfitted in riot-gear bursting into homes and businesses. The general model of militarization has involved the takeover of state, regional, and local police forces by the army and the creation of integrated units of police and military personnel. The entire top command of Mexico City's police was replaced with army officers, and active or retired military personnel now head police forces in 21 of Mexico's 31 states (Collier 1996). As the military becomes further integrated into coordinated police functions with local, state, and judicial police, efforts to fight drugs, street crime, and now counter-insurgency are increasingly being carried out by the same cast of characters.

In the 1990s, the militarization of Mexican society through the integration of police and army units has had its counterpart in the emergence of several armed guerilla movements. One of the most recent of these new groups is the Popular Revolutionary Army (EPR), which first appeared in June 1996, in Aguas Blancas, Guerrero, one year after 17 peasant activists were gunned down in the same spot by state police. During 1996, 1997, and 1998, the EPR carried out a series of coordinated armed attacks against the Mexican Army and public security forces in the states of Guerrero, Oaxaca, Puebla, Mexico, Tabasco, and Mexico City. Mexican military intelligence reports that the EPR now operates in 17 states in Mexico (Correa 1997:22). The EPR appears to have the most support in the states of Oaxaca and Guerrero. Unlike the EZLN, it has not achieved broad sympathy in Mexican society and was barred from the negotiating table. Its program of demands is quite similar to that of the EZLN in its focus on the needs of the urban and rural poor and democratizing the Mexican political system.

Increasingly, integrated operations carried out by various police units and the Mexican army combine what are often called "drug searches" with counter-insurgency. Many of these oper-ations are conducted in rural areas of the country, where Mexico's indigenous population of 5,282,347 (7.5 percent of the total) is located (Consejo Estatal de Población de Oaxaca 1994:1). In such operations, profiles are developed of those suspected of participating in armed illegal activity. In the two case studies of militarization and human rights abuses in Oaxaca and Chiapas (below), the suspects are primarily indigenous men and women suspected of participating in either the EZLN or the EPR.

National Stereotypes of Indigenous Peoples

These suspects exist not only in the concrete context of the cultural struggle to define the Mexican nation, but are also, writ large, in Mexican history. The history of the *mestizoization* (turning Mestizo) of the Mexican nation that now co-exists with the alternative vision of a multi-ethnic state carries both gendered and ethnic images. These images have deep roots in the Spanish conquest of Mexico and elsewhere in the Americas. These are best captured in the national figures of La Malinche and the Virgen de Guadalupe and are related to the Spanish doctrine known as purity of blood or *limpieza de sangre*.

The system of racial *castas* (castes) generated in Colonial Mexico through the doctrine of purity of blood and its constraints on marriage came to have a nominally important place in regulating the sexual practices of all Mexicans. In their zeal to maintain racial purity, Spanish officials and the Catholic Church shifted their focus from policing deviant forms of sexuality and gender to ensuring racial purity through monogamous marriage. Originally used to refer to the genealogical purity of Christians – purity from the blood of Jews, Muslims, and heretics – limpieza de sangre was used as a weapon of exclusion in Spain to eliminate those with "stains" on their ancestry from holding important political and clerical offices as well as from entering universities, religious orders, military orders, and certain guilds (Martínez 1997:749). The doctrine of limpieza de sangre was imported into New Spain. Because of the importance of limpieza de sangre and the social value on clean and honorable lineages, endogamous marriage and legitimate birth were critical. The ideology of racial purity focused on controlling the sexual behavior of women. As summed up by Martínez, "since it was primarily the woman, who through adultery, could introduce 'unclean' blood into a lineage, reproducing purity of blood necessitated guarding the chastity and premarital virginity of... women" (1997:750). Attempts to maintain racial purity involved a dichotomy between women whose inferior social status as members of the castas (including indigenous women) made them available to others and virtuous women – white women who were subject to severe family control over their sexuality (Stolke 1991:27). Historically, indigenous women have been projected as "available" to outsiders and invading military forces. Men can be also be feminized, sexualized, and thus also pacified and possessed by other men in miliary occupation.

The gendered implications of limpieza de sangre as implemented in Mexico neatly dovetail with the emergence of two national female icons: La Malinche and La Virgen de Guadalupe. These two dichotomous figures provided women with two clear archetypes for their sexuality: virgin and whore. Known as *la Chingada* (the fucked one), Doña Marina or Malinche was a Mayan princess from Tabasco who served as translator for Hernan Cortés and also bore a child he is said to have fathered.[4] This child was the first public member of the mestizo "race" (*raza*) in Mexico. Writer Octavio Paz (1961) describes La Malinche as the original chingada in a reference to her sexual violation by Cortés. Because of the influence of the writing of Paz, in Mexico La Malinche remains a sign of raped indigenous women.

The national gendered counterpart to La Malinche in Mexico is the Virgen de Guadalupe, an indigenous virgin who has become the patron saint of Mexico. According to Garibay (1967:821), on December 9, 1531, the Indian Juan Diego saw the Virgin Mary at Tepeyac, a hill northwest of Mexico City. Through a translator, Juan Diego informed the Bishop Zumárraga of what he had seen. The Bishop took action, ordering a shrine constructed at the site, named Guadalupe. This manifestation of the virgin casts an indigenous woman as a passive, virgin mother. Juan Diego, the indigenous man who found the Virgin of Guadalupe, is also rendered passive and silent by the Bishop's inability to understand Nahuatl and by the emerging dominance of the Spanish language (Garibay 1967:821, cited in Rodríguez 1994:18).

The particular characteristics of local indigenous communities and movements in zones of conflict reinforce national historical archetypes and influence specific patterns of militarization and political violence. In the examples that follow (drawn from occurrences in Oaxaca and Chiapas), I will discuss how stereotypes of indigenous people and challenges to ruling elites result in the assignation of "Other" to those who are victims of human rights abuses. Indeed, this is how "suspects" are created. At the same time, challenges to ethnic and gendered images slowly redefine these very images through the daily interactions of war.

Political Openings and Increased Militarization

An eye for unresolved yet constantly mobile contradictions is certainly useful in understanding the contemporary political scene in Mexico, which can be characterized succinctly as militarization within a political opening. The mid-term elections of July 1997 resulted in a significant change in the formal constitution of political power in Mexico. For the first time since the PRI's rise to power, it no longer dominated the legislature. There is now a multiparty legislature.

An important part of this story happened in Mexico City, where the first mayor of the world's largest city was elected. Formerly, the mayor was appointed by the president. In Mexico City and in two other major cities, opposition candidates won. Now more than half of Mexico's population is governed by opposition parties on both the left and right. These changes in the constellation of political power are certainly important. But how were they experienced by indigenous peoples in southern Mexico who are at the heart of the controversy raging over how to define the Mexican nation?

Since the Zapatista uprising in 1994, more than a third of Chiapas has been heavily militarized. The army has completed a major road project connecting previously inaccessible communities to main population centers to facilitate troop movement. The army has also built permanent installations in dozens of communities and significantly altered the local economy and culture. There are now 25,000 to 30,000 soldiers permanently installed in the Altos, Cañadas, and northern regions of the state that are Zapatista strongholds. In late summer of 1999, these estimates climbed to 60,000 soldiers. The army has taken over the state police forces of Chiapas, now augmented by thousands of federal and state "public security" and judicial police. There is approximately one soldier for every three or four inhabitants in many communities, and in 1997 there were four major military barracks, 17 smaller barracks, and 44 semi-permanent military installations in the conflict zone (CIACH/CONPAZ/SIPRO 1997:95). In August of 1999, even more roads and military installations were built.

As of January 1998, 12 different paramilitary groups operated in the conflict zone in Chiapas (Centro de Derechos Humanos "Fray Bartolomé de las Casas" A. C. 1998: 77, 80–84). In the two months prior to elections in July 1997, dozens of people were killed and wounded in local confrontations between the PRI, the PRD, and the violence caused by paramilitary forces and even federal police forces. In December 1997, 45 Tzotzil-speaking people, primarily women and children, were gunned down in a five-hour killing spree that began with the storming of the village church in Acteal where men, women, and children were kneeling in prayer. A paramilitary group including members of the local PRI, armed and trained by state police and an ex-soldier from the Mexican Army, carried out the Acteal massacre. In the spring and early summer of 1998, state security police along with the army carried out raids in four Zapatista communities that had declared themselves to have autonomous governments. In one of these raids, nine Zapatista sympathizers died.

Conditions in parts of Oaxaca are similar. The Zapotec region of Loxicha – sandwiched between the capital city and the coast – has been the site of intense militarization since August 1996, when the Popular Revolutionary Army (EPR) carried out a coordinated series of military actions. Most of the municipal government of San Agustín Loxicha was arrested between October and December 1996, as suspected members of the EPR. Arrests included the mayor, judges, and heads of many community committees. These officials were elected in 1995 according to local indigenous custom and succeeded in taking office. Previously, the community was governed by a group of indigenous *caciques* (bosses) aligned with the PRI and Antorcha Campesina, a reactionary peasant organization that serves primarily to divide independent peasant organizing efforts and has been linked to paramilitary violence. After the community government of San Agustín was jailed for almost two years, the caciques returned to power and occupied the town hall. Since the fall of 1996, more than 200 indigenous people – including teenagers – have been imprisoned after raids in which Federal Judicial Police entered houses and rounded people up while the army maintained watch. As of August 1999, 95 of them were still in jail. Several indigenous peasants have also disappeared according to an organization of families of political prisoners (Elizalde 1999). A paramilitary group has also made its presence known in the region.

In the fall of 1998, some 3,000 citizens from 20 communities from the country of San Agustín Loxicha were pushed to elect new local authorities because the officials they elected in 1995 continued to be jailed. Under intense militarization and the supervision of state police, the community elected a new mayor. This new mayor is an ex-state policeman who was implicated, according to the National Commission for Human Rights (government-run), in the murder of a community member. The army, along with the combined forces of the state and federal police, continues to maintain a base of operations in the community, where the search for EPR suspects continues (Ruiz Arrazola 1998).

Human rights workers estimate that up to 5,000 army troops are installed in the Loxicha region. A large sweep of several communities in the municipio of San Agustín Loxicha in November 1996 involved up to 500 people from the

Mexican army, Federal Judicial Police, State Police, preventative police, federal highway police, and local PRI-affiliated caciques who were dressed in the uniforms of Federal Judicial Police (*los Judiciales*). According to witnesses whose testimonies were collected by human rights workers (see below), local PRI-affiliated caciques identified who should be detained. Human rights workers also described this pattern of activity.

No one can give an exact number of soldiers in the area because access to San Agustín Loxicha is severely restricted. Interviews I conducted with 15 people from six different human rights organizations in Oaxaca city in August 1997 revealed that no human rights or NGO representatives had visited the area for at least three months. The state governor had let it be known that he would not guarantee the safety of anyone who visited the region, effectively giving the army and Federal Judicial Police free rein in the Loxicha region.

Hundreds of monolingual Zapotec women and children from the Loxicha region maintain a permanent presence in the center of Oaxaca trying to free their family members and community leaders from prison. They have also held marches and sit-ins in Mexico City in an attempt to bring attention to their cause. They have formed an organization called the Committee of Families of Political Prisoners of the Loxicha Region (see Elizalde 1999). Displaced from their communities and fearful of returning because of the presence of the army, Federal Judicial Police, Public Security Police, and the paramilitary group, their lives have been reduced to shuttling between the *zocalo* (central square), a few human rights organizations, the second-class bus station where some sleep, and the market in search of food. By 1999, they were also selling crafts to tourists and actively seeking support to help free political prisoners.

Militarization and Human Rights Abuses in Oaxaca and Chiapas

The most important aspect of the militarization of Mexican society has been the concentration of federal, state, and local police forces under the command of the army. In regions like southern Oaxaca and eastern Chiapas, a strategy of low-intensity war has emerged as the dominant model. The long-term engagement of the Mexican army in Chiapas and increasingly in Oaxaca and Guerrero has required the introduction of other forms of military control. In many parts of Chiapas where the army regularly carried out patrols on road networks they had built or improved, the Public Security Police now operates. The Public Security Police use army vehicles, weapons, and tactics but have blue uniforms instead of green. The extension of the domains of Public Security Police and Federal Judicial Police as well as their integration with the army has allowed for increased military coverage. This permits the army to concentrate operations in the most inaccessible parts of Chiapas and Oaxaca, usually by establishing permanent residence in rural indigenous communities.[5]

With roadblocks and permanent bases the army has established itself geographically in central spaces as a large and public presence. These permanent and mobile roadblocks force people to incorporate the army and police into their daily geographies of work and travel. The army has also established its presence through daily local patrols that pass through communities, on their perimeters, and in people's fields. Moreover, the army has established barracks that are within the boundaries of communities, often taking over community lands without permission.

The logic of low-intensity warfare includes replacing the army with the presence of police, encouraging paramilitary activity, and working to forge positive social relations between the army and local populations. Since the integration of police forces with the military in Chiapas, the army has engaged in what they call *labor social* (social work), which includes providing haircuts, dentistry, medicines, food, toys, and candy for local populations in communities where they have taken over land to set up their bases and where they run daily patrols. Groups who carry out this work post large banners reading: "They are the Mexican army carrying out social work to benefit the people of Chiapas." A significant number of the army commanders who lead the militarization of Chiapas have taken courses at the School of the Americas in Fort Benning, Georgia, where the "social work" approach is emphasized along with techniques of counterinsurgency and anti-narcotics interdiction.

The primary targets of these strategies of militarization are indigenous communities in Chiapas and Oaxaca. The fundamental result of the militarization of these regions is that local indigenous communities are forced to adjust to the lifestyles and consumption habits of thousands of young Mexican men in the army and police living in their midst. Perhaps of greater importance is the self-censorship and fear that has become part of people's lives. And then there are the hard-core human rights abuses including assassinations, kidnappings, torture, rape, and illegal detentions.

The Gendered and Ethnic Dimensions of Militarization and Human Rights Abuses

In the section that follows, I will draw on examples from Tzotzil, Tzeltal, and Tojolabal communities sympathetic to the Zapatistas and testimonies of prisoners from the Zapotec region of Loxicha in Oaxaca to discuss the gendered and ethnic patterns of human rights abuses that go hand-in-hand with the militarization of southern Mexico. My information from Chiapas stems from personal interviews I carried out during my fieldwork and those conducted by human rights and humanitarian aid delegations in which I participated. In Oaxaca, the basis of my analysis are the written testimonies of political prisoners and others who were illegally detained. Greater detail on the sources is provided below.

In cases investigated by Human Rights Watch/ Americas (1997) in Chiapas and documented by local human rights organizations in Oaxaca (Brigada Pro Derechos Humanos Observadores Por La Paz 1997), a majority (but not all) of the victims of torture, illegal detention, assassination, and disappearance are men. The particular patterns of torture and detention of men documented in both states often include asphyxiation with wet towels (held over people's noses while their mouths are blocked); the forcing of carbonated water into nasal passages (sometimes in combination with chile powder); asphyxiation with

plastic bags; electric shocks to the testicles, nipples, and other parts of the body; severe beating with a variety of implements including hoses, rifles, and sticks; ramming people's bodies against walls; sleep and food deprivation; and a lack of sanitary facilities forcing people to urinate and defecate in their cells. A variety of psychological tortures are also documented in individual testimonies and in documents referred to above, including threats of death by shooting, threats of being thrown out of helicopters and airplanes into the ocean, deliberate exposure to the cries of others under torture, and threats to kill, injure, and sexually violate family members. In addition, the ethnic identity of indigenous men is often a point of emphasis in their detention and torture.

Women are detained, but less frequently. The primary means of terror used against women is rape, gang rape, and the threat of rape. The ethnic identity of indigenous women is also used as a part of their belittlement in the process of threats, rapes, and attempted rapes through racially charged remarks.

Case one: The Zapotec men of Loxicha

The following section draws on testimonials given by 37 Zapotec men from ten different communities in the municipality of San Agustín Loxicha. These men were detained, tortured, and incarcerated in 1996 and 1997. Some have been released; many are still in jail. Most of these testimonies were tape-recorded by human rights workers from several Oaxacan human rights organizations in February 1997. They were recorded in the Ixcotel prison in Oaxaca as well as in the communities of La Sirena and Loma Bonita in the municipio of San Agustín Loxicha. The tapes were transcribed. A few of the testimonies were written by prisoners. The analysis that follows is based on the written transcripts and testimonies. Organizations from Oaxaca that participated in collecting the testimonies are the Regional Center for Human Rights *Bartolomé Carraso* (BARCA), the Center for Human Rights *Flor y Canto*, and the Center for Human Rights *Siete Príncipes*. These organizations also participate in a larger coalition titled *Brigada Pro Derechos Humanos Observadores Por la Paz* (Brigade for Human Rights, Observers for Peace). I have changed the names of those who provided testimonies to protect their identities.[6]

Originally I had hoped to visit the Loxicha area of Oaxaca while conducting fieldwork during the summer of 1997. Every person I consulted about this possibility, including many human rights workers who were themselves afraid to go, told me that it was impossible. Instead, I turned to interviewing workers from local human rights organizations in Oaxaca who generously shared their documents with me. I also inquired about whether it would be possible to visit the Ixcotel jail to interview prisoners. This was also discouraged at the time I was in Oaxaca, since not long before my field visit, a group of international human rights workers interviewing prisoners in Ixcotel prison were given 48 hours to leave the country. Without a special visa from the Mexican government, human rights workers reasoned that I was unlikely to be given permission even to enter the prison. Such a visa is also almost impossible to obtain, they noted, once a foreigner is already in Mexico.

In 1997 and 1998, the Mexican government discouraged visits from international human rights organizations. With the exception of the visit of the Special Rapporteur on Torture from the United Nations, Mexican government officials had given the cold shoulder to international human rights workers. In September 1997, top security officials canceled meetings with Pierre Sané, secretary general of Amnesty International; President Ernesto Zedillo declined to meet with him (Preston 1997:A16). In Oaxaca, human rights workers believed that a political blockade had been put in place to prevent public knowledge of human rights abuses. In the state of Chiapas, human rights organizations have more experience breaking such political blockades and are able to provide more protection for visiting human rights delegations. During 1998 and 1999, however, it became increasingly difficult to participate in human rights and humanitarian aid delegations.

A close reading of the testimonial statements given by Zapotec men from the municipio of San Agustín Loxicha reveals several significant aspects of their treatment related to their gendered and ethnic identities. In reading these

texts I made four observations. First, many of the Loxicha men who testified about their experiences were removed from their homes while their wives and children were present; in many cases, these family members were also threatened. Second, five of the men received sexually linked tortures, and others received threats that their wives and children would be sexually violated. Third, more than half of the men were monolingual in the Zapotec language and unable to understand most of the charges made against them or conversations held between their captors during their torture and detention. All were forced to sign blank pieces of paper that later appeared as signed confessions in Spanish despite obvious evidence of monolingualism and illiteracy. Fourth, the indigenous ethnic identities of many were belittled in the process of their detention, torture, and imprisonment as racial insults were yelled at them.

The violent methods used to remove men forcibly from their homes were designed to intimidate their families and to emphasize their incapacity as men to protect their families against the superior force of the men representing the state. The raids were carried out by integrated teams composed of several different federal and state police units along with the Mexican army. Those most consistently mentioned in the testimonies are the Federal Judicial Police (los Judiciales). Los Judiciales dress in black, carry machine guns, and are known to specialize in brute force and torture.

Many of the detentions described by Zapotec men now detained in Ixcotel prison occurred at four o'clock in the morning, when they were asleep at home with their families. Consider the testimony of Mario López Fuentes, who is 38 years old and was detained in November 1996:

> At four o'clock in the morning they arrived at my house, surprising us. They forced the door open and fired their guns just a few centimeters from where my children were sleeping. They pushed me out of bed practically naked (except for my underwear) and kicked me in the butt. They then kicked me in the back and stomped repeatedly on my left foot. . . . At this moment I saw that a lot of cars had arrived and were moving toward the

center of the community. They were ordered to throw me on the floor. After this they threw me handcuffed into a truck and continued to slap, punch, and kick me. They told me that I had guns in my house, things I don't even know about. I told them that I was barely able to get enough money together to feed my family. (Brigada Pro Derechos Humanos 1997:12–13)

The violent removal of Mario from his home, naked except for his underwear, and the firing of shots at his children is an explicitly gendered and sexual message. His nakedness sexualizes him and makes him vulnerable in a community where all adults keep their bodies covered at all times in public. He was feminized in front of his family because of his inability to protect his children from the gunshots of the judicial police. The constant physical punishment he describes at the hands of judicial police also serves to reinforce his powerlessness and the superior masculinity of judicial police.

The entire process of detention, torture, judicial hearings, and incarceration described in the testimonies of Zapotec men emphasizes their vulnerability as men. Constant physical punishment was augmented by electric shocks to the testicles in four cases and perhaps in more (reporting is probably low, given the difficulty of bringing up this subject with the strangers recording their testimonies). The application of electric shock to the testicles is not only a physical torture, but also is a gendered and sexual torture emphasizing the control judicial police have over their indigenous prisoners who are *agarrados por los cojones* (grabbed by the balls). Judicial police thus control the key symbolic and biological manifestation of the detained men's masculinity and sexuality. Once demasculinized, they become feminine equivalents, or genderless.

In his description of male paramilitary violence in Belfast, Allen Feldman describes how a targeted male victim is called a *cunt* prior to being killed. "Giving the message to" or killing is done to "a cunt" who becomes the feminized object of violence. In turn the *cunt* is understood as a passive recipient prior to and during the application of violence to the body (1991:69). Feldman's analysis can be extended to the treatment of male indigenous prisoners in contemporary Mexico.

The treatment of Zapotec prisoners as well as Feldman's descriptions of paramilitary violence involve the feminization of men and thereby their symbolic subordination as men to other men. It also involves the sexualization of men through enforced passivity. In *Sex and Conquest*, Richard Trexler documents the historical continuity of the relationship between forced sexuality and the construction of social and political identities, not only in the Conquest of the Americas but also in contemporary warfare and political violence (1995:173–180). Women and men are sexualized in war and sexually dominated by their conquerors. "Thus both the past and the present made politics by sexual force, showing the power of the sexual posture as a political gesture" (1995:178).[7] Indigenous Zapotec prisoners who are suspected of being members of the EPR and are interrogated primarily by Federal Judicial Police who come from Mexico City to carry out such work are clearly positioned in a relationship of subordination – not only through their demasculinization, but through the symbolic sexual control held over them by the police. As seen below, masculine control of Zapotec men by Federal Judicial Police is reinforced through the use of Spanish.

In two of the cases where men described being tortured with electric shocks, they were also threatened with the sexual violation of their wives and children, indicating an additional gendered dimension to their horrific treatment. Demasculinized and sexualized through their physical torture, this process is symbolically extended by putting them in the equivalent position of a cuckold (who has no rights over his wife) and is so lowly that his wife and children can be sexually violated. The testimony of Francisco Pérez Luna, who was detained in San Agustín Loxicha in November 1996, provides a startling example of this intertwined physical and psychological assault:

Then they threw me into another truck where there were other people from my community. They drove us toward San Bartolomé Loxicha and there they took me to an abandoned area where they took all of my clothes off. They bound my hands and feet and threw me on the floor. They covered my mouth with a wet towel and began to force dirty water into my mouth and nose at the same time that they administered electric shocks to my testicles and other private parts of my body that are very sensitive. They told me that they had already raped my wife and children and that they had carried all of this out on the order of the State Attorney. When I heard all this I was stricken with great sadness. (Brigada Pro Derechos Humanos 1997:13–14)

Francisco's testimony pulls together multiple levels of gendered and sexualized violence in which physical, psychological, and social masculinity are simultaneously assaulted – ultimately by the authoritarian power of the Oaxacan State Attorney's office, or so he was told. His great sadness seems to stem not just from his treatment, but from the statement (true or not) that this treatment was being carried out in the name of the state government, a formidable force. Francisco ends his testimony by stating from prison, "I have been in this prison since they arrested me. They have accused me of crimes I didn't carry out. I was simply carrying out my duties as a local judge in my community" (Brigada Pro Derechos Humanos 1997:14). His role as a local indigenous authority is his defense in response to the accusations of another authority and sphere of influence.

The naked lines of unequal power and authority revealed in the detention, torture, and imprisonment of rural men from San Agustín Loxicha at the hands of Federal Judicial Police and the army are further intensified by the active highlighting and insulting of their indigenous identity through language. Many of the men detained were monolingual in Zapotec and remained unclear about the accusations against them and the questions used in their interrogations under torture. The automatic use of Spanish as the language of interrogation immediately renders Zapotec invisible and useless – a non-language. In the hands of the Federal Judicial Police, Spanish becomes another weapon of control as the "suspects" are seen not even to have the capacity or right to speak because they are suspected of being subversives.

According to the testimonies and interviews carried out with human rights workers representing the prisoners from Loxicha, no efforts were made to provide translators or to ascertain whether the prisoners had any level of comprehension of Spanish. The response of one detained man is echoed by many: "Because we don't speak Spanish, the most we could do was to give our names. They asked me a lot of things, but what were they saying?" (Brigada Pro Derechos Humanos 1997:8). One bilingual man reported, "There were various people among us who didn't speak Spanish and couldn't respond to the questions. I tried to help one of them, but the judicial police told me, 'Quiet. We aren't asking you, stupid'" (Brigada Pro Derechos Humanos 1997:6). Ultimately the act of translation became irrelevant as the Federal Judicial Police created words for all of the detained, tortured, and imprisoned men. All of the men's testimonies mention that they were forced to sign blank pieces of paper and were later presented with confessions (written in perfect Spanish) they had supposedly signed, a violent supplanting of their indigenous tongue and identity for a manufactured identity in Spanish words not their own.

The final way in which the Spanish language became a weapon wielded against the prisoners was through racial slurs. In six of the 37 testimonies, there is mention of derogatory remarks made by Federal Judicial Police in reference to ethnicity. Luis López, a 36-year-old bilingual teacher, recalled in his testimony, "As we were getting on the plane to be taken to Oaxaca, they told us, 'You filthy Indians, you all smell like shit, you assholes'" (Brigada Pro Derechos Humanos 1997:6). Manuel Ramírez Mendoza, detained in Oaxaca City, reported specific mention of his Zapotec origins, stating, "They discriminated against me because of my race and made fun of my Zapotec language" (Brigada Pro Derechos Humanos 1997:21).

Thus the feminization and sexualization of Zapotec men by Federal Judicial Police was further reinforced by their racist commentary throughout torture and interrogation sessions and the silencing of many through the linguistic exclusion of Zapotec and the supplanting of false testimony in Spanish. Ironically, even in telling their stories to human rights workers, these indigenous men were reminded again of their marginal position for they had to use translators to make themselves understood.

Case two: Rape and threatened rape of women in the conflict zone of Chiapas

In Chiapas, forms of political violence used against indigenous men by security forces are similar to those in Oaxaca, particularly for men who become prisoners. Here, however, I want to focus on forms of violence perpetrated against women, primarily indigenous women, in areas of the state where women have been active in indigenous and peasant movements. In Chiapas, the primary tool of violence used against women is rape and the threat of rape. This pattern is consistent with what happens in other parts of the world where militarization is part of the context of political conflict. In their 1995 *Global Report on Women's Human Rights*, Human Rights Watch stated:

> Not until the international outcry rose in response to reports of mass rape in the former Yugoslavia did the international community confront rape as a war crime and begin to take steps to punish those responsible . . . . Investigations in the former Yugoslavia, Peru, Kashmir and Somalia reveal that rape and sexual assault on women are an integral part of conflicts whether international or internal in scope. We found that rape of women civilians has been deployed as a tactical weapon to terrorize civilian communities or to achieve "ethnic cleansing". . . . Our investigation of rape in Haiti under the former military regime of Lt. Gen. Raoul Cédras revealed that rape may also serve as a tool of political repression much as it has a weapon of war. Women activists, members of the opposition or, in many instances, the female relatives of opposition members were the focus of such attacks. (Human Rights Watch 1995:1–2)

The report documents the myriad ways that rape has been used against thousands of women in seven countries around the world. Rape by military and security forces has been documented as a common tactic of intimidation and violence in Peru (Americas Watch 1992) and Guatemala (Carmack 1988). Human rights reports on rape point out that because most state legal systems (such as those of Peru until 1991) characterize rape as a crime against honor or custom, few rape victims targeted by military or police forces receive justice (Human Rights Watch 1995:5). As Susan Hirsch points out (in her article comparing U.S. and Kenyan media depictions of an incident at a Kenyan boarding school during which many young women were raped and several killed by their male schoolmates), culturally specific "scripts of rape" and the understandings that underlie them often remain unquestioned. They often "stand in the way of efforts to envision innovative strategies to combat rape" (1994:1024–1025). One of the tasks of anthropology is to reveal the culturally and nationally based scripts of rape.

Journalists have paid a great deal of attention to rape as a tool in ethnic cleansing in Bosnia-Hercegovina, where it is described as rape with a political purpose – to intimidate, humiliate, and degrade women and others affected by their suffering. "The effect of rape is often to ensure that women and their families will flee and never return" (Helsinki Watch 1993:21). Rape in Bosnia-Hercegovina was often seen as a means of seeking revenge against the enemy (Human Rights Watch 1995:1).

In Chiapas, rape and the threat of rape have been deployed as both physical and symbolic violence to discourage women from ongoing participation in community and regional forms of organization. As noted by Cynthia Enloe, however, too often the voices of women themselves who have suffered rape are missing (1995:23). As seen in the discussion below, women in Chiapas are quite clear that *they* (not men) are the targets of rape precisely because of the specific nature of their political activity (see also Hernández Castillo 1997). Rape confirms their importance as effective political actors.

As I have written elsewhere (Stephen 1997b:35–37), women who engage in activities that are seen as disobeying government authority are cast in the role of symbolic whore by police, government security forces, and soldiers. Jennifer Schirmer has written eloquently that women are responsible not only for maintaining their own images as wives and mothers, but also for ensuring that their husbands and children do not become threats to national security (1993:54). In my work on El Salvador, I have emphasized that when large numbers of women began to take part in public actions to confront state authorities, they invoked a simultaneous image of mother, virgin, and whore. When women take over public spaces and engage in behaviour that is viewed as inappropriate for their gender or ethnicity, they are treated with suspicion. In Chiapas, they become suspected members of the EZLN.

One of the hallmarks of public demonstrations in support of the EZLN is the high level of women's participation. The armed battalions of the EZLN itself are estimated to be about 30 percent women. Civilian women who support the Zapatistas actively confront and attempt to drive the military out of their communities. They also gather in large numbers to resist men from paramilitary groups and from the PRI who are attempting to terrorize their communities. For example, when the Mexican military invaded communities held by the EZLN in February 1995, women took active roles in driving them out. They have also represented their communities' defense efforts to the press and the media. On several occasions, Tojolabal women, EZLN supporters from La Realidad, have told me about how they drove the military outside of the boundaries of the community and how they continue to monitor their activities. Lucía told me her version in June 1996.

> The army arrived on the ninth of February in 1995. We withdrew to our ejido lands behind the town. Then the army came again. They said, "We have come for peace." But that isn't true. We drove them out of town. We got together a group of women and shouted at them, "Get out. Get out of here! We are in charge here, not you. Go back to your barracks. Don't come here to frighten the women."...We kept on screaming this. This is still going on. They come here all the time. We have coffee groves where we can't go to work alone because they are there. We have to constantly be on the lookout for them because we never know when they will try to take advantage of us.

Women like Lucía are clearly stepping over the boundary of acceptable female behavior in the face of a military invasion. The fact that Lucia is indigenous Tojolabal adds another dimension to her challenge. Defiant acts such as shouting at the army until they leave the community work sharply against the stereotypical image of indigenous women. Through their actions, women such as Lucía are redefining historical images of indigenous women.

The actual rape of women and the continuously implied threat of rape is perhaps the greatest tool of terror used against women in the militarized zones of Chiapas as well as in the city of San Cristóbal (see Hernández Castillo 1997). Many NGOs supporting indigenous women in the countryside have made their home bases in San Cristóbal, often bringing indigenous women into the city for program-related activities or to live. The virtual occupation of most Zapatista communities by army encampments has resulted in a situation in which women are afraid to leave their communities to gather firewood or go to the fields, for fear of rape and sexual harassment. Women in La Realidad told me of how their piles of firewood, left by the road, were stolen by soldiers. They also related how soldiers undressed them with their eyes and told them to be careful if they were out alone. The detention and rape of four Tzeltal women at an army checkpoint in Altamirano in 1994, the rape of three nurses in San Andrés in 1995, and other acts of violence committed against women by soldiers have made rape and sexual harassment tools of war in Chiapas.

Nuns I spoke with at the San Carlos hospital in Altamirano presented other evidence of rape. San Carlos was one of the best sites for gathering information on human rights abuses in the region because many of the victims and their families came to the clinic.[8] They often arrived from long distances because they felt safe there and trusted the doctors and nurses. The sisters have run the hospital since 1976. Sister Marina provided an interesting response to a question about rape during a 1997 discussion:

> Lynn: Do you have women who report rape here at the hospital? What do you know about

accusations of rape by the military in the region?

Marina: What happens to women who are raped? They don't report it. It is very difficult to get women to talk about it. But in the past two months we have had something happen here which is quite unusual. We have had two cases of a mother and father who came in when the woman was giving birth. Afterwards, they tell us that they don't want the child. The women won't even look at them. This is very strange behavior. People here love their children to pieces. When these mothers tell me, "I don't even want to look at the child, take it away," then I have to wonder.

Women in army-occupied communities and those who work with them in health projects stated that it was highly unusual for women to report being raped by soldiers for fear of retaliation. Within militarized communities in Chiapas, the daily comings and goings of everyone in the community are closely monitored. People reported to me that when they left their communities to go to larger towns such as Altamirano, they were asked at checkpoints where they were going, with whom they were speaking, and when they would return. They also reported being asked at government health clinics in Guadalupe Tepeyac and in Altamirano what political party they supported and whether or not they were sympathetic to the EZLN.

But more than actual rape, the threat of rape and the psychological control that is exerted over communities through a male army presence is probably the strongest weapon used against indigenous women. The physical presence of the army is augmented through their surveillance tactics, which include intimidating patrols through communities with video cameras. On several occasions, I witnessed such patrols in La Realidad. At about nine o'clock in the morning, just when the sun is beginning to heat up the mud, a very slow-moving caravan of about sixteen humvees moves through La Realidad. Most of the people hide in their houses peering through the windows and doors. A few people continue their activities, ignoring the army's presence. Machine guns are mounted on top of the humvees and about four to eight soldiers sit in each vehicle. While one soldier stands behind the machine gun, another one or two in each vehicle are snapping photographs with still cameras while others are videotaping. The faces of the soldiers holding the still cameras and the video cameras are not visible. They appear as human machines mounted on the humvees, filming all that comes into their line of sight. They extend a very slow, deliberate, and intimidating gaze over the community. They travel at about two miles per hour and slow to a standstill periodically in their sojourn in the village. When they stop, everyone stops moving and is frozen in their tracks. In about fifteen minutes, they have passed through the two-block town. People come out of their houses to resume work and to complain about the military presence. Some break the tension by joking about whether or not they were really taking pictures. "They would have to spend thousands and thousands of pesos on all their film and pictures of La Realidad." Others talk about the army being able to watch them on video even when they are not driving their humvees through the town. Such a suggestion leaves a chilly pall over conversations.

The effect is quite striking over the long term. While men, women, and children in La Realidad became accustomed to the videotaping and picture-taking, they internalized it as a constant violation. Women in the town talked about "always being watched" and the "eyes of the army being everywhere." That sense of always being watched, of never being alone, has had a profound effect on women in militarized zones of Chiapas. It has heightened the constant fear of rape and harassment and creates high levels of intimidation that isolates women within their communities or homes.

In another area of Chiapas sympathetic to the EZLN, the highland Tzotzil community of San Andrés Larrainzar, women from the Artisan Cooperative Society of Women for Dignity, a Zapatista-aligned weaving cooperative, told me about their difficulties in finding a market for their goods. With a military detachment parked just outside of San Andrés, they were afraid to go to San Cristóbal de las Casas to drum up business. Clara Martínez Pérez, who has six children to support, told me, "We can't go very far to sell our goods. We are safe here, but not outside. There are a lot of soldiers here in San Andrés . . . it isn't safe to leave. We can't leave here." All of the women in the cooperative expressed fear of the surrounding soldiers, especially at night. Two days after our conversation, most of the women abandoned the cooperative building after a midnight rampage in which local PRI militants beat on the doors of their building and then went on to vandalize the city hall while shooting off their rifles. Some weeks later, two people were killed as the conflict between local PRD (Party of the Democratic Revolution)/Zapatista sympathizers and PRI hardliners escalated. Two men from the PRI were later detained and charged with the killings.

Two women from another weaving cooperative located in San Cristóbal, also sympathetic to the Zapatistas, were brutally attacked in two different incidents and threatened with rape. Gabriela López, a young Chamula woman who is part of the staff at Jolom Mayatik, told of attacks against her in the streets of San Cristóbal in January and February 1997:

> On the last day of January this year, some men approached us as we were coming home from a workshop. We were just walking down the street. They jumped on us, beating us and kicking. There was a whole group of them. We rested for ten days, hurting, trying to recover. Then again on the sixth of February we were confronted by more men on Chiapa de Corzo Street. They parked their car and six men got out. They followed us and then grabbed us saying, "You are whores. We know you sleep around with men, you know what sex is. Let's see if you want to be Zapatistas now. Let's see who will win. You are just whores on the street." Everyone on the street was listening. Imagine how we felt.

> After this happened, we decided we had to move. Now I live with my family in San Cristóbal. They all live here now. . . . Soon after, these men came to where I was living with my family. They came looking for me. My family told them, "We don't know where she is."

Then they pulled out a knife and attacked and threatened my family. . . . That is why I participate in the cooperative. We know that they don't like the fact that we are women doing what we do. . . . But we are taking action. Like on March 8th there was a march through the streets here where we said, "Get rid of the perpetrators of violence."

Gabriela has been working in the cooperative for many years and has carefully considered her role as a woman leader and its consequences in terms of both her family and herself as an individual. She and other women in the cooperative have analyzed the violence carried out against them and talk about it as directed specifically against them as women engaged in struggle.

Cristina Solís is an advisor and staff person in Jolom Mayatik. She became a full-time activist with the cooperative in 1994. She has received similar threats.

> In my case, I have received the same kinds of threats as other women here. They call up and leave messages on my answering machine saying, "We are going to rape your mother and your sisters and you are going to die. . . ." Of course we are afraid when we hear these things and sometimes it makes us feel powerless. And these threats do make us change our lives. We have to take a lot of security measures like never being alone. But the only thing we can do is to keep on struggling.

Cristina's statement captures not only her terror, but also the very real way in which such threats make women (and men who receive death threats as well) alter their behavior. The women in Jolom Mayatik as well as in the San Andrés cooperative have become accustomed to living with their fear, but acknowledge that the constant threat of rape and physical violence takes a toll on them after years of intimidating actions. Such threats have continued against them, as well as against women working in nongovernmental organizations in San Cristóbal, yet they persist in their activism.

Conclusion

The current militarization of indigenous regions of southern Mexico acknowledges the importance of regional cultural and political challenges to the legitimacy of the Mexican state (see Rubin 1997). Oaxaca and Chiapas have become the centers of strong regional indigenous and peasant organizations which in the wake of the Zapatista rebellion of 1994 have begun to operate at a national level (Hernández Navarro 1997). The heart of these movements is outside the formal political arena of electoral politics. In part because these movements offer new political forms that move the contestation for political power outside of the electoral arena, they have attracted and sustained the attention of the Mexican government.

The gendered and ethnic dimensions of human rights abuses associated with high levels of militarization in Chiapas and Oaxaca reflect, in part, the cultural and ideological perspectives of those in the occupying forces of the army, Federal Judicial Police, and Public Security Police. These in turn are rooted in the processes of military conquest, Catholic conversion, and the *mestizoization* of Mexico during and since the colonial period. National stereotypes of indigenous peoples written into the myth and vision of Mexican history continue to be played out in contemporary strategies of conquest and militarization. Tactics aimed specifically at stripping Zapotec men of their masculinity, sexualizing them, and reducing them to feminine sexual equivalents on the part of male Federal Judicial Police agents echo the findings of researchers like Trexler (1995), discussed above. The casting of Tzotzil, Tzeltal, and Tojolabal women as whore-like Malinches, as an element of sexual disciplining suggests the importance of national myths in the self-legitimating ideology underlying the behavior of men in the army and police toward women. National gendered myths are part of the cultural scripts of rape.

In Chiapas, the active and public involvement of women in repelling military invasions of community lands and in confronting PRI sympathizers who threaten their communities and families has made indigenous women particular targets of threats and abuses. Nevertheless, women in Zapatista communities, in weaving co-ops, and in nongovernmental organizations continue their work and take active stances against the military and others who try to intimi-

date them. They have publicly denounced the threats against them in the press and have continued to pressure the State Prosecutor's office to find and prosecute those carrying out the threats (Morquecho 1998a, 1998b, 1998c). By taking such a politically active stance both because of and in spite of personal danger, they are redefining indigenous femininity – they are neither active collaborators (Malinche) nor passive asexual victims (Virgen de Guadalupe). By continuing to be active, they provide an important counter-trope to the inherited colonial images of indigenous women – and this strengthens them further.

The resistance of indigenous women and men in Chiapas and efforts on the part of Zapotec and other indigenous peoples in Oaxaca to take control of their own governments is part of a coordinated national effort on the part of indigenous organizations and communities to redefine their place in the Mexican nation. This challenge involves local cultural forms that rework top-down nationalism and create a sense of local nations. Bringing nationalism down to the local level and coupling it with self-determination offers an alternative to the marginalized position of many indigenous communities in Mexican history, in national and regional politics, and in economic development schemes. In southern Mexico, this challenge has been formalized through the creation of autonomous indigenous communities and municipalities in the state of Chiapas and in other states – for example, Oaxaca. Indigenous autonomy is understood as respect for the internal practices and decision-making modes of indigenous communities and nations. Autonomy also means that indigenous communities participate in the various levels of economic, political, cultural, and legal decision-making associated with the state. Actors within the Mexican state have taken the movement for indigenous autonomy extremely seriously – at least judging from the scale of their efforts to suppress it.

More than anything, a careful analysis of militarization and human rights abuses in situations such as that of contemporary Mexico begs for a more complex analysis of politics and culture and the deployment of the tools of ethnography to illuminate such complexities. Responsible ethnography can be mobilized to illuminate crises in representation of states as well as the tactics that states use to maintain a grip on power – such as militarization, detention, torture, and constant threats of physical and symbolic violence. The tools of ethnography can be put to powerful use in exposing how dominant representations create categories of people susceptible to political violence, "suspects" who become victims of human rights abuses. By doing so, anthropologists align their own tools with those of the men and women who also draw strength from their own parallel projects of exposure and analysis.

NOTES

Acknowledgments. I am grateful to the Wenner-Gren Foundation for Anthropological Research (Grant #6168) and the Project on the Transformation of Rural Mexico administered by the Center for U.S.–Mexican Studies and in association with the Centro de Investigaciones y Estudios Superiores en Antropología Social del Occidente (CIESAS – Guadalajara) for funding the research that contributed to this paper. I thank David Amdur, Abraham Castañeda, Marta Figueroa, Gerardo González, Luis Hernández, Benjamin Maldonado Alvarado, and Anna Utech for their insights in discussing this material with me. Three anonymous reviewers for *American Ethnologist* provided wonderful suggestions for sharpening the focus and arguments of this article.

1 This definition of violence is taken from Carole Nagengast's discussion of Raymond Williams' "key word" (Nagengast 1994:11; Williams 1976).

2 See Feldman 1991 for a discussion of the feminization and sexualization of men in paramilitary violence in Belfast.

3 See Kleinman and Kleinman 1997:18–19 on the similar responsibility experts and anthropologists have in the social and health policy sphere.

4 See the work of Norma Alarcón (especially 1989) for a thoughtful discussion of Chicana feminist literature and its use of Malinche as a vindicating symbol for women.

5 The integration of state and federal police forces and their coordinated action with army troops also makes it more difficult to pinpoint blame for human rights abuses carried out in raids and confrontations. My interviews with human rights workers as well as with victims of human rights abuses in Chiapas over the past three years suggest that when both federal and state police units are involved in raids along with the military, witnesses have difficulty specifying which unit was responsible for arresting, detaining, killing, or disappearing a particular individual. Increasingly, police forces are also carrying out actions out of uniform.

6 All names in this section and throughout the article have been changed to protect those who provided testimony.

7 In her discussion of violence and the state, Carole Nagengast cites Armstrong and Tennenhouse on how masculinity is constructed in the ideological relations that relegate people into the purified and honest who do legitimate work and the politically suspect or deviant who do not. "The violent dissident must be positioned and repositioned as necessary, in a negative relationship with . . . rational masculinity, a model that ensures a relationship of dominance and subordination . . . by locking the two in a mutually defining relationship" (1989:15, 21). As noted by Gutmann in a recent review article on the anthropology of masculinity, sources of violence among men who lose control over other men are greatly undertheorized in the cultural realm (1997:399).

8 In 1998, the administration of the hospital changed, and it became a less inviting refuge for some.

REFERENCES CITED

Alarcón, Norma
1989 Traddutora, Traditora: A Paradigmatic Figure of Chicana Feminism. Cultural Critique 13:57–97.

Americas Watch
1992 Untold Terror: Violence against Women in Peru's Armed Conflict. New York: Americas Watch and the Women's Rights Project.

Aretxaga, Begoña
1997 Shattering Silence: Women, Nationalism, and Political Subjectivity in Northern Ireland. Princeton, NJ: Princeton University Press.

Armstrong, Nancy, and Leonard Tennenhouse
1989 The Violence of Representation: Literature and the History of Violence. London: Routledge.

Binford, Leigh
1996 The El Mozote Massacre: Anthropology and Human Rights. Tucson: University of Arizona Press.

Bourgois, Philippe
1991 Confronting the Ethics of Ethnography: Lessons from Fieldwork in Central America. *In* Decolonizing Anthropology: Moving Further toward an Anthropology for Liberation. Faye V. Harrison, ed. Pp. 111–126. Washington, DC: Association of Black Anthropologists and the American Anthropological Association.

Brigada Pro Derechos Humanos Observadores Por La Paz
1997 Testimonios escritos y verbales de los presos de Loxicha. Proporcionados por habitantes de las Comunidades de La Sirena, Loma Bonita, Loxicha, el diá 21 de Febrero, y por los presos (CERESO Ixcotel) el día 22 de Febrero, 1997 Oaxaca City: BARCA/Regional Center for Human Rights "Bartolomé Carraso."

Carmack, Robert M.
1988 Harvest of Violence: The Maya Indians and the Guatemalan Crisis. Norman: University of Oklahoma Press.

Centro de Derechos Humanos "Fray Bartolomé de las Casas"
1998 La legalidad y la injusticia. Centro de Derechos Humanos "Fray Bartolomé de las Casas" A.C.

CIACH/CONPAZ/SIPRO (Centro de Información Y Análisis de Chiapas/Coordinación de Organismos No Gubernamentales por la Paz/ Servicios Informativos Procesados)
1997 Para entender Chiapas: Chiapas en cifras. Mexico City: Impretei.

Collier, George, with Elizabeth Lowery Quaratiello
1994 Basta! Land and the Zapatista Rebellion in Chiapas. Oakland, CA: Food First.

Collier, Robert
1996 Out of the Barracks, Mexican Army Flexes New Muscles. San Francisco Chronicle, December 10, p. A3.

Consejo Estatal de Población de Oaxaca
1994 Población indígena de Oaxaca, 1885–1990. Oaxaca: Consejo Estatal de Población.

Correa, Guillermo
1997 Inteligencia Militar: Hasta diciembre del 96, EPR operaba ya en 17 estados y había causado 26 bajas entre soldados y policías. Proceso 1098, 16 de Noviembre, 22–28.

Daniel, E. Valentine
1996 Charred Lullabies: Chapters in an Anthropography of Violence. Princeton, NJ: Princeton University Press.

Díaz Polanco, Hector
1997 La Rebelión Zapatista y la autonomía. Mexico City: Siglo veintiuno editores.

Elizalde, Trianfo
1999 Zapotecas buscan apoyo en el DF para liberar a sus presas políticos. La Jornada, 2 de Agosto.

Enloe, Cynthia
1995 Feminism, Nationalism, and Militarism: Wariness without Paralysis? *In* Feminism, Nationalism, and Militarism. Constance R. Sutton, ed. Pp. 13–92. Arlington, VA: Association for Feminist Anthropology and the American Anthropological Association.

Esteva, Gustavo
1996 La construcción de un nuevo pacto social. Paper presented in the session "Nuevo Pacto Social," del Foro Especial para la Reforma del Estado, organized by the EZLN, San Cristóbal de las Casas, Chiapas, June 30–July 6.

Feldman, Allen
1991 Formations of Violence: The Narrative of the Body and Political Terror in Northern Ireland. Chicago: University of Chicago Press.

Garibay, Angel
1967 Our Lady of Guadalupe. *In* New Catholic Encyclopedia, 6:821–822. New York: McGraw-Hill.

Gould, Jeffrey
1996 Gender, Politics and the Triumph of *Mestizaje* in Early 20th-Century Nicaragua. Journal of Latin American Anthropology 2(1):4–33.

Gutmann, Matthew
1997 Trafficking in Men: The Anthropology of Masculinity. Annual Review of Anthropology 26:385–409.

Harvey, Neil
1994 Rebellion in Chiapas: Rural Reforms, Campesino Radicalism and the Limits to Salinismo. *In* Rebellion in Chiapas, Transformation of Rural Mexico Series, No. 5. La Jolla: Center for U.S.–Mexican Studies, University of California, San Diego.
1998 The Chiapas Rebellion: The Struggle for Land and Democracy. Durham, NC: Duke University Press.

Helsinki Watch
1993   War Crimes in Bosnia-Hercegovina, Volume II. New York: Helsinki Watch/A Division of Human Rights Watch.

Hernández Castillo, Rosalva Aída
1997   Between Hope and Despair: The Struggle of Organized Women in Chiapas since the Zapatista Uprising. Journal of Latin American Anthropology 3(1):102–120.

Hernández Navarro, Luis
1997   La CNI: Primer Aniversario. La Jornada, October 14.

Hindley, Jane
1995   Towards a Pluricultural Nation: The Limits of Indigenismo and Article 4. In Dismantling the Mexican State. Rob Aiken, Nicki Craske, Gareth A. Jones, and David Stansfield, eds. Pp. 225–243. London: Macmillan.

Hirsch, Susan
1994   Interpreting Media Representations of "a Night of Madness": Law and Culture in the Construction of Rape Identities. Law and Social Inquiry 19:1023–1058.

Howard, Rhoda
1992   Dignity, Community, and Human Rights. In Human Rights in Cross-Cultural Perspectives. Abdullah A. Anna'im, ed. Pp. 81–102. Philadelphia: University of Pennsylvania Press.

Human Rights Watch
1995   The Human Rights Watch Global Report on Women's Human Rights. New York: Human Rights Watch.

Human Rights Watch/Americas
1997   Implausible Deniability: State Responsibility for Rural Violence in Mexico. New York: Human Rights Watch.

Kleinman, Arthur, Veena Das, and Margaret Lock, eds.
1997   Social Suffering. Berkeley: University of California Press.

Kleinman, Arthur, and Joan Kleinman
1997   The Appeal of Experience; The Dismay of Images: Cultural Appropriations of Suffering in Our Time. In Social Suffering. Arthur Kleinman, Veena Das, and Margaret Lock, eds. Pp. 1–24. Berkeley: University of California Press.

Klor de Alva, J. Jorge
1995   The Postcolonization of the (Latin) American Experience: A Reconsideration of "Colonialism," "Postcolonialism," and "Mestizaje." In After

Colonialism: Imperial Histories and Postcolonial Displacements. Gyan Prakash, ed. Pp. 241–278. Princeton, NJ: Princeton University Press.

Knight, Alan
1990   Racism, Revolution and Indigenismo: Mexico 1910–1940. In The Idea of Race in Latin America. Richard Graham, ed. Pp. 71–114. Austin: University of Texas Press.

López y Rivas, Gilberto
1995   Nación y pueblos indios en el neoliberalismo. Mexico City: Plaza y Váldez Editores y la Universidad Iberoamericana.

Malkki, Liisa
1995   Purity and Exile: Violence, Memory, and National Cosmology among Hutu Refugees in Tanzania. Chicago: University of Chicago Press.

Martínez, María Elena
1997   Limpieza de Sangre. In Encyclopedia of Mexico: History, Society & Culture. Vol. I. Michael Werner, ed. Pp. 749–752. Chicago: Fitzroy Dearborn Publishers.

Mattiace, Shannan
1997   Zapata Vive: The EZLN, Indian Politics and the Autonomy Movement in Mexico. Journal of Latin American Anthropology 3(2):32–71.

Mejía Piñero, María Consuelo, and Sergio Sarmiento Silva
1987   La lucha indígena: un reto a la ortodoxia. Mexico City: Siglo Veintiuno Editores.

Messer, Ellen
1993   Anthropology and Human Rights. Annual Review of Anthropology 22:221–249.
1995   Anthropology and Human Rights in Latin America. Journal of Latin American Anthropology 1(1):48–97.

Morquecho, Gaspar
1998a   En Chiapas ya se siente "cerca de la muerte," dicen mujeres activistas. La Jornada, April 24, p. 18.
1998b   Hostigan desconocidos a mujeres miembros de ONG en Chiapas. La Jornada, April 23, p. 17.
1998c   Preocupan a ONG femenina amenazas telefónicas. La Jornada, April 25, p. 12.

Muller-Hill, Benno
1988   Murderous Science: The Elimination by Scientific Selection of Jews, Gypsies, and Others, Germany 1933–1945. New York: Oxford University Press.

Nagengast, Carole
1994   Violence, Terror, and the Crisis of the State. Annual Review of Anthropology 23:109–136.

Paz, Octavio
1961   Labyrinth of Solitude: Life and Thought in Mexico. Lysander Kemp, trans. New York: Grover Press.

Preston, Julia
1997   Mexican Snubs Visiting Head of Rights Unit. New York Times, September 25, p. A16.

Renteln, Alison Dundes
1990   International Human Rights: Universalism versus Relativism. Thousand Oaks, CA: Sage.

Rodríguez, Jeanette
1994   Our Lady of Guadalupe: Faith and Empowerment among Mexican-American Women. Austin: University of Texas Press.

Rubin, Jeffrey
1997   Decentering the Regime; Ethnicity, Radicalism, and Democracy in Juchitán, Mexico. Durham, NC: Duke University Press.

Ruiz Arrazola, Víctor
1998   Eligen indígenas a ex agente judicial como alcalde de San Agustín Loxicha. La Jornada, October 12, p. 53.

Scheper-Hughes, Nancy
1992   Death without Weeping: The Violence of Everyday Life in Brazil. Berkeley: University of California Press.

Schirmer, Jennifer
1993   The Seeking of Truth and the Gendering of Consciousness: The CO-MADRES of El Salvador and the CONAVIGUA Widows of Guatemala. In "Viva": Women and Popular Protest in Latin America. Sarah A. Radcliffe and Sallie Westwood, eds. Pp. 39–64. London: Routledge.

Stephen, Lynn
1997a   Redefined Nationalism in Building a Movement for Indigenous Autonomy. Journal of Latin American Anthropology 3(1):72–101.

1997b   Women and Social Movements in Latin America: Power from Below. Austin: University of Texas Press.

1997c   The Zapatista Opening: The Movement for Indigenous Autonomy in Mexico and State Discourses on Indigenous Rights in Mexico, 1970–1990. Journal of Latin American Anthropology 2(2):2–41.

In press Indigenous Autonomy in Mexico. In At the Risk of Being Heard: Identity, Indigenous Rights and Post Colonial States. Bartholomew Dean and Jerome Levi, eds. Ann Arbor: University of Michigan.

Stolke, Verena
1991   Conquered Women. NACLA Report on the Americas 25(5):23–28.

Taussig, Michael
1984   Culture of Terror, Space of Death. Roger Casement and the Explanation of Torture. Comparative Studies of Society and History 26:467–497.

Thompson, Richard H.
1997   Ethnic Minorities and the Case for Collective Rights. American Anthropologist 99(4):786–798.

Trexler, Richard
1995   Sex and Conquest: Gendered Violence, Political Order, and the European Conquest of the Americas. Ithaca, NY: Cornell University Press.

Warren, Kay
1993   Interpreting La Violencia in Guatemala: Shapes of Mayan Silence and Resistance. In The Violence Within: Cultural and Political Opposition in Divided Nations. Kay Warren, ed. Pp. 25–56. Boulder, CO: Westview Press.

Williams, Raymond
1976   Keywords. Oxford: Oxford University Press.

23

For Whom the Taco Bells Toll: Popular Responses to NAFTA South of the Border

Matthew C. Gutmann

News item, 1992
With CEO John Martin saying 'value and quality know no borders', Taco Bell opened its first outlet south of the border in Mexico City. (*USA Today*, 4 June 1992: A-1)
News item, 1998
According to Rocío Conejo, a spokeswoman in Mexico City for Taco Bell's new holding company (Tricon Global Restaurants, Inc., which also owns Kentucky Fried Chicken and Pizza Hut), 'because Mexican tacos are very different from Taco Bell tacos no franchises are presently in operation or planned for Mexico'. (phone interview, 6 January 1998)

Angela's Big Feet

For my friend Angela, the North American Free Trade Agreement (NAFTA) always held the promise of greater access to goods from the United States. In her case what she most wanted were size 10½-wide shoes for her grandmother's badly swollen feet. As for Angela's neighbor Tono, like most men in Colonia Santo Domingo in Mexico City, he has had a hard time finding steady employment in the 1990s.[1] To Toño the treaty represented the potential for growth of US business investment in central Mexico. Even if it meant slaving in a low-wage *maquiladora* assembly plant, Toño had high hopes for better job prospects after NAFTA went into effect on 1 January 1994.

On that fateful day, as it happens, thousands of Tzotzil, Tzeltal, Chol and other indigenous peoples made clear their very different interpretation and expectation for NAFTA: they launched an armed uprising in the southern Mexican state of Chiapas to denounce the Agreement and demand democracy, liberty, and justice for *indígenas* and all people in Mexico. Although there has to date been no Chiapas-like response to NAFTA in the *colonias populares* in Mexico City or other urban areas, and despite the views of some like Toño, disdain and contempt for the accord among the poor throughout the country have been widespread.

No matter how ambiguous and ill-defined popular opposition to NAFTA might be in the Mexican capital and in the countryside, as Chiapas has so well reminded anthropologists, we must not engage in the violence of ethnographic indifference by ignoring politically dissident moods and activities, whether they are clearly voiced or muted and confusing. By the same token, and for similar reasons, it is important regularly to assess processes such as the individualization of responses to efforts like NAFTA, as this relates to the periodic waxing and waning of popular political interest in 'politics' altogether.

Amid mountains of important analyses regarding more strictly economic and environmental aspects of NAFTA it is easy to miss critical cultural dimensions that point to equally momentous changes in the lives of millions of dispossessed on both sides of the Rio Grande/Bravo. NAFTA has meant far more than the commercial reorganization of relations between the United States, Canada and Mexico.

The announcement of Taco Bell's arrival in Mexico City in 1992, for example, was greeted as more than absurd by the capital's poor. In the *colonias populares* of Mexico City, the appearance of these franchises 'south of the border' was a symbolic tolling which heralded good times ahead for the upper middle class and elites alone. After all, the only people who could regularly patronize such establishments were the youth from these strata. The vast majority of Mexicans simply could not afford gringo fast food. Nonetheless, apparently North American tacos were too much for even these youth to stomach, which resulted in Taco Bell's evident failure to establish a foothold in Mexico. It seems that even the more affluent sectors of society took umbrage at this attempted gringo-ization of Mexico's national cuisine.[2]

In this article I address certain implications of the Free Trade Agreement for national and class identities and relations in Mexico. I examine how discontent and frustration among Mexico's urban poor are representative of contradictory political dissidence and popular nationalism, and I explore how and why these manifestations of popular political culture are both ardently felt and yet nonetheless lie dormant in all but exceptional historical moments. The tension between individual and collective strategies to oppose US domination are evidence, I conclude, of broader chaos and confusion with respect to the meanings of democratic and popular will in Mexico today.

Colonia Santo Domingo is a community that was formed by land invasion in the early 1970s, and today is home to well over 150,000 men and women, most of whom live on one to three 'minimum salaries' (the semi-official standard of poverty in Mexico). Residents of the *colonia* clean homes in wealthy neighborhoods and buildings in the nearby National University; they drive taxis and buses; and they work in factories and small enterprises throughout the capital city. Most adults are able to find paid work if they want it, yet few are able to survive on the wages from one job alone. In Santo Domingo, if someone has the temerity to ask a neighbor 'How much do you earn?' the reply is invariably 'Don't ask how much I earn, ask how much I lose!'

I am interested here in why so many men and women in working-class barrios of Mexico City today believe that defending Mexico's national sovereignty has become the duty principally of the poor because, they feel, the elites have relinquished their national loyalties, and why among the poor this is seen so often as an individual rather than a collective project. If many working-class people in Mexico City would agree that in practice the rich have generally put their own interests before those of the nation, residents in neighborhoods like Colonia Santo Domingo might nonetheless point out that the language of the elites has shifted in recent years. Now even the pretense of independence – for example, opposition to US foreign policy – has all but disappeared. It has been replaced, they say, with slogans like that of Jaime Serra Puche, the government official who called in 1991 for Mexicans to accept '*el reto de la interdependencia* [the challenge of interdependence]' between Mexico, the United States and Canada, that is, NAFTA (cited in García Canclini, 1992:5).

In this article I will also offer evidence that the perception among the poor – at least, those who worry about such matters – that defense of the Mexican nation is now their burden is related to the spreading conclusion among activists in Colonia Santo Domingo that popular social movements in the last two decades have focused too restrictively on ameliorating practical problems among the poor and in this way may have inadvertently relinquished political ground around international and global issues.[3]

Although many commentators have addressed the relationship of NAFTA to national identity, national sovereignty and political debate in Mexico, discussion of popular perceptions and responses to the treaty have been largely speculative if they have been reported at all. Ethnographic material has been sorely lacking, and thus this article also seeks to provide initial indications of popular political discourse and activity in response to the first four years of the Agreement.

Prefab Curtains and Japanese Melons

If during its initial phase Angela and especially Toño looked more benignly upon the TLC (as the accord is known in Spanish, for Tratado de Libre Comercio), Marcos, another neighbor on Huehuetzin Street in Colonia Santo Domingo in the Mexican capital, had a more typical response: 'The TLC is one more blow against the already *jodidos* [screwed]', one more instance of 'the Mexican and gringo rich fleecing *la gente humilde* [the common folks]'. Marcos works in maintenance at the National University next to Santo Domingo, and he reported that other janitors and groundskeepers felt similarly.

Other accounts of NAFTA's impact are more personal. One afternoon in late September 1994, Doña Josefina described to me what occurred to her husband, Guillermo, following Mexico's entry into the pact:

> 'Guillermo worked for many years as a *cortinero* [curtain maker] in a curtain shop', Josefina began. 'He would go to people's homes to measure their windows and then make them custom curtains. One day his *patrón* told him that because of the Tratado de Libre Comercio he was going to shut down the curtain shop.'
>
> 'But what did TLC [NAFTA] have to do with shutting down the curtain shop?' I asked.
>
> 'I think he talked about tariffs [*aranceles*]. I'm not sure if it was taxes or what. I don't know...But what it did mean was that he could no longer pay what they were charging

him, because [with the Agreement] other prefabricated curtains were going to start coming in [to Mexico]. Much cheaper ones. That's what it was. And he declared bankruptcy. He couldn't pay the workers any more, or continue in business. That's what has happened to a lot of other people, too.'

> 'Like...?'
>
> 'Like some furniture workers.'
>
> 'Have your friends who are furniture workers had problems finding work afterwards?'
>
> 'Yes, yes. And near here, as well, there was a factory that made plastic bottles. They also shut that.'
>
> 'And you're sure this had to do with NAFTA?' I pressed.
>
> 'Yes. A lot of places shut down. For example, there was an umbrella shop. They also shut that down because umbrellas from Taiwan began to arrive. So more people were out of work. Look, we know little about the Tratado de Libre Comercio. The truth is that we know little about what the Tratado was really, because they're not going to...The *patrón* tells us, "We're going to shut because of the Free Trade Agreement." But really we don't know about free trade. They don't let us in on that.'
>
> 'Do you have any idea', I continued, 'who *is* making money with the Agreement?'
>
> 'I think the ones who are importing goods here [into Mexico]. Because if you go shopping everything is from another country, radios, grills, dishes, pots, batteries, games, like that. If you go to the supermarket there's also a lot of meat from the United States.'
>
> 'Are there any Mexicans making money off the Agreement?'
>
> 'Well, maybe Serra Puche[4] and his people have gotten something. He was very optimistic [about the Agreement], because they think that it's going to make us better and do well for us. Well, no, not really! So we see how Serra Puche and all are doing very well. Yes, they have made something. We don't aspire to great things like those who have power, so much power, the owners of so much power, even over lives! We don't aspire to all that but only what's necessary. That's why there's struggle. Even if we're few in number that's

what we want: that there not be so much injustice.'

In late 1996, I also spoke about NAFTA with my good friend Jorge who spends 12–14 hours daily operating a small *tienda* corner store on Huehuetzin Street in Colonia Santo Domingo. Unlike Josefina, who went through only first grade, as an adolescent Jorge studied to be a lawyer. Today, in addition to minding the store and helping to raise his five small children, Jorge works with the local center-left Partido de la Revolución Democrática (PRD), especially at election time when he monitors polling stations in the *colonia* for vote fraud. NAFTA, gringolandia and Mexican national sovereignty are all subjects dear to Jorge's heart.

'So, my old friend, what the hell do you make of this NAFTA?' I began.

Jorge began his sermon on the impact of NAFTA among various social strata in Mexico.

'For us in the lower middle class, it's of no benefit whatsoever. It doesn't benefit us mainly because in reality, here, in the city, instead of raising employment it has lowered it. In the countryside, *campesinos* have little money to export. And let's say they try to get a loan, as I did when I went back [to Tierra Blanca, his natal *pueblo* in the western state of Guerrero]. I applied for a loan from BANRURAL.[5] I'm sure you've seen the brochures they give out, or seen their commercials on the TV where they say, "Apply for rural assistance – go to the Bank and . . .".'

'This is connected to NAFTA?' I once again asked.

'Well, yeah. Because if the banks assist *campesinos*, well, then the *campesinos* will get ahead. You know, the poor *campesinos*. There's land for planting and there's the will, too, but there's no money. NAFTA only . . . how shall I put this, it helps the *grandes* [big shots]. Those who plant on a large scale. The rich, those who have money.'

'Are gringos buying up land in Guerrero?'

'Only on the coast.'[6]

'Not to plant?'

'No, not to plant. Only on the coast. There are talks, there are rumors that the govern-

ment is going to build a dam financed by the Japanese. So there are a lot of plans. If you remember, where you entered, at the crossroads, it's all very flat there.'

Jorge was referring to an ill-fated attempt I had made several years earlier to drive to the village, Tierra Blanca, where at the time he was tending the family cows for a few months. Together with my wife, Michelle, and our infant daughter we spent the better part of a day driving over creeks, boulders and fallen logs looking for Jorge's godforsaken birthplace. To this day I tease him that Tierra Blanca probably doesn't even exist and that he invented it to make a gringo look like a fool.

In the same conversation I taunted Jorge by saying that I wanted to divulge 'the secrets' of the people from the village to my students in the United States.

'Why?' he asked. 'Because Christ never went there?'

'No, man, because no one has ever been there', I replied.

'Well, there's no gringos who go there! And, if you want,' Jorge paused before adding in a whisper, 'you can become a guerrilla there.'

'It's that easy?'

'Out there, only the goats could give you away.'

Jorge returned to his tale of Japanese-financed dams:

'So they say that the Japanese want to finance the dam and pay a little rent to grow melons (I think that's what they say) on the land. Because the Japanese really like melons and it's a lot cheaper to grow them here [Mexico] than there [Japan].'

'So are things better or worse for poor folks after the Agreement?'

'Worse. Because, based on what I understand, the small industries used to have more chance of offering work here in Mexico, but now they have to compete with transnational companies. Games, a lot of other things they used to make here. But no longer. Why? Because they shut [the plants] down. Now the big North American chains, like Home Mart and I don't know what can offer everything less expensively.'

'But people from Santo Domingo can't afford to go to Home Mart . . .'.

'Yes they can. For example, when they have some money they'll go for the sales and buy more. But for us, for the tiny merchants [*pequeñisimo comercio*], well folks are just coming to buy sodas from us. And that's what you sell the most of but earn the least from. The other thing is that my business is hurt by the Agreement simply because a lot of people are without work. So they obviously don't have money to spend in the *tienda*.'

In the wake of renewed hopes for improved economic fortunes, as part of broader democratic transformations in Mexico, Jorge and many of his friends in Santo Domingo have been frustrated in the last decade at every turn. It has become increasingly difficult to imagine fundamental changes occurring in the country's domestic economy, much less in its political sphere or in Mexican–US relations and the concomitant emigration of *paisanos* to the United States. He still works as a poll-watcher on election days, but, as Jorge himself begrudgingly admits, his distrust of political parties signals a more fundamental disenchantment with participation in collective forms of struggle and 'politics' in general.

Anti-Americanism and NAFTA

Beginning even before the Treaty of Guadalupe-Hidalgo was signed some 150 years ago, the United States has been central to debates regarding Mexico's geopolitical borders, the cultural frontiers of *lo mexicano*, and internal 'boundary' disputes involving opposing sectors of the populace. So it is no coincidence that today NAFTA is generally emblematic of contemporary US–Mexican relations.

When listening to the new transnational gospel as preached by Mexican government and business leaders – 'The purpose of Free Trade today is to allow Mexico to become the first Third World country to vault quickly into the ranks of the First World' – most in the popular urban sector of the country are more than slightly skeptical

that such a transformation will take place. A recurring and rhetorical question asked by those still actively grappling with these issues in Colonia Santo Domingo is: how can we suddenly forget about history, especially that between Mexico and '*el otro lado*' (literally, the other side, meaning the United States)? The idea that the Free Trade Agreement has instantly nullified the arrogantly unequal relations between Mexico and *el otro lado* strikes more than a few as ridiculous. Only the gringos are served by such historical myopia, they feel.[7]

Some periods in history witness greater changes and transformations in social relations than others. The present epoch and the foreseeable future have the potential to be tumultuous periods, in no small part because of significant changes associated with transnational commerce, communication and migration. But as to the possibility that profound change will impact the vast majority of the poor in Mexico, doubts persist, and they are doubts rooted in long experience with persistent poverty and marginalization.

Incredulity regarding the prospects of Mexico leaping to first-world status reflects not simply popular cynicism. The California Chamber of Commerce (1993: 14), for instance, questions 'the basis for Mexico's claim that it will soon be ready to join the group of industrialized nations'. Men and women in *colonias populares* throughout Mexico have decades of experience and opinions regarding import substitution, foreign direct investment, IMF austerity measures and *maquiladoras*. Their views on NAFTA also represent oppositional judgments about the merits of *openly* tying Mexico's economic future so thoroughly to that of the United States, as evidenced by the fact that shortly after the Agreement was ratified in Mexico, jokes began circulating in Santo Domingo that the best job prospects in the future would be those offered by the Pentagon.

If today, as John Gledhill (1997: 104) writes, for 'the majority of Mexico's growing army of deracinated urban poor, the general class opposition between "*ricos*" and "*pobres*" has greatest salience to their conditions of life', this is by no means an automatic product of historical class schisms any more than it is an inevitable consequence of class position. How people in Santo

Domingo and other *colonias populares* today view *los ricos* and *los pobres* is more particularly linked to the three remarkable and turbulent decades in which popular urban movements in Mexico, as elsewhere in Latin America, have involved millions of women and men in struggles over housing, social services, ethnic rights, domestic violence, Christian base communities, and movements around feminism, lesbian and gay rights, and ecology.[8] Especially in the 1980s, political cultures independent of the government and official parties emerged on a large scale in the popular urban sector in Mexico.

That said, it is important not to exaggerate the novelty of the cultural processes taking place. Arguments about Mexican cultural nationalism have long involved treatments of how class relates to nation, whether different classes share opposing and/or similar interests, and indeed whether and in what contexts it might be possible to speak of *a* Mexican national culture.[9] Carlos Monsiváis (1992a: 200) writes with reference to NAFTA and 'Americanization' in particular, 'The process is global, irreversible, and it must be examined from a perspective that does not characterize everything as "cultural penetration" or presume perennially virginal societies.'

Mexico entered the GATT (General Agreement on Tariffs and Trade) in 1986, in a preliminary effort to become qualitatively more 'integrated' into Washington's market schemes, while Mexican elites in the mid-1980s were still attempting to resolve the country's 1982 financial collapse and prepare the way for neoliberalism's triumph in the (widely fraudulent) elections of 1988. Especially after the fall of the Soviet system in the late 1980s, it became a matter of course for business and political leaders in Mexico to locate their country's strategy for achieving 'fast-track' modernity ever more exclusively under the North American (and NAFTA) umbrella.

With real minimum salaries in the 1990s standing at roughly the same levels as they did 30 years earlier, and workers' real earnings in 1990 less than half what they were before the 1982 crisis (see Barkin, 1991), and less still after the crisis of 1994–5, there was little confusion, or optimism, that the Agreement boded well in the short term for the poor in Mexico.

In 1993, after helping Don Armando gather hay for his animals in a rural village outside Mexico City, and after fielding his pointed questions regarding the US bombing of Iraq in January that year (see Gutmann, 1996: 7–8), I asked Armando if I could photograph him with his straw hat, deeply tanned wrinkles, and a new and nasty cut on one of his fingers. Don Armando shrugged and stared at me with his finger held up for the camera. Two days later, when I was again back in Santo Domingo, Armando's daughter came looking for me. She told me that her father was very worried about the photo I had taken. It had occurred to Armando that I might be with the CIA or DEA (Drug Enforcement Administration).[10] I had to promise never to use the picture in classes I taught and never to publish it. Why the CIA or DEA might be interested in a photograph of Don Armando and what they might do with it were not discussed.[11]

To be sure, three years later, while skimming through my ethnography of Santo Domingo, Don Armando's daughter and others noticed the photos of some family members that I had published. But I was chastised for not including Don Armando's picture, that is, for taking his accusations and admonitions seriously. My friends and acquaintances in Colonia Santo Domingo are deeply ambivalent as to how to cope with the menace and the real power of the United States.

Although the *otro lado* can be a blessing for individual Mexicans, in the view of many it remains a scourge for Mexico as a whole. Over the course of several years, while wandering familiar and unknown streets in *colonias populares* in Mexico City, I have been the target of the insult '¡*Gringo!*' on many occasions. Walking through alleys or even driving down major avenues, men, usually young men, have often yelled at me '¡*Gringo!*' or '¡*Pinche gringo!* [goddamned gringo]'. One time the accusation was accompanied by a piece of flying fruit that hit me on the head. Another time, a would-be assailant was wielding a screwdriver as if he meant to stab me. My friends Luciano and Marcos reason that this kind of cat-calling stems from simple resentment of gringos on the part of poor youth and a few adults.

What seems clear is that this kind of insult is not representative of a facile xenophobia. 'Gringos' continue to be the popular target of resentment and anger, not foreigners in general, and as often as not 'gringos' is a charge leveled against *Mexicans* who are perceived as wealthy and are unexpectedly encountered in poor neighborhoods in the capital.

On the River Plate *futbol* team made up of young men from Santo Domingo and the neighborhood of Los Reyes, an adjacent *pueblo*, most of the players had nicknames. In addition to one called Keé-kair (as in 'kicker'), Conejo (rabbit), Calaca (for a wrist cast) and Choco (as in 'chocolate', for dark brown skin), there were also Japonés (Japanese), Argentino (Argentine) and Francés (French). The name of the squad itself comes from the famous River Plate football club in Argentina. As with their middle-class compatriots, far from feeling a distaste for things foreign these young men from the poor barrios of Mexico City are especially intrigued and attracted to the exoticism of foreignness. Exoticism, too has its limits, and no one on the River Plate team has ever been nicknamed El Gringo; such a title would cross the bounds of acceptable humor and verge on gratuitous insult.

Nation-Building and the Third Millennium

How Mexico's urban poor perceive NAFTA, and whether and to whom such perceptions might ultimately matter, are questions that remain far from clear. Undoubtedly for the purposes of US commercial and foreign relations 'local' popular sentiments must be taken into account. A 1996 article in *The New York Times*, for instance, examines 'dispirited public sentiments' in Mexico with respect to NAFTA, and characterizes the overall mood among the poor as one in which 'grumpiness reigns' (see Dillon, 1996). Nonetheless, lack of enthusiasm for the Agreement on the part of the working poor is not by itself a cause for entrepreneurial worries as long as this discontent is confined to amorphous and individualized 'grumpiness'.

More disturbing to globalizing elites, perhaps, is an emerging popular judgment that although it

is increasingly easy for the rich to jet off to Houston for weekend buying sprees at the upscale Galleria shopping mall, for the vast majority of Mexicans crossing international borders still amounts to carrying out, on an individual and small-group level, the actual invasion of foreign territory. Transnationalism has not led to the withering away of the US Army or Border Patrol. In addition, whereas the same wealthy visitors are able to keep their money in dollars in Houston banks – or even in Swiss accounts – the greatest accomplishment most migrants hope to achieve is regular remittances in dollars they send back to communities wracked by peso devaluations.

The correspondence of transnationalism with rich *vendidos* (sell-outs) on the one hand, and of the Mexican nation with its poor *jodidos* (screwed) on the other, is far from casual in the minds of my neighbors in Mexico City. Many remark that the Free Trade Agreement merely confirms what they already knew to be the case: Mexico has long since lost a national sense of self, and that hereafter Mexico will not even feign national autonomy. So, with the thin façade of independence dropped, for many people in Santo Domingo, Mexico's self-reliance has become a political myth that can no longer be sustained.

Partially in response to the rupture of popular support for state institutions and the growing influence of independent urban social movements in the 1980s, the regime of Carlos Salinas de Gortari (1988–94) launched the Solidaridad/PRONASOL program early in his administration. As one government functionary put it in 1992, 'The intention behind PRONASOL is to create, through public works and services, a new urban base for the Mexican state. By the end of the 1980s the social bases of the Mexican state were unraveling' (cited in Dresser, 1994: 148).

Solidarity/PRONASOL was also designed with the Free Trade Agreement in mind. Specifically, it represented what some analysts have called 'Mexico's principal entry in the global sweepstakes to create new institutional arrangements and structures to sustain the open, market-oriented economic development strategies' of NAFTA and neoliberalism in general (Cornelius et al., 1994: 4).

Solidaridad/PRONASOL was, thus, a major federal effort designed at legitimizing the Mexican state (and the ruling PRI party) within a context of transnationalism and popular discontent. So while some men and women in Colonia Santo Domingo believe that the *maquiladoras* will shortly ride the NAFTA wave south to the capital, far more fear that the Agreement will lead to elimination of better-skilled employment through the importation of less expensive pre-fabricated products. Solidaridad/PRONASOL's rush to develop infrastructure like roads and electricity, to say nothing of a nation of consensual consumers, itself has never offered more than a few solutions to long-term employment problems in urban areas of Mexico where most of the country's population is today concentrated.[12]

As my friend Roberto contended while he re-soldered the dented radiator on my car:

> Solidaridad was meant to trick us. It's just like they come round before election time and hand things out. You know, like a bucket with the candidate's name, or a coupon for an extra [plastic] bag of milk. Well, the only difference is that the handouts are all the time. But they still don't really help if you're poor. They don't fool anyone.

Promises aside, few are still under the nationalist spell of José López Portillo's challenge during his presidency (1976–82), '¡*Preparémonos para administrar la abundancia!* [Get ready to cope with prosperity!]' The petroleum fumes that clouded the heads of so many in the 1970s have been blown away in the economic and political cataclysms that followed López Portillos's fateful words. And as petroleum promises were scattered to the winds, many contemporary premises anchoring nationalist unity suffered irreparable damage as well. Because, as Carlos Monsiváis notes, 'Nationalism depends on common and individual memories and on a minimum confidence in progress' (1992b: 71).

It is all the more remarkable therefore that despite a profound displacement of even minimal confidence in progress and even the nation-state, evidence of nationalism and nationalist consciousness persists among the poor in Mexico City. What Florencia Mallon (1995: 3) calls 'the active participation and intellectual creativity of subaltern classes' in imagining and creating nationalisms cannot be underestimated today any more than in the period in which the Mexican republic was consolidated following independence in 1821.

In many respects, of course, the nationalisms of the 21st century will be dramatically different from those of the 19th century that Mallon's study highlights. One noteworthy feature of NAFTA-era popular nationalism in Mexico is the heightened conviction on the part of many that they are unable to influence national politics, for instance, by expressing their belief that Mexico is being undermined openly and covertly by the United States. They grow less and less optimistic about Mexico's political future and increasingly disillusioned about the nature and import of democracy in their country.

The reality, most feel, is that only rarely can they control their own daily lives, and even less frequently can they influence any political process that might conceivably be regarded as democratic self-determination in Mexico. It is no surprise, then, that when they can affect either international relations, their personal existence, or both, many relish the opportunity.

In 1996, I went with Bernardino and Esther — though only in their late 20s, already veteran community militants — to a meeting to plan pre-Christmas Posada celebrations sponsored by a local chapter of the PRD. We brought along a roasted chicken and some chilies to share with the others who were to gather in an apartment in a neighboring area.

As we came into the narrow entryway into the *vecindad* (a group of single-room apartments with communal baths and sinks) we spotted two youths still in their *futbol* uniforms. After asking about the score of a nationally televised game earlier in the day, Berna asked where the meeting room was. The youths pointed us further down the walk toward some women who were washing clothes in the sinks and children in large metal washtubs. The women pointed us still further inside the *vecindad*.

Three men were already sitting in the meeting room when we arrived. Another man and a

woman arrived while I was being questioned as to
my purpose at the meeting, my political affiliations in the United States and Mexico, my relationship with the US government, and how they
could be expected to trust my intentions to 'help
the community'. They returned quickly to the
matter of my connection to the US government
– evidently there was strong suspicion that I was a
(US) federal agent of some kind.

I had seen the man who was leading the im-
promptu inquiry at collective work days in a
nearby lagoon where some community activists
met on Sundays to clean up the water and surrounding playing fields. He had seen me participating in these clean-up efforts as well. As it
appeared I was soon to be ordered out of the
meeting and the *vecindad* – two people opposed
my presence from the beginning while all but
Bernardino and Esther seemed to have serious
reservations – I decided to argue politics and
not protocol. After reiterating my ethnographic
purpose in Mexico City, my involvement as a
community and political organizer in Chicago
and Houston for many years, and my desire to
respect the wishes of all attending the meeting, I
told everyone that personally I would be aston-
ished if the United States government were interested enough in such meetings deep in the poorer
homes of the poorer neighborhoods of Mexico
City that they cared to assign a gringo agent to
investigate. I said I was fairly sure that the United
States was uninterested in such meetings.

My approach backfired immediately and I was
unceremoniously asked to leave the premises.
Bernardino escorted me to the street, apologizing
as we walked and assuring me that he would not
face untoward repercussions for having invited
me.

In retrospect, my actions and words that day
strike me later as at best naive and at worst
presumptuous. In the remainder of the article I
discuss certain issues that pertain to Mexican
popular nationalism and sovereignty as these are
developing in the late 1990s, and in the process
address recalcitrant theories of nationalism and
class, including within critical theory, that settle
for comfortable naivety and metropolitan arrogance in lieu of creative new approaches to understanding contemporary nationalism.

National Sovereignty

It turned out that for me not to consider the pre-
Posada gathering a threat to US national security
was more disrespectful of popular nationalist politics than if I had been sent to spy on the meeting
by the CIA director himself. The responses of
those in attendance that December day cannot be
reduced to knee-jerk anti-Americanism. Instead,
or in addition, I believe, they represent real frustration and bewilderment on the part of many in
the popular movements in Mexico as they try to
make contemporary sense of the Mexican nation
and of the United States.

In a process analogous to what Mercedes González de la Rocha (1991, 1994) calls the individualization and privatization of solutions to
Mexico's economic crises of the 1980s and
1990s (see also Benería, 1992), for many in the
colonias populares the defense of Mexico's nationhood and sovereignty has become a personal
rather than collective responsibility. For numerous others, of course, this goal has become illusory in the extreme; discouragement at the
possibility of defending the Mexican nation has
contributed mightily to more endemic political
malaise.

The individualization and privatization of
popular nationalism in Mexico represents in
part the fruits of two decades of social movements
among the poor that have focused rather exclusively on survival and securing rudimentary services. In the *colonias populares*, little debate has
occurred in the last 20 years on other than individual, or perhaps family and household, levels
regarding the Mexican nation and watershed developments like NAFTA. If grassroots leftist politics in the 1960s in Mexico, as elsewhere, too
often neglected daily needs and realities for the
masses of working and underemployed poor, the
pendulum in the intervening decades has not
infrequently been swung to the opposite extreme,
as recent popular social movements have customarily ignored current debate on questions of
transnationalism and nationalism.

Events such as the Chiapas uprising in 1994
and the presidential elections of 1988 and 1994
have become topics of heated discussion, of

course, including as to what these events have to do with Mexico and modernity (see Gutmann, forthcoming). This was especially true in the period around the 1988 elections. Yet fundamental pillars of Mexican nationhood – institutions like the *ejido* lands formerly held in communal trust as well as the state monopoly over basic natural resources and services like oil and telephones – have in this recent period been undermined at home and marketed abroad, all with little organized popular protest, much less rebellion. With the demise of the *ejido* and state ownership of Mexico's inheritance, says Jorge the *tienda* owner in Santo Domingo, 'Before long, only tequila, tardiness, and tourist art will carry the "Made in Mexico" stamp' of authenticity.[13]

There is still a certain desire among many ordinary Mexicans in the cities to defend what they used to regard as the collective project of Mexican sovereignty. Few of my friends and acquaintances are consistent in their feelings and actions in this respect, but most experience at least periodic bouts of anti-Americanism and patriotic fervor.

Guillermo Bonfil Batalla (1992: 175) wrote that past 'nationalization of oil, railroads, electricity, and later the banks were historic milestones which reaffirmed our national sovereignty'. Especially in the face of repeated economic crises, most recently the drastic devaluation of the peso in 1994–5, NAFTA is far more than an ideological issue alone. Now, among the other problems heightened by the Agreement, Bonfil Batalla (1992: 167–8) wrote, is that of 'cultural penetration, which translates into the imposition of the *american way of life* as a model for Mexican society'.[14]

As epitomized by the Free Trade Agreement, domestic elites are selling the country to the highest foreign bidders and making a fortune for themselves in the process.[15] Despite this popular sentiment, or perhaps in part because of it, Claudio Lomnitz (1996: 56) notes, in official venues in Mexico during this same period of crippling crisis and the auctioning off of the national patrimony, the topic of democracy has received 'obsessive attention'. As part of this discussion on democracy, Lomnitz (1996: 64–6) reports, there occurred 'a rift between state and nation' as the

state became increasingly identified with 'a small and unpopular Americanizing elite who parasitically depends on the Mexican nation' while nationalism itself became differentiated between elite and popular versions.

Whereas the Mexican upper crust has a program for transnational 'integration' into a global network headquartered in Washington, DC, Lomnitz (1996: 66) cautions, the majority of the population who seek protection of the state against the global market 'has not yet devised a political formula that can simultaneously work in a contested democratic field and provide the kind of state protection that revolutionary nationalism provided'.

The issues are complex, involving new and evolving nationalist images in Mexico and international relationships in the global arena, overnight financial catastrophes and fortunes in Mexico, and widespread opposition to Mexican immigration that continues to grow within the United States. Moreover, just as the ideas and cultural goods are reappropriated and reconfigured daily regardless of national origins or original meanings – 'LP' in Mexico signifies not only long-playing record but also '*litro de pulque*'[16] – so too can state activities inadvertently and profoundly impact national identities and awareness of international inequalities.[17]

Angela's Oil

In discussing free trade, big shoes, runaway factories, and transnationalism once again with my grandmother's friend Angela, I asked her at one point what her overall impression was of NAFTA.

'It's for the US to get more control of our *petroleo*', she replied.
'Well, I don't want your *petroleo*', I said, trying again to distance myself from the generic Gringo.
To this she responded calmly, '*Ni yo lo tengo, tampoco* [Nor do I have it, either].'

This resentment is not even particularly novel on the part of those Manuel Azuela (1939) called *los fracasados* (the failed). Over 30 years ago, Oscar Lewis (1966: 7) quotes Manuel Sánchez, one of the famous 'children of Sánchez', as saying:

> And gasoline, even though it is 'ours', eighty *centavos* a liter. *Chingao*, we were better off when the *gringos* and the English had our oil! And now that the government has nationalized electricity, too, wait and see what those bastards are going to pull on us. And there's no stealing it now . . . you're robbing the nation!

In the midst of calls in the 1990s for global trade and international interdependence there is potential for questions regarding transnational democracy and international solidarity. Weary cynicism mixes with periodic and exasperated outbursts on the streets of Colonia Santo Domingo. In the capital city a passionate desire to make sense of the madness of modernity in Mexico is as characteristic of the epoch as ennui. 'Many Mexicans now believe the train of modernity has stopped', writes Roger Bartra (1995: 144–5). 'Yet this disenchantment and delegitimation seems to be precisely what is opening the door to democracy.'

In 1994, for example, in addition to widespread political frustration and confusion in Mexico there was an armed uprising in Chiapas, the assassinations of national politicians, and presidential elections. In Santo Domingo there was, for a few months, an exhilarating sense that popular politics mattered and might just have real consequences for the political fortunes of millions of other Mexicans.[18]

Shortly after New Year's Day 1997, I asked Doña Josefina, whose husband Guillermo had lost his job as a curtain maker 'because of NAFTA', what she thought would happen in Mexico in the next few years. As a local leader of the Unión de Colonias Populares (UCP) she felt it necessary to express optimism about the future. But there was also an angry edge to her political forecasting that I had not noticed before during our six years of friendship.

> We're going to be better off. That's what we want and that's what we'll get! If it's peaceful, so much the better. But if it's not peaceful, and if there's an uprising, if nothing else, some things will change. The country will

get out of this mess, it can't continue as it is. This is too much already.

'Is it much harder to live today than before?' I asked, thinking of Josefina's early participation in founding the *colonia*, her experiences as a domestic servant beginning when she was 13 or 14, her love for reading despite her lack of formal schooling, and how she and Guillermo had eloped after Josefina's stepfather forbade them to marry.

> Yes, it's much harder today. Before, even though we were living in plastic [sheeting for housing], using oil stoves, and sometimes . . . well, actually, most of us had plastic shoes. We didn't have anything, did we? But we protected each other. If someone was sick, we helped them, or they helped us. The area was very nice then.
>
> Even if it was beans, there weren't the pressures as there are now. You can lose your job at any time now. Before, if they fired you they'd still give you some money. Now, no! Now, no contracts, no work, no nothing!
>
> So it's up to us, the *pueblo* [people], whether the change comes peacefully or in another way. But we've got to change. Having a country like Mexico and a legacy of those who struggled before us, how could we continue with the way things are? Things cannot continue as they are.

NOTES

1   Fieldwork was conducted in 1992–3, with grants from Fulbright-Hays DDRA, Wenner-Gren, National Science Foundation, Institute for Intercultural Studies, UC MEXUS, and the Center for Latin American Studies and Department of Anthropology at UC Berkeley, and 1993–5, under a grant from the National Institute for Mental Health. My gratitude to the Centro de Estudios Sociológicos and the Programa Interdisciplinario de Estudios de la Mujer, both at El Colegio de México, and to the Departamento de Antropología, Universidad Autónoma Metropolitana-Iztapalapa, for providing institutional support during fieldwork in Mexico City. Thanks also to Claudio Lomnitz, Lynn Stephen and Thomas Wilson for

comments on earlier versions of this article, and to John Gledhill for graciously accepting my endless excuses for not expanding it sooner.

2 In correspondence from Taco Bell International on 14 January 1998, I was informed that although nothing was available in Mexico, franchises were for sale elsewhere in Latin America, including in Chile, Costa Rica, the Dominican Republic, Ecuador, Guatemala, Honduras, Peru and Puerto Rico.

3 This article is thus meant to contribute to the emerging study of national culture and modernity in Mexico, for example, Claudio Lomnitz's (1996) work on contemporary Mexican nationalism and Florencia Mallon's (1995) exploration of how popular political cultures at the level of villages in Mexico and Peru interacted with regional and national arenas to construct national politics in the 19th century.

4 Jaime Serra Puche was formerly Mexico's Secretario de Comercio y Fomento Industrial, roughly equivalent to the Commerce Secretary in the United States. As indicated by his quest to engage with 'the challenge of interdependence', Serra Puche was an outspoken proponent of NAFTA in Mexico in the early 1990s.

5 BANRURAL is the Banco Nacional de Crédito Rural, the National Rural Credit Bank.

6 Guerrero's coast includes the resort areas of Acapulco, Ixtapa and Zihuatenejo.

7 During a conference for US scholars at the Chapultepec Castle in 1992, I was asked by then-US Cultural Attaché, John Dwyer, 'Do you know the history of this place?' I replied, 'You mean the Niños Héroes?' I was referring to the Mexican military cadets who, in 1847, died defending the Castle from an invading army led by US General Winfield Scott. Dwyer slapped me lightly on the shoulder and said, 'No, not *that* history.' It turned out he had been referring to the Peace Accords signed at the Castle by government and guerrilla forces from El Salvador on New Year's Eve 1991.

8 On recent social movements in the region, see especially Alvarez et al. (1998), Eckstein (1989), Escobar and Alvarez (1992), Foweraker and Craig (1990), Massolo (1992).

9 See Ramos (1962), Paz (1961), Aguilar Camín (1989), Monsiváis (1981), Bartra (1989, 1992), Lomnitz (1992, 1994).

10 The fact that the DEA is known in Mexico popularly by its acronym alone is an indication of the extent of its disrepute in Mexico.

11 Suspicions like this concerning North Americans are widespread among people in Latin America. Several acquaintances in Mexico City who are political *militantes* have asked me, 'Is there anything in your publications that the CIA can learn from?' Such concerns reflect an awareness of extensive covert activities by US agents throughout the continent as much as unwarranted paranoia. For another typical CIA allegation, this one in Nicaragua in the late 1980s, see Lancaster (1992: 75–7).

12 On Solidarity/PRONASOL's short-term infrastructure-building without long-term jobs creation, see Cornelius et al. (1994), Lustig (1994) and Dresser (1994).

13 '*Muy pronto sólo llevarán el sello "Hecho en México" el tequila, la tardanza y los Mexican curios.*'

14 Emphasis and orthography in English in original.

15 Lest we be tempted to overestimate the novelty of globalization and transnationalism, a commentary from 150 years ago:

> The bourgeoisie has through its exploitation of the world-market given a cosmopolitan character to production and consumption in every country. To the great chagrin of Reactionists, it has drawn from under the feet of industry the national ground on which it stood. All old national industries have been destroyed or are daily being destroyed . . . In place of old wants, satisfied by the productions of the country, we find new wants, requiring for their satisfaction the products of distant lands and climes. In place of the old local and national seclusion and self-sufficiency, we have intercourse in every direction, universal inter-dependence of nations. (Marx and Engels, 1969: 112)

16 A liter of *pulque*, an alcoholic beverage made from the sap of the maguey.

17 Cook (1994) discusses these issues in relation to the globalization of social movements.

18 For more on popular political culture, elections, and democracy see Gutmann (2002). For more on politics and identity in daily life in *colonias populares* in Mexico City, see Massolo (1992) and Díaz-Barriga (1998).

REFERENCES

Aguilar Camín, Héctor, ed.
(1989) *En torno a la cultura nacional*. Mexico City: Consejo Nacional para la Cultura y las Artes and Instituto Nacional Indigenista. (Orig. 1976.)

Alvarez, Sonia E., Evelina Dagnino and Arturo Escobar, eds
(1998) *Cultures of Politics/Politics of Cultures: Revisioning Latin American Social Movements*. Boulder, CO: Westview Press.

Azuela, Manuel (1939) *Los fracasados*. Mexico City: Ediciones Botas.

Barkin, David
(1991) *Un desarrollo distorsionado: La integración de México a la economía mundial*. Mexico City: Siglo Veintiuno.

Bartra, Roger
(1989) 'Culture and Political Power in Mexico', *Latin American Perspectives* 16(2): 61–9.

Bartra, Roger
(1992) *The Cage of Melancholy: Identity and Metamorphosis in the Mexican Character*, trans. Christopher J. Hall. New Brunswick: Rutgers University Press. (Orig. 1987.)

Bartra, Roger
(1995) 'South of the Border: Mexican Reflections on Distorted Images', *Telos* 103: 143–8.

Benería, Lourdes
(1992) 'The Mexican Debt Crisis: Restructuring the Economy and the Household', in Lourdes Benería and Shelley Feldman (eds) *Unequal Burden: Economic Crises, Persistent Poverty, and Women's Work*, pp. 83–104. Boulder, CO: Westview Press.

Bonfil Batalla, Guillermo
(1992) 'Dimensiones culturales del Tratado de Libre Comercio', in Gilberto Guevara Niebla and Nestór García Canclini (eds) *La educación y la cultura ante el Tratado de Libre Comercio*, pp. 157–78. Mexico City: Nexos/Nueva Imagen.

California Chamber of Commerce and California Trade and Commerce Agency (1993) *North American Free Trade Guide: The Emerging Mexican Market and Opportunities in Canada under NAFTA: Creating Jobs Through Trade*. La Jolla, CA: Center for US–Mexico Studies.

Cook, Maria Lorena
(1994) 'Regional Integration and Transnational Politics: The North American Free Trade Agreement and Popular Sector Strategies in Mexico

(DRAFT)', paper presented at Latin American Studies Association Congress, Atlanta, 10–12 March.

Cornelius, Wayne A., Ann L. Craig and Jonathan Fox
(1994) 'Mexico's National Solidarity Program: An Overview', in Wayne A. Cornelius, Ann L. Craig and Jonathan Fox (eds) *Transforming State-Society Relations in Mexico: The National Solidarity Strategy*, pp. 3–26. La Jolla, CA: Center for US–Mexico Studies.

Díaz-Barriga, Miguel
(1998) 'Beyond the Domestic and the Public: *Colonas* Participation in Urban Movements in Mexico City', in Sonia E. Alvarez, Evelina Dagnino and Arturo Escobar (eds) *Cultures of Politics/Politics of Cultures: Revisioning Latin American Social Movements*, pp. 252–77. Boulder, CO: Westview Press.

Dillon, Sam
(1996) 'Free Trade? Don't Sell Us That', *The New York Times*, 4 August: E–6.

Dresser, Denise
(1994) 'Bringing the Poor Back In: National Solidarity as a Strategy of Regime Legitimation', in Wayne A. Cornelius, Ann L. Craig and Jonathan Fox (eds) *Transforming State-Society Relations in Mexico: The National Solidarity Strategy*, pp. 143–65. La Jolla, CA: Center for US–Mexico Studies.

Eckstein, Susan, ed.
(1989) *Power and Popular Protest: Latin American Social Movements*. Berkeley: University of California Press.

Escobar, Arturo and Sonia E. Alvarez, eds
(1992) *The Making of Social Movements in Latin America: Identity, Strategy, and Democracy*. Boulder, CO: Westview Press.

Foweraker, Joe and Ann Craig, eds
(1990) *Popular Movements and Political Change in Mexico*. Boulder, CO: Lynne Rienner.

García Canclini, Néstor
(1992) 'Políticas culturales e integración norteamericana: Una perspectiva desde México', mss, Universidad Autónoma Metropolitana-Iztapalapa.

Gledhill, John
(1997) 'Liberalism, Socio-Economic Rights and the Politics of Identity: From Moral Economy to Indigenous Rights', in Richard A. Wilson (ed.) *Human Rights, Culture and Context: Anthropological Perspectives*, pp. 70–110. London: Pluto.

González de la Rocha, Mercedes
(1991) 'Family Well-Being, Food Consumption, and Survival Strategies during Mexico's Economic Crisis', in *Social Responses to Mexico's Economic Crisis of the 1980s*, Mercedes González de la Rocha and Agustín Escobar Latapí (eds), pp. 115–27. La Jolla, CA: Center for US-Mexican Studies.

González de la Rocha, Mercedes
(1994) *The Resources of Poverty: Women and Survival in a Mexican City*. Oxford: Blackwell.

Gutmann, Mathew C.
(1996) *The Meanings of Macho: Being a Man in Mexico City*. Berkeley: University of California Press.

Gutmann, Matthew C.
(2002) *The Romance of Democracy: Compliant Defiance in Contemporary Mexico*. Berkeley: University of California Press.

Lancaster, Roger N.
(1992) *Life is Hard: Machismo, Danger, and the Intimacy of Power in Nicaragua*. Berkeley: University of California Press.

Lewis, Oscar
(1966) 'A Thursday with Manuel', *New Left Review* 38: 3–21.

Lomnitz, Claudio
(1992) *Exits from the Labyrinth: Culture and Ideology in the Mexican National Space*. Berkeley: University of California Press.

Lomnitz, Claudio
(1994) 'Decadence in Times of Globalization', *Cultural Anthropology* 9(2): 257–67.

Lomnitz, Claudio
(1996) 'Fissures in Contemporary Mexican Nationalism', *Public Culture* 9: 55–68.

Lustig, Nora
(1994) 'Solidarity as a Strategy of Poverty Alleviation', in Wayne A. Cornelius, Ann L. Craig, and Jonathan Fox (eds) *Transforming State-Society Relations in Mexico: The National Solidarity Strategy*, pp. 79–96. La Jolla, CA: Center for US-Mexico Studies.

Mallon, Florencia
(1995) *Peasant and Nation: The Meaning of Postcolonial Mexico and Peru*. Berkeley: University of California Press.

Marx, Karl and Frederick Engels
(1969) 'Manifesto of the Communist Party', *Selected Works, Vol. 1*, pp. 98–137. Moscow: Progress Publishers. (Orig. 1847.)

Massolo, Alejandra
(1992) *Por amor y coraje: Mujeres en movimientos urbanos de la ciudad de México*. Mexico City: El Colegio de México.

Monsiváis, Carlos
(1981) 'Notas sobre el estado, la cultura nacional y las culturas populares en México', *Cuadernos Políticos* 30: 33–43.

Monsiváis, Carlos
(1992a) 'De la cultura mexicana en vísperas del Tratado de Libre Comercio', in Gilberto Guevara Niebla and Néstor García Canclini (eds) *La educación y la cultura ante el Tratado de Libre Comercio*, pp. 179–209. Mexico City: Nexos/Nueva Imagen.

Monsiváis, Carlos
(1992b) 'La identidad nacional ante el espejo', in José Manuel Valenzuela Arce (ed.) *Decadencia y auge de las identidades: Cultura nacional, identidad cultural y modernización*, pp. 67–72. Tijuana: El Colegio de la Frontera Norte.

Paz, Octavio
(1961) *The Labyrinth of Solitude: Life and Thought in Mexico*. trans. Lysander Kemp. New York: Grove. (Orig. 1947.)

Ramos, Samuel
(1962) *Profile of Man and Culture in Mexico*. trans. Peter G. Earle. Austin: University of Texas Press. (Orig. 1934.)

24

Immigration Reform and Nativism: The Nationalist Response to the Transnationalist Challenge

Leo R. Chavez

On November 8, 1994, the voters of California overwhelmingly passed Proposition 187, which was, in the words of its supporters, to "Save Our State" by preventing "illegal aliens in the United States from receiving benefits or public services in the State of California."[1] As with many trends that begin in California, the anti-immigrant sentiment expressed in Proposition 187 rolled across the nation, as other states, some congressional representatives, and presidential candidates expressed the need to deny health care, education, and other publicly funded benefits to immigrants.

This chapter focuses on the "rhetoric of exclusion" embedded in the contemporary discourse on immigration reform.[2] The focus on anti-immigrant discourse reflects the notion that "the occasions, spaces, and modes of representation are themselves forms of power rather than mere reflections of power residing in the real, material 'facts of life,' and the 'big structures' through which the power of class, capital, or the state are expressed."[3] At the same time, the discourse of immigration reform is situated in a space that crosses over the borders of micropolitics and macropolitics. Local immigration reform discourse can become the national discourse, but in becoming national the local can become transformed.

As California's anti-immigrant discourse flowed across the nation, the anti-"illegal alien" focus of Proposition 187 broadened considerably. Discourse about immigration reform became a way of expressing anger about demographic changes brought on by immigration, targeting anyone who might be suspected of being "immigrant," "foreign looking," "un-American," or different. By eliminating or reducing these stigmatized groups, immigration reform would, in theory, "do something" about the source of the "problems" facing U.S. citizens, problems in the economy, education system, health care, and even the relations of local governments with the federal government. To the proponents of immigration reform, illegal immigrants are not the only problem; immigration in general is a threat to the "nation" that is conceived of as a singular, predominantly Euro-American, English-speaking culture. The "new" immigrants are *trans*nationalists, or people who maintain social linkages back in the home country; they are not bound by national borders and their multiple identities are situated in communities in different nations and in communities that cross nations.[4] Transnational migrants threaten a singular vision of the "nation" because they allegedly bring "multiculturalism" and not assimilation.[5] This was clearly part of

U.S. Representative Newt Gingrich's intended message when, shortly after passage of Proposition 187, he promised that as Speaker of the House he would preside over a freewheeling congressional debate about the "cultural meanings of being American."[6]

Proponents of immigration reform, therefore, often cast their net on issues much wider than just illegal immigration. For example, flush with victory after passage of Proposition 187, the proposition's backers announced that their agenda was actually much broader and included affirmative action, bilingual education, and the promotion of English as the official language.[7] Their concerns led U.S. Representative Toby Roth (a Republican from Wisconsin) to introduce a bill that would effectively halt funding for bilingual education, abolish bilingual electoral ballots, and allow individuals to bring civil suits against institutions that violate English-only federal statutes.[8] The reason such a law is necessary, according to the bill itself, is because "It has been the longstanding national belief that full citizenship in the United States requires fluency in English."[9]

The question of who is an "American" and anti-immigrant discourse become entangled in revealing ways. For instance, on October 18, 1994, California State Senator Craven, a Republican from Oceanside, was quoted as saying "that the [California] state legislature should explore requiring all people of Hispanic descent to carry an identification card that would be used to verify legal residence."[10] By targeting "all Hispanics," citizens, legal residents, and undocumented immigrants, California Senator Craven defines all Hispanics as belonging to a suspect class. Why Senator Craven focuses only on Hispanics is not clear. After all, California's ethnic diversity includes many other ethnic groups, including undocumented Canadians and Europeans who overstay their visas. Perhaps the answer has to do with the assumptions about social evolution and progress implicit in immigration discourse. Discredited nineteenth-century scientific notions about social evolution continue to underlie present-day discourse on national encounters. This discourse positions Euro-Americans and Europeans at the top of a hierarchical ordering of civilized ("developed" and "technologically advanced" being common metaphors for this hierarchy) societies in contrast to less civilized ("less developed" and "technologically backward") societies. Senator Craven expressed these assumptions when addressing a senate hearing on migrant workers held in San Diego in February 1993; he said that "migrant workers were on a lower scale of humanity."[11]

Gifts to charitable organizations provide another example of how anti-immigrant sentiments extend beyond a concern with "illegal aliens." In Orange County, California, donors to charities are increasingly stipulating that those who receive their gifts not be illegal aliens. In some cases, the donors specifically state that the recipients should be English speaking, or even non-Latinos to ensure their citizenship status. As one director of a charitable agency said, "I had to find someone white and English-speaking" to receive the donations.[12]

Perhaps one of the clearest statements about the threat of immigration to the "complexion" of American society comes from Pat Buchanan, a presidential candidate during the 1992 and 1996 elections. Buchanan said: "A non-white majority is envisioned if today's immigration continues." Given this prognosis, he argues that America needs a "time out" from immigration.[13] Buchanan would like a moratorium on all immigration to the United States, not merely closing the borders to undocumented immigrants.

The extent to which the anti-immigrant debate is racially polarized is suggested by voting patterns in California. Proposition 187 passed with 59 percent of the votes cast. But white Californians, in particular, appeared to be expressing sentiments of unease over immigration. Two out of three voting whites in California (about 67 percent) voted for the proposition, a significantly larger proportion than the vote among African Americans and Asian Americans (about half of each group voted for it) and Latinos (only 23 percent voted for it).[14] The voting block provided by white voters ensured passage of Proposition 187. Importantly, even though whites account for about 57 percent of California's population, they account for about 80 percent of the voters, thus their views take on tremendous power. In contrast, while Latinos account for 25 percent of the state's population, they accounted for only 8 percent of those voting.[15] White voters in California appear to be sending a symbolic statement about their concern over immigration and the "new" immigrants.

Since passage of Proposition 187 by the voters of California, a number of U.S. Representatives and Senators have submitted bills dealing with the "immigration problem." Following the assumption put forward by proponents of Proposition 187, that social services, not jobs, are the magnet drawing undocumented immigrants to the United States, national immigration reform proposals target aid to immigrants.[16] For example, Representative Ron Packard (Republican from Oceanside) proposed denying illegal immigrants federal benefits offered to victims of flooding in California.[17] In June 1995, a House task force chaired by Representative Elton Gallegly (Republican from Simi Valley) submitted its report urging an approach similar to Proposition 187 at the national level. The task force recommended denying all public services, except emergency health care, to undocumented immigrants. In order for hospitals to receive reimbursement for treating undocumented immigrants, however, they would have to notify the Immigration and Naturalization Service of the patients before they are discharged.[18] The task force also recommended allowing states to cut off public education to undocumented students. One of the task force's most contentious recommendations is to amend the U.S. Constitution to end automatic citizenship for U.S.-born children whose parents are undocumented immigrants.[19]

Representative Gallegly was an early proponent of this policy. In October 1991, he introduced legislation into Congress to amend the U.S. Constitution to deny citizenship to a child born in the United States if neither of the parents are citizens and if the child's mother is not at least a legal resident.[20] His argument is that even though this is a nation of immigrants, we must reduce immigration – both legal and undocumented:

> We must recognize, however, that the United States is also a nation of finite resources and opportunities which must be available to and shared by all its citizens. Today, in many parts of this country our cities and towns

are being overrun with immigrants, both legal and undocumented, who pose major economic and law enforcement problems for local governments and place an added burden on their already strained budgets.[21]

Although Gallegly's legislation focuses on the children of undocumented immigrants, his statement clearly makes little differentiation between legal and illegal immigrants. He views immigrants generally as a "problem," as outsiders, regardless of immigration status. Thus, his attempts to stop conferring citizenship on the children of undocumented immigrants appears as but one part of a broader agenda to rid the country of all "outsiders," that is, immigrants and their U.S.-born children.

Perhaps the shift in focus from undocumented immigrants to legal immigrants became complete in June of 1995 when the U.S. Commission on Immigration Reform, headed by Barbara Jordan of Texas, recommended that legal immigration into the United States be sharply reduced.[22] President Clinton has also suggested that "You can make a good case for modest reduction of the quota on legal immigration."[23]

These emerging views on legal immigration set the context for national immigration reform proposals that target all immigrants, including those legally in the country. For example, Representative E. Clay Shaw, Jr. (a Republican from Florida) proposed that only citizens be provided benefits such as Aid to Families with Dependent Children, food stamps, and Medicaid. Denying these benefits to legal residents, would, according to Representative Shaw, take away the attraction of people to come to this country, that is, welfare and the social safety net.[24] In all, the Republican legislative program for immigration reform that was brought to the U.S. House of Representatives in Proposition 187's wake would deny sixty kinds of federal assistance to millions of legal immigrants, including health programs, Social Security, Supplementary Security Income, disability payments, housing assistance, childhood immunizations, subsidized school lunches, job training, and aid to the homeless.[25] On March 24, 1995, the House of Representatives passed the Personal Responsibility Act, which included many of these proposals to limit social services to legal immigrants.[26]

The U.S. Senate followed the House's example when it passed its own bill on welfare policy on September 19, 1995. The Senate's bill cuts fewer benefits for legal immigrants than the House's but also restricts benefits for naturalized citizens who immigrate after the bill's enactment.[27] If enacted, this would be the first time in U.S. history that government benefits were denied naturalized citizens because they were not born in the United States, thus establishing a two-tiered or segmented structure for citizenship. But even if these parts of the bill are ultimately dropped, they indicate the willingness of policy-makers to treat naturalized citizens differently from U.S.-born citizens. This is a sign of a major reconceptualization of the relationship of immigrants to the nation.

Finally, the U.S. Congress is considering legislation that would reduce the number of legal immigrants from 800,000 to about 535,000 per year. This reduction would be accomplished by eliminating several preference categories for family reunification, including the preferences for foreign adult children and parents of U.S. citizens and legal residents, and for adult brothers and sisters of U.S. citizens. The aim of eliminating these preferences is to stop the network migration of extended family members, while allowing nuclear families to continue to reunite in the United States. Eliminating these preferences would shut the door on an estimated 2.4 million foreigners – mostly Mexicans and Filipinos – waiting in queues to enter the United States on the basis of family ties.[28]

In sum, the nativist revolt against undocumented immigrants that began in California quickly reached national proportions, targeting all immigrants. The policy recommendations emanating from state and federal legislators and the discourse spewing forth from presidential candidates are of the sort not heard with such force since the nativist movements of the late 1800s and the early twentieth century. Should some of these proposals come to pass – especially such dramatic changes as a constitutional amendment to deny citizenship to children born in the United States, and distinctions between citizens by birth and those naturalized – then this round of nativism will have ushered in some of the most profound changes in how America – the United States – perceives itself as a community, as a people, and as a nation. Traditional definitions of who deserves to be an American and receive the benefits of the social contract are being challenged and redefined in unprecedented ways.

As the nation rushes along the anti-immigrant current, it is important to contemplate how we arrived at this juncture in our history and to analyze the underlying nature the attack on immigrants is taking and its implications for the future. Why this level of nativism now? Why do immigration reform proposals target mainly women and children? Or, to put it another way, why target reproduction of the immigrant labor force? And, what does this tell us about the production of immigrant labor that specific sectors of our economy have grown to depend upon?

The New Nativism in Historical Perspective

Why is anti-immigrant rhetoric so prominent in the contemporary discourse on the state of the nation? To answer this question, we must remember that Americans have always had a love-hate relationship with immigration, despite a congratulatory self-image as a "nation of immigrants." [For further treatment of the history of American nativism, see chapters 1 and 9–11 of this volume – Ed.] Because of America's history, "immigration" has become what anthropologists call a key symbol in American culture.[29] Immigration is such a central and powerful concept that it is endowed with a multiplicity of referents and meanings; it raises highly charged emotions, which can often be contradictory.[30] In short, nativism and xenophobia have been constant themes in American history, although they become prominent during specific historical moments. Contemporary anti-immigrant posturing can be traced to changes in immigration law, continued undocumented immigration, an economy undergoing repeated cycles of recession, and the end of the Cold War.[31]

In many ways, the "new" nativism sounds strikingly similar to the "old" nativism. In their book *The Immigration Time Bomb*, Richard Lamm, the ex-Governor of Colorado, and Gary Imhoff, an ex-official of the Immigration and Naturalization Service, warn about the perils of immigration in a way that is reminiscent of older laments:

> At today's massive levels, immigration has major negative consequences – economic, social, and demographic – that overwhelm its advantages.... To solve the immigration crisis, we Americans have to face our limitations. We have to face the necessity of passing laws to restrict immigration and the necessity of enforcing those laws. If we fail to do so, we shall leave a legacy of strife, violence, and joblessness to our children.[32]

More recently, Peter Brimelow, himself an immigrant from Great Britain, has vociferously echoed Lamm and Imhoff's dark scenario for a future of continued immigration.[33] America's problems, according to Brimelow, are due to immigrants who lack the cultural background of earlier European, especially British, immigrants. He argues that America needs to "rethink" immigration and calls for a "time out" from immigration.[34] Failure to restrict immigration, Brimelow warns, will lead America on the road to becoming an "alien nation."

Discourse surrounding Proposition 187 and subsequent immigration reform resonate with Lamm and Imhoff's and Brimelow's views, with their heavy emphasis on the conflict and threat to the nation posed by transnational migrants who do not respect traditional borders and the sovereignty of nation states. In arguing for the urgency of their cause, the proponents of immigration reform often characterize the immigrant as the "enemy" in metaphors of war. Immigrants become the new threat to national security and identity, filling the void left by the loss of the old enemies after the collapse of the Soviet Union and the end of the Cold War. In this respect, the anti-immigrant discourse of the 1990s corresponds to the new vision of "America First" put forward by Pat Buchanan and increasingly touted by Republican presidential candidates. The anti-internationalist stance of "America First" enthusiasts carries with it "a kind of nativistic

foreigner-bashing," according to Jeremy Rosner of the Carnegie Endowment for International Peace.[35]

Immigrants as foreigners who threatened the American way of life was a central part of the Proposition 187 campaign in California. Proponents of Proposition 187 banked on the widely held perception that an "invasion" of undocumented immigrants was the cause of California's economic problems and eroding the lifestyles of U.S. citizens to the point of reducing the nation to a "Third World" country.[36] The reference to "Third World" is a strategic marker that metaphorically alludes to social evolution and the threat of immigration leading to a de-evolution of "American civilization."

U.S. Representative Dana Rohrabacher (a Republican from Huntington Beach, California), in arguing for passage of Proposition 187 shortly before the election, carried the war metaphor even further when he said, "Unlawful immigrants represent the liberal/left foot soldiers in the next decade."[37] Another proponent of Proposition 187, Ruth Coffey, the director of Stop Immigration Now, frequently raised the specter of "multiculturalism," commenting that "I have no intention of being the object of 'conquest,' peaceful or otherwise, by Latinos, Asians, blacks, Arabs or any other groups of individuals who have claimed my country."[38] Of course, the irony of Ms. Coffey's statement appears to go unnoticed; as a result of the Mexican American War in the mid-1800s, the United States "conquered" California. An appeal to historical memory, however, can be subtle yet telling. Ronald Prince, one of the cofounders of the Save Our State (SOS) initiative, speaking to a gathering in Orange Country, explaining how Proposition 187 would stop undocumented immigration, used a metaphor that harkened back to images of frontier justice, when Mexicans were routinely hanged by vigilante mobs: "You are the posse and SOS is the rope."[39]

Glenn Spencer, founder of the Voice of Citizens Together, a San Fernando Valley-based group that was a principal grassroots backer of Proposition 187, also put his views into a war metaphor framework. Before the November elections in California, he argued for passage of Proposition 187 because illegal immigration is "part of a reconquest of the American Southwest by foreign Hispanics. Someone is going to be leaving the state. It will either be them or us."[40] After the passage of Proposition 187, at a rally to deny public education to illegal immigrants and to denounce the Clinton Administration's proposed $40-billion aid package to Mexico, Spencer said, "It boils down to this: Do we want to retain control of the Southwest more than the Mexicans want to take it from us?" He went on to compare "the conflict" to the Vietnam war: "It's a struggle between two groups of people for territory."[41] Even when confronted with academic research that suggests immigrants generally assimilate and improve their economic well-being, Spencer's comment was that "What we have in Southern California is not assimilation – It's annexation by Mexico."[42]

Immigrants as a threat to national security, sovereignty, and control of territory is central to the war metaphors as used in debates about immigration. As Bette Hammond, the head of S.T.O.P.I.T. (Stop the Out-of-Control Problems of Immigration Today), a Marin Country-based group that was an early and key organizer on behalf of Proposition 187, put it: "We've got to take back our country."[43] Newt Gingrich, speaking about immigration reform, also raised the sovereignty issue: "If they're illegal, why aren't they gone? Whatever law we have to pass to be able to protect American sovereignty and to be able to say we're not going to have illegal people in the United States, we should pass."[44]

According to Linda B. Hayes, the Proposition 187 media director in southern California, the loss of U.S. territory can occur as a result of the rapid demographic shifts caused by Mexican immigration. As she wrote in a letter to the *New York Times*,

> By flooding the state with 2 million illegal aliens to date, and increasing that figure each of the following 10 years, Mexicans in California would number 15 million to 20 million by 2004. During those to years about 5 million to 8 million Californians would have emigrated to other states. If these trends continued, a Mexico-controlled California could vote to establish Spanish as

the sole language of California, 10 million more English-speaking Californians could flee, and there could be a statewide vote to leave the Union and annex California to Mexico.[45]

Why people who left a country in search of economic opportunity and a better life would vote to return the state to that country is not explained. Nor is it clear why, in the year 2004, the children and grandchildren of immigrants – all U.S. citizens who did not grow up in Mexico and who will not have the same nostalgia for Mexico as their parents or grandparents – would vote to annex California to Mexico. Of course, such questions may be beside the point since nativist arguments rely more on emotional resonance than the marshaling of empirical evidence and support found in academic treatises.[46]

Proposition 187 and the proposals for immigration reform that followed, then, can be traced to xenophobia related to the changing complexion of immigrants, frustration with the ineffectiveness of the 1986 immigration law to control undocumented immigration, economic recessions, and a new nationalism. As anti-immigrant as the discourse appears, immigration reform targets predominantly women and children, that is, the reproduction of the immigrant labor force. Why is this and what does it mean?

Targeting Reproduction While Ignoring Production

Anthropologist Claude Meillassoux long ago reminded us of the importance of focusing on both production and reproduction when examining immigration.[47] Proposition 187 and most of the immigration reform proposals that followed it target social services, especially health care and education, as the principal attraction to immigrants, both legal and undocumented. The logic is that denial of social services to immigrants reduces the incentives for immigration and thus fewer immigrants will decide to come to the United States. This logic, however, targets reproduction – women and children – and does very little to stop the production-work of immigrant labor.

This is not to suggest that some proposals do not advocate increased funding for the Border

Patrol and that the Justice Department does not occasionally "get tough" on employers, because both of these are true.[48] Rather, the point here is that most of the proposals for immigration reform focus on social services, targeting reproduction of the immigrant family and thereby reducing the costs associated with immigrant labor while maintaining, or even increasing, the profits of that labor. It is certainly true that immigrant families have reproductive costs, some of which are subsidized by society, such as education. Immigrant workers, on the other hand, have many benefits for production, since they cost society little to produce (the costs of raising and educating them were borne by their families and home societies), are often willing to perform low-wage work, are typically young and relatively healthy, and are often afraid to pursue, or are unaware of, their rights as workers. By targeting reproduction, immigration reform does very little to undermine the lucrative and highly profitable relationship between employers and workers.

Proposition 187 and most of the immigration reform proposals discussed above do not target production. They leave immigrant workers and their employers curiously out of the picture. For example, Proposition 187 did not advocate more funds for ensuring fair labor standards and practices, thus reducing the incentive for hiring immigrant, especially undocumented, labor. As Labor Secretary Robert B. Reich noted: "One reason that employers in the United States are willing to risk employer sanctions right now and hire illegal immigrants is because they can get those illegal immigrants at less than the minimum wage, put them in squalid working conditions, and they know that those illegal immigrants are unlikely to complain."[49] Nor did the proposition propose increased enforcement of employer sanctions. The implicit message is that we are going after the reproduction of the undocumented labor force not the laborer nor the employer.

The debate surrounding Proposition 187 provides further insight into this point. The proposition's proponents targeted those who are "breaking the law" and don't deserve social service benefits. Governor Wilson argued that "Californians are justifiably fed up with those who break the law and ignore the rules that

govern a civilized society. Californians want people held accountable for their actions again – whether it's a career criminal, a deadbeat dad, or someone who violates immigration laws."[50] Proposition 187, however, targeted only undocumented immigrants' use of social services, not employers who might be breaking the law by hiring undocumented workers. Indeed, in correspondence between Pete Wilson and immigration authorities, Wilson often encouraged the immigration commissioner to stop raids on California companies, arguing that sweeping up undocumented workers caused unnecessary disruptions to business.[51] Such actions stand in marked contrast to anti-immigrant discourse, suggesting that production must be safeguarded but reproduction of the worker's family must be stopped.

Getting rid (the euphemism is "voluntary return migration") of spouses and children would reduce the costs associated with immigrant labor by removing those most likely to use social services. Parenthetically, a more cynical argument is that the objective in denying education and health care to undocumented immigrants is not to pressure them to return to their country of origin but to create a permanent underclass of low-educated, available low-wage workers. While I believe this is the practical outcome of the immigration reform proposals, I am assuming here that the goal of immigration reform is as stated: to remove the alleged incentives (social services) attracting undocumented immigrants to the United States. Research has shown, however, that undocumented immigrants come to the United States to work and rarely come to get an education.[52] It is the children of undocumented immigrants that are in the public school system. Research has also shown that immigrant women and children are more likely than immigrant men, especially among the undocumented, to use health services.[53] But even though they are more likely than adult males to use health services, immigrant women, particularly the undocumented, continue to face major health risks because they significantly underuse critical preventive medicine.[54] Despite the medical and financial implications, the first action Governor Wilson took after passage of Proposition 187 was to move to cut off prenatal care to undocumented women.[55] However, there is absolutely no evidence that if you deny health care for women and children, or deny education or school lunches for children for that matter, that it will do anything to reduce the economic magnet – jobs – that draws immigrant labor to the United States. This is true for both undocumented and legal immigration.

This relationship between production (positive) and reproduction (negative) is revealed most clearly in the proposals for a guest-worker program. At the same time that proponents of immigration reform appear to be clamoring for an end or reduction in immigration, there are serious proposals to bring foreign workers to the United States on a temporary basis to work in agriculture and highly competitive high-technology companies. Shortly after the November 1994 elections were over in California, Governor Wilson was in Washington promoting just such a new *bracero* or guest-worker program.[56] An advocate of providing California agribusiness low-cost seasonal labor (guest-workers) when he was a U.S. senator, Wilson again made his plea for a guest-worker program in an address to the Heritage Foundation. Wilson justified a guest-worker program as as a way "to alleviate the pressure for illegal immigration created by Mexico's inability to produce enough jobs for its people." Wilson clearly stated his vision of a return to a use of primarily Mexican male labor that would exclude the workers' families: "It makes sense – it has in the past, it may well continue to do so in the future – to have some sort of guest-worker program. But not the kind of thing we have been seeing where there has been massive illegal immigration, where whole families have come and where they are . . . requiring services that are paid for by state taxpayers."[57] Harold Ezzell, a coauthor of Proposition 187 and a past official of the INS, has also suggested a guest-worker program as a means of meeting labor shortages that cannot be filled by U.S. workers.[58] Even Representative Gallegly, who is so adamant about denying citizenship to children born in the United States if their parents are not legal residents, acknowledged that there may be a need for immigrants to work in temporary jobs in the United States.[59]

This is the logical next step since a guest-worker program institutionalizes the perfect cost-benefit ratio for immigrant labor: bringing foreign workers produced with no costs and who are not allowed to bring their families, thus not incurring reproductive costs (health care, education) here. In essence, production without reproduction, workers without families, sojourners not settlers.

To a certain extent we have come full circle in the debate over immigration, especially immigration from Mexico. In 1911, the Dillingham Commission, which was established to study the immigration issue, argued that Mexican migration should be promoted as the best solution to the Southwest's labor problem.[60] Unlike Japanese, Chinese, and Southern and Eastern European immigrants, the Commission argued that Mexicans were "homing pigeons" who would work for a short time in the United States and then return to their families in Mexico. It even went so far as to exempt Mexicans from the head tax for immigrants that was established under the immigration laws of 1903 and 1907. The Commission's advocacy of single male workers allowed to work on a temporary basis – without their families accompanying them – was institutionalized in contract labor programs during the 1910s and later during the Bracero Program, which lasted from 1942 to 1964. Ultimately, however, even some temporary workers manage to bring their families to join them and become settlers. As Doris Meissner, Commissioner of the INS has observed, "History shows that every contract-worker program falls victim to the inexorable goal of workers who wish to reunite with their families or to become members of the community in which they work."[61]

Even undocumented workers, our unofficial guest-workers, and their families have a remarkable capacity to develop a sense of community in the United States.[62] Although they may have come originally as temporary migrants, over time they marry or bring their spouse and children to join them in the United States, have children born here who therefore become citizens (what I have termed "binational families"), have other relatives and friends living nearby, and have important networks in the labor market.[63] These social and familial developments increase the likelihood of settlement in the United States.[64]

Final Thoughts

What is new in the "new" nativism, perhaps, is the extent to which immigrants, even those who are legal residents and citizens, are being reimagined as less deserving members of the community.[65] What began as a prairie fire against undocumented immigrants quickly ignited into a major round of immigration reform, with immigrants facing denial of many social services. The benefits immigrants have historically brought to this "nation of immigrants" have become overshadowed by the cost of immigration. To be "immigrant" today is tantamount to being a "cost" to society, a cost that must be reduced if the nation is to get its house in order and balance its budget. In the discourse of contemporary social sciences, immigrants have become the less moral, undeserving, and threatening Other in society.

In the current discourse on immigration, race matters but in a less than obvious way. As Balibar has noted, the category of immigration has replaced the notion of race. In other words, rather than speaking in terms of biological differentiation, genetic inferiority, or social evolution, proponents of immigration reform cloak a "neoracism" in a language that talks about "scales of humanity," "us and them," "conquest and sovereignty" and "a nonwhite majority."[66] Such phrasing alerts us to the fact that the "new" immigration from Latin America, particularly Mexico, and Asia is qualitatively different from the "old" immigration from Europe.

The new immigrants pose a transnationalist challenge to a narrow nationalist construction of the nation. In this sense, the current wave of immigration reform proposals reflect a nationalist response to this transnational challenge. Immigrants, it is said, are harbingers of a "nonwhite majority," multiculturalism, and an end of English dominance. As a consequence, they are depicted as posing a threat to the fiction of the "national culture" and the nationalist order of society. They undermine the notion of a singular American identity. Immigrants, as the transnational movements of people across borders – both political and cultural – underscore the dis-

order inherent in the order implied by the fiction of a singular cultural heritage.[67]

Thus enters the recurrent contradiction in America's immigration history. On the one hand, there are those who have desired immigrant labor because it provides a valuable asset to the economy. On the other hand are those Americans who believe immigrants threaten that which is "American." The specific nature of that threat may find different emphasis during any particular historical moment. In the current epoch, the threat is both cultural and fiscal. The families of immigrant workers have costs to society. Reducing society's obligations and responsibilities to immigrant families is way of balancing the budget but not necessarily a way to produce healthy and educated members of society. Nor are such policies sure to reduce the flow of immigrants, legal or otherwise. What do we get, then, from this new round of nativism? Rather than giving us an accurate portrayal of immigrant motives and behavior, the discourse of immigration reform tells us more about the fears and character of a nation under stress. In this sense, the new nativism is a lot like the old nativism.

NOTES

1 California Ballot Pamphlet 1994. On November 20, 1995, a federal district judge in Los Angeles ruled that the state of California is preempted from barring illegal immigrants from elementary and secondary education, and from federally funded health care and social welfare services. These issues are far from resolved, however, since the advocates for Proposition 187 intend to take their case to the U.S. Supreme Court. See Paul Feldman, "Parts of 187 Thrown Out," *Los Angeles Times* 21 November 1995: A1.

2 For an excellent analysis of the immigration debate in Europe, see Verena Stolcke, "Talking Culture: New Boundaries, New Rhetorics of Exclusion in Europe," *Current Anthropology* 36: 1–24, 1995.

3 Michael Peter Smith, "Postmodernism, Urban Ethnography, and the New Social Space of Ethnic Identity," *Theory and Society* 21: 493–531, 1992.

4   This view of transnational migrants converges with contemporary social theory. For example, see Linda Basch, Nina Glick Schiller, and Cristina Szanton Blanc, *Nations Unbound: Transnational Projects, Postcolonial Predicaments, and Deterritorialized Nation-States* (Amsterdam: Gordon and Breach, 1994). Also, postmodern definitions of identity critique the notion that a person must belong to only one community, geographically defined; rather, people have multiple and often contradictory identities, inhabiting a diversity of communities. See Michael Peter Smith, "Postmodernism, Urban Ethnography, and the New Social Space of Ethnic Identity," *Theory and Society* 21: 493–531, 1992. For a discussion of undocumented immigrants positioned in multiple communities, see Leo R. Chavez, "The Power of the Imagined Community: The Settlement of Undocumented Mexicans and Central Americans in the United States," *American Anthropologist* 96: 52–73, 1994; Roger Rouse, "Mexican Migration and the Social Space of Postmodernism," *Diaspora* 1: 8–23, 1991; and Michael Kearney, "Borders and Boundaries of State and Self at the End of Empire," *Journal of Historical Sociology* 4(1): 52–74, 1991.

5   Gebe Martinez and Patrick J. McDonnell, "Prop. 187 Forces Rely on Message – Not Strategy," *Los Angeles Times* 30 October 1991: A1.

6   Melissa Healy, "Gingrich Lays out Rigid GOP Agenda," *Los Angeles Times* 12 November 1994: A1.

7   Patrick J. McDonnell, "Prop. 187 Win Spotlights Voting Disparity," *Los Angeles Times* 10 November 1994: A3. See also Patrick J. McDonnell, "Is Prop. 187 Just the Beginning?" *Los Angeles Times* 28 January 1995: A1.

8   Charles King, "Too Narrow a View of Who's American," *Los Angeles Times* 21 September 1995: B11 (Orange County edition).

9   Charles King, "Too Narrow a View of Who's American," *Los Angeles Times* 21 September 1995: B11 (Orange County edition).

10 Maria C. Hunt, "Craven Says All Hispanics Should Carry I.D. Cards," *San Diego Union-Tribune* 18 October 1994: A1.

11 Maria C. Hunt, "Craven Says All Hispanics Should Carry I.D. Cards." *San Diego Union-Tribune* 18 October 1994: A1.

12 Leslie Berkman, "Some Attach Strings to the Spirit of Giving," *Los Angeles Times* 24 November 1994: B1 (Orange County edition).

13 Patrick J. Buchanan, "What Will America Be in 2050?" *Los Angeles Times* 28 October 1994: B11. See also John L. Graham, "Xenophobic Fears about a 'Nonwhite Majority' Are Nonsense," *Los Angeles Times* 27 November 1994: B17 (Orange County edition).

14 Patrick J. McDonnell, "Prop. 187 Win Spotlights Voting Disparity," *Los Angeles Times* 10 November 1994: A3. See also Philip Martin, "Proposition 187 in California," *International Migration Review* 24: 255–63, 1995.

15 Patrick J. McDonnell, "Prop. 187 Win Spotlights Voting Disparity," *Los Angeles Times* 10 November 1994: A3.

16 Kevin R. Johnson, "Public Benefits and Immigration: The Intersection of Immigration Status, Ethnicity, Gender, and Class," *UCLA Law Review* 42(6): 1509–75, 1995.

17 Lisa Richwine, "Packard Vows to Bar Illegal Immigrants from Flood Aid," *Los Angeles Times* 14 January 1995: B1 (Orange County edition).

18 Marc Lacey, "New Task Force Targets Illegal Immigration." *Los Angeles Times* 16 March 1995: A3.

19 Marc Lacey, "Immigration Report Gains Key Support," *Los Angeles Times* 30 June 1995: A34.

20 Elton Gallegly, "Gallegly Seeks to End Automatic Citizenship for Illegal Alien Children," press release of October 22, 1991, from the Office of Congressman Elton Gallegly, Washington, D.C., 1991.

21 Elton Gallegly, "Time to Amend Our Birthright Citizenship Laws," speech presented by Rep. Gallegly in the House of Representatives, October 22, 1991. Copy in author's files.

22 Janet Hook, "Immigration Cutback Urged by U.S. Panel," *Los Angeles Times* 8 June 1995: A1.

23 Alison Mitchell, "President Rebuts Some GOP Themes on Economic Woes," *New York Times* 5 September 1995: A1.

24 Elizabeth Shogren, "Plans to Cut Safety Net Leave Legal Immigrants Dangling," *Los Angeles Times* 21 November 1994: A1.

25 Aaron Epstein, "GOP Targets Legal Noncitizens," *Orange County Register* 27 December 1994: A1.

26 Elizabeth Shogren, "House OK's Welfare Overhaul that Cuts off Aid Guarantees," *Los Angeles Times* 25 March 1995: A1.

27 Elizabeth Shogren, "Senate Approves Shifting Control of Welfare to States," *Los Angeles Times* 20 September 1995: A1.

28 "Congress Moves on Immigration Reform," *Migration News* 2(10) October 1995: 1. Philip Martin, editor, *Migration News*, 1004 Eagle Place, Davis, CA 95616.

29 Clifford Geertz, *The Interpretation of Cultures* (New York: Basic Books, 1973).

30 See, generally, Stephen Steinberg, *The Ethnic Myth: Race, Ethnicity, and Class in America* (Boston: Beacon Press, 1981); John Higham, *Stragers in the Land: Patterns of American Nativism 1860–1925* (New York: Atheneum, 1985 [1955]); Stephen Jay Gould, *The Mismeasure of Man* (New York: W.W. Norton, 1981); Rita J. Simon, *Public Opinion and the Immigrant* (Lexington, MA: Lexington Books, 1985).

31 On these issues, see David M. Reimers, *Still the Golden Door: The Third World Comes to America* (New York: Columbia University Press, 1985); Frank D. Bean, Barry Edmonston, and Jeffrey S. Passel, *Undocumented Migration to the United States* (Washington, DC: Urban Institute Press, 1990); Rita J. Simon, *Public Opinion and the Immigrant* (Lexington, MA: Lexington Books, 1985); and Wayne A. Cornelius, "America in the Era of Limits," *Working Paper No. 3* (La Jolla, CA: Center for U.S.-Mexican Studies, University of California, San Diego, 1980).

32 Richard D. Lamm and Gary Imhoff, *The Immigration Time Bomb* (New York: Truman Talley Books, 1985).

33 Peter Brimelow, *Alien Nation: Common Sense About America's Immigration Disaster* (New York: Random House, 1995).

34 Peter Brimelow, "Time to Rethink Immigration?" *National Review* 22 June: 30–46, 1992.

35 Jim Mann, "GOP Candidates Warm to Anti-Foreign Policy," *Los Angeles Times* 24 September 1995: A3.

36 Gebe Martinez and Patrick J. McDonnell, "Prop. 187 Forces Rely on Message – Not Strategy," *Los Angeles Times* 30 October 1994: A1.

37 Gebe Martinez and Patrick J. McDonnell, "Prop. 187 Forces Rely on Message – Not Strategy," *Los Angeles Times* 30 October 1994: A1.

38 Gebe Martinez and Patrick J. McDonnell, "Prop. 187 Forces Rely on Message – Not Strategy," *Los Angeles Times* 30 October 1994: A1.

39 Patrick J. McDonnell, "Prop. 187 Heats up Debate over Immigration," *Los Angeles Times* 10 August 1994: A1.

40 Gebe Martinez and Patrick J. McDonnell, "Prop. 187 Forces Rely on Message – Not Strategy," *Los Angeles Times* 30 October 1994: A1.

41 Patrick J. McDonnell, "Is Prop. 187 Just the Beginning?" *Los Angeles Times* 28 January 1995: A1.

42 Spencer was quoted in Patrick J. McDonnell, "Study Disputes Immigrant Stereotypes, Cites Gains," *Los Angeles Times* 3 November 1995: A1. He was responding to the study "The Changing Immigrants of Southern California" by Dowell Myers, the first report from the research project California Immigration and the American Dream: Integration and Advancement of the New Arrivals (Los Angeles: School of Urban and Regional Planning, University of Southern California, November 1995).

43 Patrick J. McDonnell, "Prop. 187 Heats up Debate over Immigration," *Los Angeles Times* 10 August 1994: A1.

44 Melissa Healy, "House GOP Charts California Agenda," *Los Angeles Times* 13 November 1994: A1.

45 Linda B. Hayes, "Letter to the Editor: California's Prop. 187," *New York Times* 15 October 1994: 18.

46 For a discussion of the issues related to return migration among undocumented immigrants from Mexico and Central America, see Leo R. Chavez, *Shadowed Lives: Undocumented Immigrants in American Society* (Ft. Worth: Harcourt, Brace and Jovanovich College Publishers, 1992).

47 Claude Meillassoux, *Maidens, Meal and Money: Capitalism and the Domestic Community* (Cambridge: Cambridge University Press, 1975).

48 James Bornemeier, "Clinton Moves to Curb Illegal Immigration," *Los Angeles Times* 8 February 1995: A3. See also Janet Hook, "Clinton Moves to Speed Deportations," *Los Angeles Times* 7 May 1995: A1.

49 James Bornemeier, "Clinton Moves to Curb Illegal Immigration," *Los Angeles Times* 8 February 1995: A3.

50 Pete Wilson, "Sowing the Ground for a Better California," *Los Angeles Times* 4 October 1994: B11 (Orange County edition).

51 Paul Jacobs, "Wilson Often Battled INS, Letters Show," *Los Angeles Times* 25 September 1995: A3.

52 Leo R. Chavez, "Settlers and Sojourners: The Case of Mexicans in the United States," *Human Organization* 47: 95–108, 1988.

53 Leo R. Chavez, Wayne A. Cornelius, and O. W. Jones, "Mexican Immigrants and the Utilization of Health Services," *Social Science and Medicine* 21: 93–102, 1985; and Leo R. Chavez, Estevan T. Flores, and Marta Lopez-Garza, "Undocumented Latin American Immigrants and U.S. Health Services: An Approach to a Political Economy of Utilization," *Medical Anthropology Quarterly* 6: 6–26, 1992. Ruben Rumbaut, Leo R. Chavez, Robert Moser, Sheila Pickwell, and Sam Wishik, "The Politics of Migrant Health Care: A Comparative Study of Mexican Immigrants and Indochinese Refugees in San Diego," *Research in the Sociology of Medicine* 7 (Greenwich, CT: JAI Press, 1988), pp. 143–202.

54 Leo R. Chavez, Wayne A. Cornelius, and O. W. Jones, "Utilization of Health Services by Mexican Women in San Diego," *Women and Health* 11: 3–20, 1986.

55 Paul Feldman and Rich Connell, "Wilson Acts to Enforce Parts of Prop. 187; 8 Lawsuits Filed," *Los Angeles Times* 10 November 1994: A1.

56 Ronald Brownstein, "Wilson Proposes U.S. Version of Prop. 187," *Los Angeles Times* 19 November 1994: A1.

57 Ronald Brownstein, "Wilson Proposes U.S. Version of Prop. 187," *Los Angeles Times* 19 November 1994: A1.

58 Frank del Olmo, "Open the Door to Mexican Workers," *Los Angeles Times* 31 January 1995: B9 (Orange County edition).

59 Marc Lacey, "New Task Force Targets Illegal Immigration," *Los Angeles Times* 16 March 1995: A3.

60 Alejandro Portes and Robert L. Bach, *Latin Journey: Cuban and Mexican Immigrants in the United States* (Berkeley: University of California Press, 1985).

61 Doris Meissner, "Contract Workers: Human Exploitation," *Los Angeles Times* 30 January 1995: B9 (Orange County edition).

62 Leo R. Chavez, "The Power of the Imagined Community: The Settlement of Undocumented Mexicans and Central Americans in the United States," *American Anthropologist* 96: 52–73, 1994.

63 Leo R. Chavez, "Settlers and Sojourners: The Case of Mexicans in the United States," *Human Organization* 47: 95–108, 1988.

64 Leo R. Chavez, Estevan T. Flores, and Marta Lopez-Garza, "Here Today, Gone Tomorrow? Undocumented Settlers and Immigration Reform," *Human Organization* 49: 193–205, 1990.

65 Benedict Anderson, *Imagined Communities* (London: Verso, 1983).

66 Etienne Balibar, "Is There a 'Neo-Racism'?" In *Race, Nation, Class: Ambiguous Identities*, Etienne Balibar and Immanuel Wallerstein, eds. (New York: Verso, 1991), 17–28.

67 I credit Javier Inda with the notion of (dis)-order, as he discussed it in "The Anthropology of Transnationalism," 1994 mimeo.

25

The Process of Black Community Organizing in the Southern Pacific Coast Region of Colombia

Libia Grueso, Carlos Rosero, and Arturo Escobar

Ethnicity, Territory, and Politics

Since the end of the 1980s, Colombia's Pacific coast region has been undergoing an unprecedented historical process: the emergence of collective ethnic identities and their strategic positioning in culture–territory relations. This process is taking place in a complex national and international conjuncture. At the national level, the conjuncture is marked by two events: the radical opening of Colombia's economy to world markets after 1990, particularly in the ambit of the country's integration into the Pacific Basin economies; and a substantial reform of the national Constitution in 1991, which, among other things, granted the black communities of the Pacific region collective rights to the territories they have traditionally occupied. Internationally, tropical rain-forest areas, including Colombia's Pacific coast, have acquired a certain specificity in light of the fact that they are home to most of the planet's biological diversity. Confronted with the rapid destruction of these areas, the concomitant loss of species, and the potential impact of this loss on the future of humanity, scientists, environmen-

talists, governments, and non-governmental organizations (NGOs) have thrown themselves with fervor into the task of "preserving biological diversity".

The emergence of collective ethnic identities in the Colombian Pacific region and similar regions in other parts of the world thus reflects a double historical movement: the irruption of the biological, the continuity of life as we know it, as a global problem; and the irruption of the cultural and the ethnic, as highlighted by the Colombian government's decision to recognize these concepts in its desire to construct a pluriethnic and multicultural society. This double irruption of the biological and the cultural takes place in the changing contexts of capitalism and modernity that scholars have attempted to explain in terms of globalization (Robertson 1992; González Casanova 1994), postfordism (Harvey 1989), or ethnoscapes (Appadurai 1991); and in which the multiple intersections of the local and the global are no longer analyzed in terms of polarized space-time categories – such as tradition and modernity, center and periphery – but in terms of cultural hybridizations (García Canclini 1990), the local processing of global conditions (Pred and Watts 1992), alternative modernities, and postdevelopment (Escobar 1995).

The Colombian Pacific coast region, as we shall see, is defined by the local black and indigenous movements as a region-territory of ethnic groups. Based on cultural differences and the rights to identity and territory, these social movements challenge the Euro-Colombian modernity that has become dominant in the rest of the country. Black and indigenous cultural politics, in this way, challenge the conventional political culture harbored in the practices of the traditional political parties and the state, unsettle the dominant project of national identity construction, and defy the predominant orientation of development. Forces opposed to the movement – from local black elites to new agribusiness capitalists and narco-investors – continue to adhere to the same definitions of capital, development, and the political that have become entrenched in the last fifty years with disastrous consequences on the social, environmental, and cultural reality of the country. Through their appropriation of the territory and their cultural affirmation, the social movements seek to resist the onslaught of capital and development on their region.

This chapter describes and analyzes the emergence of the social movement of black communities in the southern Pacific coast region of Colombia.[1] First, we analyze the national conjuncture of the constitutional reform of 1991 that propitiated the structuration of the movement, focusing on the negotiated elaboration of the law of cultural and territorial rights for the black communities (Ley 70 of August 1993). Next, we examine the movement as an ethnocultural proposal, emphasizing the politico-organizational principles developed as a result of massive collective mobilization around Ley 70. These principles reflect important processes of black identity construction as well as novel practices and theoretical formulations concerning the relation between territory, biodiversity, culture, and development that we later analyze from the perspective of the intersection between the cultural politics of the movement and established political cultures. We conclude the chapter by suggesting ways of thinking about the political

from the perspectives of territory, nature, and culture.

The Constitutional Reform of 1991 and the End of the Invisibility of Black Cultures

From the times of conquest and slavery to today's rampant capitalism – including historical boom and bust periods of gold, platinum, precious woods, and rubber – Colombia's Pacific coast region has been affected by the forces of capitalist modernity (Whitten 1986; Leyva 1993; Aprile-Gniset 1993). Since time immemorial, this region has been seen primarily as a source of raw materials and a depository of allegedly inexhaustible natural riches, and its inhabitants have been subjected to systematic invisibility and ethnocentric representations. Perhaps because Colombia's majority Andean population sees in the Pacific region and its people an example of ineluctable cultural and economic backwardness, the social sciences have paid scant attention to the vibrant black cultures that have developed there throughout the centuries (Friedmann and Arocha 1984; Arocha 1991; Wade 1993).

This region covers a vast area (about 70,000 square kilometers) stretching from Panama to Ecuador and from the westernmost chain of the Andes to the ocean. It is a unique rain-forest region, one of the world's wettest and most diverse. About 60 percent of the region's 900,000 inhabitants (800,000 Afro-Colombians; about 50,000 Embera, Waunana, and other indigenous people; and another 50,000 mestizo colonists) live in the few larger cities and towns; the rest inhabit the margins of the more than 240 rivers in the region, most of which flow from the Andes toward the ocean. Black people have maintained distinct material and cultural practices – such as multiple subsistence and economic activities involving agriculture, fishing, hunting and gathering, and small-scale gold mining and timber collecting; extended families and matrilocal social relations; strong oral traditions and religious systems; and particular forms of knowledge and use of the diverse forest ecosystems – which are too numerous and complex to summarize here.[2] What is important to emphasize is the continued existence of important, different cultures in a region that is finally attracting the attention of the national government in its ambitious effort to participate in the alleged economic bonanza accompanying the development around the "sea of the twentieth-first century" – the Pacific Ocean.

This renewed interest on the part of the state takes place in a climate significantly different from the invisibility that characterized the region's biological and cultural reality even a decade ago. On the biological side, the debut of the discourse of biodiversity conservation in the theater of international development has substantially modified the perception of the region in the eyes of many. Culturally, the constitutional reform of 1991 transformed forever the economy of ethnic visibilities in the country. The new Constitution reversed a long-standing project of nation building; no longer the building of a racially and culturally homogeneous society (a mestizo people coded as "white"), the new goal – enshrined in the 1991 Constitution – is presented as the construction of a pluriethnic and multicultural nation.

For many sectors of society, including the black communities, the Asamblea Nacional Constituyente (ANC) – the seventy-member body entrusted with the reform of the Constitution, popularly elected in December 1990 – represented the hopes of finding a way out of the deep social and political crisis in which the country was immersed at the beginning of the decade. In the period preceding the formation of the ANC, a number of black initiatives with diverse political orientations, mostly local in character, had already been organized. These groups – which included individuals and organizations linked to Christian communities, the Left, traditional parties, government programs, and NGOs, all with experience in black issues and with a greater or lesser degree of awareness about the demands of the black communities[3] – convened in the Preconstituent Conference of Black Communities in Cali in August 1990 with the purpose of working out a proposal for action in the current conjuncture. From this conference emerged the Coordinadora Nacional de Communidades Negras (CNCN) as a mechanism to co-ordinate and implement the actions agreed upon at the conference. However, the profound divisions and the wide range of perspectives represented at the CNCN – from peasant, urban, popular, and traditional party-oriented groups to leftist and ethno-cultural movements – ensured that the CNCN was to be a short-lived experiment. When the ANC convened, each of these black sectors assessed the situation according to their own sets of interests and modes of historical insertion in the country.[4]

There was no black representation in the ANC; the plight of the black communities was brought before the assembly by one of the indigenous representatives and was finally addressed by Artículo Transitorio 55, or AT 55 (Transitory Article 55). This was not easily achieved. From the very beginning, the demands for recognition of territorial and ethnic rights for the black communities were opposed by many of the sectors represented in the ANC, even democratic sectors such as the M-19 Alliance.[5] Black communities, it was argued out of ignorance, did not conform to the definition of an "ethnic group" since they lacked their own language and forms of right and authority; they were fully integrated as citizens into the mestizo life of the country; and they had adopted alien cultural elements. Some asserted that the demand for territorial rights was a separatist position best dealt with within the framework of decentralization promoted by the new Constitution. The inclusion of AT 55 was thus possible only after a massive lobbying campaign that even included the takeover of buildings.[6]

The constitutional reform is, in this way, the first important space of black community organizing on the basis of cultural, ethnic, and territorial demands; it entailed the construction of an alternative proposal by the black communities centered on ethnic and cultural rights. Once the 1991 Constitution went into effect, a number of black organizations came together to evaluate the results of the ANC and to discuss their participation in the election of representatives of ethnic groups to Congress, as stipulated by the Constitution. From then on, a rift grew between those who favored the construction of a movement for political participation in the established institutions and those who believed in a social movement in which electoral participation was only one possibility and not the central element.

This difference marked the definitive distancing between the nucleus of activists who remained within the CNCN and the black sectors closer to the traditional Liberal and Conservative Parties. CNCN members dedicated their efforts from then on to regulating AT 55 (the negotiated process of specifying its contents until its enactment into law, which took place in August 1993); to strengthening community organizing; and to reaching out to peasant organizations in Chocó Province. From this dynamic there emerged in October 1993, as a national organizational response, the Proceso de Comunidades Negras, or PCN (Process of Black Communities), a network of more than 120 local organizations that assumed the regulation of AT 55 and the consolidation of responses from local organizations. The distance from those who emphasized political or bureaucratic representation deepened.[7] At the same time, the collective construction of mechanisms and forms of participation in the interior of the movement made possible the consolidation of at least minimal political and ideological agreements and halted the organizational dispersal that had been occurring previously.

The ethno-cultural character of the movement that surfaced during the ANC; the promulgation of AT 55, with its recognition of collective rights to traditional territories; and the ensuing threats to the black people of the Pacific region and their territories were the main factors determining the nature of the organizing work being done in rural areas. This emphasis reflected the importance attributed by the PCN to maintaining social control of territory and natural resources as a precondition for the survival, re-creation, and strengthening of culture. Among the riverine populations, activists geared their efforts toward advancing a pedagogical process with and within the communities on the meaning of the new Constitution; reinforcing the fundamental concepts of territory, development, traditional production practices, and use of natural resources; and strengthening the organizational capacity of these communities. This sustained effort during the 1991–1993 period served to lay down the

basis for the elaboration of a proposal for the law called for by AT 55 and also to firm up a series of politico-organizational principles, as we will discuss later in this chapter. It also helped PCN activists recognize the various tendencies, trajectories, and styles of work found among the array of black organizations involved with the debate on, and regulation of, what was to become Ley 70.

The collective elaboration of the proposal for Ley 70 was another decisive space for the development of the movement. This process was advanced at two levels, one centered on the daily life and practices of the black communities of the Pacific, the other on the ideological and political reflections of the activists. The first level – carried out under the rubric of what was referred to as "the logic of the river" – relied on the broad participation of local people in the articulation of their own rights, aspirations, and dreams. The second level, although using the rivers and their settlements as referents, sought to transcend the rural domain and raise the broader issues involving black people as an ethnic group, even beyond what could be granted by the law. This level entailed a rearticulation of the notions of territory, development, and the social relations of black communities with the rest of Colombian society. Despite differences and the manipulation of the process by black politicians linked to the Liberal Party, an agreement was reached on the text of the law to be negotiated with the government.[8]

In this context, negotiations with the government entailed a double effort of constructing agreements between, on the one hand, organizations and communities, and on the other, these groups and the government. Given the forceful implementation of the neoliberal opening of the economy and the growing currency of discussions on biodiversity and genetic resources, these negotiations became ever more tense; while the government became more intransigent as its awareness of the capacity of their black interlocutors grew, the black organizing groups grew stronger in structure, experience, coordination, and awareness of their rights. Government officials realized that the demands of the organizing process went well beyond the desire for integration and racial equality, as had been maintained until then by other sectors of the black community. Besides, black organizations mounted a strategy of persuasion and consciousness raising among the delegates to the special high commission appointed by the government for the regulation of AT 55. The entire process constituted a veritable social construction of protest (Klandermans 1992) that was to culminate in the approval by the Senate of the version of the law (Ley 70) negotiated with the communities. However, it is important to recognize that during and after the convening of the ANC, there were a variety of ideological and political tendencies among black organizations. It was for this reason that the black communities' proposal was presented by an indigenous representative.[9]

The Social Movement of Black Communities and the Ethno-Cultural Proposal of the Process of Black Communities

Black communities in Colombia are far from being homogenous – culturally, historically, or politically. There are at least six sociocultural regions with an important black presence: the Caribbean coast, the Pacific coast, the Magdalena, the Cauca and Patía river valleys, and the Archipelago of San Andrés and Providencia. These communities comprise a vast spectrum of political positions, experiences of mobilization, and conceptions of the struggle that motivate, in turn, continuous tensions, alliances, and realignments of forces, depending on the particular situation. Historically speaking, there have been periods of black convergence and unification; the construction of a movement on the basis of ethno-cultural rights in the wake of the ANC is one of these exceptional experiences.

The first Asamblea Nacional de Comunidades Negras, or ANCN (National Conference of Black Communities) took place in July 1992 in the predominantly black city of Tumaco (100,000 inhabitants) with representatives from all over the Pacific, the Caribbean and the Norte del Cauca regions. Its principal conclusions were geared toward laying down a framework for the regulation of AT 55 and building the necessary organizational and operational mechanisms to this end. At the ANCN's second national conference in May 1993, delegates revised and approved the law's text as negotiated by government and black community representatives in the ambit of the High Commission created for this purpose by the Constitution.

The third national conference was convened in September 1993 in Puerto Tejada, another predominantly black town, south of Cali in the Norte del Cauca region. With more than 300 delegates attending, the conference debated the politico-organizational situation of black communities in 1993. At that time, black sectors linked to the traditional liberal and conservative parties – eager to capitalize on the unprecedented legal mechanisms favorable to black communities that had been achieved by the mobilization and social construction of protest – had begun to adopt a confused and opportunistic discourse on "blackness" that usually did not go beyond the question of skin color. Recognizing the existence of these sectors and the diversity among the social movements of black communities, the conference proposed to characterize its own identity as "a sector of the social movement of black communities composed of people and organizations with diverse experiences and goals, but united around a set of principles, criteria and objectives that set us apart from other sectors of the movement. In the same vein, we represent a proposal to the entire black community of the country, and aspire to construct a unified movement of black communities able to encompass their rights and aspirations."[10]

The objective of the organizing process was stated as "the consolidation of a social movement of black communities for the reconstruction and affirmation of cultural identity," leading to an autonomous organizing strategy "for the achievement of cultural, social, economic, political and territorial rights and for the defense of natural resources and the environment." A central feature of the conference was the adoption of a set of politico-organizational principles formulated out of the practice, lifeworld vision, and desires of the black communities. These principles concern the key issues of identity, territory, autonomy, and development:

1. *The reaffirmation of identity* (the right to be black). In the first place, we conceive of being black from the perspective of our cultural logic and lifeworld in all of its social, economic, and political dimensions. This logic counters the logic of domination that intends to exploit and subject our people. Our cultural vision opposes a model of society that requires uniformity for its continued dominance. Being black thus cannot be restricted to particular moments but should encompass our entire lives. Second, our cultural affirmation entails an inner struggle with our consciousness; the affirmation of our being is not easy, since we are taught in many ways and through multiple media that we are all equal. This is the great lie of the logic of domination.

This first principle clearly identifies culture and identity as the organizational axes of both daily life and political practice. As we will see later in this chapter, despite its seemingly essentialist tone, this principle also partakes of a conception of identity as constructed.

2. *The right to territory* (the right to space for being). As a vital space, territory is a necessary condition for the re-creation and development of our cultural vision. We cannot be if we do not have a space for living in accordance with what we think and desire as a form of life. It follows that we see territory as a habitat and space where black people develop their being in harmony with nature.

3. *Autonomy* (the right to the exercise of being-identity). We understand autonomy in relation to the dominant society, other ethnic groups, and political parties. It arises out of our cultural logic. Thus understood, we are autonomous internally in the political realm and aspire to social and economic autonomy.

4. *Construction of an autonomous perspective of the future.* We intend to construct an autonomous vision of economic and social development based on our culture and traditional forms of production and social organization. The dominant society has systematically imposed on us a vision of development that responds to their own interests and worldview. We have the right to give others the vision of our world, as we want to construct it.

5. *Declaration of solidarity.* We are part of the struggle for the rights of black people throughout the world. From our own particularity, the social movement of black communities shall contribute to the efforts of those who struggle for alternative life projects.

This declaration of principles constituted a rupture with the political and developmentalist formulations of the Left, including black urban organizations and traditional liberal political sectors. It responded to the specific situation of the black communities of the Pacific and, while demanding a solution to their pressing problems, placed greater emphasis on the nature and content of the possible solutions. The declaration also cast into relief the growing gap between the PCN and other organized black sectors. These differences arose over four main issues: (a) the perception of history and identity; (b) the views and demands concerning natural resources, territory, and development; (c) the types of political representation and participation of the communities involved in black mobilization, and the relationship between the latter and the rest of society; and (d) the conception of organizational strategy and modes of construction of the movement.

With this strategy, the PCN sought to pursue various goals: to become a source of power for black communities vis-à-vis the state and other social actors; to advance the social movement of black communities; and to contribute to the search for more just and viable societal options for the country as a whole. From then on, the PCN strategy and its successive transformations were to depend on the activists' investigation and assessment, on the one hand of the historical and cultural reality of the communities and on the other of the balance of forces – from the local to the international level – between the communities, the social movement, and other social sectors, economic groups, and centers of power.

As a result of this new situation, the basic agreement that existed with the organizations of Chocó Province broke down shortly after the approval of

Ley 70. Article 66 of the law created a special electoral district for black communities, reserving two seats for black candidates in the chamber of representatives. The ensuing electoral process also divided the organizations of Chocó itself and spurred a national explosion of candidate lists. Article 66 had been regulated by the High Commission without taking into account the proposal of the organized communities, thus favoring black traditional party politicians and their clientelistic networks. In the end, one of the seats was occupied by a politician from the conservative party who usurped the name "social movement of black communities" for his campaign, confusing public opinion, and who declared thereafter that the time of grassroots organizing was over. The second seat went to a representative of the Chocó organizations who had participated in the regulation of Ley 70 and who was elected with the support of factions of the indigenous, socialist, and women's movements and of some government institutions. Although this candidate had participated actively in ethno-cultural organizations, once elected she shifted her position from the ethnic approach to emphasizing the country's marginalized peoples as a whole.

Conveniently, the government began to question the PCN's representation, legitimacy, and achievements by arguing that there were other organized sectors of the black community. Depending on the specific situation and its interests at the moment, the government would lend support to the positions of the two black Congress members as "legitimate representatives" of the black community. The political practices of these members did indeed conform to the conventional clientelistic scheme so characteristic of Colombian party politics, to the extent that their efforts focused on public jobs for their constituencies, bureaucratic representation, the creation of institutional spaces, and the use of public funds to ensure their reelection and political survival. Coupled with the government's accommodating manipulation of the situation, their actions distorted the meaning of the demands raised by the black communities and constrained the role of ethno-cultural organizations in negotiations with the state on vital matters such as territory and natural resources.

For some activists, the election of the black candidates to Congress represented a step backward for black communities. Nevertheless, and even if the traditional black politicans succeeded in permeating wide sectors of the black community, the ethno-cultural movement remained as an important organizational dynamic at the national level. Its assessment of the Pacific coast region as Colombia's most significant black region and as a strategic ethnic and ecological unit – with the concomitant emphasis placed on the defense of the territory – was one of its most pertinent accomplishments. In a similar vein, it has been the ethno-cultural sector of the movement that has trained the majority of activists to effectively carry out a critical dialogue and collective negotiations with the state, and that has attempted to endow river communities with a tool kit for the defense of their rights within the framework of Ley 70 and Ley 121 of 1991. These accomplishments have become key components of the political practice of the entire black community.[11]

The 1995–1996 period saw the appearance of new organized black sectors with different, and at times conflicting, agendas, seeking to capitalize on the space earlier created for black people's rights. During these two years, the number of organized sectors of black communities increased significantly.[12] The conflicts and contradictions among all of these groups have impinged upon important issues such as the composition and work of the High Commission, the formulation of the National Development Plan for Black Communities, and the regulation of Ley 70, weakening the bargaining position of communities vis-à-vis the government. Given that many of these groups do not have a developed political or ideological position, and considering that their actions focus on gaining access to institutional and bureaucratic spaces, it is still difficult to attempt a characterization or assessment of the groups that exist at present.

Territory, Identity, and Strategy: From Cultural Politics to Political Culture

The social movement of the Pacific black communities is endowed with very particular features arising from the historical, cultural, ecological, and economic specificity of the region. The movement constitutes a complex process of construction of ethnic and cultural identity in relation to novel variables such as territory, biodiversity, and alternative development. In this section, we will highlight some of these complexities from the perspective of the effect that the cultural politics set into motion by the movement is having or might have on notions and practices of collective identity, political culture, biodiversity, and alternative development.

The construction of a collective identity

For many years, the approach to the reality of black people in Colombia was shaped by three basic concepts: marginality, discrimination, and equality. Black identity was largely conceived in terms of equality before the law. The ambiguous character of this formulation has been pointed out by many, to the extent that the assertion "we are all equal before the law" – which denies the existence of discrimination and promulgates the elite ideology of "racial democracy" prevalent in most of Latin America – makes impossible the articulation of an oppositional ethnic discourse (Wade 1993). Until recently, black opposition emphasized a common past grounded in slavery and in the forms of resistance to it, especially in the *palenques*. In this vision, history was chiefly commemorative and was indelibly tainted by the representation of a past always diminished by domination.[13] In contrast, the PCN adamantly asserts that the invocation of a common past must be accompanied by a parallel identification of lessons for the present and a project for the future. This emphasis constitutes a rupture with black organizing efforts of the 1970–1990 period that called for integration as a way to overcome racial discrimination and oppression. This earlier theory of the struggle arose out of the economic and political marginalization of the region and shared some similarities with black civil rights struggles in other parts of the world, particularly in the United States.

In the late 1970s, the state itself began to foster the process of the "integration" of the Pacific region into the rest of the country, particularly through ambitious development plans (Escobar and Pedrosa 1996). These attempts at integration into national culture and economic markets have had devastating effects on the values and aspirations of local cultures. It is for this reason that the ethno-cultural approach highlights the importance of reconstructing and exercising cultural differences as a mechanism for eradicating socio-economic and political inequality. The new focus entails a significant redefinition of the relationship between the black communities and the rest of society and reflects an important trend in the black movement. For the activists who share this vision, the historical resistance of black communities in the Pacific and other parts of the country suggests a certain intentional distancing on the part of these communities as a way of constructing their own social and cultural forms of organization. This would explain the persistence of distinct cultural features in the Pacific and other regions such as the different sense of time, the lack of interest in accumulation, and the social and economic role of kindred and extended family. Some of these cultural practices are recovered and invoked by activists as basic elements of the organizing process. Even if the Pacific coast region has been integrated into the world economy for centuries as provider of raw materials (Whitten 1986), the river communities never strove for a full integration into Colombia's economy.[14]

In sum, if integrationist approaches seek the incorporation of black communities into national life, ethno-cultural approaches construct the relation between national and minority cultures and their corresponding projects as problematic. These overall approaches reflect diverging readings of the history, living conditions, and cultural expressions of the black communities of the Pacific; they maintain a tension that shapes organizing processes to this day. According to the ethnocultural process, the movement must be constructed on the basis of broad demands for territory, identity, autonomy, and the right to its own vision of development and the future. Similarly, ethno-cultural activists espouse a view of blackness that goes well beyond issues of skin color and the racial aspects of identity.

The black communities' social movement is embarked on a process of collective identity construction that bears similarities to the construction of Caribbean and Afro-British identities analyzed by Stuart Hall (1990). For Hall, ethnic identity construction entails cultural, economic, and political negotiations characterized by a certain "doubleness." On the one hand, identity is thought of as rooted in shared cultural practices, a collective self of sorts; this conception of identity has played an important role in anticolonial struggles and involves an imaginative rediscovery of culture that lends coherence to the experience of fragmentation dispersal, and oppression. On the other hand, identity is seen in terms of the differences created by history; this aspect of identity construction emphasizes becoming rather than being, positioning rather than essence, and discontinuity as well as continuity at the cultural level. In this way, the coexistence of difference and sameness constitutes the doubleness of identity today; it recognizes the dialogues of power and resistance generated by the various encounters between European modernity and other cultural forms and – in the context of the "New World" – the fact that cultural identity is always creolized and characterized by difference, heterogeneity, and hybridization (see also García Canclini 1990).

The doubleness of identity can be seen at play in the ethno-cultural approach of the Pacific coast black movement. For the activists, the defense of certain cultural practices of the river communities is a strategic question to the extent that these communities are seen as embodying not only resistance to capitalism and modernity but also possibilities for alternative constructions. Although often couched in culturalist language, this defense is not intransigent or essentializing to the extent that it responds to an interpretation of the challenges faced by the communities and the possibilities presented by a cautious opening toward forms of modernity such as biodiversity conservation and alternative development. Identity is thus seen in both ways: as an anchor of "traditional" practices and forms of knowledge and as an ever changing project of cultural and political construction. In this way, the movement builds upon the river communities' submerged networks of cultural practices and meanings as well as their active construction of lifeworlds

(Melucci 1989); it sees such practices in their transformative capacity of the biophysical and social environments; and it attempts to articulate, as we shall see in the following sections, a practical project of territorial defense and alternative modes of development.

To the fixed, static, and conventional notion of identity implicit in the new Constitution, the movement thus opposes a more fluid notion of identity as political construction. Although this identity is constructed in novel terms of culture and ecology, it is also traversed by class. Most black elites of the Pacific coast, in fact, resent Ley 70 not only because they feel that the law treats them like "Indians" but because they want to integrate and be treated as regular Colombians – that is, they do not want to be singled out as an "ethnic minority" at all.[15]

As an important aspect of identity construction, gender is also progressively becoming a salient aspect in the agenda of ethno-cultural organizations, although it is still given insufficient attention. The fact that many of the top leaders and activists of the movement are women who are committed to the ethno-cultural approach and who are increasingly interested in advancing gender questions is acting as a catalyst for the articulation of gender issues. These leanings were already felt in 1994, when the need to embrace gender as an integral part of the movement – as opposed to promoting the creation of separate women's organizations – was recognized.[16] The organization of black women is beginning to overflow the boundaries of the larger movement and to take on a dynamic of its own. In 1992, the first meeting of black women of the Pacific coast already attracted over 500 participants; a network of black women's organizations exists and is gaining visibility in various domains of activity particularly since 1995 (Rojas 1996); and discourses of gender and biodiversity are also slowly emerging (Camacho 1996). Although most of these efforts are still couched in conventional "women in development" terms (Lozano 1996), the number of activists committed to gender mobilization is increasing. Studies of the black women's mobilization are already under way, particularly from the perspective of the intersection of gender and the ethnic constructions of identity and political strategy that have been dominant until now.[17]

Reformulating the political

One may think that the biophysical, social, and cultural characteristics of the Pacific coast region would lend themselves to a nontraditional approach to politics; however, this has hardly been the case. Until recently, conditions in the region have been used to strengthen a conventional system based on political *clientilismo* that articulates with traditional social relations – established on the basis of extended families and kinship groups – and with particular geographical spaces. Votes and favors are exchanged and circulate, budgets are negotiated, and regional and local bureaucracies and programs are enacted, all on the basis of these articulations. As in many other parts of the country, local bosses control political groups and participate, in turn, in wider political clientelistic networks controlled by more important bosses. Coupled with the fact that the Pacific region is composed of four provinces, three of which have capitals that lie in the Andean region (the exception being the northern Chocó Province), this clientele-based system ensures that decisions are made outside the region. These two factors – the difference between the northern Chocó and the central and southern provinces, and the clientelistic system – have militated against the political construction of the Pacific as an ecological and cultural region and against the emergence of significant social movements.

As in other parts of Latin America, the absence of black movements is related to racial miscegenation, democracy, the political control mechanisms initiated during colonial times, and elite ideological constructions of various kinds, such as notions of racial democracy (Serbin 1991). Black demands have generally been tied to those of economically subordinate sectors and channeled through their political organizations without any ethnic specificity. Blacks' attempts at organizing in racially defined terms have not been completely absent in Colombia.[18] However, ethnic organizing remained latent until 1991, when black groups of all persuasions – whether linked to community organizations or to conventional political parties – began to see black identification as a means to access spaces from which they were previously excluded.

Few of these efforts have succeeded in breaking away from traditional political practices. For the PCN, it was a question of convincing communities of their right to participate in a gamut of mechanisms of representation and negotiation with the state, such as the electoral process. In contrast to traditional *clientilismo*, PCN activists have sought to foster more daring proposals along with broad mechanisms of decisionmaking and degrees of political consciousness that go well beyond each individual group or river community. At the basis of this strategy is the conviction that the link between the ethnic and the political must be constructed. In this way, for instance, electoral processes are geared to the formulation of ideals and the elaboration of lists of candidates who represent community needs and aspirations, in contradistinction to the usual strategy of exchanging votes for favors or state programs. Traditional politicians have responded angrily to this strategy by blocking community initiatives, reinforcing elite coalitions, and pointing their fingers in accusation at movement activists.

The PCN's strategy of constructing the political, in sum, seeks to irrupt in a field that was previously off limits to nonconventional actors and to provide – at the same time that it chips away at the power base of traditional politicians – alternative political nuclei. This strategy was first attempted in 1992 (after the ANC) in the black city of Buenaventura and was implemented on various other occasions, such as during the 1992 and 1994 elections. Even if Ley 70 fostered an explosion of candidate lists for black representatives in Congress, the lists themselves and the bulk of the mobilization for the electoral process did not correspond to the ethno-cultural orientation of the movement but to political forces linked to the traditional political parties, who eagerly seized these unprecedented electoral opportunities. Despite this outcome, it is possible to assert that the ethno-cultural movement of black communities, with its alternative participatory practices articulated on the notion of cultural difference, has begun to transform the conventional political culture in Colombia's Pacific region and beyond.

Cultural politics, territory, and biodiversity

Because of its rich natural resources, Colombia's Pacific coast region is currently in the mire of both the national and the international development establishment. It is also a territory of ethnic groups, who constitute 93 percent of its population and whose active mobilization in recent years has become a preoccupation for government agencies and politicians alike. An important aspect of this mobilization is the involvement of black and indigenous groups in discussions about biodiversity conservation, genetic resources, and the control and management of natural resources. For the social movement of black communities, these issues cannot be dissociated from the question of territorial control. In fact, the relationships between culture, territory, and natural resources constitute a central axis of discussion and strategy building both within movement organizations and in their dealings with the state. Conversely, disagreements in the conceptualization of the culture/territory/natural resource relationship have created tensions among community organizations and between some community sectors and ethno-cultural organizations.

These tensions are related to the overall intensification of development, capitalism, and modernity in the region (Escobar and Pedrosa 1996). First, the growing migration to the Pacific of peasants, proletarians, and entrepreneurs displaced from the interior of the country is having a visible socioeconomic, ecological, and cultural impact arising chiefly from the different cultural logic that these actors bring with them. Second, the government continues to insist on implementing conventional development plans for the region, intended to create infrastructure for the large-scale arrival of capital. Third, government policies for the protection of natural resources have consisted of conventional measures of expansion of natural parks or social forestry programs with little or no community participation. Only one small, but symbolically important, project for the conservation of biological diversity has attempted – even if in ambiguous ways – to incorporate the demands of the organized black

communities.[19] Finally, the drug cartels are also entering the region in the form of large-scale mining, agro-industrial, and tourist projects, with enormous consequences that are still difficult to discern.[20]

In addition to highlighting these factors, it is necessary to point out that the organizational level of the black communities in the central and southern Pacific region is still low. Their vulnerability has been revealed in a variety of environmental, social, and cultural conflicts between local communities and timber, mining, and agro-industrial interests that have increased in number and intensity since the approval of Ley 70; nevertheless, movement organizations have extracted partial but important victories in some of these conflicts.[21] These cases have made manifest several important aspects of environmental policy and conflict. They have made evident not only the weakness of the state agencies in charge of the protection of natural resources but also the not infrequent collusion between their functionaries and the private interests exploiting the same resources they are mandated to protect. In a handful of cases, state functionaries have allied themselves with local businesses to repress movement organizations. Also, local government officials are hesitant to address the severe environmental problems that sometimes affect the communities under their jurisdiction. Finally, government measures aimed at controlling environmental abuses are frequently late and insufficient, or require the perpetrators to make only minor corrections to their environmentally destructive activities.[22]

It is important to highlight some of the conceptions of territory and biodiversity developed by the movement in their interaction with community, state, political, and academic sectors. As was already mentioned in the earlier discussion of the movement's principles, the territory is seen as a fundamental and multidimensional space for the creation and re-creation of the social, economic, and cultural values and practices of the communities. The defense of the territory is thus assumed within a historical perspective linking past and future. In the past, communities maintained a certain autonomy; they relied on forms of knowledge, worldviews, and ways of life conducive to certain uses of natural resources. Meanings and practices of nature go side by side in all cultures, producing particular "uses" and effects. This relationship between meanings and practices – and the social relations in which they are embedded – is being transformed today by the developmentalist onslaught that forces the loss of knowledge, territory, and cultural practices and that reduces nature into a commodity. Confronted with national and international pressures concerning the biodiversity, the natural and genetic resources, of the region, the organized black communities are preparing themselves for an unequal and strategic struggle to maintain control over the only remaining territorial space over which they still exert a significant cultural and social influence.

As part of their strategy for the demarcation of collective territories, activists have developed an important conception of the territory that highlights articulations between patterns of settlement, use of spaces, and practices of meaning-use of resources. Riverine settlements, for instance, evidence a longitudinal and discontinuous pattern along the rivers in which multiple economic activities (fishing, agriculture, small-scale mining and forestry, hunting and gathering, and subsistence and market activities) are combined and articulated according to the location of the settlement in the upper, middle, or lower segment of the river. This longitudinal dimension articulates with a horizontal axis regulated by the knowledge and utilization of multiple resources, from those close to the river margin that have been domesticated – including medicinal herbs and food crops – to the undomesticated species found in the various layers of forest away from the river. A vertical axis – from the infraworld to the supraworld, populated by benevolent as well as dangerous spirits – also contributes to articulating the patterns of meaning-use of resources. These various axes also depend on maintaining social relations between communities, which in some parts of the Pacific entail interethnic relations between black and indigenous communities.[23]

The defense of the territory entails the defense of this intricate pattern of social relations and cultural constructions, and is understood by movement activists in this light. It also implies the creation of a new sense of belonging linked to the political construction of a collective life project and the redefinition of relations with the dominant society. In the vision of the PCN, this possibility is more real in those communities encompassed under particular *palenques*, or networks of black organizations. At stake with Ley 70, in this way, is not "land" or even the territory of this or that community but the concept of territoriality itself as a central element in the political construction of reality on the basis of black experience. The struggle for territory is thus a cultural struggle for autonomy and self-determination. This explains why for many people of the Pacific the loss of territory would amount to a return to slavery or, worse perhaps, to becoming "common citizens."

The definition of "biodiversity" as "territory plus culture" made by movement activists incarnates an entire political ecology. This definition and the political practice that surrounds it are important contributions to today's intellectual ferment on the nature-society relation. It finds echo in current trends in political ecology concerning concepts such as territory, landscape, biodiversity, and "nature" itself. If territory is to be thought of as "the ensemble of projects and representations where a whole series of behaviors and investments can pragmatically emerge, in time and in social, cultural, aesthetic and cognitive space" – as an existential space of self-reference where "dissident subjectivities" can emerge (Guattari 1995, 23, 24) – it is clear that this project is being advanced by the social movements of the Pacific. Similarly, the definition of biodiversity proposed by the movement provides elements for reorienting biodiversity discourses according to local principles of autonomy, knowledge, identity, and economy (Shiva 1994). Finally, from the activists' efforts at theorizing local practices of use of resources, we learn that "landscapes" are not only surface phenomena but that they involve multiple worlds (Bender 1993), and that "nature" itself is not an entity "out there" existing outside human history but that it is produced in deep conjunction with the collective practice of humans who see themselves as integrally connected to it.

The Question of Development

From the PCN's perspective, development plans for the Colombian Pacific region have amounted to no more than material interventions on behalf of national and international economic interests. From the very first development plan for the region – the Plan for the Integral Development of the Pacific Coast, or PLADEICOP (DNP 1983), implemented between 1983 and 1993 – to today's Plan Pacífico for Sustainable Development (DNP 1992), state intervention has been geared toward rationalizing the extraction of natural resources and structured by a homogenizing development discourse; it has in no way taken into account the diversity of cultures of the region, and actually acted against this diversity.[24]

As most other countries in Latin America and the world, Colombia has opened up its doors to the transnationalization of the economy. Despite the recognition of ethnic and territorial rights, the contradiction between the *apertura* policies and the interests of the black communities is clear, particularly in light of the geopolitical location of the region in the context of Pacific Basin integration and the wealth of its natural resources. Notwithstanding the protection afforded by the new Constitution, it is market forces that continue to determine the goals of development, including what has been rightly called "the merchandising of biodiversity" (Martínez-Alier 1996). The conflict between market-driven interests and the interests of ethnic groups is more visible in the Pacific rain-forest region than anywhere else in Colombia.

For the ethno-cultural organizations, development must be guided by principles derived from the rights and aspirations of the local communities and must propend for the affirmation of cultures and the protection of natural environments. These principles – compensation, equity, autonomy, self-determination, affirmation of identity, and sustainability[25] – also point toward restoring a sense of balance between the cultural, social, economic, and ecological contributions of black communities to the country and the scarce contributions made to the country by the central government. Similarly, development

strategies must foster the communities' ethnic identity and decisionmaking capacity, including their creativity, solidarity, pride in their traditions, consciousness of their rights and forms of knowledge, and attachment to their territory. Any development alternative must articulate a vision of both a present and a future based on collective aspirations. It must go well beyond the creation of infrastructure and the improvement of material conditions to the strengthening of local cultures and languages.

PCN activists are by no means dismissive of goals such as health, education, communications, overall economic productivity, and distributing a fair share of public resources. These goals, however, are seen from the perspective of the need to defend the ancestral territories and maintain control over them, the rights of the communities to determine planning processes, and the overall goal of preserving cultural and organizational differences. "Sustainability" is not only an ecological, economic, and technological issue; it involves all of the principles stated above. It reflects the way in which the black communities of the Pacific continue to trust that life, peace, and democracy in Colombia will sacrifice neither nature nor cultural diversity (PCN 1994). The articulation of the ecological, the cultural, and the economic that underlies this vision constitutes a political ecology for the reconstruction of the relations between culture, nature, and society in this important part of the world. It also aims at a postdevelopment moment in which the unidimensional character of development – as an economistic project of social, cultural, and ecological transformation – is called into question.[26]

Conclusion

The Colombian Pacific coast region is witnessing the development of an important social movement, explicitly conceived from an ethno-cultural perspective. This movement has emerged at a particular moment in the regional, national, and international histories of the economic and the biological, and has been growing steadily in scope and complexity. The social movement of black communities is struggling against forces of Euro-Andean modernity – from colonizers to developers and narco-investors – that seek to impose in the region an extractivist regime. The movement constitutes, in this way, an important manifestation of the historical struggle for the autonomy of minority cultures and subjectivities, and for alternative regimes of nature construction – of weaving together the ecological, the cultural, and the techno-economic.

We have argued in this chapter that the social movement of black communities embodies a politicization of culture – a cultural politics – that has visible effects on established political cultures. The social and political crisis that Colombia – and most of Latin America – is undergoing finds in this movement a series of elements for reordering its imaginary and reorienting its project of nation building. The firm and radical yet pluralistic and nonviolent position of the movement can contribute toward processes of peace and solidarity with nature and each other so needed in the country. Despite the forces opposing the movement, in the current climate of certain favorable ecological and cultural conjunctures it is not far-fetched to think that the social movement of black communities actually represents a real defense of the social and biophysical landscapes of the Pacific region.

This defense advances through a slow and laborious construction of Afro-Colombian identities that articulate with alternative constructions of development, territory, and biodiversity conservation. The social movement of black communities can be described as one of cultural and ecological attachment to a territory, even as an attempt at creating new existential territories. Its reinterpretation of the history of local knowledge and practices; its critique of mainstream representations of blackness and of the Pacific region itself; and its articulation – still incipient and precarious, and yet illuminating – of alternative views of the link between culture, nature, and development, are all important elements for this project. In the long run, the movement can be seen as an attempt to demonstrate that social life, work, nature, and culture can be organized differently than as mandated by the dominant models of culture and the economy. The desires of an entire collectivity and even life itself are at stake.

NOTES

1 We should make clear from the outset that our analysis refers only to the central and southern parts of the Pacific region, and to one movement strand only (the ethno-cultural organizations). This qualification will become clear as the chapter unfolds.

2 The number and quality of studies of black cultures of the Pacific region is increasing. For an introduction to the anthropological literature, see Friedemann and Arocha 1984; Arocha 1991; and Whitten 1986. For a critical assessment of the anthropological discourse on black culture, see Restrepo 1996.

3 Among the earlier expressions linked to the church was the Golconda movement promoted by the Bishop of Buenaventura, Gerado Valencia Cano – known as "the red bishop" – whose social doctrine contributed to an incipient black consciousness; his legacy is strongly felt today among those sectors that work within the framework of the Afro-American pastoral. In urban and student circles, two organizations – the National Movement for the Rights of the Black Communities (Cimarrón) and Presencia Negra – succeeded in articulating a series of demands and in forming an urban militant base. Some of these aspects of the black movement in Colombia are discussed in Wade 1995.

4 The differences among black groups can be considered from various angles, such as the basis for mobilization (rural or urban), relations to traditional parties and the Left, the intellectual training of the activists, and geographical location. One of the main differences occurs between the organizations of the northern province of Chocó and its capital, Quibdó; and the southern provinces of Valle del Cauca, Cauca, and Nariño, with the port cities of Buenaventura, Guapi, and Tumaco, respectively, as their main black centers. As the only majority black province in Colombia, Chocó has an older and stronger link to the state and to traditional political parties than the rest of the region. Another important area of black mobilization is in the Norte del Cauca region, south of Cali.

5 The M-19 Alliance was formed as a result of the peace process of the late 1980s and the return to civilian politics of the M-19 guerrilla group. The

development of this movement prior to 1991 is chronicled in Fals Borda 1992.

6   AT 55 stated that, within two years of the approval of the new Constitution, the Congress had to elaborate and approve "a law that recognizes the right to collective property to the black communities that have occupied *tierras baldías* ['empty,' 'unused,' or public lands] in the rural riverine areas, in accordance with their traditional production practices.... The same law shall establish mechanisms for the protection of the rights and cultural identity of the same communities, and for the promotion of their social and economic development." The article also stipulated the establishment of a commission to draft the law, with the participation of the black communities, and the possibility of applying the law to other areas of the country with similar conditions.

7   The PCN is composed of regional *palenques*; a national coordinating committee; and technical teams at national and, in some cases, regional levels. Originally designating the autonomous territories of maroons or freed slaves in colonial times, today's *palenques* are spaces for discussion, decisionmaking, and policy orientation established in each of the regions with substantial black populations. They operate in conjunction with the Asamblea Nacional de Comunidades Negras, or ANCN (National Conference of Black Communities) and, together, constitute the Consejo Nacional de Palenques. Regional *palenques* are composed of two representatives from each of the region's organizations. The National Coordinating Committee is in charge of coordinating actions, implementing the decisions of the ANCN, and representing the PCN in national and international forums. The committee also coordinates the technical teams and the *palenque* representatives to the high-level commission in charge of regulating Ley 70. The technical teams contribute technical advice toward policy decisions in economic, development, environmental, and ethno-educational matters.

8   In an intelligent maneuver, a black senator from the Liberal Party got hold of the draft proposal for the enactment of AT 55 into law, prepared through the massive organizing process detailed here, and presented a version of it to Congress as her own.

9   Ley 70 is composed of sixty-eight articles distributed among eight chapters. Besides recognizing the rights to collective ownership of territory and to natural resources, Ley 70 explicitly recognizes Colombian blacks as an ethnic group with rights to its own identity and culturally appropriate education, and requires the state to adopt social and economic measures in accordance with black culture. Similarly, according to the law, any program on behalf of black communities must enlist their participation and respond to their particular needs, the preservation of the environment, and the development of local production practices. Development and the eradication of poverty should equally reflect black community aspirations. The law also outlined participatory mechanisms for its regulation and implementation (particularly the High Consultative Commission and its regional counterparts, with the participation of both government and black representatives) and created a special electoral system for electing two black candidates to the Chamber of Representatives. Some of these features are unprecedented in Latin America.

Ley 70 defines the black community as "the ensemble of families of Afro-Colombian descent possessing their own culture, sharing a history, and practicing their own traditions and customs within the rural-town relationship, who exhibit and maintain a consciousness of identity that sets them apart from other ethnic groups."

10   This and the succeeding quotations in this section are from the proceedings of the ANCN's Puerto Tejada conference held in September 1993.

11   Law 121 ratified the International Labor Organization's Agreement 169 concerning indigenous and tribal communities.

12   These include the Process of Black Communities (with which this part of the chapter is primarily concerned); the Working Group of Chocó Organizations; the Afro-Colombian Social Movement; the Social Movement of Black Communities; the Cimarrón National Movement; the National Afro-Colombian Home; the Afro-Colombian Social Alliance; Afro-South; Afro-Antioquia; Malcom; the Cali Black Community Council; Vanguard 21 of May; Raizales; and the Federation of Organizations of the Cauca Coast.

13   The problematic character of this view of the black experience has already been analyzed by Fanon in his discussion of a national culture (1968, 206–248).

14   The activists' interpretation of certain features of the river communities as showing a lack of interest in accumulation is in accordance with Marx's observation that only with the development of the class structure of capitalism does "accumulation for accumulation's sake" become a cultural imperative.

15   This articulation of movement strategy around culture and identity resonates with that of Mayan activists in Guatemala as discussed by Warren [in *Cultures of Politics/ Politics of Cultures: Re-visioning Latin American Social Movements*. Eds. Sonia E. Alvarez, Evelina Dagnino, Arturo Escobar. Boulder: Co: Westview Press]. Black activists of the Pacific have also been criticized for their cultural approach in terms similar to criticisms of their Guatemalan counterparts, even if in Colombia the logic of "popular" leftist organizing is significantly different. There is much to be learned from comparative analyses of ethno-cultural mobilizations taking place in many parts of Latin America today (from the Zapatistas to the Mapuche and from the Pacific to the Amazon) in the context of the emergence of ethnic consciousness, constitutional reforms, Left-Right and class realignments, and particular processes of globalization.

16   See the day-long interview conducted by Arturo Escobar and co-researchers with leaders of the movement, including the two authors of this chapter, in which the question of gender occupied a prominent place, mostly as it was advanced by Libia Grueso, Leyla Arroyo, and other women activists. The interview took place in Buenaventura on January 3, 1994 (Escobar and Pedrosa 1996, chap. 10).

17   See, for example, Camacho's work (1996) and the dissertation in progress by Kiran Asher (1997).

18   One example is the effort spearheaded by the black writer Manuel Zapata Olivella in the 1960s.

19   This is the Proyecto Biopacífico for biodiversity conservation (see GEF/PNUD 1993). The project – conceived as a Global Environment Facility (GEF) program and funded by the Swiss government and the United Nations Development Program (UNDP) – has allowed a certain degree of participation by black organizations. Its initial three-year budget of US$9 million, however, is ridiculously low compared with the budget of the large-scale development plan, Plan Pacífico for Sustainable Development, during the same period ($256 million). One of the authors of this chapter, Libia Grueso, was the regional project coordinator for Proyecto Biopacífico in Buenaventura. For an analysis of the meaning of this project in the strategies of conservationist capital, see Escobar 1997.

20   In fact, movement activists feel the least equipped to deal with this tremendous force, which has already brought widespread changes to Colombia and elsewhere.

21   Some of these cases involved the construction of an oil pipeline ending in the port of Buenaventura; the suspension by the Ministry of the Environment of industrial gold mining in the Buenaventura area; the closing of a hearts of palm canning operation in the same area; and the design of a reforestation program in the south Pacific region (a particularly important ecological zone that suffers from intense timber activity). In all of these instances, despite tensions with other community organizations, the social movements achieved partial but important victories. For a discussion of these cases and their impact on the movement, see Grueso 1995.

22   Juan Martínez-Alier (1995) suggests that the study of environmental conflict and its distributional effects should be a central task of political ecology. To this extent, the Pacific region of Colombia – and other rain-forest areas – have particularly important lessons for the field.

23   This brief presentation of what could be called "local models of nature" in the Pacific region is highly inadequate, and could be the topic of a separate study. Suffice it to say that the ensemble of meanings-practices (or "local models") of nature at play here are very different from modern systems. For a theoretical and political discussion of the importance of this difference, see Shiva 1994. For a detailed study of one such model in the Pacific, see Restrepo and del Valle 1996.

24   For an in-depth analysis of these plans, see Escobar and Pedrosa 1996.

25 These principles were laid out in February 1994 as part of the collective analysis by the PCN of the National Plan for the Development of Black Communities elaborated by the Colombian Department of National Planning (DNP). While there was some black representation in the commission that drafted the plan – including representatives from the PCN – the government rejected the PCN's request to have its own panel of experts and advisors included in the deliberations. As a result, the technocratic vision of the DNP and of conventional black politicians and experts prevailed in the overall conceptualization of the plan. This battle for the first "development plan for black communities" was thus lost by the movement, although not entirely, to the extent that some of their views were included.

26 The potential role of biodiversity conservation in the formulation of alternatives to development is analyzed by Escobar (1997).

REFERENCES

Appadurai, Arjun
1991. "Global Ethnoscapes." In *Recapturing Anthropology*, ed. R. Fox, 191–210. Santa Fe, N.Mex.: School of American Research.

Aprile-Gniset, Jacques
1993. *Poblamiento, Hábitats y Pueblos del Pacífico*. Cali: Universidad del Valle.

Arocha, Jaime
1991. "La Ensenada de Tumaco: Invisibilidad, Incertidumbre e Innovación." *América Negra* 1:87–112.

Asher, Kiran
1997. "Constructing Afro-Colombia: Ethnicity and Territory in the Pacific Lowlands." Ph.D. diss., Department of Political Science, University of Florida.

Bender, Barbara, ed.
1993. *Landscape: Politics and Perspectives*. Oxford: Berg.

Camacho, Juana
1996. "Black Women and Biodiversity in the Tribugá Golf, Chocó, Colombia." Final report presented to the MacArthur Foundation, Bogotá.

DNP (Departamento Nacional de Planeación de Colombia)
1983. *Plan de Desarrollo Integral para la Costa Pacífica, PLADEICOP*. Cali: DNP/CVC.
——— 1992. *Plan Pacífico. Una Estrategia de Desarrollo Sostenible para la Costa Pacífica Colombiana*. Bogotá: DNP.

Escobar, Arturo
1995. *Encountering Development: The Making and Unmaking of the Third World*. Princeton: Princeton University Press.
———. 1997. "Cultural Politics and Biological Diversity: State, Capital, and Social Movements in the Pacific Coast of Colombia." In *Between Resistance and Revolution: Cultural Politics and Social Protest*, ed. R. Fox and O. Starn, 40–64. New Brunswick, N.J.: Rutgers University Press.

Escobar, Arturo, and Alvaro Pedrosa, eds
1996. *Pacífico: Desarrollo o Diversidad? Estado, Capital y Movimientos Sociales en el Pacífico Colombiano*. Bogotá: CEREC/Ecofondo.

Fals Borda, Orlando
1992. "Social Movements and Political Power in Latin America." In *The Making of Social Movements in Latin America: Identity, Strategy, and Democracy*, ed. A. Escobar and S. Alvarez, 303–316. Boulder: Westview Press.

Fanon, Frantz
1968. *The Wretched of the Earth*. New York: Grove Press.

Friedemann, Nina S. de, and Jaime Arocha, eds
1984. *Un Siglo de Investigación Social en Colombia*. Bogotá: Etno.

García Canclini, Néstor
1990. *Culturas Híbridas: Estrategias para Entrar y Salir de la Modernidad*. Mexico City: Grijalbo.

GEF/PNUD (Global Environment Facility/ United Nations Development Program)
1993. *Conservación de la Biodiversidad del Chocó Biogeográfico. Proyecto Biopacífico*. Bogotá: DNP/Biopacífico.

González Casanova, Pablo
1994. *Globalidad, Neoliberalismo y Democracia*. Mexico City: UNAM.

Grueso, Libia
1995. "Diagnósticos, Propuestas y Perspectivas de la Región del Chocó Biogeográfico en Relación con la Conservación y Uso Sostenido de la Biodiversidad." Unpublished report to Proyecto Biopacífico, Bogotá.

Guattari, Félix
1995. *Chaosophy*. New York: Semiotext[e].

Hall, Stuart
1990. "Cultural Identity and Diaspora." In *Identity, Community, Culture, Difference*, ed. J. Rutherford, 392–403. London: Lawrence and Wishart.

Harvey, David
1989. *The Condition of Postmodernity*. Oxford: Blackwell.

Klandermans, Bert
1992. "La Construcción Social de la Protesta y los Campos Pluriorganizativos." In *The Frontiers in Social Movement Theory*, ed. A. Morris and C. Mueller. New Haven: Yale University Press. Unpublished Spanish translation.

Leyva, Pablo, ed
1993. *Colombia Pacífico*. Bogotá: Fondo FEN.

Lozano, Betty Ruth
1996. "Mujer y Desarrollo." In *Pacífico: Desarrollo o Biodiversidad?* ed. A. Escobar and A. Pedrosa, 176–204. Bogotá: CEREC/Ecofondo.

Martínez-Alier, Juan
1995. "Political Ecology, Distributional Conflicts, and Ecological Incommensurability." *New Left Review* 211:70–88.
———. 1996. "Merchandising Biodiversity." *Capitalism, Nature, Socialism* 7 (1):37–54.

Melucci, Alberto
1989. *Nomads of the Present*. Philadelphia: Temple University Press.

PCN (Proceso de Comunidades Negras)
1994. *Documento para Discusión Frente al Plan Nacional de Desarrollo para Comunidades Negras*. Unpublished manuscript.

Pred, Alan, and Michael Watts
1992. *Reworking Modernity*. New Brunswick, N.J.: Rutgers University Press.

Restrepo, Eduardo
1996. "Economía y Simbolismo en el Pacífico Negro." Undergraduate anthropology thesis, Universidad de Antioquia, Medellín.

Restrepo, Eduardo, and Jorge I. del Valle, eds
1996. *Renacientes del Guandal*. Bogotá: Biopacífico.

Robertson, Roland
1992. *Globalization*. London: Sage.

Rojas, Jeannette
1996. "Las Mujeres en Movimiento. Crónicas de Otras Miradas." In *Pacífico: Desarrollo o Diversidad?* ed. A. Escobar and A. Pedrosa, 205–219. Bogotá: CEREC/Ecofondo.

Serbin, Andrés
1991. "Por Qué no Existe el Poder Negro en América Latina?" *Nueva Sociedad* 111: 148–165.

Shiva, Vandana
1994. *Monocultures of the Mind*. London: Zed Books.

Wade, Peter
1993. *Blackness and Race Mixture: The Dynamics of Racial Identity in Colombia*. Baltimore: Johns Hopkins University Press.
———. 1995. "The Cultural Politics of Blackness in Colombia." *American Ethnologist* 22(2):341–357.

Whitten, Norman
1986. *Black Frontiersmen: Afro-Hispanic Culture of Ecuador and Colombia*. Prospect Heights, Ill.: Waveland Press.

Index